mediaguardian

Who's Who in the media

lian

eters

First published in 2006 by Guardian Books,
An imprint of Guardian Newspapers Ltd.

A CIP record for this book is available from the British Library

ISBN: 0 85265 055 8

Text design: Bryony Newhouse
Cover design: Two Associates

Printed by Cambridge University Press

Welcome to **Who's Who in the Media**, a guide to the most influential people working in the British media today.

From newspaper editors to advertising executives, foreign correspondents to marketing gurus, we compiled the book by inviting hundreds of people to submit information about themselves. Among other things, we asked what they read, who inspired them, what their career highlights had been. Entrants submitted as much or as little as they considered appropriate.

For those who felt that they didn't have time to respond, we researched an entry for them from information in the public domain.

Whether you want more insight into the personalities at the top of the media tree, or need to know the contact details of someone in a particular job, **Who's Who in the Media** is a unique and invaluable resource.

Jenny Abramsky

7.10.46

Room 2811, BBC Broadcasting House, Portland Place, London W1A 1AA

T 020 7765 4561
E Jenny.Abramsky@bbc.co.uk

Occupation: Director of Radio and Music, BBC

Other positions: Economic and Social Research Council, 1992-96; News International Visiting Professor of Broadcast Media, Oxford University, 2002; Director, RAJAR 1996-present; Honorary MA, Salford University, 1997; Chairman, Hampstead Theatre 2005 (director 2003-05); Fellow, Radio Academy, 1998. Council of the British Film Institute, 2000. Deputy Chair, Digital Radio Devpt Bureau (DRDB) 2002-present; Member, Board of Governers, BFI, 2000-present.
Awards: Woman of Distinction award, Jewish Care, 1990; Special Award, Radio 5 Live, Sony Radio Awards 1995; UK Station of the Year, Sony Radio Awards, 1996; CBE, 2001; Honorary Professor, Thames Valley University, 1994.
Education: Holland Park School; University of East Anglia
Career highlights: Joined BBC in 1969 as Programmes Operations Assistant, moving to The World At One as a producer in 1973; 1974, jointly responsible for BBC Radio's special coverage of the Nixon Watergate scandal; successfully relaunched PM as Editor in 1978; returned to The World At One as Editor in 1981; 1978-86 responsible for Radio 4 Budget Programme; Editor, Today Programme 1986, persuaded John Humphrys to become a presenter; Editor, News and Current Affairs Radio, 1987-93; 1991, set up Radio 4's Gulf FM network for duration of Gulf War; Founding Controller, Radio 5 Live, 1994, winning Sony Station of the Year Award 1996; Head of Ceefax 1994-96, Director, Continuous News 1996-98; Director, BBC Radio 1998-2000, Director BBC Radio and Music 2000-present.

» **Relaxing to:** *Theatre, music.* » *Married, 2 children*

Paul Adams

22.3.65

Room 2505 BBC TV Centre, Wood Lane, London W12 7RJ

T 020 8624 8547
E Paul.Adams@bbc.co.uk

Occupation: Chief Diplomatic Correspondent, BBC News 24

Other positions: Defence Correspondent, BBC; Middle East Correspondent, BBC; Belgrade Correspondent, BBC; Jerusalem Correspondent, BBC.
Awards: Amnesty International UK TV News Award, 2001.
Education: Sevenoaks School; York University

» *Married, 2 children*

Jan Adcock

72 Broadwick Street, London W1F 9EP

T 020 7439 5691
E jan.adcock@natmags.co.uk

Occupation: Publishing Director, Cosmopolitan Group, The National Magazine Company

Other positions: Advertisement Director, Elle (Hachette), Company (NatMags); Publisher, Company, NatMags Group Publisher, Parenting titles, NatMags.
Publications: Options, Mirabella, Elle, Company, Cosmopolitan.
Education: Non-graduate
Career highlights: I have worked with many amazingly talented people and teams including Mandi Norwood, Duncan Edwards, Sue Phipps, Fiona McIntosh, Lorraine Candy and Sam Baker, all of whom have been both an inspiration and fantastic fun to work with. Most recent highlights on Cosmopolitan, where I have worked for 5 years, have been reaching our 30th birthday in 2002 and maintaining market leadership, launching CosmoGIRL!, leading the first above-the-line brand campaign for Cosmo since 1972, receiving the P&G Award for Magazine that has best supported the beauty industry, launching the Cosmo Group Beauty Awards, achieving the highest ABC for Cosmo in 23 years (January-December 2004) and getting Cosmopolitan SuperBrand status in 2005. And finally, being appointed to the NatMag board in 2002.
Mentor: I've had many, most of which are listed above.
Big break: My first job at NatMags, Ad Director of Company Magazine. I have been at NatMags now for 13 years and loved every minute.
Big mistake: Not reading any business management books - I think it might be my eventual downfall.

» **Reading:** *As many magazines as I can from anywhere in the world, the Guardian, the Week, FT and trade press.* **Watching:** *A healthy combination of weekly trash and current affairs. Fantasy favourite, Grand Designs.* **Listening:** *Husband and kids dominate radio stations so whatever they have on, usually Radio 5.* **Relaxing to:** *Being with friends, my kids and my husband, beauty treatments, the cinema.* » *Married, 2 children*

Aaquil Ahmed

6.6.73

Channel 4, 124 Horseferry Road, London SW1P 2TX

T 020 7306 8065
E aahmed@channel4.co.uk

Occupation: Commissioning Editor, Religion, Channel 4

Other positions: Executive Producer, BBC Religion & Ethics; Series Producer, Producer, BBC Current Affairs.
Awards: Personally I was awarded an Achievement in Media award in 2005 from the Muslim News. The BBC season Islam UK won numerous awards. Inside the Mind of the Suicide Bomber won an Indy for best current affairs.
Education: Deane School, Bolton; University of Westminster

Career highlights: The Islam season for the BBC in 2001 was the first major event I helped shape. With documentaries on diverse subjects such as Islamophobia, football and music, it was a unique moment to try and shape how a faith as large as Islam should be seen. Broadcast a few weeks before 9/11, the tone of it was definitely a one-off. Joining Channel 4 and being allowed to commission projects like Inside the Mind of the Suicide Bomber, Children of Abraham and Priest Idol has been the ultimate highlight of my career so far. Reinventing religion on the channel so that it feels important is something I am very proud of. The support of Kevin Lygo has made it possible and I get excited when I think about those films and others such as The Cult of the Suicide Bomber and Immigration is a Time Bomb - they have all delivered for the channel and if I am honest when I took the job I didn't think things would work out so well. I expected graveyard slots and dwindling budgets - the opposite has happened and beating this will be a challenge.
Mentor: No great individual mentor but lots of people who have helped shape my career. Ruth Pitt - she has been a great supporter of mine since we worked together on the Islam season. Chris Choi - much as I hate to say this as he is a friend but producing him made me a better journalist. Kevin Lygo - I shouldn't say this as we still work together but he makes me feel like I am doing an important job and I know from working in religion elsewhere that's not always the case. A good skill that I have learnt from.
Big break: Impressing Linda Mitchell, the former Diversity Head at the BBC, at a seminar enough for her to push me forward to help run the BBC Islam UK season.
Big mistake: Staying in Birmingham in the BBC Asian Programmes Unit about a year to 18 months too long.

» **Reading:** *The Independent, political biographies, GQ, the Tablet, BBC sports website.* **Watching:** *The Simpsons, Soccer am - Sky Sports full stop in fact, Top Gear, Spooks, anything with Peter Kay in.* **Listening:** *Anything from Paul Weller, The Small Faces, Two Tone records, The Clash - all on the iPod these days.* **Relaxing to:** *Cycle, gym, spend time with the kids, championship manager on the computer, watch TV, DIY, gardening, follow the fortunes of Bolton Wanderers.* » *Married, 3 children*

Dawn Airey

15.11.61

British Sky Broadcasting, Grant Way, Isleworth, Middlesex TW7 5QD
T 020 7705 3131
E dawn.airey@bskyb.com

Occupation: Managing Director, Sky Networks

Other positions: Trustee, the Media Trust; Member, Board, UK Film Council; Vice President, Royal Television Society; Executive Chair, Media Guardian Edinburgh International Television Festival; Member, Board, International Emmy Awards; Non-executive Director, EasyJet plc; Honorary Committee Member, Monte Carlo Television Festival.
Awards: FRTS; Brownies badge for gymnastics.
Education: Girton College, Cambridge
Career highlights: A definite highlight is the role I am currently playing in helping to transition television from being a linear service to a new and exciting medium for the digital age, available on different platforms and devices. I am also very proud of having been part of the Channel Five team that was able to take an abstract concept and turn it into one of the nation's most popular channels. Most of all, as one of those rare creatures in our industry that enjoys all telly, from the populist to the highbrow, I am gratified to have been able to play some small role in shepherding to the screen programmes of the calibre of Father Ted, Hollyoaks and Five News. Former roles, various positions at Central Television, including Director of Programme Planning, 1985-93; Controller of Network Children's and Daytime, ITV, 1993-94; Controller of Arts and Entertainment, Channel 4, 1994-96; Director of Programmes, Channel 5, 1996-2000; Governor, Banff TV Festival, 1999; Chief Executive, Channel 5, 2000-03.
Mentor: Andy Allan, Director of Programming, Central TV.
Big break: Smashing my ankle on an Outward Bound course ... coming into TV as a trainee at Central TV in the 80s.
Big mistake: I was told never to admit to these ... being conned by an ex-CEO.

» **Reading:** *Anything and everything.* **Watching:** *A lot of mainstream fare.* **Listening:** *I'm addicted to Radio 4 going to sleep.* **Relaxing to:** *In Oxford with my cat Cleo.* » *Living in sin with partner, no children*

George Alagiah

22.11.55

BBC News, Room 2254, BBC Television Centre, Wood Lane, London W12 7RJ
T 020 8624 9929
E george.alagiah@bbc.co.uk

Occupation: Presenter, BBC Six O'Clock News

Publications: A Passage to Africa (2001).
Awards: Monte Carlo TV Festival and RTS awards for Somalia reports, 1993; BAFTA, commendation for Newsnight Kurdistan reports, 1994; Amnesty International Press Awards, Journalist of the Year, 1994; Broadcasting Press Guild, Journalist of the Year, 1994; James Cameron Memorial Trust Award, 1995; One World Broadcasting Trust, TV News Premier Award, 1995; Bayeux War Reporting Award, 1996; Ethnic Minority Media Awards, Media Personality of the Year, 1998; Asian Film and TV, Best TV Journalist, 1999.
Education: St John's College, Southsea; University of Durham
Career highlights: South Magazine, London 1981-89; Foreign Affairs Correspondent, BBC, 1989-94; Africa Correspondent, 1995-98; Presenter BBC News 24, 1998; Presenter BBC TV News 1999-present; BBC news reports/documentaries include trade in human organs in India, street children in Brazil, civil war in Liberia, famine and civil war in Somalia, persecution of Kurds in Iraq, effects on developing countries of GATT Agreement, ethnic conflict in Burundi, civil war in

Afghanistan, genocide in Rwanda, Kosovo crisis, East Timor, Asian tsunami.

» **Relaxing to:** *Sport, tennis, music, hiking.* » *Married, 2 sons*

Charles Allen

5.1.61

ITV plc, The London Television Centre, Upper Ground, London SE1 9LT

T 020 7261 3001
E charles.allen@itv.com

Occupation: Chief Executive, ITV plc

Other positions: Vice Chairman, London 2012
Awards: CBE in the Queen's New Years Honours 2003; Honorary Doctorate, MMU; Degree of Doctor of Letters Honoris Causa, Salford University.
Education: Bellshill Academy, Lanarkshire
Career highlights: Chairman, Granada plc; Chairman, Forte plc; Chairman, 2002 Commonwealth Games.
Mentor: Bruce Allen, MD Grandmet International; Gerry Robinson, Chairman Granada plc.
Big break: Being appointed MD of Grandmet Vending.
Big mistake: Cancelling holidays.

» **Reading:** *The Times, Telegraph, FT, Guardian, Independent.* **Watching:** *ITV programmes!* **Listening:** *BBC Radio 4.* **Relaxing to:** *Friends, family and travel.* » *Single*

Karen Allen

25.6.72

BBC Nairobi Bureau, 5th floor Longonot Place, PO Box 58621, Nairobi 00200, Kenya

T +254 20 222 637 / 215 490
E karen.allen@bbc.co.uk

Occupation: BBC East Africa Correspondent

Other positions: BBC Senior Health Correspondent
Education: University of Manchester
Career highlights: As a health correspondent most closely associated with covering the global spread of HIV/Aids. Reported from Durban at the time when the South African government was facing international pressure to recognise the link between HIV and Aids and extensively reported the fight to secure anti-retroviral drugs worldwide. Among key figures interviewed are the UN Secretary-General Kofi Annan and Microsoft billionaire Bill Gates. In 2003 stepped out of role as health correspondent to cover the Iraq war, one of the few domestic correspondents to be sent, and was embedded with the RAF for the duration of the war. Returned to report from Baghdad a year later during the capture of the British hostage Ken Bigley, and now devoted to foreign news as the BBC's East Africa Correspondent based in Nairobi, reporting for both BBC TV and Radio.
Mentor: The BBC's former India Correspondent Mark Tully was my inspiration. I first heard him report on a cholera epidemic in Delhi in 1987 just hours before I was about to set off on a student trip to Delhi myself. His reporting was so evocative that it cemented my desire to go into journalism. Up until that point it had been 50/50 whether I'd pursue a career as a reporter or use my economics background to work for the UN. I've never regretted my choice.
Big break: Being the first broadcast journalist to interview Bill Gates on his philanthropic ambitions. Being one of the few domestic journalists to be sent to cover the Iraq war.
Big mistake: Not getting Bill Gates' personal mobile phone number!

» **Reading:** *Mainly newspapers and current affairs magazines. Like most journalists there's a pang of guilt if I read anything else. But when I do get a chance to relax I enjoy biographies and travel writing.* **Watching:** *BBC TV News, Casualty, Silent Witness.* **Listening:** *I am a huge World Music fan so I listen to a lot of music from Senegal as well as flamenco and bhangra. Being based in Nairobi I am also a regular listener to BBC World Service.* **Relaxing to:** *Travelling. Eating good food in fine restaurants. Listening to music and going out dancing with my friends. Diving.* » *Single*

Kenton Allen

17.6.71

Room 4030 BBC TV Centre, Wood Lane, London W12 7RJ

T 020 8576 7978
E kenton.allen@bbc.co.uk

Occupation: Creative Head of Comedy Talent and Comedy North, BBC

Other positions: Editor BBC Comed,y 2003-05; Creative Director, Shine, 2000-03; Producer, Granada TV, 1997-2000; Head of Development, Granada Entertainment, 1994-97.
Publications: Funland, BBC3, 2005; I'm With Stupid, BBC3, 2005; Six Shooter, Film Four, 2005; Ideal, series 1 and 2, BBC3, 2004 and 2005; The Royle Family, BBC1; A Many Splintered Thing, BBC1; Lucky Numbers, ITV; Saturday Zoo, Channel 4; Tonight with Jonathan Ross, Channel 4.
Awards: BAFTA nomination, Best Short Film, Six Shooter 2005; BAFTA, Best Comedy: The Royle Family 2000; RTS, Best Situation Comedy: The Royle Family 2000; National Television Award, Best Comedy, The Royle Family 2000; Broadcast Award, Best Comedy 2000.
Education: Yes
Career highlights: Young upstart from Birmingham moves to London and meets Jonathan Ross and Caroline Aherne and gets very lucky.
Big break: Meeting Jonathan Ross, who plucked me from the relative sanity of BBC Radio and introduced me to the joyful evils of television.
Big mistake: The 3.30 at Kempton, November 2004.

» **Reading:** *Scripts and books and mags. And then some more scripts.* **Watching:** *As much as possible. Mainly comedy, drama and sport.* **Listening:** *Radio 4 before 9am, Radio 5 during the day, Radio 4 from 6 to 8, then Xfm or Magic or Radio 1.* **Relaxing to:** *Sailing, or reading magazines about yachts I can't afford.* » *Married, 2 children*

Kevin Allen

18.9.58

7-11 Herbrand Street, London WC1N 1EX
T 020 7961 2381
E kevin.allen@europe.mccann.com

Occupation: Executive Vice-President, Director of Worldwide Accounts, McCann Erickson

Other positions: Chief Growth Officer, Interpublic.
Publications: Led the development of the Priceless campaign for MasterCard now in 97 countries.
Awards: Awarded McCann's highest honour, the Harrison K. McCann Leadership Award, in 1995, and shortly thereafter the McCann NY General Manager's Award; Certificate of Recognition from Rudy Giuliani, Mayor of New York.
Education: Dowling College, New York; Queen Mary College, University of London; Adelphi University, New York
Career highlights: Chief Growth Officer for the Interpublic Group, McCann's parent company; Executive VP, Director of Corporate Development of McCann Worldgroup from 2002; in both positions responsible for spearheading multinational new business initiatives and the expansion of key global clients across marketing disciplines; held a similar post in McCann's EMEA (Europe, Middle East, Africa) region, based in London, with regional responsibility for the development of Worldgroup's integrated communications offering and for institutionalizing new business programmes, yielding a doubling of new business performance to over $600 million and contributing to multiple European and worldwide Agency of the Year honours.
Mentor: Dennison Young, Senior Council for Rudy Giuliani, Mayor of New York.
Big break: Joining McCann Erickson.
Big mistake: Not to have returned to London sooner.

» **Reading:** *Military history, a constant stream of management lessons. Just finished The Reason Why: The Story of the Fatal Charge of the Light Brigade (purchased at book sale for $1.00), a very good deal...* **Watching:** *Every old movie I can get my hands on, still flip over Wizard of Oz.* **Listening:** *Music from the roaring 20s, have a double motor Victrola and stacks of 78s, favourite is Time on my Hands by Rudy Vallee.* **Relaxing to:** *With a gaggle of friends (more eccentric the better) around me for a Sunday lunch that goes on so long it turns into dinner...* » *Single, no children*

Lord Waheed Ali

16.11.64

House of Lords, London SW1A 0AA
T 020 7219 3000

Occupation: Television producer and politician

Other positions: Non-executive Director, Shine Limited 2000-present; Chairman, Chorion Plc 2002-present; Patron, Skillset (National Training Organisation for Broadcast, Film, Video and Multimedia); Patron, Family Planning Association; Patron, Naz Foundation; Patron, The Albert Kennedy Trust; Director, Elton John Aids Foundation; Vice-President, UNICEF UK Trusts; Trustee, London School of Economics.
Awards: Life Peerage, 1998.
Education: Norbury Manor School, South London; Stanley Technical High School
Career highlights: Research Wootton Publications Ltd, 1982-85; Head of investment research, Save and Prosper Investment, 1985-88; Marketing Director, United Trade Press Ltd, 1988-89; Publisher, United Trade Press Ltd, 1989-91; Management Consultant, Bacon and Woodrow, 1991-92; Managing Director, Planet 24 Productions Ltd, 1992-99; Director, Carlton Media Group, 1999-2000.

» *Partner*

Nick Allsop

10.5.73

DDB London, 12 Bishop's Bridge Road W2 6AA
T 020 7258 3979
E nick.allsop@ddblondon.com

Occupation: Art Director, DDB London

Other positions: Launch campaign and identity, More4; national teacher recruitment campaign; TV and press advertisments for the Guardian; campaigns for Volkswagen, including Cops and King Kong ads for VW Polo.
Awards: 2005 D&AD silver pencil, poster advertising; 2004 Cannes gold Lion for press advertising; 2005 Campaign poster gold; 2004 Campaign press gold; 2004 One Show, NYC, gold; 2004 Clio Awards, Miami, gold.
Education: Burnham Grammar School, Bucks; Christ Church, Oxford; St. Martin's School Of Art and Design, London
Career highlights: Getting hired by ad agency BMP DDB [now DDB London]. Writing the most awarded press ad in the world in 2004. Winning Cannes Gold Lion last year and D&AD pencil this year. Being invited to set briefs for advertising course at St. Martin's. Helping young creative teams get their first jobs in the industry.
Mentor: Mark Reddy
Big break: Meeting my copywriter Simon Veksner 9 years ago (I wouldn't have a career without him).
Big mistake: Not arguing more with people who didn't like my ideas.

» **Reading:** *Cookery books, NME, Mojo, the Guardian.* **Watching:** *Birds.* **Listening:** *Radio 4 and 5, any 'indie' music.* **Relaxing to:** *Run around Hampstead Heath, make bad music.* » *Single*

Tess Alps

14.11.57

The Telephone Exchange, 5 North Crescent, Chenies Street, London WC1E 7PH
T 020 7446 0555
E talps@phd.co.uk

Occupation: Chairman, PHD Group UK

Other positions: General Media Panel for the ASA; Executive Committee for MediaGuardian Edinburgh International TV Festival.
Publications: Major clients include AA, Adidas, BBC, bmi, BMW, BT, COI, eBay, the Economist, Expedia, Flextech, Guardian Newspapers, McCain, O2, Prudential, Sainsbury's, Warner Bros, Yell.

Education: Retford High School; Durham University; Mountview Theatre School
Career highlights: Joined ATV selling TV airtime in 1978 and ended up as Sales Director for ITV in Yorkshire and Tyne-Tees; joined PHD in 1993 as Broadcast Director; set up Drum PHD 1996; became Deputy Chairman in 2000 and Chairman in 2003.
Mentor: The divine late Craig Pearman. A giant in every sense: intellect, affection, forgiveness, optimism.
Big break: Finding my natural home at PHD.
Big mistake: Eating that last biscuit.

» **Reading:** *For pleasure: the Guardian, Observer, Private Eye, The English Garden, Country Life, Radio Times, Dickens, Barnes, Yeats, Eliot etc and my favourite blogs such as Willie Lupin, Quinquireme, James and the Blue Cat, Grammar Puss and Wyndham the Triffid. For work: Campaign, Marketing Week, Marketing, Media Week, the Economist plus every paper and mag under the sun at some point.* **Watching:** *On TV Green Wing, Black Books, Malcolm in the Middle, Brainiac, Newsnight, X Factor, Takeshi's Castle, Six Feet Under, The Simpsons, Foyle's War, House, everything on BBC4, and posh dramas such as 2000 Streets Under The Sky. Professionally, I try to catch everything at least once. At the cinema, whatever The Rex at Berkhamsted shows. Online, film trailers and virals from trusted sources.* **Listening:** *My iPod (mainly Bach, Rameau, Beethoven, Mahler, Monteverdi, Britten), Radio 3 and 4 (especially the 6.30pm comedies), Classic FM and LBC.* **Relaxing to:** *Growing flowers and vegetables. Singing. Cheering on the Pitstone and Ivinghoe Pumas.*
» *Married, 1 son*

Roger Alton
21.12.51

The Observer, 3-7 Herbal Hill, London EC1R 5EJ
T 020 7713 4744
E roger.alton@observer.co.uk

Occupation: Editor, the Observer

Other positions: The Guardian: Assistant Editor, Features Editor, Weekend Magazine Editor, Arts Editor, Deputy Sports Editor, Chief Subeditor News; Liverpool Post: Deputy Features Editor, Graduate Trainee.
Awards: Editor of the Year - What the papers say Awards 2000; GQ Editor of the Year 2005.
Education: Clifton; Exeter College, Oxford
Career highlights: See awards
Mentor: Peter Preston
Big mistake: Countless. Running a millennium campaign to change the name of Heathrow Airport was a great success ... just drive down the M4.

» **Reading:** *Not enough.* **Watching:** *Films, TV.* **Relaxing to:** *Playing and watching sport, skiing, climbing, lying in the sun.*
» *Divorced, 1 daughter*

Matthew Anderson
9.9.70

Euro RSCG London, Cupola House, 15 Alfred Place, London WC1 7EB
T 020 8467 9281
E matthew.anderson@eurorscg.com

Occupation: Senior Copywriter, Euro RSCG London

Publications: Citroen C4, Transformer; Bounty, Strong Housewives; London Underground, unNOTICED; Launched Bmibaby, VirginOne.
Awards: D&AD Pencil; Creative Circle gold; 4 Creative Circle silvers; Cannes bronze; Campaign Posters silver; Shark Awards gold; BTA Awards gold plus loads of others from weird worldwide awards.
Education: Ardingly College, Sussex
Career highlights: Started as a despatch boy at Dorlands. Was an account man for about a year - still have nightmares. Saatchi & Saatchi; learnt trade, met wife; Simons Palmer, nice agency. Merged with TBWA; Joined Partners BDDH, which merged with EURO RSCG, where I made an ad that the Sun rates as 'the best ad ever made'.
Mentor: My father
Big break: Being a crap account exec, the client asked for me to be removed from the account; at the same time the agency was looking for a junior art director.
Big mistake: Losing a cheque for £4.2 million while working as a despatch boy at Dorlands - the interest accrued overnight would have been more than my salary.

» **Reading:** *20th century modern classics like Graham Greene, Mark Twain, Vladimir Nabokov, Aldous Huxley, George Orwell etc, BBC online, Popbitch, the Sun, Telegraph (only for the cryptic crossword), Beano, Gruffalo - to my kids.* **Watching:** *Not X factor, Wife Swap, Strictly Come Dancing, anything on ITV. Give me University Challenge any day. Oh and any sport.* **Listening:** *Radio 5 live, Planet Rock (DAB station devoted to AC/DC, The Who, Pink Floyd etc), Indie music (Kasabian, Snow Patrol, Elbow, Franz Ferdinand etc) Chill out. Bob Dylan.* **Relaxing to:** *Play sport a lot, golf, football, tennis, gym, squash, read, bike rides with wife and kids.* » *Married, 3 children*

Hilary Andersson
24.9.71

c/o Newsgathering, BBC Television Centre, Wood Lane, London W12 7RJ
T +2782 453 5208
E Hilary.Andersson.01@bbc.co.uk

Occupation: BBC Overseas Correspondent

Publications: Mozambique: A War Against the People (Macmillan 1991).
Awards: RTS Specialist Journalist of the Year, 2004; RTS News Event of the Year, 2005; Peabody Award, 2005; BAMMF Award, 2005; Amnesty International Award, Best Documentary, 2005.
Education: Cheltenham; University of Edinburgh
Career highlights: Freelance writer for South African newspapers, 1989-90; BBC World Service Radio Reporter/Producer, 1990-93; BBC Television Producer, London, 1994-96; BBC Lagos Correspondent, 1997-99; BBC Jerusalem

Correspondent, 1999-2001; BBC Africa Correspondent, 2001-05; Panorama, Secrets of the Camps, 2004; Panorama, The New Killing Fields, 2003.
Mentor: No one!
Big break: My first report on the 10 O'Clock News in 1997 on brutal treatment of mentally ill people in Nigeria.

» **Reading:** *Favourite authors include John Steinbeck and Cormac McCarthy.* **Watching:** *All sorts.* **Listening:** *All sorts.* **Relaxing to:** *Off-piste skiing, windsurfing, cooking.*
» *Single, no children*

Phil Angell

9.6.69

UKRD, Wilson Way, Redruth, Cornwall TR15 3XX
T 01209 314400
E philangell@aol.com

Occupation: Group Programme Director, UKRD

Other positions: Programme Director, Pirate FM; Programme Director, Fox FM; Assistant Traffic Manager, LBC.
Publications: Bugger all (though was the person in 1988 who came up with the Sunday Sport's strapline 'Where else can you get it so often?').
Awards: Bugger all (though was the breakfast jock when Fox FM won Sony Station of the Year in 1993).
Education: University of East Anglia (History)
Career highlights: I was the first person to broadcast from Fox FM's travel helicopter, then called the Unipart Flying Fox. I then hosted the breakfast show on Fox, became its PD and ran away to Cornwall to do a similar job at Pirate FM. Won the raffle to be UKRD's Group PD and I am now a practising alcoholic.
Mentor: Too many to name, but my boss William Rogers, Mark Beever, Phil Dowse, and Tracker are amongst the main ones.
Big break: Probably when Tom Hunter put me in Fox FM's helicopter to do the travel reports.
Big mistake: Getting my first job after university by replying to one of those ads in the Guardian wanting 'graduate trainees' to work in the media. I ended up selling advertising on Computing magazine. What a sucker!

» **Reading:** *Any history books. Hate most novels unless it's Dickens or Steinbeck.* **Watching:** *Top Gear, history programmes, sport, Sky News, QI.* **Listening:** *Pink Floyd and generally the sort of old man rock that Jeremy Clarkson likes. God knows why I'm doing the job I am!* **Relaxing to:** *Read history books, and am writing a book for my family only on what my Dad did during World War 2.* » *Living with partner of 16 years (female by the way!), no children I'm aware of*

Alex Armitage

18.5.62

19 Denmark Street, London WC2H 8NJ
t 020 7836 3941
E aarmitage@noelgay.com

Occupation: CEO, Noel Gay

Other positions: Various other directorships and trustee postions.
Awards: Best decorated potato (Toothill flower show 1964).
Education: Eton
Career highlights: Agent for Mary Nightingale, Sir David Frost, Jeremy Vine, Danny Baker, Rageh Omaar, Johnnie Walker, Sarah Montague, Julian Worricker, Richard Littlejohn, Mark Pougatch, Sian Williams, Richard Stilgoe, Kate Silverton, etc etc. Founder Noel Gay Television, Theatre producer of Me and My Girl.
Mentor: Richard Armitage, Bill Cotton and Russell Harty.
Big break: My ankle, 4 ribs and my wrist at the same time.
Big mistake: Not becoming a farmer.

» **Reading:** *Anything and everything.* **Watching:** *My clients, The Simpsons, House, Seinfeld, fishing programmes, my weight and my language.* **Listening:** *My clients, Radio 2, The Arrow, Woman's Hour, Planet Rock, my children.* **Relaxing to:** *My children, wine, painting, raising chickens and cooking them.*
» *Divorced, 4 children*

Charlotte Ashton

24.5.67

2nd Floor, 160 Great Portland Street, London W1W 5QA
T 020 8765 2043
E charlotte.ashton@uktv.co.uk

Occupation: Director of Network Programmes, UKTV

Other positions: Head of Factual, UKTV; Channel Executive, BBC Two; Director, Media Guardian Edinburgh International Television Festival.
Publications: 1,000 Years of History; V For Victory season.
Awards: MGEITF New Channel of the Year Award 2003 (UKTV History).
Education: Polytechnic of Central London
Leading the launch of the new UKTV factual portfolio taking in UKTV History, UKTV Documentary and UKTV People.
Mentor: Sophie Turner-Laing
Big break: Being given the Directorship of the TV Festival.
Big mistake: Not spending a few years in coal-face production before moving into channel management.

» **Reading:** *The Guardian, Observer, Elle Decoration.* **Watching:** *Everything.* **Listening:** *Whatever my iPod shuffle gives me at the time.* **Relaxing to:** *Doing up houses – the more wrecked the better.* » *Single, 1 child*

Clive Aslet

16.2.59

Country Life, King's Reach Tower, Stamford Street, London SE1 9LS

E clive_aslet@ipcmedia.com

Occupation: Editor, Country Life

Publications: Books include The Last Country Houses, Yale University Press, 1982; The American Country House, Yale University Press, 1990; Anyone for England?, Little Brown, 1997; Inside the House of Lords, HarperCollins 1998; The Landmarks of Britain, Hodder and Stoughton 2005.

Awards: BSME Editor of the Year, 1997; PPA Campaign of the Year, 1994.

Education: Peterhouse, Cambridge

Career highlights: Since 1993, Editor of Country Life magazine. Also Editor-in-Chief Country Life Books and Editor-in-Chief Country Life Online, the award-winning website. I began my working life on Country Life as an architectural writer in 1977. I have also taken part in many radio and television programmes, including Any Questions, Newsnight, The Moral Maze, various chat shows, etc. I have contributed to The Times, Sunday Times, Financial Times, Daily Telegraph, Sunday Telegraph, Daily Mail, Mail on Sunday, Independent, Economist, Spectator, etc.

Mentor: Frank Miles, my English teacher at school.

Big break: Landing my first job. It was at Country Life and I've been here ever since.

Big mistake: Going to the Isle of Man.

» **Reading:** *Biography, history, novels.* **Watching:** *Mostly the children's cartoons.* **Listening:** *Radio 3.* **Relaxing to:** *Eating, drinking, talking, reading, preferably in Ramsgate.*

» *Married, 3 children*

John Atkin

7.9.71

PO Box 104.5, Derby DE1 3HL

T 01332 375001

E john.atkin@bbc.co.uk

Occupation: News Editor, BBC Radio Derby

Other positions: Managing news, sport, online presence.

Awards: 2005 Frank Gillard Awards, Sports Coverage; 2003 Sony Radio Academy Gold Award, Coverage of a News Story; 2003 Frank Gillard Awards, Breakfast Show, News Story.

Education: Hull University

Career highlights: 10 years in local newspapers in Derby, Oxford and Stoke followed by a move to the BBC in 1998.

Mentor: Mike Lowe, ex-Derby Evening Telegraph. Alison Ford, HRLP for BBC in the East Midlands.

Sir David Attenborough

8.5.26

5 Park Road, Richmond, Surrey TW10 6NS

Occupation: Vice-President, Royal Television Society; naturalist, traveller, broadcaster and writer

Other positions: Trustee, Learning Through Landscapes 1990-present; Trustee, British Museum 1980-present.

Publications: Zoo Quest to Guiana (1956); Zoo Quest for a Dragon (1957); Zoo Quest in Paraguay (1959); Quest in Paradise (1960); Zoo Quest to Madagascar (1961); Quest under Capricorn (1963); The Tribal Eye (1976); Life on Earth (1979); The Living Planet (1984); The First Eden (1987); The Trials of Life (1990); The Private Life of Plants (1995); The Life of Birds (1998); The Blue Planet (2001); Life on Air (2002); Life of Mammals (2002).

Awards: Special Award, SFTA 1961; Silver Medal, Zoological Society of London 1966; Silver Medal, RTS 1966; Desmond Davis Award, SFTA 1970; Cherry Keaton Medal, RGS 1972; Kalinga Prize. UNESCO 1981; Washburn Award, Boston Museum of Science, 1983; Hopper Day Medal, Academy of Natural Sciences, Philadelphia, 1983; Founder's Gold Medal, RGS, 1985; International Emmy Award, 1985; Encyclopaedia Britannica Award, 1987; Livingstone Medal, RSGS, 1990; Honorary Freeman, City of Leicester, 1990; Honorary Fellow, Manchester Poly 1976, UMIST 1980; Hon DLitt, Univ of Leicester 1970, City University, 1972; Honorary Fellow, University of London, 1980; Honorary Fellow, University of Birmingham, 1982; Honorary LLD, University of Bristol, 1977; Honorary LLD, University of Glasgow, 1980; Honorary DSc, University of Liverpool, 1974; Honorary DSc, Heriot-Watt University, 1978; Honorary DSc, University of Sussex, 1979; Honorary DSc, University of Bath, 1981; Honorary DSc, Ulster University, 1982; Honorary DSc, University of Durham, 1982; Honorary DSc, Keele University, 1986; Honorary DSc, University of Oxford, 1988; Honorary DUniv, Open University, 1980; Honorary DUniv, University of Essex, 1987; Honorary ScD, University of Cambridge, 1984; Commander of the Golden Ark (Netherlands), 1983; Honorary FRCP 1991, FRS 1983; Fellow, BAFTA 1980.

Education: Wyggeston Grammar School for Boys, Leicester; Clare College, Cambridge

Career highlights: Served Royal Navy, 1947-49; editorial assistant in an educational publishing house, 1949-52; Producer, talks and documentary programmes, BBC 1952; Controller, BBC2 1965-68; Director of Programmes TV and Member, Board of Management, BBC 1969-72; zoological and ethnographic filming expeditions to: Sierra Leone 1954, British Guiana 1955, Indonesia 1956, New Guinea 1957, Paraguay and Argentina 1958, South West Pacific 1959, Madagascar 1960, Northern Territory Australia 1962, Zambesi 1964, Bali 1969, Central New Guinea 1971, Celebes 1973, Borneo 1973, Peru 1973, Columbia 1973, Mali 1974, British Columbia 1974, Iran 1974, Solomon Islands 1974, Nigeria 1975; writer and presenter BBC series: Zoo Quest 1954-64, Tribal Eye 1976, Life on Earth 1979, The Living Planet 1984, The First Eden 1987, Lost Worlds Vanished Lives 1989, The Trials of Life

1990, The Private Life of Plants 1995, The Life of Birds 1998, The Blue Planet 2001; trustee: World Wildlife Fund UK 1965-69, 1972-82 and 1984-90, World Wildlife Fund Int 1979-86, Science Museum 1984-87, Royal Botanic Gardens Kew 1986-92; member, Nature Conservancy Council 1973-82, corresponding member, American Museum of Natural History, 1985, Huw Wheldon Memorial Lecture RTS, 1987.

» **Reading:** *Tribal art, natural history.*

Rachel Attwell

5.5.55

BBC Television Centre, Wood Lane, London W12 6RJ
T 020 8576 4416
E rachel.attwell@bbc.co.uk

Occupation: Deputy Head, BBC Television News

Other positions: Editor, London Plus; Deputy Editor, Breakfast News; Editor, World News, Channel 4 Daily (ITN); Head, BBC World; Deputy Head, TV News Channels.
Education: University of Warwick
Career highlights: Two biggest highlights would be being offered the opportunity to take responsibility first of BBC World Service TV News, see it through to the launch of BBC World and it being considered a force in global news broadcasting, and then taking over BBC News 24. It had had a difficult launch and the team and I were able to turn that around to the point where the channel is taking on Sky News with greater and greater success.
Mentor: David Lloyd, both as my boss at the BBC and as my Commissioning Editor at Channel Four.
Big break: Being moved from an Assistant Producer to Day Editor almost overnight to Breakfast mostly as a result of a successful D-Day anniversary outside broadcast. After that other senior editorial opportunities followed.
Big mistake: Dozens of them but for me personally I wish I had been out of the BBC for a bit longer before I returned to BBC World Service TV News.

» **Reading:** *Modern history, trashy novels.* **Watching:** *West Wing, Spooks, House, history docs and I am still loyal to EastEnders.* **Listening:** *Ella, Sinatra, Gershwin, Sondheim. Very old fashioned.* **Relaxing to:** *With my friends with good food and drink.* » *Single, no children*

Mark Austin

2.11.62

200 Gray's Inn Road, London WC1X 8HF
T 020 7833 3000
E mark.austin@itn.co.uk

Occupation: Presenter, News at Ten Thirty

Other positions: Senior Correspondent, 1998-2002; Asia Correspondent, 1990-94, 1996-98; Africa Correspondent, 1994-96; Sports Correspondent, 1987-90.
Awards: International Emmy Award 2000, Mozambique; Golden Nymph Monte Carlo 2000, Mozambique; Golden Nymph Monte Carlo, Bosnia.
Education: Bournemouth Grammar School
Career highlights: From school to local newspaper, Bournemouth Evening Echo. From Echo to Evening Mail, West London to BBC World Service as subeditor. In 1981 to BBC Television News as reporter aged 23. In 1986 joined ITN.
Mentor: Chris Cramer and Ron Neil at BBC plus the Home News editor in the early eighties, John Exelby, a real pro with great humour. At ITN, Nigel Hancock, one of the great news enthusiasts. Now, David Mannion, a top journalist and a top man.
Big break: Being made a national TV reporter at the BBC at the age of 23.
Big mistake: Telling the cameraman to film armed white right-wingers in South Africa. They took all our gear and marched myself and the producer into a field at gunpoint. We had to kneel there for what seemed like ages with a gun at my temple. Ghastly.

» **Reading:** *Biographies political and military, cricket books.* **Watching:** *Current affairs and sport.* **Listening:** *Miles Davis, Hugh Masekela, Van Morrison.* **Relaxing to:** *With three kids you can't.* » *Married, 3 children*

Sylvia Auton

9.6.53

IPC Media, King's Reach Tower, Stamford Street, London SE1 9LS
T 020 7261 6396
E sylvia_auton@ipcmedia.com

Occupation: Chief Executive, IPC Media

Other positions: Director, PPA Ltd, 2003-present; Chairman, IPC Media Pension Trustee Ltd, 2000-present; Managing Director, IPC Country & Leisure Media, 1998-2003; Publishing Director, New Scientist 1990-98.
Education: Southampton University
Career highlights: Joined IPC in 1977 as a marketer, and held several new media and publishing positions including Publishing Director of New Scientist and Head of New Media; as Managing Director of IPC Country & Leisure Media, grew its diverse portfolio of specialist titles; in October 2001 was one of the Board team that led the sale to Time Warner for £1.15bn, the biggest ever transatlantic media deal; appointed CEO of IPC Media in March 2003.
Mentor: Linda Genower, the best leader I have ever worked with.
Big break: Getting my first IPC marketing job, Marketing Executive for Country Life.
Big mistake: It seems to have gone OK so far.

» **Reading:** *Everything I can lay my hands on, the Spectator, Economist, Time, Country Life, Woman & Home, Sunday Times, FT.* **Watching:** *The 10 O'Clock News, Love Soup and The X Factor!* **Listening:** *Jonathan Ross on Saturday morning.* **Relaxing to:** *Travelling, walking, gardening, friends and family.* » *Married, 2 sons*

Sly Bailey 25.1.66

1 Canada Square, Canary Wharf, London E14 5AP
T 020 7293 2203
E sly.bailey@trinitymirror.com

Occupation: Chief Executive, Trinity Mirror plc

Other positions: IPC Magazines: joined 1989, Advertising Sales Director, 1990-97; Board Director, 1994-2002; MD IPC tx, 1997-99, Chief Executive IPC Media 1999-2002.
Awards: Marcus Morris Award, PPA, 2002.
Education: St Saviour's and St Olave's Grammar School for Girls

» *Married*

John Baish 15.7.72

Classic Gold Digital, 50 Lisson Street, London NW1 5DF
T 01582 676200
E john.baish@ubcmedia.com

Occupation: Managing Director, Classic Gold Digital Ltd (part of UBC Media Group)

Other positions: Programme Director, Jazz FM (1996-2002); News Editor (Broadcasting), Press Association (1996); Producer, Head of International Programmes, Classic FM (1993-1996); Presenter, Head of Music, Deputy Programme Controller, Radio 210 (1989-1993).
Publications: Classic Gold Digital, Music That Still Fits, 2004; Jazz FM Smooth Jazz relaunch, including the Robbie Vincent breakfast show (1998); Tony Blackburn's Big Soul Night (1999) and the Late Lounge (2001); PA Broadcasting launch (1996); Classic FM's evening news programme launch (1995); Classic FM's international operations (1994); Radio 210's relaunch as 2-Ten FM, introduction of music research and listener-focused formatting (1992).
Awards: Sony-nominated five times at Jazz FM, 1997-2002; Student Broadcaster of the Year, 1987.
Education: Exeter University
Career highlights: For a while, it seemed that I was destined to work in IT for a chocolate company, but instead I took it into my head to become a DJ in Reading. After several years in local radio, I moved to Classic FM, which was going through a highly exciting period of development. After a foray overseas, working in Holland, Finland and New York, I returned to work on Classic's relaunched evening news programme. The move to the Press Association, at the time when the company was moving into broadcasting for the first time, seemed like a natural step, but before long I was back in music radio, running Jazz FM's output in London and Manchester. In my time there we doubled our market share, and increased the valuation of the business seven-fold. Now, at Classic Gold Digital, I'm working across 18 stations with some of Britain's best known broadcasters.
Mentor: Tim Blackmore was a real inspiration.
Big break: Making the leap to Classic FM was a perfect piece of luck, giving me the chance to work with some great people - presenters like Susannah Simons, Henry Kelly, Alan Freeman and Hugh Macpherson, and behind the scenes with Michael Bukht and Chris Vezey.
Big mistake: Assuming that there was nothing left to go wrong with my B-reg Renault 5.

» **Reading:** *Everything, all the time, particularly biographies and political memoirs, fiction bestsellers at random, and the Economist each week.* **Watching:** *All the TV news channels, documentaries (particularly historical), and crime drama.* **Listening:** *Apart from our own great network, 5 Live, Radio 4 and bits of Radio 2, plus Planet Rock on DAB.* **Relaxing to:** *Playing silly games with my three young boys, and watching Southampton FC's march back to glory.* » *Married, 3 children*

Alistair Baker 26.7.62

Microsoft Ltd, Thames Valley Park, Reading RG6 1WG
T 0118 909 3118
E abaker@microsoft.com

Occupation: Managing Director, Microsoft Ltd

Other positions: Vice-President, Microsoft EMEA
Awards: FRSA
Education: BSc Hons Computing and Informatics; Postgraduate Diploma
Career highlights: Joined IBM, 1985; various roles, IBM, Hewlett Packard, Morse Computers, 1985-96; joined Microsoft, 1996; Country Manager, Scotland, 1996-2000; Group Director, Microsoft Services Organisation, 2000-02; General Manager, Small and Mid-Market Solutions and Partners, 2002-04.

» **Relaxing to:** *Cycling, snow-boarding, guitar.* » *3 children*

James Baker 8.6.64

BskyB, Grant Way, Isleworth, Middlesex TW7 5QD
T 020 7705 3000
E james.baker@bskyb.com

Occupation: Managing Director, Sky Networked Media

Education: Haberdashers' Aske's School, Elstree
Career highlights: Presenter and Producer, TV-am Children's Department, 1982-1988; Producer, Sky News, 1989; Programme Producer and Editor, TV-am, 1990-1993; Head of Programmes/Head of International Programmes, Nickelodeon, 1993-1996; Head of Programmes, Sky One, 1996-1999; Head of Programming Projects, Sky Networks, 2000-2003; Controller, Sky One, 2003-2005; Managing Director, Sky Networked Media, 2006-present.
Mentor: Bruce Gyngell, Gerry Laybourne, Dawn Airey.
Big break: Barefoot Hyde Park interview with Head of Nickelodeon.

Big mistake: Poor operation of Roland Rat's left paw....

» **Reading:** *Wired, New Yorker, Observer Food Monthly.* **Watching:** *Simpsons, 24, Life on Mars.* **Listening:** *Anything my iPod offers up on shuffle.* **Relaxing to:** *Bad guitar, average exercise, sleep.* » *Married, 2 children*

Mike Baker

17.2.61

Room 1502, BBC TV Centre, Wood Lane, London W12 7RJ

T 020 8624 9023
E mike.baker@bbc.co.uk

Occupation: BBC Education Correspondent

Other positions: Columnist for BBC News Online and Times Educational Supplement.
Publications: Books: Who Rules Our Schools (Hodder); A Parents' Guide to the New Curriculum (BBC); Visiting Professor, Institute of Education, 1999-2001; Reuters Fellow, Oxford University, 1992; Michigan Journalism Fellow, 1999.
Awards: Edexcel Education Correspondent Award, 2003; Shortlisted Race in Media Awards, 2004.
Education: Colchester Royal Grammar School; Cambridge University; Kingston University (MA)
Career highlights: Being a political correspondent during the Thatcher years, including covering the Brighton bomb, and filling in as Moscow Correspondent during the Yeltsin years. The A-level marking crisis when we had many scoops, including the exclusive interview (with Sir William Stubbs) which led to Estelle Morris's resignation.
Mentor: I learned a lot as a young political correspondent when working under BBC Political Editor, John Cole, and with fellow Political Correspondent, the late John Harrison.
Big break: Writing articles for my local newspaper, the Braintree & Witham Times, while still at school and getting onto the BBC graduate trainee scheme.
Big mistake: Too many to mention but usually involving something technical like forgetting to press the record button on tape machines.

» **Reading:** *BBC News Online, the TES, and the Guardian's education supplement. For general news the Independent is a favourite. Any books on social and economic history.* **Watching:** *The Ten O'Clock News and Match of the Day.* **Listening:** *Divided loyalties between Radio 5 and Radio 4. Smooth FM on the rare occasions when it still plays jazz. BBC Radio Suffolk (on the web) for football commentaries.* **Relaxing to:** *Cycling and watching Ipswich Town FC losing.* » *Married, 2 daughters*

Sam Baker

8.7.70

72 Broadwick Street, London W1F 9EP

T 020 7439 5442
E sam.baker@natmags.co.uk

Occupation: Editor, Cosmopolitan magazine

Other positions: None currently
Publications: Fashion Victim, Orion Books, 2005.
Education: Birmingham University
Career highlights: Born in Hampshire, studied politics at Birmingham University; rejected by the London College of Printing for not having 'what it takes' and got big break on Chat magazine; became a writer on Take a Break before moving to Emap where as Features Editor and then Deputy Editor of New Woman, worked on the launch dummies of Red, relaunched Just Seventeen as J17 and edited minx; After five hugely successful years as Editor of the Natmags title Company magazine, where sales increased by 50%, signed a six-figure, two-novel deal on both sides of the Atlantic, the first of which, Fashion Victim, was published in 2005 by Orion Books; Editor of Cosmopolitan for just over a year, during which time instigated Cosmo's high profile High Heel Vote campaign to engage young women with the political process.
Mentor: Ian Birch, previously Editor-in-chief, EMAP plc.
Big break: Going to Chat magazine as a temp PA to the Editor and never leaving.
Big mistake: As a writer on Take A Break, I scooped the nationals by securing an interview with the Taylor sisters on their release from prison after their conviction for murder was overturned. When the Press Gazette wanted to interview me about my scoop, I turned them down because I was too shy! I've obviously learnt the error of my ways since then!

» **Reading:** *Everything – I skim most papers every morning, but always the Guardian, Mail and Evening Standard. I flick through literally hundreds of magazines every month, from Heat to Vogue to the New Statesman. But actually read? Sadly, not so often.* **Watching:** *In the office, Sky news. At home, if I'm in, the TV's on. I'm hooked on American imports from Lost, Desperate Housewives and West Wing to the Daily with Jon Stewart. More4 is my new obsession. I also love the new Trinny and Susannah (the format is inspired – I swear the one on divorcees made me cry), Grand Designs, Hell's Kitchen ... and I'll give most detective series a try at least once. I also tune into Newsnight several nights a week. If I had my way, I'd never go out.* **Listening:** *I'm not a huge radio listener, but when I do it's Radio 4. I usually wake up to Today.* **Relaxing to:** *That's a novel concept.* » *Married, 1 stepson*

Joan Bakewell

17.4.37

c/o Knight Ayton Management, 114 St Martins Lane, London WC2N 4BE

T 0207 836 5333
E info@knightayton.co.uk

Occupation: Broadcaster and writer

Other positions: Chair of the National Campaign for the Arts.
Publications: The Complete Traveller; The New Priesthood; The Heart of Heart of the Matter; The Centre of the Bed; Belief.
Awards: BAFTA; Richard Dimbleby Award 1993.
Education: Stockport High School for Girls; Newham College, Cambridge
Career highlights: Late Night Line Up; Reports Action; Newsnight; Heart of the Matter; My Generation; Taboo.
Mentor: None
Big break: Late Night Line Up in 1965.

» *Twice married, twice divorced, 1 boy and 1 girl*

Kevin Bakhurst

11.12.69

Room 1640, BBC TV Centre, Wood Lane, London W12 7RJ
T 020 8624 9999
E kevin.bakhurst@bbc.co.uk

Occupation: Editor, BBC Ten O'Clock News

Awards: BAFTA, TV News Coverage 2004; RTS, TV News Programme of the Year 2004; RTS, News Event 2004 (Darfur).
Education: Haberdashers' Aske's, Elstree; St John's College, Cambridge
Career highlights: Started as Researcher on Business Breakfast in 1989. Producer, Nine O'Clock News; Europe Producer; Political Producer, Nine O'Clock News; Assistant Editor, Nine and Ten O'Clock News; Evenings Editor, News 24; Editor, Ten O'Clock News Sept 2003-present; Producer, Hong Kong Handover; covered many US elections in last 15 years; sent to US to cover September 11th.
Mentor: Paul Gibbs and Mark Damazer for much of my early career. Now I also look up to the great correspondents I work with.
Big break: Getting a Researcher job on Business Breakfast and then getting the chance to make a series of films around Europe due to my languages and despite huge inexperience.
Big mistake: Letting Robin Oakley broadcast a 6-minute lead report on the Nine O'Clock News with a frog in his throat.

» **Reading:** *I love a range of books - but have limited time. Novels, historical and political autobiography in particular. Papers - I read most of them during the week and the Economist.* **Watching:** *Films; football, rugby and cricket. Most news outlets during the week. The X Factor.* **Listening:** *Today programme and Five Live. I hear the Radio 4 Midnight News most nights - but rush to turn off Sailing By. A good range of music.* **Relaxing to:** *Cinema; cooking for family and friends. Reading. Going to Chelsea as often as I can (often thanks to Jeremy Vine). Travel is my favourite and we often visit France.*
» *Married, 3 children*

Michiel Bakker

MTV, Hawley Crescent, London NW1 8TT
T 020 7284 7777
E michiel.bakker@mtvne.co.uk

Occupation: Managing Director, MTV Networks UK, Ireland and Nordic

Career highlights: Joined MTV and set up MTV Europe's Amsterdam office, 1987; established MTV Europe's Benelux operations with an office in Brussels, 1989; appointed Senior Vice-President, Network Development; oversaw launch of VH1 in the UK, 1994; Managing Director, MTV Networks UK and Ireland, 1996; oversaw launch of MTV2, MTV Base, MTV Hits, MTV Dance and VH1 Classic, 1999; established MTV Networks UK's sales arm Viacom Brand Solutions, 2000; launched The Music Factory on Freeview, 2000; MTV won non-terrestrial channel of the year, Media Guardian Edinburgh International TV festival, 2003; launched VH2, 2003; Executive Vice-President, MD MTV Networks UK, Ireland and Nordic, 2003-present.

Jeff Barak

27.4.65

25 Furnival Street, London EC4A 1JT
T 020 7415 1500
E jeffbarak@thejc.com

Occupation: Managing Editor, the Jewish Chronicle

Other positions: Editor, the Jerusalem Post, 1996-2002.
Publications: The Jewish Chronicle, Jerusalem Post and a sabbatical year (1999-2000) at the Daily Telegraph.
Education: University of Newcastle upon Tyne
Career highlights: Being the first journalist to get an Israeli Prime Minister (Ehud Barak) on record as saying there would be two Jerusalems - East Jerusalem for the Palestinians, West Jerusalem for the Jews. Unfortunately, two days later the intifada broke out and the peace process was destroyed.
Mentor: Charles Moore
Big break: Avoiding the mass walk-out at the Jerusalem Post soon after Hollinger's takeover of the paper. I was in the middle of my compulsory military service in the Israeli Army.
Big mistake: Publishing an obituary of someone very much alive.

» **Reading:** *The Times, Guardian, Telegraph, Ha'aretz, Yediot Ahronot, Sunday Times.* **Watching:** *Sky News, News at 10, West Wing, Sopranos, Match of the Day, live football and cricket.* **Listening:** *Today Programme, then Radio 2 in the car.* **Relaxing to:** *Watching live sport, family holidays.*
» *Married, 3 children*

Dave Barber

8.4.58

09-071, BBC Birmingham B1 1RF
T 0121 567 6340
E david.barber@bbc.co.uk

Occupation: Head of Specialist Music and Compliance, BBC Radio 2

Other positions: Reporter, the Star, Sheffield, 1979-84; Producer/Assistant News Editor, Northwest Tonight, BBC1 regional, 1984-91; Series Producer, Close Up North, BBC 2 regional, 1992-94; Assistant Editor, BBC Radio 5 Live, 1994-96; Assistant Editor, The Really Useful Show, BBC1,1996-98; Editor, Countryfile, BBC1,1999-2000.
Publications: Lost Boy, In Search of Nick Drake, BBC Radio 2; Countryfile, BBC1; The Really Useful Show, BBC1; Sybil Ruscoe/The Magazine, BBC Radio 5 Live; Close Up North, BBC2 regional; North West Tonight, BBC1 regional.
Awards: Sony Radio Station of the Year, BBC Radio 2, 2001, 2002, 2005 ; Sony Radio Station of the Year, BBC Radio 5 Live, 1996; Sony Silver, Best Phone In, The Magazine, BBC Radio 5 Live, 1996; British Environment and Media Awards, Best TV Documentary, Badgering The Diggers, 1992; Royal Television Society Journalism Awards, Special Commendation, After Hillsborough, 1989.
Education: Wirral Grammar School; University of Leeds
Career highlights: Working through the night to produce a special edition of the Sheffield Star

marking the missile attack on HMS Sheffield during the Falklands War; seeing my by-lined front page story for the Sheffield Star about Princess Diana visiting Derbyshire turned into a 'readers offer' tea towel; working with Stuart Hall on Northwest Tonight, and Brian Redhead on Close Up North, stars in very different ways. Winning a Special Commendation from the Royal Television Society for a BBC Northwest and BBC North joint programme about the Hillsborough disaster.

Mentor: Lots of people have helped me down the years. Peter Goodman at the Sheffield Star, Olwyn Hocking at BBC North West, Bill Rodgers at 5 Live, Andrew Thorman at Countryfile, Jim Moir and now Lesley Douglas at Radio 2.

Big break: Having music as a hobby. It helped get me my job in Radio 2.

Big mistake: Not realising that the very tall BBC trainee sent to work on The Really Useful Show (day-time BBC1 consumer show) was a comic genius. We sent Stephen Merchant out on OBs!

» **Reading:** *Guardian Unlimited, bbc.co.uk, Saturday Telegraph, and which ever Sunday newspaper has made it to our local newsagent with all (or most) of its supplements. Assorted magazines – the Word, the Week.* **Watching:** *Comedy, documentaries, and design shows. Grand Designs Abroad, then No Direction Home followed by Extras (the Les Dennis episode) would be a perfect evening.* **Listening:** *All sorts of music for pleasure. Radio 2 obviously. Late Junction on Radio 3. Radio 4 and 5 Live for news and speech. Alan Green on 5 Live for the best footie phone-in anywhere, Ricky Gervais and Stephen Merchant on Xfm, Adrian Goldberg on Radio West Midlands.* **Relaxing to:** *Singing with the City of Birmingham Symphony Chorus, staggering around the British countryside, taking regular 'refreshment' breaks in pubs and cafés.*
» *Married, no children*

Lynn Barber

22.5.44

The Observer, 3–7 Herbal Hill, London EC1R 5EJ
T 020 7278 2332
E lynnbaba@aol.com

Occupation: Journalist and author

Publications: How to Improve Your Man in Bed (1973); The Single Woman's Sex Book (1975); The Heyday of Natural History (1980); Mostly Men (1991); Demon Barber (1998).

Awards: British Press Awards, Magazine Writer of the Year, 1986 and 1987 (commended 1992), Feature Writer of the Year 1990, Interviewer of the Year 1997 and 2002; What the Papers Say Award, Interviewer of the Year, 1990.

Education: The Lady Eleanor Holles School; St Anne's College, Oxford

Career highlights: Assistant Editor, Penthouse Magazine, 1967–72; Staff Writer, Sunday Express Magazine, 1984–89; Feature Writer, Independent on Sunday, 1990–93; Contributing Editor, Vanity Fair, 1992; Columnist, Sunday Times, 1993; currently Feature Writer, the Observer.

» **Relaxing to:** *Gossip.* » *Widowed, 2 daughters*

Andrew Barnes

27.11.59

124 Horseferry Road, London SW1P 2TX
T 020 7306 8200
E abarnes@channel4.co.uk

Occupation: Sales Director, Channel 4

Other positions: Chairman of the BACC; Member of the Advertising Association Council; Sit on the Board of Thinkbox.

Education: Hatfield Polytechnic

Career highlights: Joined Southern Television September 1979 and was appointed Deputy Sales Director in 1984, Head of Sales, C4 in 1991 and Sales Director in 1997. Greatest achievement is setting up the C4 sales department from scratch and endeavouring to sell and trade airtime in a different way against a dominant and powerful competitor. Over time developing the sell further and endeavouring to take brand leader status against a still dominant player.

Mentor: John Fox (TVS), Ron Miller (LWT) and Stewart Butterfield (C4).

Big break: Getting into television at an early age.

Big mistake: Always trying to attain a consensus.

» **Reading:** *The Sun, Observer, Arsenal programmes.* **Watching:** *Channel 4 and Sky Sports.* **Listening:** *My iPod which has a pretty wide selection of music on it. Radio – I flick between Capital, Heart and Virgin – Chris Moyles is a must in the morning.* **Relaxing to:** *Watching the Arsenal.* » *Married, 3 children*

Brian Barron

28.4.1940

98 Riverside Drive, 7a, New York, New York 10024, USA
T 001 917 69248 61
E brian.barron@bbc.co.uk

Occupation: BBC Correspondent based in New York

Other positions: Reporter, Western Daily Press, Bristol 1956–60; Subeditor, Evening World, Bristol 1961; Subeditor, Daily Mirror, London, 1962; Editor, Bristol Observer Weekly, 1963; Chief Subeditor, BBC External Services News, London, 1965; BBC Aden Correspondent, 1967; BBC Cairo Correspondent, 1968; BBC South East Asia Correspondent, 1969; BBC TV Reporter, London, 1972; BBC Far East Correspondent, 1974; BBC Africa Correspondent, 1977; BBC Ireland Correspondent, 1981; BBC Washington Correspondent, 1982; BBC Asia Correspondent, 1986; BBC New York Correspondent,1994; BBC Rome Correspondent, 2000; return to New York, 2005.

Publications: Many documentaries for BBC TV including the Fall of Saigon, 1975; the End of the Rhino, 1980; the Secret History of Mongolia, 1989; the Bridge of No Return (North Korea), 1991; the Iron Rice Bowl (Northern China), 1992.

Awards: Royal Television Society Journalist of the Year, 1980, for coverage of the overthrow of Idi Amin; ditto the coup that toppled Emperor Bokassar in central Africa; Royal Television Society International Reporting Award, 1986, for coverage of the volcanic eruption in Bolivia.

Education: Bristol Grammar School
Career highlights: After being an apprentice reporter on the Western Daily Press in the 50s, one year behind Tom Stoppard, I eventually joined the BBC in my mid-20s and quickly became a foreign correspondent and have remained one over a span of five decades; I spent six years off and on covering the Vietnam War and was there as the Northern Vietnamese tanks captured Saigon, and destroyed our camera car in the process. Between 1967 and 2003 I covered many wars and coups, including the Tiananmen Square democracy uprising in Beijing where I was arrested twice by the secret police and forced to write confessions of guilt before eventually being expelled; I covered both Gulf Wars and the final phase of the war to overthrow the Taliban (in Kandahar).
Mentor: Ernie Averis of the Evening World Bristol, and Kenneth Fairfax, Editor of BBC External Services News.
Big break: The single biggest exclusives were being the first foreign correspondent into liberated Kampala as Idi Amin fled in 1979, and 18 months later tracking him down internationally to his hideaway in Saudi Arabia, secretly agreeing to interview him, and smuggling our TV gear into Jeddah to do so.
Big mistake: Reporting the US military might have concealed heavy casualties in the invasion of Grenada in 1983 based on an exclusive interview with a British Defence Attaché with the US forces who got it wrong.

» **Reading:** *New York Times, Wall Street Journal, Financial Times, Guardian, Telegraph sometimes, Economist, Art Review, New Yorker, New York Review.* **Watching:** *News programmes, old movies, 24, international tennis.* **Listening:** *In New York, jazz and classical channels. In the UK, Radios 3 and 4.* **Relaxing to:** *Jogging very regularly, tennis, swimming in the summer, opera and classical music concerts, post-war art on both sides of the Atlantic.* » *Married to Angela, 1 daughter, Fleur*

John Bartle 23.8.48

Woodland, 214 Amersham Road, Hazlemere, High Wycombe, Bucks HP15 7QT
T 01494 558 196
E jb@john-bartle.com

Occupation: Non-executive and advisory roles with Guardian Media Group, Dare, i-Level, Garner International and Barnardo's

Other positions: Several advertising book contributions and many ad campaigns, especially at Bartle Bogle Hegarty (BBH).
Awards: CBE; FIPA; F.CAM; BA.
Education: Roundhay Grammar School, Leeds; Nottingham University
Career highlights: A founding partner of ad agency TBWA's London office in 1973. Starting BBH - several times agency of the year - in 1982 with my two partners; President of IPA 1995-97 and President of NABS, the charity for the communications industry, 2001-04.
Mentor: John Harvey (Cadbury Schweppes) and Stanley Pollitt (BMP).
Big break: Being invited to move from Cadbury Schweppes to the agency world in 1973.
Big mistake: Deciding that two newcomers - Hello magazine and IKEA - wouldn't succeed in the UK.

» **Reading:** *Guardian, Observer, Campaign, BBC History Magazine, Golf World, Leeds United programmes and lots of books.* **Watching:** *Sport, more sport, films and Spooks.* **Listening:** *The great American songbook and singers, and jazz.* **Relaxing to:** *Playing (golf) and watching sport, reading, and my 4 granddaughters.* » *Married, 2 children*

Brian Barwick 21.6.54

Football Association, 25 Soho Square, W1D 4FA
T 020 7745 4545

Occupation: Chief Executive, Football Association

Education: Rudston Road County Primary School; Quarry Bank Comprehensive School; Liverpool University
Career highlights: Journalist/Subeditor, North Western Evening Mail, Barrow-in-Furness, 1976-79; BBC Television (Sport), Assistant Producer, 1979-84; Producer, Football Focus, 1982-84; Assistant Editor, Grandstand, 1984-88; Editor, Match of the Day, 1988-95; Sportsnight, 1990-94; World Cup coverage, 1990 and 1994; Olympics, 1992 and 1996; Sports Review of the Year, 1991-95; Head, Sport Production, 1995-97; Controller, ITV Sport, 1998-2004; Director of Programming, ITV2, 1998-2001.

» **Watching:** *Sport, football, boxing and cricket, British TV comedy.* **Listening:** *Contemporary music.* **Relaxing to:** *Sports and comedy memorabilia collecting, holidaying with family.* » *Married, 2 children*

Peter Bazalgette 23.5.57

Shepherds Building Central, Charecroft Way, Shepherds Bush, London W14 0EE
T 020 8222 4453
E peter.bazalgette@endemoluk.com

Occupation: Chairman, Endemol UK; Chief Creative Officer, Endemol Group

Other positions: Non-Exec Director, YouGov; Deputy Chairman, National Film and Television School; Board Member, English National Opera.
Publications: Most recent book: Billion Dollar Game, (Time Warner 2005).
Awards: Fellow, BAFTA, 2000; Fellow, RTS, 2002; RTS, Judges Award 2003.
Education: Dulwich College; Fitzwilliam College, Cambridge
Career highlights: BBC News trainee 1977; Researcher, That's Life, 1978; Producer, Food and Drink; set up Bazal Productions in 1987, sold to Guardian Media Group 1990; joined Endemol 1998; McTaggart Lecture 1998; RTS Wheldon Lecture 2001.
Mentor: Esther Rantzen and Will Wyatt.
Big break: Creating Ready Steady Cook.
Big mistake: Not owning my own company at the time.

» **Reading:** *Guardian, FT, Spectator, Private Eye, plus fiction and non-fiction, widely.* **Watching:** *News, current affairs,* *drama and of course, reality.* **Listening:** *Radio 4, Magic, my children's iPods, classical CDs.* **Relaxing to:** *At the English National Opera or in my wine cellar.* » *Married, 2 children*

Claire Beale

27.11.70

174 Hammersmith Road, London W6 7JP
T 020 8267 4683
E claire.beale@haynet.com

Occupation: Editor, Campaign

Education: Manchester University
Career highlights: Media Editor, Marketing magazine; Deputy Editor, Campaign, 2000; Editor, Campaign, 2004.

» **Reading:** *Anything I can get my hands on.* **Watching:** *BBC2 comedies, Newsnight, CBeebies.* **Listening:** *The Today Programme, Radio 4.* **Relaxing to:** *A hot bath and early night.* » *Partner Martin, son Emerson*

Trevor Beattie

16 Short's Gardens, London WC2H 9AU
T 020 7632 0400
E trevor@bmbagency.com

Occupation: Founding Partner, Beattie McGuinness Bungay

Other positions: Chairman and Creative Director, TBWA Advertising.
Publications: Ad campaigns for Wonderbra, Hello Boys; French Connection, FCUK; Labour Party, Hague in Thatcher's Wig; Playstation; McCain; John Smiths.
Awards: None recently
Education: Wolverhampton Polytechnic
Career highlights: Weetabix If you know what's good for you; Bovver Boys TV ad campaign, 1980s; Hello Boys billboard campaign for Playtex Wonderbra, 1993; relaunching and rebranding French Connection UK as FCUK in 1997 and riding the ensuing media rollercoaster; working with Nelson Mandela and Muhammad Ali on UNICEF in 2000; working as Creative Director for TBWA for 14 years; working with Tony Blair on 3 consecutive Labour Election victories, creative highlight was presenting image of Hague in Thatcher's Wig to Blair at 10 Downing Street; writing for the Guardian and G2; setting up Beattie McGuinness Bungay (BMB) on Election Day 2005; planning the future of commercial space flight with Richard Branson and Virgin Galactic; travelling to space myself in 2008!
Mentor: Muhammad Ali
Big break: Getting a job in advertising.
Big mistake: Drinking my bodyweight in Chablis before being introduced to Natalie Imbruglia (I recently secured the patent on my TimeMachine© and will be popping back there soon to put things right).

» **Reading:** *Every newspaper I can get my hands on.* **Watching:** *Everything. I have Sky+, the world's greatest invention.* **Listening:** *My elders, and Test Match Special.* » *Gardening, flying*

Kevin Beatty

Associated Newspapers, Northcliffe House, 2 Derry Street, London W8 5TT
T 020 7938 6000
E jeni.jakovleva@md.assocnews.co.uk

Occupation: Managing Director, Associated Newspapers Ltd

Career highlights: Managing Director, Mail on Sunday, 1996-99; Managing Director, Evening Standard, 1999-2001; Managing Director, Associated Newspapers, 2001-present.

Dawn Bebe

17.4.66

Emap Elan, 4th Floor, Endeavour House, 189 Shaftesbury Avenue, Covent Garden, London WC2
T 020 7437 9011
E dawn.bebe@ecm.emap.com

Occupation: Managing Director, EMAP Elan

Other positions: Committee Member, British Society of Magazine Editors.
Awards: Winner, Magazine of the Year, PPA Awards, 1998; Most Improved Publication, EMAP Awards, 1998.
Education: Diploma in Journalism
Career highlights: Feature Writer, South Wales Echo, Just 17; Editor, Big!, Bliss, New Woman; Publishing Director, Red, 1999-2000; Publishing Director, New Woman, 1999-2000; Managing Director, Emap Elan Women's Media, 2000-02; Managing Director, Emap Elan, 2002-present.

Elaine Bedell

BBC Television Centre, Wood Lane, London W12 7RJ
T 020 8752 5592
E Elaine.bedell@bbc.co.uk

Occupation: Commissioning Editor, Features and Factual Entertainment, BBC

Awards: BAFTA (Best Entertainment Programme); British Comedy Award.
Education: Valentine's High School; Leeds University
Career highlights: BBC Trainee Producer; Producer, Start The Week, MidWeek (Radio 4); Series Producer, Clive James (BBC2); Producer, New Year's Eve shows (BBC1), Assignment (BBC2); Head of Factual Entertainment, Tiger Aspect. Set up own independent production company, Watchmaker Productions, to produce comedy, entertainment and factual programmes including Clarkson (BBC2), What a Performance (ITV), Clive James Show (ITV), Collins & Maccine's Movie Show (ITV), The Unforgettables (ITV), Rich Kids (Sky One), The Showbiz Set (C4). Following sale of Watchmaker to Chrysalis Group, became Managing Director Chrysalis Entertainment. Returned to BBC as Independent Executive to manage relationship between indies and BBC. Became Commissioning Editor, Features and Factual Entertainment in August 2005.

» **Relaxing to:** *Failing to cook, sleeping.*

Keith Beech

26.6.69

BBC WM, The Mailbox, Birmingham B1 1RF

T 0121 567 6025
E keith.beech@bbc.co.uk

Occupation: Managing Editor, BBC West Midlands

Other positions: Managing Editor, BBC Radio Suffolk; TV Producer, Bristol News; Editor, Radio Gloucestershire; Sports Editor, Radio Bristol.
Awards: Prevous winner of Sony gold for Station of the Year; Frank Gillard Awards; two golds at the British Diversity Awards.
Education: King Edward VI High School, Stafford
Career highlights: Lots of challenges over the years. Moving BBC WM to our new building here at The Mailbox was a pretty big task which went well. I was the News Editor at Radio Gloucestershire throughout the Fred West case and then trial. When I was Sports Editor in Bristol I was lucky enough to be main rugby commentator when Bath ruled on the rugby pitch, which was a great thrill.
Mentor: David Holdsworth gave me my first management job and is now again my boss in the West Midlands.
Big break: In a morbid way the Fred West story was a big break for me, and covering the story was a great experience.
Big mistake: When I was a rookie sports reporter I once announced that a cup game was called off because of bad weather only to later find out that the game was to be played. Several fans blamed me for missing the game.

» **Reading:** *To be honest I don't find the time to read as often as I should or I'd like.* **Watching:** *Sport remains a passion of mine so I watch a good match when I can. Currently Spooks is among my favourites and I was brought up with Coronation Street and still like to get a fix at least once a week.* **Listening:** *BBC WM of course!* **Relaxing to:** *I play rugby every Saturday which is an excellent distraction from the day job.* » *Married, 2 children*

Steve Beech

16.9.71

BBC Radio Nottingham, London Road, Nottingham NG2 4UU

T 0115 9021890
E steve.beech@bbc.co.uk

Occupation: News Editor, BBC Radio Nottingham

Education: University of Nottingham

» **Reading:** *The Times, Press Gazette.* **Watching:** *Shameless.* » *Married, 1 child*

Paul Belford

21.4.66

E p.belford@blueyonder.co.uk

Occupation: Advertising Creative Director and Art Director, freelance

Other positions: Ad campaigns for Waterstone's, Tate Gallery, Nissan, Sony Playstation, Oddbins, Le Creuset, Guinness Extra Cold, RSPCA, Snickers, the Economist.
Awards: Over 150 major advertising awards. In 2005, a Silver Nomination at D&AD. Gold at Cannes, Gold at The One Show and Gold at Campaign Poster Awards.
Education: Imperial College, University of London
Career highlights: After completing a PhD in Biochemistry, I began a career as an advertising art director in 1988; since then I've worked at some of London's top agencies, reaching the position of Creative Director at both Ogilvy and AMV BBDO; I'm often invited to judge awards schemes, lecture, write and teach all over the world, and last year was voted onto the D&AD Executive Committee by industry peers; I left AMV BBDO in autumn 2005.
Big break: Joining Leagas Delaney 10 years ago.

» **Reading:** *Currently reading Robert Brownjohn, Sex and Typography.* **Watching:** *More internet than TV.* **Listening:** *A very diverse 20Gb iTunes library.* **Relaxing to:** *Art, design, photography books.* » *Married*

Emily Bell

15.9.69

Guardian Unlimited, 119 Farringdon Road EC1R 3ER

T 020 7278 2332
E emily.bell@guardian.co.uk

Occupation: Editor-in-Chief, Guardian Unlimited

Other positions: Media Columnist for Guardian and Broadcast Magazine 1998-2000; Business Editor, the Observer.
Awards: AOP Editor of the Year 2003; 1999-2005 NPA Best newspaper website; 2005 Webby, Best newspaper website.
Education: King Edward VI, Louth; Christ Church, Oxford
Career highlights: Started at excellent magazine Big Farm Weekly (1987) straight out of college. Spent a year there and then 18 months at Campaign Magazine. Moved to the Observer in 1990, working as a business journalist. Became Business Editor for the Observer in 1998. In 2000 moved to Guardian Unlimited to set up mediaguardian.co.uk then became GU Editor-in-Chief in 2001.
Big break: Melvyn Marckus, Business Editor of the Observer giving me a job in 1990, after an interview that felt more like a gossip (very canny hiring technique).
Big mistake: Long long ago, following the direction of a useless editor to 'do a hatchet job'.

» **Reading:** *Not enough books - too many websites and newspapers.* **Watching:** *Everything (part of the job). Highlights - X Factor, Newsnight, Six Feet Under, Channel 4 News, Curb Your Enthusiasm, Weeds, Thick of It.* **Listening:** *Radio 4 - Today, Woman's Hour, Broadcasting House and The Archers; Radio 2 - Jonathan Ross & Janice Lory; Radio 3 - almost anything - even modern squeaky banging composers; Radio 1 - anything except Chris Moyles; World Service (past midnight); any of the many thousand tracks in the iTunes library.* **Relaxing to:** *By playing cards (badly) with friends, taking the kids to the galleries (relaxes me - but I suspect not the other art goers), running very very slowly, cooking, generously allowing my husband to wait on me hand and foot.* » *Married to Ed Crooks, 3 sons*

Nick Bell

15.1.61

JWT Ltd, 1 Knightsbridge Green, London SW1X 7NW

T 020 7656 7247
E nick.bell@jwt.com

Occupation: Executive Creative Director, JWT London

Other positions: Executive Creative Director, Leo Burnett; President, D&AD.
Publications: Mercedes, McDonalds, Heinz, John West, Ikea, the Economist, RSPCA, Smirnoff, Vodafone.
Awards: 2 D&AD silver Pencils, Cannes Grand Prix, 5 Cannes gold Lions, Andy Award of Excellence, 2 Clio golds, 10 Campaign Press silvers.
Education: Lancing College
Career highlights: First job, Post Boy, Ogilvy Benson and Mather; first proper job, Writer, Ted Bates 1986; big break, landing job as Writer at Abbott Mead Vickers 1987; joined Leo Burnett as Group Head, 1996; won D&AD silver and Cannes Grand Prix in 1997; appointed Deputy Executive Creative Director, 1998 and then Executive Creative Director, 1999. Won Campaign Advertiser of the Year for McDonalds, 1998, and Heinz, 2000; Leo Burnett won 3 D&AD silver awards and 3 Cannes Gold Lions in 2001 and became most awarded agency in world in film, 2001; elected President of D&AD by industry peers, 2003; in same year appointed Executive Creative Director of J Walter Thompson, London; part of team that won HSBC worldwide, 2004.
Mentor: Richard Foster, David Abbott (Abbott Mead Vickers).
Big break: Joining Abbott Mead Vickers.

» **Reading:** *Varied, though currently Stephen Fry. Other than that, hundreds upon hundreds of scripts.* **Watching:** *Film, documentary, news and too much sport.* **Listening:** *iPod shuffle while running and cycling.* **Relaxing to:** *With my wife, Angie and children, Tiffany, Elly-May and Charlie.*
» *Married, 3 children*

Zoe Bell

5.3.70

Biscuit Building, 10 Redchurch Street, London E2 7DD

T 020 7012 1999
E zoe@motherlondon.com

Occupation: Head of TV Production, Mother Advertising

Other positions: TV Producer; Production Assistant.
Publications: Tango, Pot Noodles, AA, Supernoodles, Cup-a-soup, Egg, Orange, Miller Genuine Draft.
Awards: BTAA; D&AD; Creative Circle; APA 50.
Education: Our Lady of Sion Convent, Worthing
Career highlights: Being hired at HHCL when it was the hottest creative shop in town; running my own company; joining Mother early on and being part of the whole growth experience; working on challenging projects that seemed insurmountable; Working with great talent; travelling the world.
Mentor: Steve Henry was, my husband is.
Big break: Being hired by HHCL when I was 25 and made Head of TV 6 months later.
Big mistake: Leaving HHCL just before they sold.

» **Reading:** *Sunday Times, books, trade press, magazines, children's books.* **Watching:** *Films, documentaries, comedy, comedy dramas, dramas.* **Listening:** *Anything.* **Relaxing to:** *Weekends in Norfolk with my husband and children, dinner with friends, massage, bathing – where I do most of my thinking.* » *Married, 3 children*

Julian Bellamy

1971

BBC Three, Television Centre, Wood Lane, London W12 7RJ

T 020 8743 8000
E julian.bellamy@bbc.co.uk

Occupation: Controller, BBC Three

Education: Sussex University; Cambridge University
Career highlights: Started television career as a freelance Assistant Producer working for Channel 4 and for ITV on investigative documentaries, then for Channel 4's Dispatches and ITV's The Big Story; Editor of Current Affairs, including The Mark Thomas Comedy Product, Channel 4, 1998-2001; Commissioning Editor, Factual in the Nations and Regions, including Football Stories, How To Rob A Bank and Football's Fight Club, and Commissioning Editor, Big Brother and Celebrity Big Brother, Channel 4, 2001-03; Head of Factual Entertainment, continued responsibility for Big Brother and Celebrity Big Brother, other credits include The Salon, Brat Camp, The Unteachables, Bollywood Star, The Sex Inspectors and The Banned Season, Channel 4, 2003-05; Head of E4 in addition to Factual Entertainment role, 2005-06; Controller, BBC Three, 2006-present.

Antony Bellekom

7.10.58

BBC Broadcasting House, London W1A 1AA

T 020 7765 4612
E antony.bellekom@bbc.co.uk

Occupation: Managing Editor, BBC Radio 2 and 6 Music

Education: MA City University, London; BSc Reading University
Career highlights: After a career in music and theatre production that encompassed work with punk bands, directing theatre in the hold of a cargo ship and producing opera in a cathedral, radio beckoned. Since the mid-80s radio work has included producing The Archers, being Managing Editor at BBC Radio Nottingham, Programme Director at talkSPORT and then back to the BBC to be the founding Managing Editor for 6 Music, and subsequently joining Radio 2.

» **Reading:** *Simenon, Leonard, Orwell ... as only one is alive and he is in his 80s, I seem to be catching up.* **Watching:** *American Football.* **Listening:** *Endless and reckless ... Ramones, Richard Thompson, Gotan Project, Michael Nesmith ... and almost ignored heroines from the 70s Judee Sill, Bridget St John, Mandy More.* **Relaxing to:** *Family, swim, garden, travel.* » *Married, 2 children*

Andy Benham

30.4.65

14th Floor, Tower House, Fairfax Street,
Bristol BS1 3BN
T 0117 9279009
E andybenham@originpublishing.co.uk

Occupation: Publisher, Origin Publishing

Other positions: Publishing Director, Emap Active; Publisher, Dennis Publishing.
Publications: BBC Music; BBC History; BBC Gardens Illustrated; BBC Wildlife; BBC Sky at Night; BBC Focus.
Awards: Don't believe in them, primarily because I've never won one.
Education: Imperial College
Career highlights: Moving the BBC specialist magazines to Bristol has been fun; recruiting new teams, almost from scratch, sorting out all the production issues and ensuring that the readers don't notice the difference has been interesting. Coming up with the idea, and then launching Home Entertainment magazine was fantastic, and I'm also really proud of launching Living History, and, more recently, Sky at Night. Although niche, specialist titles, they both manage to punch way above their weights. Probably the nicest thing about a career in publishing is that I've had the chance to work on over 50 titles, in loads of different markets, and you get to see the market dynamics of hugely different industries.
Mentor: I learnt most about publishing during my 7 years working with Felix Dennis, without doubt the best 'gut feel' publisher I've ever worked with.
Big break: As an editor at Dennis Publishing I forgot to remove my Emap visitor's badge coming back after an interview for the editor's job on Garden Answers; I was promoted to Publisher the next day.
Big mistake: Probably filling in this bloody survey.

» **Reading:** *Specialist magazines, the more obscure the better. The occasional Guardian on the train up to London, and, hopefully, everything I publish!* **Watching:** *Horizon, quality US soaps such as reruns of Hillstreet Blues, Grand Designs, almost anything historical.* **Listening:** *Wogan, Ross and Evans, plus a bit of Radio 3.* **Relaxing to:** *I'm a keen renovator of old buildings and really chill out by applying lime plaster.*
» *Married, no children*

David Benjamin

21.12.75

164 Deansgate, Manchester M60 2RD
T 0161 211 2266
E david.benjamin@men-news.co.uk

Occupation: Chief Operating Officer, GMG Regional Newspapers

Other positions: Managing Director, Manchester Evening News; Finance Director, GMG Regional Newspapers; Finance Director, Manchester Evening News.
Publications: Manchester Evening News; Metro; MEN Lite.
Education: BA (Hons) European Business; MBA
Career highlights: Appointed to the board of the Manchester Evening News as Finance Director aged 25; appointed Managing Director of Manchester Evening News aged 30; launched MEN Lite transforming MEN into part paid, part free newspaper; launched morning edition of MEN improving circulation by 5%; delivered successive increases in profitability to record levels.
Mentor: Fiona Parashar, founder of Leadership Coaching.
Big break: Being recruited by the Manchester Evening News as Financial Analyst.
Big mistake: Failing to anticipate the pace of migration of print advertising to online media.

» **Reading:** *Harvard Business Review, Economist, Guardian.* **Watching:** *Current affairs, Sky sports.* **Listening:** *Radio 5 live, Radio 2.* **Relaxing to:** *Eating out, playing with son, golf.*
» *Co-habiting, 1 child*

Roger Bennett

30.5.46

ELSPA, 167 Wardour Street, London W1F 8WL
T 020 7534 0580
E roger.bennett@elspa.com

Occupation: Director General, Entertainment & Leisure Software Publishers Association (ELSPA)

Other positions: Director, Newsfield Publications; Sales Manager, Birmingham Post and Evening Mail.
Publications: A number of White Papers, Annual International Games Industry Summit Conference; GameStars Live Consumer Show and Trade Expo; major anti-piracy campaign.
Awards: Annual Award 2001, person who has contributed most to the industry; Special Media Award, Successfully defending industry from disingenuous media frenzy!
Education: Kimbolton, Cambs
Career highlights: 1994, launch of new Computer & Video Games Voluntary Age Rating System; 2003, negotiating successful introduction of Pan European Age Ratings System, based on previous UK System; writing and developing Industry support for new European representative trade body constitution; initiating new industry charity, Entertainment Software Charity (ESC); starting and developing a very successful dedicated Anti-Piracy Unit team of 14 investigative and administrative staff.
Mentor: None
Big break: Joining Newsfield Publications, who specialised in dedicated computer games consumer magazines, which led directly to my present position.
Big mistake: Employing someone as a senior member of staff who subsequently created major staff problems and costs to the company.

» **Reading:** *Most daily and Sunday newspapers, the industry weekly trade paper, MCV, biographies, and when possible, good novels.* **Watching:** *Horse racing (NH), rugby, boxing, soccer, on TV political commentary, documentaries, movies, drama, comedy.* **Listening:** *Classic FM, Radio 4, Radio 5 Live.* **Relaxing to:** *Horse riding, gardening, reading, cooking, watching sport.* » *Divorced, 1 child*

Zai Bennett 6.5.78

200 Gray's Inn Road, London WC1X 8HF
T 020 7843 8332
E zai.bennett@itv.com

Occupation: Editor, ITV2

Education: University of London

» **Reading:** *Guardian, Heat, Time Out, Arena, Radio Times, TV Times.* **Watching:** *The Simpsons, the West Wing, Arrested Development and Larry Sanders.* **Listening:** *Radios 1 and 4.* » *Single*

Peter Bennett-Jones 12.3.59

7 Soho Street, London W1D 3DQ
T 020 7434 6700
E pbj@tigeraspect.co.uk

Occupation: Chairman, Tiger Aspect Group, PBJ Management and KBJ Management

Other positions: Chair, Comic Relief and Sport Relief; Director, Oxford Playhouse and theatreshare plc.
Publications: Exec producer and producer credits include Mr Bean, Harry Enfield Shows, The Vicar of Dibley, Blackadder Back and Forth, Gimme Gimme Gimme, The Thin Blue Line, The League of Gentlemen's Apocalypse, Kevin and Perry Go Large, Our House, and Lenny Henry.
Awards: For Tiger Aspect awards include BAFTAs, RTS, EMMY, International EMMY, Olivier, Golden Roses and Annecy Animation.
Education: Winchester; Cambridge
Career highlights: Representing many of the country's most talented writer-performers and presenters; building Tiger Aspect into the UK's leading multi-genre independent production company with a reputation for quality, integrity and a magnet for talent; chairing Comic Relief since 1997; winning Olivier Award for Best New Musical in 2003.
Mentor: Beryl Vertue, Richard Curtis and uber lawyer Mark Devereux.
Big break: Sharing a theatre at the Edinburgh Fringe with Atkinson and Curtis in 1976.
Big mistake: Producing a West End musical. Ouch.

» **Reading:** *A great deal - fiction, biography, history and anything disposable.* **Watching:** *Loads of television, especially comedy.* **Listening:** *Radios 2,4 and Five Live. Classic FM when running.* **Relaxing to:** *With difficulty but sometimes in a small boat on the high seas.* » *Married, 3 children*

Lee Bennion 21.11.78

BBC Radio Merseyside, 55 Paradise Street, Liverpool L1 3BP
T 0151 708 6161
E lee.bennion@bbc.co.uk

Occupation: Presenter, Merseyside Breakfast on BBC Radio Merseyside

Other positions: Senior Broadcast Journalist
Awards: Sony bronze, Boris and Bigley for News Story of the year 2005. Station won it but I was News Editor at the time.
Education: Chester Catholic High School; Cheltenham and Gloucester College of HE; University of Central England (postgrad)
Career highlights: Personal highlight in my career is getting an exclusive interview with Sir Paul McCartney. Other career highlights include becoming drive-time presenter at BBC Radio Merseyside at 25, working for the One O'Clock and Six O'Clock News as producer, covering stories from 9/11 to the Burnley Riots. Becoming News Editor at BBC Radio Merseyside, then becoming Breakfast Presenter in June 2005.
Mentor: Biggest influence on my career is my former News Editor Ruby Williams.
Big break: Difficult to say, but I suppose getting my first freelance reporter shift got the ball rolling.
Big mistake: Too many to mention - nothing major though!

» **Reading:** *Independent, Mirror, Observer. I enjoy reading biographies.* **Watching:** *Most sports, especially football. News programmes. New comedy and music channels.* **Listening:** *Radiowise, BBC Five Live, Radio 1, Radio 2 and of course Radio Merseyside! Musically I like Indie Rock.* **Relaxing to:** *Music, reading, TV, eating, drinking, sleeping...* » *Married, no children*

Glenwyn Benson 24.11.51

Room 3220 White City, 201 Wood Lane, London W12 7TS
T 020 8752 6178
E glenwyn.benson@bbc.co.uk

Occupation: Controller, BBC Factual TV

Other positions: Joint Director, BBC Factual and Learning
Publications: BBC Learning Campaigns, especially computer literacy in the mid-1990s.
Awards: BBC News and Factual Award 2004, awarded by Women in Film and Television.
Education: Cambridge University; Harvard; Charles University, Prague
Career highlights: Began in local newspaper journalism, spent most of my TV career in journalism at LWT and then the BBC. Head of Science and Specialist Factual from the mid-1990s.
Mentor: Jana Bennett
Big break: Becoming Editor of Panorama.
Big mistake: Don't dwell on it!

» **Reading:** *History.* **Watching:** *Drama, especially 24.* **Listening:** *Radio 4 on weekend mornings.* **Relaxing to:** *Walking in Hyde Park.* » *Married, 2 children*

Laurie Benson

Brettenham House, Lancaster Place, London WC2E 7TL
T 020 7322 1205
E laurie_benson@timemagazine.com

Occupation: Publishing Director, Time Magazine, Europe, Middle East and Africa

Other positions: Formerly Senior Vice-President Sales, Home and Garden Television; Senior Vice-President Sales, Oxygen Media.
Education: University of Minnesota
Mentor: Jon Mandel, Co-CEO Mediacom.
Big break: My first job at CNN.
Big mistake: Leaving CNN

» **Reading:** *International newspapers, Time magazine.* **Watching:** *International news channels, Channel 4, More4.* **Listening:** *Music from all over the world.* **Relaxing to:** *Yoga, horse riding.* » *Single, no children*

Josh Berger

Warner House, 98 Theobolds Road, London WC1X 8W
T 020 7984 5000

Occupation: Executive Vice-President and Managing Director, Warner Bros UK

Other positions: Member, Young Presidents Organization; Member, Council on Foreign Relations; Board Member, CanalSatellite Digital, Spain.
Education: Harvard University
Career highlights: Sales Executive, Warner Bros International Television Distribution (WBITD), France, 1989-91; Managing Director, WBITD Spain and Portugal, including Business Development, Europe, 1991-95; Vice-President, WBITD Spain and Portugal, 1994-97; Vice-President, Licensing and Business Development, Europe, 1997-99; Senior Vice-President, International Sales and Business Development, and Managing Director, Warner Bros Europe, 1999-2002; Executive Vice-President and Managing Director, Warner Bros UK, 2002-present.

David Bergg

ITV Broadcasting, 200 Gray's Inn Road, London WC1X 8HF
T 020 7843 8000
E dutyoffice@itv.com

Occupation: Director of Programme Strategy, ITV

Career highlights: Qualified as PE teacher; began broadcasting career in the mid-1980s in audience research departments at Ulster, Grampian, Tyne Tees, LWT and TV-am; subsequently Head of Programme Acquisition, TV-am; Controller of Marketing and Research, GMTV; Scheduler, BBC1, 1994-96; Launch Controller of Planning and Programme Acquisition, Channel 5, 1996-97; Director of Planning and Strategy, ITV Network Centre, 1997-2000; General Manager, Sky One, 2000-01; Director of Programmes, ITV2, 2001-02; Director of Programme Strategy, ITV, 2002-present.

Ralph Bernard

11.2.53

Classic FM House, Swallow Place, London W1B 2AG
T 020 7343 9000
E shona.harvey@gcapmedia.com

Occupation: Executive Chairman, GWR Group plc

Other positions: Chairman, London News Radio (LBC and News Direct), 1996-2001; Chairman, Campaign Board, Great Western Hospital, Swindon, 2000-02; Chairman, Digital One Ltd, 1998-present; Director, Independent Radio News, 1994-present.
Awards: Fellow, Radio Academy, 1999; Sony Gold Award, 2000.
Education: Caterham High School, Ilford
Career highlights: Copy Boy, London News Service, 1970-71; Reporter, Express and Independent, Leytonstone, 1971-72; Stratford Express, 1972-73; Cambridge Evening News, 1973-75; Radio Journalist, 1975-78, Documentaries Editor, 1978-80, Radio Hallam, Sheffield; News Editor, Hereward Radio, Peterborough, 1980-82; Programme Controller, 1982-83, Managing Director, Wiltshire Radio, 1983-85; Pre-launch Manager, Classic FM, 1991.

» **Listening:** *Most music.* **Relaxing to:** *Walking, newspaper originals, cricket.* » *Married, 4 daughters*

Michael Betton

4.2.62

Lincs fm Group Limited, Witham Park, Waterside South, Lincoln LN5 7JN
T 01522 549900
E janeriddle@lincsfm.co.uk

Occupation: Chief Executive, Lincs fm Group Limited

Education: Ipswich School; St Edmund Hall Oxford; Open University
Career highlights: Management Trainee, Suffolk Group Radio, 1984-85; Station Co-ordinator, Saxon Radio, 1985-86; Ocean Sound, Programme Controller, 1986-89; Programme Director, 1989; Prog Director and Deputy Managing Director, 1989-90; Managing Director, 1990; Lincs fm, Managing Director, 1991-98; Chief Executive, 1998-present.

» **Relaxing to:** *Travel, tennis, food and drink.*
» *Married, 3 children*

Hilary Bevan Jones

British Academy of Film and Television Arts, 195 Piccadilly, London W1J 9LN
T 020 7734 0022
E info@bafta.org

Occupation: Deputy Chairman, BAFTA

Other positions: Founder, Tightrope Pictures, 2003.
Publications: Drama Producer credits include Cracker, Far From the Madding Crowd, Frank Stubbs Promotes, The Secret World of Michael Fry, Butterfly Collectors, May 33rd, Dad, and State Of Play. As Producer, Red Dwarf, Not The Nine

O'Clock News, Blackadder, Merlin, Shakespeare, Open Golf, Blue Peter and Top of the Pops.
Awards: Sony Pictures Television International Contribution to the Medium Award, Women in Film, 2004.
Career highlights: Teacher, Essex County Council; Assistant Floor Manager, BBC, 1979; Producer, BBC, 1988; Producer, Granada Television; Producer, State of Play, 2003; Co-founder, Endor Productions, 1994; Co-founder, Tightrope Pictures, 2003.

Peter Biles 16.12.58

BBC News, 1 Park Road, Richmond 2092, Johannesburg, South Africa
T + 27 11 482 2305
E peter.biles@bbc.co.uk

Occupation: BBC Southern Africa Correspondent

Education: University of Natal, Durban
Career highlights: Prior to becoming BBC Southern Africa Correspondent, I was a World Affairs Correspondent based in London. Joined the BBC in 1984, working as a reporter for The World At One, PM and The World This Weekend. A lifelong passion for Africa drew me to Kenya in 1989 where I was a correspondent for the BBC, the Guardian and the Observer. During three tumultuous years in East Africa, I witnessed the climax to 30 years of war in Ethiopia and Eritrea with the fall of the Mengistu regime, and the political disintegration of Somalia after the overthrow of Siad Barre's dictatorship. I have taken a close interest in the career of Nelson Mandela and was at ANC headquarters in Zambia on the day of Mandela's release from prison in 1990. Also reported from South Africa in 1994 during the country's first democratic elections when Mandela became President. As a foreign affairs specialist, reported from more than 60 countries for the BBC.
» **Listening:** *BBC World Service.* **Relaxing to:** *Listening to African jazz.* » *Married, 2 children*

Hugh Birley 7.11.58

8 Bolsover Street, London W1W 6AB
T 020 7908 6488
E hbirley@lexispr.com

Occupation: Chief Executive, Lexis Public Relations

Other positions: Chairman, PRCA Best Practice Committee.
Publications: Dove Real Women, Domino's franchising, Barclays Premiership.
Awards: Marketing Magazine's PR Agency of the Year, 2004; Marketing Society Marketing Communications award, 2005; Sunday Times Top 10 Best Small Companies to Work For, 2004; PR Week Campaign of the Year award, 2004.
Education: Winchester College; London University
Career highlights: Started my career in the music industry as a publicist representing many artists including David Bowie, The Specials and Blondie; in 1990 moved into PR consultancy and joined Scope: communications as Director Consumer Brands with clients including Carlsberg, Allied Domecq, McDonalds and BT; joined the Lexis board in 1995 and in the next five years helped the company grow to become one of the most successful independents in the UK; led a management buy-out of the founders in 2002 and the expansion of the agency into sports, healthcare and public sector specialisms; with extensive experience of brand, corporate and sponsorship communications I currently advise clients including NTL, Diageo, Hutchison 3G mobile (Three), William Grant and Sons, eSure and Music Choice, a digital satellite music channel.
Mentor: James Maxwell and Richard Aldwinckle at Scope showed me how to be more than a publicist.
Big break: Getting my first job as a label-licker in the Decca records press office; then years later being asked by Bill Jones and Tim Adams, the founders of Lexis, to help them grow and run the business.
» **Reading:** *I consume newspapers and magazines of all kinds – all human life is there! And I collect old fishing and motorcycling books.* **Watching:** *CSI, Discovery Real Time, news and movies.* **Listening:** *CD compilations my daughter makes me and lots of vinyl from a large collection accumulated mostly free when I worked in the record business.* **Relaxing to:** *Fishing, walking, pubbing, motorcycling and talking to my charming and very talented wife and family.* » *Married, 2 children*

Lord John Birt 10.12.44

House of Lords, London SW1A 0PW
T 020 7219 3000
E cloudsdalel@parliament.uk

Occupation: Broadcaster

Other positions: Member, Wilton Park Academic Council 1980-83; Vice-President, Royal Television Society 1994-2001; Visiting Fellow, Nuffield College, Oxford 1991-99.
Publications: The Harder Path (autobiography), 2002; various articles in newspapers and journals.
Awards: Emmy Award, US National Academy of Television, Arts and Sciences 1995; Honorary Fellow, University of Wales, Cardiff, 1997; Honorary D Litt, Liverpool John Moores, 1992; City, 1998; Honorary D Litt, Bradford, 1999.
Education: St Mary's College, Liverpool; St Catherine's College, Oxford
Career highlights: Producer, Nice Time, Granada Television, 1968-69; Joint Editor, World in Action, Granada Television, 1969-70; Producer, The Frost Programme, LWT,1971-72; Executive Producer, Weekend World, LWT, 1972-74; Head of Current Affairs, LWT, 1974-77; Co-Producer, The Nixon Interviews, 1977; Controller of Features and Current Affairs, LWT, 1977-81; Director of Programmes, LWT, 1982-87; Deputy Director-General, BBC, 1987-92; Dir-General, BBC, 1992-2000; Adviser, McKinsey & Co., 2000-05; Chairman, Lynx New Media, subsequently Lynx Capital Ventures, 2000-03; Non-executive Director, PayPal (Europe) Ltd, 2004-present; Adviser to Prime Minister on Criminal Justice, 2000-01; Personal Adviser to the Prime Minister (Blue Skies Thinking) 2001-05; Member, Cabinet Office Strategy Board, 2003-2005; Member, Media Law Group, 1983-94; Opportunity 2000 (formerly

Women's Economic) Target Team, BITC, 1991-98; International Council, Museum of TV and Radio, New York, 1999. Broadcasting Research Unit: Member, Working Party on the New Technologies, 1981-83; Member, Executive Committee, 1983-87; FIEE (CompIEE 1998).

» **Relaxing to:** *Football, walking, cinema.* » *2 children*

Christopher Bisco 30.12.50

Newspaper House, Dalston Road, Carlisle CA2 5UA
T 01228 612266
E chris.bisco@cngroup.co.uk

Occupation: Managing Director, Publishing Division, CN Group

Other positions: Chairman, Cumbria Creative Industries Partnership; Director, Association of British Choral Directors; Trustee, Austin Friars St. Monica's School.
Education: Gilberd School, Colchester
Career highlights: Managing Director (Publishing Division), CN Group Ltd, since 2001; responsible for the newspaper publishing and associated activities of the CN Group in Cumbria, Northumbria and Scotland; previously Deputy Managing Director, Portsmouth Publishing & Printing Limited and MD of West Sussex Newspapers; worked for Robert Maxwell as Commercial Director of British Newspaper Printing Corporation plc and at Mirror Group Newspapers; prior to joining Portsmouth Publishing & Printing Limited, worked as a management consultant on general management and finance assignments for KPMG, including a spell overseas in Pakistan; earlier career in convenience food industry as a market accountant and commercial manager, with Cadbury-Schweppes Foods and Unilever, developing very well-known consumer brands; before that with the Official Receiver's department as Examiner in Companies Winding-up, and at NatWest Bank; Fellow, Chartered Association of Certified Accountants; Member, Institute of Management Consultants.
Mentor: Mr Ambridge, primary school teacher, and John Jordan, Partner, Peat Marwick Mitchell & Co.
Big break: Joining Unilever as a market accountant.
Big mistake: Joining Robert Maxwell at Mirror Group.

» **Reading:** *Mostly newspapers.* **Watching:** *Rain falling in Cumbria.* **Listening:** *Ditto.* **Relaxing to:** *What's that?* » *Married, 3 children*

Simon Blackmore 30.11.74

50 Lisson Street, London NW1 5DF
T 020 7453 1600
E simon.blackmore@oneword.co.uk

Occupation: Managing Director, Oneword Radio Limited

Other positions: Managing Director, Unique Facilities; Business Development, BBC Music Entertainment; Operations Director, Sonic Arts; Production, Heart 106.2; Studio Manager, Chop Em Out.
Awards: The Clarion Award for radio broadcasting won by Oneword Radio.
Education: Hayes School, Kent
Career highlights: Left school in 1987 and started as a tech op at audio production house, Chop Em Out; after nine years went to Heart 106.2 as part of the launch team and left two years later to help set up Sonic Arts; moved to the BBC working within the Music Entertainment department before joining UBC Media Group in 2000 as Operations Director for their studio operation, Unique Facilities; moved to the MD role in 2001 and in 2004 took responsibility for UBC's national digital radio station Oneword; following the sale of a 51% stake in Oneword to Channel 4, became MD of Oneword in April 2005.
Mentor: Tim Blackmore
Big break: Being given the opportunity to be part of the launch of Heart 106.2.
Big mistake: Leaving Rick Dees' Heart 106.2 weekend show in my locked drawer while I went on a weekend away in deepest Wales where mobile phones didn't work.

» **Reading:** *BBC News online, Guardian Unlimited, the Week, Broadcast, Radio Magazine, Independent on Sunday and Management Today.* **Watching:** *Spooks, The West Wing, Sopranos, Grand Designs and the odd soap.* **Listening:** *BBC Radios 1, 2 and 4, LBC, Virgin, Xfm and Oneword.* **Relaxing to:** *TV, curry and a glass of red.* » *Married, 3 children*

Tim Blackmore 4.7.48

UBC Media Group, 50 Lisson Street, London NW1 5DF
T 020 8987 9673
E tim@timblackmore.com

Occupation: Editorial Director, UBC Media Group

Other positions: Chairman, CGDL; Chairman, Smooth Operations; Director, Oneword Ltd; Chairman, The Unique Broadcasting Company Ltd; Chairman, Sony Radio; Academy Awards.
Awards: MBE; Fellowship of the Radio Academy.
Education: King's School Pontefract; Blyth Grammar School
Career highlights: One of four people hired by the BBC's Gramophone Department to launch Radio One in 1987; Noel Edmonds' first radio producer; wrote and produced the 26 part Story of Pop before joining Capital Radio as Head of Programmes; left in 1983 to become the first Director of the Radio Academy; in 1989 founded the Unique Broadcasting Company with Simon Cole which floated as UBC in 2000; for 21 years wrote and produced the annual Ivor Novello Awards Show and in the late 80s produced the BRITS Show.
Mentor: The late Teddy Warrick.
Big break: Being hired for the launch of Radio 1.
Big mistake: Staying at Capital Radio when they refused to appoint me to the board.

» **Reading:** *Biographies, social and political history, the Week, Private Eye, Guardian and Independent.* **Watching:** *Lots of news and The West Wing.* **Listening:** *The Today Progamme, documentaries on Radio Two, Chris Evans, Between the Lines on Oneword.* **Relaxing to:** *DIY, drinking wine, and six grandchildren.* » *Married, 2 children*

Mike Blair

16.4.64

ITV Central, Gas Street, Birmingham B1 2JT
T 0121 634 4212
E Mike.Blair@itv.com

Occupation: Controller, News and Regional Programmes, ITV Central

Other positions: Head of Factual, Oxford Scientific Films/Southern Star; Head of Regional Programmes, Carlton TV (Midlands).
Publications: Central Regional programme schedule ... and Central News × 3.
Awards: A few but I don't like to show off.
Education: Harraby Comprehensive, Carlisle
Career highlights: Working at Raymonds News Agency. Leaving Raymonds News Agency. Reading the news on Radio Trent and reporting for local and network radio on the miners' strike. Getting a reporter's job at Central Television. Making my first network documentary for ITV while still in the newsroom. Reporting from Israel during the first Gulf War. Switching codes and working for Central's Current Affairs and Documentary department. Devising Motorway, Trauma, Flying Medics, Waterworld and Landladies for the regional schedule. Heading Carlton's Regional Programming Department. Joining Oxford Scientific Films as Head of Factual, making wildlife films for BBC, Channel 4, Discovery and National Geographic. Taking over as Controller of News and Regional Programming for ITV Central.
Big break: Getting an exclusive interview for a local news programme which led to a one hour network documentary, several awards, plaudits from the company (and no wage rise).
Big mistake: Trying to get rid of a cough during a live radio bulletin by drinking the nearest thing to hand ... it turned out to be a cup of cold coffee filled with cigarette butts.

» **Reading:** *Selection of papers during the week (Guardian on a Monday!). Family commitments permitting, a selection of papers at the weekend. Lots of books late into the night.* **Watching:** *X Factor or anything starring Ant and Dec with the children. Dramas and documentaries with the wife. Sport with 'the lads'.* **Listening:** *Radio 5 for news while travelling, Radio 4 comedy, Radio 2 on a Saturday, and the (current) 1200 songs on my iPod.* **Relaxing to:** *Time out with the family, going to the gym and playing 70s punk on the above-mentioned iPod at full volume.* » *Married, 2 children*

Sir Maurice (Victor) Blank

9.11.42

Trinity Mirror, 1 Canada Square, London E14 5AP
T 020 7293 3000
E lora.fitzsimons@gusplc.com

Occupation: Chairman, Trinity Mirror plc (to May 2006)

Other positions: Chairman, GUS plc; Chairman, Williams plc; Chairman, WellBeing of Women (formerly Birthright) 1989-present; Member, Council, University of Oxford 2000-present; Member, Financial Reporting Council, 2003-present; Member, Advisory Council, Orchestra of the Age of Enlightenment.
Publications: Weinberg and Blank on Takeovers and Mergers.
Awards: Honorary Fellow, St. Catherine's College, Oxford; Honorary Fellow, Royal College of Obstetricians and Gynacologists, 1998; Freeman, City of London.
Education: Stockport Grammar School; St Catherine's College, Oxford
Career highlights: Partner, Clifford-Turner (solicitors), 1969-81; Charterhouse plc, Head of Corporate Finance and Managing Director, Charterhouse Bank Ltd, 1981-85; Chief Executive, 1985-96; Chairman, 1991-97; Chairman, Charterhouse Bank Ltd, 1985-97; Chairman, Mirror Group, 1998-99, Chairman, Trinity Mirror plc, 1999-present; Deputy Chairman, Coats plc (formerly Coats Viyella plc), 1999-2003 (Non-executive director 1989-2003); GUS plc (formerly The Great Universal Stores plc), Non-executive Director, 1993-present; Deputy Chairman, 1996-2000, Chairman, 2000-present; Non-executive director, Williams plc 1995-2000, Chubb plc 2000-04; Industrial and Development Advisory Board, 1999-2004; Trustee, Oxford University Law Foundation, 1998-2001; Adviser, Oxford Environmental Change Unit; RSA; Vice-President, Oxford Philomusica; Chairman of Governors, UCS; Member, City of London Solicitors' Company, Law Society; CIMgt.

» **Relaxing to:** *Family, cricket, tennis, theatre.*
» *Married, 3 children*

Helen Boaden

2.3.60

Room 5601 Television Centre, Wood Lane, London W12 7RJ
T 020 8743 8000
E helen.boaden@bbc.co.uk

Occupation: Director, BBC News

Other positions: Radio Tees and Radio Aire, 1981-83; BBC Radio Leeds, News Producer, 1983; Reporter then Editor of Radio 4's File on 4; presented Woman's Hour and produced and presented features and documentaries for Radio 4; Reporter on Brass Tacks, BBC2; appointed Head of Business Programmes, BBC, 1997; appointed Head of Current Affairs, BBC, 1998; appointed Controller, Radio 4, 2000; appointed Controller, BBC7 (as well as Radio 4) 2002; appointed Director, BBC News, 2004.
Awards: 2 Sony Gold awards for File on 4; 2 Sony Gold awards, Radio Station of the Year, Radio 4, 2003 & 2004; Radio Industrial Journalist of the Year and Campaigning Industrial Journalist of the Year.
Education: University of Sussex; London College of Printing

» *Married*

Murray Boland

Celador Productions, 39 Long Acre, London WC2 9LG
T 020 7845 6999
E tvhits@celador.co.uk

Occupation: Head of Factual Entertainment, Celador Productions

Career highlights: Began career in broadcasting as a reporter on a range of entertainment and factual programmes including Network 7; Assistant Producer, BBC; Producer, The Big Breakfast pilot, Channel 4, 1991; Co-deviser and Producer, The Sunday Show, BBC 2; Producer, The Word, Channel 4; Director of Programmes, MTV, including Video Clash, Cribs, Fanatic and Singled Out; Head of Programmes, E4, 2002-05; Head of Digital Programming, 2003-05, E4, including Infamous Fives, A Wife for William, The Pilot Show, Your Face or Mine, Desperate Housewives, The OC, Six Feet Under, Curb Your Enthusiasm, and Lost; Advisory Chair, Edinburgh International TV Festival, 2004; Head of Factual Entertainment, Celador Productions, 2005-present.

Paul Boon

29.7.57

25 High Street, Rothwell, Northants NN14 6AD
T 01536 418558
E paul.boon@theradiomagazine.co.uk

Occupation: Managing Editor and Director, The Radio Magazine

Other positions: Previously Chair of The Association for Broadcasting Development; radio presenter; producer; licence application consultant and various TV and radio production positions.
Publications: The weekly production of the radio industry's news magazine.
Education: Gloucestershire College of Art and Technology; South West London College
Career highlights: Starting off in pirate radio in the early 1980s I went on to chair a radio deregulation lobby group, The Association for Broadcasting Development. The ABD was credited by the Home Office for the cessation of punitive needle-time restrictions and with the lifting of the ban on UK commercial radio stations playing American-produced Station IDs, at a time when the BBC could. But my biggest achievement here was to create the framework which led the way to the country's first new tier of specialist radio stations. Acknowledged by the Home Secretary of the day, it led to Jazz fm, Melody, Kiss 100, Sunrise Radio and other stations taking to the air; I produced the first ever Mrs Merton radio script, which was declined by the agency! I recorded a fly-on-the-wall documentary on Formula 1 for Radio 5 Live and later flew around the world with Bernie Ecclestone's digital TV company.
Mentor: My old boss in my last 9-5 job, who taught me the value of the written word.
Big break: Having a serving Cabinet Minister as my local MP at a time when lobbying for more, less-regulated commercial radio.

» **Reading:** *The Guardian, Sunday Times, Private Eye and books - generally but not exclusively about music.* **Watching:** *Mostly contemporary TV comedy.* **Listening:** *Radio 4, Radio 2, 6 Music, my local GCap station and Virgin, but mostly songs from my iTunes selection.* **Relaxing to:** *When not drinking a glass of red wine with good friends - looking around record shops. I enjoy the tactile experience not afforded by the world of the download.* » *Married, 3 children*

Mark Borkowski

71 Kingsway, London WC2B 6ST
T 020 7404 3000
E Sarahb@borkowski.co.uk

Occupation: Owner and Operator, Borkowski PR

Other positions: Pork pie salesman, theatre publicist; freelance PR and entrepreneur.
Publications: Relaunch of Action Man; relaunch of Cliff Richard; launch of Smart Car; relaunch of Hovis, Horlicks, Complan; launch of Trevor Beattie's FCUK campaign; relaunch of Selfridges; launch of alcopops - Bacardi Breezer and Smirnoff Ice.
Awards: Various PR Week awards that are now gathering dust.
Education: None
Career highlights: I seem to have an ability to generate stories which grab the headlines, and as a result have developed a firm belief in challenging orthodox public relations theory. My agency is founded on a culture of radical, innovative thinking and thrives on linking creativity to commercial needs. I really appreciate good showmanship. In the Barnum tradition, I walked across the Alps with Ian Botham and two elephants, and generated the only interesting event ever to be held in the Millennium Dome - a world record custard pie fight involving 1000 people. My first freelance work was as a publicist to a single-seat theatre on the sidecar of a 750cc motorcycle, and whilst the youngest publicist in the West End, I handled Brenda Blethyn and six other naked actresses in a swimming pool on stage. And once sacked Michael Jackson, all in the interests of promoting product. Clients, products and events include Prince, Graham Norton, Eddie Izzard and Joan Rivers.
Mentor: Philip Hedley, the ex-Director of the Theatre Royal, Stratford East. He taught me everything about bravery and risk.
Big break: Persuading someone to give me a job in theatre and having a boss who allowed me to do whatever I wanted to do.
Big mistake: Promoting alcopops.

» **Reading:** *Every newspaper daily, key media blogs, GQ, Condé Nast Traveller, Harry Crews, Philip K Dick.* **Watching:** *The Simpsons, the Sopranos, Lost, Curb Your Enthusiasm, Dick and Dom in Da Bungalow, Soccer am.* **Listening:** *Depends on my mood. Killers and Razorlight, Clash to Neil Young, Terry Allen to Marvyn Gaye via Miles Davies and Led Zeppelin.* **Relaxing to:** *Adventures with my wife and children, collecting anecdotes.* » *Married, with 2 children, Janek and Joe*

Bridget Boseley

30.12.69

200 Gray's Inn Road, London WC1X 8HF
T 020 7843 8297
E bridget.boseley@itv.com

Occupation: Controller of Factual Programmes, ITV1

Other positions: Controller of Features, Granada North; Editor, Network Entertainment and Features, BBC Manchester.
Publications: Exec produced 100 Greatest ... strand, After They Were Famous specials, Spoilt Rotten; commissioned Bad Lads Army, Holiday Showdown, Ladette to Lady, Deep Jungle, 49 Up, Real Life strand.
Awards: RTS Award - Holiday Showdown, Features and Factual, 2004; BAFTA Nomination for After They Were Famous: The Sound of Music Children, 2004.
Education: Nottingham High School for Girls; University of Sussex
Career highlights: Highlights include working in the BBC's Youth Department, particularly on Rough Guide, as it enabled me to travel all over the world in my early 20s. The department was a very exciting environment to work in. It was hard work and very tough but it gave young people real opportunities and breaks that they would have had to wait years for in other areas of television. As an exec at the BBC, highlights include a Theme Night for BBC2 on George Best, of which I was very proud, and working with the likes of Peter Kay and Paul Kaye (Dennis Pennis) and loads of other new talent on the Sunday Show. Building a Features Department into a thriving business at Yorkshire Television was another highlight. I had a great team and I hope I gave opportunities to talented people in the North to work on quality output. Becoming Controller of Factual Programmes at ITV was both thrilling and terrifying - and still is. There have been many highlights but commissioning here is like a rollercoaster ride, and you need a strong stomach!
Big break: Getting a researcher job on Rough Guides in Janet Street-Porter's 'yoof' department at the BBC.
Big mistake: Applying for and being offered a job in local radio as a roving reporter and then telling them I couldn't drive.

» **Reading:** *Mainly contemporary fiction. I am in a book club and have just read The Kite Runner (Khaled Hosseini) and Small Island (Andrea Levy). I'm also a magazine junkie.* **Watching:** *Coronation Street, West Wing, Desperate Housewives, The X Factor, I'm A Celebrity Get Me Out of Here, Jamie's School Dinners, 49 Up, Bleak House.* **Listening:** *Oasis, Coldplay, REM, Stevie Wonder, KT Tunstall, James Blunt.* **Relaxing to:** *At home with my family, having friends to stay, eating and drinking too much. Occasionally play tennis.*
» *Married, 2 girls, Grace and Flora*

Anna Botting

Sky News, British Sky Broadcasting, Grant Way, Isleworth, Middlesex TW7 5QD
T 0870 240 3000
E anna.botting@bskyb.com

Occupation: News Presenter, Sky News

Other positions: Originally a Reporter at Sky, before that Reporter/ Presenter at BBC Look North, in Newcastle, and Reporter at BBC Radio stations York, Humberside, Leeds, Cumbria. Began life as a Researcher on Granada Action, Granada TV.
Education: Ricards Lodge Comprehensive School, Wimbledon; Esher 6th Form College; St Edmund Hall, Oxford University; School of Journalism, Cardiff University
Career highlights: I worked in the North East at a time of momentous change. I stood outside the pits as the last five deep coal mines closed, the last shipyard closed, and the call centres moved in to absorb the unemployed. Moving to Sky News I've been on air during all the big recent wars - Kosovo, Afghanistan, Iraq, and for the downfall of some of the infamous leaders - Slobodan Milosovic and Saddam Hussein. I was the first person reporting outside Kensington Palace on the day Diana died, as double-decker bus drivers shouted in disgust, tarring us all with the paparazzi brush. I witnessed the same public mourning, presenting live in Krakow, in Poland for the death of Pope John Paul II, heading on to Rome for his extraordinary funeral. Followed the Lib Dems in the 1997 election campaign, and more recently was on air for each of David Blunkett's resignations. Separately from news, took part in a 'celebrity' Oxford and Cambridge boat race, for BBC1 and BBC3, and filmed my participation in the Fastnet race for Sky.
Mentor: All fluent journalists who can tell a great story.
Big break: An IRA bomb attack, a derailed train, and a hijacked plane - all in the first half hour of my first presenting shift at Sky. One of my bosses happened to be watching.
Big mistake: So many! Is it cumulative?

» **Reading:** *Wires, daily, hundreds of pages of them.* **Watching:** *Lots of news and lots of escapist TV. Love films.* **Listening:** *Five Live, Xfm, Virgin.* **Relaxing to:** *Going up mountains, sailing.*

Adam Boulton

15.2.59

Sky News, 2nd Floor, 4 Millbank, London SW1P 3JA
T 020 7705 5500
E adam.boulton@bskyb.com

Occupation: Political Editor and Presenter, Sky News

Awards: RTS Judges Award, 2002; Plain English Society Programme of the Year, 2001.
Education: Johns Hopkins School of Advanced International Studies; Christ Church, Oxford
Career highlights: Political Editor, TV-am; Talks Writer, BBC External Services.

» *Divorced, 3 daughters - Lucy Moorehead, 24, Hannah, 18, Blaise, 15*

Tim Bowdler 17.5.51

Johnston Press plc, 53 Manor Place, Edinburgh EH3 7EG
T 0131 225 3361
E tbowdler@johnstonpress.co.uk

Occupation: Chief Executive, Johnston Press plc

Other positions: Director, Press Standards Board of Finance Ltd, 2000-present; Non-Executive Director, Associated British Ports Holdings plc, 2001-present; Non-Executive Director, The Press Association, 2001-present; Non-executive Director, The Miller Group, 2004-present.
Education: London Business School; Birmingham University; Wrekin College
Career highlights: Graduated as a production engineer spending early years of career in the engineering sector with GKN; after studying for MBA at London Business School, held a series of commercial and then general management positions in various UK manufacturing businesses; headhunted to join Johnston Press plc as Group Managing Director in 1994, becoming Chief Executive in 1997; during the last 12 years, Johnston Press has achieved considerable growth, most notably the acquisition of Emap's newspaper interests in 1996, Portsmouth & Sunderland Newspapers in 1999 and Regional Independent Media, publishers of the Yorkshire Post, in 2002; in mid-2005, Johnston Press entered the Irish market for the first time with three substantial acquisitions, giving it a strong position in both Northern Ireland and the Republic of Ireland; whilst at Johnston Press the market capitalisation of the Group has grown from £170m to £1,318m.
Mentor: I have lots ... the industry is full of people who know more than me!
Big break: Joining Johnston Press.
Big mistake: Not joining the media sector sooner.

» **Reading:** *Newspapers, lots of them!* **Watching:** *Sport, news and current affairs.* **Listening:** *Radio 4, I'm a news junkie!* **Relaxing to:** *Playing golf.* » *Married, 2 daughters*

Jeremy Bowen 7.2.64

c/o BBC News, Television Centre, London W12 7RJ
T 020 8743 8000
E jeremy.bowen@bbc.co.uk

Occupation: BBC Middle East Editor

Publications: Six Days: how the 1967 war shaped the Middle East.
Awards: In teams that won awards from Monte Carlo TV Festival, NY TV Festival, Sony Gold Award, RTS, BAFTA and EMMA.
Education: Cardiff High School; University College London, School of Advanced International Studies; Johns Hopkins University, Bologna and Washington DC

Martin Bowley 28.3.59

56-60 Hallam Street, London W1W 6JL
T 020 7907 4444
E martin@ktlondon.co.uk

Occupation: Head of Media, Kendall Tarrant Worldwide

Other positions: Chairman, British Television Awards; Director, Future Marketing Awards; Director, Atlantic FM.
Education: Torquay Boys' Grammar School
Career highlights: Joining and launching Carlton Television in 1993; launching gaming channel in 4 weeks; chairing Media Business Course; hosting Cannes Advertising Awards for five years; opening virtual sales office in the USA just before start of dot.com revenue boom, small judgement, massive luck!
Mentor: Harry Turner, Ron Miller and Jeremy Bullmore.
Big break: Harry Turner employing me as a regional sales executive at Westward Television.
Big mistake: Who on earth is going to pay to sit on a boat for four days declining to take part, ie pay to take part in the now world-famous Marketing Forum ship experiences?

» **Reading:** *Mojo, Q, Rolling Stone Magazine, Campaign, The Times, Sun, Brand Republic, Media Guardian.* **Watching:** *News, Sunday am, sport, The X Factor, movies, Later with Jools Holland, Top of the Pops.* **Listening:** *Radio 4, Radio 5 Live, Jonathan Ross on Radio 2, Xfm, rock music.* **Relaxing to:** *Shooting, golf, rock concerts, Sunday lunch with the family.* » *Married, 2 children*

Rosie Boycott 14.5.55

16 Leamington Road Villas, London W11 1HS
T 020 7229 1507
E rosieboycott@hotmail.com

Occupation: Broadcaster, writer and smallholder

Other positions: Founder of Spare Rib Magazine and Virago Books; Editor of Esquire, Independent on Sunday, Independent, Daily Express; Broadcaster, Moral Maze, Late Review, Politics Show, Question Time; Writer; Board member, Hay-on-Wye festival and international festival commitee; Trustee of Street Smart, The Old Vic, Warchild; smallholder, speaker and teacher.
Publications: First woman editor of a broadsheet and first woman editor of a daily tabloid.
Awards: Magazine Editor of the Year 1994 and 1995.
Education: Cheltenham Ladies' College; Kent University
Career highlights: I think my career has been very unpredictable - I've been lucky enough to have done some extraordinary things, largely through being in the right place at the right time. Founding Spare Rib at the age of 20 was both lucky and priviliged - it is only in hindsight that I am able to see that we did something with relative ease that at another time and place might have been impossible. I never thought for one second that I would become a newspaper editor: apart from a three-month stint at the Telegraph, I hadn't

worked for a newspaper until I became editor of the IOS. I was unprepared for how much I would come to like it! I've been lucky to be able to combine politics and arts in what I do, and also lucky to be able to take up something completely new (farming) in my 50s and be able to not only do it, but write about it as well.

Mentor: Martha Gellhorn was, until her death in 1997, my mentor and inspiration.

Big break: There were two: being 19 in 1970 and at the forefront of the feminist movement, which led to the founding of Spare Rib, and being the editor of Esquire in the 1990s and the subject of a rumour, begun in the Guardian, that I was going to be the editor of the Independent on Sunday. There was no truth in the rumour, but because of it, I was given the job 18 months later.

Big mistake: Hard to admit to, but probably to leave the Independent on Sunday for the daily paper. When I left, we were selling 300,000 copies, the Observer wasn't going great guns, and I was just getting used to the job!

» **Reading:** *Times, Guardian, the Week, LRB, Keep Media (a website which provides the best of the US magazines each week), New York Times online. Currently, I read no fiction, just books on farming as I now have a smallholding.* **Watching:** *The news on any channel, but preferably C4. Historical series, films, soaps like Desperate Housewives, West Wing and Weed.* **Listening:** *Radio 4 whenever in the car, and on Saturday mornings in the kitchen. 60s and 70s music, hymns, and an assortment of classical.* **Relaxing to:** *I live part of my life in Somerset where I have a small farm, with 14 pigs, 300 chickens, vegetables and plants. It's the best relaxant I've ever found!* » *Married, 1 child, 4 stepchildren*

Alan Boyd

Fremantle Media Limited, 1 Stephen Street, London W1T 1AL

T 020 7691 6502
E alan.boyd@fremantlemedia.com

Occupation: President, Worldwide Entertainment, Fremantle Media Production, Fremantle Media Limited

Other positions: 1968-80, BBC Producer/Director in BBC Light Entertainment and Sciences and Features Department; 1980-82, London Weekend Television, Head of Entertainment; 1982-87, London Weekend Television, Controller of Entertainment; 1987-92, TVS Television, Director of Programmes/ITV Network Scheduler; 1992-94, Reg Grundy Productions, Senior Vice-President, Light Entertainment; 1994-97, Reg Grundy Productions (GB), Ltd, Chief Executive; 1997-2001 Pearson Television UK Productions, Chief Executive; 2001-02 Thames Television (UK production division of FremantleMedia Ltd), Chief Executive; 2002-present Fremantle Media Production, President Worldwide Entertainment.

Mentor: Bill Cotton

» *Married*

Tom Bradby

14.1.71

Press Gallery, House of Commons, London SW1A 0AA

T 020 7430 4991
E tom.bradby@itn.co.uk

Occupation: Political Editor, ITV News

Other positions: Ireland Correspondent; Political Correspondent; Asia Correspondent; Royal Correspondent; UK Editor (all with ITN).

Publications: Five novels, all published by Transworld: Shadow Dancer, The Sleep of the Dead, The Master of Rain, The White Russian, The God of Chaos.

Awards: Shortlisted for Thriller of the Year 2003 and Historical Novel of the Year in 2004 and 2005.

Education: Sherborne School; Edinburgh University

Career highlights: Being Ireland Correspondent for ITN as the peace process began to emerge in the early nineties; traveling around the world as Asia Correspondent between 1998 and 2001 to cover natural disasters, conflicts and diplomatic bust-ups in China, India, Indonesia, Kosovo and many other places besides; making a documentary on Aids orphans in Lesotho with Prince Harry in 2004; setting up the new UK bureau at ITN in 2003; being made Political Editor in 2005; the publication of my first novel, Shadow Dancer, in 1998, and striking my first deal in America with The Master of Rain in 2003 (with the editor at Doubleday who was busy buying The Da Vinci Code at the same time). Career lows; being shot in Jakarta in October 1999, which hurt a lot and still does.

Mentor: In television, Nick Pollard and, especially, David Mannion. In the literary world, Mark Lucas and Bill Scott-Kerr.

Big break: Becoming Ireland Correspondent at a very young age in 1993. It was a big step at the time. Dave Mannion took a gamble on me. I hope it's paid off.

Big mistake: Getting shot. I ended up coming back to London and being rather out of sorts for a while.

» **Reading:** *All the newspapers, every day, Private Eye, The Spectator, The New Statesman, The Economist. Political books and non-fiction history books for novel research. Fiction on holiday, when I have time.* **Watching:** *ITV drama, BBC comedy, the news on all channels, films.* **Listening:** *Radio 4, Capital, Heart etc.* **Relaxing to:** *With my family, or writing.* » *Married, 3 children*

Lord Melvyn Bragg

6.10.39

The South Bank Show, The London Television Centre, Upper Ground, London SE1 9LT

T 020 7261 3128

Occupation: Vice-President, Royal Television Society; journalist, broadcaster and author

Other positions: Governor, LSE 1997-present, Chancellor, University of Leeds 1999-present; President, MIND 2002-present

Publications: For Want of a Nail (1965); The Second Inheritance (1966); Without a City Wall (1968); The Hired Man (1969); A Place in England (1970);

The Nerve (1971); Josh Lawton (1972); The Silken Net (1974); A Christmas Child (1977); Autumn Manoeuvres (1978); Kingdom Come (1980); Love and Glory (1983); The Cumbrian Trilogy (1984, comprising The Hired Man, A Place in England and Kingdom Come); The Maid of Buttermere (1987); A Time to Dance (1991, BBC TV series 1992); Crystal Rooms (1992); Credo: An Epic Tale of Dark Age Britain (1996); The Soldier's Return (1999, W H Smith Literary Award 2000); A Son of War (2001); Crossing the Lines (2003); non-fiction: Land of the Lakes (1983); Laurence Olivier (1984); Rich (1988, biog of Richard Burton); Speak for England - oral history of England since 1900 (1976); Ingmar Bergman: The Seventh Seal (1996); On Giants' Shoulders (1998); The Adventure of English (2003); Musicals Mardi Gras, Orion (TV, 1976); The Hired Man (W End 1985, Ivor Novello Award 1985); screenplays for Isadora, Jesus Christ Superstar, The Music Lovers, Clouds of Glory, Play Dirty; stage play, King Lear in New York 1992.

Awards: John Llewelyn Rhys Award and PEN Awards for Fiction; BAFTA Richard Dimbleby Award for Outstanding Contribution to TV 1987; RTS Gold Medal 1989; winner BAFTA Huw Wheldon Award for Best Arts Programme or Series (for An Interview with Dennis Potter) 1994; winner BAFTA for Debussy film (with Ken Russell); Radio Broadcaster of the Year (for In Our Time and Routes of English) Broadcasting Press Guild Radio Awards 1999; VLV Award - Best Individual Contributor to Radio (for In Our Time and Routes of English) 2000; VLV Award - Best New Radio Series (for Routes of English) 2000; Honorary DUniv, Open Univ 1988; Honorary LLD, Univ of St Andrews 1993; Honorary DLitt, Liverpool 1986; Honorary DLitt, Lancaster 1990; Honorary DLitt, CNAA, 1990; Honorary DLitt, South Bank University, 1997; Honorary DLitt, University of Leeds, 2000; Honorary DLitt, University of Bradford, 2000; Honorary DCL, University of Northumbria, 1994; Honorary DSc, UMIST 1998; Honorary DSc, Brunel Univ 2000; Honorary DA, University of Sunderland, 2001; Honorary Fellow, Lancashire Polytechnic; Domus Fellow, St Catherine's College, Oxford 1990; Honorary Fellow, Library Association, 1994; Honorary Fellow, Wadham College, Oxford 1995; Honorary Fellow, University of Wales, Cardiff, 1996; FRSL, FRTS, Life Peerage, 1998.

Education: Nelson Thomlinson Grammar School, Wigton; Wadham College, Oxford

Career highlights: General traineeship, BBC 1961; Producer, Monitor (BBC) 1963; Editor, BBC 2, 1964; New Release (arts magazine latterly called Review, then Arena); Writers World (documentary); Take It or Leave It (literary programme); Presenter, In The Picture (Tyne Tees), 1971; 2nd House (BBC) 1973-77; Start the Week (BBC Radio 4; TRIC Award 1990 and 1994) 1988-98; In Our Time (BBC Radio 4) 1998-present; Routes of English (BBC Radio 4) 1999-present; Presenter and Editor; Read All About It (BBC) 1976-77; South Bank Show (ITV) 1978-present (BAFTA Prix Italia 5 times, TV Music and Arts Programme of the Year, TV and Radio Industry Awards 2000); Adventure of English (also Writer, ITV); Director, LWT Productions 1992; Controller, Arts Department, LWT, 1990-present (Head of Arts 1982-90); Chairman, Border Television 1990-96 (Dep Chm 1985-90); occasional contributor, Observer, Sunday Times and Guardian; weekly column Times 1996-98; member, RSL 1977-80; president, National Campaign for the Arts.

» **Relaxing to:** *Walking, books.* » *Married, 3 children*

David Brain 16.6.66

1st Floor, Haymarket House, 28-29 Haymarket, London SW1Y 4SP

T 020 7344 1203
E david.brain@edelman.com

Occupation: President and CEO, Edelman Europe

Other positions: Joint CEO UK, Weber Shandwick; CEO BSMG UK

Publications: Microsoft; Shell; London Mayor's Office; Inbev.

Awards: Include PR Week Best International Campaigns for Unilever and for Jim Beam.

Education: University of East Anglia

Career highlights: After training as a journalist in Newcastle, I moved to then PR hot shop Paragon Communications, winner of more awards than any other firm of the day. A seven-year stint in Asia Pacific saw spells in-house at Visa International and as a brand planner at WPPs Batey Ads (now red cell) before returning to the UK and the PR fold with Burson-Marsteller. After three years spent fixing Weber Shandwick with my business partner Colin Byrne (still CEO at WS) I became head of Europe for Edelman.

Big break: Being given joint management of the UK's biggest PR firm (Weber Shandwick) when it was very broken and putting it together again over the next three years.

Big mistake: I was a dotcom believer.

» **Reading:** *Four UK national newspapers (vary) every day. Economist, Wallpaper, European Wall Street Journal and FourFourTwo.* **Watching:** *CNBC.* **Listening:** *Radio 4 and 5.* **Relaxing to:** *Family and football.* » *Married, 2 children*

Charles Brand 1.7.54

Tiger Aspect Productions, 5 Soho Square, London W1V 5DE

T 020 7544 1688
E charlesbrand@tigeraspect.co.uk

Occupation: Managing Director, Tiger Aspect Productions

Other positions: Member, Board, Tiger Aspect Productions, 1993-present; Member, Executive Committee, MediaGuardian Edinburgh International Television Festival, 2002-present; Member, Development Board, YCTV; Chair, Channel of the Year Awards.

Awards: BAFTA, 1990; FRTS, 2004.

Education: Bryanston; University of Reading

Career highlights: Researcher and Producer, including Sunday Sunday, James Bond - The First 21 Years, An Audience with Mel Brooks, The World According to Smith and Jones, LWT, 1977-87; Freelance Producer, Free Nelson Mandela Concert,

1987; Producer, including The Movie Life of George, Clive James Meets Jane Fonda, The Driven Man, Life of Python, Funny Business, Tiger Television, 1988-93; Managing Director and Member, Board, Tiger Aspect Productions, including Executive Producer Kid in the Corner, Births Marriages and Deaths, Playing the Field, Howard Goodall's Big Bangs, Country House, Streetmate, 1993-present; Director, Specialist Factual and US Director Documentary and Factual Programming, including Human Mutants, TV Revolution, Virtual History, Westminster Wannabees, The Monastery, Tiger Aspect, 2002-present; Executive Producer, Billy Elliott, 2000; Executive Producer, Liberal Democrat Party political broadcasts; Chair, International Edinburgh Television Festival, 2002.

» **Relaxing to:** *Walking, bicycling, tennis.*

» *Married, 2 children*

Colin Brazier

28.3.68

Sky News, Grant Way, Isleworth TW7 5QD
T 020 7705 3000
E colin.brazier@bskyb.com

Occupation: News Correspondent and Presenter, Sky News

Other positions: Europe Correspondent; Political Correspondent.
Awards: Gold Medal, New York TV Festival for coverage of war in Afghanistan, 2002.
Education: University College, Cardiff
Career highlights: First British journalist to enter Iraq and reach Baghdad during 2003 invasion while embedded with US Third Infantry Division.

» *Married, 4 children*

Juliet Bremner

4.7.67

IPC, 1/18, Boulevard Charlemagne, Brussels 1041, Belgium
T 0032 2 230 6930
E juliet.bremner@itn.co.uk

Occupation: Europe Correspondent, ITV News

Other positions: BBC News Correspondent; Channel 5 Diplomatic Editor; News Correspondent ITV News.
Education: Harrogate College, North Yorkshire

» *Married, no children*

Adrian Britton

13.7.66

200 Gray's Inn Road, London WC1X 8XZ
T 020 7833 3000
E adrian.britton@itn.co.uk

Occupation: News Correspondent

Other positions: Midlands Correspondent; Political Correspondent; South of England Correspondent.
Awards: Royal Television Society, 1994 Best Home News Story, kidnap of baby Abbie Humphries.
Education: Homefield, Christchurch; National Broadcasting School, London
Career highlights: As an A-level student working part-time as a radio station security guard (it was a way in!) I was sponsored as a trainee journalist to attend the National Broadcasting School. Six years followed in independent radio as a reporter, news reader and presenter. After a year off in Brazil teaching English, I made the break into regional television in the South of England and then Birmingham. My move into national television came in 1992 when ITN asked to 'borrow me' for 3 months from Central TV. I was never returned! It's been a worldwide tour covering compelling stories ever since. From the dying days of the Soviet Union to the Bali bombings, from Baghdad to the Californian trial of Michael Jackson and from the tsunami in Thailand to some of the most notorious child murders in the UK, my ITN career has seen the lows and triumphs of humanity.
Mentor: Childhood mentor ... Alan Whicker.
Big break: As a new boy in the Television South newsroom I asked the man I thought was selling sandwiches for a 'tuna mayonnaise on brown'. He was in fact the Head of News clutching lunch snacks for a few staff! He accepted the apologies spluttered from a red face, then asked me, 'Have you had a screen test yet?' I presented the following weekend bulletins.
Big mistake: Declining an on camera interview with Ian Huntley for News at Ten ... the night before he was arrested for the Soham murders. Ooops!

» **Reading:** *For work, as many newspapers as time permits and the Economist (a great explainer!). For leisure, novels that make me laugh out loud on trains - I'm a great Tom Sharpe fan.* **Watching:** *For work, a regular diet of news programmes. For sheer non-thinking leisure value, on sofa, shoes off, glass of white wine in hand, it's The Bill and Will and Grace.* **Listening:** *Driving during worktime, Radio 5. Peter Allen is superb. At home, music, Coldplay, Jack Johnson, Morcheeba, Trance (before clubbing), James Blunt, Keene, REM, and Queen.* **Relaxing to:** *Cycling in my beautiful home town of Bournemouth. Gym when I can muster the energy to get there. Otherwise, and too often, socialising with friends at home or out on the scene, just chatting away to the small hours. Very sad but I'm a born-again clubber and after a few glasses of wine I believe I can dance. No photos please!*

» *Divorced, 2 young girls. My loves.*

Annabel Brog

30.3.76

Sugar, 64 North Row, London W1K 7LL
T 020 7150 7074
E annabelbrog@hf-uk.com

Occupation: Editor, Sugar Magazine

Other positions: Deputy Editor, Bliss; Features Editor, J-17; Features Editor, Shine; Features Assistant, Tatler.
Publications: Over the years have freelanced for lots of mass-market titles: Cosmo, More, FHM, She etc. Launched the Sugar Stand Up, Speak Out anti-bullying campaign. Got Sugar into every national paper and on all main breakfast TV shows. Had about 20,000 teen girls sign the manifesto so far. Produced 400,000 SUSO posters which girls have pinned up around the country.
Awards: Nada. Shortlisted for BSME Editor of the Year (Youth) 2005; and Editor's Editor of the Year 2005.

Education: North London Collegiate School; University of Sussex
Career highlights: Taking five angry and opinionated teenage girls to Downing Street to grill Tony Blair on what he intends to do about bullying, crime, teenage depression, sex education and the environment. He handled himself OK, until he came to Laura, 16, Yorkshire, who told him she'd had one sex education lesson in her life, three months earlier. Which, considering three girls in her year were pregnant at 12, and the rest were doing it by 13, was a little too late. All he could think of to ask was what happened to the babies. 'Two girls had them,' said Laura, 'the third lost it in a fight.' The look on his face was priceless. I then made him stand next to me for a photograph, while he held up a copy of my magazine which had a big, beaming picture of Jordan on the cover!
Mentor: David Bostock - a completely ego-free appreciation and understanding of magazines, plus someone who can spot and develop less experienced journos. Helen Johnston - former editor of Bliss, now on Grazia. Brilliant journalist, people manager, and idea generator.
Big break: Securing an 'advice' column for FHM when I was just starting out. As one of the three FHM Angels, it involved being photographed wrapped in a sheet and doling out advice to unfortunate FHM readers with girlfriend problems (that would be most of them, then). High points included a letter of proposal from a 14-year-old (he called me Miss Annabel) and a death threat from Borstal ('Don't you know, women LIE.' Wonder what he was banged up for?).
Big mistake: I'm sure I've made plenty, but I'm very happy now so none of them have had long-lasting effects. In fact, I'm sure they've all contributed to my career in a positive way.

» **Reading:** *Books whenever I possibly can. The Sun and the Guardian, US Glamour and US Cosmo, US Weekly (possibly the best magazine of the planet), Grazia, Elle, Cosmo, Chat, Nuts, Empire - I try and dip into all mags from all genres.* **Watching:** *As little as possible. Top Gear is brilliant. I dip into popular US TV series (Lost, Desperate Housewives etc) for work, ditto UK soaps. I don't have the time to commit to series, but have loved (infrequently) Shameless, Little Britain, America's Next Top Model, Blackpool.* **Listening:** *Virgin, Radio 1, Radio 4. Terrible middle-aged pop rock like Meatloaf and Cher, Guns 'n' Roses, Elvis. Plus non-R&B pop stuff, Greenday and Good Charlotte, Daniel Powter, James Blunt.* **Relaxing to:** *I read To Kill a Mockingbird. But because I limit myself to only reading it every three years, I also read other books. As many as I possibly can. Have recently fallen in love with The Kite Runner, The Time Traveller's Wife, Property, Running with Scissors.* » *Single, no children*

Sophie Brooks

30.6.72

7 Albion Court, Galena Road, Hammersmith, London W6 0QT
T 020 8846 8338
E sophie.brooks@augustone.com

Occupation: Managing Director, August One Communications London

Other positions: Client Strategy Director, August One, 2001-04; Communications UK CEO, August One Communications Worldwide and Regional Director, August One Asia Pacific 1999-2001 - stepped down following maternity leave and move to part time Client Services Director; Text 100 Asia Pacific, 1998-99; Associate Director, Text 100 UK, 1996-98; Account Executive, Manager and Director, Text 100 UK, 1992-96; PR & Marketing Manager, Real Life Estates South East, 1990-92; Research Manager, IDC Australia, 1989-90.
Publications: Jordans Cereals Corporate, 2005; Home Office Child Protection on the Internet, 2003; Office of the e-Envoy - ESummit, 2002; Microsoft Corporate - Asia Pacific (Hong Kong), 1999-2001; Cisco Europe (managing corporate communications and 17 agencies across the continent), 1996-97; Microsoft Corporate UK,1996-98; Microsoft Windows 95 Launch, 1993-95.
Education: Imberhorne School, West Sussex; Westfield College; University of London
Career highlights: In 2003 I began work on what was to become a watershed event in the marketing landscape - the pre-launch of Microsoft's Windows 95. Using PR alone, this campaign was the first IT product to break through the traditional trade media and successfully penetrated national and broadcast press, leading the way for other technology brands to do the same. The PR campaign, which I led for the UK, was so successful that when the product came to market in Aug 1995, there were already one million pre-orders. It won wide recognition in the PR and marketing industry for its ground-breaking results which included almost constant presence in the national press for months running up to the launch, and blanket broadcast coverage in the UK on the day of launch.
Mentor: Mark Adams - Founder and Director of Text 100 and winner of the IPR Lifetime Achievement Award in 2004. I worked with Mark for about five years mainly on pan-European campaigns. His 'take no prisoners' consultancy style constantly amazed and impressed me though I never managed to emulate it! Andrew Lees - Product Marketing Director/Director of Desktop Products at Microsoft UK during my formative years in media relations. He was both my toughest and most rewarding client to date, constantly challenging me to reach for the skies when it came to results and always testing my advice to the nth degree to ensure my thinking was more than just gut feeling.
Big break: Being offered the opportunity to become CEO of a global PR company with over 130 staff, the majority of whom were based in London, whilst I was based in Sydney, Australia!
Big mistake: Trying to grow a business in Asia Pacific during the post-apocalyptic 2001-02 based

too heavily around one major client - one of the largest and most demanding in the world.

*» **Reading:** The Independent during the week, BBC News Online in the mornings, the Observer on Sundays, PR Week (for my sins), Marketing Week (for my clients), the Economist (not as often as I should), Waitrose Food Illustrated and Homes & Gardens (for my indulgence). **Watching:** EastEnders (on Sky+ series link!), The West Wing, Spooks. **Listening:** Radio 4 Today (religiously), Virgin Radio. **Relaxing to:** Cooking and Iyengar Yoga. » Married to Matthew Ravden, 2 children, Owen (2) and Callum (4)*

Ben Brown

27.5.64

Room 2505, BBC Television Centre, Wood Lane, London W12 7RJ

T 020 8624 8542
E ben.brown@bbc.co.uk

Occupation: Special Correspondent, BBC Television News

Other positions: World Affairs Correspondent, BBC News; Moscow Correspondent, BBC News.
Publications: All Necessary Means (book, published in 1991, with David Shukman).
Awards: Royal Television Society International News award, Zimbabwe; Bayeux War Correspondent of the Year award (twice), Chechnya and Israel; Golden Nymph, Monte Carlo, Chechnya; BAFTA, team award for Kosovo.
Education: Sutton Valence, Kent; Keble College, Oxford
Career highlights: Since joining the BBC in 1988, I have covered most of the major international news events of the last two decades including the fall of the Berlin wall, both Gulf Wars, September the 11th and the invasion of Afghanistan. I have worked extensively in Africa, covering Rwanda, Burundi, Somalia, Sudan and Zimbabwe, where I won an RTS award after being trapped inside a white-owned farm as armed black militants took it over. As the BBC's Moscow Correspondent, I covered the collapse of communism in 1991 and the war in Chechnya. I'm currently the BBC's Special Correspondent, deployed on major domestic and international stories.
Mentor: Martin Bell
Big break: Applying for a reporter's job at the BBC that was advertised in the Guardian - and getting it!
Big mistake: When I was in local radio in Glasgow, on the first anniversary of the Falklands War I rebroadcast a clip of the news announcement that the islands had been invaded. The listeners thought it had happened all over again.

*» **Reading:** Modern novels - Ian McEwan, Sebastian Faulks, Alan Hollinghurst. **Watching:** A lot of football. **Listening:** Radio 5 Live. **Relaxing to:** Playing and watching football, and jogging. » Married, 3 children*

Craig Brown

23.5.57

c/o PFD, Drury House, 34-43 Russell Street, London WC2B 5HA

T 020 7344 1000
E jedelstein@pfd.co.uk

Occupation: Satirist

Other positions: The Marsh-Marlowe Letters (1983); A Year Inside (1988); The Agreeable World of Wallace Arnold (1990); Rear Columns (1992); Welcome to My Worlds (1993); Craig Brown's Greatest Hits (1993); The Hounding of John Thenos (1994); The Private Eye Book of Craig Brown Parodies (1995); The Marsh-Marlowe Letters (2001); This is Craig Brown (2003); Craig Brown's Imaginary Friends: The Collected Parodies 2000-2004 (2004); 1966 and All That (2005); This is Tony's Britain: Craig Brown's Blair Years (2005).
Education: Eton; University of Bristol
Career highlights: Articles for numerous newspapers and magazines including New Statesman, Observer, TLS, Mail on Sunday, New York, Stern, Corriere della Sera; columnist; The Times Parliamentary Sketch Writer, 1987-88; Restaurant Critic, Sunday Times 1988-93; Columnist (as Wallace Arnold), the Spectator, Private Eye, Independent on Sunday; Columnist, Evening Standard (as Craig Brown), 1993-present, the Guardian (as Bel Littlejohn) 1995-2001.

*» **Relaxing to:** Flower arrangement, needlework, tidying, deportment, macramé. » Married, 2 children*

Jane Bruton

21.3.68

189 Shaftesbury Avenue, London WC2H 8JG

T 020 7520 6401
E jane.bruton@emap.com

Occupation: Editor, Grazia

Other positions: Formerly Deputy Editor, Wedding and Home; Associate Editor, Prima; Editor, Livingetc; Editor, eve Magazine.
Awards: BSME Editor of the Year, 2004; Grazia also won Best Designed Launch at the MDA Awards.
Education: Byrchall High School, Wigan; Nottingham University; City University
Career highlights: Doubling circulation of Livingetc within 6 months. Successfully re-launching eve Magazine (for which I won BSME Editor of the Year); launching Grazia, which has revolutionised the women's glossy market and just posted a 10% pop circulation rise. Having Madonna ring Grazia to offer us her only UK interview; abusing my position as Editor to party with Prince at the Brits; most recently, beating every national magazine and newspaper in Britain to get the first interview with Camille Aznar (the dumped fiancée of Celebrity Big Brother's Preston).
Mentor: Jo Foley
Big break: Coming up with my own magazine idea at IPC. I presented it to Sally O'Sullivan who sent me off into a cupboard with five other people for six months. The idea never saw the light of day (do they ever?) but the experience put me in

the frame for my first editorship at Livingetc.
Big mistake: Putting Coleen on the cover of Grazia - let's just say it wasn't our best-selling issue!

» **Reading:** *Proofs, proofs and more proofs. We're churning out up to 100 editorial pages a week.* **Watching:** *Everything from Lost to The Catherine Tate Show to My Name Is Earl (plus Coronation Street as a guilty pleasure).* **Listening:** *Jonathan Ross on Radio Two, Ricky Gervais whenever he's on Xfm and, er, Take That and Wham after a few drinks.* **Relaxing to:** *Sorry - I've got two small children. I don't understand the question!*

» *Married, 2 children*

John Bryant

25.04.44

1 Canada Square, London E14 5DT
T 0207 538 6300

Occupation: Editor-in-Chief, The Daily and Sunday Telegraph

Education: Sexey's School, Somerset; Queen's College, Oxford University
Other positions: Daily Mail 1971-86; Managing Editor 1986-88, and Deputy Editor, 1988-1990, The Times; Editor, Sunday Correspondent 1990; Editor, The European 1991; Deputy Editor, The Times, 1991-2000; Consultant Editor, Daily Mail, 2000-2005

» *Married, two sons*

Nick Bryant

18.6.72

BBC South Asia Bureau, AIFACS Building, 1 Rafi Marg, New Delhi 110 001
T 00 91 11 2335 5751
E nick.bryant@bbc.co.uk

Occupation: BBC South Asia Correspondent

Other positions: BBC Washington Correspondent, 1998-2003; BBC Five Live Reporter, 1995-98; BBC News Trainee 1994-95; Freelance writer for the Daily Mail, The Times, the Independent.
Publications: I am working on a book to be published in June 2006 - The Bystander: John F. Kennedy and the Struggle for Black Equality (Basic Books, New York).
Awards: I helped the Five Live breakfast programme win a Sony in 1998 with a series of reports on proportional representation, remarkably enough.
Education: Wellsway Comprehensive, Bristol; Churchill College, Cambridge; Balliol College, Oxford; Massachusetts Institute of Technology, Boston
Career highlights: An extraordinarily newsy five years in Washington provided many of the highlights - a presidential impeachment trial, a disputed election, 9/11, the Washington sniper killings, and the build-up to the Iraq war. But I've thoroughly enjoyed South Asia, which in many ways has been more rewarding journalistically (at times in Washington, it almost felt as if you were shackled to the rooftop camera position overlooking the White House). The patch here is brilliant. Kashmir, Afghanistan, Pakistan, Sri Lanka, Nepal - all of our troublespots are in such beautiful places. And occasionally I get to cover Indo-Pakistan cricket series, which has been a joy. In earlier days, I covered Northern Ireland before and after the Good Friday agreement, which was fascinating. I used to very much enjoy presidential trips abroad with Clinton and Bush, which took in some really fascinating places, such as the DMZ on the Korean Peninsula.
Mentor: A lot of my BBC bosses and colleagues have been very helpful and kind. Mark Sandell and Phil Longman, two of my first bosses at Five Live, kept on sending me to fun places abroad, and Jenny Baxter, the former Head of Foreign Newsgathering, seemed very keen for me to go to Washington. I really enjoyed working alongside Stephen Sackur, Paul Reynolds, Richard Lister, Rob Watson and Matt Frei in the States, and like working with Paul Danahar, our Bureau Editor in Delhi. Nikki Millard, our main cameraman here in Delhi, is fantastically talented, as is Vivek Raj, my main producer.
Big break: Three days after joining Five Live, they packed me off to Jerusalem to cover the assassination of Yitzak Rabin, which was helpful early on. But my biggest break was to be sent to Washington in late 1998 just as the impeachment proceedings against Bill Clinton cranked into action.
Big mistake: Deciding to go on holiday during the first two weeks of September 2001, which meant I slept through 9/11, and was stranded 3000 miles away from Washington or New York (I also slept through the tsunami, the 7/7 bombs and, most recently, the Delhi bombs).

» **Reading:** *The New York Times, New Yorker, Atlantic Monthly, Vanity Fair, Outlook, India Today, Washington Post, Economist, Time, Newsweek, Drudge, Foreign Affairs and the BBC website.* **Watching:** *Any cricket or international rugby on television, West Wing, Desperate Housewives, BBC World, NDTV, an Indian news channel, a lot of movies and the ever-brilliant Bollywood dance sequences (especially those filmed in the 1970s).* **Listening:** *I still can't work out how to use my iPod, but there's a lot of William Walton, Elvis, John Rutter, Tom Jones, Mahalia Jackson and Grimethorpe Colliery Band waiting to be loaded.* **Relaxing to:** *I try to swim a lot, work out at the gym and play cricket. I love eating out. But I've been finishing a book for the past 12 months, and it's been harder to relax.*

» *Single, no children*

Deborah Bull

23.3.67

Royal Opera House, Covent Garden, London WC2E 9DD
T 020 7240 1200
E Deborah.Bull@bbc.co.uk

Occupation: Creative Director, ROH2, Royal Opera House; BBC Governor

Other positions: Additional work in broadcasting (writing, presenting).
Publications: BBC TV: Dancers Body (BBC2, 2002); Travels With My Tutu (BBC2 1999); presenting work on BBC1, 2 and 4. BBC Radio: Breaking the Law (Radio 4); Law in Order (Radio 4); Leaving Barons Court (Radio 4); A Dance Through Time (Radio 4). Books: Vitality Plan (Dorling Kindersley, 1998), Dancing Away (Methuen, 1999), Faber Guide to Classical Ballets (Faber, 2005). Speeches / lectures / debates: debated at the Oxford Union in 1996, speaking against the motion 'This house

believes the National Lottery gives too much money to the elitist arts'; 1996 Arts Council Annual Lecture (From private patronage to public purse); lectured at the Royal Institution, 2003.
Awards: CBE, 1999; Honorary Doctorates from Sheffield Hallam, Derby and the Open University.
Education: Royal Ballet School
Career highlights: Danced with the Royal Ballet from 1981-2001 (Principal Dancer from 1991). Established and now direct the ROH2 programme at the Royal Opera House, utilising the small-scale theatres to develop new art, new artists and new audiences. Sat on Arts Council England from 1998-2005 and joined the BBC Board of Governors in 2003.
Big break: Speaking at the Oxford Union in 1996. Almost everything I do now can be traced back to that occasion.

» **Reading:** *The Week, the Guardian, Time Out - and anything else that catches my eye.* **Watching:** *Small-scale and interesting productions of dance and opera; dance, and dance and music theatre; television - especially arts and documentaries...* **Listening:** *Radio 4; dance music (no, not ballet music).* **Relaxing to:** *With friends. In private.*
» *Married, no children*

(John) Jeremy David Bullmore

21.11.29

WPP, 27 Farm St, London W1J 5RJ
T 020 7408 2204
E jjeremyb@aol.com

Occupation: Member WPP Advisory Group; columnist Guardian, Management Today, Campaign, Market Leader, President MRS (Market Research Society)

Other positions: Occasional LibDem advisor.
Publications: Behind the Scenes Advertising, Ask Jeremy, Another Bad Day at the Office? Apples, Insights and Mad Inventors.
Awards: CBE
Education: Harrow/Oxford (no degree)
Career highlights: Career highlights 1954-1987 J Walter Thompson London: copywriter, creative director, chairman. Member of JWT Worldwide Board. 1982-87, Chairman Advertising Association. 1988-2001, Non-Executive Director Guardian Media Group; 1988-2004 Non-Executive Director WPP.
Mentor: No one person.
Big break: Getting first job at JWT.
Big mistake: Not telling.

» **Reading:** *Too many newspapers; trade mags, political weeklies, novels, occasional biographies.* **Watching:** *News, Bremner B & F, son's and daughter's things. At least one film a month.* **Listening:** *Radio 4, Classic FM, mostly morning and car.* **Relaxing to:** *Slumping, reading, mowing grass*
» *Married, 3 children*

Robin Burgess

31.1.51

C N Group Ltd, Dalston Road, Carlisle, Cumbria CA2 5UA
T 01228 612600
E robin.burgess@cngroup.co.uk

Occupation: Chief Executive, Cumbrian Newspapers Group Ltd

Other positions: High Sheriff of Cumbria, March 2006 onward; Director, Cumberland and Westmorland Herald Ltd 1985-present.
Education: Trinity College, Glenalmond
Career highlights: 2nd Lieutenant, The King's Own Royal Border Regiment, 1969-72; Chief Executive, C N Group Ltd, 1985-present, 4th generation of family to be involved in business; President, Newspaper Society 1996-97; Director, Border TV plc, 1987-2000.

» *Married, 4 children*

Patrick Burgoyne

14.3.70

50 Poland Street, London W1F 7AX
T 020 7970 6273
E patrick.burgoyne@centaur.co.uk

Occupation: Editor, Creative Review

Other positions: Stockroom Assistant, The Body Shop, Oxford Street; Fruit Packer, Turners of Soham, Suffolk; Wheelie-Bin Delivery Operative, Bury St Edmunds Council, Suffolk. Staff Writer, Senior Writer, Deputy Editor at Creative Review.
Publications: D&AD Annual, 2005.
Education: Sudbury Upper School, Sudbury, Suffolk; Thomas Mills High School, Framlingham, Suffolk; University of Southampton (Politics and International Studies)
Career highlights: Our redesign earlier this year which finally got the magazine somewhere close to where I'd like it to be; getting the magazine into the D&AD Annual for the first time; sharing a dinner table with Jonathan Ive and Stephen Fry.
Big break: Getting a spec piece published in Midweek magazine (it was on the incredibly original theme of the joys of sharing a flat; I did a better one on how awful employment agencies are but they wouldn't publish it due to advertiser sensitivities, an early lesson in how magazines work). Answering an ad in the Guardian for a Staff Writer on Creative Review.
Big mistake: The usual misspellings, misunderstandings and cock-ups but probably the worst was missing out several pages from last year's Annual issue and replacing them with random pages from a feature running elsewhere in the same issue. Plus we spelled February wrong on the cover once.

» **Reading:** *The competition plus (predictably) the Guardian, Observer, Independent; New Yorker and Economist in pathetic attempt to look good on planes; The Onion; Popbitch; football365; Design Observer and various other blogs/message boards; whichever books my son has brought home from school.* **Watching:** *Whatever my son is watching plus (if he'll let me near the remote) Curb Your Enthusiasm; re-runs of Marion and Geoff and Spaced on Homechoice video-on-*

demand; sport; and am finding myself increasingly drawn to Coronation Street (a worry). **Listening:** *Today Programme; BBC 6 Music; a whole host of bands from the 80s which I wasn't cool enough to like at the time but now pretend that I did.* **Relaxing to:** *I haven't relaxed since 1999.* » *Living with long-term partner, with 1 child*

Kay Burley

Sky News, Grant Way, Isleworth, Middlesex TW7 5QD
T 0870 240 3000
E kay.burley@bskyb.com

Occupation: Presenter, Sky News

Other positions: Sky News Lunchtime Live
Awards: BAFTA News Award (part of Sky News team)
Career highlights: Reporter, Sunday Mirror; Newsreader and Presenter, TV-am, 1985-88; joined Sky Television, 1988; live coverage of stories including both Iraq wars, the deaths of Diana Princess of Wales, the Queen Mother and Princess Margaret, the Concorde crash, the fall of the Berlin Wall, and the September 11 attacks. As an interviewer work includes an array of names from the world of politics, sport and entertainment, most recently Rebecca Loos, David Beckham's former PA.
» *1 child*

Sir Andrew Burns

22.7.47

British Broadcasting Corporation, Room 211, 35 Marylebone High Street, London W1U 4AA
T 020 7208 9519
E Andrew.Burns@bbc.co.uk

Occupation: International Governor, BBC

Other positions: Currently Chairman of Council of Royal Holloway, University of London; Director of the JP Morgan Chinese Investment Trust; Formerly HM Diplomatic Service, British High Commissioner to Canada, British Consul-General in Hong Kong and Macau, British Ambassador to Israel.
Awards: KCMG
Education: Highgate School; Trinity College Cambridge
Career highlights: Over a diplomatic career of 38 years I have represented Queen and country in India in the 60s, Romania in the 70s during the Cold War, and Washington and New York in the 80s. In the US I ran the British Information Services and that led in due time to a Press Secretary job in London. In more recent years I became involved in the Middle East Peace Process during my time as Ambassador to Israel during the second Rabin Prime Ministership and the Oslo Agreements; and for over ten years I played an active part in the negotiations with China over the handover of sovereignty in Hong Kong, going out to Hong Kong in 1997 to re-establish the British position after the departure of the Governor. My final posting was to Canada, one of Britain's closest allies, where I came up against many of the challenging realities caused by climate change.
Mentor: George Malcolm Thomson, a journalist and author of huge talent and influence in the post-war years.
Big break: Choosing a career that suited my talents.
Big mistake: Too many to recall.
» **Reading:** *Widely and eclectically, but mainly history and biography and the literature of Canada.* **Watching:** *More and more of the excellent output from the BBC across all channels including BBC World.* **Listening:** *News and current affairs on Radio 4 and the World Service; music on Radio 3.* **Relaxing to:** *Walking on Exmoor and singing in choirs.* » *Married, 2 sons and 1 stepdaughter*

Sir Peter Burt

6.4.44

Gleacher Shacklock Ltd, 33 King Street, London SW1Y 6RJ
T 020 7484 1127

Occupation: Non-executive Chairman, ITV plc

Other positions: Non-executive Director, Shell Transport and Trading Company plc, 2002; Director, Templeton Emerging Markets Investment Trust plc, 2004.
Education: Merchiston Castle School, Edinburgh; University of St Andrews; University of Pennsylvania
Career highlights: Hewlett Packard Company, Palo Alto, California, 1968-70; Conversational Software Ltd, Edinburgh, 1970-74; Edward Bates & Sons, Edinburgh, 1974; Bank of Scotland, joined 1975, Assistant General Manager, International Division, 1979-84; Divisional General Manager, International Division, 1984-85; Joint General Manager, International Division, 1985-88; Treasurer and Chief General Manager, 1988-96; appointed Main Board Director, 1995; Chief Executive, 1996-2001; Deputy Chairman, HBOS plc 2001-03; Non-executive Chairman, ITV plc, 2004-present; FCIB (Scotland); Chairman, Gleacher Shacklock UK Ltd, 2000-05; Executive Deputy Chairman, HBOS plc, 2001-03; Governor of The Bank of Scotland, Group Chief Executive, 1996-2000.
» **Relaxing to:** *Golf, tennis, skiing, reading.*
» *Married, 3 sons*

Andy Bush

21.9.67

Brettenham House, Lancaster Place, London WC1 7TL
T 020 7322 1594
E andy_bush@fortunemail.com

Occupation: Publishing Director, Fortune magazine

Other positions: The Fortune Money Group; Fortune, leading global fortnightly business magazine; Fortune Small, leading US magazine for small business owners; B2.0, leading cutting edge monthly for business entrepreneurs; Money Magazine, leading personal finance and lifestyle monthly; CNNMoney.com, newly launched website combining the power of the above listed brands and the newsgathering force of CNN.
Awards: Campaign, Ranked in Top 10 Most Respected/Trusted International Salespeople,

2005; Media & Marketing Europe, Ranked in Europe's '40 under 40' Young Achievers, 2005.
Education: King's School, Canterbury
Career highlights: Began career at Saatchi & Saatchi in 1986, initially in the postroom, subsequently International Research Department, then promoted to Media Planner/Buyer; moved to Saatchi's independent media-buying arm, Zenith, 1988; Advertising Sales, the Sunday Correspondent, 1989-90; travelled and worked around the world, including Saatchi & Saatchi, New Zealand, 1990-93; Advertising Sales, Mail on Sunday, 1993-97; joined Time Inc as International Sales Manager, Time Magazine, Europe, 1997; relocated to New York as US East Coast Sales Manager, Time International, 1998; Fortune US Sales team, 1999-present.
Mentor: A fairly unique combination of a butcher, a Federal US agent, and a Pole. They all know the way.
Big break: Landing the postroom job at Saatchi & Saatchi in 1987. I subsequently wore a bright red jumper to work every day for three months, which got me noticed everywhere within the Saatchi offices. This included the top floor boardrooms where Maurice and Charles resided, all the way down to the postroom which was appropriately called 'Dispatch'. As a result was soon recruited into the Saatchi Media Research department.
Big mistake: Leaving that postroom job.

» **Reading:** *Everything I can from daily newspapers, to a terrific fortnightly global business magazine called Fortune, and all leisure magazines and books suited to my life's passions.* **Watching:** *My expanding waistline.* **Listening:** *My wife.* **Relaxing to:** *Ideally on skis, on water, on golf courses, or up in remote hills, ie preferably anywhere that various handheld devices do not, or are not allowed to function.* » *Married, 3 children*

Adam Buxton 8.6.73

c/o Jennifer Rhodes, PBJ Management, 7 Soho Street, London W1D 3DQ
T 020 7287 1112
E jennifer@pbjmgt.co.uk

Occupation: Writer and performer

Other positions: Busboy, bartender, DJ.
Awards: Royal Television Society Best Newcomer, 1997.
Education: Westminster School; Sir John Cass School of Art; Cheltenham College of Higher Education
Career highlights: With school friend Joe Cornish made four series of The Adam and Joe Show, a home-made pop culture review show for Channel 4 between 1996 and 2001. The show was celebrated for its stuffed toy parodies of films and TV shows as well as reviews of youth culture from Adam's father Nigel as BaaadDad. Thereafter a few of Adam and Joe's jobs have included presenting BBC3's Glastonbury coverage on 2000 and 2002; making two series about animation for Channel 4 (Adam and Joe's Wonky World Of Animation and Adam & Joe's American Animation Adventure); talking rubbish over two series' worth of porno clips on E4's Shock Video; reporting on Japanese pop culture on BBC3's Adam and Joe Go Tokyo; presenting a Saturday afternoon show on London's Xfm. Solo efforts include a half hour documentary about The League Of Gentlemen; co-writing and starring in the Channel 4 sitcom The Last Chancers about the travails of a shit band based in Brighton; a one-man show at the Edinburgh Festival 2005.
Mentor: Joe Cornish was my mentor.
Big break: Meeting Fenton Bailey and Randy Barabato who run World Of Wonder. They thought we should be on TV and let us do exaclty what we wanted to get there.
Big mistake: Doing exactly what we wanted a little too long maybe. I've got no complaints though.

» **Reading:** *Books about music – 'like dancing about architecture' as Frank Zappa accurately said.* **Watching:** *A lot of TV, all the time feeling like John Peel sifting hopefully through piles of shite in the hope that the next thing might be great and new. Sopranos can't be beat.* **Listening:** *A lot of music, much more frequently rewarding than watching TV.* **Relaxing to:** *Play my guitar and sing badly. Go to the carwash with my son Frank.* » *Married, 2 children*

Mark Byford 13.6.58

BBC Media Centre, Media Village, 201 Wood Lane, London W12 7TQ
T 020 8008 1400
E mark.byford@bbc.co.uk

Occupation: Deputy Director-General and Head of Journalism, BBC

Other positions: Director, World Service and Global News, 1998-2003; Director, Nations and Regions, 1996-98.
Awards: RTS Journalism Awards 1980, 1982, 1989; Sony Radio Award 2001; Fellow, Radio Academy.
Education: University of Leeds
Career highlights: Started in 1979 at BBC Leeds as a Holiday Relief Programme Assistant during the summer holidays working on Look North, the regional television news programme. I'm still here with the BBC! Producer, Documentary Producer, Editor, Head of News and Current Affairs in Bristol and Yorkshire Region; Head of all Regional Journalism across UK; Director of Nations and Regions; Director of World Service and Global News; Deputy Director-General, BBC, 2003-present; Head of all BBC Journalism, 2004-present.

» **Reading:** *All newspapers, many journals and magazines, rock and pop magazines including Q and Mojo. I surf the net regularly. I read both novels and non-fiction including biography.* **Watching:** *A lot! News, current affairs, documentaries, music, sport and drama.* » *Married, 5 children*

Colin Byrne

26.2.61

Weber Shandwick, Fox Court, 14 Gray's Inn Road, London WC1X 8WS
T 020 7067 0000
E cbyrne@webershandwick.com

Occupation: CEO, UK and Ireland, Weber Shandwick

Other positions: MD, Shandwick Public Affairs; Communications Director, The Prince of Wales Business Leaders Forum; Chief Press Officer, The Labour Party; Press Officer, National Union of Students.
Publications: My agency works for many of the UK's and the world's top brands and organisations and my clients range from Coca-Cola to the Department for Education and Skills. I was delighted also to work as a consultant for Peter Mandelson on Labour's historic 1997 election campaign.
Awards: PR Week Award for leading work on big merger in the media sector; GQ's top 100 influential blokes survey in 2003 and 2004.
Education: University of Kingston upon Thames
Career highlights: Blagged way into PR as graduate (English Lit) on strength of editing student newspaper and publishing own punk fanzine; worked on last successful campaign against student loans for NUS in early 1980s; recruited by Peter Mandelson to work for Labour in 1986. Ended up as his deputy and worked for Tony Blair, Gordon Brown and Jack Straw as press officer; went to work on Prince Charles' CSR interests; hired as lobbyist by Shandwick in 1995 and ended up as CEO of UK's largest PR firm, Weber Shandwick.
Mentor: Peter Mandelson
Big break: Working with Peter Mandelson, Tony Blair, Gordon Brown and Neil Kinnock - the four politicians who did most to create New Labour.
Big mistake: Not taking Art A-level.

» ***Reading:*** *The Sun, The Times and the FT on a daily basis. The Guardian on a Monday, Tuesday and Saturday. The Independent on a Monday. The Sunday Times, News of the World and the Observer. The Economist and all the PR and marketing trade media every week. GQ Magazine every month. Private Eye.* ***Watching:*** *BBC news output, Coronation Street (I was born in Salford!), The X Factor, Lost, EastEnders, The History Channel. Hugely enjoyed BBC 2's The Space Race series.* ***Listening:*** *Manchester bands from the 70s and 80s, the Beatles, early Oasis, early Dylan, Mahler, anything at all by Sinead O'Connor, Leftfield, U2, Chet Baker, early choral music, The Clash, early Bowie, Beethoven, early Pink Floyd (with Syd Barrett).* ***Relaxing to:*** *Cooking, painting, gardening, reading, watching movies and Dr Who DVDs with my five-year-old son, Gabriel.* » *Married, 2 children from previous marriages*

C

Mark Calvert

17.5.66

Sky, Unit 1, Grant Way, Isleworth TW7 5QD
T 020 7800 2700
E mark.calvert@bskyb.com

Occupation: Editor, Five News

Education: Heath Grammar School, Yorkshire
Career highlights: Two highlights, both programme launches, both very different experiences, but both invaluable. First, and best, re-launching Five News for Sky. Wrestling the contract from ITN was fantastic. Then being given the freedom to start afresh with a new team producing new programmes in a new studio was a great privilege. More than a year on, running Five News is a daily joy. The other highlight was being Sky's man on the launch of RI:SE for Channel Four, working in partnership with an independent producer. Total nightmare. Too many masters, each and every one of them with a different and daily view of how we should re-invent the show. But it didn't kill me, and I learned invaluable lessons about how to manage programmes and people. And how not to.
Mentor: Brian Steele, my first-ever News Editor, on the Rotherham Advertiser in 1985. He taught me the importance in news of real people, and gave me a lifelong aversion to 'issues'.
Big break: Being sent to cover the Lockerbie air disaster.
Big mistake: Underestimating the foot and mouth outbreak as a story. I was too young to recall the first crisis, so struggled to care about poorly sheep.

» ***Reading:*** *Every newspaper, every day.* ***Watching:*** *Every news bulletin, every day, and 24. And, thanks to my partner, anything featuring Tyra Banks.* ***Listening:*** *My own voice, far too much. Will somebody else say something, please?* ***Relaxing to:*** *Tyra Banks.* » *Living with partner, 2 children*

Fiona Campbell

30.1.74

Channel 4 News, ITN, 200 Grays Inn Road, London WC1X 8XZ
T 020 7833 3000
E Fiona.Campbell@itn.co.uk

Occupation: Commissioning Editor, Channel 4 News Independents Fund

Other positions: Series Producer, BBC Current Affairs; Executive Producer, Network Development BBC Northern Ireland; Producer, Panorama BBC.
Publications: Election Unspun: What They'll Never Tell You, Channel 4; Fergie and Son, BBC3/BBC1; Crooked Britain and Lifting the Bonnet, BBC2; Panorama: Battle for Basra, BBC1; Panorama: Gap and Nike No Sweat, BBC1.
Education: Fortwilliam Belfast; Cambridge University; SAIS Johns Hopkins University, Italy

Career highlights: I am most proud of the team I assembled on the BBC2 investigative series Lifting the Bonnet and Crooked Britain. I hired BBC Current Affairs' brightest assistant producers and gave them the opportunity to direct their first long form programmes. It was a brillant team who supported each other and had a great laugh. We delivered BBC2 a successful series and all of my team went on to be recognised as long form producers and directors in their own right. I will also always remember the Panoramas I worked on in hostile environments such as Kosovo, Afghanistan and Iraq. Being in these places in times of war and meeting the people who lived there has made me appreciate my own life infinitely more. One of my first Panoramas was an undercover investigation exposing child labour in factories manufacturing Gap and Nike clothing in Cambodia. We took on the huge PR operations of Nike and Gap and I even had the US Ambassador to Cambodia phoning me late at night asking me to change the content of the programme. The programme made headline news and was shown on Capitol Hill.
Mentor: Peter Horrocks, Head of BBC News for being calm in a crisis and letting me loose on some great programmes, and Jane Corbin, Panorama Correspondent, for teaching me the meaning of getting your foot in the door and keeping it there with a smile.
Big break: Convincing Peter Horrocks to promote me from Assistant Producer on Panorama to Permanent Producer - something that was unheard of at the time.
Big mistake: An infamous night at the RTS awards - that's all I'll say.

» **Reading:** *Political books like Bob Woodward on Bush or Seymour Hersh on Abu Ghraib. Or fiction about countries I am travelling to like Carlo Levi, When Christ Stopped at Eboli.* **Watching:** *Channel 4 News; More4 every night at 21:00 it seems. Dispatches, West Wing - I love CJ.* **Listening:** *Radio 4 - Today, World at One, PM; BBC World - Newshour, From Our Own Correspondent; Talk Sport - James Whale - I love the phone-ins; Depeche Mode and the Black Crows.* **Relaxing to:** *Yoga and drinking beer in The Harbour Bar in Donegal.* » *No children*

Robert Campbell

8.10.62

7-11 Herbrand Street, London WC1N 1EX
T 020 7961 2266
E robert.campbell@europe.mccann.com

Occupation: Executive Creative Director, McCann Erickson UK and Emea

Other positions: Vice-Chairman, Y&R Europe; Creative Partner, Rainey Kelly Campbell Roalfe, Y&R.
Publications: D&AD, British Television, Cannes, Campaign Press, Campaign Posters.
Education: Bristol University
Career highlights: Famous work for Volvo, RSPCA, Virgin, Times, Sunday Times, Marks and Spencer, Miller beer, Coca-Cola, Land Rover, Jaguar, Lego, Ford, Toblerone, Mastercard, American Airlines, Bisto, Nesquik, MTV, VH1, X Box. Starting several high-profile advertising / direct marketing companies.
Mentor: David Abbott
Big break: A £25-a-week job as a copywriter in 1982 at an agency that's long gone out of business.
Big mistake: Selling Rainey Kelly Campbell Roalfe to Y&R.

» **Reading:** *The Guardian.* **Watching:** *My computer screen.* **Listening:** *Children's nursery songs.* **Relaxing to:** *Scuba diving, motor bikes, sex.* » *Married, 1 boy*

Lorraine Candy

9.7.72

64 North Row, London W1K 7LL
T 020 7150 7353
E lorraine.candy@hf-uk.com

Occupation: Editor-in-Chief, Elle UK

Other positions: Editor-in-Chief, Cosmopolitan; Features Editor, The Times; Editor, B Magazine; Deputy Editor, The Times Saturday magazine; Associate Editor, Marie Claire; Woman's Editor, the Sun and Today; Feature Writer, the Daily Mirror; Reporter, the Wimbledon News; Editorial Assistant, the Cornish Times.
Awards: BSME Editor of the Year, Cosmo; BSME Innovation of the Year, Cosmo campaign.
Education: Liskeard Comprehensive, Cornwall; no university
Career highlights: I left school at 16 with ambitions to work on the Daily Mirror. Getting a staff job at the Mirror at 21 is the highlight of my career - I was so young and so grateful and enjoyed every minute of it, travelling the world to do interviews and news backgrounders; meeting Helen Gurley Brown, the founder of Cosmo, in my first week in the job (in the Bahamas!) is the most memorable highlight of my career alongside winning Editor of the Year at Cosmo in my first year in the job when Glamour launched against us at half our price.
Mentor: Mac Ifill, the old-school Wimbledon News Editor who tortured me and Piers Morgan as cub reporters in the best possible way. Richard Stott, Daily Mirror/Today Editor who taught me how to sell a good feature to the reader. Mary Riddell, columnist, Gill Morgan, The Times Saturday magazine Editor, Cosmo's Helen Gurley Brown.
Big break: Writing to hundreds of local London newspapers at 16 expecting them all to take my request to make tea and do any job on offer seriously - Andrew Palmer gave me the break as a 17-year-old from Cornwall on the Wimbledon News.
Big mistake: Too many to admit to in public.

» **Reading:** *News of the World, Mirror, The Times, Observer, every US and UK glossy monthly under the sun, Heat, OK, Hello, Elle Deco.* **Watching:** *Everything on Channel 4 before 10pm - I have had no sleep for three years due to children so go to bed very early. All repeats of Seinfeld, Little Angels, Super nanny, Wife Swap, 321 on Living Channel.* **Listening:** *Radio 4's Today Programme every day religiously, music my team tell me I should have on the iPod.* **Relaxing to:** *With husband James, my girls and our dog. Drinking copious amounts of red wine with friends forced to eat my appalling cooking in the garden in the summer.* » *Married, 2 daughters*

Joce Capper 2.10.69

66 Old Compton Street, London W1D 4UH
T 020 7437 8676
E joce@rushes.co.uk

Occupation: Managing Director, Rushes Postproduction Ltd

Other positions: General Manager; Senior Producer. We've worked on campaigns for all major advertisers including Virgin, Ford, Land Rover, M&S, as well as on groundbreaking music promos, feature films, longform and other broadcast work.
Awards: I'm proud to say that during the time I've worked here, Rushes has won nearly every major advertising award from D&ADs to CADs and Clios.
Education: Clare Park Secondary
Career highlights: Something I am most proud of is launching the Rushes Soho Shorts Film Festival, which is now a major event on the international short film circuit. We never dreamt that the festival would become so incredibly respected and popular - it's hugely rewarding and a demonstration of Rushes' absolute commitment to the creative industries.
Mentor: John Taylor, a very clever and wise Scottish accountant.
Big break: Discovering the world of post production through a temp agency in 1985. It was an immediate love affair.
Big mistake: Mistake? Perhaps I've led a charmed life, but I can't think of a work one. Personal? An odd taste in men sometimes!

» **Reading:** *I'm an avid reader, I enjoy The Times and, recently, the Independent as well as a lot of contemporary fiction, biographies and the occasional copy of OK!* **Watching:** *I don't get a lot of time to watch television (apart from the ads), but I'm a big black-and-white film fan. And Coronation Street of course, it makes me laugh.* **Listening:** *I stand by my most recent liking for Anthony and the Johnsons!* **Relaxing to:** *Walking, good food, good friends, good wine and good films.* » *Single*

Phil Carrodus 3.10.60

ITV Westcountry, Western Wood Way, Langage Science Park, Plymouth PL7 5BQ
T 01752 333044
E phil.carrodus@itv.com

Occupation: Controller, ITV Westcountry News

Other positions: Editor, Central News, Abingdon; Assistant Editor, BBC Look East; Deputy Editor, Bermuda Broadcasting Company; Political Correspondent, the Royal Gazette, Bermuda; Reporter, Coventry Evening Telegraph.
Career highlights: I started as a trainee reporter on the Coventry Evening Telegraph before heading off to Bermuda to work for the daily paper. That's where I got my first break into television, working variously as Deputy Editor, Co-anchor and Political Reporter for the island's television service. After returning to England, a few short term contracts were followed by four years at the BBC in Norwich, producing Look East. I moved to ITV in 1990, joining Central in Abingdon, first as News Editor then Producer and finally Editor of Central News South. I joined ITV Westcountry in 2001.
Mentor: Laurie Upshon, my Head of News at Central. He was a great boss and a loyal friend.
Big break: Landing a job at the Bermuda Broadcasting Company - it might not sound like much, but it was my first taste of broadcast journalism and I loved it.
Big mistake: Ordering a club sandwich at a lunch with a government minister in Bermuda. I only realised it had a toothpick in it after biting through it - rather than admit my mistake, I went on to eat the rest of the toothpick as well.

» **Reading:** *Modern fiction.* **Watching:** *News and almost any sport - I even got hooked on women's curling at the last Winter Olympics.* **Listening:** *Bob Marley, Groove Armada, Aretha Franklin, early reggae and ska, Joao Gilberto - all sorts.* **Relaxing to:** *Walking with my family on the beach, or on Dartmoor, running, playing tennis, cooking, eating, drinking red wine.* » *Married, 3 children*

Gillian Carter 19.12.63

BBC Worldwide, 80 Wood Lane, London W12 0TT
T 020 8433 3777
E gillian.carter@bbc.co.uk

Occupation: Editor, BBC Good Food Magazine

Other positions: Features Editor, More!; Deputy Editor, Woman; Editor, Family Circle.
Publications: BBC Good Food Vegetarian Christmas.
Awards: Shortlisted, Best Food magazine, World Food Media Awards 2005; Lifestyle Magazine of the Year, BSME, 2005.
Education: Jersey College for Girls; Oxford Polytechnic
Career highlights: The highlights are the people I've been lucky enough to work with: Orlando Murrin (ex-Editor and Editor-in-Chief) and Nicki Hill (Food Group Publisher), and Elaine Stocks (my Deputy Editor) all at BBC Worldwide. Also Carole Russell (ex-Editor, Woman) Sally Morris (ex Sunday Mirror, now freelance) and Sian James (ex Sunday Mirror and now Features Editor, Mail on Sunday); and dozens more brilliant people who've supported and inspired me.
Mentor: Orlando Murrin
Big break: Giving him a call when I knew he was looking for a number two on Good Food.
Big mistake: Probably, not calling earlier.

» **Reading:** *Too many emails.* **Watching:** *Whatever's on between 9 and 11pm.* **Listening:** *Radio 4.* **Relaxing to:** *Yoga, eating in.* » *Married*

Mark Carter 29.12.77

Broadcasting Centre, Guildford GU2 7AP
T 01483 306306
E mark.carter@bbc.co.uk

Occupation: Head of Output, BBC Southern Counties Radio

Other positions: Presenter and journalist at other radio stations including Star FM, Neptune Radio and Channel Travel Radio.
Awards: In the pipeline, I'm sure.
Education: Kingston University

» *Single*

Stephen Carter
12.2.64

Ofcom, Riverside House, 2a Southwark Bridge Road SE1 9HA

T 020 7981 3500
E stephen.carter@ofcom.org.uk

Occupation: Chief Executive Officer, Ofcom

Education: Aberdeen University; Harvard Business School
Career highlights: Chief Executive, J W Thompson, 1986-99; Chief Operating Officer and Managing Director, ntl, UK and Ireland, 1999-2002.

» *Married, 2 children*

Sam Cartmell
27.9.72

60 Sloane Avenue, London SW3 3XB

T 020 7894 5548
E sam.cartmell@loweworldwide.com

Occupation: Creative Head/Copywriter, Lowe Worldwide

Publications: Tesco, Stella Artois, HSBC.
Awards: 3 D&AD Pencils; 2 Campaign Press gold; Creative Circle; Eurobest; Cannes Lion.
Education: Bedford School; Cardiff University
Career highlights: Started as a local journalist. Sports commentator for BBC. Worked briefly at the Sun. Moved to Hong Kong and someone generously gave me a job as a copywriter. Since returning to UK have created campaigns for Tesco, Stella and HSBC.
Mentor: Paul Weinberger, Chairman of Lowe.
Big break: Making the cut when APL merged with Lowe.
Big mistake: Mis-spelling both names of 'Allo 'Allo's Gordon Kaye while working at the Sun - still not 100% sure of the correct spelling. It brings me out in a cold sweat even now.

» **Reading:** *Dickens, Campaign, Guardian (Berliner format), Daily Telegraph, Topsy and Tim books to my children.* **Watching:** *Channel 4 news, BBC, Spooks, live cricket and rugby.* **Listening:** *The Today Programme, Five Live.* **Relaxing to:** *Playing rugby, swimming, going home.*
» *Married, 3 daughters*

Andrew Caspari

Room 5016, Broadcasting House, Portland Place, London W1A 1AA

T 020 7765 2660
E andrew.caspari@bbc.co.uk

Occupation: Commissioning Editor, Specialist Factual, BBC Radio 4

Other positions: Commissioning Editor, Weekday Evenings, BBC Radio 4; Deputy Editor, PM and World at One, Duty Editor, Radio 4; Producer, Today, BBC Radio 4; Presenter, Morning Merseyside, BBC Radio Merseyside.
Awards: Sony Golds (1, and 2 others as part of teams); Broadcasting Press Guild.
Education: Haberdashers' Aske's School for Boys; Elstree and Van Mildert College; Durham University
Career highlights: As Presenter of Morning Merseyside for nearly three years I covered many of the key events in the region in the mid-80's from Hatton to Heysel; I spent nearly six years on Today and edited the programmes in Berlin covering the fall of the Berlin Wall, the end of Margaret Thatcher's time as Prime Minister, the Moscow White House siege (Sony Gold Award Winner), two weeks at the Rio Earth Summit and an election results morning; when I was at PM it was the biggest non-breakfast programme in UK Radio. At Radio 4 I was one of the architects of the new schedule launched in 1998 by James Boyle and as such was part of the team that oversaw the creation of staples such as Front Row, The Film Programme, The Westminster Hour, Broadcasting House, Home Truths, The Now Show and many others; recent highlights include the Reith Lectures, the migrations event, the season of programmes marking the anniversary of the end of World War Two and winning Sony Station of the Year in 2003 and 2004.
Big break: Professionally: being asked to do an audition for Radio Merseyside after appearing as a contributor whilst working as an Events and Entertainments Manager in Liverpool. Personally: meeting my wife.
Big mistake: Best kept private!

» **Reading:** *Newspapers, magazines and biography mainly.* **Watching:** *Sport, drama (contemporary and classic), current affairs and documentaries, film (DVD or cinema rather than TV).* **Listening:** *Radio 4 and the competition. Test Match Special. When I have had enough speech any music station playing a tune I like.* **Relaxing to:** *Playing with my children, going to the theatre and watching sport. I am a churchwarden which takes up another portion of my non-work time.*
» *Married, 2 children*

Dan Chambers
13.9.69

Five TV, 22 Long Acre, London WC2E 9LY

T 020 7550 5555
E dan.chambers@five.tv

Occupation: Director of Programmes, Five TV

Other positions: Controller of Factual, Five; Editor, Science, C4.
Education: University College School; Brasenose College, Oxford
Career highlights: When I was Controller of Factual at Five I was very proud of helping to create series such as Extraordinary People, Revealed and Stranger Than Fiction. Since I've been Director of Programmes my proudest achievement has been to expand the range and improve the quality of the shows in Five's schedule.
Mentor: First David Cohen, Documentary and Feature Film Producer, later Sara Ramsden, then Commissioning Editor for Science and Education at C4.
Big break: Becoming Deputy Commissioning Editor of Science at C4.
Big mistake: Saying yes to a biggish reality show at C4 which didn't rate.

» **Reading:** *American and Canadian non-fiction, eg anything by Malcolm Gladwell, Urban Tribes, Freakonomics, No Brow, plus wide variety of magazines.* **Watching:** *All Five's output,* *plus good comedy eg Curb Your Enthusiasm, Extras.* **Listening:** *Unhealthy amounts of Nick Cave.* **Relaxing to:** *With my family.* » *Single, 1 child*

Will Chambers

29.10.71

Capital Disney, GCap Media plc,
30 Leicester Square, London WC2H 7LA
T 020 7766 6415
E will.chambers@capitalradio.com

Occupation: Programme Manager and Head of Music, Capital Disney

Other positions: Radio Presenter for Capital Disney, Spirit FM and StormLive. TV Breakfast Presenter for Disneychannel UK. Freelance voiceover, producer and writer.
Publications: 2004, Central Office of Information Safe Surfing Week, a week-long series of evening shows with advice on safe use of the internet; FurbyStar 2005, a joint campaign between Capital Disney, MTV and Hasbro to promote the new toy range run across all dayparts with individual presenters acting as mentors to their own Furby. Each Furby had recorded a song and listeners voted by text and web for their Furbystar.
Awards: NTL Commercial Radio Digital Station of the Year, 2004; Sony Radio Academy Awards Station of the Year, Digital Terrestrial, 2005.
Education: Pocklington Grammar School
Career highlights: I never had a career plan in my early 20s although I always liked the idea of working in radio. After years in sales roles I decided to go for it! Highlights include that first pro show doing an overnight, landing the Disney channel breakfast show and now running my own radio station.
Mentor: I have a huge amount of respect and admiration for Paul Robinson. He's got so much experience of UK TV and radio from on-air to senior management. Always there with some advice when I need it!
Big break: Without doubt, getting a national audience on Disney Channel UK.
Big mistake: I sometimes regret not entering the media industry until nearly 30, but then again I've got a wealth of life experience from all the other things I've done.

» **Reading:** *The Independent, MediaGuardian, Broadcast, Music Week, Marketing Week, also flick through the red tops for the lighter stuff. Love a good book for the train, particularly enjoyed Piers Morgan's The Insider.* **Watching:** *Corry, Hollyoaks, Sky News, Midsomer Murders, Little Britain, Dr Who (essential family viewing), T4 and various music channels. Plus I love a good investigative documentary.* **Listening:** *Radio and lots of it! From Capital Disney to Radio 4. At home my CD collection covers early Genesis, Steve Hackett and Pink Floyd through to Nickelback and McFly – something for every mood.* **Relaxing to:** *Good bottle of wine and a film! Time out with the kids, watching motor racing and DIY.* » *Married, 2 daughters aged 8 and 3*

David Chance

22.4.57

ITV plc, 200 Gray's Inn Road, London WC1X 8HF
T 020 7843 8000
E David.Chance@itv.com

Occupation: Non-executive Director, ITV plc

Other positions: Non-executive Director, Sunderland plc, 1998-present; Non-executive Director, 1998, Chairman, Modern Times Group, 2003-present; Chairman, Top UP TV Limited, 2002-present; Non-executive Director, Viasat Broadcasting UK Ltd, 2003-present; Non-executive Director, Transmission Facilities Limited, 2003-present; Non-executive Director, mmO2 plc, 2003-present.
Education: Shrewsbury School; University of North Carolina
Career highlights: Scientific Atlanta, 1981-86; Grass Valley Group, 1986-88; SES Astra, 1988-89; BSkyB, 1989-98, appointed Deputy Chief Executive, 1993; Co-founder of Top-Up TV with former BSkyB Executive Ian West.

» **Relaxing to:** *Gym, watching Sunderland FC, running property development company in North Carolina.*
» *Living with partner*

Peter Charlton

PO Box 168, Wellington Street, Leeds LS1 1RF
T 0113 243 2701
E yp.editor@ypn.co.uk

Occupation: Editor, Yorkshire Post

Other positions: Formerly Editor, the Star, Sheffield; Editor, Lancashire Evening Post; Editor, Blackpool Gazette.
Publications: Campaigns currently under way in the YP include pressing for better NHS dental services, better transport funding for Yorkshire, and supporting the York Minster restoration appeal.

» **Reading:** *The national newspapers, plus the business/financial press, as the business sector is a key constituency for the Yorkshire Post.* **Watching:** *Sheffield United*

Barbara Charone

The Wellington Building, 28–32 Wellington Road, St John's Wood, London NW8 9SP
T 020 7483 9205
E Barbara@mbcpr.com

Occupation: Publicist and writer

Publications: Keith Richards, 1979; Keith Richards: Life as a Rolling Stone, 1982
Education: Northwestern University
Career highlights: Writer, Chicago Sun-Times; Sounds (Writer, then Features Editor, then Deputy Editor); NME; Creem; formerly Staff Writer, Press Officer, Press Manager, Head of Press, Director of Press, Warner Brothers, 1981-; Madonna's UK spokeswoman, other clients include REM, Elvis Costello, Jennifer Lopez, Christina Aguilera and James Blunt.

Neil Christie

10.7.66

16 Hanbury Street, London E1 6QR
T 020 7194 7000
E neil.christie@wk.com

Occupation: Managing Director, Wieden + Kennedy London

Education: Aberdeen University
Career highlights: Becoming MD of Wieden + Kennedy London in 2004 and in 2005 seeing the agency become IPA agency of the year and win the Grand Prix at Cannes.
Big break: The Wieden + Kennedy pitch for Honda's business.
Big mistake: The plastic trousers.

» **Reading:** *Depressing contemporary fiction.* **Watching:** *Obscure foreign films.* **Listening:** *The Fall, Black Dice, Animal Collective, Boredoms – anything from the fringes, preferably with guitars.* **Relaxing to:** *Travel, reading, sleeping, a cold beer and the soothing sounds of the Fall.*
» *Married, 2 children*

Louise Chunn

25.7.60

Kings Reach Tower, Stamford Street, London SE1 9LS
T 020 7261 4756
E louise_chunn@instyleuk.com

Occupation: Editor, Good Housekeeping

Other positions: Editor, In Style magazine; Editor, ES Magazine; Deputy Editor, Vogue; Editor, Guardian women's page, style page and parents' page; Deputy Editor, Elle; Editor, Just Seventeen.
Publications: Irish portfolio for Vogue with Bruce Weber featuring everyone from Seamus Heaney through to Bono. Regularly commissioning the likes of Suzanne Moore, Jan Moir, Susie Mackenzie and Michele Hanson for Guardian women's page features.
Awards: In Style, magazine of the year, 2004; PPA Awards Writer of the Year, EMAP Awards, 1984.
Education: University of Auckland, New Zealand (BA History)
Career highlights: I worked on Just Seventeen from the launch. It was a landmark, the first grown-up teen magazine. From there it was on to Elle, which was very much the trendy women's fashion magazine of the 80s where I commissioned the likes of Germaine Greer, Tony Parsons and Julie Burchill. On to the Guardian for five years where I edited the women's pages, giving Suzanne Moore her first weekly column, regularly using Michele Hanson, Susie Mackenzie, Jan Moir, and Mark Haddon (he co-wrote Men: A User's Guide). I instituted regular events like a team of undergraduates editing the section for a week, summer fiction specials, and also edited the style and parents' pages. I left for a job at Vogue where I was brought in to beef up the features. I tackled everything from reporting Rosemary West's trial to celebrities on ageing and anorexic teens on food, plus using excellent writers from Zoe Heller to Janine di Giovanni. Working with Alexandra Shulman and Robin Derrick was inspirational.
Mentor: Dave Hepworth (now at Development Hell). When he edited Just Seventeen he employed me – I was then working on a trade magazine as a lowly reporter – as Features Editor and knocked at least some of the pretensions out of me.
Big break: Probably getting the Guardian job though it came about because someone else got the job I wanted (editorship of Elle). It seemed like an anomaly – women's pages? why? – but it was a golden opportunity for creating great features from a female perspective. There was also less celebrity pressure at the time, for which I am grateful.

» **Reading:** *The Guardian every day, Telegraph on Saturday, Observer on Sunday, occasionally Telegraph, Times or Indy. Magazines have become 'work' so I have transferred that passion to my airmail copy of the New York Times Sunday edition, especially Sunday Styles, even more especially the weddings section. Light-as-a-feather relief. Otherwise, books: I loved Zadie Smith's On Beauty, Lionel Shriver's We Have to Talk About Kevin, Sarah Dunant's The Birth of Venus.* **Watching:** *Am still mourning the end of Six Feet Under, but have started a new batch: Rome, Bleak House, Lost. Will also watch documentaries and news, but mostly if something is breaking.* **Listening:** *Yawn ... Today Programme though I get annoyed with tetchiness of Humphries et al, Jonathan Ross on Saturday Radio 2, Front Row (especially with Mark Lawson), Saturday Review, The Archers (but not religiously).* **Relaxing to:** *Paying a lot of money to have a massage in my sitting room on a Friday night. Failing that, reading in bed, or lying on the floor after a run.*
» *Married to Andrew Anthony, 3 children*

Liz Citron

10.5.64

Syzygy UK Ltd, 4th Floor, Elsley House, 24-30 Great Titchfield Street, London W1W 8BF
T 020 7460 4080
E l.citron@syzygy.net

Occupation: Head of User Experience at Syzygy, London

Other positions: Chair of BIMA (British Interactive Media Association) 2002-06; Associate Lecturer, Open University Business School.
Awards: None recent enough to note.
Education: Camberwell School of Art (BA); Open University (MBA); halfway through MSc in HCI at UCL
Career highlights: Getting a job at Wired magazine felt like a 'finger on the pulse' moment, followed by helping to establish the Guardian's New Media Lab (forerunner to Guardian Unlimited). Setting up a design agency with people who I loved to work with and seeing it blossom and grow. Getting an MBA at the same time. Being asked to be the Chair of BIMA for three consecutive years.
Mentor: I have had a lot of support from all sorts of people as I have made my way through my working life. Most recently, my children and my partner have probably had the biggest impact and have taught me things that I take to work every day. They are persistent enough to make sure I get the message.
Big break: Getting a job at Wired magazine when I returned to work after taking time off to have children. It is hard getting things started when

you haven't got a recent track record. It was a really buzzy place to be and I learned a lot.
Big mistake: Thinking life would just fall into place when I was younger. I have had to do a lot of work to rectify the damage done by wasted time.

» **Reading:** *I love reading fiction and usually find that my favorites are by women authors. I do judge a book by its cover (and maybe a sample page or two) and am rarely disappointed.* **Watching:** *Not much. If anything just very light comedy, stuff you don't really have to commit to because I rarely see a whole programme, let alone a series.* **Listening:** *A wide range of music from acoustic to drum 'n' bass.* **Relaxing to:** *Usually by reading, pottering in the garden, spending time with good friends or having a siesta. But the best way to relax usually includes a glass of wine.* » *Divorced, 2 children*

David Clayton

20.11.56

BBC Radio Norfolk, The Forum,
Millennium Plain, Norwich NR2 1BH
T 01603 617411
E david.clayton@bbc.co.uk

Occupation: Editor, BBC Radio Norfolk

Other positions: Freelance Radio Presenter, Radio 4; Norfolk TV Presenter, Anglia TV, BBC East.
Awards: Sony Award
Education: Great Yarmouth Grammar School
Career highlights: Hospital radio, BBC Radio Norfolk as a freelance presenter. TV Announcer/Newsreader Anglia, then BBC East. Won Sony Award for best magazine programme in 1986 then to Radio 4 as Co-presenter of the Local Network and other programmes. Deputy Editor of BBC Radio Norfolk 1991, Editor 1998.
Mentor: Ian Masters
Big break: Standing in on a one-off election special mid-morning show on Radio Norfolk, then being offered a permanent show.
Big mistake: Not sending in a winning pools coupon.

» **Reading:** *Broadcasting and showbiz biographies. The Eastern Daily Press before I leave home of a morning.* **Watching:** *Football, Coronation Street, documentaries and regional news programmes - Look East.* **Listening:** *Radio Norfolk, Five Live.* **Relaxing to:** *Write, listen to 70s disco hits, walk in the Yorkshire Dales.* » *Married, 3 children*

Alan Clements

28.5.65

St George's Studios, 93–97 St George's Road,
Glasgow G3 6JA
T 0141 353 8438
E alan.clements@iwcmedia.co.uk

Occupation: Creative Director, IWC Media

Publications: Author, Restless Nation.
Education: Stranraer Academy; University of Glasgow; University of Pennsylvania
Career highlights: Previously journalist at BBC Scotland 1987-90; Managing Director at Wark Clements, 1991-2003.
Mentor: Lots of great and inspirational support through the years but not one mentor.
Big break: Getting a runner's job at the BBC.
Big mistake: Lots of mistakes but none yet fatal.

» **Reading:** *History books.* **Watching:** *Biggest treat is The West Wing.* **Listening:** *Maria Callas when working and everything from Elvis Presley to the Black Eyed Peas when not.* **Relaxing to:** *Five-a-side football, tennis, swimming and running with the labrador.* » *Married, 2 children*

Polly Cochrane

6.4.68

124 Horseferry Road, London SW1
T 020 7396 4444
E pcochrane@channel4.co.uk

Occupation: Director of Marketing, Channel 4

Other positions: Head of Advertising and Promotions, Channel 5; Manager, Guardian Development Unit; Marketing Manager, The Observer; UK Communications Manager, Vanity Fair; Account Director, Cowan Kemsley Taylor; Account Manager, WCRS.
Awards: I have had management responsibility for creative teams and departments over the years that have won numerous awards for advertising, channel identity and on-air promotion but I wouldn't want to claim any of them as my own. Most recently the Channel 4 idents won a D&AD Black Pencil and the Shameless poster produced by 4 Creative won a Campaign gold. We have also won a healthy number of media awards with our agencies M&B and OMD over the years.
Education: St Paul's Girls' School; Cambridge
Career highlights: Being in the room when the Squirrel and Dambusters ads were presented to Bass for Carling Black Label. Promoting the pregnant Demi Moore issue of Vanity Fair. Being part of the launch of the Observer under Guardian Media Group's ownership. Being part of the launch of Channel 5/retuning the nation. Seven years at Channel 4.
Mentor: David Brook
Big break: Moving from an ad agency to run communications for Vanity Fair in the UK probably required the greatest leap of faith by any employer I've had and triggered my subsequent career in the media.
Big mistake: Buying a complicated ad concept for a campaign with a small budget.

» **Reading:** *The Guardian, Observer, Broadcast, MediaGuardian.co.uk, Vogue, Condé Nast Traveller, strategy documents, children's books.* **Watching:** *Channel 4, More4 and anything by Ricky Gervais and Stephen Merchant.* **Listening:** *Radio 4, the soundtrack to Shrek and every once in a while some opera.* **Relaxing to:** *With difficulty - must try harder.* » *Married, 2 children*

James Coghill

8.3.60

Hylton Road, Worcester WR2 5WW
T 01905 748485
E james.coghill@bbc.co.uk

Occupation: Station Manager, BBC Hereford and Worcester (radio, online, television)

Other positions: Reporter, Northwich Guardian; Reporter, RTV, Hong Kong; Reporter and News Producer, BRMB Radio; News Editor, BBC Hereford and Worcester; Producer, Sybil Ruscoe Show, R5L.

Awards: Sony bronze 1993, Response to News Event; Sony silver 1995, Response to News Event.
Education: Denstone College, Uttoxeter; Leicester Polytechnic
Career highlights: A lowlight really - covering the Tory Party Conference and getting called back to the BRMB newsroom the evening before the IRA bombed The Grand Hotel in Brighton, on the grounds that 'it's all over bar the shouting - you'll be more use here'.
Mentor: Too many to mention.
Big break: My Dad serving in the Korean War with Trevor Buckley, who was later Editor in Chief of the Warrington Guardian Series - the pulled string got me an interview which got me my first job in journalism.
Big mistake: Forgetting to give the outcue while doing a live to camera for RTV in HK, and then standing there for what seemed like forever on live telly tongue-tied and looking like a penis.

» **Reading:** *The Guardian, Uncut, Songlines, Private Eye, books.* **Watching:** *Footy and cricket, various stuff mostly on BBC2, BBC4 and C4.* **Listening:** *My own radio station, and a variety of others when I'm travelling. Rock and roll, world, punk, dance, old vinyl.* **Relaxing to:** *Like a newt.*
» *Married, 2 children*

Danny Cohen

Channel 4, 124 Horseferry Road, London SW1P 2TX
T 020 7396 4444
E dcohen@channel4.co.uk

Occupation: Head of Documentaries, Channel 4

Other positions: Commissioning Editor, Documentaries, Channel 4; Commissioning Editor, Factual Programmes, E4.
Publications: Cutting Edge, Supernanny, Born With Two Mothers, Fat Kids, The Games, Extraordinary Families.
Education: Oxford University

Professor Peter Cole 16.12.45

Department of Journalism Studies, University of Sheffield, Minalloy House, Regent Street, Sheffield S1 3NJ
T 0114 222 2500
E journalism@ sheffield.ac.uk

Occupation: Professor of Journalism, University of Sheffield

Publications: Can You Positively Identify This Man? (with Peter Pringle), 1975.
Education: Tonbridge School; Queens' College, Cambridge
Career highlights: Reporter, Evening News, 1968-72; Diary Editor, Evening Standard, 1976-78; News Editor, Deputy Editor, the Guardian, 1978-88; Editor, Sunday Correspondent, 1988-90; News Review Editor, Sunday Times, 1990-93; Professor of Journalism, University of Central Lancashire, 1993-2000.
» *Married, 4 children*

Nicholas Coleridge 4.3.57

Condé Nast, Vogue House, Hanover Square, London W1S 1JU
T 020 7499 9080

Occupation: Managing Director, Condé Nast Publications

Other positions: Chairman, Periodical Publishers Association
Publications: Tunnel Vision (collected journalism), 1982; Shooting Stars (1984); Around the World in 78 Days (1984); The Fashion Conspiracy (1988); How I Met My Wife and Other Stories (1991); Paper Tigers (1993); With Friends Like These (1997); Streetsmart (1999); Godchildren (2002).
Awards: Young Journalist of the Year, 1984; Mark Boxer Award for Lifetime Achievement and Editorial Excellence, 2001.
Education: Eton; Trinity College, Cambridge
Career highlights: Associate Editor, Tatler, 1980-82; Columnist, Evening Standard, 1982-84; Editor, Harpers and Queen, 1986-89 (Assoc Ed 1984-86); Managing Director, Condé Nast Publications (Editorial Dir 1989); Member, Council, Royal College of Art 1995-2000; Chairman, British Fashion Council, 2000-03; Chairman, Fashion Rocks, Prince's Trust, 2003.
» **Relaxing to:** *Travel, shuttlecock.* » *Married, 4 children*

Malcolm Coles 19.1.74

2 Marylebone Road, London NW1 4DF
T 020 7770 7226
E malcolm.coles@which.co.uk

Occupation: Editor, Online at Which?

Other positions: Editor, Which? magazine; Editor, Computing Which?; various other jobs at Which?; Researcher at Hurlstons Consultancy.
Publications: www.which.co.uk
Awards: AOP Online Publisher of the Year 2004 (Consumer).
Education: St Albans School; York University
Career highlights: My first job involved doing research to say nice things about the credit card industry. I then moved to Which? in 1995 where I started out doing research to reveal the truth about the credit card industry. Since then I've been an Assistant Editor on Which?, launched and edited Computing Which?, come back to Which? magazine as Managing Editor, and combined being Editor of Which? magazine and Which? Online at the same time. This role was recently split into two again, and I've stayed as the Editor of Online, making it my sixth job here in ten years.
Mentor: Helen Parker, Editorial Director, who's managed me for many years at Which? in several different roles.
Big break: Getting a job at a research/PR consultancy straight out of university. When I think of some of the other jobs I applied for...
Big mistake: Changing a website that ended in .cc to .co.uk without checking it. We had to reprint Computing Which? that month as I'd changed it to a porn site. And I once walked off the set of This

Morning in front of the (still rolling) cameras, thinking they'd gone to a video (I'm still waiting for the call from Dennis Norden).

›› **Reading:** *Print: Guardian, Arena, Heat; Online: news.bbc.co.uk, www.sacfc.co.uk, www.mattcutts.com.* **Watching:** *Sky+ means I watch far too much on E4 and Sky One, OC, Scrubs, Friends, Lost etc.* **Listening:** *Radio 5, Radio 7 and my iPod.* **Relaxing to:** *TV and football.* ›› *Married, no children*

Ron Coles 18.7.44

Manor Farm, Main Street, Upton, Newark, Nottinghamshire NG23 5ST
T 01636 812289
E ron.coles@saga.co.uk

Occupation: Managing Director, Saga Radio

Awards: FRSA, 2001
Education: Wellingborough Grammar School; Sunderland College of Education; University of Leeds.
Career highlights: BBC Radio: Producer, local and network radio, 1969-75; Training Instructor, radio production techniques, 1975-76; Programme Organiser, Nottingham, 1976-78; Manager, Sheffield, 1978-80; Managing Director, Radio Trent Ltd, 1980-89; Midlands Radio plc, 1989-92; radio consultant, 1992-present; Managing Director, Investors In Radio Ltd, 1996-98; Radio 106fm Ltd, 1996-98; Director of Radio, Saga Group 1999-present; Association of Independent Radio Contractors, Chairman, Labour Relations Committee, 1982-83, elected to Council, 1982-92 (Chairman 1986-87), Chairman of Finance 1988-92; Chairman, Radio Academy, 1995-98 (Council Member, 1989-98, Vice-Chairman 1994-95, Fellow 1998-present); Member, Rare Breeds Survival Trust, Notts Beekeepers Association; Editor, The Beekeepers' Annual 1993-97.

›› **Relaxing to:** *Beekeeping, bearded collie dogs.*
›› *Married, 2 children*

Stephen Cook 6.4.60

160 Great Portland Street, London W1W 5QA
T 020 7299 5000

Occupation: Director, Flextech Television

Other positions: Consultant, Wiggin & Co, 1998-present; Director, Telewest plc, 2000-present.
Education: Duncanrig School, East Kilbride; University of Aberdeen
Career highlights: Trainee, Moncrieff Warren Patterson Glasgow, 1982-84; Assistant, McGrigor Donald, 1984-87; Partner, Herbert Smith, London, 1991-93 (Asst 1987-91); Head, Company Department, McGrigor Donald, 1994-96; Member, Law Society of Scotland, 1984; Law Society of England and Wales, 1989.

›› **Relaxing to:** *Medieval history, walking the dog, wine.*
›› *Married, 2 children*

Belinda Cooper 19.6.72

King's Reach Tower, Stamford Street, London SE1 9LS
T 020 7261 6379
E belinda_cooper@ipcmedia.com

Occupation: Publisher, IPC Media

Other positions: Publisher, Hobsons plc.
Publications: Homes & Gardens; Country Homes & Interiors; 25 Beautiful Kitchens.
Education: St Paul's Girls' School; Central St Martin's

›› **Reading:** *A magazine junkie - but always Time Out, Uncut and Vogue...*

Ben Cooper 9.12.73

Yalding House, 152/156 Great Portland Street, London W1N 6AJ
T 020 7765 2236
E sarah.ansah@bbc.co.uk

Occupation: Head of Mainstream Programming, BBC Radio 1

Other positions: Sony Radio Academy Awards Committee member.
Education: Brighton University
Career highlights: Following the completion of studies at Brighton, began career at BBC Hereford and Worcester as a runner before securing a slot as presenter of the early morning breakfast show. One year on, trained as a journalist and spent two years working as a reporter on the station. In 1994 returned to presenting on BBC Three Counties Radio hosting the drivetime show before moving into a producer role a year later. In 1997 moved to Radio 1 and produced a variety of shows including Nicky Campbell, Jo Whiley and Chris Moyles. Following this period as one of the station's most successful and innovative producers, moved to Capital Radio as Executive Producer, a post held for two years before returning to Radio 1 as Head of Mainstream in January 2003. Overhauled the whole of Radio 1's daytime line up including installing Chris Moyles at breakfast, Colin and Edith at lunchtime and Scott Mills at drive.
Big break: Making cups of tea for Jane Garvey on BBC Hereford and Worcester before she got her job at BBC Radio 5 Live.

›› **Reading:** *The Guardian or Independent, Sun and Observer newspapers, Music Week, NME, Q magazine, Wallpaper magazine.* **Watching:** *On TV I watch Spooks, The West Wing and Lost. Online I click on MTV Overdrive, but usually I spend my time watching the latest film releases on DVD.* **Listening:** *Radio 1.* ›› *Engaged, no children*

Andy Coulson

1969

News of the World, 1 Virginia Street, London E98 1NW
T 020 7782 4000
E andy.coulson@notw.co.uk

Occupation: Editor, News of the World

Awards: Scoop of the Year (Beckham's Secret Affair), British Press Awards, 2005; Newspaper of the Year, British Press Awards, 2005.
Career highlights: Junior Reporter, Basildon Evening Echo; Editor, Bizarre pages, the Sun, 1988; Assistant Editor, then Associate Editor, the Sun; set up page3.com; joined News of the World, 2000; Editor, News of the World, 2003-present.
» *Married, 2 children*

Barry Cox

25.5.42

Channel 4 Television Corporation, 124 Horseferry Road, London SW1P 2TX
T 020 7396 4444
E barry.cox@channel4.co.uk

Occupation: Deputy Chairman, Channel 4 Television

Other positions: Chairman, Digital TV Stakeholders Group 2002-04; Chairman, Switch Co Ltd 2005-present; Consultant, United Broadcasting & Entertainment, 1998-2001; Consultant, ITN, 1998-present; Member, Council, Institute of Education, 2000-present; Governor, European Institute for the Media, 1999-2001; Chairman, Oval House, 2001-present; Visiting Professor of Broadcast Media, University of Oxford, 2003.
Publications: Civil Liberties In Britain (1975); The Fall of Scotland Yard (jointly, 1977); Free for All? (2004).
Awards: FRTS
Education: Tiffin School, Kingston upon Thames; Magdalen College, Oxford
Career highlights: Journalist, The Scotsman, 1965-67; Journalist, Sunday Telegraph, 1967-70; Reporter and Producer, Granada TV, 1970-74; Editor, London Weekend Television, 1974-77; Head of Current Affairs, London Weekend Television, 1977-81; Controller of Features and Current Affairs, London Weekend Television, 1981-87; Director of Corporate Affairs, London Weekend Television, 1987-94; Special Adviser to Chief Executive, London Weekend Television, 1994-95; Director, ITV Association, 1995-98; Deputy Chairman, Channel 4, 1999-present.
» *4 children*

Jon Craig

9.8.57

Sky News, 2nd Floor, 4 Millbank, London SW1P 3JA
T 020 7705 5505
E jon.craig@bskyb.com

Occupation: Political Correspondent, Sky News

Education: King's School, Macclesfield; Wetherby High School; Tadcaster Grammar School
Career highlights: Political Correspondent, Thomson Regional Newspapers, 1982-86; Home Affairs Correspondent, Sunday Times, 1986-89; Political Correspondent, Today, 1989-92; Political Editor, Daily Express, 1992-96, Deputy Political Editor, the Express, 1996-98; Political Editor, Sunday Express, 1998-2001; Political Editor, BBC London, 2001-2003.
» *Divorced, no children*

Jeremy Craigen

8.5.67

DDB London, 12 Bishops Bridge Road, London W2 6AA
T 020 7258 3979
E jeremy.craigen@ddblondon.com

Occupation: Executive Creative Director, DDB London

Other positions: Board Director, BTAA; Education Council member, D&AD.
Publications: VW: UFO, Protection, Demon Baby, Smile; Sony: Unexpected, Power of TV; American Airlines: Seats.
Awards: Cannes, D&AD, Clio; BTAA, Campaign Press and Poster, One Show; helping put DDB London at the top of the Gunn Report over the last six years.
Education: Radley College
Career highlights: Joined Ted Bates as a Junior Copywriter in 1984, merged with Dorlands 1988. Joined BMP DDB in 1990. Made Director of Creativity in 1996. Deputy Creative Director in 2001, Joint Creative Director in 2002 and Executive Creative Director in 2005.
Mentor: Bill Bernbach
Big break: Tony Cox hiring me to work at BMP DDB.
Big mistake: Lots of little ones, yet to make a really big one though I'm sure it will happen.
» **Reading:** *In-flight magazines.* **Watching:** *Sky sports, any food programme.* **Listening:** *Talk Sport, Pete Tong, Tim Westwood.* **Relaxing to:** *Golf, travel, wine.* » *Married, 1 child*

Graham Creelman

20.5.48

ITV Anglia, Anglia House, Norwich NR1 3JG
T 01603 752241
E graham.creelman@itv.com

Occupation: Managing Director, ITV Anglia

Other positions: Chair, Screen East; Chair, Regional Cultural Consortium.
Awards: Several international and UK awards for production and direction of natural history films (Survival).
Education: Greenock Academy; University of Sussex
Career highlights: A Founding Producer of BBC Scotland's hugely successful Good Morning Scotland show; inititating European debate on oil pollution at sea with ITV documentary On Troubled Waters; warning UK politicians about the dangers of an Argentine invasion of the Falklands in More British than the British (ITV) - fat lot of notice they took; changing UK attitude towards withdrawing British Citizenship from St Helena (Island in Exile); achieving record late-night audience for The Last Frontier, ITV documentary which discussed the dangers facing Antarctica; many international awards for films which married natural history with informed political/environmental debate. On the

strength of this, stopped making films and became Director of Programmes at Anglia and, in 1996, Managing Director.
Mentor: The late Jim Herd of BBC Scotland.
Big break: Anglia TV's brave decision that you didn't need to be a zoologist to run Survival, ITV's long-running natural history series.
Big mistake: Not going to the US for a stint when I was offered a job there.

» **Reading:** *The Guardian, Observer, Eastern Daily Press, Broadcast, New Scientist, Trout and Salmon and Trout Fisherman. Books, constantly re-read John Buchan.* **Watching:** *Old films on TCM, anything scaly and slimy on the Sci-fi channel, Newsnight's ITV Anglia Regional news and programmes, most of ITV's drama output, footy on Sky.* **Listening:** *Radio 4 and Radio 3.* **Relaxing to:** *Fishing and walking.* » *Married, 4 daughters, 2 stepchildren*

Sara Cremer
19.4.66

eve Magazine, Haymarket Style,
174 Hammersmith Road, London W6 7JP
T 020 8267 5000
E Sara.Cremer@Haynet.com

Occupation: Editor, eve Magazine

Other positions: Committee Member, British Society of Magazine Editors; Committee Member, Editorial Training Consultant Committee.
Awards: BSME New Editor of the Year, 2001; ECM Editor of the Year, 2001; ECM Magazine of the Year, 2002.
Education: Hextable School, Kent; University of York
Career highlights: I started on FHM as Promotions and Grooming Editor in 1993; moved to Men's Health in 1995 working my way up to Deputy and then Managing Editor; I moved into women's magazines in 1999 as Deputy Editor of New Woman and was promoted to Editor in 2000, taking the magazine to its highest ever ABC and winning three awards in my time there; in 2004 I was promoted to Editorial Director of New Product Development of Emap Elan; I was appointed Editor of eve in December 2004.
Mentor: Phil Hilton
Big break: Getting my first job at FHM.
Big mistake: A men's fashion feature on cardigans.

» **Reading:** *Vanity Fair, the Guardian, Condé Nast Traveller, Country Living and hundreds of British and American women's magazines.* **Watching:** *Bleak House, Lost, The West Wing, Doc Martin, Gray's Anatomy, What Not to Wear, Strictly Come Dancing, Top Gear.* **Listening:** *Radio 4.* **Relaxing to:** *With husband, friends and wine.* » *Married, no children*

Susan Crewe
31.8.49

House and Garden, Vogue House, Hanover Square, London W1S 1HA
T 020 7499 9080
E susan.crewe@condenast.co.uk

Occupation: Editor, House and Garden magazine

Other positions: Founder, Friends of the Rehabilitation of Addictive Prisoners Trust (RAPT); Vice-patron, Royal Society of Sculptors.
Education: St Mary's School, Wantage; Cheshire College of Agriculture
Career highlights: Journalist, freelance writer and broadcaster; Contributor, The Times, Daily Telegraph, Evening Standard, Literary Review; Social Editor, Harpers & Queen, 1991-92; Editor, House and Garden 1994-present.

» **Relaxing to:** *Gardening, riding, travelling, theatre and music.* » *Divorced, 2 children*

Michael Crick
22.5.62

Room G680, BBC Television Centre, Wood Lane, London W12 7RJ
T 020 8624 9820
E Michael.Crick@bbc.co.uk

Occupation: Reporter, BBC Newsnight

Other positions: Writer of biographies and other books; Shareholder, Oxford Student Publications Ltd; Former Vice-Chair, Shareholders United.
Publications: Books: Militant, 1984; Scargill and the Miners, 1985; Manchester United: The Betrayal of a Legend (with David Smith), 1989; Jeffrey Archer: Stranger than Fiction, 1995; The Complete Manchester United Trivia Factbook, 1996; Michael Heseltine: A Biography, 1997; The Boss: The Many Sides of Alex Ferguson, 2002; In Search of Michael Howard, 2005.
Awards: RTS awards: 1989 for the Bush Tapes; 2002 for Jeffrey Archer: A Life of Lies.
Education: Manchester Grammar School; New College, Oxford University
Career highlights: Career as a journalist began on the school newspaper The Mancunian; at Oxford I edited Cherwell, and founded the Oxford Handbook and the Oxbridge Careers Handbook; joined ITN as a trainee in January 1980, and worked as a producer in Poland in 1981 and Lebanon in 1982; founder member of ITN's Channel 4 News in 1982, and in 1984 became a reporter; Washington Correspondent for Channel 4 News, 1988-90; joined the BBC in 1990; Reporter, BBC Panorama 1990-92, and BBC Newsnight 1992 to date; occasional programmes for Radio 4; since 1984 I have combined TV with writing books, mostly biographies, of which the most successful in terms of sales were those on Jeffrey Archer and Alex Ferguson.
Mentor: The late Paul McKee, former Deputy Chief Executive of ITN.
Big break: In 1983, when Andrew Franklin, then of Faber and Faber, commissioned my first book, on the Militant tendency, for an advance of £1,500.
Big mistake: Joined Panorama in 1990 at the height of Birtism within the BBC. TV reporters are like runners, each with his ideal distance. I soon discovered I do not have the patience or stamina for long programmes which take several months. I prefer 'middle-distance' reporting for programmes like Channel 4 News and Newsnight.

» **Reading:** *Guardian, Telegraph, Times, Sunday Telegraph, Observer, Spectator, Tribune, the Week, Private Eye, When Saturday Comes and far too much material about Manchester United. Biographies and modern novels.* **Watching:** *Manchester United, West End theatre, the Edinburgh Fringe festival. On TV it is mainly news, current affairs, football, comedy and documentaries.* **Listening:** *Radios 4 and 5.* **Relaxing to:** *Walking, swimming, collecting football and political books and memorabilia.* » *Separated, 1 daughter, Catherine*

David Croft 2.4.55

Flat 51, 3 Concordia Street, Leeds LS1 4ES
T 0113 243 8283
E david.croft@itv.com

Occupation: Managing Director, Yorkshire Television Ltd

Education: Epsom College; Magdalen College, Oxford
Career highlights: Ocean Transport & Trading; NFC; Thames TV; Channel Four TV; Director, Tyne Tees TV, 1998-present; Director, Granada TV, 1998-present; Director, Meridian Broadcasting, 2001-present; Director, Border TV, 2001-present; Director, Anglia TV, 2001-present; Director, Granada Enterprise, 2002-present.

» **Relaxing to:** *Golf, horseracing, travel.* » *Married, 1 son*

Paul Crompton 10.7.67

New Horizons Court 1, Grant Way, Isleworth, Middlesex TW7 5QD
T 020 7805 8482
E paul.crompton@bskyb.com

Occupation: Commissioning Editor, Popular Factual, Sky One

Other positions: Welder, Draughtsman, Freelance TV Producer.
Publications: Conspiracies, Darts Players' Wives, Rock Stars' Wives, Danny Wallace's Hoax Files, The Bigamists, Secret Life of Suburbia.
Education: University of Manchester Institute of Science and Technology
Career highlights: One of my biggest highlights was my very first job in television. I was 25 and had been through a string of unexceptional jobs and hadn't once thought of working in TV. I was lucky to be asked to present a short report on Granada for a new strand where 'real people' have their say on issues of the day. I talked about the repeal of the licensing laws, but that was irrelevant because all I wanted was to plug my band's new single on a T-shirt I wore. The single didn't sell much but I'd found my true vocation; I packed in the band and spent several years working as a researcher and then a director on a range of regional programming, from news and current affairs to comedy and art shows. The arts programming lead to a snazzy job offer to work for CNN as the Series Producer on an international arts magazine show. It also meant leaving Manchester to live in London. After two and a half years jet-setting for CNN I went freelance and worked for a number of indies on a wide range of documentaries and factual programming; three years ago I was asked to become a Commissioner for Sky One and I'm still here. I believe that working in TV is one of the best jobs in the world but I'd give it all up to get my band on Top of the Pops. Possibly.
Mentor: Tosh Ryan, video artist and founder of Rabid Records.
Big break: Being asked to be a commissioner after spending most of my life either locked in edit suites or running around with a camera crew persuading people to divulge huge chunks of their personal lives in the name of television.

» **Reading:** *Atlantic Monthly, Record Collector, The Times, Guardian, Observer, Mirror.* **Watching:** *Curb Your Enthusiasm, Seinfeld and Larry Sanders re-runs (they're out there somewhere), The Simpsons, Jon Stewart, Celebrity Big Brother and The Late Review.* **Listening:** *Johnny Cash, Miles Davis, The Libertines, Flaming Lips, Badly Drawn Boy, Adam and Joe on Xfm, Andrew Collins on BBC 6Music and Eamonn Holmes' show on Radio Five Live.* **Relaxing to:** *I have a radio in every room, all of which are usually switched on, and I also like the sound of horse racing on TV.* » *Married, 3 children*

Dominic Crossley-Holland 8.4.71

200 Gray's Inn Road, London WC1X 8HF
T 020 7843 8073
E dominic.crossley-holland@itv.com

Occupation: Controller of Current Affairs, Arts and Religion, ITV

Other positions: Producer, ITV Daytime News programmes; Producer, News at Ten; Deputy Editor, News at Ten; News Editor, ITN Westminster; Editor, News at Ten; Editor, ITV News Channel.
Publications: Co-author Penguin Guide to Employment Rights.
Awards: Shared in a range of RTS awards for coverage at ITN over 16 years.
Education: Bryanston School; York University
Career highlights: I joined ITN as a trainee straight from York University. Over 16 years I covered a range of foreign stories and progressed to produce then edit all ITV News programmes, became a news editor, and edited a range of network specials from Royal Weddings to Budgets and Elections. In 2001 I went on to run ITN's 24-hour News Channel. In 2004 joined ITV as Controller of Current Affairs, Arts and Religion responsible for a range of programming from News Specials, elections and political programming, Tonight with Trevor McDonald and The South Bank Show.
Mentor: I've learnt a huge amount from one of the best reporters of his generation, Norman Rees, and David Mannion, Editor-in-Chief, ITV News. My father is always an inspired sounding board.
Big break: Scraping onto the ITN trainee scheme straight from university. It was a wonderful scheme that gave me the basics, from law for journalists to rudimentary camera operator. Typically it was really hands-on and opened up opportunities we'd never have had elsewhere. It's a real shame the trainee scheme has gone.
Big mistake: Too numerous to mention. One that springs to mind is leading News at Ten on a newspaper front page that had been biked round to us. Only problem was the paper didn't go with the story ... and we did.

» **Reading:** *I try and keep up with most newspapers and magazines. The Tablet is a stimulating weekly. thepaperboy.com is great for international newspapers.* **Watching:** *The West Wing, though it's not quite the same post-Sorkin. I'm a newsaholic so I expose myself to far more rolling news than is good for me. Contrary to exaggerated reports of their death I think current affairs are alive and kicking on British TV and I'm an avid consumer.*

Listening: *An eclectic CD collection and Radios 4 & 5.* **Relaxing to:** *Gardening and walking and cycling are good therapy. That and reading for so long the bath goes cold.* » *Married, no children*

Robert Crozier 17.10.53

36–38 Piccadilly, London W11 0DP
T 020 7534 3900
E rcrozier@forbes.com

Occupation: Managing Director, EMEA Forbes Magazine

Other positions: President, Interactive Bureau; President, Time Magazine, EMEA; Partner, GMT Communications Partners.
Education: Denison University, Ohio, USA
Career highlights: After moving to London in 1989 as Publisher of Departures Magazine, I served as President of Time Magazine/EMEA; later became a venture capitalist with GMT Communications Partners, launched and sold a successful dot.com business in 1999, and since then have been Managing Director of Forbes Magazine/EMEA.
Mentor: My father, who encouraged me to launch my own magazine after leaving university, my current boss and best friend in the business, Jim Berrien, President of Forbes Magazine Group, and Tom Ryder, Chairman of Reader's Digest, who sent me to London in 1989.
Big break: Being introduced to Alan Patricof, founder of the venture capital firm, APAX partners, who helped me get my first paycheck job at The Village Voice Newspaper in 1974.
Big mistake: Not accepting a promotion to a corporate role at CBS Publishing and working with John Suhler, who later started his own very successful venture capital firm specialising in media - so I could 'retire' for a couple of years when I was 27 years old.

» **Reading:** *The international business press, most of the quality UK newspapers, plus Forbes.com, the New York TImes.com, and various media trade websites.* **Watching:** *BBC and CNN News, plus whatever my 17 year-old-daughter watches.* **Listening:** *Radio 3 and jazz CDs.* **Relaxing to:** *Listen to music, with a good read and a glass of wine, or socialise with wife and friends.* » *Married, 2 children*

Mark Cunnington 11.5.74

Tabernacle Court, 16–28 Tabernacle Street, London EC2A 4DD
T 020 7382 8268
E mark.cunnington@ft.com

Occupation: Publishing Director, Financial Times Business

Publications: Investors Chronicle; Digital business development.
Education: Liverpool and London
Career highlights: After completing academic studies, joined the FT newspaper as an Advertising Sales Executive. Worked in various sales roles and joined the magazine division in early 2000 as a Sales Manager. Appointed to the FT Business board in October 2002.
Mentor: Most recent was Helen Fraser, MD, Penguin.
Big break: Joining the FT group.
Big mistake: I try not to make them.

» **Reading:** *Aside from the obvious media (ie FT), I love Haruki Murakami.* **Watching:** *Motor racing.* **Listening:** *Pretty eclectic mix generally - anything from Coltrane to Coldplay.* **Relaxing to:** *With my family. It may not be deemed relaxation but also I enjoy racing cars when I can!* » *Married, 2 children*

Lord David Currie 9.12.46

Ofcom, Riverside House, 2a Southwark Bridge Road SE1 9HA
T 020 7981 3500
E kate.lee@ofcom.org.uk

Occupation: Chairman, Ofcom

Other positions: Dean, Cass Business School, City University, 2001-present.
Publications: Advances in Monetary Economics (editor, 1985); The Operation and Regulation of Financial Markets (editor, 1986); Macroeconomic Interactions between North and South (editor, 1988); Macroeconomic Policies in an Interdependent World (editor, 1989); Rules, Reputation and Macroeconomic Policy Coordination (1993); EMU: Problems in the Transition to a Single European Currency (editor, 1995); North-South Linkages and International Macroeconomic Policy (editor, 1995); The Pros and Cons of EMU (1997); Will the Euro Work? (1998).
Awards: Honorary D Litt, University of Glasgow, 1998; Honorary Fellow, Queen Mary College, London; Member, Royal Economic Society.
Education: Battersea Grammar School; University of Manchester; University of Birmingham; University of London
Career highlights: Hoare and Govett Co, 1971-72, Economic Models, 1972; QMC London, Lecturer, 1972-79; Reader, 1979-81; Professor of Economics, 1981-88; London Business School, Professor of Economics 1988-2000; Director, Centre for Economic Forecasting, 1988-95; Deputy Principal, 1992-95; Deputy Dean, External Relations, 1999-2000; Chairman, Ofcom 2002-present; Non-executive Director, Abbey National plc 2001-02; Member, HM Treasury Panel of Independent Forecasters, 1992-95; Member, Advisory Board for the Research Councils, 1992-93; Member, Advisory Commission, RPI, 1992-93; Member, Management Board, Ofgem, 1999-2002; Trustee, Joseph Rowntree Reform Trust, 1991-2002.

» **Relaxing to:** *Music, literature, swimming.*
» *Married, 2 children*

Paul Dacre
14.11.48

The Daily Mail, Northcliffe House, 2 Derry Street, London W8 5TT
T 020 7938 6000
E katy.farnell@dailymail.co.uk

Occupation: Editor, Daily Mail

Other positions: Director, Associated Newspaper Holdings 1991-present; Director, DMGT 1998-present; Director, Teletext Holdings Ltd 2000-present; Member, Press Complaints Commission, 1998-present; Member, Press Standards Board of Finanace 2004-present.
Education: University College School, London; University of Leeds
Career highlights: Daily Express, Reporter Manchester, 1970-71; Reporter, Feature Writer and Associate Features Editor, London, 1971-76; New York Correspondent, 1976-79; Daily Mail, Bureau Chief New York 1980; Deputy News Editor, London, 1981; News Editor, 1983, Assistant Editor, News and Foreign, 1986; Assistant Editor, Features, 1987; Executive Editor, 1988; Associate Editor, 1989-91; Editor, Evening Standard 1991-92; Daily Mail 1992-present; Editor-In-Chief, Associated Newspapers, 1998-present.

» *Married, 2 children*

Peter Dale
26.7.59

Channel 4, 124 Horseferry Road, London SW1P 2TX
T 020 7306 8314
E pdale@channel4.co.uk

Occupation: Head of More4

Other positions: Head of Documentaries, Channel 4 Television; Producer BBC Documentaries.
Awards: RTS Single Documentary Award 1994; RTS Documentary Series Award 1996; Grierson Documentary Award 1996.
Education: King Henry VIII School, Coventry
Career highlights: 1977 sweeping up in a Goldhawk Road cutting room; Assistant Editor freelance, then inside the BBC; Trainee Director in BBC Children's, BBC Trainee Researcher Scheme; Producer/Director BBC Television; 1998 Commissioning Editor, Documentaries at Channel 4, then Head of Documentaries; 2005 Head of More4.
Mentor: Never really had one. Wish I had.
Big break: Running More4.
Big mistake: Not forcing the BBC to let me join the pension scheme.

» **Reading:** *Books. A healthy mix of modern fiction and non-fiction.* **Watching:** *More4, Channel 4, BBC4 and anything else with a 4 in it - except ITV4.* **Listening:** *My children learning to play the guitar, piano and the violin. And when they're not, Bob Dylan, John Tavener and Nina Simone.* **Relaxing to:** *Sleeping and sailing.* » *Married, 3 children*

Mark Damazer
16.4.59

Broadcasting House, Portland Place, London W1A 1AA
T 020 7765 3836
E mark.damazer@bbc.co.uk

Occupation: Controller, BBC Radio 4 and BBC 7

Other positions: Vice-Chairman, International Press Institute Board, Institute of Contemporary History (London University).
Publications: Articles in newspapers and magazines, seminar articles.
Awards: Harkness Fellow, 1977-79; US Political Science Congressional Fellow, 1979; RTS Programme of the Year, Home News Story of the Year, 1993.
Education: Haberdashers' Aske's, Elstree; Cambridge
Career highlights: Film trip with Charles Wheeler to the Soviet Union in 1987. Extraordinary time. Interview with Boris Yeltsin (1988). Editing 9 O'Clock News 1990-93; Head of Current Affairs; Head of Political Programmes.
Mentor: Inspirational schoolteacher Bernard Barker. Inspirational university don Vic Gatrell. At the BBC, Peter Snow (intellectual generosity).
Big break: Producer of first interview with Boris Yeltsin after he had been demoted and sidelined by Mikhail Gorbachev (1988).
Big mistake: Many

» **Reading:** *History, biography, books about Italy, medley of papers and magazines.* **Watching:** *Football - lots, news and current affairs, Have I Got News for You, West Wing.* **Listening:** *Many hours of Radio 4 - a pleasure. But also some R3, R5 and R2.* **Relaxing to:** *Family, Italian art, football, occasional terrible tennis, opera.* » *Married, 2 children*

Matthew d'Ancona
27.1.68

The Spectator, 56 Doughty Street, London WC1N 2LL
T 020 7405 1706
E editor@spectator.co.uk

Occupation: Editor, Spectator; Political Columnist, Sunday Telegraph

Other positions: Formerly Deputy Editor, Sunday Telegraph, 1998-2006; Deputy Editor (Comment), Sunday Telegraph, 1996-98; The Times 1991-95 becoming Assistant Editor; Board Member, Centre for Policy Studies, Index on Censorship; Member, Millennium Commission.
Publications: Books: The Jesus Papyrus (with CP Thiede) 1996; The Quest for the True Cross (with CP Thiede), 2000; Going East, 2003; Tabatha's Code, 2006.
Awards: Political Journalist of the Year, British Press Awards, 2004; Charles Douglas-Home Memorial Trust Prize, 1995; elected Fellow of All Souls College, Oxford, 1989.
Education: St Dunstan's College; Magdalen College, Oxford
Career highlights: In 1994, I disclosed the remarkable claims of the German papyrologist, Carsten Thiede, that manuscript fragments of the Gospel according to St Matthew in Oxford were written before 70 AD and within the lifetime of eyewitnesses to the life of Jesus - a claim that

became a bestselling book and a television documentary; in 1995, I reported the contents of the Anglo-Irish joint framework document – a story which was very controversial and was also hailed as one of the best political scoops of the decade; in 1996, Tony Blair gave me what is still his only extensive interview on the link between his politics and his faith; in 2004, I was named Political Journalist of the Year in the British Press Awards. In the same year, I was named one of Britain's top 100 public intellectuals by Prospect magazine and one of the 80 most influential young British people by the Observer.
Mentor: Sir Peter Stothard, Dominic Lawson, Sarah Sands.
Big break: Being hired as a Graduate Trainee by The Times in 1991.
Big mistake: Writing that Jo Grimond was dead, well before his actual death in 1993.

» **Reading:** *All newspapers and weekly magazines. Also American titles, the Weekly Standard, New Yorker, American Interest, New Republic. Film magazines, political journals.* **Watching:** *Rolling news channels, Newsnight. As many films as I can physically get to. 24 on DVD, Curb Your Enthusiasm, anything with Ricky Gervais in it.* **Listening:** *Music of all sorts on my iPod.* **Relaxing to:** *Time with my wife and children. Movie-going.* » *Married, 2 sons, Zac and Teddy*

Antony Davidson 26.2.68

16 Hanbury Street, London E1 6QR
T 020 7194 7000
E natalie.brown@wk.com

Occupation: Creative Director, Wieden & Kennedy UK

Other positions: Used watch battery buyer.
Publications: 5 Nike Run London campaigns; The Honda Power of Dreams Campaign; Flat Eric.
Awards: Junior Art Prize, Lawrence Sherrif Grammar School.
Education: Leamington Hastings Primary
Career highlights: Building a company of 60 people who care about each other and what they do.
Mentor: Everybody I've ever come into contact with who inspired me. Far too many to mention in this small space.
Big break: You make your own luck, but meeting Kim Papworth, my creative partner of 17 years, has been a big influence on my career and life.
Big mistake: Not making enough mistakes.

» **Reading:** *Email.* **Watching:** *The internet.* **Listening:** *Smart people who are not in my industry and my girlfriend.* **Relaxing to:** *Sleep.* » *Single, no children*

Paul Davidson

Newsquest Media Group, 58 Church Street, Weybridge, Surrey KT13 8DP
T 01932 821212
E pdavidson@london.newsquest.co.uk

Occupation: Chairman and Chief Executive, Newsquest Media Group

Career highlights: Ran own training company; various positions for Thomson Regional Newspapers; joined Newsquest in 1988; Group Director, Newsquest, 1994-present; senior positions at Newsquest include Regional Managing Director, London and Deputy Chief Executive/Group Managing Director.

David Davies

Endeavour House, 189 Shaftesbury Avenue, London WC2H 8JG
T 020 7437 9011
E david.davies@emap.com

Occupation: Managing Director, Grazia and POP

Other positions: Managing Director, Emap Elan; Editor, FHM; Managing Director, Emap Men's; Managing Director, Emap Elan East; Editorial Director, Heat; Editor, Q; Managing Director, DMC Publishing Ltd; Editor, Mixmag.
Awards: Emap Editor Of The Year, 2003.
Education: Polytechnic of Central London

» **Reading:** *Snowmail.* » *Married, 3 children*

Evan Davis 8.4.62

Room 4220, BBC Television Centre, Wood Lane, London W12 7RJ
T 020 8624 9843
E evan.davis@bbc.co.uk

Occupation: Economics Editor, BBC News

Education: The Ashcombe School, Dorking; St John's College, Oxford; Kennedy School of Government, Harvard University

Moz Dee 14.9.70

Room 6200, Television Centre, Wood Lane, London W12 7RJ
T 020 8624 8956
E moz.dee@bbc.co.uk

Occupation: Commissioning Editor, BBC Radio Five Live

Other positions: Commissioning Editor, Sport; Editorial Executive, Sports Rights and Programming.
Awards: Sony Radio Award winner.
Education: Cardinal Newman School, Coventry
Career highlights: Currently Deputy to Controller at Five Live. Prior to joining the BBC was Director of Programmes at talksport. Prior to that was Head of Sport at Talk Radio and was a presenter with the station for three years. As a rights negotiator won broadcast rights to Manchester United, Chelsea, Football League and World Cup 98 and Pakistan and India cricket tours, taking them away from the BBC for the first time ever. As a writer have written three plays and all have been performed, as an actor have appeared in film and TV and on stage.
Mentor: Bob Shennan, current Controller of Five Live.
Big break: Being asked to present the Breakfast Show on Talk Radio UK.
Big mistake: Telling Jenny Abramsky, the Director of Radio BBC, that the licence fee was a fundamentally

flawed idea. I was working at Talk Radio at the time. Two years later I was working for her.

» **Reading:** *Most things - it's the job.* **Watching:** *West Wing is my favourite. House is brilliant. Love cooking travelogues.* **Listening:** *Five Live ... er ... Five Live, and a bit of Radio 2, 4, 1.* **Relaxing to:** *My children help. Also play golf and walk.*
» *Married, 2 children*

Baroness Ruth Deech 30.4.47

Thames Tower, Station Road, Reading RG1 1LX
T 01189 599813
E ruth.deech@oiahe.org.uk

Occupation: Independent Adjudicator for Higher Education; BBC Governor

Other positions: Rhodes Trustee, Mandela/Rhodes Trustee; Bencher of Inner Temple.
Publications: Publications on law and bioethics.
Awards: DBE 2002; Life Peerage 2005; Hon LLD Strathclyde 2003; Hon Fellow, St Anne's College, Oxford.
Education: Christ's Hospital; St Anne's College, Oxford
Career highlights: Called to the Bar 1967; taught law at Oxford and abroad 1970-1991; Senior Proctor and Chair of Admissions, Oxford; chaired Human Fertilisation and Embryology Authority during period of introduction of stem cell research, therapeutic cloning and preimplantation genetic diagnosis; Principal of St Anne's College, Oxford; first Independent Adjudicator for Higher Education.
Mentor: No one
Big break: The 11+ and excellent free education all the way. Being chosen to be a fellow and tutor in law at a women's college where there was a full time day nursery for babies - I was able to get on with my career and be a mother.
Big mistake: Only having one child.

» **Reading:** *Newspapers, weeklies, news magazines, BBC Board papers.* **Watching:** *News and documentaries.* **Listening:** *Radio 4, Classic FM, opera.* **Relaxing to:** *Travel, cooking, music, walking, sudoku.* » *Married, 1 daughter*

Tim Delaney 12.3.46

Leagas Delaney, 1 Alfred Place, London WC1E 7EB
T 020 7758 1758
E tim_delaney@leagasdelaney.com

Occupation: Chairman, Leagas Delaney

Publications: BBC, Adidas, Nationwide, Patek Philippe, Barclays InterContinental.
Awards: British Television Awards Lifetime Achievement Award; D&AD President's Award; Nelson Mandela Children's Fund Lifetime Achievement Award.
Education: Chandos Secondary, Middlesex
Career highlights: Started in a mail room at 15; began copywriting at 19; Creative Director at 27; MD of BBDO at 31; started Leagas Delaney aged 34.
Mentor: Bill Bernbach, taught everyone everything about mass communication.
Big break: Someone said what do you want to do, and I replied 'be a copywriter'.
Big mistake: Re-hiring someone who I thought had changed and then finding out he hadn't.

» **Reading:** *Books and newspapers.* **Watching:** *Soccer, the news, TCM and MTV.* **Listening:** *BBC Radio 4, BBC World Service and music, from the Killers to Mahler.* **Relaxing to:** *Cooking, eating, reading, going to the cinema and playing a Fender Telecaster loudly and badly.*
» *Single, 2 children*

Barry Dennis 20.9.52

Prospect House, Rouen Road, Norwich, Norfolk NR1 1RE
T 01603 772848
E barry.dennis@archant.co.uk

Occupation: Managing Director, Archant Norfolk

Other positions: Director, Archant Regional Board; Director, Norfolk Chamber of Commerce; Member, Norfolk Common Purpose Advisory Board; Member, Norwich Economic Round Table; Director, Norwich Radio Group; Associate Director, Norwich City Football Club.
Publications: Eastern Daily Press; Norwich Evening News; 12 Norfolk weeklies including Great Yarmouth Mercury and the Norwich Advertiser.
Education: Wisbech Grammar School
Career highlights: Began as a junior reporter with Emap on a weekly newspaper; Chief Sub-Editor, Peterborough Evening Telegraph; Editor of Angling Times; Publishing Director, Emap Magazines; Managing Director, Emap Pursuit (sports and outdoor leisure magazines) for 12 years; MD, Archant Norfolk for past six years.
Mentor: Robin Miller, former Chief Exec of Emap.
Big break: Having the opportunity to join the Emap magazine division when it was starting to develop in the 1970s under Robin Miller's leadership. The big break came when he appointed me MD of Emap Pursuit.
Big mistake: Being the first publisher to covermount a golf ball on the launch edition of Today's Golfer without checking that the protective cover would stick properly. All 180,000 fell off and we had to employ an army of people to sellotape them back on in newsagents.

» **Reading:** *Loads of local newspapers.* **Watching:** *Very little TV apart from news channels first thing in the morning. DVDs occasionally at home, but prefer the cinema.* **Listening:** *Van Morrison.* **Relaxing to:** *Golf, walking, music, watching Norwich City and trying to learn to play guitar.* » *Separated, 2 children*

Fiona Dent 8.8.71

IPC Media, Room 2103, King's Reach Tower, Stamford Street, London SE1 9LS
T 020 7261 5568
E fiona_dent@ipcmedia.com

Occupation: Publishing Director, Country Life and Horse & Hound

Other positions: Commercial Director, Web User (2000-03); Publisher, IPC Photography and Gardening magazines (1997-2000); Marketing Manager, New Scientist (1996-97); Marketing Manager, IPC Photography magazines (1994-96).
Awards: Highly Commended, PPA Publisher of the Year 2002 for the launch of Web User.

Career highlights: My dream publishing job - working on Country Life and Horse & Hound, which are truly iconic weekly magazine brands, and taking them on to even greater success. Being given the opportunity to use my online knowledge to be the launch publisher of Web User which was launched simultaneously in print and online and became the UK's market leading internet magazine from launch. Working on New Scientist during the early excitement of the web, and helping evolve its website.
Mentor: Sylvia Auton who gave me my first publishing role and taught me that you can't succeed without your team.
Big break: Becoming Marketing Manager of New Scientist and working on the development of its website in the early days of the web being a commercial medium.
Big mistake: Mistakes are a part of learning and we all make them, but I thankfully can't think of a really major mistake.

» **Reading:** *I devour magazines, anything from the Economist and the Week to Vogue, and of course Horse & Hound and Country Life. Just finished reading Consolations of Philosophy by Alain de Botton.* **Watching:** *Lots of world cinema and classic films. Apart from news and current affairs, not much TV.* **Listening:** *Various radio stations in the morning; my CD and record collection.* **Relaxing to:** *Skiing or walking, dancing, speaking and learning other languages, travelling off the beaten track, taking photographs when time allows.*

Katie Derham
18.6.70

ITN, 200 Gray's Inn Road, London WC1X 8XZ
T 020 7833 3000
E katie.derham@itn.co.uk

Occupation: Presenter, ITV Lunchtime News, London Tonight, Classic fm Hall of Fame.

Education: Cheadle Hulme School; Magdalene College Cambridge
Career highlights: Media and Arts Editor, ITV News 1998-2003; Journalist, BBC Business programmes, TV and Radio, 1993-97; Reporter, Barry Norman's Film 96, 97, 98; Presenter, Classical Brit Awards 2001-04.

» *Married, 2 daughters*

Richard Desmond
8.12.51

Northern & Shell Building, 10 Lower Thames Street, London EC3R 6EN
T 0871 4341010
E charlie.slade@express.co.uk

Occupation: Chairman, Express Newspapers

Other positions: Publisher of numerous magazines in areas including leisure, music, hi-tech, fitness, cooking, environment, business, automative, and men's and women's lifestyle.
Education: Christ's College, Finchley
Career highlights: Musician, 1967; Advertisement Executive, Thomson Group, 1967-68; Group Advertisement Manager, Beat Publications Ltd, 1968-74; launched International Musician, 1974 (editions in US, Europe, Australia and Japan); De Monde Advertising Ltd, 1976-89; launched OK! magazine, 1993; Fantasy Channel, 1995; OK! TV, 1999; Daily Star Sunday, 2002; New! magazine, and Star magazine, 2003.

» **Relaxing to:** *Music, fitness.* » *Married, 1 child*

Richard Deverell
5.12.69

10th Floor, East Tower, BBC Television Centre, London W12 7RJ
T 020 8576 4575
E richard.deverell@bbc.co.uk

Occupation: Chief Operating Officer, BBC Children's

Other positions: Head of BBC News Interactive; Head of Strategy and Marketing, BBC News.
Education: St Mary's College, Southampton; Cambridge
Career highlights: Back in the mid 1990s I worked for John Birt in BBC Corporate Strategy. We did a lot of very interesting work on the way the world was changing with the arrival of multi-channel and digital TV and the implications and opportunities for the BBC. I also wrote John's first report on the internet that sketched out what the BBC might do with this new medium. Running BBC News Interactive was a great job; we launched the separate global and domestic editions of the BBC News website, and worked hard to boost the originality and ambition of our journalism - including persuading the BBC's star correspondents to write for the site. We launched mobile editions and broadband services - and we won many, many awards. We also managed to change the way we worked to free up a lot of savings that helped fund our journalism. It was a great team.
Mentor: Tony Hall at BBC News and Alison Sharman at CBBC.
Big break: Tony Hall letting me run the BBC News website back in 2000.
Big mistake: Being too reasonable when faced with arguments why we should not change the status quo.

» **Reading:** *A lot. History, science, biography and the Economist. Anything lucid on how and why the world is changing. Any and every newspaper.* **Watching:** *Lots of children's programmes, anything to do with natural history or current affairs, Bad Lads Army, Bleak House and old episodes of Frasier.* **Listening:** *Radio 4 and my iPod.* **Relaxing to:** *Running, making bread, hot baths.* » *Married, 3 children*

David Dimbleby
29.10.42

c/o PFD, Drury House, 34-43 Russell Street, London WC2B 5HA
T 020 7344 1010
E rhamilton@pfd.co.uk

Occupation: Freelance broadcaster

Publications: A Picture of Britain; An Ocean Apart.
Education: Charterhouse; Oxford University
Career highlights: Chairman, BBC Question Time; Anchor, BBC Election Nights since 1979; Presenter, Panorama; various documentary series including The White Tribe of Africa, An Ocean Apart, A Picture of Britain.

» **Relaxing to:** *Sailing and drawing.* » *Married, 4 children*

Jonathan Dimbleby

31.7.44

c/o David Higham Associates, 5-8 Lower John Street, Golden Square, London W1F 9HA

T 020 7434 5900
E fb@dimblebypartners.co.uk

Occupation: Writer, broadcaster and film-maker

Other positions: President, Voluntary Service Overseas; President, Soil Association; Vice-President, Council for the Protection of Rural England; Trustee, Richard Dimbleby Cancer Fund; Trustee, Dimbleby Cancer Care; Trustee, Susan Chilcott Scholarship.
Publications: Richard Dimbleby (1975); The Palestinians (1979); The Prince of Wales (1994); and The Last Governor (1997).
Education: University College, London
Career highlights: Presenter, ITV's flagship weekly political programme, Jonathan Dimbleby; Presenter, Any Questions? and Any Answers? for BBC Radio 4 1987-present; Main Presenter, ITV's General Election coverage.

» **Relaxing to:** *Tennis, riding, music and rural life.*
» *Separated, 2 children*

Carl Dinnen

18.9.74

C4 News Midlands, The Old Vicarage, Market Square, Castle Donington DE74 2JB

T 01332 856 968
E carl.dinnen@itn.co.uk

Occupation: Midlands Correspondent, Channel Four News

Other positions: Occasional Presenter More4 News; Ireland Correspondent, GMTV; Sports Producer, Channel Four News; General Producer, Channel Four News; ITN Trainee.
Awards: Nominated for the 2005 Mental Health Media Awards.
Education: Methodist College Belfast; Trinity Hall, Cambridge
Career highlights: Producing for Gaby Rado in Eastern Europe in the 90s and C4's coverage of the Hong Kong handover in 1997; working for GMTV in New York after September 11th; being embedded with the US Army during the invasion of Iraq and with the Black Watch at Camp Dogwood; and I once interviewed Jennifer Lopez.
Mentor: I've produced for Gaby Rado and Alex Thomson (and even, on occasion, Jon Snow).
Big break: Getting into CNN's London office as a script runnner. The first step is the most difficult.
Big mistake: Rushing into on-screen reporting instead of producing in more interesting places. I don't think I've made a complete fool of myself on telly but there's time yet.

» **Reading:** *All the papers and as many newsy websites as I can. Books are harder with a new baby; he's more interesting.* **Watching:** *News 24 and Sky News in the office. American glossies (The West Wing/Desperate Housewives) but British comedy (Green Wing and Monkey Dust). Channel Four/More4 News when I'm home in time.* **Listening:** *The Today Programme in the morning, 5 Live in the car and the kitchen.* **Relaxing to:** *I'm trying to learn Arabic. I may never have it 'learned' but the process is interesting. I play football enthusiastically and atrociously.* » *Married, 1 child*

Matt Doman

10.7.77

AMV BBDO Ltd, 151 Marylebone Road, London NW1 5QE

T 020 7616 3642
E domanm@amvbbdo.com

Occupation: Art Director, Abbott Mead Vickers BBDO

Other positions: Board Director
Publications: Guinness, the Economist, Samaritans, Bells, the Observer.
Awards: 24 D&AD entries; Silver BTAA; Bronze Cannes Lion; Gold, Silver and Bronze Creative Circle; Bronze One Show; Gold and Silver Campaign Poster; 8 times Campaign poster finalist; twice Campaign press finalist.
Education: Sir William Ramsay School, Hazlemere, Bucks
Career highlights: See awards
Mentor: Derek Hass, Steve Dunn, and Paul Belford.
Big break: Working under Paul Belford and Nigel Roberts at Ogilvy and Mather.
Big mistake: TBA

» **Reading:** *Metro, the Guardian, Sunday Times, Creative Review.* **Watching:** *Everything and anything.* **Listening:** *Hip-hop, rock, jazz.* **Relaxing to:** *Cabernet Sauvignon.* » *Single, no children*

Lesley Douglas

1963

BBC Radio 2, Western House, 99 Great Portland Street, London W1A 1AA

T 020 7765 3493
E lesley.douglas@bbc.co.uk

Occupation: Controller, BBC Radio 2 and 6 Music

Other positions: Trustee, Children In Need.
Awards: BBC Radio 2 voted Sony UK Radio Station Of The Year, 2005; 6 Music voted Best Radio Station at the UK 2005 BT Digital Music Awards; Music Industry Woman Of The Year Award, 2004; Fellow, Radio Academy; Chair, Radio Festival Steering Committee, twice.
Education: Manchester University
Career highlights: Production Assistant, BBC 1986; Promotions Assistant, BBC, 1987; Producer, BBC Music Department, 1988, working on the Gloria Hunniford show, the David Jacobs show, the Ken Bruce show and Brian Matthew's Round Midnight; Producer, Promotions, 1990; Editor, BBC Radio 2 Presentation and Planning, 1993; Managing Editor, BBC Radio 2, 1997; Head of Programmes, BBC Radio 2, 2000-present.

Torin Douglas 25.9.54

Room G640, BBC Television Centre, Wood Lane, London W12 7RJ

T 020 8624 9052
E torin.douglas@bbc.co.uk

Occupation: BBC Media Correspondent

Other positions: Former Chairman, Broadcasting Press Guild; Fellow, Communications Advertising and Marketing Foundation.
Publications: Author, The Complete Guide to Advertising.
Education: Eastbourne College; University of Warwick

» *Married, 3 children*

Mark Douglas-Home 1.9.55

200 Renfield Street, Glasgow G2 3QB

T 0141 302 7004
E mark.douglashome@theherald.co.uk

Occupation: Editor, The Herald, Glasgow

Other positions: Scotland Editor, Sunday Times; Deputy Editor, Scotland on Sunday; Assistant Editor, the Scotsman; News Editor, the Scotsman; Scottish Correspondent, Independent.
Education: Eton College, Windsor; University of the Witwatersrand, Johannesburg

» *Married, 1 daughter, 1 son*

Mark Downie 27.6.72

Channel 4, 124 Horseferry Road, London SW1P 2TX

T 020 7306 8034
E mdownie@channel4.co.uk

Occupation: Editor, Daytime, Channel 4

Education: St Ninian's High School, Giffnock, Glasgow; University of Glasgow
Career highlights: Editor, Daytime, Channel 4, 2002-present.

» *Unmarried, no children*

Sarah Drummond 21.6.70

BBC Local TV, Level 9, The Mailbox, Birmingham B1 1RF

T 0121 5676767
E sarah.drummond@bbc.co.uk

Occupation: Hub Editor, BBC West Midlands Local TV pilot (secondment)

Other positions: Regional Charter Review Coordinator, BBC North East and Cumbria, 2004-05; Managing Editor, BBC Radio Newcastle, 1999-2004; Senior Broadcast Journalist, BBC Midlands Today, 1998-99; Senior Broadcast Journalist, BBC Radio Stoke, 1997-99.
Education: University of East Anglia
Career highlights: Gaining a place in the BBC Local TV pilot team in September 2005 - it's the future! My systematic overhaul of BBC Radio Newcastle's schedules and positioning - 'The station that loves the North East'.
Mentor: The BBC is full of inspiring people - too many to mention. Outside the BBC it's got to be John Myers.
Big break: This latest one - becoming Hub Editor of the BBC's Local TV pilot in the West Midlands - we will make a fresh kind of television, with all eyes upon us (for a range of reasons).
Big mistake: Listening to my school careers teacher. He told me a comprehensive girl could never become a radio DJ. I let that derail me for a few years. To be fair he was technically right. I didn't become a DJ, I became the manager.

» **Reading:** *In no particular order, Guardian, Mirror, Times, Mail, local newspapers (a must-read and always will be), BBC websites, trade press such as Broadcast, Radio Mag, UKPG. For leisure it's usually Top 10 intellectual novels. Every two years I have to re-read Italo Calvino's If On A Winter's Night A Traveller - genius.* **Watching:** *In my multi-channel household, TV news across the channels, Corrie and EastEnders, adult comedy. I love the movies, but no gore thank you.* **Listening:** *BBC Local Radio wherever I am in the country, BBC R2 for being iconic, Talksport. I'm so into radio that I don't have a very large music collection, nor woofers and tweeters. I still always listen to my Mum.* **Relaxing to:** *Long brisk walk by the sea with my favourite person towards a fish and chip shop and pub.* » *Divorced, with no children*

Andy Duncan 31.7.62

Channel 4, 124-126 Horseferry Road, London SW1P 2TX

T 020 7396 4444
E aduncan@channel4.co.uk

Occupation: Chief Executive, Channel 4

Other positions: Director of Marketing, Communications and Audience, BBC; Senior General Management positions, Unilever.
Publications: Flora sponsorship of London Marathon; Freeview, BBC Digital TV and Radio launches.
Education: University of Manchester Institute of Science and Technology
Career highlights: CEO, Channel 4, 2004-present; have begun to implement strategy to secure Channel 4's future post digital switchover, directing record investment into public service output on Channel 4, extending the company's presence in multi-channel and launching the 4 brand on new media platforms; Channel 4 was the only terrestrial network to maintain audience share in 2005 and grow audiences in peak; E4 has more than doubled its share of viewing year-on-year since its launch on Freeview and More4 has instantly established itself as the most upmarket of all digital channels; Channel4.com has been fully broadband enabled allowing for the launch of new services including documentary channel, 4Docs; marketing spend across Channel 4's network has doubled to £50 million; also announced a move into radio, in support of Channel 4's ambition to put its unique brand of public service on every media platform. Prior to joining Channel 4, spent three years at the BBC, as Director of Marketing, Communications and Audience; oversaw the launch of all the BBC's digital TV and radio services and was a co-architect of Freeview and led its

launch; joined the BBC from Unilever, having worked for nearly 17 years in a variety of senior general management and marketing roles.
Mentor: Not mentor, but greatest influence, wife and kids - great at keeping my feet on the ground.
Big break: Leading the Freeview project.
Big mistake: An orange T-shirt I bought last year.

» **Reading:** *The Channel 4 duty log. All human life is there and it's a brilliant reminder of the impact that the channel has on the lives of its viewers.* **Watching:** *Anything on Channel 4.* **Listening:** *The Smiths, the Strokes and the Arctic Monkeys (at the moment).* **Relaxing to:** *Family and playing sport.*
» *Married, 2 children*

Greg Dyke

20.5.47

Royal Television Society, 5th Floor, Kildare House, 3 Dorset Rise, London EC4Y 8EN
T 020 7822 2810
E info@rts.org.uk

Occupation: Vice-President, Royal Television Society

Other positions: Chairman, HIT Entertainment, 2005-present; Member, Media Advisory Board, Apax Partners, 2004-present; Chancellor, University of York, 2004-present.
Awards: FRTS, 1998
Education: Hayes Grammar School; University of York
Career highlights: Journalist, LWT 1977; Editor-in-Chief, TV-am, 1983-84; Director of Programmes, TVS 1984-87; London Weekend Television, Director of Programmes, 1987-90; Managing Director, 1990; Group Chief Executive, LWT (Holdings) plc, 1991-94; Chairman, Independent Television Association, 1992-94; Executive Chairman, GMTV, 1993-94; Chief Executive, Pearson Television, 1995-99; Main Board Director, Pearson plc, 1996-99; Chairman, Channel 5 Broadcasting Ltd, 1997-99 (Non-executive Director, 1996-99); Director-General, BBC, 2000-04; Non-executive Director, Channel Four Television, 1988-90; Non-executive Director, ITN Ltd until 1992.

» **Relaxing to:** *Football, riding, skiing.* » *Married, 2 children*

Nigel Dyson

29.8.59

BBC Radio Cumbria, Annetwell Street, Carlisle, Cumbria CA13 9PL
T 01228 592444
E nigel.dyson@bbc.co.uk

Occupation: Managing Editor, BBC Cumbria

Other positions: Assistant Editor, BBC Radio Northampton; Managing Editor, BBC Three Counties Radio; Managing Editor, BBC Radio Cambridgeshire.
Awards: Sony Gold Station Of The Year, 2001; Frank Gillard Gold Station Of The Year, 2001; Frank Gillard Gold Station Of The Year, 2005.
Education: Lancaster Royal Grammar School; Hull University
Career highlights: Started at BBC Radio Humberside while a student in 1974; BBC Radio Blackburn, 1976-81; BBC Radio Northampton, 1981-85; BBC Radio Cumbria, 1985-88; Programme Organiser, BBC Northampton, 1988-1994; Editor, Three Counties Radio, 1994-95; Editor, BBC Radio Cambridgeshire, 1995-98; Editor, BBC Radio Cumbria, 1998-present.
Mentor: Gerald Jackson taught me all I know about radio. Brian Salmon, history master at school. Wise man.
Big break: At Uni getting the chance to present a weekly programme at the local BBC station.
Big mistake: Interviewing the Glitter Band with the microphone switched off!

» **Reading:** *Biographies, history, general novels, old and new constantly.* **Watching:** *News 24, news in general, good drama.* **Listening:** *BBC Radio Cumbria! BBC Local Radio and commercial radio across the country. Radio 2 and Radio 4.* **Relaxing to:** *Walking, reading, films.* » *Married, 3 children*

Steve Dyson

6.3.72

Birmingham Mail, Weaman Street, Birmingham B4 6AX
T 0121 236 3366
E steve_dyson@mrn.co.uk

Occupation: Editor, Birmingham Mail

Other positions: Editor, Evening Gazette, Teesside, 2002-05; Deputy Editor, Assistant Editor, Head of News, Features Editor, Deputy News Editor and Industrial Correspondent, Birmingham Evening Mail, 1994-2002; Reporter, Sunday Mercury (B'ham), 1993; Birmingham Metro News, 1992; Caters News Agency, 1991.
Publications: Campaigns - various community and industrial campaigns, eg Birmingham Evening Mail Don't Let Rover Die, 2000; Evening Gazette, Teesside: Kerb the Crawlers, 2002-05; Save Our Steel, 2003-04; Let the Boats Come In (so-called ghostships issue) 2004.
Awards: Business Journalist of the Year, BT Regional Awards, 1995; North East Newspaper of the Year, Tom Cordner Awards, 2003.
Education: Primrose Hill Secondary, Birmingham; Matthew Boulton Technical College, Birmingham; Lancaster University (Politics and International Relations, 2:1); Lancashire Polytechnic (Journalism Dip).
Career highlights: Hooked on journalism aged 14 in 1982 with The Cut, a community news sheet in south Birmingham. Helped write, photocopy, staple and deliver the title. Trained locally and joined Evening Mail as Industrial Correspondent in 1993. Award-winning coverage of Rover, Jaguar, the rail strike and the greed of former utility bosses in the 'fat cats' media frenzy of 1994 followed. Then served as Deputy News Editor, Features Editor, Head of News, Assistant Editor and Deputy Editor at the Evening Mail before heading north to edit the Evening Gazette on Teesside in early 2002. By this stage both papers had become part of Trinity Mirror. A defiant community newspaper, the Gazette scored three ABC pluses out of the next seven, won Newspaper of the Year 2003 in the North East Press Awards, and switched from broadsheet to tabloid in a 2004 relaunch. In July 2005, promoted to Editor of the Evening Mail and returned to Birmingham to reestablish local grassroots reporting as the title's main raison d'être.
Mentor: Various including Ian Dowell, MBE, Editor

of the Evening Mail 1989-2003, and the late Tony Dumphy, the old chief sub at the Evening Gazette, Teesside until 2004.

Big break: Confidential tip from insider on MEB electricity boss Bryan Townsend's 24-hour retirement to trigger six-figure pension on top of salary. Fat cat of the year, 1994!

Big mistake: That last pint of Pedigree on Friday night...

›› **Reading:** *Local papers wherever I am. The Sun, Guardian, Private Eye, When Saturday Comes, Graham Greene, Barry Hines, JB Priestley, Jonathan Coe and any other Brummie novelists.* **Watching:** *News, Have I Got News for You, Little Britain.* **Listening:** *Radio 5 and local radio.* **Relaxing to:** *Family, friends, beer, curry, walking.* ›› *Married, 3 boys*

Mark Easton

13.3.63

Room 1508, BBC Television Centre, London W12 7RJ
T 020 7624 9051
E mark.easton@bbc.co.uk

Occupation: BBC Home Editor

Awards: Bar Council Legal Journalist of the Year (Broadcast) 2004; Winner, Mental Health Media Awards (TV & Radio News) 2004; Joint Winner, International News Coverage Emmy at Channel Four News 2003.

Education: Peter Symonds Grammar School, Winchester

Career highlights: Cub reporter on the Southern Evening Echo in Southampton in 1978 but quickly moved into local radio - Radio Victory in Portsmouth followed by Radio Aire in Leeds. Moving to London in 1981, I produced the Dave Loyn programme on LBC before becoming an IRN reporter. In 1986 I moved to the BBC - first on London Plus, then Breakfast News, Newsnight and the BBC1 current affairs programme Here and Now. In 1996 appointed Political Editor at the new Channel 5 television where I also made a three-part documentary series Perfect Babies on genetics. In 1999 appointed Home Affairs and Social Affairs Editor at Channel Four News. I also worked on more than twenty documentaries including the award-winning Judges in the Dock for Dispatches. In 2004 I was appointed Home Editor at the BBC, heading the Social Affairs Unit and working across all media.

Mentor: I have had many but I would single out Tim Gardam and Peter Horrocks.

Big break: When on the Southern Evening Echo I covered an industrial tribunal about a teacher who couldn't control her class. It made the splash on the Daily Mail and led to a job on a local news agency from which I moved into broadcasting.

Big mistake: I am so delighted and surprised to be where I am, even things which seemed disastrous at the time have worked out for the best.

›› **Reading:** *These days, I get most of my written news and analysis from the internet, surfing from news sites to wherever my interest takes me. If I buy a single paper, more often than not it is The Times or Sunday Times. I tend to read factual books rather than fiction.* **Watching:** *Everything and anything - although I am not a big soap opera fan. Too much shouting.* **Listening:** *Five Live and Radio 4 mostly. Victoria Darbyshire phone-in on Five Live and the 1800 news on Radio 4 are must-hear.* **Relaxing to:** *Family life is hugely important to me and I am never happier than sitting down for a big Sunday lunch with my wife, all my children and close friends.* ›› *Married, 3 girls and a boy*

Clark Edwards

29.11.78

Flat 5, 29 York Street, Twickenham TW1 3JZ
T 07831 759 163
E clark.edwards@leoburnett.co.uk

Occupation: Copywriter/Art Director, Leo Burnett

Publications: Heinz, John West, Daz, Washington Mutual.
Awards: Creative Circle Gold 2005; Creative Circle Silver 2005; Campaign Poster Silver 2005 × 3; D&AD Silver Nomination 2005; Campaign Press Commended 2004; Campaign Press Commended 2005; Cannes Finalist 2004; Cannes Finalist 2005 × 2.
Education: University of Sheffield
Career highlights: This year's D&AD silver nomination and our 3 Campaign Poster silvers.
Mentor: Nick Hastings, Jim Thornton, Dave Beverley.
Big break: Being given my first creative job without any real kind of creative book.
Big mistake: Doing geography at college.

» **Reading:** *Bruce Robinson, Raymond Carver, Sam Shepard.* **Watching:** *Curb Your Enthusiasm, Family Guy, The Mighty Boosh, Ray Mears.* **Listening:** *Beck, David Holmes, Super Furry Animals, 70s Stevie Wonder.* **Relaxing to:** *Writing stuff, taking pics, biking.* » *Single, no children*

Duncan Edwards

29.3.68

National Magazine House, 72 Broadwick Street, London W1F 9EP
T 020 7439 5000
E suzie.carradice@natmags.co.uk

Occupation: Chief Executive, The National Magazine Company

Publications: Cosmopolitan; CosmoGIRL!; Cosmo Hair & Beauty; Company; She; Zest; Esquire; Harpers & Queen; Country Living; Coast; Cosmopolitan Bride; You & Your Wedding; Good Housekeeping; Best; Reveal; Prima; Prima Baby; House Beautiful; Men's Health; Runner's World.
Education: Merchant Taylors' School; Sheffield University

» **Reading:** *Lots of magazines, newspapers and books.* **Watching:** *Sport and DVD box sets.* **Listening:** *Radio 4 and my zen.* **Relaxing to:** *Running, triathlon, the hills, my caravan in Suffolk.* » *Married, 2 children*

Ed Edwards

9.1.74

60 Kingly Street, London W1B 5DS
T 020 7453 4205
E ed.edwards@bbh.co.uk

Occupation: Creative, Bartle Bogle Hegarty

Publications: Volkswagen press and poster campaigns; creating the Ben & Jerry's poster campaign; the Sony Hollywood says Thank You campaign; Skoda TV campaign; BBC Radio 1 Love of Live campaign; Levi's Ice Cream commercial.
Awards: D&AD pencil; 2 Creative Circle silvers/golds; BTAA gold and silver; 2 Cannes Lions; 2 Campaign Poster silvers; 4 Campaign Posters; 3 One Show Pencils.
Education: Bucks College
Career highlights: So far: getting hired at BMP DDB, winning a string of major awards for campaigns for Volkswagen, London Transport and Marmite; winning our first D&AD Pencil for BBC Radio 1; creating campaigns for Sony, Skoda and probably the first toilet roll advert to win a BTAA God Arrow with Double Velvet; moving to BBH and creating campaigns on Levi's, Boddingtons and Lynx.
Mentor: Dave Morris
Big break: Getting a job at BMP DDB.
Big mistake: Being vegetarian for 15 years.

» **Reading:** *Anything.* **Watching:** *Anything.* **Listening:** *Anything.* **Relaxing to:** *Photography.* » *Married*

Huw Edwards

19.8.65

BBC News, BBC TV Centre, London W12 7RJ
T 020 8743 8000
E huw.edwards@bbc.co.uk

Occupation: Presenter, BBC Ten O'Clock News

Awards: Honorary Fellow, University of Wales, Cardiff; BAFTA Cymru Presenter of the Year 2001, 2002, 2003, 2004.
Education: University of Wales, Cardiff
Career highlights: Started as a BBC News Trainee in 1984, and served as BBC Political Correspondent from 1988-97; after a stint as Chief Political Correspondent 1997-99 became Presenter, BBC Six O'Clock News 1999-2003; by now also providing commentary on the Festival of Remembrance, the State Opening of Parliament, Trooping the Colour and other major events including 60th anniversary of D-Day, funeral of Pope John-Paul II, the 200th anniversary of Trafalgar; have co-presented two general election results programmes on Radio 4, and BAFTA-winning documentaries for BBC Wales and BBC Four.
Mentor: David Dimbleby for his supreme broadcasting skills and his relaxed authority. John Cole for his ability to bring politics alive for millions of viewers.
Big break: Being appointed the youngest-ever BBC Political Correspondent by John Cole.

» **Reading:** *Novels, political biographies, and books on 19th century Welsh history.* **Watching:** *Comedy (The Thick of It is brilliant) or drama (The Way We Live Now was irresistible).* **Listening:** *Charles Trenet makes me feel good. Mozart always energises.* **Relaxing to:** *I have 5 young children...* » *Married, 5 children*

Nick Elliott

21.5.44

ITV Broadcasting, 200 Gray's Inn Road, London WC1X 8HF
T 020 7843 8201
E dutyoffice@itv.com

Occupation: Director of Drama, ITV

Education: St Edmund Hall, Oxford
Career highlights: Started as Graduate Trainee for Granada, 1966; Editor, Weekend World, 1974-77; Head of Features, LWT, 1977-82; Controller of

Drama, LWT, 1982-92; Head of Drama Series, BBC; Managing Director, LWT Productions, 1992; Controller, ITV Network Drama, 1995-present.

» *Married, 2 adult children*

Tony Elliott

7.1.47

Universal House,
251 Tottenham Court Road W1T 7AB

T 020 7813 6130
E tonyelliott@timeout.com

Occupation: Chairman and Owner, Time Out Group Ltd.

Publications: Time Out weeklies in London, New York and Chicago; Eating & Drinking Guide to London and many other London guides; international city guides to over 50 worldwide destinations; licensed Time Outs throughout world including Moscow, Dubai, Mumbai, Tel Aviv, Istanbul, Cyprus, Mexico City, St Petersburg, Beijing and Shanghai.
Awards: Marcus Morris Award, 1999.
Education: Stowe School; Westminster College; Keele University
Career highlights: Started Time Out in summer of 1968 whilst still a student at Keele University. Quit being a student at Christmas 1968 as I found I was doing what I really wanted to do. Continued the ever-expanding project from then to present day.
Mentor: Little bits from lots of people. Working with Pearce Marchbank, the graphic designer, from 1971-1980 was very influential on myself and the company's overall output.
Big break: Starting Time Out in London in August 1968.
Big mistake: Not changing the monthly Paris Passion magazine into a totally 100% Time Out product when we took it over in 1988.

» **Reading:** *Newspapers and some magazines. Rarely read books, regrettably.* **Watching:** *TV (lots of CSI!) and decent films at cinema.* **Listening:** *Whatever's current as I like to keep in touch.* **Relaxing to:** *Going to bed to read or watch TV.*
» *Married, 3 children*

Frances Ellis

30.6.69

60 Kingly Street, London W1B 5DS

T 020 7453 4342
E Frances.Royle@bbh.co.uk

Occupation: Head of TV Production, BBH

Publications: Audi, Levi's, Boddingtons.
Awards: Various creative awards including Cannes Lions, D&AD, British Television; in 2005 we were voted Agency of the Year by the British Television Advertising Association (who are specifically interested in TV production). This is the fourth time we have won this award and makes us the only agency in history to have won it four times; featured in Media and Marketing Europe magazine's Top 40 under-40 list 2003.
Education: St Patrick's RC, Eccles, Manchester
Career highlights: Left school at 16 and became secretary in pipe factory in Swinton, Manchester; moved into modelling and signed up with top London Agency, and was featured in Harpers and Queen! Swiftly got bored of modelling, moved to Marbella and sold timeshare in Puerto Banus for six months; returned to London with a small fortune and sold shirts around Soho cold calling door to door; discovered advertising and BBH in November 1989. Joined as temporary secretary, made permanent three months later. Transferred to TV Production as TV Secretary. Promoted to Production Assistant after six months, first job was Levis ad starring an unknown Brad Pitt. Promoted to Producer in 1992. Discovered Melanie Sykes for Boddingtons, and produced award-winning work for Audi. Set up an initiative at BBH called Mint Source which finds young directors and shows their work to the creative department. This led to previously unknown directors getting big breaks on brands like Levi's and Audi. In 2005 we launched Cutlets which gives young directors the chance to pitch for scripts; after eight years of producing, working with top directors such as Jonathan Glazer, Frank Budgen and Danny Kleinman, was promoted to Head of Television Production in 2000.
Mentor: Mark Collier and Paul Bagnall.
Big break: Joining BBH
Big mistake: Selling my TVR Griffith.

» **Reading:** *Campaign, Creativity, Marketing, Creative Review, Eventing, Horse & Hound. No.1 Ladies Detective Agency book series, inspiring biographies!* **Watching:** *Films, CSI Vegas, House, equestrian DVDs, Coronation Street if I'm home in time!* **Listening:** *Dance music, Kanye West, 50 Cent, Goldfrapp.* **Relaxing to:** *Horse riding, eventing and running.*
» *Divorced*

Laura Ellis

18.1.71

Canal Walk, Level 10, BBC, Mailbox,
Birmingham BR1 1RF

T 0121 567 6242
E laura.ellis@bbc.co.uk

Occupation: Business Manager, BBC English Regions

Other positions: Head of Region, BBC South East; Head of Region, BBC West Midlands; Editor, Television, Bristol.
Education: Rydal School, North Wales; Nottingham University
Mentor: I'm lucky enough to have several.
Big break: Getting my first editor job in Bristol.
Big mistake: All my mistakes come from being too optimistic!

» **Reading:** *Crime fiction, thrillers, good biographies.* **Watching:** *Anything newsy, Spooks, Waking the Dead, Casualty, Holby, contemporary drama, UKTV Food.* **Listening:** *Loads of Local Radio, Radio 4, anything I come across that sounds interesting. I'm a manic channel-hopper.* **Relaxing to:** *Running, riding, reading.* » *Married, 1 son*

Steve Ellis

Write Image, 271 Regent Street, London W1B 2BP
T 020 7959 5400
E steve@write-image.co.uk

Occupation: Chief Executive, Write Image

Other positions: Director, Finextra Research
Education: London School of Economics
Career highlights: I've only ever had one proper job, so I guess that has been my career. 18 years ago we founded an agency called Write Image. The simple idea was to help technology companies build better structured, more systematic and more measurable PR and marketing programs. During this period we have helped companies like Microsoft, HP, BT and Dell grow their core businesses, expand into new markets, improve their marketing operations, build communities among customers and partners, engage internal stakeholders and develop their citizenship credentials. Today I work with 200 talented, entrepreneurial people - marketeers, writers, developers, creatives, PRs. We have four offices around the world. Revenues are around £15m. The programs we run are usually multi-country, often use software applications to automate core marketing processes, they scale massively, create efficiencies, and are always repeatable, measurable and designed to contribute to the bottom line. As an agency we don't look or behave like most others. We often work inside the client organisation, becoming part of their marketing resource and part of the fabric of their marketing operations. Our term for this arena is Marketing Process Optimization.
Mentor: We've been really lucky to work with some great clients who have shared very openly with us. That has given us a privileged insight into how other businesses operate. We've shamelessly always tried to copy what's good and learn from their experiences.
Big break: Missing out on the absurdities of the dotcom era.
Big mistake: Missing out on the absurdities of the dotcom era.

» **Reading:** *Minimsft.blogspot.com, microsoft-watch.com, timesofindia.com, bbc.co.uk, Ovum Holway.*
Watching: *CBeebies.* **Listening:** *Radio 4, Radio 5 Live.*
Relaxing to: *Being a dad. I love it.*

Jane Ellison

29.5.62

BBC Radio 4, Broadcasting House, Portland Place, London W1A 1AA
T 020 7765 4615
E jane.ellison@bbc.co.uk

Occupation: Commissioning Editor, General Factual, BBC Radio 4

Education: Farnborough Hill School; Newnham College, Cambridge

» *Married, 1 child*

Jo Elvin

22.2.74

6-8 Old Bond Street, London W1S 4PH
T 020 7499 9080
E jelvin@condenast.co.uk

Occupation: Editor, Glamour magazine

Other positions: Editor, New Woman magazine; Editor, B magazine; Editor, Sugar magazine.
Publications: Glamour
Awards: 1995 BSME Editor of the Year (women's magazines) Sugar; 1996 BSME Editor of the Year Sugar; 2001 Launch Editor of the Year, Glamour; 2002 Editor of the Year, Glamour; 2002 Editors' Editor of the Year, Glamour; 2003 Achievers Award, Cosmetic Executive Women.
Education: University of Western Sydney, Australia
Career highlights: Obviously Glamour has been an incredible highlight - it's amazing to work on something that's so successful, influential and fun. Also, Sugar was a real career milestone. It changed the way teenage magazines in this country were produced and I'm still very close friends with many of the people I worked with.
Mentor: I don't really have a mentor, but I think at one time it would have been Kath Brown, my Editor-in-Chief on Sugar (now at Marie Claire). She taught me how to be an editor. Condé Nast's Managing Director Nicholas Coleridge is an inspiration. I've never worked with anyone with so much energy and enthusiasm for what they do.
Big break: Definitely Sugar - it was my first job as an editor, aged 24. Granted, I had an editor in chief, but to be appointed to that position was an enormous vote of confidence from Kath that set my career on its course.
Big mistake: I've made so many embarrassing mistakes, I can't bear to list any of them here!

» **Reading:** *I dip in and out of everything.* **Watching:** *Far too much. At the moment I can't get enough of Arrested Development, the funniest TV show ever written. And I'm already grieving over the loss of Six Feet Under.* **Listening:** *Besides Jonathan Ross's Radio 2 show, all the hip-hop my husband can inflict upon me. It's a lot of fun making him cringe as I sing along with Kanye.* **Relaxing to:** *Drink.*
» *Married, 1 child*

Bill Emmott

7.8.60

25 St James's Street, London SW1A 1HG
T 020 7830 7032
E be@economist.com

Occupation: Editor, The Economist

Other positions: Brussels Correspondent, the Economist 1980-82; Economics Correspondent, 1982-83; Tokyo Correspondent, 1983-86; Finance Editor 1986-89, Business Affairs Editor 1989-93.
Publications: The Sun Also Sets: Why Japan will not be Number One, 1989; Japan's Global Reach (1992); 20:21 Vision: 20th-century lessons for the 21st century, 2003.
Awards: Amex Bank Essay prize in international economics 1989 (first prize); honorary degrees Warwick University, City University; Honorary Fellowship, Magdalen College, Oxford.

Education: Latymer Upper School; Oxford University
» **Reading:** *Financial Times, International Herald Tribune.*
Relaxing to: *Living on Exmoor, dog-walking, journalism.*
» *Married*

Donald Emslie

8.5.57

SMG, 200 Renfield Street, Glasgow G2 3PR
T 0141 300 3300
E donald.emslie@smg.plc.uk

Occupation: Chief Executive, SMG Television

Other positions: Chairman, ITV Network Ltd; Chairman, Royal Lyceum Theatre Company; Chairman, Scottish Industry Skills Panel; Member, Board, Skillset and Scottish Screen; Fellow and Vice-President, RTS.
Education: Inverness High School; Jordanhill College of Education
Career highlights: Chief Executive of the Television Division of SMG plc, on the SMG plc Board since 1999; previously Managing Director of Broadcasting for SMG; TV career started 20 years ago in the Sales Department in Glasgow, then spent 10 years in London working for Scottish TV's sales house and in JV sales houses with companies like HTV and Granada. Now have responsibility for Broadcasting (Scottish TV and Grampian TV), SMG TV Productions (SMG's network producer) and the company's new production facilities business, SMG Broadcast and Event Solutions; responsible for the integration of Grampian TV and Ginger Television into the Television Division.
Mentor: My father was the biggest influence.
Big break: Being appointed the Director responsible for the integration of Scottish TV and Grampian TV.
Big mistake: Not being radical enough when instigating changes in the organisation.
» **Reading:** *The Times, Scotsman and Sun most weekdays. Also subscribe to the Economist and enjoy reading it over the course of the week on various trains and planes. Also read many autobiographies about people in the media business.* **Watching:** *Very varied as you would expect, but particularly drawn to news, sport and original UK drama.* **Listening:** *Many different types of music, most of them on the Virgin Radio playlist. Favourites at the moment are Oasis' new album and Razorlight, but also Texas' new album.* **Relaxing to:** *Walking, cinema, tennis and spending time with family and friends.*
» *Married, 2 daughters*

Jane Ennis

IPC Media, King's Reach Tower,
Stamford Street SE1 9LS
T 020 7261 6273
E Jane_ennis@ipcmedia.com

Occupation: Editor, NOW Magazine

Other positions: Features Editor, Sunday Mirror; Assistant Editor, Features, Today newspaper; Editor, Here magazine; Deputy Editor, Best magazine; Deputy Editor, TV Quick magazine; Features Editor, TV Times magazine; Feature Writer, Daily Mail, NOVA magazine, Honey, Petticoat; Consumer Editor, Detroit Free Press; Roving Editor, Melody Maker.
Publications: As above
Awards: 1998, 1999, 2000, 2002 winner, BSME Editor of the Year, Women's Weekly Magazines Award; 2003, winner, PPA Editor of the Year, Consumer Magazines Award; 1993, winner, Race In The Media Award.
Education: Mayfield Girls School, Putney
Career highlights: Winning the awards listed above and some of the features I wrote for the original NOVA magazine.
Mentor: My father, John Ennis, a lifelong journalist and author. Martin Dunn, current Editor of the New York Daily News and my editor on Today newspaper.
Big break: Getting off a local paper onto the launch of Petticoat and Honey magazines as a teenager. Getting off magazines onto the Daily Mail.
Big mistake: My marriage
» **Reading:** *19th-century literature, modern novels. Love David Mitchell.* **Watching:** *Ordinary people, my back, reality TV programmes for work, regular theatre goer.* **Listening:** *Jeff Buckley, Antony and The Johnsons, Moloko, The Flaming Lips, Rufus Wainwright, Blind Boys of Alabama, Coleman Hawkins, Clifford Brown, Art Tatum, Motown stuff.* **Relaxing to:** *Pilates, Tai Chi, online chess, reading, going out with friends.* » *Single, 1 child*

George Entwistle

8.7.62

BBC, White City, 201 Wood Lane, London W12 7TS
T 020 8752 4467
E george.entwistle@bbc.co.uk

Occupation: Head of Television Current Affairs, BBC

Awards: Newsnight, RTS Awards for Best News Programme, for Innovation with the Baghdad Blogger programme, and twice winner in the Home News category; Broadcast Award for Best News Programme.
Education: Silcoates School, Wakefield; University of Durham
Career highlights: Began career as a print journalist with Haymarket Magazines; BBC Broadcast Journalist Trainee, 1989; Assistant Producer, Panorama, including coverage of first Gulf War, fall of Margaret Thatcher and aftermath of Tiananmen Square protest, 1991-93; Producer, On the Record, BBC, 1993-94; Producer, Newsnight, BBC, 1994-97; Assistant Editor, Newsnight, BBC, 1997-99; Deputy Editor, Tomorrow's World, BBC, 1999-2000; Deputy Editor, Newsnight, BBC, 2000-01; Editor, Newsnight, BBC, 2002-04; Executive Editor, topical arts, BBC2 and BBC4; Launch Editor of The Culture Show on BBC 2, 2004-05; Head of Television Current Affairs, BBC, 2005-present.

Caroline Evans

9.11.72

Hachette Filipacchi (UK) Ltd, 64 North Row, London W1K 7LL
T 020 7150 7075
E carolineevans@hf-uk.com

Occupation: Publisher, Sugar and B magazines

Other positions: Associate Publisher, Marie Claire, In Style, Woman & Home, Ideal Home and others; Publisher, TV7; Assistant Publisher, T3; Circulation Manager, G+J of the UK; Group Account Manager, COMAG; Product Manager, EMAP; Metro (Q, Mojo, Empire, Premiere); Researcher, EMAP; Ad Sales Executive, EMAP Nationals, Car and Performance Car; Ad Sales Executive, Hi Fi Choice.

Publications: Sugar, B, Marie Claire, In Style, Woman & Home, Essentials, Family Circle, Ideal Home, Homes & Gardens, Living etc, 25 Beautiful Homes, Country Homes & Interiors, T3, Prima, Best, Your Home, Prima Baby, DJ, Health & Fitness, Rosemary Conley Diet & Fitness, Q, Mojo, Empire, Car, Performance Car, Hi-Fi Choice and many more...

Awards: Can't remember - over the years lots of mags made the shortlist and a couple of wins too - it only seems to matter up until the actual event!

Education: Leek High School, Staffs; Salford University

Career highlights: Relaunching Sugar in May 2005 - still the original and best teen mag by far; successful launch of Rosemary Conley Diet & Fitness magazine - a dream client!; proving (despite our client, ITV Digital's demise) that a large-circulation weekly TV magazine can work on subscription; agreeing to launch a magazine about WAP in six weeks - before I knew what WAP was!

Mentor: Probably my first great boss Carolyn Morgan who was Business Development Director at EMAP - good teacher, worked hard, very clever, led by example, showed me off and was relaxed and great fun - not often you get all that at once...

Big break: Not so much a break as an eye opener - leaving ad sales meant I could learn about printing, marketing, distribution, balance sheets (joy!), acquisitions and get to see what was going on right at the top of EMAP rather than just one division - only spent a year there but learnt so much and knew from then on that I wanted to be in general management.

Big mistake: Assuming that filling in this questionnaire before leaving the office was only going to take me two minutes! Seriously - maybe I should have stayed in ad sales a bit longer - would have got to senior level faster but only in one specialism - either that or taken a law degree instead of languages and marketing.

» **Reading:** *Magazines! I only have time for books on holiday. Media Guardian (Monday paper and daily email updates), Sunday Times, BBC news online. Also unmissable are Popbitch/Holy Moly.* **Watching:** *Coronation Street - that's all anyone needs to watch, surely? I am brilliant at the lyric round in Never Mind the Buzzcocks but maybe that's a function of my age...* **Listening:** *Xfm and Radio 4. Wide selection of music on iPod but mostly indie rock.* **Relaxing to:** *Alone: Coronation Street. With others: eating, drinking, dancing, travelling, going to festivals.* » *Single, no children*

Tim Ewart

7.2.53

200 Gray's Inn Road, London WC1X 8XZ
T 07971 130244
E tim.ewart@itn.co.uk

Occupation: Sports Editor, ITV News

Other positions: At ITN, Warsaw Correspondent, Washington Correspondent, Moscow Correspondent, Africa Correspondent; previously, reporter on various newspapers; News Editor Radio Orwell, Ipswich; Reporter/Presenter BBC TV Look North, Leeds; Reporter/Presenter Thames News, London; Presenter BBC Newsroom South East.

Awards: New York Television Awards silver medal for coverage of Zimbabwe.

Education: Gresham's School; Ipswich Civic College

Career highlights: I started in 1967 on a weekly newspaper in Suffolk, the Bury Free Press, and went via the Leicester Mercury to work in Bermuda on newspapers and TV in 1970. I arrived at ITN in 1981 after jobs in local radio and regional television, and have been there since apart from a three-year spell presenting BBC Newsroom South East in the mid-90s. I covered martial law in Poland, US-Soviet summits and the end of the Cold War in Washington, the demise of Gorbachev and the collapse of the Soviet Union in Moscow; and famine in Sudan and the crisis in Zimbabwe while I was based in Johannesburg.

Mentor: I didn't have a mentor, but I was inspired by various ITN reporters, notably Jon Snow (in my opinion the best British television reporter in his day) and Norman Rees.

Big break: Having an insider on the interview board for the Washington bureau job in 1986, knowing the questions - and the correct answers - in advance, and getting the job.

Big mistake: Stepping drunk in front of a taxi in the middle of the night in Montevideo, Uruguay, during the Falklands war. I spent a week in hospital and was sent home.

» **Reading:** *Elmore Leonard, John Le Carré etc.* **Watching:** *Old DVDs of Fawlty Towers and Inspector Morse and Ipswich Town FC home games.* **Listening:** *Steve Earl and the Dukes, Buckwheat Zydeco, Brenda Fassi.* **Relaxing to:** *Golf, running and, most importantly, walking my black labrador Charlie (a good dog).* » *Married, 5 children*

Maire Fahey

10.10.59

National Magazine Company, 72 Broadwick Street, London W1F 9EP
T 020 7312 4114
E maire.fahey@natmags.co.uk

Occupation: Editor, Prima magazine

Other positions: Formerly Editor, Best magazine; Launch Editor, For Me magazine, Sydney; Editorial Director, Attic Futura; Deputy Editor, Take a Break; Deputy Editor, Chat magazine.
Education: Loreto College, St Albans; Harlow Technical College; National Council for the Training of Journalists
Career highlights: Biggest thrill was my first editorship at Best at the age of 33, then totally revamping the title and putting 15% sales on in the first year. Also launching a new weekly in Australia - having to recruit a team from scratch and hit the shelves within seven months of stepping off the plane. And most recently, achieving success for Prima - defying the market trend and actually putting on sales!
Big break: Landing a job as Subeditor on the new launch of Chat magazine - my first job on a national after doing my time on local papers.
Big mistake: Trying out contract publishing for a brief 10 weeks - never again.

» **Reading:** *Anything I can get my hands on - novels, preferably as magazines are more like work, newspapers (the Guardian and Observer at weekends) and cereal boxes if there's nothing else to hand.* **Watching:** *The only TV programme I currently can't miss is Shameless.* **Listening:** *Too wide-ranging to list, but not drum'n'bass if I can avoid it.* **Relaxing to:** *Drinking and dancing (sometimes at the same time).* » *Single, 1 child*

Ivor Falvey

6.8.75

174 Hammersmith Road, London W6 7JP
T 020 8267 8025
E Ivor.Falvey@haynet.com

Occupation: Commercial Director, MediaWeek, Portfolio, Media 360

Other positions: Associate Publisher, MediaWeek; Advertisement Manager, Packaging News; Advertisement Manager, CTN.
Publications: MediaWeek, MediaWeek Awards, Media 360, AOL Online Planning Awards, GCAP Radio Planning Awards, Various Supplements - Ireland/Targeting Kids/ Targeting Commuters.
Awards: Are there awards for salespeople?
Education: University College, Dublin
Career highlights: Relaunched MediaWeek in 2004; launched Media 360 in 2004; launched TV Planning Awards in 2001; launched Radio Planning Awards in 2002; launched the Online Planning Awards in 2004.
Mentor: My father still plays a huge part in how I approach life and work and play.
Big break: Getting into Emap and getting the best training around at an early point in my career.
Big mistake: Leaving Emap - the title I worked on was taken over!

» **Reading:** *Lots of newspapers online, Metro, Sun, an occasional book.* **Watching:** *Any sport, property programmes, my new baby daughter trying to roll over.* **Listening:** *Mostly BBC Radio 1 in the car or Classic FM if I want to wind down.* **Relaxing to:** *Playing golf, gym, earphones with The Red Hot Chilli Peppers playing loudly.* » *Married, 1 daughter*

Andy Farrant

9.1.59

PO Box 219, Newport, Lincoln LN1 3XY
T 07764 354942
E andy.farrant@bbc.co.uk

Occupation: Assistant Editor, BBC Radio Lincolnshire

Other positions: Various news and sports journalist posts in newspapers and radio, including BBC World Service Sport.
Education: Newquay Grammar School; Sheffield Hallam University
Career highlights: Commentating on the closing stages of Kenya beating West Indies in the 1996 World Cup in India. It's the only BBC sound archive of that famous cup upset. Interviewing Chris Patten in Government House in Hong Kong. Working with the best talent around in local radio.
Big break: Getting my first reporter's job on a free newspaper.
Big mistake: Getting my first reporter's job on a free newspaper.

» **Reading:** *Scripts, cues, the Racing Post and The Good Beer Guide.* **Watching:** *My horses losing and my pints going down.* **Listening:** *BBC Radio Lincolnshire, and as much other radio as I can.* **Relaxing to:** *Smashing a little white ball around and talking about it in the bar.* » *Single, no children*

Jane Featherstone

24.3.69

Kudos Film and TV Ltd, 12-14 Amwell Street, London EC1R 1UQ
T 020 7812 3278
E michellef@kudosfilmandtv.com

Occupation: Head of Drama, Kudos Film and Television Ltd

Awards: BAFTA nomination, Best Drama Series and RTS Social Award nomination, Best Behind the Scenes Newcomer for Touching Evil 1 and 2; BAFTA nomination, Best Single Film for Sex 'n' Death; various awards at festivals including Berlin, Emden and BIFA for Pure; for Spooks 1, 2, and 3 include BAFTA Best Drama Series, Broadcast Award, Best Drama Series 2003 (nomination 2004), RTS Award Best Drama Series 2004 (nomination 2003); nomination, Banff Rockie Award, Best Continuing Series 2003 and 2004, nomination, Indie Award, Best Production of the Year and Best

Drama, nomination BAFTA Craft Award Editing Fiction/Entertainment.
Education: Old Palace School, Croydon; University of Leeds
Career highlights: Joint Managing Director, Kudos Film and TV Ltd; Producer, Touching Evil 1 and 2 (ITV), Sex 'n' Death (BBC2), Glasgow Kiss (BBC1); Executive Producer, Pure, Spooks (MI5) 1, 2, and 3 (BBC1), Pleasureland (Channel 4), Comfortably Numb (Channel 4), Hustle 1 (BBC1), Hustle 2 (BBC1), Spooks 4 (BBC1); Member, BAFTA 1996-present.
» **Watching:** *Cinema.* **Relaxing to:** *Sailing, skiing, riding.*

Peter Fincham 27.7.60

Room 6239, BBC Television Centre, Wood Lane, London W12 6RJ
T 020 8576 1622
E peter.fincham@bbc.co.uk

Occupation: Controller, BBC One

Other positions: CEO, talkbackTHAMES.
Publications: Broadcast; Media Guardian.
Awards: 2001 Indie Award for the individual who has made an outstanding contribution to the independent sector of the industry.
Education: Cambridge
Career highlights: Joined the BBC as Controller BBC One in May 2005; appointed Chief Executive of talkbackTHAMES in February 2003, when Talkback and Thames, two of the best known brands in UK television were brought together to create the UK's biggest, best known and most diverse independent production company. Responsible for bringing the two companies together while maintaining their individual cultures. Talkback productions include The Lost Prince, The Apprentice (UK), Look Around You, Essential Poems, QI, Grand Designs, Jamie's Kitchen, House Doctor, and How Clean Is Your House? Thames credits include The X Factor, Pop Idol, The Bill, Family Affairs and Murder Investigation Team. At Talkback, executive producer credits have included shows for the BBC such as music-based quiz Never Mind the Buzzcocks, long-running sporting quiz They Think It's All Over, comedy series I'm Alan Partridge, the BAFTA award-winning drama Perfect Strangers and The Lost Prince.
» **Watching:** *BBC One programmes.* » *Married, 4 children*

Elly Fiorentini 9.8.67

BBC Radio York, 20 Bootham Row, York YO30 7BR
T 01904 641351
E elly.fiorentini@bbc.co.uk

Occupation: Presenter and Producer of weekday show Elly on BBC Radio York.

Other positions: News Editor, Selby Reporter; former Breakfast Presenter.
Publications: Getting listeners to hold coffee mornings to raise money for water in Africa.
Awards: Sony Gold for producing coverage of floods in November 2000; Bronze in the Gillard Awards for coverage of the Great Heck Train Crash.
Education: The Bar Convent, York; Harrow College of Higher Education
Career highlights: Life for me started as a secretary in the BBC. Highlights include working on major news stories - North Yorkshire's 2002 floods, the Great Heck Train Crash, the murder of Caroline Stuttle and getting the first radio interview with her mum. Producing coverage of the Queen's first visit to York for nearly 20 years, and meeting some great people over the years.
Mentor: Chris Choi (now ITV news) always encouraged people to take risks and his enthusiasm for radio inspired me to continue down the presentation road.
Big break: Being asked to present my first ever three hour show!
Big mistake: Not sure about this one - I have made many but hopefully I have learned from them!
» **Reading:** *Most newspapers, I have to for research purposes, and glossy magazines. I love car magazines too!* **Watching:** *Spooks is my all-time favourite drama - but why are so many of them getting killed off? And I love Corrie - a great escape from all those stresses of the day!* **Listening:** *U2 and Bon Jovi.* **Relaxing to:** *Sleeping, and spending time with my friends. Living life to the full! I also enjoy days at the races - York has a fantastic racecourse. And eating in friends' restaurants.* » *Single, no children*

Andrew Flanagan 15.3.56

200 Renfield Street, Glasgow G2 3PR
T 0141 300 3000
E sandra.macvarish@smg.plc.uk

Occupation: Chief Executive, SMG plc

Other positions: Non-executive Director, Scottish Rugby Union 2000-05; MICAS.
Education: Hillhead High School, Glasgow; University of Glasgow
Career highlights: Articled Clerk, Touche Ross, 1976-79; Audit Supervisor, Price Waterhouse 1979-81; Finance Manager, ITT Europe Inc, 1981-86; Director of Finance, Europe, PA Consulting Group, 1986-91; Group Finance Director, The BIS Group Ltd, 1991-93; SMG plc (formerly Scottish Television plc then Scottish Media Group plc), Group Finance Director, 1994-96; Managing Director, 1996; currently Chief Executive.
» **Watching:** *Cinema.* **Relaxing to:** *Golf, jogging, skiing, reading, television.* » *Married, 3 children*

Kim Fletcher 17.9.56

10 Caithness Road, London W14 0JB
T 07747 635580
E kim.fletcher@dsl.pipex.com

Occupation: Chairman, National Council for the Training of Journalists, journalist and media consultant

Other positions: Deputy Editor, the Sunday Telegraph; Editor, the Independent on Sunday; Editorial Director, Hollinger Telegraph New Media; Editorial Director, Telegraph Group Limited.

Awards: Reporter of the Year, 1981 (awarded to Sunday Times team).
Education: Heversham Grammar School, Westmorland; Hertford College, Oxford; University College, Cardiff
Career highlights: Working on the Star, Sheffield, the night the Yorkshire Ripper was arrested in the city; reporting on the burning oilfields of Iraq in the first Gulf War; selling off the Telegraph Group after the departure of Conrad Black.
Mentor: Tony Bambridge, late Managing Editor, the Sunday Times.
Big break: Answering the phone and being available to rush in for a news shift at the Sunday Times the day someone shot a starting pistol at the Queen during Trooping the Colour.
Big mistake: Not working harder when I was younger.

» **Reading:** *All newspapers, many magazines and not enough books.* **Watching:** *The Simpsons, football and stuff I think I ought to.* **Listening:** *Radio 4, Five Live and whatever the children put on in the car.* **Relaxing to:** *Running.*
» *Married, 3 children*

Miles Flint

Royal Television Society, 5th Floor, Kildare House, 3 Dorset Rise, London EC4Y 8EN
T 020 7822 2810
E info@rts.org.uk

Occupation: Vice-President, Royal Television Society

Other positions: President, Sony Broadcast and Professional, Europe; Managing Director, Sony UK Ltd.
Education: London University; Cranfield Institute of Technology
Career highlights: Held marketing and product development roles at ICL and then at STC; joined Sony as Managing Director of Sony Broadcast and Professional UK, 1991; Regional Director, North, 1993; Deputy Managing Director, 1996; President of Sony Broadcast and Professional, Europe, 2000; appointed to the Board of Sony Europe, 2001; Managing Director, Sony UK Ltd, 2001-present.

Dee Forbes 5.2.71

16 Great Marlborough Street, London W1F 7HS
T 020 7693 1134
E dee.forbes@turner.com

Occupation: SVP and GM Turner Entertainment Networks UK/Ireland

Other positions: SVP and GM, Turner Entertainment Networks Nordic, Eastern Europe, Africa; SVP, Advertising Sales, Turner Entertainment Networks Europe; Account Director, Media Audits; Account Manager, Young and Rubicam Media in Europe.
Education: Convent of Mercy, Clonakilty, Co. Cork; University College, Dublin
Career highlights: Began at Y and R Media in Europe as Media Exec in 1989 and cut my teeth in the media world there. Went on to join Media Audits where I was part of the team that opened up their Dublin office. From there I joined Turner in a sales role for Cartoon Network and progressed to leading the European sales team as well as channel management.
Mentor: Charles Courtier, Y and R (now Media Edge), Mick Buckley, CNBC.
Big break: Adding channel management for Nordic, Eastern Europe and Africa to my ad sales role.
Big mistake: Placing a £100 bet on the Lions to win their last tour!

» **Reading:** *The Guardian and Observer, the Week, Vanity Fair, Wallpaper, Condé Nast Traveller, Irish Arts Review.* **Watching:** *Rugby, Waking the Dead, Prime Suspect, Grand Designs, Lost, TCM.* **Listening:** *Kaiser Chiefs, Hotel Costes, Burt Bacharach, Paul Weller.* **Relaxing to:** *A weekend in West Cork with friends and family enjoying great food and wine.*

Matt Ford 3.9.77

1-5 Wandsworth Road, London SW8 2LN
T 020 7526 3327
E matt.ford@bigissue.com

Occupation: Editor, The Big Issue

Other positions: Content Editor, Timeout.com
Education: Birmingham University; post-grad Bristol University
Career highlights: The first time my work was published in a broadsheet - the Independent - was a big moment for me, and helped me believe things were on track for me as a writer. Seeing anything I've written in print is still a joy, but by far my biggest achievement has been helping return the Big Issue to profitability. After six years of declining sales, the magazine is now redesigned, reinvigorated and has booming sales. It's been a huge effort personally and professionally made great fun by brilliant colleagues.
Mentor: I've never really had one - but Matthew Collins, the previous editor of the Big Issue and author of This Is Serbia Calling, was an inspiring boss and is a great journalist.
Big break: Being shortlisted for the Observer Young Travel Writer competition in 1999 - it really convinced me I could be a good journalist.
Big mistake: Believing the hype once or twice too often.

» **Reading:** *I've always read everything and anything, as many papers and magazines as I can, lots of non-fiction, fiction books when I have the time and I'm constantly grazing for stories on the internet. Before I was a journalist I was a historian and archaeologist and I still love history of all periods.* **Watching:** *Films. Whether it's a strange four-hour Serbo-Croat epic, a meandering US indie, a Jamie Stewart comedy or a blockbuster superhero adaptation - I can usually find some joy in most genres. On TV the BBC is the backbone for me, but I can also often be found slumped in front of UKTV History or UKTV Food.* **Listening:** *My heart's in the 1970s and I'm a bit of a Mojo man, but my head's in the present and I listen to loads of new music. I'm an obsessive fan and most places I spend any time become surrounded by piles of CDs from beardie-weirdie psychedelia to 1970s rock, American punk and odd bits of jazz and indie.* **Relaxing to:** *On foot, or on my bike, in the woods or up a hill somewhere.* » *Very attached but not married, no children*

Adam Foulkes

16.9.70

Nexus Productions, 113–114 Shoreditch High Street, London E1 6JN
T 020 7749 7500
E adam@nexusproductions.com

Occupation: One half of directing duo Smith & Foulkes

Other positions: Commercial work includes Honda Grrr, NSPCC Speech Bubble and the Observer Music Monthly From Abba to Zappa; film work includes The Littlest Elf opening sequence to the Dreamworks/Paramount film A Series of Unfortunate Events and the main titles for the Working Title/Universal film Thunderbirds; we also worked on sketches and the titles for the BBC animated comedy show Monkey Dust.
Awards: British Animation Awards, Best Direction in a Commercial, 2000; Rushes Soho Shorts, Best Title Sequence, 2002; British Television Advertising Craft Awards, Best Animation, 2004, 2005; British Television Advertising Awards, Best Commecial, Gold, Silver, 2005; D&AD Golds, 4 Silvers, 2005; Cannes Grand Prix, Titanium, Journalists' Award, 2005.
Education: WSCAD, Farnham; Royal College of Art
Big break: Straight from college we directed some work for the U2 Popmart Tour. It was shown on the world's biggest screen all over the world.
Big mistake: The world's biggest screen means big mistakes.

» **Reading:** *Recently I enjoyed Never Let Me Go by Kazuo Ishiguro. The daily instalments of The Fiver on the Guardian website are always a welcome treat.* **Watching:** *Shameless is one programme I try not to miss.* **Listening:** *There's music on constantly in our studio. At the moment it's Miles Davis, Brian Eno, Eels and the Bugsy Malone soundtrack. At home it's Radio 5 Live.* **Relaxing to:** *Running around the football pitch for Green Park Rangers every Sunday.* » *Single, no children*

Jerry Fowden

26.6.60

Trader Media Group, Unit 6 Thatcham Business Village, Thatcham, Berkshire RG19 4LW
T 01635 588500
E jerry.fowden@tradermedia.co.uk

Occupation: Chief Executive, Trader Media Group

Other positions: Non-Executive Director, Chesapeake Corporation (USA Multinational Packaging company); Member of Board of Governors, Dame Alice Owens School; Member of Chartered Institute of Marketing.
Publications: Auto Trader, Ad Trader, Autotrader.co.uk, and 50+ other titles in UK, Holland, Italy and South Africa.
Awards: Various advertising awards achieved in companies I ran for Stella Artois, Caffreys, Irish Ale, Carling Black Label, etc. But the thanks go to all the team and happy customers.
Education: Dame Alice Owens School, London; Kings College (formerly Queen Elizabeth College), University of London, BSc (Hons) Food Science and Management Studies; IMD, Switzerland Summer Programme.
Career highlights: I have had the benefit of working with the largest, most successful public and private blue chip corporations in the world such as Mars, PepsiCo, InBev etc. Career highlights involve successful brand launches such as Hooch and Caffreys at Bass, acquisitions and disposals of multi-billion dollar companies like Becks and Coors while at InBev. I believe in an unrelenting focus on the customer and meeting their needs and wants, with excellent customer service, a low cost base and a motivated aligned management team.
Mentor: Terry Riley, a senior manager in the Mars Group when I first started work as a graduate on Mars' Management Through Sales programme.
Big break: When I moved from Pepsi Europe to Bass in 1991 to manage Customer Service and Sales, eventually becoming Chief Operating Officer and then CEO of this £1.5bn-plus turnover business. Also sales of PepsiCo soft drinks to all Gulf War I troops via a network of Middle East bottlers delivering the PR of Pepsi, Diet Pepsi and Mirinda on Storming Norman's peace signing table in the desert tent in Kuwait.
Big mistake: Being involved in the relaunch of Butlins while on the board of The Rank Group plc. This brand was beyond saving.

» **Reading:** *Apart from work papers (and newspapers of course) my reading is mainly property related/real estate magazines and journals.* **Watching:** *News at 10.* **Listening:** *Enya, Celine Dion, Voice (Belgium Archipelago Group).* **Relaxing to:** *Lane swimming at least 3 times a week.* » *Married, 2 children*

Tim Franks

15.5.72

BBC, IPC Boulevard Charlemagne 1, Boite 50, 1041 Brussels, Belgium
T 00 32 2 230 2120
E tim.franks@bbc.co.uk

Occupation: BBC Europe Correspondent

Other positions: Presenter, World at One, BBC Radio 4
Publications: Contributor to various newspapers and magazines on topics such as music, food and books.
Education: Wadham College, Oxford
Career highlights: Six months as Washington Correspondent covering the aftermath of the September 11 attacks; reported on the assassination of the Dutch politician Pim Fortuyn, the earthquake in southern Italy in November 2002, and the enlargement of the EU.

Peter Franzen

8.5.51

Eastern Daily Press, Prospect House, Rouen Road, Norwich NR1 1RE
T 01603 772400
E peter.franzen@archant.co.uk

Occupation: Editor, Eastern Daily Press

Publications: Eastern Daily Press raised £1m for carers in Norfolk in four years to set up trust fund; work overseas setting up children's homes in Sarajevo, Sierra Leone, Rumania and Mozambique with money raised by readers; biggest regional contribution by any newspaper for tsunami.

Awards: OBE in 2005 New Year's Honours for services to journalism; Daily Regional Newspaper of the Year, 1998; Plain English award (best regional), 1989; Regional Front Page of the Year, 2002.
Education: The William Penn School
Career highlights: NCTJ Young Journalist of Year; Chief Sub Eastern Evening News; Group Production Editor, News Editor, Eastern Daily Press and Eastern Evening News; Editor, Great Yarmouth Mercury; Editor, Eastern Daily Press.
Mentor: Alfred Jenner, former Editorial Director of Eastern Counties Newspapers and Stuart Garner, former Editor-in-Chief of TRN.
Big break: First editorship, Great Yarmouth Mercury as stepping stone to Eastern Daily Press editorship.
Big mistake: Delaying too long in taking a marketing diploma - only then could I intelligently sift the bullshit.

» **Reading:** *All national dailies, and assorted regionals that come my way. Read Dan Brown fiction while on holiday.* **Watching:** *West Wing, Spooks, Have I got News for You, Question of Sport, University Challenge (I sometimes get a couple right!), news channels, Sky, football.* **Listening:** *Five Live, Today Programme, Jonathan Ross.* **Relaxing to:** *Watch Norwich City (but not very relaxing of late!), gardening, drink wine, take holidays.* » *Married, 2 children, Oliver 24, Sam 21*

Mark Freeland

Hartswood Films Ltd, Twickenham Studios, The Barons, St Margarets, Twickenham, Middlesex TW1 2AW
T 020 8607 8736
E films.tv@hartswoodfilms.co.uk

Occupation: Producer, Hartswood Films

Education: Exeter University
Career highlights: Production Assistant, LWT; Assistant Floor Manager, Thames TV, 1988-94; Writer and Senior Producer, The Big Breakfast, Planet 24, 1994-96; Development Producer, Planet 24, including Nothing But the Truth, Survivor, 1996-97; Executive Producer, including Naked in Westminster, Cream, 16, Weekender, co-wrote You Are Here (C4), Writer on Trigger Happy, Script Editor on Stressed Eric, 1997-2000; Head of Original Programming, Drama and Comedy, Sky One, including Dream Team, Time Gentlemen Please, Mile High, The Bombmaker, Do or Die, Now You See Her, Harry Enfield's Brand Spanking New Show, Jumpers for Goalposts, 2000-02; Executive Producer, BBC, including Early Doors, Marion and Geoff, Look Around You, The Keith Barret Show, The Catherine Tate Show, Nighty Night, QI, The Lenny Henry Show, The Big Impression, The Kumars, The Mighty Boosh, The Worst Week of My Life, Carrie and Barry, Shirley Ghostman, All About Me, Rich Hall's Fishing Show, Vic and Bob in Catterick, Supernova, Sensitive Skin, Mock the Week, 2002-05; Producer, Hartswood Films, 2005-present.

Matt Frei

26.11.63

Suite 350, 2030 Main Street NW, Washington, DC 20036, USA
T 202 223 2050
E Matt.Frei@bbc.co.uk

Occupation: Chief Washington Correspondent, BBC

Publications: Italy: the unfinished revolution (1996); regular contributor, the Spectator, London Review of Books, Wall Street Journal.
Awards: RTS Award, 2000.
Education: Westminster School; St Peter's College, Oxford
Career highlights: Disc Jockey, German Service, BBC Radio, 1986-87; Producer, Current Affairs, World Service, BBC Radio, 1987-88; Reporter, Jerusalem, BBC Radio, 1988-89; Correspondent, Bonn, BBC Radio, 1989-91; Correspondent, Foreign Affairs, BBC Television, 1991-92; Correspondent, South Europe and Rome, BBC Television, 1992-96; Asia Correspondent, BBC Television, 1996-2002; Washington Correspondent, 2002-present.

» **Relaxing to:** *Painting*

Matthew Freud

2.11.63

Freud Communications Ltd, 19-21 Mortimer Street, London W1T 3DX
T 020 7580 2626
E matthew@freud.com

Occupation: Chairman, Freud Communications

Other positions: Trustee, Comic Relief.
Education: Westminster; Pimlico
Career highlights: Chairman, Freud Communications 1990-present.

» *Married, 3 children*

Mark Frith

22.5.70

7th Floor, Endeavour House, 189 Shaftesbury Avenue, London WC2H 8JG
T 020 7437 9011
E mark.frith@emap.com

Occupation: Editor, Heat magazine

Awards: PPA Consumer Magazine Editor of the Year 2001 and 2002.
Education: Gleadless Valley School, Sheffield; University of East London
Career highlights: Editor, college magazine, Overdraft, 1989-90 (Writer 1988-89); Smash Hits, Writer 1990-93, Features Editor 1993-94, Editor 1994-96; Editor; Sky magazine 1996-97; Editor, Special Projects, 1997-98; Editor, Heat Magazine, 1999-present.

Ben Frow

14.07.61

Five TV, 22 Long Acre, London WC2E 9LY
T 020 7550 5555
E ben.frow@five.tv

Occupation: Controller, Features and Entertainment, Five TV

Other positions: Head of Features, Factual Entertainment and Daytime, C4, 2002-03; Head of Features and Daytime, C4 Television, 2001-02; Head of Features, C4 Television, 1999-01; Executive Producer, BBC TV, 1998-99.
Education: St Paul's Cathedral Choir School; Woodberry Down Comprehensive School; London College of Fashion
Career highlights: Being voted Best Newcomer at the 1985 British Fashion Design Show when I was setting out as a Fashion Designer. Launching 9 O'Clock Live and Lorraine Live at GMTV (1995-7); establishing a successful Features Department at Channel Four that regularly delivered the highest viewing figures across the channel with programmes that included Property Ladder, How Clean Is Your House, Location Location, Relocation, Grand Designs, No Going Back and Sex Tips For Girls; bringing Nigella Lawson to TV with Nigella Bites; re-inventing Jamie Oliver with Jamie's Kitchen; creating a vibrant Features and Entertainment Department at Five Television that brings a solid audience to the channel week after week with such programmes as Build A New Life, Cosmetic Surgery Live, How To Be A Property Developer, How Not To Decorate, The Hotel Inspector, The Diet Doctors and Swinging; Rebecca Loos and 'that pig' on The Farm and Cosmetic Surgery Live - both for Five Commissioning.
Mentor: Richard Madeley and Judy Finnigan when I worked at This Morning, Peter McHugh when I worked at GMTV, and Tim Gardam (ex Director of Programmes, C4).
Big break: Being hired to look after Richard and Judy's wardrobe on This Morning in September 1990.
Big mistake: Not setting up my own Independent company five years ago. I'd be a lot richer!

» **Reading:** *The Daily Mail, Mirror, Sunday Times, Patricia Highsmith and Truman Capote.* **Watching:** *America's Next Top Model, Will and Grace, Bad Girls, Footballers' Wives, Coronation Street, the News, Desperate Housewives, The XFactor.* **Listening:** *Kate Bush, ABBA, Dolly Parton, Mozart, and a wide selection of musicals (sorry!).* **Relaxing to:** *I bake cakes, arrange flowers and shop for things I don't need.* » *Single, no children*

Anthony Fry

21.6.59

25 Bank Street, London E14 5LE
T 020 7102 1300
E anthony.fry@lehman.com

Occupation: Managing Director, Head of UK Investment Banking; Chairman, Media Group, Lehman Brothers.

Other positions: Non-executive Director, Mowlem plc. Board, Edinburgh International Television Festival; Board, LAMDA; Board, The Sixteen.
Education: Magdalen College, Oxford
Career highlights: The UK privatisations of the 1980s whilst an Executive Director of Rothschilds; running a bid for the newly created National Lottery in 1994; creating Europe's leading media investment banking business in late 1990s at CSFB.
Mentor: Russell Edey taught me to put my banking career into a life context.
Big break: Being sent by Rothschilds to Australia at the age of 25.
Big mistake: Getting the structure of the Rothschild Tattersalls bid for the National Lottery in 1994 wrong - with some modest compromise it would have been us.

» **Reading:** *Modern novelists such as Sebastian Faulks, history - currently American Civil War, Financial Times, Times, Daily Telegraph, Media Guardian, Economist, Spectator, Vogue.* **Watching:** *Theatre, opera, sport - particularly rugby and cricket, films, current affairs, black comedies.* **Listening:** *Classical - 16th century choral, Bruckner, Mozart operas, Handel, Sibelius, Nielsen, Barber; Rock - Coldplay, KT Tunstall, Genesis, Elton John, Men at Work; soft rock - The Corrs, Katie Melua, David Gray; Jazz - Amy Winehouse.* **Relaxing to:** *At house in Oxfordshire by a roaring fire listening to Bach and reading a great book; playing cricket on a perfect English summer's afternoon on a typical English village green; watching my children play sport; tennis, rugby, cricket, football.* » *Married, 1 daughter and 2 sons*

Eric Fuller

9.2.56

IPC Media, King's Reach Tower, Stamford Street, London SE1 9LS
T 020 7261 5675
E eric_fuller@ipcmedia.com

Occupation: Group Publishing Director, IPC ignite!

Other positions: Publishing Director, Dennis Publishing & United Consumer Magazines; Publisher at Emap.
Publications: Nuts and NME.
Awards: Highly Commended for Publisher of the Year at PPA Awards 1996, 1997, 1998, 2002, 2003, 2005.
Education: University of Sussex
Career highlights: Editor of Sounds, then Publishing Director of Kerrang! Launch Publishing Director of Maxim and Stuff at Dennis, and Nuts at IPC.
Mentor: Alan Lewis and Mike Sharman at Spotlight Publications, back in the 1970s.
Big break: Switching from editor to publisher in 1984, a time when journalists were generally dismissed as airheads who couldn't even manage money, let alone make it. Not like today, of course.
Big mistake: Brief flirtation with pipe smoking (a very long time ago).

» **Reading:** *For work, every magazine I see. For pleasure, luxurious books about classic English motorcycles.* **Watching:** *Sarah Beeny, all variants of CSI and anything with clips of vintage rock 'n' roll.* **Listening:** *A small but blissful selection of blues, reggae and soul.* **Relaxing to:** *In ways not always recommended by doctors.* » *Married, no children*

G

Richard Galpin 1.10.67

c/o BBC Television Centre, Wood Lane, London W12 6RJ
T 0030 6974 339773
E richard.galpin@bbc.co.uk

Occupation: BBC Athens Correspondent

Other positions: BBC Jakarta Correspondent; Freelance Correspondent in Pakistan for the BBC and the Guardian; BBC Dhaka Correspondent; Senior Producer, BBC World Service Radio, London.
Education: Oundle School; Oxford University
Career highlights: Being part of the BBC team covering Iraq since April 2003. Covering the Bali, Istanbul and Madrid bombings. Covering the Israeli/Palestinian conflict in 2003. Covering Indonesia and East Timor from 1999-2002. Covering the Athens Olympics 2004.
Big break: Joining the BBC in 1988.

» **Reading:** *Everything I can lay my hand on.* **Watching:** *Whatever is available in the country where I'm based.* **Listening:** *As above.* **Relaxing to:** *Taking my family out or playing football or cooking.* » *Married, 2 children*

Dominic Gardiner 20.11.74

16 Great Marlborough Street, London W1F 7HS
T 020 7693 1090
E dominic.gardiner@turner.com

Occupation: Channel Manager, Cartoon Network UK

Other positions: Various programming jobs for Turner, Flextech and Playboy, also worked in Tokyo for Cartoon Network Japan.
Publications: CN's current Where Cartoons Live campaign.
Awards: Kids BAFTA for Best Website; New Media Age Awards, Best Use of Multiple Channels for CNX: TV That Keeps You Up.
Education: University of Liverpool, Engineering Science & MGT.
Career highlights: Getting the job at Cartoon Network and sitting next to Dan Balaam, 'wacky' channel manager of Boomerang.
Mentor: This position is currently vacant. Please send me your CVs.
Big break: Getting a proper telly job in 'that London', working for TVI facilities making tea and toast.
Big mistake: Not being able to convince the head of The Adult Channel that he could make millions from putting their content on the internet.

» **Reading:** *National Geographic, newspapers (any), cereal packets.* **Watching:** *Everything I can. Sky+ has ruined my life.* **Listening:** *Neil Young, AC/DC, Terry Wogan, Jonathan Ross.* **Relaxing to:** *Horizontal on a beanbag with a can of Stella and family bag of peanuts watching Deadwood (best show on telly).* » *Married to Tracie, 3-year-old daughter, Zoe*

Frank Gardner 1.8.65

BBC Television Centre, Wood Lane, London W12 7RJ
T 020 8743 8000
E frank.gardner@bbc.co.uk

Occupation: BBC Security Correspondent

Other positions: Former BBC Middle East Correspondent
Awards: Order of British Empire (OBE); McWhirter Award.
Education: Exeter University
Career highlights: In-depth TV and radio reports and analysis from Saudi Arabia, Yemen, Afghanistan and the Middle East.
Mentor: No one
Big break: Getting unpaid work experience in the BBC World newsroom in 1995.
Big mistake: Trusting the Saudi Ministry of Information minders to look after us in Riyadh.

» **Reading:** *The Times, Economist, New Yorker, online publications.* **Watching:** *BBC, Channel 4, Al-Jazeera.* **Listening:** *Virgin, Classic FM, Radio 4.* **Relaxing to:** *By exploring mountains, jungles and deserts when I can.* » *Married, 2 children*

Julie Gardner 5.6.73

BBC Wales Drama, 2nd Floor, BH Llandaff, Cardiff CF5
T 02920 323908
E julie.gardner@bbc.co.uk

Occupation: Head of Drama, BBC Wales

Other positions: Executive Producer, Dr Who, Torchwood, Life on Mars, New Street Law, Rocket Man.
Education: Queen Mary & Westfield; University of London
Career highlights: I'm proud of getting Casanova commissioned at the BBC. It was a script I loved and it was a complicated path to a green light. I'm also grateful that the return of Dr Who has meant so much to its audience, particularly children. It's the greatest show in the world to work on. I've never worked so hard nor had so much fun.
Mentor: Russell T Davies and Jane Tranter are the two people I've learnt the most from. Both have brilliant minds, passion and know how to have fun. They make everything possible.
Big break: Co-producing Othello with Anne Pivcevic for ITV. Hardly anyone watched but the ambition for the piece made me realise anything was possible. Undoubtedly though, my biggest break was being offered the job of Head of Drama, BBC Wales and being able to work with Russell T Davies on Dr Who.
Big mistake: I don't think there's been one, single, big mistake - or if there has been, I haven't been found out yet! There are lots of little ones where I've made a wrong choice or editorial judgement. You never escape these mistakes. They haunt you.

» **Reading:** *Everything I read currently seems to be on A4 paper, bound by a daisy clip. I'm longing for a good book* *at Christmas.* **Watching:** *I have a huge appetite for TV – British and US drama, reality shows, news. I'm happiest on a wet Sunday afternoon with a DVD box set of something…* **Listening:** *This week it's been Virgin Radio in the car, Jeff Buckley, The Kaiser Chiefs, Franz Ferdinand, Murray Gold and U2. I LOVE Bono.* **Relaxing to:** *I watch TV, I eat out, drink lychee martinis. Mostly I work. It's the best thing.*

Wayne Garvie 10.9.67

Room 4025, Television Centre, Wood Lane, London W12 7RJ
T 020 8576 8010
E wayne.garvie@bbc.co.uk

Occupation: Head of Entertainment Group, BBC

Other positions: Director of Broadcasting, Granada Television; Producer, Granada Television.
Education: University of Kent at Canterbury; University of Sheffield
Career highlights: Transforming BBC Entertainment; Strictly Come Dancing; Dragon's Den; making Dancing with the Stars in the US; revitalising Question of Sport; co-creating the I Love brand; blagging way into World Cup Final 1990; killing off The Krypton Factor.
Mentor: Chris Pye
Big break: Getting the job as Director of Broadcasting at Granada.
Big mistake: Agreeing to make A Question of TV and Class of … never do a controller or a commissioner a favour if you don't believe in it.
» **Reading:** *Guardian, When Saturday Comes, Heat, Private Eye, William Boyd, books on Roman history and modern British history.* **Watching:** *Seinfeld DVDs, American drama, esp Deadwood, Sopranos, West Wing; anything written by Paul Abbott; anything produced by Nicky Shindler and Jeff Pope; history documentaries, especially by Lawrence Rees; anything Pat Llewellyn makes and anything at all Michael Winterbottom gets involved in.* **Listening:** *Everything I can cadge from the Later and Top of the Pops teams.* **Relaxing to:** *Listening to the free CDs I cadge from the Later and Top of the Pops teams and larking around with my daughters.* » *Married, 2 children*

Rupert Gavin

Royal Television Society, 5th Floor, Kildare House, 3 Dorset Rise, London EC4Y 8EN
T 020 7822 2810
E info@rts.org.uk

Occupation: Vice-President, Royal Television Society

Other positions: Director, Incidental Colman 1981-present; Director, Ambassador Theatre Group, 1999-present; Founder, Kingdom Media, 2004; Chairman, Contender Entertainment Group, 2004-present; Chief Executive, Odeon/UCI Cinemas Group 2005-present; Non-executive Director, Virgin Mobile, 2004-present.
Awards: Olivier Award for Best Entertainment 1998, 1999 and 2001; FRTS.
Career highlights: Copywriter, Account Director, Equity Partner, Director of Sharps (later Saatchi & Saatchi), 1976-87; Executive Vice-President, Dixons US 1987-89; Commercial Director, Dixons Group plc, 1989-92; Deputy Managing Director, Dixons Stores Group, 1992-94; BT plc, 1994-98, Director of Information, Communications and Entertainment, Director of Multimedia Services, Managing Director, Consumer Division; Chief Executive, BBC Worldwide, 1998-2004.
» **Relaxing to:** *Theatre producer, lyricist, gardener.*

Martin Geissler 1.3.75

ITV News Scotland Bureau, 10 George Street, Edinburgh EH2 2DU
T 0131 200 8065
E martin.geissler@itn.co.uk

Occupation: Scotland Correspondent, ITV News

Education: George Watson's College, Edinburgh
Career highlights: I began work in 1990 as a freelance covering Scotland for the fledgling Sky News. From there, the lure of newsdesk experience (and regular money) led me around various ITV regions. I joined Scottish TV in 1994, left to join Sky Sports as Scotland Correspondent in 1999. I joined ITN as ITV's Scotland Correspondent in 2002. The job has afforded me a series of fantastic opportunities, I've covered the Middle East from Kuwait, Iraq and Israel, as well as being sent to cover the tsunami and the New Orleans floods…
Mentor: Andrew Fyall, Foreign Correspondent for the Daily Express in the 1960s, was my Bureau Chief at Scottish Television … now retired but still an inspiration.
Big break: Being asked to join ITN on secondment from Scottish TV in 2002. By chance Scottish news hit a purple patch shortly after, a busy couple of months followed and I was given the job full time.
Big mistake: No regrets
» **Reading:** *Could be anything, this week Hemingway, last week Ian Rankin. Big fan of travel writing – and the sports pages!* **Watching:** *Television news and Heart of Midlothian Football Club.* **Listening:** *Very eclectic music taste, but the Stone Roses are never far from the stereo.* **Relaxing to:** *Keeping the children happy, running, and watching Hearts FC.* » *Married, 2 children*

Sir Bob Geldof 5.10.54

c/o Jukes Productions, PO Box 13995, London W9 2FL
T 020 7286 9532

Occupation: Musician, campaigner against debt

Awards: UN World Hunger Award, Irish Peace Prize, Rose d'Or Charity Award, 2005; Lifetime Achievement Award, Brit Awards, 2005; Hon Doctor of Law, University of Dundee, 2002, University College Dublin, 2004; Honorary DCL, University of East Anglia, 2004.
Education: Blackrock College, Dublin
Career highlights: Former Journalist with Georgia Straight Canada, NME and Melody Maker; Founder, Boomtown Rats, 1975-86; Organiser, Live Aid 1985, Live 8 2005; Chairman, Band Aid

Trust 1985-present; former Co-owner, Planet 24; Co-founder, Ten Alps Communications, 1999; Founder, Deckchair.com, WapWorld; Campaigner against Third World debt and supporter of numerous charities including Make Poverty History and Drop the Debt; Singles Co-writer (with Midge Ure) Do They Know It's Christmas? (Band Aid), 1984, Do They Know It's Christmas? (Band Aid II), 1989, Do They Know It's Christmas? (Band Aid 20), 2004; albums, The Boomtown Rats: The Boomtown Rats, 1977, Tonic for the Troops, 1978, The Fine Art of Surfacing, 1979, Mondo Bongo, 1980, V Deep, 1982, In the Long Grass, 1984, The Best of The Boomtown Rats, 2003; solo: Deep In the Heart of Nowhere, 1986, The Vegetarians of Love, 1990, The Happy Club, 1992, Sex, Age & Death, 2001; television, Grumpy Old Men (BBC), 2003, Geldof in Africa (BBC), 2005; film, Pink in Pink Floyd's The Wall, 1982.

›› *Divorced, 3 daughters, 1 adopted daughter*

Shiulie Ghosh 29.9.71

ITV News, 200 Gray's Inn Road, London WC1X 8XZ
T 020 7833 3000
E shiulie.ghosh@itn.co.uk

Occupation: Newscaster and News Correspondent, ITV News

Other positions: Home Affairs Editor, ITV News; Reporter / Presenter, BBC South East; Reporter / Presenter, BBC CountryFile; Reporter / Presenter, BBC East Midlands.
Awards: Best TV News Journalist 2001; British Telecom EMMA Awards.
Education: Teesside High School, Eaglescliffe; St Mary's Sixth Form College, Middlesbrough; University of Kent
Career highlights: Since joining ITN I have extensively covered many national and international stories including the immediate aftermath of the 9/11 attack, the Stephen Lawrence inquiry, the Queen Mother's death, the RAF Harriers campaign during the Kosovo conflict, the tsunami disaster in Thailand and the severe flooding in Europe. I have also anchored a range of news bulletins on ITV News and the ITV Newschannel.
Big break: As always, being in the right place at the right time. I was a BBC news trainee completing an attachment at Pebble Mill in Birmingham when the management decided to open a new regional TV station in Nottingham. They needed staff, I needed a job. The rest is history.
Big mistake: Forgetting my words through nerves during a live broadcast when I'd just started at ITN.

›› **Reading:** *Crime fiction, real-life dramas, sci-fi.* **Watching:** *News, drama, news, comedy.* **Listening:** *Morning reports on Five Live.* **Relaxing to:** *Holidays with my family, scuba-diving, skiing, anything that doesn't involve watching the news.*
›› *Married, 1 daughter*

Gary Gibbon 16.3.69

Channel 4 News, Parliamentary Press Gallery, House of Commons, London SW1A 0AA
T 020 7430 4990/1/2
E gary.gibbon@itn.co.uk

Occupation: Political Editor, Channel 4 News

Education: John Lyon School, Harrow; Balliol College, Oxford
Career highlights: A trip to the Balkans as producer to a great reporter, Channel 4 News Foreign Correspondent, the late Gaby Rado. I've rarely laughed and learnt so much. All the last four general elections, especially the last one when we had the Attorney General's legal advice on war in Iraq to report on Channel 4 News. The Hutton Inquiry was a fascinating insight into the workings of government.
Mentor: Elinor Goodman, a model political journalist and great fun too.
Big break: Just after I graduated, the former BBC veteran Political Reporter Vincent Hanna gave me a job in his independent production company, making videos for trade unions and programmes for Channel 4. It was pure luck - my letter landed on his desk just as a vacancy opened up.
Big mistake: The worst is yet to come.

›› **Reading:** *People, road signs, books and newspapers.* **Watching:** *Channel 4, of course. Religiously.* **Listening:** *My sons' voices, with occasional bits of Radio 3 and Radio 4 filtering through.* **Relaxing to:** *With great ease.*
›› *Married, 2 children*

Jessica Gibson 18.4.68

eve Magazine, Haymarket, 174 Hammersmith Road, London W6 7JP
T 020 8267 8202
E jessica.gibson@haynet.com

Occupation: Publisher, eve Magazine

Other positions: Publisher, What to Wear magazine; Group Publisher, Music Division, BBC Worldwide; Publisher, BBC Music magazine; Publisher, Southbank magazine; Managing Editor, BBC Music magazine.
Publications: eve magazine; What to Wear magazine; BBC Music magazine; Southbank magazine; Old Grey Whistle Test 30th anniversary DVD, Bob Harris - The Whispering Years; Steve Lamacq - Going Deaf for a Living.
Education: Warwick University, Classical Civilisation
Career highlights: I started in theatre programmes, where I learnt to sub and write. I moved to a contract publishers working on a range of magazines including sport, parenting, food and B2B. I became Managing Editor just as DTP was coming in (a wonderful way to spend £1m) and then jumped ship for Managing Editor at BBC Magazines to run a small but beautiful title on classical music. I mistakenly thought swapping 66 titles for just one might be slightly easier and I spent 10 years on the title, ending up as Publisher. Whilst running the Music genre at BBCW I tried my

hand at book and DVD publishing but the lure of magazines proved too strong and I was delighted to swap classical music for Jimmy Choos when I joined eve in 2002. Highlights have been taking OGWT out of the BBC archives (which took three years) where it went straight to number one in the best-seller list in its first week, and taking BBC Music into profit in under two years to be the world's best-selling classical music title.

Mentor: Hard to say - I've worked for so many great people over the years and I've learnt something different from each of them...

Big break: Making the move from Managing Editor on BBC Music to Associate Publisher - everyone in editorial thought I was mad but I was determined to experience the cut and thrust of the commercial side of publishing. And I rather liked being in charge...

Big mistake: Choosing scented candles as a cover gift for eve - they got removed at some airports as a security hazard, just in case someone might want to hijack a plane armed with citronella or very berry candles!

» **Reading:** *Everything and anything. Regularly the Indie, the Sunday papers and all the women's mags (which takes a while) and then when I have time books, books, books. Mostly biographies, thrillers and armchair travelling...* **Watching:** *The sad truth is I adore Corrie and Spooks plus USA's finest such as Gray's Anatomy, America's Next Top Model and Lost. Can't beat a BBC drama either or when in doubt a Hollywood musical.* **Listening:** *Radio 4, LBC, Heart, Virgin, Radio 3 and Smooth - mostly when I'm driving - and a bit of Radio 7 at the weekends. Music is quite random from Graham Parker, Randy Newman, Fleetwood Mac to Oscar Peterson, Jane Siberry and the Dubliners.* **Relaxing to:** *Not easily! The kids are great fun and my husband's taken up the drums during his mid-life crisis so it's not a quiet household. So, really it's either pub with mates, piano with family or curled up with a book on my own.* » *Married, 2 children*

Nick Gill

25.9.65

BBH, 60 Kingly Street W1B 5DS
T 020 7453 4222
E nick.gill@bbh.co.uk

Occupation: Creative Director, Bartle Bogle Hegarty

Other positions: Inadequate Art Director, then Copywriter.

Publications: Lynx 24/7, Getting Dressed; Levi's, Doorman, Hispanic and Midsummer; KFC Soul Food campaign, VW Passat, Obsessive Designers.

Awards: 5 Cannes gold Lions; 1 Cannes silver Lion; 7 D&AD silver pencils; 7 British Television Advertising Awards golds; 7 BTAA silvers; 4 Campaign poster silvers; 2 Campaign press silvers.

Education: Manchester Poly

Career highlights: I get a lot of satisfaction out of making people like brands through memorable advertising, any time I've been successful at this would constitute a career highlight; I suppose the single piece of work I'm most proud of is Lynx Getting Dressed. It's the story of a young man and woman who wake up in bed together. They start to get dressed, but we soon discover that their clothes are scattered right across the city. The last shoe sits by two opposite-facing shopping trolleys in a supermarket aisle. The couple met there only hours ago. The man, it transpires, was wearing lynx 24/7 body spray; I was also involved in the first dialogue-based work for Levi's. One ad features a young man who refuses himself entry into a club because the place isn't cool enough for 501s, another features two men discussing the merits of loose-fitting denim in unintelligible Hispanic, and a third is a reworking of A Midsummer Night's Dream set in modern LA.

Mentor: When I was a young writer I was lucky enough to work with the great John Webster, who was a big influence on me.

Big break: When I joined Manchester Poly in 1981 I thought I'd been accepted on the graphic design course, only to find that they'd got me down for advertising. That took some coming to terms with.

Big mistake: Not learning to play a musical instrument.

» **Reading:** *I've just been reading Jack Kerouac, On the Road and Desolation Angels.* **Watching:** *The last thing that had a real impact on me was Shameless. Paul Abbott is a big talent.* **Listening:** *A huge amount of music. I've just bought a CD (which I believe is a reissue) by a band called The Wrens. I haven't played it yet, so I can't tell you what it's like, but I'm very optimistic.* **Relaxing to:** *With great difficulty these days.* » *Married to Laura, 2 children, Sara and Jack*

Margaret Gilmore

10.2.60

Room 1264, BBC TV Centre, Wood Lane, London W12 7RJ
T 020 8624 9054
E margaret.gilmore@bbc.co.uk

Occupation: BBC Home Affairs Correspondent

Other positions: Environment Correspondent, BBC News; Reporter, Panorama, This Week, Newsnight, BBC Northern Ireland, Independent Radio News, Kensington News and Post.

Awards: British Environment and Media (BEMA) TV News Journalist of the Year 1997.

Education: North London Collegiate School; Westfield College; London University

Career highlights: Being in East Germany during the fall of the Berlin Wall; the freeing of the Guildford Four; reporting in Jerusalem, the West Bank and Northern Iraq in the 1990s; interviewing people like Gorbachev and Arafat amongst others; reporting from Northern Ireland through the 1980s; covering BSE, global warming and GM crops as new stories in the late 1990s; covering terrorism for BBC TV News in the UK culminating in the July 2005 London bombings.

Mentor: Too many people I admire to mention.

Big break: Being made redundant from the Kingston Advertiser (my first job) - I landed a job the next day on the Kensington News and Post and never looked back.

Big mistake: Far too many to mention.

» **Reading:** *Mainly novels, occasionally autobiographies.* **Watching:** *TV News, including News 24, Jonathan Ross, modern comedies.* **Listening:** *Radio 5, Radio 4, Radio 3, Radio 2, and CDs of modern music.* **Relaxing to:** *Being with my friends and family and in particular my seven-year-old son, playing the piano, swimming, playing bridge.* » *Married, 1 child*

Jon Gisby

28.5.72

Yahoo!, 125 Shaftesbury Avenue, London WC2H 8AD
T 020 7131 1400
E jong@yahoo-inc.com

Occupation: MD Yahoo! UK and Ireland, and VP Media Yahoo! Europe

Other positions: MD Portals, Freeserve/Wanadoo UK; Senior Adviser Corporate Strategy, BBC.
Publications: While at Freeserve I led our involvement in the BAFTA award-winning drama Online Caroline.
Awards: Fulbright Scholar
Education: Oxford; Johns Hopkins; Harvard Business School
Career highlights: I transitioned into digital media about 10 years ago, having been in the US when AOL and Netscape were exploding onto the scene; on my return I initially joined the BBC, and enjoyed a productive stint helping to plan the BBC's digital services but took the opportunity to return to the commercial sector and joined Freeserve during its dramatic growth into one of the most significant online businesses in the UK; I ran the online sites and services, and over five years transformed the performance of the business, and helped launch some of the most innovative content in the UK; I'm now at Yahoo! where I run the UK business, and also lead our media business across Europe. It's an exciting place at an exciting time: online as a medium is coming of age, and the pace of change is as fast as ever. Many services that will be commonplace in 10 years' time have yet to be invented, and Yahoo! is well placed to invent and champion them.
Mentor: Many and varied, but John Pluthero stands out for having taken a risk in giving me a big role.
Big break: I joined Freeserve to do business development, but with an expectation that I could run a piece of the business within a year. It happened after six weeks.
Big mistake: They're always about people. Half of them are making premature judgements on what people are capable of. The other half is believing for too long that someone can change.

» **Reading:** *Beyond the inevitable trade press, I read the Guardian, Economist and New Yorker, and whatever is left on the train by previous passengers. Books currently range from Collapse to Harry Potter and Postman Pat, depending on who else is in the room.* **Watching:** *Broadcast news and sport, or whatever's on the Sky+ box: currently the West Wing, Spooks and some documentaries that I keep hoping to find time for.* **Listening:** *The Archers (is George really Ed's son?), and the John Mayer fan station on Yahoo! Music. Forgive the plug, but our music service is extraordinary.* **Relaxing to:** *I have three children ranging from seven to two. So I relax in very small doses.* » *Married, 3 children*

Fi Glover

27.2.69

BBC Radio 4, Broadcasting House, Portland Place, London W1A 1AA
T 020 7580 4468
E fi.glover@bbc.co.uk

Occupation: Journalist and Presenter, BBC

Publications: I'm an Oil Tanker: Travels with my Radio (Ebury Press, 2000).
Education: University of Kent
Career highlights: Began radio career on local radio in Canterbury whilst at university; joined BBC as reporter on various local radio stations including BBC Somerset Sound, Humberside, Northampton and GLR, 1993-97; Key Broadcaster in news and political coverage, BBC Radio Five Live, 1997-2003; Reporter, BBC 2's The Travel Show, 2003-04; Host of BBC Radio 4's Sunday morning news analysis programme Broadcasting House, 2004-present; occasional stand-in for Jeremy Vine on lunchtime show on Radio 2.

Stephen Glover

13.1.52

c/o Gillon Aitken Associates, 18-21 Cavaye Place, SW10 9PT
T 020 7373 8672
E recep@gillonaitken.co.uk

Occupation: Journalist and author

Other positions: Director, Newspaper Publishing plc, 1986-92; Visiting Professor of Journalism, St Andrews University, 1992.
Publications: Paper Dreams (1993); Editor, Secrets of the Press (1999).
Education: Shrewsbury School; Mansfield College, Oxford
Career highlights: Leader and Feature Writer, Daily Telegraph, 1978-85, including Parliamentary Sketch Writer, 1979-81; Founding Foreign Editor, the Independent, 1986-89; Founder and Editor, the Independent on Sunday, 1990-91; Associate Editor, Politics, Evening Standard, 1992-95; Columnist, Daily Telegraph, 1996-98; Columnist, the Spectator, 1996-2005; Columnist, Daily Mail, 1998-present; Columnist, the Independent, 2005-present.

Jon Godel

22.7.75

200 Gray's Inn Road, London WC1X 8XZ
T 020 7403 4814
E jon.godel@itn.co.uk

Occupation: Editor, Independent Radio News; Editor, ITN Multimedia

Other positions: ITN Core News Editor; News Editor, IRN; Editor, Kiss FM; News Editor, Northants FM; News Editor, Bedfordshire on Sunday; Reporter, Bedfordshire on Sunday; Reporter, Bedfordshire Times; Reporter, Biggleswade Chronicle.
Publications: IRN (news content for 270 commercial radio stations); Classic FM News, Magic FM News, Kiss FM News, video bulletins for Yahoo! News and entertainment content for Vodafone Live.
Awards: NTL Radio Awards, Technical Innovation

2005; World Communication Awards, Best Content 2005; New York Festival, Best Radio Bulletins 2002.
Career highlights: Editor of the UK's leading supplier of news to UK Commercial radio combined with running ITN Multimedia; overseeing an operation which provides news content and bulletins to 270 radio stations with teams based at ITN. Began career as a newspaper journalist in Bedfordshire before moving to radio as News Editor at Northants FM; specialise in radio news for young people; appointed Group News Controller for the Kiss Network in 1996, responsible for news output in Manchester, Leeds and London; joined IRN in London as News Editor in 1997 and moved to ITN as a News Editor; appointed Editor of IRN in 2000; Since taking charge at IRN have radically reshaped the service to introduce additional targeted bulletins, new distribution technology and improved communication with IRN's client base; in 2005 brief was expanded to ITN's growing Multimedia business supplying content to businesses including Vodafone and Yahoo!.
Mentor: Nicholas Wheeler - he believed I could do it!
Big break: Walking through the door at ITN.

» **Reading:** *Autobiographies - you can learn so much from how other people 'did it'.* **Watching:** *All the video content on my mobile phone.* **Listening:** *My iPod.* **Relaxing to:** *Walking in Norfolk - with my iPod!* » *Partner, no children*

Alex Godfrey
22.4.74

30 Cleveland Street, London W1T 4JD
T 020 7907 6000
E alex_godfrey@dennis.co.uk

Occupation: Editor, Bizarre magazine

Other positions: Previously Hotdog magazine, Editorial Assistant, Staff Writer, Reviews Editor, Features Editor, Deputy Editor; Jack magazine, Film Editor.
Awards: Shortlisted for PTC New Journalist Of The Year 2001 ... no awards.
Education: Bournemouth University

» *Single, no children*

Jo Godman
29.5.44

10a Belmont Street, London NW1 8HH
T 020 7428 2288

Occupation: Founder, Godman Ltd

Awards: Numerous commercials winning awards at D&AD, British TV Awards, Cannes and Clio, New York.
Education: Camden School for Girls; Holborn College of Law, Languages and Commerce
Career highlights: Girl Friday, Chapman Raper TV commercials production company, 1965-67; Production Assistant, Geoffrey Forster Associates, 1967-71; Producer for Tom Bussmann, Bussmann Llewelyn, 1972-80 (Prodn Asst 1971-72); Co-founder, Patterson Godman Ltd., 1980-83; Managing Director, Ridley Scott Associates Film Ltd, 1983-96; Founder, Godman Ltd 1997-present.

» **Relaxing to:** *Cinema, gardening, ballet, cooking, swimming.*
» *Married*

Joe Godwin

BBC Television Centre, Wood Lane, London W12 7RJ
T 020 8743 8000
E joe.godwin@bbc.co.uk

Occupation: Head of CBBC Entertainment, BBC

Other positions: Chair, Committee of Television and Young People, the educational arm of the Edinburgh Festival; Member, Advisory Panel on Children's Viewing, BBFC.
Career highlights: Joined BBC as Regional News Floor Manager, 1986; Studio Director and Producer, Going Live, Record Breakers, Live and Kicking and Blue Peter, subsequently Editor, Children's Presentation, BBC, 1989-2000; Nickelodeon UK, becoming VP Operations and Interactive Director, 2000-05; Head of Entertainment, including Dick and Dom in Da Bungalow, Smart, and Chucklevision, CBBC, 2005-present.

Nik Goodman
19.11.76

30 Leicester Square, London WC2H 7LA
T 020 7766 6000
E nik.goodman@capitalradio.com

Occupation: Programme Director, 95.8 Capital FM, London

Other positions: Programme Director, Radio Forth; Producer, Bam Bam Breakfast, Kiss 100; Deputy Programme Director, Virgin Radio; Head of Music, Virgin Radio; Head of Music, 103.2 Power FM; Presenter/Producer, Radio City.
Awards: Sony Gold, 2004
Education: Merchant Taylors' School, Liverpool; Bournemouth University
Career highlights: Joining Virgin Radio when Chris Evans owned the station was fantastic. It was a brilliant time to be at Virgin, with a great team to work with. Bam Bam is a creative genius and every day I worked with him was a highlight! Being Programme Director at Capital has to be one of the top jobs in radio programming in the UK and is my current highlight!
Mentor: Pete Waterman, because he understands better than anyone what mainstream popular taste is all about.
Big break: Getting my very first job on air at Radio City.
Big mistake: Booking Billie Piper onto Chris Evans' Breakfast Show at Virgin!

» **Reading:** *Evening Standard, Sunday Times, News of the World, Media Guardian, Music Week and The Hungry Caterpillar with my daughters.* **Watching:** *The Daily Show with Jon Stewart, The West Wing, Channel 4 News and Balamory.* **Listening:** *Lots of radio every single day and plenty of Northern Soul on my iPod whenever possible.* **Relaxing to:** *By writing really bad pop songs on my piano and going for long walks with my wife and kids in Windsor Great Park.*
» *Married, 2 children*

Lord James Gordon 18.5.40

House of Lords, London SW1A 0PW
T 07711 223149
E gordonj@parliament.uk

Occupation: Member of the House of Lords; Chairman, RAJAR; Director, Johnston Press, Active Capital Trust.

Awards: Sony Gold Award for outstanding service to Radio, 1984; CBE,1984; Fellow Radio Academy, 1994; Life Peerage, 1997.
Education: St. Aloysius' College; University of Glasgow
Career highlights: Political Editor, Scottish TV, 1964-73; Managing Director, Radio Clyde, 1972-96; Chief Executive, Scottish Radio Holdings, 1991-96; Chairman, 1996-2005; Non Exec Director, Johnston Press, 1996-present.
Mentor: Ian Chapman
Big break: Winning Observer Mace National Debating Tournament 1957.
Big mistake: Buying BuzzFM

» **Reading:** *The Week.* **Watching:** *Comedies and documentaries.* **Listening:** *Clyde 2, Radio 4.* **Relaxing to:** *Skiing, walking.* » *Married, 1 daughter and 2 sons*

Elliott Gotkine 26.12.79

BBC White City, 201 Wood Lane, London W12 7TS
T 020 8576 7572
E elliott.gotkine@bbc.co.uk

Occupation: BBC Business Producer/Reporter

Other positions: BBC South America Correspondent; Lima Correspondent; Video Journalist; Deputy Stock Market Editor, UK-invest.com; Reporter, Euromoney.
Education: Haberdashers' Aske's; University of Nottingham
Career highlights: Covering political crises in Bolivia from October 2003 to June 2005; interviewing Presidents Hugo Chavez (Venezuela), Lucio Gutierrez (Ecuador), Eduardo Rodriguez (Bolivia), Alejandro Toledo (Peru); and interviewing world-renowned novelist, Mario Vargas Llosa.
Big break: Taking a year out from the BBC to freelance in Peru.

» **Reading:** *Louis de Bernières, Patrick Neate, Mario Vargas Llosa, Gabriel Garcia Marquez et al.* **Watching:** *West Wing, Simpsons, ER, Newsnight.* **Listening:** *Xfm, BBC World Service, Radio 4.* **Relaxing to:** *Reading, cinema, cycling, water polo, poker, travelling.* » *Single*

Lizie Gower 29.6.62

16 West Central Street, London WC1A 1JJ
T 020 7395 4155
E lizie@academyfims.com

Occupation: Managing Director, Academy Productions

Publications: Advertisements for Guinness, Surfer, Swimback; ads for Stella Artois, Skating Priests, Last Orders; Campaigns for VW, Levi's, Coke; music videos for Madonna, Massive Attack, Richard Ashcroft, Radiohead, etc.
Awards: 52 British Television Advertising Arrow awards; 6 MTV awards for Best Video; 11 Cads, Music Week; 10 Cannes Lions, 32 D&AD pencils; Best Production Company, Televisual and Campaign magazines; winner of Best Television Commercial Ever Made, Sunday Times for Guinness Surfer.
Education: Royal School, Bath; New College of Speech and Drama
Mentor: My Dad
Big break: Breaking my leg and not continuing with my acting career.

» **Reading:** *The Times, News of the World, Campaign, Time Out, Variety, Screen International, Condé Nast Traveller, National Geographic...* **Watching:** *News and any makeover programme, MTV, Match of the Day and X Factor with my sons.* » *2 sons, Harrison and Luke*

Michael Grade 8.3.43

BBC Television Centre, Wood Lane, London W12 7RJ
T 020 8743 8000
E michael.grade@bbc.co.uk

Occupation: Chairman of Governors, BBC

Other positions: Vice-President, Bafta, June 2004-present; Non-executive Chairman, Pinewood Shepperton; Chairman, Hemscott Group plc, 2000; Member, Council, Royal Albert Hall; Director, Charlton Athletic Football Club; Chairman, Working Group on the Fear of Crime, 1989; Member, National Commission of Inquiry into the Prevention of Child Abuse, 1994-96; Chairman, Index on Censorship 2000-04.
Publications: It Seemed Like a Good Idea At The Time (autobiography, Pan, 2000); At the BBC, A Special Tommy Steele (ITV, 1973); Two's Company (1975-79); The Fosters (1976-77); The South Bank Show (1978-present); The Professionals (1977-83); EastEnders (1985-present); at Channel 4, Cutting Edge (1990-present); GBH (Alan Bleasdale, 1991); The Big Breakfast (1992-2002); Film on Four, Four Weddings and a Funeral (directed Mike Newell, 1994) and The Madness of King George (directed Nicholas Hytner, 1994).
Awards: FRTS, 1991; Fellow, Bafta, 1994; CBE, 1998; Honorary Professor, Thames Valley University; Honorary LLD, Nottingham University.
Education: Stowe School; St. Dunstan's School London
Career highlights: Sports Columnist, Daily Mirror, 1960-66; Joint Managing Director, London Management (theatrical agency), 1966-73; Deputy Controller of entertainment Programmes, LWT, 1973-81; President, Embassy TV, Hollywood, California, 1981-84; Controller, BBC One, 1984; Director of Programmes, BBC Television, 1986; Chief Executive, Channel 4, 1988-97; Executive Chairman, First Leisure, 1997-2000; Chairman, Pinewood-Shepperton studios, 1999; Chairman, Camelot, 2002-04; Chairman, BBC, 2004-present.

» *Married, 3 children*

Roger Graef 19.4.40

Films of Record, 2 Elgin Avenue, London W9 3QP
T 020 7286 0333
E rogerg@filmsofrecord.com

Occupation: Film maker

Other positions: Criminologist
Publications: Malaria: Fever Road, Murder Blues, The Secret Policeman's Ball, Panorama: What Future for Kurt.
Awards: Fellowship of the British Academy of Film and Television in 2004.

» Married, 2 children

Douglas Graham 18.2.30

Express and Star, Queen Street, Wolverhampton, West Midlands WV1 1ES
T 01902 313131
E scoyle@expressandstar.co.uk

Occupation: Chairman, Midland News Association Ltd

Other positions: President, Young Newspapermen's Association, 1969; West Midlands Newspaper Society, 1973-74; Chairman, Evening Newspaper Advertising Bureau 1978-79.
Education: Shrewsbury School
Career highlights: Chairman, Claverley Co 1993; The Midland News Association Ltd 1984-present; Express & Star Ltd; Shropshire Newspapers Ltd 1980-present; Stars News Shops Ltd 1994-present; Director, Guiton Group CI 2004

» **Relaxing to:** *Shooting.* *» Married, 2 stepchildren*

Damian Grammaticus 1.6.70

c/o BBC News Centre, London W12 8QT
T 020 8743 8000
E damian.grammaticus@bbc.co.uk

Occupation: Moscow Correspondent, BBC

Education: Corpus Christi College, Cambridge; Cardiff University
Career highlights: Trainee Reporter, BBC Television News, 1994; Reporter, BBC Look East and BBC Radio, 1995-97; Launch Producer, BBC News 24, 1997; London-based Reporter covering British, European and International News for BBC World Television, BBC News 24 and BBC Television News, 1998; currently Moscow Correspondent, BBC.

Chris Green 14.9.55

Wellington Street, Leeds LS1 1RF
T 0113 23432701
E chrisg@ypn.co.uk

Occupation: Divsional Managing Director, Johnston Newspapers North; Managing Director, Yorkshire Post Newspapers Ltd.

Other positions: Director of Halifax Courier Holdings Ltd; Yorkshire Weekly Newspaper Group Ltd; The Yeller Publications Ltd: Leeds Weekly News Ltd; Yorkshire Post Magazines Ltd; Yorkshire Regional Newspapers Ltd; The Reporter Ltd; Ackrill Newspapers Ltd; Yorkshire News Ltd; Marketing Leeds Ltd.

» Married, 3 children

Michael Green 2.12.47

113-117 Wardour Street, London W1F 0UL
T 020 7434 1441

Occupation: Chairman, Tangent Industries

Other positions: Chairman, The Media Trust; Chairman, Tangent Charitable Trust; Trustee, Sainsbury Centre for Mental Health.
Education: Haberdashers' Aske's School
Career highlights: Chairman, Carlton Communications plc, 1983-2003; Director, Tangent Industries Ltd; Non-executive Director, Reuters Holdings plc, 1992-99; Non-executive Director, Independent Television News Ltd; Non-executive Director, Thomson; Non-executive Director, GMTV Ltd.

» **Relaxing to:** *Bridge, television.* *» Married, 5 children*

Germaine Greer 29.1.39

c/o Gillon Aitken Associates, 18-21 Cavaye Place, London SW10 9PT
T 020 7373 8672
E recep@gillonaitken.co.uk

Occupation: Writer, broadcaster and academic

Other positions: Founder and Editor, Tulsa Studies in Women's Literature, 1981; Founder and Director, Tulsa Centre for the Study of Women's Literature.
Awards: Honorary Doctorate, University of Griffith 1996; Honorary Doctorate, University of York, Toronto, 1999; Honorary Doctorate, UMIST, 2000; Honorary degree, University of Essex, 2003; Honorary D Litt, Anglia Polytechnic University, 2003; Degree of Laws, University of Melbourne, 2003.
Education: Star of the Sea Convent, Gardenvale; University of Melbourne; University of Sydney; University of Cambridge
Career highlights: Broadcaster, journalist, columnist and reviewer 1972-present; Senior Tutor in English, University of Sydney, 1963-64; Assistant Lecturer, then Lecturer in English, University of Warwick, 1967-72; Lecturer throughout North America, American Program Bureau, 1973-78; Visiting Professor, Graduate Faculty of Modern Letters, University of Tulsa, 1979; Lecturer to raise funds for Tulsa Bursary and Fellowship Scheme, 1980-83; Professor of Modern Letters, University of Tulsa, 1980-83; Director, Stump Cross Books, 1988-present; Special Lecturer and unofficial Fellow, Newnham College, Cambridge, 1989-98; Professor of English and Comparative Literary Studies, University of Warwick, 1998-2003.

Geordie Greig
1961

Tatler, Vogue House, Hanover Square, London W1S 1JU
T 020 7499 9080
E Geordie.Greig@condenast.co.uk

Occupation: Editor, Tatler magazine

Publications: Louis and the Prince: A Story of Politics, Intrigue and Royal Friendship (Coronet, 2000).
Education: Eton; St Peter's College, Oxford
Career highlights: Variously war reporter, crime reporter, fashion writer, New York Correspondent, literary editor; South East London and Kentish Mercury, Deptford; Daily Mail; Sunday Today; Sunday Times, 1987-99; Editor, Tatler, 1999-present.
» **Reading:** *Samuel Menashe and Anthony Trollope.*

Gagan Grewal
21.8.82

BBC Asian Network, St. Nicholas Place, Leicester LE1 5LB
T 0116 201 6781
E gagan@bbc.co.uk

Occupation: Breakfast Presenter, BBC Asian Network

Other positions: Was part of the network during the transition from local to national BBC station; tsunami appeal; Pakistan earthquake appeal and coverage.
Awards: None as yet but fingers crossed!
Education: Thames Valley, London
Career highlights: I've been presenting a breakfast show of some kind for the last 10 years so have been lucky enough to cover the biggest news stories around in recent times from the death of Diana to the Pakistani coup and the tsunami.
Mentor: My Mum (another radio presenter, Sunrise Radio, London), Jo Wiley.
Big break: At the age of 21 getting the job as Asian Network Breakfast Presenter.
Big mistake: Falling asleep on the radio desk on a nightshift leaving almost an hour of dead air! (it was in the middle of my A levels!)
» **Reading:** *I love to read horror or thriller novels, James Herbert is one of my favourite authors. I also love to read books set in or based around south Asia.* **Watching:** *EastEnders has been great recently. I watch a lot of the satellite news channels and Asian music stations.* **Listening:** *I appreciate all south Asian music in particular, but do listen to R 'n' B sometimes. Sufi music and Qawaali is my favourite genre, with the late Nusrat Fateh Ali Khan the best performer ever!* **Relaxing to:** *Walk my dog (Kane, 15-month-old Rottweiler!) on local heath. Travel anywhere anytime! Study extreme weather. Music.* » *Single, no children*

Andy Griffee
26.8.65

BBC, Level 10, The Mailbox, Birmingham B1 1XL
T 07711 032842
E andy.griffee@bbc.co.uk

Occupation: Controller, BBC English Regions

Other positions: Local Newspaper Reporter; Assistant News Editor, BBC Bristol; Editor NCA, BBC South; Head of Centre, BBC South.
Education: Duke of York's Royal Military School; University of Manchester
Mentor: David Flintham, Mark Byford, Pat Loughrey, Helen Griffee.
Big break: Blagging a Broadcast Journalist job at BBC Bristol (Points West) from local newspapers and becoming Controller English Regions.
Big mistake: Opting back to network for an announcement that the Queen Mother had died only to discover it was a rehearsal.
» **Reading:** *Latest fiction and Bleak House once a year.* **Watching:** *News, Spooks, natural history and more news.* **Listening:** *40 BBC Local Radio stations.* **Relaxing to:** *Watching my son play rugby, my daughter play hockey and my wife Helen.* » *Married, 2 children*

Krishnan Guru-Murthy
6.4.74

Channel 4 News, 200 Gray's Inn Road, London WC1X 8XZ
T 020 7833 3000
E news@channel4.com

Occupation: Main Presenter, Channel 4 News at Noon; Columnist, Metro

Other positions: 2005 Exorcism Live, C4, Election Unspun, C4, UK Leaders Live, commercial radio; 2003-4 The KGM Show, LBC 97.3 Radio; 2003 C4 News War Report, The Channel 4 Political Awards; 2001-03 Powerhouse, C4; 2002 The Autopsy, C4, Think TV, C4; 2001 Morning News Specials, C4; 2000 The Difference Debate, C4; 1997-98 BBC News 24; 1994-97 Newsnight, BBC Two; 1995 The National Lottery Live, BBC One, BBC World TV News; 1991-94 Newsround, BBC One; 1993 Going Live, BBC One; 1990-91 Network East, BBC Two; 1990 Posh Frocks and New Trousers, ITV; 1989-90 Network East, BBC Two; 1988-89 Reportage, BBC Two; 1988 Open to Question, BBC Two.
Education: Queen Elizabeth's Grammar School, Blackburn; Hertford College, Oxford University
Career highlights: I was incredibly lucky to get a job on screen on BBC 2 when I was leaving school in 1988. My first programme was a half-hour grilling of John Prescott. But I really started learning about TV journalism on the children's programme Newsround, where I learned to report things like the Bosnian war and the break-up of the Soviet Union in an understandable way. I learned about analysis and rigour at Newsnight, whose editor threw me at everything from the Dunblane massacre to the Pakistani elections and the 1997 general election. And Channel 4 News has been a liberation – a place where ideas flourish and stories get broken by bosses who

understand about causing trouble, poking the establishment and challenging received wisdom.
Mentor: I don't have one, but I wouldn't have got my first job in television in 1988 presenting the youth discussion programme Open to Question on BBC 2 were it not for the help and guidance of the man I took over from - John Nicolson, who left to cover Westminster for the BBC and now presents ITV News.
Big break: Being asked to step out of the audience to take over as Presenter of BBC Two's Open to Question at the age of 18 and one week before my A-level results came out.
Big mistake: Falling asleep for a split second while reading the news on BBC World wasn't my finest moment.

» **Reading:** *All the newspaper websites get a glance online most mornings including the New York Times, Washington Post and the Times of India. I read the Sun, Guardian and Times newspapers on the way to work. At the weekend I get the Observer, Sunday Telegraph and News of the World delivered. I might read the others if I get a chance. The Spectator, New Statesman and Newsweek get flicked through from time to time. I read political biographies after being given them at Christmas, novels on holiday and have a hitherto secret liking for technology and car magazines.* **Watching:** *Everything, I am a TV junkie. Loads of news of all flavours - Sky and News 24 mostly but I keep an eye on Fox, Al Jazeera, CNN and Star News. For fun lots of E4 and lots of movies. I pick one or two dramas to get into, like 24 or Lost, but don't have time for soaps any more. Plus the occasional classic Yes Minister or Only Fools and Horses if it crops up on the EPG. I love Question Time and have endless admiration for Richard and Judy.* **Listening:** *At home I only listen to the radio between 8 and 8.30 in the morning for the Today Programme. If I'm in the car I either listen to music or Radio 4. Nick Clarke on The World at One is my favourite news man. I switch to Five Live when Radio 4 gets too pompous or boring. I'm Sorry I haven't a Clue and the News Quiz keep me amused at weekends. For music in the car it has to be Virgin. At home it's something from my large and varied iTunes folder.* **Relaxing to:** *I relax by playing with my baby girl, eating and cooking food, playing rock and roll in a band of fellow TV-types and occasionally playing golf. Watching TV and listening to music help too. And sleep.*
» *Married, 1 daughter*

H

Janice Hadlow

BBC Television Centre, Wood Lane, London W12 7RJ
T 020 8743 8000
E janice.hadlow@bbc.co.uk

Occupation: Controller, BBC Four

Other positions: BBC Head of Specialist Factual; Joint Head, History Unit, Channel 4; Editor, Late Show, BBC TV.
Publications: Niall Fergusson's Empire; David Starkey's 6 Wives; 1940s House; Edwardian Country House; Simon Schama's History Of Britain.
Education: Swanley School; University of London
Career highlights: See above
Mentor: Michael Jackson
Big break: Being asked to join the Late Show as an Associate Producer.
Big mistake: Not working in the US when I had the chance.

» **Reading:** *18th century diaries. Every weekly magazine I can get my hands on. Evelyn Waugh, Robert Graves, and Jane Austen over and over again. Hollywood biographies.* **Watching:** *Anything with a strong opinion. Clever comedy. Medical dramas. Almost any history.* **Listening:** *Usual iPod fodder.* **Relaxing to:** *Gazing out of the window.* » *Married, 2 children*

Bobby Hain

13.7.67

200 Renfield Street, Glasgow G2 3PR
T 0141 300 3460
E bobby.hain@smg.plc.uk

Occupation: Managing Director, Broadcasting, SMG Television

Other positions: Managing Director, Scottish TV; Business Development Director, SMG radio; Managing Director, Beat 106; Programme Director, Virgin Radio.
Education: Craigmount High, Edinburgh

Liam Halligan

29.4.69

Channel 4 News, ITN, 200 Gray's Inn Road, London WC1X 8XZ
T 020 7430 4601
E liam.halligan@itn.co.uk

Occupation: Economics Correspondent, Channel 4 News; Business Columnist, Sunday Telegraph

Other positions: Member, Advisory Council, Social Market Foundation; Member, Risk Commission, Royal Society of Arts.
Publications: Whose Pension are you Paying?, Channel 4, 30 Minutes documentary, 2006; How Safe is Your Pension?, Channel 4, 30 Minutes

documentary, 2004; Lessons of Russia's Stabilisation Programmes, Social Market Foundation pamphlet, 1996; A Guide to Russia's Parliamentary Elections, Economist Intelligence Unit, 1995; Europe Isn't Working, with Frank Field MP and Matthew Owen, Institute of Community Studies pamphlet, 1994; Beyond Unemployment, with Robert Skidelsky, Social Market Foundation pamphlet, 1994; Another Great Depression, with Robert Skidelsky, Social Market Foundation pamphlet, 1993.

Awards: Business Journalist of the Year, Broadcast category, 2004; Aon Investment Writer of the Year, highly commended, 2004; Foreign Press Association, Best Financial Submission, runner-up, 2004; Bradford and Bingley Personal Finance Awards, Broadcaster of the Year, 2003; WorkWorld Programme of the Year, 2004, 2003 and 2001; Workworld Broadcaster of the Year, highly commended, 2002; Industrial Society Programme of the Year, 1999; Wincott Business Broadcaster of the Year, 1999; Business Journalist of the Year Awards (shortlisted in 7 categories), 1999-2004.

Education: John Lyon School, Harrow; Warwick University; St. Antony's College, Oxford

Career highlights: I started out as an academic economist, holding posts at The London School of Economics and the International Monetary Fund. In the early 1990s I moved to Moscow, to help start a journal called Russian Economic Trends. While I was there - through a chance meeting at a party, and some fast-talking by me - I ended up writing an OpEd piece for the Wall Street Journal. It was a life-changing moment. My academic 'career' was put on hold and I started a weekly column for the Moscow Times. That led to work on the Economist and then, in 1996, I returned to London to join the Financial Times as a Political Reporter - covering the death throes of John Major's government and the upsurge of New Labour. Being in the FT's lobby team brought some TV work - morning paper reviews and late-night political programmes. Then, in 1999, I got a call from Channel 4 News, jumped ship, and have been the programme's Economics Correspondent ever since. While predominantly a broadcast journalist, I have kept a toe-hold in print - as a Columnist for Sunday Business and, now, the Sunday Telegraph.

Big break: Being asked by the Economist to cover the 1996 Russian Presidential Elections.

Big mistake: Thinking that Britain was (is) a meritocracy.

» **Reading:** *My job involves so much reading of factual material, that I find it hard not to feel guilty when I read fiction. But, when I do, I enjoy complex novels, especially by the Victorian masters such as Dickens, Hardy and Wilkie Collins. I also read a lot of biography, particularly political biography. In my view, it is impossible to cover economics effectively without a firm grasp of who's who in politics.* **Watching:** *Not too much TV outside news and current affairs. Good quality films, mainly. I also confess to watching some sport on TV, but only as and when the domestic chaos allows.* **Listening:** *Modern jazz (Chick Corea, Herbie Hancock, Miles Davis et al), Hendrix, Pink Floyd, Lynyrd Skynyrd, Irish/ English/US folk music. Also quite a bit of classical, mainly mid-to-late 19th century, but I like the bouncy Baroque stuff too.* **Relaxing to:** *See previous two entries, plus tennis, sailing and playing musical instruments with my kids.* » *Co-habiting, 2 girls (Ailis and Maeve) and a boy (Ned)*

Trish Halpin

22.5.71

64 North Row, London W1 1LK
T 020 7150 7000
E gabrielle.nathan@hf-uk.com

Occupation: Editor, Red magazine

Other positions: Deputy Editor, Red, 1999-2000; Deputy Editor, New Woman 1997-99; Deputy Editor, more!, 1996-97; Chief Sub, more!, 1994-96; Subeditor, Screen International 1992-94.

Awards: 2003 BSME Editor of the Year, women's non-weekly.

Career highlights: Editor of Red is probably one of the most coveted jobs in women's glossies, so it's no surprise that it has been the most enjoyable and rewarding of my career; since I took the helm in 2000, circulation has risen from 155k to 220k (and is still on the way up in an increasingly competitive market). We've been shortlisted three times for the Periodical Publishers Association (PPA) Magazine of the Year award, and three times (winning once) for the British Society of Magazine Editors (BSME) Editor of the Year award.

Mentor: Ian Birch, former Editor-in-chief at Emap Elan, and Marie O'Riordan, Editor of Marie Claire.

Big break: Moving from business publishing to women's magazines. When I joined more! in 1994 it was the first time that I actually looked forward to going into work each day - and it's still like that now.

Big mistake: No major gaffes, so far.

» **Reading:** *For news the Independent, Guardian Weekend, Observer. For gossip the Daily Mirror, Grazia. For pleasure Anne Tyler, Barbara Kingsolver, Kate Atkinson, Jonathan Franzen, Philip Roth.* **Watching:** *Coronation Street, Six Feet Under, ER, The Sopranos, Property Ladder and any kind of costume drama.* **Listening:** *Radio 4, Virgin, Red Hot Chilli Peppers, Manic Street Preachers, Green Day, Gorillaz, Madonna.* **Relaxing to:** *When I have the time and energy, swimming and walking. When I don't, flaking out on the sofa with a glass of red (which, with two-year-old twins, is more likely to be the case these days).* » *Married to photographer Neil Cooper, twins Esmé and Kit*

Paul Hammersley

23.5.66

12 Bishops Bridge Road, London W2 6AA
T 020 7258 4091
E paul.hammersley@ddblondon.com

Occupation: Chairman and CEO, DDB London

Education: Exeter

Career highlights: Spent the first nine years of working life at Saatchi's in London, rising from Graduate Trainee to Executive Board Member, from the heady days of the early 80s to the disasters of the early 90s. Most of the time it was fantastic, but then most of the time was spent working on Castlemaine XXXX and Tetley Bitter; lured away in 1993 by the exciting cocktail of Frank Lowe, Coca Cola and New York and went to work at the nascent Lowe New York; returned to London in 1997 to be MD of Lowe Howard-Spink and after the global merger with Ammirati Puris Lintas became CEO of Lowe Lintas London, winning Campaign's

and AdAge's Agency of the Year in 2000; moved back to New York in 2001 to be CEO of Lowe North America and left Lowe in 2003; moved back to London in March 2004 to be Chairman/CEO of DDB London, managing the recently rebranded legacy of BMP.
Mentor: I've been fortunate enough to have many; and luckier still not to need them any more.
Big break: My current role.
Big mistake: Lowe New York, second time.
» **Reading:** *Guardian, FT, the Week, Newsweek, Private Eye, Living etc.* **Watching:** *Rugby, cricket, Lost.* **Listening:** *Five Live.* **Relaxing to:** *My kids.* » *Married, 3 children*

Brian Hanrahan
23.3.53

Room 2505, BBC TV Centre, Wood Lane, London W12 7RJ
T 020 8624 8543
E brian.hanrahan@bbc.co.uk

Occupation: Diplomatic Editor, BBC News
Other positions: Far East Correspondent; Moscow Correspondent.
Education: Essex University
» *Married, 1 child*

Michael Hapgood
22.10.51

BBC South East, The Great Hall, Mount Pleasant, Tunbridge Wells, Kent TN1 1QQ
T 01892 670000
E mike.hapgood@bbc.co.uk

Occupation: Head of regional and local programmes, BBC South East
Other positions: Managing Editor, BBC Radio Bristol 1992-98; Managing Editor, BBC Southern Counties Radio 1998-2004.
Education: University of York
» *Married, 3 children*

Tony Hardcastle
27.7.65

151 Marylebone Road, London NW1 5QE
T 020 7616 3500
E hardcastlet@amvbbdo.com

Occupation: Senior Art Director, AMV BBDO
Publications: 118 118 campaign, Nectar card launch, Economist posters, BBC.
Awards: Campaign of the Year, 118 118; Gold awards at British Television; Creative Circle, Campaign Posters and Epica; D&AD Silver nomination.
Education: Blackpool; Fylde College of Art
Career highlights: See awards
Mentor: Dave Trott, Malcom Gluck, Dave Waters, Mark Reddy.
Big break: Working with Chris Moss at The Number. Perversely getting made redundant at WCRS.
Big mistake: Not taking a job at GGT when it was offered.
» **Reading:** *Biographies, Campaign, Creative Review, the Standard, Economist, FT.* **Watching:** *Upminster Park Rovers, West Ham United, anything from Ridley Scott, Alan Parker and Aardman.* **Listening:** *Whatever Mark Tweddell (copywriter) puts on.* **Relaxing to:** *Running an under-8s football team, life drawing, drinking good wine.* » *Married, 4 children, Chloe, Beth, Eleanor and Charlie*

Andrew Harding
15.5.71

BBC Asia Bureau, Shaw Towers, 100 Beach Road, Singapore
T +65 62957699
E andrew.harding@bbc.co.uk

Occupation: BBC Asia Correspondent
Other positions: BBC East Africa Correspondent 2000-2004; BBC Moscow Correspondent 1996-2000; BBC Caucasus Correspondent (freelance post) 1994-1996; Freelancer in Moscow 1991-1994.
Awards: 2004 Bayeux War Correspondents and Foreign Press Association radio awards for coverage of conflict in Northern Uganda.
Education: Emmanuel College, Cambridge
Career highlights: Covering the tsunami in Aceh; undercover in Burma; embedded in Iraq; Afghanistan; exposing corruption in Kenya; wars in Darfur, eastern Congo, southern Sudan, Northern Uganda, Liberia, Somalia; in Russia, covering both Chechen wars, the rise of the oligarchs, and the 1993 parliamentary rebellion.
» *Married, 3 children*

Bert Hardy
13.12.28

Northcliffe House, 2 Derry Street, London W8 5EE
T 020 7938 6000
E bert.hardy@assocnews.co.uk

Occupation: Managing Director, Evening Standard
Other positions: Advertisement Director, Odhams Press (Daily Herald); Advertisement Director, News of the World and The Sun; Chief Executive, News International; Director, Townsend Hook (newsprint manufacturers); Deputy Chairman, Convoys Transport; Chief Executive, Radio 210; Director, London Weekend Television; Director, Hutchinsons Books Publishers; Chief Executive and Chairman, Evening Standard; Managing Director, Associated Newspapers Limited; Director, LBC; Director, Channel One Television; Deputy Chairman, Channel 4 Television; Chief Executive and Deputy Chairman, Press Holdings; Managing Director, Scotsman Publications; Director, Evening Standard.
Education: Royal Military Academy, Sandhurst
Mentor: Rupert Murdoch
Big break: Hugh Cudlipp's decision to bring me back to London from Manchester.
Big mistake: Still to come.
» **Reading:** *All the dailies.* **Watching:** *News and sport.* **Listening:** *BBC Radio 4 and Humphrey Littleton's radio show, 'I'm sorry I haven't a clue'.* **Relaxing to:** *Reading business homework.* » *Married, 1 child*

Paddy Harverson 9.11.66

Clarence House, London SW1A 1BA
T 020 7024 5506
E paddy.harverson@royal.gsx.gov.uk

Occupation: Communications Secretary to the Prince of Wales and the Duchess of Cornwall

Education: London School of Economics
Career highlights: Communications Director, Manchester United, 2000-04; Financial Times Reporter, 1988-2000 working as Economics Reporter, New York Correspondent, and finally Sports Correspondent.

» **Reading:** *All daily and Sunday newspapers, many magazines, leading news websites.* **Watching:** *News, sport, comedy.* **Listening:** *Radio 5 and Radio 4.* » *Married, no children*

Georgina Harvey (nee Crace) 20.8.68

One Canada Square, Canary Wharf, London E14 5AP
T 020 7293 2690
E georgina.harvey@trinitymirror.com

Occupation: Managing Director, Regional Newspapers, Trinity Mirror plc

Other positions: Managing Director, Wallpaper* Group, IPC Media; Managing Director, IPC Advertising, IPC Media; Director of Sales, IPC Media; Group Ad Sales Director, Southbank Publishing, IPC Magazines; Ad Director, Daily Express, Express Newspapers; Ad Manager, Daily Star, Express Newspapers.
Publications: Liverpool Echo, Birmingham Mail, Evening Chronicle (Newcastle), Welsh Daily Post, Western Mail (Cardiff), The Journal (Newcastle), Sunday Mercury (Birmingham), Sunday Sun (Newcastle).
Awards: Media Week Media Sales Team of the Year, 2001.
Education: York College (Leeds University)
Career highlights: In February 2005 I joined Trinity Mirror plc - the UK's largest newspaper publisher - as Managing Director, Regional Newspapers. The Regionals division publishes some 240 local and regional titles across the UK. I moved from IPC Media, where I was MD of Wallpaper* Group. This included Wallpaper* magazine, the iconic international design and lifestyle magazine. In addition to this role, I was also MD of IPC Advertising. I created IPC Advertising in order to harness the power of the IPC magazine brands and to answer customers' need for greater accountability and increased trading efficiencies. At IPC Advertising I initiated a major shake-up in sales strategy, drove through significant change and delivered results that out-performed the market and competitors. This drove IPC's overall top-line business growth and helped attract AOL Time Warner to look at the company as a potential acquisition target. I was appointed to the Board of IPC Media in 2000.
Mentor: Sly Bailey, Chief Executive, Trinity Mirror plc.
Big break: When, in addition to my job as MD of IPC Advertising, I was made MD of Wallpaper* Group. This represented a significant broadening of my role, from functional Head to General Manager of a publishing business.

» **Reading:** *All the papers, plus fashion, celebrity and home magazines and as many of our own regional titles as possible.* **Watching:** *Lost, Spooks, Sunday am. The House of Tiny Tearaways, Supernanny and Nanny 911 - in preparation for the worst!* **Listening:** *Virgin, my iPod, with my favourites being T69 and Oasis.* **Relaxing to:** *Spending time with my husband (for example, eating out) and 16-month-old son (for example, the playground). Regular trips to South Africa.* » *Married, 1 child*

Mark Haskell 12.11.59

ITV Westcountry, Western Wood Way, Langage Science Park, Plymouth, Devon PL7 5BQ
T 01752 333333
E mark.haskell@itv.com

Occupation: Managing Director, ITV Westcountry

Other positions: Governor, Falmouth College of Arts 1998-present; Trustee, Frank Copplestone Trust, Devon Community Foundation.
Awards: ACA 1984; FRSA.
Education: Poole Grammar School; University of Warwick
Career highlights: Chartered Accountant, KPMG 1981-92; Finance Director, ITV Westcountry, 1992-97; Managing Director, ITV Westcountry 1997-present; Managing Director, ITV West 2004-present.

» **Relaxing to:** *Golf, flat-coated retrievers.* » *Married*

Jocelyn Hay 30.7.27

Voice of the Listener & Viewer Ltd (VLV), 101 Kings Drive, Gravesend, Kent DA12 5BQ
T 01474 352835
E info@vlv.org.uk

Occupation: Founder and Chair, Voice of the Listener & Viewer

Other positions: A freelance writer and broadcaster for over 40 years; founded and directed the training agency London Media Workshops, 1978-94; President, European Alliance of Listeners' & Viewers' Associations (EURALVA), 1994-present.
Publications: Numerous audio and television broadcasts on BBC Radio (national and local), BBC World Service, Forces Broadcasting Service and some commercial stations. Many newspaper and magazine articles, mainly on broadcasting but also on other subjects.
Awards: MBE for services to broadcasting, 1999; Commonwealth Broadcasting Association's Elizabeth R Award for outstanding contribution to public service broadcasting, 1999; CBE for services to broadcasting, 2005.
Education: Open University
Career highlights: Started as a volunteer in Forces Broadcasting Service, have worked as a freelance writer, broadcaster and photographer for over

40 years. Through the short course programme of London Media Workshops have met and helped scores of writers, directors and producers to develop a career in broadcasting; Member, Society of Authors Radiowriters Group, 1969–75; gave up broadcasting in own right when founded Voice of the Listener & Viewer (VLV) in 1983, an independent association working for quality, independence and diversity in British broadcasting and to support the principles of public service in broadcasting worldwide. VLV is free from political, commercial and sectarian affiliations and concerned with the regulation, structures, funding and institutions that underpin the British broadcasting system. VLV holds about a dozen public events thoughout the UK each year which provide an accessible forum where all with an interest in broadcasting can meet on equal terms. VLV also produces briefing papers and a quarterly Bulletin of topical news. VLV does not handle complaints and has no relationship with the former National Viewers' and Listeners' Association founded by Mary Whitehouse. Member, Council of European Institute for the Media, early 1990s; Member, Steering Group, European Commission Information Society Forum, 1995–2000; Member, UK Digital Stakeholders' Group, 2000–present.

Mentor: Ian Woolf of Forces Broadcasting Service in first place but then too many over the years to mention. I am grateful to all.

Big break: Starting out as a volunteer in Forces Radio.

Big mistake: Hard to say.

» **Reading:** *Classics and modern (including foreign) authors. In the past year, Birds without Wings by Louis de Bernières, A Suitable Boy by Vikram Seth, Fathers and Sons by Ivan Turgenev, Shadow of the Wind by Carlos Ruiz Zafon, Falling by Elizabeth Jane Howard.* **Watching:** *Any arts programme with Tim Marlow, Waldemar Januszak, Andrew Graham-Dixon; any programme with Judi Dench – especially As Time Goes By; comedy including Have I Got News for You; Channel 4 News; classic drama; would like more Auf Wiedersehen Pet.* **Listening:** *Radio 4, sometimes Radio 2, occasionally World Service and Radio Kent.* **Relaxing to:** *At home, TV, reading, walking, gardening, and when out visiting galleries and exhibitions.* » *Married, 2 daughters, 4 grandchildren*

Alan Hayling

BBC TV, White City Building, 201 Wood Lane W12 7TS
T 020 8752 6501
E alan.hayling@bbc.co.uk

Occupation: Head of Documentaries, BBC

Career highlights: Editorial Director, Mentorn; Commissioning Editor, Channel 4, including Secret History, Secret Lives, Undercover Britain, The Awful Truth; worked with Michael Moore on early stages of Bowling for Columbine; Head of Documentaries, BBC, including One Life, Secret Policeman, Secret Agent, Whistleblower, Dunkirk and Derailed, 2004–present.

Fru Hazlitt

Virgin Radio, 1 Golden Square, London W1F 9DJ
T 020 7434 1215
E fru.hazlitt@virginradio.co.uk

Occupation: Chief Executive, Virgin Radio

Other positions: Non-executive Director, Betfair; Non-executive Director, Woolworths plc; regular speaker at business forums and seminars; Member, Government's Digital Inclusion Panel; formerly Managing Director, Yahoo UK!; Sales and Marketing Director, Yahoo! Europe; Sales Director, Capital Radio.

Publications: Contributor, Sonic Branding by Daniel Jackson.

Awards: Media Week Sales Team of the Year, 1999; CBI First Woman Award, 2005.

Education: Downe House; London University

Career highlights: I joined Virgin Radio as Chief Executive in 2005. I have 18 years of sales and marketing experience within the media sector across magazines, newspapers and radio, most notably at the Guardian Media Group and Capital Radio. At Yahoo! UK & Ireland I arrived at a time when dotcoms were moving from boom to bust. Having faced this challenge I had a clear vision of the future of interactive technology, the opportunity it presents, the creativity it can inspire and the need to listen to a generation who have grown up with the web.

Mentor: Richard Eyre

Big break: Joining Yahoo! at a time when the dotcom bubble looked set to go on forever.

Big mistake: Joining Yahoo! a year too late and missing all those millions!

» **Reading:** *Books, anything and everything, Charles Dickens through to Harry Potter.* **Watching:** *24.* **Listening:** *What do you think!* **Relaxing to:** *I don't! I have 3 children under 4 years old.* » *Single, 3 children*

Ian Heartfield

21.9.76

151 Marylebone Road, London NW1 5QE
T 020 7616 3547
E heartfieldi@amvbbdo.com

Occupation: Advertising Copywriter, AMV BBDO

Publications: Guinness, Samaritans, Bells, the Economist.

Awards: 24 D&AD entries; silver BTAA; bronze Cannes Lion; gold, silver and bronze Creative Circle; bronze One Show; gold Campaign Poster; silver Campaign Poster; eight times Campaign Poster finalist; twice Campaign Press finalist.

Education: Buckinghamshire University

Career highlights: See awards

Mentor: Dave Trott, Tim Delaney, Nigel Roberts, and Dave Morris.

Big break: Nigel Roberts and Paul Belford arriving as my new bosses at Ogilvy and Mather in 2001.

Big mistake: Buying a CCM (an obscure and now defunct British motorcycle).

» **Reading:** *The Guardian, Zen and the Art of Motorcycle Maintenance at least once a year.* **Watching:** *Motorcycle racing, Balamory.* **Listening:** *BBC 6, the Balamory theme tune.* **Relaxing to:** *Pottering around the garden (where you can't hear the Balamory theme tune).* » *Married, 1 child*

Lorraine Heggessey 16.11.56

talkbackTHAMES, 20-21 Newman Street, London W1T 1PG
T 020 7861 8017
E lorraine.heggessey@talkbackthames.tv

Occupation: CEO, talkbackTHAMES

Education: Durham University
Career highlights: Became CEO of talkbackTHAMES in May 2005; prior to this I was the first female Controller of BBC One, a position I took up in October 2000, where I oversaw the channel's re-branding and a comprehensive shake-up of its schedule; I started my BBC career as a News Trainee and went on to work both inside and outside the BBC on a range of flagship current affairs and popular factual programmes. In 1997 I became Head of BBC Children's and in 1999 I became BBC Production's Director of Programmes.
Mentor: I've been lucky enough to work with several inspiring people at every stage of my career.
Big break: Getting to produce and direct a 50-minute Panorama film in the Falklands when I was 25 and had never made a film before.

» **Reading:** *Several national newspapers, Heat, Broadcast, Private Eye, novels when I have the time.* **Watching:** *As much as possible.* **Listening:** *Whatever my husband has downloaded onto my iPod.* **Relaxing to:** *Exercise, ski, spend time with my family.* » *Married, 2 children*

Darren Henley

Classic FM, 7 Swallow Place, London W1B 2AG
T 020 7343 9000
E darren.henley@classicfm.com

Occupation: Managing Editor, Classic FM

Other positions: Editorial Consultant, Classic FM magazine, 1996-present; Member, Broadcast Journalism Training Council, 2000-present; regular speaker, Media Trust, 2001-present; Chairman of Judges, Radio Documentary Category, Prix Italia 2000; Judge, Sony Radio Academy Awards 2001 and 2002; Member, Board of Judges and Advisors, New York International Radio Festival 2001-present; Director, Canterbury Festival and Theatre Trust, 2001-present; Member South East Regional Council, Arts Council, England 2002-present; Member, Founder Partners Board, The Beacon Fellowship 2003-present.
Publications: 3 volumes, Classic FM Pocket Book series, Boosey & Hawkes.
Awards: FRSA, 1998; UN Gold medal 2000; Gold medal, Arts and Culture New York International Radio Festival 2000.
Education: St Edmund's School, Canterbury; University of Hull
Career highlights: Freelance Radio Journalist for Invicta, LBC, IRN, Classic FM and BBC GLR 1989-92; Senior Broadcast Journalist, ITN Radio 1992-95; Classic FM, Programme Editor, Classic Newsnight 1995-96; News Manager, 1997-99; News and Programme Manager, 1999-2000; Managing Editor, 2000-04; Station Manager, 2004-present.

» **Listening:** *Classical music.* **Relaxing to:** *Horse racing, food.*
» *Married, 2 children*

Jeff Henry 15.6.65

200 Gray's Inn Road, London WC1X 8HF
T 020 7396 6051
E jeff.henry@itv.com

Occupation: Chief Executive, ITV Consumer

Other positions: 1980 Touche Ross, Accountant; 1983 BBC, Assistant Contracts Executive, Scotland; 1988 Scottish Television Enterprises, Director and General Manager; 1994 NYNEX CableComms, Executive Director Marketing and Programming; 1996 London News Network, Managing Director; 1998 Granada Sky Broadcasting, Chief Executive; 2000 Chief Executive, The Hallmark Channel, Europe, Middle East and Africa, Crown Digital Worldwide; 2005 Chief Executive, ITV Consumer Division.

» *Married, 2 children*

David Hepworth 28.7.54

90 Pentonville Road, London N1 9HS
T 020 7520 8625
E mail@davidhepworth.com

Occupation: Editorial Director and Partner, Development Hell Ltd

Other positions: Magazine consultant, broadcaster, writer, speaker.
Publications: NME, Sounds, Smash Hits, Just Seventeen, Q, More, Empire, Mojo, FHM, Heat, Word.
Awards: Periodical Publishers Association Editor Of The Year and Writer of the Year; British Society Of Magazine Editors Mark Boxer Award for Editorial Excellence.
Education: Queen Elizabeth Grammar School, Wakefield; Trent Park College of Education, Middlesex
Career highlights: Began writing for music magazines in mid-70s while working in the music business; joined Smash Hits in 1978; launched various magazines as Editorial Director of EMAP Consumer Magazines; in 2002 launched independent magazine publisher Development Hell Ltd with Jerry Perkins. Have also broadcast regularly. Experience here includes period presenting BBC TV's Whistle Test (I was one of the anchors of BBC's coverage of Live Aid); a weekly music show on BBC GLR and regular contributions to Radio 4 and Five Live.
Mentor: No one mentor but lots of people to whom I owe a lot including Fred Dellar, Nick Logan, Peter Strong and Tom Moloney.
Big break: Ringing up Nick Logan, the Editor of Smash Hits, in the very week he was looking for a Deputy. Drunkenly haranguing the Producer of Whistle Test in the very week he was looking for a Presenter. As Shakespeare put it in a rare flash of insight, 'Ripeness is all'.
Big mistake: Waiting so long to start my own company.

» **Reading:** *19th century novels, history, current affairs, war, PG Wodehouse, the New Yorker.* **Watching:** *BBC4.* **Listening:** *Louis Armstrong, the Beatles, Blind Willie McTell,*

Jacqueline Du Pré, Bob Dylan, Elgar, Joni Mitchell, Bob Marley, Randy Newman, Miles Davis, Hank Williams, Richard Thompson and anything sung at the beginning of a rugby match. **Relaxing to:** *Walking.* » *Married, 3 children*

Tony Herrington

20.9.65

The Wire magazine, 23 Jack's Place, 6 Corbet Place, London E1 6NN

T 020 7422 5010
E tony@thewire.co.uk

Occupation: Editor-in-Chief and Publisher, The Wire magazine

Other positions: Director, The Wire Magazine Ltd; Director, Current Media Ltd.
Publications: The Wire magazine. But keep your eyes peeled for Open, which will, er, open a window onto a world of underground film, literature and visual art that other, existing and so-called 'art and culture' publications don't even know exists.
Awards: The Wire: Magazine of the Year, Music Und Maschine International Techno Fair and Congress, Berlin, 2002.
Education: Kirkham Grammar School, Lancs; London College of Printing
Career highlights: Arrived in London on my 30th birthday to attend the London College of Printing's one year post-graduate course, having talked my way onto it (that is, I'm not a graduate, having left school at the ripe old age of 16). Weeks out of the LCP, am offered the Deputy Editor's job at The Wire magazine. Within a year I am appointed Editor, then Editor and Publisher, then I appoint myself Editor-in-Chief and Publisher. Then I head a management buyout of the title from its owners, Naim Attalah's Namara Group. The rest is hysterie.
Mentor: Richard Cook, former editor of The Wire.
Big break: Being dumped by my live-in girlfriend in Manchester in 1991, which led directly to me fleeing a city where I had failed to make a success of anything, landing up in London, where, against all expectations, I seem to have made a success of most things.
Big mistake: Not moving to London sooner.

» **Reading:** *Nihilistic cult novelists, 19th century European Romantics and 17th century English history.* **Watching:** *My back.* **Listening:** *Formless noise issued on hand-painted CD-Rs in editions of 25 by a bunch of freaks and outsiders that you've never heard of. Unless you read The Wire that is.* **Relaxing to:** *Lying in a deep, warm bath for at least 15 minutes every morning.* » *Single, 1 child*

Nick Hewat

10.2.69

Virgin Radio, 1 Golden Square, London W1F 9DJ

T 020 7432 3340
E nick.hewat@virginradio.co.uk

Occupation: Sales Director, Virgin Radio

Other positions: Formerly various management positions at Capital Radio.
Awards: Part of the Media Week Sales Team of the Year at Capital; part of the 3 times winners of the CRCA's National Sales Team of the Year.
Education: Chesham High School; Birmingham Polytechnic
Mentor: John Tulley, now at emap, who taught me 3 golden rules of media: we're not saving lives working in a hospital; you can't kid a kidder; men should always wear a belt.
Big break: Joining Virgin Radio in September 2005. It's liberating to be part of a team making decisions which directly affect the future of the business.
Big mistake: Youth is wasted on the young, and I was a bit of a know-it-all, a cocky bastard. It took Morag Blazey to put the phone down on me (rightly) to make me wise up.

» **Reading:** *The Economist, Private Eye and the Independent. For books, I always consult the Economist Book of the Year list - never read a duff book from it yet.* **Watching:** *Curb Your Enthusiasm, Seinfeld, Shameless, West Wing, Coronation Street (a Hewat family institution), Match of the Day and Six Feet Under. Too much actually.* **Listening:** *60 hours of Virgin Radio each week. Guilty pleasure is Radio 5's Sportsweek on Sunday morning. Favourite music at the moment includes Nada Surf, Elbow and Johnny Cash.* **Relaxing to:** *Not my speciality but weekends help as they are devoted to my little family - love 'em to bits.* » *Living with partner, 2 sons*

Gavin Hewitt

BBC TV Centre, Room 2505, Television Centre, Wood Lane, London W12 7RJ

T 020 8624 8554
E gavin.hewitt@bbc.co.uk

Occupation: Special Correspondent, BBC News

Publications: Books, A Soul on Ice; Terry Waite: Why was he kidnapped?
Awards: Royal Television Society Award, for coverage of the Oldham Riots, 2001; Broadcast Award for England's Shame, an investigation into football hooliganism at Euro 2000; BAFTA award for report on the Madrid Bombings.
Education: Durham University
Career highlights: Worked as Correspondent for BBC News, the Canadian Broadcasting Corporation and BBC Panorama; became Special Correspondent for BBC News in 2000; in 2005 covered the tsunami and reported on Hurricane Katrina; did the main reports on the London bombings for the 10 O'Clock News; in 2004 presented Crisis Command: Can you run the country?; in 1997 wrote and presented the BBC One tribute to Princess Diana; made two programmes for the BBC's Natural History Unit called the Land of the Tiger; while working at Panorama made the Case of India One which led to the largest investigation into police corruption in this country.

» **Reading:** *The Observer and Sunday Times at weekends. The New York Times most days and the Evening Standard.* **Watching:** *The 10 O'Clock News and Channel 4 News when I can.*

Steve Hewlett

9.8.62

6 St. Andrews Avenue, Harpenden, Hertfordshire AL5 2RA
T 07887 632740
E lange.hewlett@btinternet.com

Occupation: Writer, broadcaster and broadcasting consultant

Other positions: Non-exec Director, Tiger Aspect Productions; Visiting Professor (Journalism and Broadcasting Policy) Salford University; Chair, Sheffield International Documentary Festival; Fellow, Royal Television Society.
Awards: RTS Programme of the Year; RTS Best Home Current Affairs programme; BAFTA, various; Broadcasting Press Guild.
Education: University of Manchester
Career highlights: BBC Nationwide, 1982; Friday Alternative, C4, 1983; BBC Brass Tacks 1987; BBC Documentaries, 1989; Editor BBC Inside Story, 1992-94; Editor BBC Panorama, 1995-97; Head of Factual Programmes Channel 4 TV, 1997-98; Director of Programmes and Managing Director, Production, Carlton Television, 1998-2004; 2004-present, writer, broadcaster and broadcasting consultant.
Mentor: Key people have been Roger Bolton, Colin Cameron, Paul Hamann and Clive Jones.
Big break: Getting the Diana interview on to Panorama.
Big mistake: Hard to say - there have been so many!

» **Reading:** *Elmore Leonard, Carl Hiaasen, the Guardian and The Times.* **Watching:** *Drama, comedy, Newsnight and occasional documentaries and current affairs programmes. Oh, and cricket!* **Listening:** *Radio 4.* **Relaxing to:** *Sailing, cricket and organising rugby for kids.* » *Living with partner, 3 children*

Jon Hewson

16.2.71

CN Radio, Watch Close, Spon Street, Coventry CV1 3LN
T 07776 404040
E jon.hewson@cngroup.co.uk

Occupation: Managing Director, CN Radio

Other positions: Group Sales Director, GMG Radio; Sales Director, Century Radio; Managing Director, Sun FM; Sales Manager, CFM.
Publications: Citybeat 96.7FM, The Bay, Lakeland Radio, Abbey FM, Oak 107FM, Centre FM, Kix 96 FM, The Bear 102FM, Banbury FM, Touch FM.
Awards: NTL/Aquiva Local Sales Team Of the Year 2005; Sony gold Speech Award 2004; Sony Gold Interactive Award 2004; Scottish Sales Team Of the Year 2003.
Education: Harrogate Grammar School
Career highlights: Moved on from generating record revenues at CFM to develop the commercial side of Century FM with Border TV plc. Left Border to set up Guardian Media Group plc's radio business. Won and launched Real Radio in Wales and Yorkshire. Relaunched Scot FM as Real Radio. Grew GMG from scratch to be one of the largest radio groups in the UK. Developed commercial aspect of Jazz FM. Project managed sales and revenue growth for 22 radio stations in Radio Investments portfolio. Won new FM licences in Banbury and Barrow for CN Radio and acquired Lakeland Radio. Moved CN Radio into operational profit with record audiences and revenue.
Mentor: John Myers
Big break: Winning the South Wales regional radio licence for Guardian Media Group.
Big mistake: Still waiting to make it!

» **Reading:** *Any good book, The Times, Mediaweek and Radio Ink (The US Radio rag).* **Watching:** *Football!* **Listening:** *Local commercial radio, BBC Radio 2, Five Live, Talksport and my iPod.* **Relaxing to:** *Over a few beers!* » *Single, 3 children*

Nick Higham

2.6.58

Room G640, BBC Television Centre, Wood Lane, London W12 7RJ
T 020 8624 9261
E nick.higham@bbc.co.uk

Occupation: BBC News Correspondent and Presenter, Factfile, BBC News 24

Other positions: Arts and Media Correspondent, BBC News, 1988-2003; freelance journalist 1978-88 (writing for Broadcast, The Times, Sunday Times, Listener, Observer, Guardian).

Ashley Highfield

4.10.69

5th Floor Broadcast Centre, BBC Media Village, 201 Wood Lane, London W12 7TP
T 020 8008 5051
E ashley.highfield@bbc.co.uk

Occupation: Director, New Media and Technology, BBC

Other positions: Executive VP and GM, Flextech Interactive; Head of IT and New Media, NBC Europe; Consultant, Coopers and Lybrand Management Services. Professional bodies: Science Museum Trustee Sub-Committee, RSA Advisory Council, Broadband Stakeholders Group.
Publications: Launch of Interactive TV programming; Integrated Media Player (IMP) bringing New Media to the centre of the BBC's thinking as it prepares for broadcasting in the digital age.
Awards: In 2004 was awarded the Digital Innovator internet award by the Sunday Times, and named 'most influential individual in technology' by online technology news site Silicon.com; in 2005 voted No.1 Digital Marketeer by Revolution Magazine.
Education: Elizabeth College, Guernsey; City University Business School
Career highlights: The number of UK adults visiting bbc.co.uk has more than trebled from 4.6 million to 14.4 million monthly users, and page impressions have increased 10-fold to over two billion a month. Alongside this, bbc.co.uk has also received numerous awards including several Webbys and BAFTAs and AOP Awards. BBCi, the digital interactive TV service accessed from the red button, is now regularly used in over 50% of all

digital TV homes by around 10 million users, up from one million in 2000.
Mentor: Adam Singer, formally CEO Telewest plc and now CEO MCPS-PRS Alliance.
Big break: Moving into this emerging business called IT while at NBC Europe.
Big mistake: Working as a consultant for Coopers and Lybrand in South Africa I attended a discussion on the introduction of SMS and I said it would never catch on!

» **Reading:** *The Daily Telegraph, Sunday Times, reading Home first, then driving, then News Review. Also enjoy Condé Nast Traveller, Car and Evo.* **Watching:** *I don't watch much TV but Sky+ quite a lot of stuff and catch up on some of it during the week. Top Gear and F1 are the only appointments to view. Apprentice, Dragon's Den, QI and Dr Who when they were on, and Lost.* **Listening:** *I listen to the radio on the drive into work (Radios 1 or 4, leaving the easy listening on my iTripped-up iPod for the drive home).* **Relaxing to:** *Playing with gadgets or a round of golf.* » *Married*

David Hill 1.2.48

Prime Minister's Office, 10 Downing Street, London SW1A 2AA
T 020 7219 4272
E david.hill@pmo.gov.uk

Occupation: Director of Communications, Prime Minister's Office

Education: King Edward VI School, Birmingham; Brasenose College, Oxford
Career highlights: Assistant to Rt Hon Roy Hattersley, MP, 1972-76; Political Adviser, Dept of Prices and Consumer Protection, 1976-79; Head of Staff, Roy Hattersley, 1979-83; Deputy Leader of Labour Party's Office, 1983-91; Director of Campaigns and Communications, Labour Party, 1991-93; Chief Spokesperson for Labour Party, 1993-98; Director, Good Relations, 1998-2003; Managing Director, Keith McDowall Associates, subsequently Good Relations Political Communications, 2000-03.

» **Watching:** *Sport, cinema.* **Relaxing to:** *Foreign travel.* » *Divorced, 2 children*

Peter Hill 6.4.45

Daily Express, 10 Lower Thames Street, London EC3R 6EN
T 0871 4341010
E janice.vye@express.co.uk

Occupation: Editor, Daily Express

Other positions: Member, Press Complaints Commission, 2003-present.
Education: Hulme Grammar School, Oldham; Manchester University
Career highlights: Reporter, Colne Valley Guardian, 1961-62; Subeditor, Huddersfield Examiner, 1962-63; Manchester Evening News, 1963-65; Leader Writer, Oldham Evening Chronicle, 1965-67; Subeditor, Daily Telegraph, 1967-74; Subeditor, Daily Mirror, 1974-78; Chief Subeditor, Sunday People, 1970-80; Chief Subeditor, Night Editor, Associate Editor, and Deputy Editor, 1978-98, Editor, 1998-2003, Daily Star.

» **Relaxing to:** *Sailing, tennis, skiing, conversation, making mischief.* » *Married, 2 children*

Lindsey Hilsum 4.8.62

ITN, 200 Gray's Inn Road, London WC1X 8XZ
T 020 7833 3000
E lindsey.hilsum@itn.co.uk

Occupation: International Editor, Channel 4 News

Other positions: Columnist, New Statesman; previously freelance journalist for Guardian, Observer, BBC and others; BBC World Service Radio Producer 1989-93; BBC and Guardian stringer in East Africa, 1986-89; worked for UNICEF (East Africa) and Oxfam (Central America) in earlier incarnations.
Publications: 1996, The Betrayal, a Channel 4 documentary about genocide in Rwanda; essays in Granta, Where is Kigali?, 1996, Two Farms, 2002, We Love China, 2005.
Awards: 2005, Royal Television Society Journalist of the Year, James Cameron Award, Women in Film and Television; 2004 Amnesty, One World, Voice of Viewer and Listener; 2003, RTS Specialist Journalist of the Year; 1996, Amnesty.
Education: Exeter University; Worcester Girls' Grammar School
Career highlights: I covered the war in Iraq and its aftermath from Baghdad and beyond, and have also reported extensively from elsewhere in the Middle East including Iran and Israel/Palestinian territories. With Tim Lambon (cameraman/ producer), I was in the first group of journalists to reach the Palestinian refugee enclave of Jenin after the Israeli assault in 2002; during the NATO bombing of Serbia, I was in Belgrade and Kosovo; I covered the 1994 genocide in Rwanda as a freelance for the BBC and the Guardian, and have also reported from Zimbabwe and elsewhere in Africa, including Equatorial Guinea and Ethiopia/Eritrea.
Mentor: Mike Wooldridge, BBC East Africa Correspondent in the mid-1980s. He was the correspondent; I was the stringer.
Big break: It sounds terrible, but the genocide in Rwanda was my biggest break. In early 1994, my career was on the ropes, so I went to Rwanda to work for UNICEF. That was how I happened to be the only English-speaking foreign correspondent in Rwanda when the genocide started.
Big mistake: Not understanding early enough that the slaughter going on around me in Rwanda was genocide - in other words, that the killing wasn't in any way spontaneous but was a planned, organised campaign of murder.

» **Reading:** *Too many journals, newspapers and current affairs magazines. Not enough books. Fiction when I have time, poetry when I don't.* **Watching:** *Very little. Channel 4 News, obviously, Newsnight occasionally. Sometimes documentaries, but the good ones are on too late and the video broke down years ago.* **Listening:** *Birdsong.* **Relaxing to:** *Fitfully.* » *Neither single nor married*

Boyd Hilton

9.12.67

Heat, Endeavour House, 189 Shaftesbury Avenue, London WC2H 8JG
T 020 7859 8654
E boyd.hilton@emap.com

Occupation: TV Editor, Heat magazine

Other positions: Formerly Editor, PA Listings.
Education: Ilford County High; Sussex University; University of Massachusetts, Amherst
Career highlights: My interview with Elton John for Heat in autumn 2004 made international headlines when he expressed controversially honest thoughts about George Michael, the Beckhams and Robbie Williams. George Michael was so angered by Elton's comments that he wrote an open letter to Heat to put his side of the story. Our less incendiary, half-hour conversation about the genius of Elvis Costello didn't make it into the final piece, but is a cherished memory nonetheless. I also think I'm the only writer Elton's shown his 'porn cupboard' to. Or at least the one in his Atlanta apartment which has stacks and stacks of Czech gay porn treats. I'm also inordinately proud of being the only journalist (to my knowledge) ever allowed to visit the set of The Office where I witnessed the filming of the Comic Relief episode and managed to nick a few genuine David Brent business cards.
Mentor: Colin Vine, my school teacher, Samuel R Delaney at the University of Massachusetts, and Mark Frith my boss.
Big break: When Emap was thinking of putting a weekly TV guide in 'project J' (which eventually became Heat) they came to see me at PA to ask how it was done. Then they employed me to do it.
Big mistake: Recording a two-hour exclusive interview with Richard and Judy and leaving the tape recorder (and tape) in the back of a cab.

» **Reading:** *Dozens of magazines but especially Entertainment Weekly, Vanity Fair and Mojo, the Guardian, and two new novels a week (for the Simon Mayo Radio 5 Live book panel).* **Watching:** *Woody Allen films, Curb Your Enthusiasm and Seinfeld with alarming regularity, and every major new show on TV for work.* **Listening:** *Morrissey, Bob Dylan, Neil Young, Nanci Griffith.* **Relaxing to:** *By watching Curb Your Enthusiasm, walking and visiting Vancouver.*
» *Single, no children*

Phil Hilton

7.2.68

Nuts, IPC Media, King's Reach Tower, Stamford Street, London SE1 9LS
T 020 7261 5660
E Phil_hilton@ipcmedia.com

Occupation: Editor, Nuts

Other positions: Reporter/Editor FHM; Editor in Chief, FHM Bionic; Editor, Later; Editor, Men's Health; Deputy and Features Editor, FHM; Reporter, Personnel Management; Reporter, Datalink.
Awards: BSME launch of the year for Later; BSME launch of the year for Nuts; IPC Media launch of the year for Nuts; IPC Media magazine of the year for 120,000 circ and above for Nuts.
Education: Caterham High School; University College London
Career highlights: Nuts breaking 300,000 circulation; the first few issues of Later; the learning and general hilarity while Mike Soutar's deputy at FHM; success of Men's Health.
Mentor: I'm very grateful to Mike Soutar, IPC Editorial Director, and Mike Lafavore, formerly US Editor of Men's Health.
Big break: Being given the editorship of Nuts from launch.
Big mistake: I make many medium-sized mistakes but am far too namby and cautious to make a really big one.

» **Reading:** *Sun, Mirror, Star, Guardian, Observer, Mojo, Uncut, Kerrang!, Closer, Heat, Amis, Easton Ellis, crime fiction.* **Watching:** *Peep Show, Green Wing, Curb Your Enthusiasm, Ultimate Fighting, Xtreme Sports Channel, Scuzz, Newsnight, Match of the Day, most of BBC4.* **Listening:** *Virgin Classic Rock, Radio 4, Radio 3, Kerrang Radio, Xfm, anything by System of a Down and Slayer.* **Relaxing to:** *Kick boxing, weight training, red wine, crisps, heavy music.* » *Cohabiting, 2 children*

Tim Hincks

Endemol UK, Shepherds Studios Central, Charecroft Way, London W14 0EE
T 0870 333 1700
E june.clements@endemoluk.com

Occupation: Chief Creative Officer, Endemol UK

Other positions: Member, Governing Council, Edinburgh International Television Festival; Chair, 2005.
Publications: Endemol content includes Space Cadets, Fame Academy, The Salon, The Games, Fear Factor, Restoration, Big Brother, 8 Out of 10 Cats, The Law of the Playground, Deal or No Deal, and Millionaire Manor.
Career highlights: Began television career in 1990 producing BBC Two's Food and Drink programme for Bazal (now Endemol UK Productions) and working on current affairs programmes Newsnight and BBC Westminster; Deputy Creative Director, GMG Endemol (now Endemol UK), 1999-2002; Creative Director, Endemol UK, 2002-05; Chief Creative Officer, Endemol UK, 2005-present.

» **Relaxing to:** *Playing guitar*

Les Hinton

19.2.44

News International, 1 Virginia Street, London E98 1EX
T 020 7782 6000

Occupation: Executive Chairman, News International

Other positions: Director, British Sky Broadcasting plc, 1999-2003; Director, Press Association, 1996-present; Chairman, PCC Code of Practice Committee, 1998-present; Chair, Commonwealth Press Union, 1999-present; Member, Board of Trustees, American School in London 1999-present.
Education: British Army Schools in Germany, Libya, Egypt, Ethiopia and Singapore

Career highlights: Reporter, Adelaide News, 1960-65; Desk Editor, British United Press, London, 1965-66; Reporter, the Sun, 1966-69; Writer, Editor, Adelaide News 1969-70; Reporter, the Sun, 1971-76; US Correspondent, News International, New York, 1976-78; The Star, New York, News Editor, 1978-80; Managing Editor, 1980-82; Associate Editor, Boston Herald 1982-85; Murdoch Magazines, Editor-in-Chief, Star magazine 1985-87; Executive Vice-President, 1987-90; President, 1990-91; President and CEO, News America Publishing Inc, New York, 1991-93; Chairman and CEO, Fox TV Stations Inc and Fox News Inc LA 1993-95; Executive Chairman, News International plc 1995; Member, News International Executive Committee.

» *Married, 5 children*

Peter Hitchens 29.10.55

Mail on Sunday, 2 Derry Street, London W8 5TS
T 020 7938 7073
E peter.hitchens@mailonsunday.co.uk

Occupation: Columnist, Mail on Sunday

Other positions: Socialist Worker,1972; Swindon Evening Advertiser, 1973-76; Coventry Evening Telegraph, Industrial Reporter, 1976; Daily Express (sometime Industrial Reporter, Labour correspondent, Deputy Political Editor, Defence and Diplomatic Correspondent, Moscow correspondent, Washington correspondent, Assistant Editor) 1977-2001.
Publications: Author of The Abolition of Britain, 1999; Monday Morning Blues, 2000; A Brief History of Crime, 2003; The Abolition of Liberty, 2004.
Awards: Golden Bollock, Labour and Industrial Correspondents' Group, 1982; Columnist of the Year, British Press Awards 2005.
Education: University of York

» *Married, 1 daughter and 2 sons*

Julia Hobsbawm 15.8.64

41 Cheverton Road, London N19 3BA
T 020 7272 8898
E Julia@editorialintelligence.com

Occupation: PR Consultant and Founder, Editorial Intelligence Ltd

Other positions: Founded Hobsbawm Macaulay Communications in 1993 which became Hobsbawm Media and Marketing Communications in 2002; Labour Party's High Value Donor Consultant before the 1992 General Election.
Publications: Cosmopolitan Guide to Working in PR and Advertising (co-author, Penguin, 1996); Where the Truth Lies: Trust and Morality in PR and Journalism (Editor, Atlantic, 2006).
Education: Camden School for Girls; Polytechnic of Central London, now the University of Westminster
Career highlights: I developed the first high value donor fundraising programme for Labour and handed the Shadow Cabinet what was then their largest single donation by cheque the day the 1992 General Election started; I then started my PR business - Julia Hobsbawm Associates - in 1992 with the stated aim to only ever take on clients I believed in and felt I could represent well, and I kept to this policy; I became George Soros' external PR Adviser in 1992 when he donated $50 million to Bosnia and handled the PR strategy for announcing this with aid agencies, generating my first front page stories; created the global PR strategy for Christie's Holocaust restitution art sale, the Mauerbach Sale, in 1996 which raised five times its pre-sale estimate; ran launch PR for Wallpaper* magazine and Prospect Magazine; I was made London's first Professor of PR in 2002 after I started the MA in Public Relations at the London College of Communications, University of the Arts.
Mentor: I was inspired by Lynne Franks when I was still a teenager. She had great energy and flair, and she still does today. The late Theo Cowan, who was Britain's gentle, great giant of entertainment PR. The TV producer John Tagholm gave me invaluable advice and insight into the media over a number of years. And my first big client, someone who taught me and inspired me in equal measure: Maya Angelou.
Big break: Getting plucked from an obscure medical publishing house to work in Penguin's publicity department in the early 1980s when there was an unlimited budget to network with authors and journalists.
Big mistake: I regret not going to university. In business any mistake is always bad but learning from them is always good. The most embarrassing was definitely when I accidentally emailed my entire address book with a private financial memo.

» **Reading:** *All the titles monitored by Editorial Intelligence, ie all the dailies, Sundays and key weekly print titles. For relaxation it's Grazia and the National Enquirer and I'm afraid I'm a shopping catalogue addict, especially Mitty James. I collect PR books, my favourite being one with the unbelievable title 'Tight skirts and a short smile won't do'.* **Watching:** *West Wing (addictively), Morgan and Platell, Question Time, the Week, Discovery Kid's Mysteries, CBeebies, Spooks on BBC 1 and MTV's Pimp My Ride. Detective movies and thrillers on DVD.* **Listening:** *Radio 4 a lot: Today, Moral Maze. Absolute favourite is Peter Day's In Business. I prefer Classic FM to Radio 3. Steve Wright on Radio 2 has made me laugh most of my adult life. Jo Wiley on Radio 1, who is on at an impossible slot in the morning, is also fantastic. In the car we listen to audio books like Lemony Snicket and my idea of desert island music is early Joni Mitchell or a bit of Brahms.* **Relaxing to:** *Cuddling the children and listening to them download their amazing thoughts and feelings.*

» *Married, 3 children, 2 stepchildren*

Neil Hodgkinson 29.5.64

Wellington Street, Leeds LS1 1RF
T 0113 2432701
E eped@ypn.co.uk

Occupation: Editor, Yorkshire Evening Post

Other positions: Editor, Lancashire Evening Post 1996-99; Deputy Editor, Yorkshire Evening Post, 1992-96.
Publications: Life In Leeds campaign to encourage investment in inner-city areas.
Awards: Yorkshire Newspaper of the Year, 2005; CRE Local Paper of the Year, 2005; UK Evening Newspaper of the Year, 2001; Johnston Press Newspaper of the Year, 2002-04; BT North West Paper of the Year, 1997.
Education: Baines Grammar School, Lancs; Preston Polytechnic
Career highlights: Winning the UK Evening Newspaper of the Year. It was a great moment made even more enjoyable by the sheer pride and joy in the faces of the team who work very hard. Being given the CRE award this year for work that included our aggressive stance against the BNP in Yorkshire.
Mentor: No one mentor. Learned (and still learning) from some excellent professionals.
Big break: Getting my current job.
Big mistake: Haven't made it yet!

» **Reading:** *Various from Steinbeck to J K Rowling.* **Watching:** *A fixation with news programmes and documentaries. Plus an unhealthy (according to my wife) obsession with American crime series.* **Listening:** *Again various depending on the mood. Velvet Revolver currently meeting Katie Melua in the car CD collection.* **Relaxing to:** *Playing with my 5-year-old son. Brings everything back to reality.* » *Married, 1 child*

Dame Patricia Hodgson 19.1.47

Royal Television Society, 5th Floor, Kildare House, 3 Dorset Rise, London EC4Y 8EN
T 020 7822 2810
E info@rts.org.uk

Occupation: Vice-President, Royal Television Society

Other positions: Member, Statistics Commission, 2000-present; Member, Council, Competition Commission, 2003-present; Member, Committee on Standards in Public Life, 2004-present; Member, Board, HEFCE 2005-present; Governor, Wellcome Trust, 2004-present; Non-executive Director, GWR Group plc, 2004-present; Chair, Higher Education Regulatory Review Group, 2004-present.
Education: Brentwood County High School; Newnham College, Cambridge
Career highlights: Conservative Research Dept 1968-70; Producer, BBC Open University (specialising in history and philosophy), 1970-82; TV series including English Urban History 1978, Conflict in Modern Europe 1980, Rome in the Age of Augustus 1981; broadcaster and freelance journalist in UK and USA, Editor, Crossbow, 1976-80; BBC Deputy Secretary, 1982-83; Theological Secretary, 1985-87; Head, Policy and Planning Unit, 1987-92; Director of Policy and Planning, 1993-99; Director, Public Policy, 2000; Chief Executive, ITC, 2000-03; Chairman, Bow Group, 1975-76; Director, BARB, 1987-98; Member, Monopolies & Mergers Commission, 1993-99; Member, London Arts Board 1991-96; Parliamentary Candidate (Cons), Islington, 1974; Visiting Bye-fellow, Newnham College, Cambridge, 2004, (Associate Fellow, 1994-96).

» **Relaxing to:** *Quietness.* » *Married, 1 son*

Lord Clive Hollick 20.5.45

House of Lords SW1A 0PW
T 020 7219 3000

Occupation: Chairman, United Business Media

Other positions: Director, DIAGEO plc 2001-present; Chairman, South Bank Centre 2002-present; Director, Honeywell International Inc 2003-present; Managing Director, Kohlberg Kravis Roberts 2005-present; Founder, Institute for Public Policy Research, 1988; Governor, London School of Economics and Political Science 1997-present.
Education: Taunton's School, Southampton; University of Nottingham
Career highlights: Joined Hambros Bank 1967, Director 1973-96; Managing Director, MAI plc 1974-96; Director, Mills and Allen Ltd 1975-89; Chairman, Shepperton Studios Ltd 1976-84; Member, National Bus Company 1984-91; Director, Logica plc 1987-91, Avenir Havas Media SA (France) 1988-92, National Opinion Polls Ltd. 1989-97, Satellite Information Services 1990-94; Chairman, Meridian Broadcasting 1991-96; Director, British Aerospace 1992-97; Member, Financial Law Panel 1993-97; Director, Anglia Television 1994-97; Member, Commission on Public Policy and British Business 1995-97; Chairman, United Broadcasting and Entertainment Ltd 1995-2000;Chief Executive, United Business Media plc 1996-2005; Special Adviser to Margaret Beckett as President of the Board of Trade 1997-98; Director, Express Newspapers plc 1998-2000; Director, TRW Inc 2000-02.

» **Relaxing to:** *Reading, countryside, cinema, theatre, tennis.* » *Married, 3 daughters*

Mike Hollingsworth 25.11.52

TVTimes, 10th Floor, Kings Reach Tower, Stamford Street, London SE1 9LS
T 020 7261 7740
E mike_hollingsworth@ipcmedia.com

Occupation: Editor, TVTimes

Other positions: Editor, What's On TV; Launch Editor Soaplife; Managing Editor on Bauer TV mag launch; Deputy Editor Screen International; variety of TV freelance work on national and evening newspapers; radio; after training on Recorder Newspapers, East London.
Awards: As Editor of What's On TV, 1992 Consumer Mag of the Year; 1994 PPA Consumer Mag of the

Year; 1996 BSME Editor of the Year, General Interest Mags.
Education: Left school at 16
Career highlights: Getting the jobs when they mattered, especially the move to Bauer which led to the move to What's On TV.
Mentor: Never had one.
Big break: Liking the film Last Tango in Paris (God only knows why I did but I did), when being interviewed for the Screen International job. The owner of the mag had sat through the interview and hadn't said a word after an hour when he suddenly piped up and asked my opinion. I burbled something to the effect of liking it for its lighting (or some such nonsense) and he said he did too. Apparently, I was the only candidate who agreed with him and I promptly got the job!
Big mistake: Far too many to mention.

» **Reading:** *Rival TV mags; the sport pages mainly, particularly the Sun, Guardian and Telegraph. Novels when I get the chance. Big fan of Rebus.* **Watching:** *A wide range of telly to get the feel of what people like. Sport, particularly football and cricket. Guilty pleasure is game shows, Bullseye is the all-time great.* **Listening:** *Less than I used to. The White Stripes are my only modern band. The rest pass me by, I'm afraid, though my daughter tries her best to keep me informed.* **Relaxing to:** *Play badminton, read, going walking.*
» *Married, 2 children*

Corinne Hollingworth 25.5.52

ITV Network Centre, 200 Gray's Inn Road, London WC1X 8HF
T 020 7843 8000
E corinne.hollingworth@itv.com

Occupation: Head of Continuing Series, ITV

Awards: Member, BAFTA, 1996; Member, RTS, 1996.
Education: Sherwood Hall Grammar School; University of Bristol; Webber Douglas Academy of Dramatic Art.
Career highlights: Producer, EastEnders, BBC, 1988-91; Producer, Eldorado, BBC, 1992-93; Producer, Casualty, BBC, 1993-95; Executive Producer, EastEnders, 1994-96; Controller of Drama, Channel 5, 1996-2002; Head of Continuing Series, ITV, 2002-present.

» *Married, 1 child*

Mark Hollinshead 17.6.60

1 Central Quay, Glasgow G3 8DA
T 0141 309 3288
E m.hollinshead@dailyrecord.co.uk

Occupation: Managing Director, Scottish Daily Record & Sunday Mail Ltd

Other positions: Daily Record, Sunday Mail, Scottish Metro, Glaswegian, Insider Magazine, The One directory series.
Education: University of East Anglia
Career highlights: Managing Director, Midland Weekly Media; Marketing Director, Midland Independent Newspapers plc; Business Development Director, Thomson Regional Newspapers; Marketing Services Manager, Thomson Regional Newspapers; Research Manager, Express & Star Ltd.
Mentor: Thomas Hollinshead
Big break: Getting a job at the Express & Star in Wolverhampton.
Big mistake: Supporting Wolverhampton Wanderers.

» **Reading:** *Daily Record, Sunday Mail, the Herald.* **Watching:** *Big Brother, Desperate Housewives, Question Time.* **Listening:** *BBC Radio Scotland.* **Relaxing to:** *I run.* » *Married, 3 children*

Paul Horrocks 19.12.53

Manchester Evening News, 164 Deansgate, Manchester M3 3RN
T 0161 832 7200
E paul.horrocks@men-news.co.uk

Occupation: Editor, Manchester Evening News

Other positions: Vice-President, Community Foundation for Greater Manchester, 2000-present; Member, Organising Council, Commonwealth Games, Manchester 2002; Patron, Francis House Children's Hospice, 1999-present.
Education: Bolton School
Career highlights: Reporter, Daily Mail, 1974; Manchester Evening News, Reporter, 1975-80; Crime Correspondent, 1980-87; News Editor, 1987-91; Assistant Editor, 1991-95; Deputy Editor, 1995-97. Director, Society of Editors, 2001-present; Member, PCC, 2002-present.

» **Relaxing to:** *Sailing, golf, rugby union.*
» *Married, 3 children, 1 stepchild*

Nina Hossain 15.12.73

ITN, 200 Gray's Inn Road, London WC1X 8HF
T 07841 047116
E nina.hossain@itn.co.uk

Occupation: ITN Newscaster

Other positions: Producer, reporter
Education: Durham University
Career highlights: Surviving! My ambition to become a journalist began 20 years ago, and this year I will celebrate a decade's worth of hard work and incredibly lucky breaks. It is a pretty impossible industry to get into, and equally difficult to continue to climb the slippery career ladder which is television news. Every day I broadcast, there is some highlight, be that grilling a prominent politician, doing a sensitive interview with someone who has experienced something traumatic, writing a link to a story that works, meeting people I admire (Matthew Parris, Simon Le Bon, Tracy Chapman), or reporting from places only journalists get to visit. It is a rich and varied job on a day-to-day basis, and it is a privilege to do it.
Mentor: Sandy Smith, formerly Editor of BBC London, now Editor of Watchdog.
Big break: Being poached by Deborah Turness, Editor of ITV News, from BBC London to present the ITV Evening News.
Big mistake: Trying to combine being a perfectionist with the imperfect world of live television news.

» **Reading:** *The Guardian, Daily Mirror, Mail, Indy and Telegraph, some Saturday papers, the majority of the*

Sunday papers, and lots of books (William Boyd, Armistead Maupin, Haruki Murakami, Phillip Pullman). **Watching:** *BBC Ten O'Clock News, ITV News at Ten Thirty, Sky News, The West Wing and Six Feet Under (thank goodness for DVDs and Sky Plus).* **Listening:** *For work, the Today Programme, for pleasure Five Live (breakfast programme, Victoria Derbyshire, Simon Mayo), for lazy days and holidays Radio 1 (Chris Moyles, Vernon Kay), Radio 2 (Chris Evans).* **Relaxing to:** *Snowboarding, reading, going to gigs and making endless playlists for my iPod.* » *Single, no children*

Ilse Howling

17.8.69

Freeview, Broadcast Centre (BC3 D5), Media Village, 201 Wood Lane, London W12 7TP
T 020 8008 2397
E ilse.howling@bbc.co.uk

Occupation: General Manager, Freeview

Other positions: Head of Digital Marketing and Communications, BBC; Board member of the BBC's programme-making division, BBC Production; Chief Assistant to the Director of Radio and Head of Internal Communications at BBC News Producer, Radio Five Live.
Publications: Led the BBC digital Changing face of TV and Teach an Old Dog New Tricks campaigns.
Awards: 2004, Winner, Marketing Society New Brand Award and Marketing Society Consumer Insight Awards for Freeview/BBC Digital campaigns.
Education: University of Leeds, BA International History and Politics; MA Research History
Career highlights: I joined Freeview as General Manager in October 2005. Before joining Freeview I worked at the BBC where I led the corporation's award-winning digital promotion which launched Freeview and helped grow take up of the BBC's six extra digital television channels by more than two-thirds in three years. I was one of the main architects of the Freeview consumer proposition and was on the board of Freeview from the launch in 2002; previously, I was Controller of Marketing and Strategy on the board of the BBC's programme-making division BBC Production; other roles within the BBC have included Chief Assistant to the Director of Radio and Head of Internal Communications in BBC News. I also worked as a producer on Radio Five Live. Before joining the BBC in 1993, I worked for US telecoms operator NYNEX, heading up corporate and internal communication for its European subsidiary; my first job was for a venture capital funded online start up heading customer services and marketing in the UK and US.
Mentor: David Docherty and Andy Duncan.
Big break: Launching Freeview. It was the first time I had the chance to put the consumer right at the heart of the proposition - and all our decisions flowed from there. The results have been way beyond what any of us imagined.
Big mistake: Cutting off the presenter live on air when in the studio producing the Radio Five Live Morning Show!

» **Reading:** *Modern novels.* **Watching:** *Six Feet Under, The West Wing.* **Listening:** *BBC World Service.* **Relaxing to:** *Painting with my 4-year-old son.* » *Long-term partner, 1 son*

Gill Hudson

BBC, 80 Wood Lane, London W12 OTT
T 020 8433 2235
E gill.hudson@bbc.co.uk

Occupation: Editor, Radio Times

Other positions: Member, PTC Editorial Training Consultants Committee.
Awards: BBC Magazines Editor of the Year 2005; BSME Entertainment Magazine Editor of the Year 2003; BSME Men's Magazine Editor of the Year 1997.
Education: University of Sussex
Career highlights: Editor, Radio Times, BBC Magazines, 2002-present; Launch Editor, eve, BBC Magazines 1999-2002; Editor in Chief, Maxim (Launch Editor), Stuff and Ministry magazines Dennis Publishing, 1994-99; Editor, New Woman, Hachette/EMAP (formerly Murdoch Magazines), 1990-94; Deputy Editor and then Editor, Company magazine, National Magazine Company, 1987-90; Editor, Cook's Weekly, Marshall Cavendish, 1986-87; Deputy Editor then Editor, Fitness, Stonehart, 1984-86; Contributing Editor, Oracle Teletext, LWT 1983; Editor, Home & Country, Women's Institute, 1981-83.
Mentor: Maggie Goodman (Company/Hello). She proved that being a good editor doesn't mean you have to play the bitch from hell.
Big break: Going straight in as Editor of the WI Magazine Home & Country. No climbing-the-ladder stage at all. It was a total fluke, and as learning curves go it was vertical. Brilliant experience, though.
Big mistake: In an early incarnation of phone services, the company we were using on the magazine mixed up the line for a recipe with that for a sex line. Readers hoping for Shepherd's Pie were asked if they wanted to last for the whole three minutes, while those wanting a good time were told to start chopping an onion. Made me laugh, anyway. But that wasn't really my mistake.

» **Reading:** *The Week - brilliant, simple digest of the week's news that is my one must-and-always read. Plus whatever our book group is tackling: Ian McEwan, Salman Rushdie, Zadie Smith, Lionel Shriver...* **Watching:** *Absolutely bloody anything and everything, of course. It's my job. Bleak House and Dr Who stand out a mile, though.* **Listening:** *Radio 4, Wogan, classic piano concertos, and everything Phill Jupitus recommends in his weekly Radio Times music column - fantastically eclectic, contemporary and educational - which means I can nod knowingly (and, OK, smugly) when my daughter says she likes Elbow.* **Relaxing to:** *Going for a run. Works every time.* » *1 child*

Dominic Hughes 13.7.71

Room 2253, BBC TV Centre, Wood Lane, London W12 7RJ
T 020 8576 2035
E dominic.hughes@bbc.co.uk

Occupation: Correspondent, The World Today, BBC World

Other positions: BBC Sydney Correspondent 1999-2003; British Affairs Correspondent, BBC World Service 1997-1999; Political Producer, BBC World Service, Millbank 1996-97.
Education: Bristol University
Career highlights: An Antarctic expedition in 2000; Sydney Olympics 2000; World Cup in South Korea 2002; Iraq war.
Big break: Falconio murder - broke the story to UK audiences after it hit the ABC Sydney newsroom and I happened to be there.
Big mistake: Missing the Fiji coup because of a family wedding back in the UK. Not renewing my Crystal Palace season ticket.
» **Reading:** *What I can.* **Watching:** *As above.* **Listening:** *5 Live, Today Programme, lots of music.* **Relaxing to:** *Family, football, running, walking, music.* » *Married, 1 child*

John Humphrys 18.8.47

c/o BBC News, Television Centre, London W12 7RJ
T 020 8743 8000
E john.humphrys@bbc.co.uk

Occupation: Presenter, Today Programme; Presenter, Mastermind

Other positions: Foreign correspondent; television newsreader; newspaper columnist.
Awards: Most recently, Sony Gold Medal for lifetime service to radio.
Education: Cardiff High School
Career highlights: Journalist since the age of 15.
Mentor: Nobody
Big break: Arriving in the USA a few days before Watergate started happening.
Big mistake: Too numerous to mention.
» **Reading:** *Everything.* **Watching:** *Almost nothing.* **Listening:** *Radio 4.* **Relaxing to:** *Reading, walking, gardening, being with small child.* » *Unmarried, 3 children*

Peter Hunt 1963

BBC Television Centre, Wood Lane, London W12 7RJ
T 020 8743 8000
E Peter.Hunt@bbc.co.uk

Occupation: Royal Correspondent, BBC

Education: University of York
Career highlights: Joined BBC as News Trainee, 1988; National Reporter,1990; Deputy, then Royal Correspondent; reported from Coalition Headquarters in Qatar throughout 2003 war in Iraq; have also reported from Kuwait, Croatia, Moscow, New York, South Africa and Hong Kong, and have worked extensively in Northern Ireland and across the UK; as Deputy Royal Correspondent covered the death of the Queen Mother, the Jubilee weekend celebrations and the Paul Burrell trial; as Royal Correspondent conducted first television interview with Prince William and the first radio interview with Prince Harry; also presented the PM programme on BBC Radio 4 and also worked as a presenter on BBC Radio Five Live.

Richard Huntingford 15.5.60

The Chrysalis Building, Bramley Road, London W10 6SP
T 020 7470 1057
E richard.huntingford@chrysalis.com

Occupation: Chief Executive, Chrysalis Group plc

Awards: Still waiting!
Education: Radley College
Career highlights: Trained as a Chartered Accountant with KPMG working across a broad range of clients for 12 years, including working out of Nestlé's corporate HQ in Switzerland for 3 years. Joined Chrysalis Group plc in 1987 as Corporate Development Director with the brief to diversify the company from its music roots. Responsible for Chrysalis's move into the radio sector, initially taking a 20% shareholding (and board seat) in Metro Radio plc. Originated the Heart brand and successfully launched it into the competitive Midlands and London markets in 1994 and 1995. Appointed Chief Executive of Chrysalis Radio in 1994 and built the business through licence wins and acquisition into one of the UK's leading, brand-led commercial radio companies (Heart, Galaxy, LBC, Arrow). Promoted to Chief Executive of Chrysalis Group plc in December 2000.
Mentor: Don't have one other than my own ambition.
Big break: Winning the London FM licence for Heart in October 1994 (from an applicant field of over 40).
Big mistake: Ignoring my gut instinct during the crazy days of dotcom investment.
» **Reading:** *The Guardian, MediaGuardian, Daily Telegraph, Sunday Times, Music Week, Media Week, Campaign, Broadcast, Marketing.* **Watching:** *The Chrysalis share price, Sky News, Sky Sports.* **Listening:** *Heart, LBC, Arrow, Xfm on the radio and Exile on Main Street on the iPod.* **Relaxing to:** *Playing tennis, watching cricket, fine dining.* » *Married, 3 children*

Mark Hurrell 1.8.58

BBC, London Road, Gloucester GL1 1SW
T 01452 308585
E mark.hurrell@bbc.co.uk

Occupation: Managing Editor, BBC Radio Gloucestershire

Other positions: Managing Editor at BBC Radio Stoke; News Journalist and Presenter, BBC Points West TV; Programme Organiser, BBC Radio Gloucestershire; Trainer, BBC Training; Presenter/Producer Radio Cambridgeshire; Head of Programmes, Centre Radio, Leicester.
Publications: The last long form interview with

Cotswold-based author Laurie Lee before he died; leading the team that took Radio Stoke to 38.3% reach; coaching and developing colleagues.
Education: King's College Taunton; Grenoble University (France)
Career highlights: I joined the BBC in 1978 and lived out of a suitcase for three years travelling the world of local radio as a locum. However I did appear briefly on Radio One during that time sitting in for Mike Read! Before that I had jocked on the Voice of Peace (off the Israeli coast), enjoyed hospital radio in Weybridge and endured a night-time career spinning discs in numerous west London discos! In 1981 I joined Centre Radio in Leicester doing mid-morning and eventually the Head of Programmes job. When Centre closed I returned to the BBC in Cambridge and lunchtimes. After three years as a trainer (86-89) I moved to Radio Bristol briefly before settling in Gloucester (1990) as Number Two. Three years later found myself back in Bristol but in regional TV ... a new set of skills and a fresh challenge. I returned to radio and my first Managing Editor's job at Stoke in 1998. Moved the station from what Greg Dyke called 'the worst building in the BBC' before returning to Gloucester (2002).
Mentor: No one individual. There are a handful of people in and outside the industry that I take advice from but my family has always given me support and encouragement.
Big break: Joining the BBC in 1978.
Big mistake: Nothing significant ... hindsight is a wonderful thing.

» **Reading:** *Local evening paper The Citizen, weekend Telegraph, Cotswold Life, www.bbc.co.uk/Gloucestershire, dailies as and when.* **Watching:** *Sport - rugby on Sky, Match of the Day; news - mostly BBC and Channel 4; drama - anything in the Spooks/Taggart mould; comedy - Little Britain etc; history programmes. Not a soap watcher.* **Listening:** *My own station, R4, R2, Five Live, Classic FM, Smooth, US radio, choral music, jazz.* **Relaxing to:** *Watching rugby, singing, walking the dog, food and drink.* » *Married, 2 sons*

Monica Iglesias

4.5.75

Oxford House, 76 Oxford Street, London W1D 1BS
T 020 7307 6650
E monica.iglesias@nbcuni.com

Occupation: Head of Acquisitions, Sci-Fi Channel Europe

Other positions: Manager Programming and Acquisitions, Calle 13, Spain; Director of Children and Documentaries, Planeta 2010/DeAPlaneta, Spain; Sales Director, BRB International SA, Spain.
Education: UNNE, Madrid; Roehampton Institute, London; Universidad Carlos III, Madrid
Career highlights: In my first job I was based in Madrid and stayed for 8 years. It was in distribution, responsible for worldwide sales of children's animation, which allowed me to travel everywhere and make many friends that I am still in contact with; then moved to Barcelona to join the Planeta Group, a good experience, and then I joined Universal Studios Networks (now NBCUniversal Global Networks) in Spain where I worked for two years before I moved to London to join the UK team.
Mentor: Dan Marks, former President of the Sci-Fi channel in the UK, now Head of BT Entertainment as CEO.
Big break: I am not sure I've ever had a proper break...
Big mistake: Can't remember...

» **Reading:** *Historical novels, travel writing.* **Watching:** *The Sci-Fi Channel, of course, then news, some documentaries, music video clips and, when it comes to movies, romantic comedies and spy/secret agent movies are my favourite!* **Listening:** *I have a wide taste but, in general, R&B/Urban music. I also like reggae, Latin music (specially salsa and boleros) and classic/opera. I love Prince, Frank Sinatra, James Brown, Sade and Simply Red amongst others.* **Relaxing to:** *Bikram yoga, listening to chill-out music and a nice bath or massage.* » *Single, no children*

Charles Inge

10.6.65

7-9 Rathbone Street, London W1T 1LY
T 020 7462 8514
E charles.inge@chiadvertising.com

Occupation: Creative Partner, CHI (Clemmow Hornby Inge)

Other positions: Creative Director, Lowe
Publications: Originated Tesco Prunella Scales TV campaign, and Stella Artois Jean de Florette campaign at Lowe. Currently Carphone Warehouse, Talk Talk, Telegraph and Tango amongst others.
Awards: Over 70 Gold and Silver Awards in the major Advertising Award Festivals, including the Grand Prix at the Cannes Advertising Festival.
Education: Oxford University
Career highlights: In my two years as Creative

Director at Lowe, I oversaw two consecutive Cannes Grand Prix (Independent TV 1999, Stella Artois press 2000). Our Tesco campaign won the IPA effectiveness Grand Prix, and Lowe were awarded Campaign Agency Of The Year, Ad Age European Agency Of The Year, and the British Television Advertising Agency of the Year (2003), and Marketing Magazine's Creative Agency of the Year (2004).

Mentor: John Hunt, Global Creative Director, TBWA Worldwide.

Big break: Starting CHI with Simon Clemmow and Johnny Hornby.

Big mistake: Not doing it sooner!

» **Reading:** *The Daily Telegraph, the Week.* **Watching:** *Very little. I need a longer day.* **Listening:** *Radio 4.* **Relaxing to:** *Painting, walking, reading.* » *Married, 3 girls*

Richard Ingrams

19.8.37

The Oldie Magazine, 45-46 Poland Street, London W1V 4AU

T 020 7734 2225
E megmendez@theoldie.co.uk

Occupation: Editor, the Oldie

Other positions: Chairman, Private Eye.

Publications: (With Christopher Booker and William Rushton) Private Eye on London, 1962; Private Eye's Romantic England, 1963; (with John Wells) Mrs Wilson's Diary, 1965; Mrs Wilson's 2nd Diary, 1966; The Tale of Driver Grope, 1968; (with Barry Fantoni) The Bible for Motorists, 1970; (Editor) The Life and Times of Private Eye, 1971; (as Philip Reid, with Andrew Osmond) Harris in Wonderland, 1973; (Editor) Cobbett's Country Book, 1974; (Editor) Beachcomber: the works of J B Morton, 1974; The Best of Private Eye, 1974; God's Apology, 1977; Goldenballs, 1979; (with Fay Godwin) Romney Marsh and the Royal Military Canal, 1980; (with John Wells) Dear Bill: the collected letters of Denis Thatcher, 1980; (with John Wells) The Other Half: further letters of Denis Thatcher, 1981; (with John Wells) One for the Road, 1982; (with John Piper) Piper's Places, 1983; (Editor) The Penguin Book of Private Eye Cartoons, 1983; (with John Wells) My Round!, 1983; (Editor) Dr Johnson by Mrs Thrale, 1984; (with John Wells) Down the Hatch, 1985; (with John Wells) Just the One, 1986; John Stewart Collis: a memoir, 1986; (with John Wells) The Best of Dear Bill, 1986; (with John Wells) Mud in Your Eye, 1987; The Ridgeway, 1988; You Might As Well Be Dead, 1988; England (anthology), 1989; (with John Wells) Number 10, 1989; On and On..., 1990; (Editor) The Oldie Annual, 1993; (Editor) The Oldie Annual 2, 1994; Malcolm Muggeridge: the authorized biography, 1995; (Editor) I Once Met, 1996; (Editor) The Oldie Annual 3, 1997; (Editor) Jesus: authors take sides (anthology), 1999; (Editor) The Oldie Annual 4, 1999; The Life and Adventures of William Cobbett, 2005.

Education: Shrewsbury School; University College, Oxford

Career highlights: Editor, Private Eye 1963-86 (Chairman, 1974-present); Columnist, the Observer, 1988-2006; Founder and Editor, The Oldie magazine, 1992-present.

» **Relaxing to:** *Piano.* » *Married, 1 son*

Mark Iremonger

43-44 Hoxton Square, London N1 6PB

T 020 7613 3330
E mark@iremonger.co.uk

Occupation: Managing Director, unit9.creative.production

Other positions: MD, Sleeper (a Blink/Deepend partnership); Head of Film and Video, Maritz; Producer, Interlink; Producer, Diverse Image.

Awards: D&AD, BIMA, LIAA, IVCA, Design Week, Biz Net, One Show, D&ADC.

Education: Wesley College, Dublin; Dublin City University

Career highlights: Grew up in Dublin, graduating from Dublin City University with a BA (Hons) in Communications Studies; after university, joined communications agency Diverse Image in Dublin; moved to London in 1992, and joined marketing services agency, Interlink; produced the award-winning TV magazine, Express Yourself, with Emma Freud for DHL; left Interlink in 1996 to become Head of Film and Video at the brand experience agency Maritz Communications; highlights included award-winning work for Fiat, Thorn, Nissan, and Microsoft's New Home; left Maritz in 2000 to set up the cross-platform, interactive production company Sleeper as a joint venture.

Mentor: James Studholme, Blink; Mike MacLeod, Imagination.

Big mistake: Ignoring that lump for so long before getting it investigated...

» **Reading:** *Independent, The Times, FT, NMA, Campaign, Marketing Week.* **Watching:** *My diet and my kids.* » *Married, 2 children*

John Irvine

3.6.67

ITN, Penthouse Floor, The Maneeya Centre, 518 Ploenchit Road, Bangkok 10330, Thailand

T +66 98952751
E john.irvine@itn.co.uk

Occupation: Asia Correspondent, ITV News

Other positions: Middle East Correspondent, ITV News; Ireland Correspondent, ITV News; General Reporter, Ulster Televison, Belfast; General Reporter, The Tyrone Constitution, Omagh, Co. Tyrone (weekly newspaper).

Awards: Royal Television Society Journalist of the Year 2002-03 for coverage of Iraq; Royal Television Society News-International Award 2002-03 for Welcome to Baghdad (first journalist to meet American soldiers coming into the city); New York Festival Silver Medal 2002-03 for coverage of the Iraq War.

Education: Campbell College, Belfast; College of Business Studies, Belfast

Career highlights: Reporting the end of the troubles in Northern Ireland; being in the position to cover the Omagh bomb (my career began in Omagh and my knowledge of the town made me the right person for this difficult job). Exclusives including an IRA Army Convention ratifying the ceasefire

and the capture of the border sniper in South Armagh; following a hunch and going to Jerusalem's Temple Mount for prayers on Sept 29 - rioting marked the start of the Palestinian intifada; covering the Iraq War from Baghdad; reporting on the tsunami as someone who had been through it.
Mentor: Michael Macmillan, former BBC Middle East Correspondent.
Big break: Getting my first job.
Big mistake: Running to get my camera when the tsunami approached our Thai beach, rather than running away immediately with my wife and children!

» **Reading:** *All the British papers online, International Herald Tribune, the Spectator, Car and Top Gear magazines, thriller novels.* **Watching:** *All available English-speaking news programmes here in Thailand.* **Relaxing to:** *Spending time with my wife and children, golf, swimming, tennis.*
» *Married to Libby, 2 children, Elizabeth (10) and Peter (6)*

Faisal Islam

30.5.81

Channel 4 News, ITN, 200 Gray's Inn Road, London WC1X 8XZ
T 020 7430 4008
E faisal.islam@itn.co.uk

Occupation: Business Correspondent, Channel 4 News

Other positions: Economics Correspondent, the Observer 2001-04.
Publications: Channel 4 News, the Observer.
Awards: 2000 Young Financial Journalist of the Year, Harold Wincott Awards; 2001 Young Journalist of the Year (shortlist), British Press Awards; 2005 Business Programme of the Year, Workworld Awards; 2005 Story of the Year (shortlist), Business Journalist of the Year Awards.
Education: Cambridge University
Career highlights: Newspaper interviews with Gordon Brown, George Soros, Steve Jobs, James Wolfensohn; occasional leader-writing and columns while at the Observer.
Mentor: Emily Bell
Big break: Compiling the contextualised schools league tables in the Observer, 1998.
Big mistake: Agreeing to compile the contextualised schools league tables in the Observer, 1998.

» **Reading:** *All the papers. Many internet sites on the computer, and on my PDA. Redissue.co.uk.* **Listening:** *Five Live, Today.* **Relaxing to:** *Football (Manchester United), electronica, gadgets.*

J

Ian Jack

8.2.49

2/3 Hanover Yard, Noel Road, London N1 8BE
T 020 7704 9776
E ijack@granta.com

Occupation: Editor, Granta and Guardian Columnist

Other positions: Foreign Correspondent, Sunday Times; Editor, Independent on Sunday.
Awards: Journalist, Reporter, Editor of the Year.
Education: Dunfermline High School
Career highlights: Started as a trainee journalist with the Glasgow Herald, then moved via local papers to the Scottish Daily Express in Glasgow before joining the Sunday Times; Highlights include covering India for the Sunday Times; editing the Independent on Sunday (1991-1995); writing for Granta (especially pieces on the Gibraltar shootings and the Hatfield train crash).
Mentor: Several, including Harold Evans and Don Berry.
Big break: Being hired by Harold Evans in 1970 when he was Editor of The Sunday Times.
Big mistake: Thinking the Falklands war would never happen and declining the chance to board SS Canberra.

» **Reading:** *The Guardian regularly, plus little bits of everything else.* **Watching:** *Ditto, plus old films when I can.* **Listening:** *Many things my children do, plus Schubert, Kathleen Ferrier etc.* **Relaxing to:** *By thinking of the Firth of Clyde, or being on it with my family.* » *Married, 2 children*

Paul Jackson

8.7.69

Virgin Radio, 1 Golden Square, London W1F 9DJ
T 020 7434 1215
E paul.jackson@virginradio.co.uk

Occupation: Programme Director, Virgin Radio

Other positions: Formerly Regional Programme Director, Capital Radio Group; Programme Director, BRMB.
Education: Glasgow Academy
Mentor: I have met many people who I regularly seek advice from, but my life mentor has been my Dad.
Big break: Getting the opportunity to programme BRMB. I felt that it was my chance to prove I could turn a big station around.
Big mistake: I think most of us make mistakes regularly, hopefully not too impactful though, but on reflection I made a few too many changes too quickly when I was at Century Radio.

» **Reading:** *Enid Blyton mostly each night with the kids! I am always reading two or three books at once, right now it's The Knowledge Company by Nonaka, Blink by Malcolm Gladwell and 44 Scotland St by Alexander McCall Smith.* **Watching:** *Sky Sports, Sky News, Sky Movies. Life on Mars, Hustle, Spooks, 24 and of course The Jeremy Kyle Show.* **Listening:** *I listen up and down the dial to all stations all the* *time. My favourites are Virgin Radio, BBC Radio 5 Live and Magic.* **Relaxing to:** *I love to be with my wife, three kids and dog at Virginia Water and my ever-growing extended family; also, I play a lot of golf and go to football matches every week.* » *Married, 3 children*

Andrew Jeffries

30.3.76

Kiss 100, Mappin House, 4 Winsley Street, London W1W 8HF
T 020 7182 8157
E andrew.jeffries@kiss100.com

Occupation: Programme Director, Kiss 100 London

Other positions: Programme Director, Kerrang! Radio (from launch); Programme Director, Nova 937, Perth, Australia (from launch); Programme Director, Galaxy 105, Yorkshire, and Galaxy 102, Manchester; Programme Director, Beat 106, Scotland; Programme Director, Southern FM, Brighton; Programme Director, More FM, Dunedin, New Zealand; Breakfast Host and Programme Director, Classic Hits 99FM, Timaru, New Zealand; Head of Music, Classic Hits 89FM, Morning Presenter on Classic Rock 96FM, Hawkes Bay, New Zealand; Drive Presenter, Radio Marlborough, New Zealand; Evening Presenter, River City Radio, Wanganui, New Zealand.
Awards: BRA UK Programmer 2005; BRA West Mids Programmer 2005; BRA North West Programmer 2003; NTL Programmer 2002; NTL Station of the Year - Galaxy 105 2003; Arqiva Gold Award 2005 - Kerrang! Radio; Arqiva Digital Station 2005 - Kerrang! Radio.
Education: Wanganui College, New Zealand
Career highlights: Started on air in New Zealand at 15, worked through a number of markets there in presentation, production and programming capacity. Left NZ in 1999 on an extended holiday with my wife, arrived in England, landed at Heathrow with no job. Found a bar in Hammersmith, worked there four days and quit. Sent CV to Clive Dickens and Richard Park at Capital. Had a great run in the UK since then, played a small part in a host of industry awards for the teams on stations I was working with. Really pleased with where I am now.
Mentor: Hard to pin it down. Richard Park, Mark Story, Alan Burns, Tracy Johnston and from New Zealand Don Douglas and Pat Grace.
Big break: Actually getting meaningful employment back in radio when arriving in the UK. The antipodean cliché of working in a bar did not suit me beyond four days. Since then it has been a great run.
Big mistake: Thinking I know it all. Get to that phase and you are set for a fall. Everyone goes through it, but be humble and learn from others' experiences ... they are not where they are now by being fools.

» **Reading:** *Jet Skier Magazine, R&R, Rolling Stone, Kerrang! FHM, F1 mag, and anything to do with the All Blacks.* **Watching:** *I love music videos on TV. The range of stations inside EMAP cut across most of my commercial musical tastes! My wife has me hooked on ER and Lost. Never miss the rugby (don't mention the Lions tour) or Formula 1.* **Listening:** *I love what I work with, so currently the Urban and Dance scene is doing it for me most of the time. However to really switch off and relax, Pink Floyd, Split Enz, Kate Bush, XTC, Alice Cooper, Daft Punk, Snoop Dogg and The Who. Pretty much anything really.* **Relaxing to:** *Along with going to Big Space (soft play area for kids and dads!) with my family, music is a massive relaxation, it's on constantly. Jet skiing most weekends, riding or driving anything motorised really, watching the telly and the PSP is working at the moment!* » *Married, 1 little dude*

Blair Jenkins

9.1.61

Queen Margaret Drive, Glasgow G12 8DG
T 0141 338 2450
E blair.jenkins@bbc.co.uk

Occupation: Head of News and Current Affairs, BBC Scotland

Education: Elgin Academy, Edinburgh University
Career highlights: Began career as a reporter with the Evening Express in Aberdeen and was Young Journalist of the Year in the Scottish Press Awards in 1977. Joined BBC News in London in 1980 and became a Producer on the Nine O'Clock News before returning to Scotland to produce Reporting Scotland in 1984. Joined Scottish Television in 1986 and was successively Controller of News and Current Affairs, Head of Regional Programmes and Director of Broadcasting. Was Chairman of BAFTA Scotland from 1998-2004. Rejoined BBC in Scotland as Head of News and Current Affairs in 2000.
Mentor: Several important influences, no single mentor.
Big break: Joining the BBC in 1980.
Big mistake: No big ones yet.

» **Reading:** *The Herald, Scotsman, Daily Record, Daily Mail, Guardian, Sunday Times, Sunday Herald, Scotland on Sunday, Sunday Mail.* **Watching:** *Lots of news.* **Listening:** *Radio Scotland.* **Relaxing to:** *Movies, walking, books, restaurants.* » *Married to Carol Sinclair, 3 children from first marriage*

Sir Simon Jenkins

10.6.43

c/o The Guardian, 119 Farringdon Road EC1R 3ER
T 020 7278 2332

Occupation: Columnist and author

Other positions: Chairman, Buildings Books Trust 1995-present.
Publications: A City at Risk (1971); Landlords of London (1974); Insight on Portugal (Editor, 1975); Newspapers: The Power and The Money (1979); The Companion Guide to Outer London (1981); The Battle for the Falklands (with Max Hastings, 1983); Images of Hampstead (1983); With Respect Ambassador (with Anne Sloman, 1985); The Market for Glory (1986); The Selling of Mary Davies and Other Writings (1993); Accountable to None (1995); England's Thousand Best Churches (1999); England's Thousand Best Houses (2003).
Awards: Journalist of the Year, 1988; British Press Awards Columnist of the Year, 1993; Honorary Doctorate, University of East Anglia, 1998; Honorary Doctorate, University of London 2000; Honorary Doctorate, City University 2001.
Education: Mill Hill School, London; St John's College, Oxford

Career highlights: Journalist, Country Life, 1965; News Editor, Times Education Supplement, 1966-68; Columnist, Evening Standard, 1968-74; Insight Editor, Sunday Times 1974-75; Editor, Evening Standard, 1976-78 (Deputy Editor 1975-76); Political Editor, the Economist, 1979-86; Columnist, Sunday Times, 1986-90 (Editor, Books Section, 1988-89; Journalist of the Year, 1988); The Times, Editor, 1990-92; Columnist, 1992-2005 (British Press Awards Columnist of the Year, 1993); Columnist, the Guardian, 2005-present; Member, Board, BR 1979-90; Member, Millennium Commission, 1994-2000; Deputy Chairman, English Heritage, 1989-90.

» *Married, 1 son, 1 stepson*

Jane Johnson

189 Shaftesbury Avenue, London WC2H 8JG
T 020 7437 6570

Occupation: Editor, Closer magazine

Other positions: BSME Editor of the Year (Weekly), 2005; Emap Awards, Editor of the Year, 2005; PPA Awards, Magazine of the Year (weekly), 2005; BSME Awards, Editor of the Year (weekly), 2004; PPA Awards, Editor of the Year, 2004; Emap Awards, Magazine of the Year, 2004; BSME Awards, Fiona Macpherson New Editor, 2003.
Education: Brasenose College, Oxford
Career highlights: Started out as a local paper reporter, later worked as Women's Editor on the Mirror and launched Closer in 2002.
Mentor: Ian Birch and Fiona McIntosh.
Big break: Launching Closer
Big mistake: There are lots! But fortunately the successes outweigh the mistakes!

» **Reading:** *Everything. All the papers, magazines and modern fiction.* **Watching:** *Strictly Come Dancing and Newsnight.* **Listening:** *Radio 4 and Five Live.* **Relaxing to:** *Pilates and horse riding.*

Paul Johnson

2.11.28

29 Newton Road, London W2 5JR
T 020 7229 3859

Occupation: Columnist and author

Publications: A History of Christianity (1976), A History of the Modern World (1983), A History of the Jews (1987), Intellectuals (1988), The Birth of the Modern World - World Society 1815-1830 (1992).
Awards: Include Yorkshire Post Book of the Year award, 1975; Francis Boyer award for services to public policy, 1979; Krug award for excellence (literature), 1982.
Education: Stonyhurst College; Magdalen College, Oxford
Career highlights: National Service, Captain, Army, 1949-51; Assistant Executive Editor, Realities, Paris, 1952-55; Editor, New Statesman, London, 1964-70 (Assistant Editor then Deputy Editor, 1955-64); Member, Board, New Statesman Publishing Co, 1964-76; contributor, The Times, Daily Telegraph, Daily Mail, Wall Street Journal, New York Times, Washington Post, and various other newspapers and periodicals, frequently involved in broadcasting and the production of TV documentaries; international lecturer to academic, government and business audiences; De Witt Wallace Professor of Communications, American Institute for Public Policy Research, Washington, 1980; Member, Royal Commission on the Press, 1974-77; Member, Cable Authority, 1984-90.

» **Relaxing to:** *Hill walking, painting.* » *Married, 4 children*

Paul Johnson

21.11.53

119 Farringdon Road, London EC1R 3ER
T 020 7239 9704
E paul.johnson@guardian.co.uk

Occupation: Deputy Editor, Guardian

Other positions: Deputy Editor (News), News Editor, Ireland Correspondent, Midlands correspondent, Guardian. Leader writer/feature writer, Western Mail.
Awards: British Press Awards: Reporter of the Year, runner up, twice member of the winning team award, received Front Page of the Year.
Education: Wellington Grammar School, Shropshire/ Cardiff University.
Mentor: Peter Cole, formerly of the Guardian and the Sunday Correspondent.
Big break: Getting into newspapers as a graduate trainee.
Big mistake: Deciding at the age of seven to support Wolverhampton Wanderers.

» **Reading:** *The weekly magazines, history and anything about Irish politics.* **Watching:** *Too much news and too much sport.* **Listening:** *Radio 4 and Radio Five Live.* **Relaxing to:** *Playing with the children, cricket, swimming, water-skiing, cooking.* » *Single, 2 children*

Richard Johnstone

20.3.77

Wallpaper*, Brettenham House, Lancaster Place, London WC2E 7TL
T 020 7322 1177
E richard_johnstone@wallpaper.com

Occupation: Publishing Director, Wallpaper Group

Other positions: Publisher, Loaded and Later, IPC Media; Publisher, Ministry, Ministry of Sound; Senior Sales, Stuff and Maxim, Dennis Publishing; Sales Exec, Smash Hits.
Publications: Wallpaper*, wallpaper.com, Loaded, upoaded, Later, Ministry, Hip Hop Connection.
Awards: Various magazine and website awards and commendations on Wallpaper* and Ministry; Highly Commended Publisher of Year at Ministry.
Education: Roehampton Institute; Surrey University
Career highlights: Recently, managing Wallpaper* back to its best and turning around the business in the process has been fantastically rewarding and a great success, as has launching editions of Wallpaper* in Russia and Thailand and taking the brand online via wallpaper.com. All have proved to be financially successful and well-received creatively, therefore satisfying my creative and commercial ambitions whilst also keeping the

bosses happy! Going further back, publishing a special Ibiza in a Box edition of Ministry that remains (to my knowledge) the best-selling dance music magazine ever, and proved to be a turning point for the magazine through taking market leadership, and also a great lesson for me; working on fantastic brands with great teams gives you the freedom and opportunity to try things. Sometimes it worked, other times it didn't, but I have always had fun trying to work it out.

Mentor: There have been too many important people at important times to mention just one.

Big break: Firstly, being giving the opportunity and freedom to publish Wallpaper* how I wanted to. Secondly, becoming Publisher of Ministry at just 25 as the popularity of dance music went through the roof.

Big mistake: Taking agency reps to Ibiza to 'enjoy' the clubbing experience and thinking I could control them!

» **Reading:** *Too many magazines to mention, ranging from Vanity Fair via Heat to Blender. Guardian, Telegraph, Sun.* **Watching:** *West Wing and Match of the Day.* **Listening:** *My iPod constantly.* **Relaxing to:** *Spend time with my family, sport and eating out.* » *Married, 1 child*

Clive Jones

10.1.49

ITN, 200 Gray's Inn Road, London WC1X 8HF
T 020 7843 8395
E clive.jones@itv.com

Occupation: Chief Executive, ITV News and Regions

Other positions: Oversee sport, broadcast operations, transmission and compliance on ITV; Chairman, Skillset; Chairman, YCTV; Chairman, Welsh Creative Industries IP Fund; Governor, NFTS; Board Member, Young Vic Theatre.

Education: Newbridge Grammar School; London School of Economics

Career highlights: Eight years in newspapers, I began life as a Yorkshire Post Trainee; 28 years in ITV spanning YTV, TV-AM, TVS, LNN, Central, Carlton and now ITV plc. I've now done most jobs in telly and I still can't believe we get paid for having so much fun.

Mentor: My friends have always saved that role.

Big break: Joining YTV from newspapers.

Big mistake: Not getting into TV straight from university.

» **Reading:** *Newspapers endlessly, novels steadily, Chandler repeatedly.* **Watching:** *Television drama, theatre, cinema, soccer, rugby and athletics.* **Listening:** *Currently the Magic Numbers.* **Relaxing to:** *With my kids.* » *Married, 6 children and 1 stepson*

Dylan Jones

19.1.65

GQ, Vogue House, Hanover Square, London W1S 1JU
T 020 7499 9080
E dylan.jones@condenast.co.uk

Occupation: Editor of British GQ, Editor-In-Chief GQ Style

Other positions: Editor-At-Large, the Sunday Times; Associate Editor, the Sunday Times Magazine; Associate Editor, the Observer Magazine; Group Editor, The Face, Arena and Arena Homme Plus; Editor, Arena; Contributing Editor, The Face; Editor, i-D.

Awards: BSME Men's Magazine Editor of the Year 1992, 2001, 2002, 2004.

Education: Chelsea School of Art; St Martin's School of Art

Career highlights: I'm most proud of the fact that while I've been editing GQ, the magazine has won more awards than any other men's magazine (16).

Mentor: Terry Jones, editor of i-D.

Big break: Terry Jones asking me to come and work at i-D when I was an unemployed photographer.

Big mistake: Taking the occasional job for money (always a mistake).

» **Reading:** *The small print.* **Watching:** *News, sport, The Sopranos, anything my kids watch.* **Listening:** *The 6,432 songs on my iPod.* **Relaxing to:** *Running.* » *Married, 2 children*

Heather Jones

1.8.74

180 Oxford Street, London W1D 1DS
T 020 7478 5208
E heather.jones@paramountcomedy.com

Occupation: Managing Director, Paramount Comedy Channels

Other positions: Director of Programming, Paramount Comedy; Channel Editor, Trouble TV; Producer/Director, Flextech TV; Producer/Director, Buena Vista Productions.

Publications: Most of our content is acquired. Currently in production with two shows that we have co-commissioned with Five.

Education: University of Wales, Aberystwyth; University of California, Irvine

Career highlights: I'm proudest of my recent activities at Paramount Comedy, including launching Paramount Comedy 2 and Paramount Comedy 1 +1, totally rebranding the channels and radically changing both channels' remits and content. Commissioning and exec-producing Cruel Summer was probably the highlight of my role at Trouble TV.

Mentor: My first producer, Miles Ross, taught me a lot about the art of production. Lisa Opie guided me through the pitfalls of broadcasting in my early days at Trouble.

Big break: Being asked to write and produce an entire kids' programme after working in TV for less than six weeks! (courtesy of Miles Ross).

Big mistake: Acquiring Young Americans for Trouble TV at great expense. The show was cancelled after seven episodes.

» **Reading:** *The Guardian, Sun, Broadcast and all the classic novels I didn't get to read when I was at school.*

Watching: *Lots of Channel Four and More4, and all good comedies on any network.* **Listening:** *Radio 2 and Radio 4 in the car. Trashy pop, funk and R 'n' B on my iPod.* **Relaxing to:** *Singing in the English Baroque Choir, dancing at any opportunity, and playing in the park with my kids.* » *Married, 2 children*

Tessa Jowell 17.9.47

House of Commons, London SW1A 0AA
T 020 7219 3000
E jowellt@parliament.uk

Occupation: Secretary of State for Culture, Media and Sport

Other positions: Minister for Women; Vice-Chairman then Chairman, Social Services Comittee, Association of Metropolitan Authorities, 1978-86; Campaigner for Mental Health Act 1985-90; Governor, National Institute for Social Work 1985-97; Visiting Fellow, Nuffield College, Oxford 1993-2002; Visiting Senior Fellow, Policy Studies Institute, 1986-90; Visiting Senior Fellow, King's Fund 1990-92.
Education: St Margaret's School, Aberdeen; University of Aberdeen; University of Edinburgh; Goldsmiths College, London
Career highlights: Child Care Officer, London Borough of Lambeth, 1969-71; Councillor, London Borough of Camden 1971-86; Psychiatric Social Worker, The Maudsley Hospital, Camberwell, 1972-74; Assistant Director, MIND, 1974-86; Director, Community Care Special Action Project Birmingham, 1987-90; Director, Joseph Rowntree Foundation Community Care Programme, 1990-92; Parliamentary Candidate, Ilford North, 1979; MP (Lab), Dulwich 1992-97, Dulwich and West Norwood 1997-present; Minister of State for Public Health and Spokesperson for Women in the Commons, 1997-99; Minister of State for Employment, 1999-2001; Secretary of State for Culture, Media and Sport 2001-present; Minister for Women 2005-present.
» *Separated, 2 children, 3 stepchildren*

Judith Judd 19.4.53

Admiral House, 66-68 East Smithfield, London E1W 1BX
T 020 7782 3280
E judith.judd@tes.co.uk

Occupation: Editor, Times Educational Supplement

Other positions: Reporter and Education Correspondent, Birmingham Post; Reporter and News Editor, Times Higher Education Supplement; General Reporter, Religious Affairs Correspondent and Education Correspondent, the Observer; Education Editor, Independent and Independent on Sunday.
Education: Bolton School; Oxford University
Career highlights: I enjoyed interviewing Robert Runcie, then Archbishop of Canterbury for the Observer. I wrote the first story about Margaret Thatcher's interference in education when she was trying to persuade Kenneth Baker that children didn't need to know anything except the three Rs. She later wrote about their rows in her autobiography. I was the first journalist to be allowed to sit in on a series of Cambridge interviews as the university tried to prove that it was being fair to state school candidates. Private school heads were outraged when they discovered what was happening. My biggest education scoop was based on a tape, sent to me anonymously, in which Chris Woodhead, then Chief Inspector of Schools, told a group of trainee teachers that an affair between a pupil and a teacher could be 'educative and experiential'.
Mentor: Peter Wilby, former Editor of the New Statesman and education journalist.
Big break: Being told by Linda Christmas when I was her secretary at the Guardian that I didn't really want to be a journalist or I'd have tried harder to get a reporting job. I started sending off applications straight away.
Big mistake: A story in the Times Higher Education Supplement - my first job in London - saying that three colleges were going to close. They weren't.
» **Reading:** *Newspapers, novels, crime fiction, biography, gardening books. Re-read George Eliot and Jane Austen.* **Watching:** *Detective dramas, history documentaries on TV, films that aren't X-rated or obscure.* **Listening:** *Anything as long as it has a tune. Especially pre-twentieth century classical music - Mozart, Haydn and Beethoven.* **Relaxing to:** *Gardening.* » *Married, 2 children*

Phill Jupitus 6.3.62

BBC 6 Music, Western House, 99 Great Portland Street, London W1A 1AA
E phill.6music@bbc.co.uk

Occupation: Presenter, BBC 6 Music Breakfast Show

Publications: Directed video for Sexuality by Billy Bragg.
Career highlights: Rose through alternative comedy ranks as Porky The Poet; worked extensively with Billy Bragg in the heyday of the late 80s Red Wedge movement; directed videos for Bragg and Kirsty MacColl; former Press Officer and MC for The Housemartins; collaborated with Madness and Ian Dury, performing Reasons To Be Cheerful with The Blockheads at the Brixton Academy in 2000; toured with The Nutty Boys; regular appearances on television and radio panel shows, including BBC Radio 4's I'm Sorry I Haven't A Clue and BBC Two/BBC Four's QI; team captain, BBC Two's Never Mind The Buzzcocks; DJ on the radio and at clubs and festivals, including presenting BBC radio's coverage of the Glastonbury Festival; currently Presenter, Breakfast Show, BBC 6 Music.
» **Watching:** *Boston Red Sox.*

K

John Kampfner 28.12.66

3rd Floor, 52 Grosvenor Gardens SW1W 0AU
T 020 7881 5676
E john@newstatesman.co.uk

Occupation: Editor, New Statesman

Other positions: New Statesman, Daily Telegraph, Reuters.
Awards: Journalist of the Year 2002, Foreign Press Association Awards.
Education: Westminster; Queen's College, Oxford
Career highlights: Reuters, 1984-89; Foreign Correspondent, Bonn, Moscow, Daily Telegraph 1989-94, Berlin, Moscow 1994-98; Financial Times Chief Political Correspondent 1998-2000; BBC R4 Today Programme Political Corespondent 2002-05; New Statesman Political Editor, May 2005, New Statesman Editor.
Mentor: Nigel Wade, Foreign Editor, Daily Telegraph, late 80s, early 90s.
Big break: Sent to Berlin to cover protests a few weeks before the Berlin Wall came down.
Big mistake: Sending an alert in 1986 from Moscow on Reuters on an extension of the Chernobyl exclusion zone, and getting it wrong - then having to kill it.

» **Reading:** *All newspapers, plus New Yorker and Atlantic Monthly.* **Watching:** *Documentaries, Desperate Housewives.* **Listening:** *Radio 4.* **Relaxing to:** *Kids, travel, tennis, Chelsea season ticket.* » *Married, 2 daughters*

Pranab Kapadia 30.3.76

Unit 7, Belvue Business Centre, Belvue Road, Northolt UB5 5QQ
T 020 8839 4027
E pranab.kapadia@zeetv.co.uk

Occupation: Head of Programming and Operations, Zee Network UK

Publications: Zee Cine Awards campaign across underground stations.
Awards: EMMA Award for Most Entertaining Asian Channel.
Education: Bombay University
Career highlights: Master of Management Studies from Bombay University majoring in finance. Eight years' experience in operations, programming and distribution areas of entertainment software creation, broadcast and reach to end consumer.

» **Reading:** *Biographies and personal profiles of eminent industrialists and sports persons.* **Watching:** *Terrestrial TV mainly Channel 4, on satellite Sky News, of course all the cricket featuring England.* **Listening:** *Radio, Magic and LBC, music, soul, jazz and ballads.* **Relaxing to:** *PS2.*
» *Married, 2 children*

Natasha Kaplinsky 7.9.72

BBC Television Centre, Wood Lane, London W12 7RJ
T 020 8743 8000
E natasha.kaplinsky@bbc.co.uk

Occupation: Presenter, BBC Six O'Clock News

Awards: Newscaster of the Year, Television and Radio Industry Awards, 2005.
Education: Hertford College, Oxford
Career highlights: Worked in the press offices of Neil Kinnock and John Smith after university; Presenter, Talk TV, with Paul Ross and Sacha B, now better known as Ali G, 1997; Anchor, evening news, Meridian, 1997-98; Host, London Today, London Tonight and Seven Days, Carlton, 1998; Co-presenter with Jeremy Thompson, Live At Five, and Presenter, Sunrise, Carlton, 1998-2000; Presenter, Sky News, 2000-02; Presenter, BBC Breakfast, 2002-05; with dancing partner Brendan Cole won first series of Strictly Come Dancing, and co-hosted second series with Bruce Forsyth, 2004; Main Anchor, Six O'Clock News, BBC, 2005-present; appearances in a number of episodes of the sitcom My Hero; Host, BBC Children In Need charity telethon, alongside Fearne Cotton and Sir Terry Wogan, 2005; Presenter, New Year Live, BBC 2006.

» *Married*

Trevor Kavanagh 20.1.47

1 Virginia Street, Wapping, London E98 1XY
T 020 7782 4121
E trevor.kavanagh@the-sun.co.uk

Occupation: Political Editor, the Sun

Other positions: Assistant Editor, the Sun
Publications: The Sun Campaigns: Keeping Britain out of the Euro and the EU Constitution.
Awards: UKPG Journalist of the Year, 1998; UKPG Political Journalist of the Year, 1998; What The Papers Say Scoop of the Year, twice; Political Studies Association Journalist of the Year, 2005; UKPG Reporter of the Year, 2005.
Education: Reigate Grammar School
Career highlights: Started work as trainee on Surrey Mirror after leaving school; worked for two years on Hereford Evening News; later with the Bristol Evening Post; lived and worked in print and broadcasting journalism in Australia; joined Sun in 1997, worked on news desk until joining industrial team; Political Editor since 1983.
Mentor: Various editors plus Ken Donlan, News Editor of the Sun.
Big break: Deciding to go into journalism, rather than the police force. Then being sent to Canberra to witness the last six months of the collapsing Whitlam government. A formative introduction to political journalism.
Big mistake: Too many to mention.

» **Reading:** *Non-fiction, biographies, political memoirs. Most recently, Bernard Lewis on Islam.* **Watching:** *I use Sky+ to record innumerable good TV programmes to watch at my leisure.* **Listening:** *Voice radio, mainly Radio 4, but for music a combination of classics and jazz.* **Relaxing to:** *Play golf, swim a couple of kilometres fairly regularly, enjoy meals with friends and spend time with my family.* » *Married, 2 sons*

Fergal Keane

7.1.65

World Affairs Unit, BBC News, Wood Lane, London W12 7RJ
T 020 8743 8000
E fergal.keane@bbc.co.uk

Occupation: Special Correspondent, BBC News

Other positions: Asia Correspondent, BBC News; Southern Africa Correspondent, BBC News; Ireland Correspondent, BBC News.
Publications: All of These People - a memoir (2005); A Stranger's Eye (2002); Letters Home (2000); Letter to Daniel (1997); Season of Blood (1995); The Bondage of Fear (1994).
Awards: Royal Television Society Reporter of the Year, 1994; Sony Radio Reporter of the Year, 1994; BAFTA, 1998; James Cameron Prize, 1995; Amnesty Human Rights Reporter of The Year,1993; Edward R Murrow Award, 1998; Bayeux Prize for War Correspondents, 1999; Foreign Press Association prize for best TV documentary; Index on Censorship Prize for Commitment to Journalistic Integrity. Honorary degrees from Queens University Belfast; University of Strathclyde; Staffordshire University; Bournemouth University; Open University.
Education: Presentation College, Cork
Career highlights: Covering the South African transition to democracy and the handover of Hong Kong to China in 1997.
Mentor: There've been a few great mentors. Brendan Halligan, Editor of my first paper, the Limerick Leader; Paul Dunne who was News Editor on the Irish Press in Dublin and David Harrison, one of the great BBC producers who turned me into a proper television reporter.
Big break: I think being given the job of BBC Southern Africa Correspondent.
Big mistake: While being trained on the BBC computer I typed in a joke story about Ian Paisley resigning from politics. It was minutes away from broadcast when I noticed the error.

» **Reading:** *Good fiction like Philip Roth and Don DeLillo, the poetry of Robert Lowell and Michael Longley, and lots of history. Tom Collins book on the Roman Republic was a recent favourite.* **Watching:** *Good documentaries mostly and a lot of children's television. My two-year-old daughter insists I sit through CBBC's morning output. I am an expert on the plots and sub-plots of Balymory.* **Listening:** *Bob Dylan, the Band, Kate Rusby, Townes Van Zandt as well as the piano works of Field and Chopin.* **Relaxing to:** *Not enough is the answer. My ideal relaxation is to head for our cottage in Ireland and walk, fish and swim with the kids.* » *Married, 2 children*

Martha Kearney

8.10.57

BBC Television Centre, Wood Lane, London W12 7RJ
T 020 8624 9800
E martha.kearney@bbc.co.uk

Occupation: Political Editor, BBC Newsnight; Presenter, Newsnight Review and Woman's Hour

Other positions: Reporter, On The Record, Panorama.
Awards: TRIC House Magazine Political Commentator of the Year, 2005; Sony Bronze Award, Radio Presenter of the Year, 2004.
Education: Watsons Edinburgh; Oxford
Career highlights: Woman's Hour special in Afghanistan; General Election campaigns; film with Jack Straw when he shook hands with Mugabe.
Mentor: Vivien Fowle at LBC Radio.
Big break: When I was at LBC Radio, the police shot a man in a yellow Mini near my house and I was able to cover because I had a tape recorder at home. That was my first chance at reporting.
Big mistake: Again at LBC I did police calls in the morning and was told they'd found human remains in a drain in Muswell Hill. I thought it was too gruesome to run at breakfast time, but the Dennis Nielsen murders did turn into a bit of a story.

» **Reading:** *Mainly modern novels, though political biographies gather dust by my bed.* **Watching:** *The West Wing, House, Bleak House, Lost, Six Feet Under. Oh, and Newsnight.* **Listening:** *At the moment Anthony and the Johnsons, Arctic Monkeys, Arcade Fire and Editors.* **Relaxing to:** *Reading, tennis, making chutney and beekeeping.* » *Married, no children*

Roland (Roly) Keating

6.8.65

BBC, Television Centre, Wood Lane, London W12 7RJ
T 020 8225 6621
E roly.keating@bbc.co.uk

Occupation: Controller, BBC Two

Education: Westminster School; Balliol College, Oxford
Career highlights: BBC General Trainee including attachments to Radio Ulster, Kaleidoscope, Everyman and Newsnight, 1983; Producer and Director, Bookmark, Omnibus, Arena and numerous music and arts programmes including Made in Ealing and Philip Roth - My True Story, 1985; founder Producer, The Late Show, 1988; Editor, The Late Show, 1990; winner BP Arts Journalism Award, Editor, Bookmark, 1992; winner BAFTA Best Documentary award and International Emmy nomination, Executive Producer of series including A History of British Art, The House Detectives and How Buildings Learn, 1993; devised and launched Heritage Magazine, One Foot in the Past for BBC2, Head of Development, Music and Arts with special responsibility for New Services BBC, 1995; seconded to BBC Broadcast to develop factual channel propositions for BBC Worldwide/ Flextech joint venture, Head of Programming UKTV, 1997; overseer all new services including BBC Choice and BBC Knowledge, Controller Digital Channels BBC, 1999; Controller, arts commissioning for all BBC TV channels, 2000; Controller, BBC4, 2001-04; Controller, BBC2, 2004-.

» *Married, 1 son, 2 daughters*

John Keeling 3.2.66

160 Great Portland Street, London W1W 5QA
T 020 7765 1999
E john.keeling@bbc.co.uk

Occupation: Controller, UKTV

Publications: UKTV Gold; UKTV Gardens; UKTV G2; UKTV Bright Ideas; UKTV Drama; UKTV History; UKTV Style; UKTV Documentary; UKTV Food; UKTV People.
Education: Downside School
Career highlights: Worked on over 100 music videos and concert films in the 1980s, followed by the launch of MTV; several years' attendance producing TV programmes from Film Festivals across Europe; being appointed Head of the Movie Channels at BSKYB at the age of 30; the launch of the Disney Channel, the launch of Film Four and then joining the BBC in 2001.
Mentor: Now, Dick Emery, CEO UKTV. Was Sam Chisolm, CEO BSkyB.
Big break: Landing a job on the launch team of MTV Europe.

» **Reading:** *Newspapers, magazines and contemporary fiction.* **Watching:** *Movies, lots of TV and more movies.* **Listening:** *As much music as I can, my iPod has revolutionised my listening.* **Relaxing to:** *Alcohol, cigarettes and laughter.*
» *Married, 3 children*

Simon Kelner 9.12.57

The Independent, Independent House, 191 Marsh Wall, London E14 9RS
T 020 7005 2000
E simon.kelner@independent.co.uk

Occupation: Editor, the Independent

Publications: To Jerusalem and Back, 1996
Awards: Honorary Fellow, University of Central Lancashire, 1999; Editor of the Year, What the Papers Say Awards, 1999, 2003; Edgar Wallace Award, London Press Club, 2000, 2004; Editor of the Year, GQ Awards, 2004; Media Achiever of the Year, Campaign Media Awards, 2004; Marketeer of the Year, Marketing Week Effectiveness Awards, 2004.
Education: Bury Grammar School; Preston Polytechnic
Career highlights: Trainee Reporter, Neath Guardian, 1976-79; Sports Reporter, Extel, 1979-80; Sports Editor, Kent Evening Post, 1980-83; Assistant Sports Editor, Observer, 1983-86; Deputy Sports Editor, Independent, 1986-89; Sports Editor, Sunday Correspondent, 1989-90; Observer, 1990-91; Editor, Observer Magazine, 1991-93; Sports Editor, Independent on Sunday, 1993-95; Night Editor, 1995, Features Editor, 1995-96, Independent; Editor, Night & Day magazine, Mail on Sunday, 1996-98.

» **Relaxing to:** *Supporting Swinton RFC.*
» *Married, 1 daughter*

Adam Kemp 3.1.66

Room 2156, White City, 201 Wood Lane, London W12 7TS
T 020 8752 6391
E alia.choudhury@bbc.co.uk

Occupation: BBC Commissioning Editor, Arts, Music, Performance and Religion

Other positions: Editorial Executive BBC One; Head of Independent Commissioning for Arts, Specialist Factual and Current Affairs.
Publications: M.Litt thesis Labour and the Bomb (1986)
Awards: International Emmy Winner; Primetime Emmy Winner; 2 BAFTA Craft Winners; 2 Wildscreen Winners; 5 RTS Craft Winners; Grierson Winner.
Education: Shrewsbury School; Southampton University; Oxford University
Career highlights: Appointed Commissioning Editor of Arts, Music, Performance and Religion in April 2005; initiated several of the BBC's landmark factual dramas including D-Day, Dunkirk, Hawking and Pompeii and executive produced over seventy BBC factual series and specials including the Emmy and BAFTA award-winning Walking with Dinosaurs specials, George Orwell: A Life in Pictures, Christopher Reeve, Killing Hitler, Elephants: Spy in the Herd, Two Fat Ladies, Century Road, Children of Crime, Country Parish, D-Day, Animal Games, Space Odyssey, The Last Tommy and The Queen's Castle.
Mentor: Peter Salmon, Michael Atwell and Sean McPhilemy.
Big break: Joining the BBC in 1994 at the birth of indie commissioning.
Big mistake: Not flying out for the England vs. Australia Rugby World Cup Final.

» **Reading:** *Non-fiction, especially biography, comics, New Yorker, New York Review of Books, all broadsheets.* **Watching:** *A great deal! All specialist and as much quality drama and entertainment as I can.* **Listening:** *Wire, Ian Brown, White Stripes, Kasabian, Faithless, Coldplay, plus the usual suspects in classical music.* **Relaxing to:** *Vets football; coaching mini rugby; going to ballet and theatre; visiting museums and galleries; Sunday walks in the woods.*
» *Married, 1 child*

Bridget Kendall 28.4.60

Room 2505, BBC TV Centre, Wood Lane, London W12 7RJ
T 020 8743 8000
E bridget.kendall@bbc.co.uk

Occupation: BBC Diplomatic Correspondent

Other positions: BBC Moscow Correspondent; BBC Washington Correspondent.
Awards: James Cameron Award, 1992; VLV award for radio, 1993; MBE, 1994.
Education: Perse Girls, Cambridge; Lady Margaret Hall, Oxford; Harvard; St Antony's, Oxford; Moscow State University
Career highlights: Been a producer and reporter in BBC news and current affairs since 1983; spent 10

years abroad for BBC in Moscow and Washington, now cover main diplomatic and foreign policy analysis stories for BBC domestic TV and radio news and current affairs programmes. Also Presenter for World Service flagship programme Talking Point-global interactive phone and email - in programme live simultaneously on radio, TV and online.
Mentor: An early mentor was John Tusa who I worked alongside on Newsnight in 1983-84 and subsequently became my boss at BBC World Service.
Big break: Being BBC Moscow Correspondent to witness end of Soviet Communism and collapse of the USSR.
Big mistake: Dipped my toe into TV presenting too early - after only six months in the business. But the on-air experience was invaluable later.

» **Reading:** *Loads of everything. Classic 19th and 20th century novels, modern fiction, historical novels, science fiction and fantasy.* **Watching:** *High-grade TV dramas from Bleak House to Doctor Who to Six Feet Under to Lost. Lots of movies (box office hits, art house and European cinema - I go about once a week).* **Listening:** *Classical music, early English, alternative folk, American country, some jazz.* **Relaxing to:** *Reading, movies, gardening, listening to music, tennis, hiking, cooking, playing with the cat.* » *Single*

Colin Kennedy 16.11.72

Mappin House, 4 Winsley Street, London W1W 8HF
T 020 7182 8781
E colin.kennedy@emap.com

Occupation: Editor-in-Chief and Acting Publisher, Empire

Other positions: Formerly Editor, Empire; Features Editor, Empire; Commissioning Editor, Smash Hits; TV & Films Editor, Smash Hits.
Publications: Empire magazine
Awards: Emap Consumer Media Editor Of The Year, 2004; BSME Entertainment Editor Of The Year, 2004; BSME Innovation Of The Year 2005.
Education: Hertford College, Oxford University
Career highlights: Joined Empire in January 2000 after graduating from Smash Hits finishing school. Became Empire Editor in September 2002 and added 20% to the ABC figure over the next three years, culminating in a record high of 205,984 posted July 2005. Significant achievements include investigating and where necessary inventing a number of technical breakthroughs that resulted in a series of award-winning covers: the first mass market holographic cover (The Matrix Reloaded, May 2003); the first lenticular 3-D cover (Spiderman 2, June 2004) and the first sound effects cover (Revenge Of The Sith, May 2005). Was made Editor-in-Chief in May 2005, taking operational control of and overseeing efforts to extend the Empire brand even further. In early 2004, took operational control of Empire Online, the UK's leading movie website, and began the complete integration of the online and offline arms, both teams and content, an innovation that was acknowledged by the Association Of Online Publishers in 2004 (Best Integration Of Media). Was appointed as Acting Publisher of Empire, along with existing duties, in January 2006.
Mentor: Emap legends past and present Ian Birch, Barry McIlheney and Mark Ellen were all big influences at different stages but it was former Empire Editor Emma Cochrane who took a chance on me, not once but twice, hiring me for Smash Hits and then inviting me to apply for Empire Features Editor.
Big break: Meeting Emma in 1996. I was a failed novelist/rock band manager at the time, for some reason she thought I had the makings of a good journalist.
Big mistake: Apart from a series of instantly regrettable covers (Pearl Harbor, Van Helsing, The Island) my biggest mistake was divorcing myself too much from the day-to-day editing of the magazine in an attempt to concentrate on brand extensions and 'blue-sky' thinking. I was persuaded that a foolproof plan was in place and that the magazine could run itself; neither proved to be true and I learned the hard way that the fundamentals need constant attention.

» **Reading:** *The Guardian and Observer religiously, The Times most of the time. I scan all the tabloids daily and check the film coverage in most papers. Websites: empireonline, bbc.co.uk, guardian unlimited, aintitcool.co.uk, the imdb, amazon.com and a constantly changing parade of new discoveries - currently I like What Would Tyler Durden Do (www.wwtdd.com) a celebrity gossip site that's like FHM meets Heat. Magazines: for work, pretty much everything, but for pleasure I like the New Yorker, Vanity Fair, Wired, New Scientist, Esquire (US) and Entertainment Weekly.* **Watching:** *All cool American drama and British comedy and occasionally vice versa. Current obsessions include Curb Your Enthusiasm, Lost, The Wire, 24, Extras, The West Wing, Weeds and Peep Show. Reality TV like America's Next Top Model and Extreme Makeover: Home Edition are not-so-guilty pleasures.* **Listening:** *Everything, although I know shamefully little about classical music. Otherwise, hugely catholic tastes take in the best of rap, jazz, pop, dance, rock plus absolutely all shades of indie grey. I have always been a sucker for literary singer-songwriters from Bob Dylan and Elvis Costello to Sufjan Stevens and Rufus Wainwright. Current favourite band is The Arcade Fire.* **Relaxing to:** *Reading, watching and listening to everything listed above takes up most of my time. I do occasionally go to the cinema outside of work but mostly go out to music and comedy gigs, the theatre when I can afford it and the odd club when I can find the energy. I try to keep fit and still play football, albeit on smaller 5-a-side pitches these days. That said I also drink too much, especially with the same college friends I have known for 14 years.* » *Single, no children*

Nigel Kennedy 2.2.56

Grayling, 1 Bedford Avenue, London WC1B 3AU
T 020 7255 1100
E zannie.abbott@uk.grayling.com

Occupation: Chief Executive, Grayling

Education: Ardingly; Trinity College, Oxford
Career highlights: Public Affairs Officer, Mobil, 1979-81; Total Oil, 1981-84; Co-ordinator (Northern Europe) Total Compagnie Française des Pétroles, Paris, 1984-86; Director, the Communication

Group plc, 1986-93; Managing Director, Grayling, 1993-99; Group Chief Executive, Grayling 1999-present.

» **Relaxing to:** *Soccer, cricket, tennis, squash, and travel.*

» *Married, 4 children*

Duncan Kenworthy 9.9.49

British Academy of Film and Television Arts, 195 Piccadilly, London W1J 9LN

T 020 7734 0022
E info@bafta.org

Occupation: Chairman, BAFTA

Other positions: Managing Director, Toledo Productions Ltd, 1995-present; Director, DNA Films Ltd, 1997-present; Chairman, Film Policy Review Group, 1997-99; Director, Film Council, 1999-2003; Chairman, Film Advisory Committee, British Council, 1999-present; Governor, National Film and Television School, 2001-present.

Awards: Outstanding Children's Programming, Emmy Award, 1983; Best Children's Programme, BAFTA, 1989; Outstanding Mini-series, Emmy Award, 1996; Best Children's Programme, Emmy Award, 1990; Best Film, and Lloyd's Bank Peoples' Choice Award, BAFTA, 1994; Best Foreign Film, César Award, 1994; Orange Audience Award, BAFTA, 2000; British Producer of the Year, London Film Critics, 1994; OBE, 1999; FRSA, 2000.

Education: Rydal School; Christ's College, Cambridge; Annenberg School; University of Pennsylvania.

Career highlights: Children's Television Workshop, New York, 1973-76; Consulting Producer, Arabic Sesame Street, Kuwait, 1977-79; Producer and Executive, Jim Henson Productions, London, 1979-95; Associate Producer, The Dark Crystal (film), 1980; Producer, Fraggle Rock, 1982 (Outstanding Children's Programming, Emmy Award, 1983); Producer, The Storyteller, 1986-88 (Best Children's Programme, BAFTA, 1989); Producer, Living with Dinosaurs, 1988 (Best Children's Programme, Emmy Award, 1990); Producer, Monster Maker, 1988; Producer, Greek Myths, 1990 (Best Children's Fictional Programme, BAFTA, 1991); Producer, Gulliver's Travels, 1996 (Outstanding Mini-series, Emmy Award, 1996); Producer, Four Weddings and a Funeral, 1994 (Best Film, and Lloyd's Bank Peoples' Choice Award), BAFTA, 1994); Best Foreign Film, César Award, 1994); Producer, Lawn Dogs, 1997; Producer, Notting Hill, 1999 (Orange Audience Award, BAFTA, 2000); Producer, The Parole Officer, 2001; Producer, Love Actually, 2003; Chairman, Film, 2002-04; Chairman, BAFTA, 2004-present.

Nicholas Kenyon 1951

BBC Radio 3, Broadcasting House, Portland Place, London W1A 1AA

T 020 7765 5887
E nicholas.kenyon@bbc.co.uk

Occupation: Controller, proms, events and TV classical music, BBC Radio 3

Other positions: Member, Board, English National Opera; Governor, Wellington School; Governor, Guildhall School of Music and Drama; Member, Board of Management, Arts and Humanities Research Board (AHRB); Trustee, Dartington Hall Trust.

Publications: The BBC Symphony Orchestra: the first fifty years, (1981); Authenticity and Early Music (editor, 1987); Viking/Penguin Opera Guide (Co-editor); Simon Rattle: from Birmingham to Berlin (2001); BBC Proms Pocket Guide to Great Symphonies (Editor, 2002); BBC Proms Pocket Guide to Great Concertos (Editor, 2002).

Awards: Royal Philharmonic Society award, Mozart Now, 1991; award-winning seasons Fairest Isle (1995) and Sounding the Century (1997-99); CBE, 2001.

Education: Balliol College, Oxford

Career highlights: Music Critic, the New Yorker, 1979-82; Music Critic, The Times, 1982; Music Editor, the Listener; Editor, Early Music, 1983-87; Chief Music Critic, the Observer, 1987-91; Artistic Adviser to the South Bank Centre's festival Mozart Now, 1991; Controller, BBC Radio 3, 1992-96; Director, BBC Proms 1996-98; Controller, BBC Proms and Millennium Programmes, 1998-2000; Controller, BBC Proms, Live Events and Television Classical Music, 2000-present.

» *Married, 4 children*

David Kermode 19.2.76

Room 1605, BBC Television Centre, London W12 7RJ

T 020 8624 9660
E david.kermode@bbc.co.uk

Occupation: Editor, BBC Breakfast

Other positions: Weekend Editor, BBC newsroom; Strand Editor, BBC News 24.

Education: Highbury College, Portsmouth

Career highlights: Editor of BBC Breakfast since November 04 - the highlights have included our election coverage, led by Declan Curry, and Natasha's presentation of the programme from Kenya for the Africa Lives season. Previous highlights include various News 24 network specials, my favourite being Concorde's Final Flight because of the picture power.

Mentor: Chris Carnegy, former MD of TLRC and founder of various radio stations. An inspirational manager of people.

Big break: Getting a job at Sky News when I had no TV experience. An editor - Steve Bennedik - took a punt on me.

Big mistake: It's usually the same one - speaking before thinking.

» **Reading:** *The papers, obviously. The Economist, Spectator,*

Condé Nast Traveller, Elle Decoration and World of Interiors. **Watching:** *BBC Breakfast, obviously. The Ten O'Clock News, Newsnight when there's a big political story. Lots of BBC News 24, some Sky News. Otherwise, Crimewatch, Grand Designs, Location Location Location, Little Britain and repeats of Frasier.* **Listening:** *Favourites are Eddie Mair on PM, Kevin Greening on Smooth fm and Scott Mills on Radio 1.* **Relaxing to:** *Socialising with friends, gardening, shopping.* » *Living with partner, no children*

Justine Kershaw

29.1.67

Five TV, 22 Long Acre, London WC2E 9LY
T 020 7550 5555
E Justine.kershaw@five.tv

Occupation: Controller of Science, Five

Other positions: Deputy Controller, Factual, Five; Company Director, Tigress Productions; Head of Science, Tigress Productions; Exec Producer, Series Producer; Producer Director (Tigress, Tiger Aspect, BBC); News Producer, Visnews.
Publications: On location for news during Reunification, Romanian Elections 1990, Kurdish Refugee Crisis, Moscow Coup, 1991; Slovenian War of Independence, 1991; Key Productions, Eyewitness, 1999, Nature Detectives, The Big Trip (BBC); In The Wild: The Galapagos with Richard Dreyfuss; Cheetahs with Holly Hunter; Pandas with Debra Winger (ITV); Operation Lemur with John Cleese (BBC); Secrets of The Dead: Riddle of The Plague Survivors (C4); Howard Goodall's Big Bangs (C4); Monkey Business (Meridian/Granada/National Geographic); Journey of Man (National Geographic/PBS); Ewan McGregor: The Bear Facts (BBC3/PBS).
Awards: BAFTA nominations, Panda Award, Mountain Films awards for Operation Lemur with John Cleese; Emmy nomination, BAFTA winner, Howard Goodall's Big Bangs; Emmy Winner, Eyewitness Guides series; Independents Awards, Ewan McGregor: The Bear Facts.
Education: St Mary's Cambridge; Brasenose College Oxford
Career highlights: 1990 Visnews (Reuters Television) Producer covering breaking stories from the Kurdish refugees to the Moscow coup and the start of the Bosnian conflict; 1992-94 I made seven films at the BBC's Natural History Unit in Bristol including Killing for a Living, narrated by Sir Anthony Hopkins, which drew an audience of 8.2 million; 1995 at Tigress Productions I produced and directed several 'In The Wild' celebrity wildlife docs with Richard Dreyfuss, Holly Hunter, Whoopi Goldberg, Ewan Macgregor and won a BAFTA nomination for Operation Lemur with John Cleese; I became a Company Director at Tigress in 1999 and set up a science unit, making films for National Geographic, PBS and Channel 4; In 2002 I moved to Channel Five as Deputy Factual Controller. My first commission was a strand called Extraordinary People, which is now in its fifth run and has become the most successful factual strand in the Channel's history; In 2004 I became the Channel's first Controller of Science and commission approximately 90 hours of programming a year. Programmes include The Royal Institution Christmas Lectures, The Big Question with Stephen Hawking, The Gadget Show, Aircrash Investigations, Real Wife Swaps, Megastructures, and returning strands Stranger Than Fiction and Extraordinary People.
Big break: Being dumped on the news-desk after my first interview and told 'if you're still here in a week you've got the job'.
Big mistake: Falling off a cliff.

» **Reading:** *Selection of newspapers or The Week to catch up. Modern novels.* **Watching:** *Comedy, satire, US Dramas, period dramas, rival programming.* **Listening:** *Radio 4 in the morning, Radio 2 in the car. Eclectic mix of CDs collected over the years.* **Relaxing to:** *Playing with one-year-old baby, watching TV, playing the piano (badly), dinner with friends, dancing, swimming.* » *Married, 1 child*

Liz Kershaw

National Magazine House, 72 Broadwick Street, London W1 9EP
T 020 7439 5279
E liz.kershaw@natmags.co.uk

Occupation: Executive Group Publishing Director, the National Magazine Company

Other positions: Group Publishing Director, Harpers and Queen, Esquire, Cosmopolitan, Country Living, Good Housekeeping, Coast.
Awards: PPA Publisher of the Year; Media Week Publishers' Publisher.
Education: Sheffield University
Career highlights: Every month when whatever titles I am involved with sell more advertising, more copies, or make more money than they have before is a career highlight.
Mentor: Sally O'Sullivan
Big break: Joining the National Magazine Company.
Big mistake: Too hideous to think about.

» **Reading:** *Apart from huge quantities of magazines, most of the Sunday papers.* **Watching:** *Sport, when time permits.* **Listening:** *Radio 4.* **Relaxing to:** *Shooting, gardening, going on 'adventures'.* » *Single, 1 child*

Simon Kippin

29.3.55

6-8 Old Bond Street, London W1S 4PH
T 020 7152 3526
E skippin@condenast.co.uk

Occupation: Publishing Director, Glamour Magazine

Other positions: Publisher, Company, Cosmopolitan and Good Housekeeping.
Publications: Glamour Magazine
Awards: PPA Publisher of the Year 2002.
Education: Hall Mead School, Upminster
Career highlights: My career in advertising began at J Walter Thompson as Media Planner/Buyer on the Unilever Accounts, and continued in JWT in Toronto Canada as Media Supervisor; my media owner career began at IPC working firstly on the young women's titles in space sales, culminating in a group head position on the big women's weekly titles. The following 16 years were spent

at The National Magazine Company, becoming Publisher of Company Magazine, followed by eight years as Publisher of Cosmopolitan with promotion in due course to the board of the company; I then became Publishing Director of Good Housekeeping for two years before leaving to launch Glamour for the Condé Nast Company in 2000. Glamour is really the zenith for me, number one in the UK and Europe within a year of its launch, it has changed the face of monthly magazine publishing!

Mentor: Nicholas Coleridge, the MD of Condé Nast UK, and my publishing colleagues past and present.

Big break: The opportunity of launching Glamour, and working for Condé Nast.

Big mistake: So many mistakes, I cannot list them.

» **Reading:** *Almost everything I can get hold of from the Innovations catalogue to Dickens novels.* **Watching:** *Coronation Street whenever I can, and great drama like Bleak House.* **Listening:** *Radio 4, LBC (Nick Ferrari), Classic FM.* **Relaxing to:** *Fly fishing as often as I can.* » *Married, 2 children*

Jenny Lacey

22.7.53

PO Box 194, Bristol BS99 7QT

T 01179 741111

E jenny.lacey@bbc.co.uk

Occupation: Managing Editor, BBC Radio Bristol and Somerset Sound

Other positions: Presenter, LBC; Education Correspondent, BBC in the West; Managing Editor, BBC Radio Gloucestershire.

Awards: Variety Club Independent Radio Personality of the Year 1982.

Career highlights: Started in BBC Schools Radio as a Broadcast Assistant and then moved to BBC Radio London. Became a presenter and joined LBC to present late night phone-ins in 1979. Also presented Weekend am for two years. Came to Bristol in 1988 to work for GWR and moved back to the BBC to present the morning show for BBC Radio Bristol in 1990. Became BBC Education Correspondent for television and radio for the West Country and then went into management at BBC Radio Gloucestershire. Have managed BBC Radio Bristol for around eight years.

Mentor: Ron Onions at LBC, John Shearer at the BBC.

Big break: Being asked to present late night phone-ins at LBC in 1979 ... possibly the first regular woman phone-in host.

Big mistake: Mistaking our cricket correspondent for a caller on air and quizzing him about Elvis for five minutes as he got more and more perplexed. And lots of others!

» **Reading:** *The Guardian, the Observer.* **Watching:** *The West Wing.* **Listening:** *BBC Radio Bristol, BBC Radio 5 Live, BBC Radio 2.* **Relaxing to:** *Swimming and gardening.* » *Married, 4 children*

Stephen Lambert

23.3.63

RDF Media Group plc, Gloucester Building, Kensington Village, Avonmore Road, London W14 8RF

T 020 7013 4275

E stephen.lambert@rdfmedia.com

Occupation: Chief Creative Officer, RDF Media Group plc

Other positions: Director of Programmes, RDF Media; Editor, Real Life, ITV; Editor, Modern Times, BBC2; Executive Producer, BBC Documentaries; Producer/Director, BBC Documentaries.

Publications: Wife Swap, Faking It, Shipwrecked, Perfect Match, The Power of Nightmares and The Century of the Self, Real Life, Modern Times, Inside Story, 40 Minutes.

Awards: 4 BAFTAs, 2 Rose D'Or, International Emmy, Monte Carlo Golden Nymph, 3 RTS, 7 Broadcast Awards, 3 Indie, 3 BPG, NTA.
Education: University of East Anglia, Norwich; Nuffield College, Oxford
Career highlights: 16 years in the BBC Documentaries Department going anywhere in the world that was interesting. Since 1998, being part of RDF Media, possibly the most exciting place to be in independent television production.
Mentor: Eddie Mirzoeff and Paul Hamann.
Big break: When I was a 21-year-old postgraduate student, being asked by Anthony Smith, then director of the BFI, to write a book on the origins of Channel 4 to coincide with the launch of the channel in 1982.
Big mistake: Being too honest filling in questionnaires.

» **Reading:** *Everything I can find time to read, but also having a wife who actually reads everything and tells me what I must read.* **Watching:** *Everything, or at least, try to make it seem like I've watched everything.* **Listening:** *Radio 4 when it's intelligent, Radio 3 or Classic FM when they play something I like.* **Relaxing to:** *Walk, talk, sleep.* » *Married, 1 daughter, 1 son*

Jeremy Langmead

4.11.69

Wallpaper*, Brettenham House, Ground Floor, Lancaster Place, London WC2E 7TL
T 020 7322 1591
E contact@wallpaper.com

Occupation: Editor-in-chief, Wallpaper* magazine

Other positions: Editor of the Life&Style section, Evening Standard; Editor of Nova magazine; Editor of Sunday Times Style magazine.
Awards: Shortlisted for BSME Lifestyle Magazine Editor, 2004; PPA Consumer Lifestyle Magazine of the Year, 2004; BSME Editor's Editor of the Year, 2005.
Education: Central Saint Martin's School of Art
Career highlights: My ambition, since college, had been to edit the Style section at the Sunday Times. When that came to pass, along with the chance to relaunch it as a glossy(ish) magazine, I was thrilled. I spent six successful and very happy years there.
Mentor: I have had many mentors. Liz Jones gave me my first job in journalism, at Mirabella magazine, for which I'll always be grateful; Alison McDonald, my boss when I first joined the Sunday Times Style section, who taught me to always check the facts and question the statements in every piece of copy, whoever the writer; John Witherow, the Editor of the Sunday Times, who gave me the Style Editor's job when Alison left. He took a chance on me and I will always appreciate that. And my ex-wife, India Knight, who has always been extraordinarily supportive.
Big break: Answering the phone in the college secretary's office when I was about to graduate from Central Saint Martins and being asked if I could recommend a student to join Mirabella magazine as a junior sub-editor. I recommended myself even though I didn't know what a sub-editor was. I got the job and soon learnt.
Big mistake: Agreeing to edit Nova magazine. It was only a few days after I joined that I realised what a mess the business was in. But it taught me to do my homework properly before signing on the dotted line the next time.

» **Reading:** *Books. Lots of them. My family all reads at least one or two novels a week and I have to try and keep up.* **Watching:** *I go to the theatre and the cinema regularly. And watch a reasonable amount of TV. If you work in the media, it's very important that you are tuned into all aspects of it. They all feed off each other.* **Listening:** *I'm afraid I'm a Radio 4 fan: the Today Programme, Front Row, Midweek, Desert Island Discs, Any Questions and, of course, The Archers.* **Relaxing to:** *Reading, radio, CDs, hanging out with my kids and planning how I'll decorate my next apartment.*
» *Single, 2 children*

Richard Last

20.7.31

Tiverton, The Ridge, Woking, Surrey GU22 7EQ
T 01483 764 895

Occupation: Retired; freelance contributions to various publications

Other positions: Membership Secretary, Broadcasting Press Guild.
Publications: Provincial newspapers, 1949-59; sang with former Carl Rosa Opera Company, 1954-55; Daily Herald, 1959-64; IPC Sun, Reporter, Music Critic, 1964-69; Daily Telegraph, Feature writer, deputy TV critic, Deputy TV Critic and Broadcasting Correspondent, 1970-86; Chief TV Critic, 1986-92.
Awards: Rose Bowl (supreme vocal trophy), Cheltenham Competitive festival, 1956.
Education: St. George's College, Weybridge, Surrey
Career highlights: Hearing and reviewing the first four performances in Coventry and London of Benjamin Britten's War Requiem in 1962, the outstanding musical event of my adult lifetime; covering the Edinburgh International Festival, 1961-64, and music festivals at Bath, Aldeburgh, and Bayreuth; covering 23 Golden Rose of Montreux Festivals and seven Prix Italia, including one in Capri; regular participation in conferences organised by the Royal Television Society from 1972 onwards; contributing around 2,700 television reviews to the Daily Telegraph, 1970-92; helping to found the Broadcasting Press Guild in 1974 and playing a leading role in setting up critic's viewings at BAFTA; Chairman, BPG, 1984-85; organiser of the annual BPG Television and Radio Awards, 1992-2005; being invited to defend the role of television in contemporary society at an Oxford Union debate; in-depth interviews with (among many others) Russian cellist Mstislav Rostropovich, Wagnerian bass Hans Hotter, and Colin Davis.
Mentor: Peter Black, TV critic, Daily Mail, 1953-74.
Big break: Standing in for Nancy Banks-Smith, then star TV reviewer for the IPC Sun, which led to my job on the Daily Telegraph.
Big mistake: Not trying hard enough to develop a radio career alongside my Fleet Street career.

» **Reading:** *Daily Telegraph, the Week, novels, biographies, history.* **Watching:** *University Challenge, Channel 4 News, The Daily Politics, Newsnight, Foyle's War, The Bill, repeats* *of vintage comedy, any promising documentary not smothered in background music.* **Listening:** *Today and other news sequences, The Archers, Counterpoint, The Week in Westminster, classic serials and occasional one-off drama on Radio 4; the Proms (most nights) on Radio 3, plus Classic FM and the occasional French station (in the forlorn hope of understanding it).* **Relaxing to:** *Listening to Bruckner, playing patience on the computer, re-reading favourite authors (Trollope, P G Wodehouse, Conan Doyle, David Lodge), eating at favourite pubs, playing with grandchildren.* ›› *Married, 5 daughters, 8 grandchildren*

Jason Lawes

2.5.74

60 Sloane Avenue, London SW3 3XB
T 020 7584 5033
E jason.lawes@loweworldwide.com

Occupation: Creative Head, Lowe and Partners

Other positions: Captain of Bedfont FC.
Publications: Tesco, Every Little Helps campaign; Stella Artois (Pilot); HSBC (Hole in One).
Awards: 3 D&AD pencils; 2 gold and 4 silver Campaign Press; 2 Creative Circle gold; Eurobest gold; Cannes Lion gold; 3 BTAA silver awards, plus a few other bits and pieces.
Education: West Thames Polytechnic
Career highlights: My most satisfying acheivement has, up to now, been to develop a good relationship with Tesco enabling us to produce work to a high creative standard which has had a positive impact on their business. At the same time proving that good work can come from anywhere, even the retail sector! I suppose the other has to be finally getting my first job in a proper creative department and so resigning my post as dispatch boy.
Mentor: Frank Lowe and Paul Weinberger.
Big break: Frank Lowe once came to me and said 'I've got a little job for you, can you see if you can come up with a new campaign for Tesco.'

›› **Reading:** *Autobiographies mostly, and football magazines.* **Watching:** *The Simpsons* **Listening:** *At the moment Kaiser Chiefs, but more often than not Radiohead.* **Relaxing to:** *Sailing with my son, playing Sunday morning football (keeps me sane).* ›› *Single, 3 children*

Mark Lawson

11.4.62

c/o The Guardian, 119 Farringdon Road EC1R 3ER
T 020 7239 9959

Occupation: Journalist, broadcaster and author

Publications: Bloody Margaret, 1991; The Battle for Room Service, 1993; Idlewild, 1995; John Keane, 1995; Going Out Live, 2001; Enough Is Enough, 2005.
Awards: British Press Award, 1987; TV Critic of the Year, 1989 and 1990.
Education: St Columba's College, St Albans; University College, London
Career highlights: Junior Reporter and TV Critic, The Universe, 1984-85; TV Previewer, Sunday Times, 1985-86; TV critic, Parliamentary sketchwriter, feature writer, columnist, The Independent/Independent on Sunday (1986-1995); Columnist, the Guardian, 1995-present; Presenter for radio and TV, 1990-present, including Late Review, Newsnight Review (BBC2) (1993-2005); Front Row (Radio 4), 1998-present; Never Ending Stories (BBC2); Mark Lawson Talks To... (BBC4) since 2004; Scriptwriter for radio and TV, including The Vision Thing (BBC2), 1993; The Man Who Had 10,000 Women, 2002; St Graham and St Evelyn, Pray for Us, 2003 (Radio 4); Absolute Power (BBC2), 2003-05; The Third Soldier Holds His Thighs, 2005; London, this is Washington (2006).

›› **Watching:** *Theatre.* **Relaxing to:** *Cricket, tennis, wine, reading.* ›› *Married, 3 children*

Nigella Lawson

6.1.60

c/o Jacquie Drewe, Curtis Brown, Haymarket House, 28-29 Haymarket, London SW1Y 4SP
T 020 7360 7384

Occupation: Journalist and broadcaster

Publications: How to Eat (1998); How to be a Domestic Goddess (2000); Nigella Bites (2001); Forever Summer (2002); Feast (2004).
Awards: Nigella Bites, Television Broadcast of the Year, Guild of Food Writers Awards, 2001; Forever Summer 2002, Author of the Year, British Book Awards, 2001.
Education: Godolphin and Latymer Schools; Lady Margaret Hall, Oxford
Career highlights: Editor, Quartet Books, 1982-84; Sunday Times, Assistant on Arts and Review section, 1984-86; Deputy Literary Editor, 1986-88; Arts Writer, 1988-89; Restaurant Columnist, the Spectator, 1985-96; Columnist, Evening Standard, 1989-94; The Times, 1995-98; the Observer, 1998-2001; Food Writer, Vogue 1996-2002; Channel 4 television, Nigella Bites, 2000 and 2001.

›› *Married, 2 children*

Norman Lebrecht

11.7.1948

020 7938 6000
norman.lebrecht@standard.co.uk

Occupation: Assistant Editor, Evening Standard

Other positions: Presenter lebrecht.live, BBC Radio 3
Awards: Whitbread Award, First Novel, 2002 for The Song of Names.
Publications: 11 books including: Mahler Remembered (1987); The Maestro Myth (1991); When the Music Stops (1996); Covent Garden: The Untold Story (2000); The Complete Companion to 20th Century Music (2000); The Song of Names (2001)
Education: Hasmonean, London; Bar-Ilan, Israel
Career highlights: After spending my 20s in radio and television news, I gravitated into writing about the arts for the Sunday Times, graduated to a column on the Daily Telegraph and was hired by Veronica Wadley in 2002 to reconstruct the arts section of the Evening Standard, where I also write a weekly column. Broadcasting has always been an important strand of my work and I am never without two books on the go. My principal themes have been the corruption and decline of classical music; the volatile relationship between the state

and the arts; the importance of art in education and national identity.
Mentor: The late composer Berthold Goldschmidt in terms of what the Germans call 'Bildung' - general cultural perspective. Don Berry at the Sunday Times. The late Andre Deutsch in publishing.
Big break: First book contract, 1979.
Big mistake: Wait for the memoirs.

» **Reading:** *Everything I can lay hands on in four languages - fiction, memoirs, history, musicology.* **Watching:** *Ever-worsening television, soaps for structural discipline, occasional BBC drama.* **Listening:** *Lots of music, classical and contemporary, whatever my youngest daughter is into on her i-pod.* **Relaxing to:** *With family and friends, around a table.* » *Married 1977, to Elbie. Three daughters*

Ana Leddy

1.6.57

RTÉ, Donnybrook, Dublin 4, Ireland
T 0035 31 208 3111
E ana.leddy@rte.ie

Occupation: Head of RTÉ Radio 1, Ireland

Other positions: Coffee-maker and Freelance, BBC Radio Sheffield, 1979-81; Assistant Producer, Radio Aire, Leeds (ILR), 1981-83; Reporter, BBC Radio Stoke, 1983-89; Producer, BBC Radio 4 Woman's Hour and You and Yours, 1989-95; Senior Producer, BBC Radio 4 medium wave, 1995-98; Managing Editor, BBC Radio Foyle, 1998-2006.
Awards: 1999-2005, 13 Sony Radio Award nominations; Station of the Year Award, 2005; Station of the Year Award, 2004; Station of the Year Award, 2001; Station of the Year Award, 2000; Breakfast News and Talk Award, 2000.
Education: St. Louis Convent, Monaghan, Ireland; Trinity College Dublin, Ireland
Career highlights: An instant passion for radio and hard work got me from making the coffee in BBC Radio Sheffield into freelancing. The adrenalin rush of being a reporter on the ground being first with the story back in my days at Radio Stoke, then the buzz of getting into BBC Radio 4 and learning a whole new level of production and creative deconstruction and working with brilliant people and legendary broadcasters like Vincent Hanna, then going to BBC Radio Foyle and having a whole radio station to produce was a dream come true; we got 13 Sony nominations between 1999 and 2005 with an unbroken run of seven station of the year nominations; my new post as Head of RTÉ Radio 1 is a whole new adventure and my biggest challenge.

» **Reading:** *Republic of Ireland, Northern Ireland and England newspapers, fiction.* **Watching:** *News and current affairs although I get most of this from the radio, which is my first love. Also I really enjoy documentaries, movies, drama and comedy and soaps when my daughter is home. Currently addicted to CSI Miami and always the Simpsons.* » *Divorced, 3 children*

Laurence Lee

13.11.67

T 07850 920326
E laurencelee99@hotmail.com

Occupation: Moscow Correspondent, Sky News

Awards: Russian Media Union TV award winner, 2004; part of Sky News BAFTA and RTS winning entries on September 11th.
Education: Coventry School; Birmingham University
Career highlights: 8 years in BBC Radio and TV followed by Sky News from 1998. Covered home and international events, including two years on and off in the Middle East, before becoming Moscow Correspondent in 2003.
Mentor: My wife
Big break: Being in the right place at the right time during the May Day riots one year. Almost got run over by a police horse.
Big mistake: Thinking that TV news is more about what you say than what you look like.

» **Reading:** *Guardian, Indy, Economist, the Onion website.* **Watching:** *Sky, Shameless, Channel Four News.* **Listening:** *Turin Brakes, Belle and Sebastian.* **Relaxing to:** *In the pub, or cooking.* » *Married, 1 child*

Peter Levelle

5.5.45

34 Murray Road, London SW19 4PE
T 020 8241 9006
E levelle@blueyonder.co.uk

Occupation: Director, BTAA

Other positions: Governor, King's College School, Wimbledon.
Publications: Barclays Bank, Benson & Hedges, Cinzano Bianco, Condor Tobacco, Economist, EMI, Fiat, Hamlet Cigars, Texaco, Olympus Cameras, Parker Pens, Shredded Wheat, Vauxhall, Whitbread.
Awards: BTAA (Director): 2 gold, 3 silver, 5 bronze; Cannes (Director): 3 gold, 1 silver, 1 bronze; Eurobest: 1 gold; BTAA (Producer): 5 gold, 6 silver, 7 bronze; D&ADA (Producer): 3 gold, 5 silver.
Education: Queen Elizabeth's School, Crediton; Queen Mary College, London
Career highlights: The traditional mid-60s launching pad of the postroom (Charles Hobson & Grey's) led to a first career as an advertising film producer. Rapid progress saw launch of first production company, Picture Palace Productions, with Malcolm Craddock and John Crome in 1972. Collett Dickenson Pearce, however, was London's creative powerhouse so Frank Lowe and John Salmon's invitation to join as Head of TV in 1977 proved irresistible. The agency only worked with the very best directors (Alan Parker, Hugh Hudson, Ridley and Tony Scott, Bob Brooks) and over the next five years produced most of the classic commercials that defined what is now acknowledged as the golden period of British advertising. A second career as a director started with the launch of Beechurst Film Productions in 1982. The company (colleagues included Michael Apted and Joe Sedelmaier) was one of only a handful of London outfits to open a successful

outpost in the USA and forged co-production links in Paris, Milan and Rome. A key figure in the creation of the British Television Advertising Awards in 1976, retired from active film-making to chair the organisation 2000-03.
Mentor: Frank Lowe, Alan Parker and Alan Marshall.
Big break: Being asked by John Salmon in 1980 to switch from producer to director on a low-budget CDP Daily Express commercial featuring Brian Clough.
Big mistake: Turning down the Oxo Katie campaign.
» **Reading:** *The Independent, the Week, Spectator, National Geographic, Patrick O'Brian, John Le Carré, Martin Cruz Smith, biographies in general, Hello! (in the hairdresser's).* **Watching:** *Movies, TV documentaries and news, the Simpsons.* **Listening:** *Radio 4.* **Relaxing to:** *Play golf.*
» *Married to Liz, 2 sons, James and Michael*

Jon Leyne 1.3.62

World Affairs Unit, BBC Television Centre, Wood Lane, London
T 020 8743 8000
E jon.leyne@bbc.co.uk

Occupation: BBC Amman Correspondent

Other positions: BBC State Deputy Correspondent; BBC World Affairs Correspondent in London; BBC United Nations Correspondent; BBC Rowing Correspondent; Reporter, Radio Ulster; Reporter, Cambridge Evening News; Reporter, The Yorkshire Evening Press.
Awards: Shared in a Sony award for 1992 Barcelona Olympics Coverage.
Education: Winchester College; Exeter University; Oriel College, Oxford
Big break: I tend to be in the right place when bad things happen.
Big mistake: On my first radio job they faded me off air when I started burbling.
» **Reading:** *The Herald Tribune, cheap thrillers, Saki.* **Watching:** *DVDs of Father Ted.* **Listening:** *Chopin, Beethoven, Stravinsky, Debussy, Ravel, Wanda Landowska, Alfred Cortot.* **Relaxing to:** *Marathon running, anything to do with boats, playing the piano and the bassoon, kite flying.*
» *Married, 2 stepchildren*

David Liddiment 20.9.52

The Old Vic, The Cut, London SE1 8NB
T 020 7928 2651
E david.liddiment@oldvictheatre.com

Occupation: Creative Director, All3Media Ltd

Other positions: Producer, Old Vic Theatre
Awards: RTS Gold Medal.
Education: Huddersfield New College; Liverpool University
Career highlights: Researcher, Producer, Director, Granada TV; Executive Producer, Coronation Street, 1987-92; Director of Programmes, Granada TV; Head of Entertainment, BBC TV; Director of Programmes, LWT; Director of Programmes, ITV; Producer, The Old Vic Theatre Company; Columnist, MediaGuardian.
Mentor: Mike Scott and Joyce Wooler.
Big break: Taking over production of Albion Market.
Big mistake: Turning down Big Brother.
» **Reading:** *Anything by Carol Ann Duffy.* **Watching:** *Coronation Street.* **Listening:** *Joni Mitchell.* **Relaxing to:** *Listening to Joni Mitchell.* » *Partner, 1 child*

Rod Liddle 1.4.60

c/o Noel Gay, 19 Denmark Street, London WC2H 8NA
T 020 7836 3941
E rliddlemonkey@hotmail.com

Occupation: Journalist and author

Other positions: Associate Editor, the Spectator
Publications: Columnist, Sunday Times; contributor to Arena and GQ magazines; television work includes Evangelism, Channel 4, 2005, Authored Presenter; Infidelity, Sky, 2005, Authored Presenter; Immigration is a Time Bomb, Channel 4, 2005, Presenter; Some Of My Best Friends Are..., Lion Television/Channel 4, 2004, Presenter; Call My Bluff, BBC, 2003-04, Team Captain; Question Time, BBC, 2004, Regular Contributor; Weekend, with Rod Liddle and Kate Silverton, BBC2, 2003, Presenter.
Awards: As Editor of the Today Programme, Sony Silver, 2002; Sony Bronze, 2003; Amnesty International Media Award, 2003.
Education: Laurence Jackson Comprehensive School; Leeds University; London School of Economics
Career highlights: Trainee, South Wales Echo; Speechwriter/Researcher, Labour Party,1983-87; joined BBC as Trainee Producer; Editor, the Today Programme, 1997-2002.
» *Divorced, 2 children*

Jane Lighting 22.12.56

Channel Five Broadcasting, 22 Long Acre WC2E 9LY
T 020 7550 5555
E jane.lighting@five.tv

Occupation: Chief Executive Officer, Channel Five Broadcasting Ltd

Other positions: Member, Executive Committee, Edinburgh International Television Festival; Governor, National Film and Television School, 2001-present; Founder and Chairman, British Television Distributors Association, 1995-96; former Member, Exports Group, Creative Industries Taskforce.
Awards: Business Woman of the Year, Women in Film and Television Awards, 2000.
Career highlights: Began with distribution business Crown Cassette Communications, 1976; Video Arts Television, becoming Managing Director, 1987-95; Founder and Managing Director, Minotaur International, 1995-99; Managing Director, Broadcast and Television, Flextech, 1999-2002; CEO, Flextech, 2002-03; Chief Executive, Five Television, 2003-present.
» **Relaxing to:** *Painting, escaping to the country.*

Matthew Line
22.4.58

SHE magazine, National Magazines,
72 Broadwick Street, London W1F 9EP

T 020 7312 3757
E matthew.line@natmags.co.uk

Occupation: Former Editor, SHE magazine

Other positions: CEO, The Prince's Foundation; Editor, Homes & Gardens; Group Editor, Homes Interest Titles, Redwood Publishing.
Publications: Created H&G Classic Design Awards in association with The Prince of Wales and V&A Museum, 1999; set up first international conference and exhibition of the New Urbanism in UK, 2002.
Awards: PPA/BSME
Education: Chiswick School; Exeter University
Career highlights: Started out as an actor and began freelance writing as a second string in 1987, progressing to full time in 1990; Editor of a county magazine for Oxfordshire, 1992 and left to edit a number of customer magazines for Redwood Publishing, 1993; won PPA award for best customer magazine four years running; joined IPC Media in 1997 as Editor of Homes & Gardens and won many awards for the contemporary reinvention of the title, doubling its revenue, and (from the BSME) for creating the Homes & Gardens Classic Design Awards with V&A Museum; left to join the The Prince's Foundation as Chief Executive in 2002. Developed the organisation creating separate charities in the fields of art, design, architecture and urbanism and long-term strategies for development. Set up pan-UK building advisory team and postgraduate education programme in urbanism. In 2003 launched first international conference and exhibition of the New Urbanism with the Office of the Deputy Prime Minister and HRH Prince of Wales; invited by National Magazines to develop a new women's magazine which assumed the established title SHE and launched in November 2005.
Mentor: Felicity Green
Big break: Walking in to Carlton magazines as an out-of-work actor to do a day's temporary dogsbody work and coming out with my first commission.
Big mistake: Far too many to mention, though I sometimes regret turning down some very lucrative senior editorial positions in the US when offered.

» *Married, 2 children*

Alan Little

BBC Newsgathering, Television Centre, Wood Lane, London W12 7RJ

T 020 8743 8000
E allan.little@bbc.co.uk

Occupation: BBC Correspondent

Publications: Death of Yugoslavia (with L Silber, Penguin, 1995).
Awards: Sony Reporter of the Year; Amnesty International Award; Grierson TV Documentary award; Bayeux War Correspondent of the Year.
Education: University of Edinburgh
Career highlights: BBC Radio and Television Reporter since 1987; reported Gulf War from Baghdad in 1991, 4 years in former Yugoslavia, then postings in Africa (twice), Moscow and Paris; have also presented Radio 4 Today programme, PM and The World Tonight, and Newsnight on BBC2.

» **Reading:** *Fiction, especially 20th century American and lots of Scottish. Poetry, George McKay Brown. History, 17th and 18th century British and European.* **Watching:** *Been living abroad so out of touch with UK TV. But BBC World is excellent, as is CNN International. Also the History Channel and BBC documentaries on DVD. Some American comedy.* **Listening:** *French radio news, Radio 4 on longwave, BBC World Service. And music - love the great twentieth century Russian composers.* **Relaxing to:** *Long walks, and long hot baths with a good book.*

Howard Litton

Nickelodeon, 15–18 Rathbone Place, London W1T 1HU

T 020 7462 1000
E howard.litton @nickelodeon.co.uk

Occupation: Senior Vice-President, General Manager, Director of Channels - Nickelodeon UK

Other positions: Member, BAFTA Children's Committee.
Publications: Writer and producer, The Grimleys (BBC), 1997.
Awards: BAFTA, Nick News, 1999
Career highlights: Head of Business Affairs, Executive Producer of Magic Adventures of Mumfie, Britt Allcroft; joined Nickelodeon in 1995 as Acquisitions Manager, responsible for acquisitions of Sabrina the Teenage Witch, Sister Sister and Teletubbies; currently oversee programming and creative strategies for Nickelodeon, Nick Jr and Nicktoons; played key role in launches of Nicktoons and Nick Jr; involved in a number of BAFTA Award-winning productions, including Nick News; recent creative and ratings successes include the re-facing of Nicktoons, the launch of weekday breakfast show, The Crunch, and the development of Nickelodeon's pre-school channel Nick Jr.

John Lloyd
15.4.46

Financial Times, One Southwark Bridge, London SE1 9HL

T 020 7873 3000
E rakhee.shah@ft.com

Occupation: Editor, Financial Times magazine

Other positions: Senior Associate Fellow, Kennedy School, Harvard, 1995; Senior Associate Member, St Antony's College, Oxford, 1996-99.
Publications: (With Ian Benson) The Politics of Industrial Change, 1982; (with Martin Adeney) The Miners' Strike: loss without limit, 1986; (with Charles Leadbeater) In Search of Work, 1987; (contributor) Counterblasts, 1989; Rebirth of a Nation: an anatomy of Russia, 1998; Re-engaging Russia, 2000; The Protest Ethic, 2001.

Awards: Journalist of the Year, Granada Awards, 1984; Specialist Writer of the Year, IPC Awards, 1985; Rio Tinto David Watt Memorial Prize, 1997.
Education: Waid Comprehensive School; Edinburgh University
Career highlights: Editor, Time Out, 1972-73; Reporter, London Programme, 1974-76; Producer, Weekend World, 1976-77; Industrial Reporter, Labour Correspondent, Industrial and Labour Editor, Financial Times, 1977-86; Editor, New Statesman, 1986-87; re-joined Financial Times, 1987; European Editor, 1987-90; Moscow Correspondent, 1991-95; Associate Editor, New Statesman and Society, subsequently New Statesman, 1996-2003; Columnist, The Times, 1997-98. Director: East-West Institute, New York, 1997-present; Foreign Policy Centre, 1999-present.

» **Listening:** *Opera.* **Relaxing to:** *Hill walking.*
» *Divorced, 1 child*

Joan Lofts

Occupation: Director of Television, Contender Entertainment Group

Other positions: Chair, Cardiff International Festival; Member, Junior BAFTA Comittee.
Career highlights: Film Librarian, ITN, 1964-69; Researcher and Associate Producer, Thames TV, 1969-74; Social Worker, Kent County Council, 1975-85; Animation/Acquisition Executive, TVS, 1985-90; Deputy Head of Acquisitions and Development, Children's Department, BBC, 1990-93; Head of Acquisition and Development, TCC, 1993-94; Head of Programming, TCC, 1994-96; Director of Programming, TCC, 1996-97; Consultant, Polygram Visual Programming, 1997-98; Director of Programmes and Acquisitions, Disney Channel UK, 1998-99; Head of TV, Contender Entertainments Group, 1999-present.

Martin Long 22.7.71

Golley Slater Public Relations, Wharton Place, Wharton Street, Cardiff CF10 1GS
T 029 2038 8621
E mlong@golleyslater.co.uk

Occupation: Managing Director, Golley Slater Public Relations

Other positions: Board Member, Drive; External Examiner, Postgraduate Diploma in Public & Media Relations, Cardiff University.
Education: Rugby School; Kings College, London; Cardiff University

» *Married, 3 children*

Mark Longhurst 7.5.57

Sky News, 6 Centaurs Business Park, Grant Way, Isleworth, Middlesex TW7 5QD
T 020 7585 4451
E mark.longhurst@bskyb.com

Occupation: Presenter, Sky News

Other positions: Formerly TV am, BBC World, ITN, BBC South, Channel Four Daily.
Awards: RTS Home News nomination; RTS News Channel of the Year.
Education: Midhurst Grammar School; University of London
Career highlights: Scooping Kate Adie on one of my first foreign assignments for TV am. We were all chasing a murder suspect across France, and it was believed he was trying to join the Foreign Legion down in Marseille. I was in the next bedroom to hers at a hotel in Lyon and I can still remember her cameraman banging on her door to get moving after we had filed footage of the arrest some five hours earlier. Delicious. Also seven trips to Berlin before, during and after the wall came down and managing to witness one of those 'first draft of history' moments. Apologies though to the Trabant factory in Zwickau for driving one of their appalling cars into the bike sheds when a Jeremy Clarkson style piece to camera went horribly wrong.
Mentor: Ivan Howlett, News Editor at BBC Radio Sussex who could edit quarter-inch tape with a surgeon's skill. He also taught me how to broadcast rather than just report.
Big break: Getting into Thames Television just at the end of the Golden Years. I can still remember ordering crème brulée at the staff restaurant on my first day. I had been used to a 15p luncheon voucher at the Beeb.
Big mistake: To stop writing once I had got into television ... and selling my LWT shares before Greg Dyke did.

» **Reading:** *Anything that's lying about or whatever looks interesting at my local second-hand bookshop. I am also a closet classic car enthusiast so I like Car Porn.* **Watching:** *Everything, including the junk. I am curiously addicted to re-runs of Top Gear and seeing how Jeremy Clarkson's bald patch disappears and mysteriously reappears when he goes faster.* **Listening:** *My wife, for obvious reasons.* **Relaxing to:** *By shouting at other drivers on the M25 on my drive home.*
» *Married, 3 children*

Angie Lopez 1.7.74

8th Floor, 1 Stephen Street, London W1T 1AL
T 07974 575529
E angie.lopez@lycos-europe.com

Occupation: MD Sales, Lycos UK

Other positions: Consultant, Sales; Account Director.
Publications: First ever Global online Sony Ericsson campaign, Pirates of the Caribbean for Disney, first ever UK McDonalds online ad campaign.
Education: Business School, London

Career highlights: I originally joined Lycos UK in February 1998 as Key Account Director. Over the last 7 years I have held a number of positions, increasing in responsibility, within the European business development and commercial team. I was promoted to Managing Director (Sales) in January 2005. In this role I am responsible for developing and maintaining strategic business relationships with the aim of ensuring consistency of revenue streams for Lycos UK. I also play an integral role in the planning and development of Pan-European partnerships. Prior to joining Lycos UK, I held management positions within Sales and Project Management divisions for Frost and Sullivan in both Germany and London. Previously I worked for an investment bank in Hong Kong.
Mentor: My colleagues' creativity and everyone I have met in this industry who truly believe in what they do.
Big break: Maternity leave!
Big mistake: Not learning Chinese during my stint in Hong Kong - also I sometimes understimate the power of my gut feeling on certain elements of the job. My gut feeling more than often turns out right.

» **Reading:** *Most morning papers, Marketing Week, Time, the Economist, Marie Claire and Vogue magazines.* **Watching:** *News at Ten, Jonathan Ross, Michael Parkinson, X Factor - Maria to win, and Bremner, Bird and Fortune, Panorama and Chelsea with my son.* **Listening:** *I listen to my mother, my husband and my bank manager. Also love classical music and Rolling Stones.* **Relaxing to:** *Long sunny weekends spent with my family in my house in Spain, drinking fine Spanish wine with my husband and friends over long dinners.* » *Married, 2 children*

Pat Loughrey

30.12.59

Media Centre (MC4 A4), BBC White City, 201 Wood Lane, London W12 7TQ
T 020 8008 1220
E pat.loughrey@bbc.co.uk

Occupation: Director, BBC Nations and Regions

Other positions: Head of Programmes, Northern Ireland; Controller, BBC Northern Ireland.
Publications: The People of Ireland (radio series and subsequent publication); Making a Difference (a celebration of Northern Ireland's unsung heroes).
Awards: Fellow of the Radio Academy.
Education: University of Ulster; Queen's University, Belfast; Trent University, Ontario
Career highlights: The highlight when Head of Programmes BBC Northern Ireland was in 1994 when BBC Radio Ulster and Foyle won six Sony golds from six nominations. It was a real privilege, after many dark days in Ulster, to be Controller Northern Ireland for the signing of the Good Friday agreement. As Director Nations and Regions there have been many highs; the first was the move in 2002 of English Regions current affairs programmes from BBC Two to BBC One. Audiences subsequently trebled but that outcome was not guaranteed! I'm also proud of the part I played in creating decent and accessible BBC offices right across the country and of the Open Centres and buses. Perhaps the most significant achievement is the ever-growing number of programmes made in Scotland, Wales, Northern Ireland and English Regions for the BBC networks. The triumph of Dr Who (BBC Wales) is evidence of what can be achieved.
Mentor: I'm lucky enough to have two mentors: the film-maker David Hammond and my predecessor as Controller Northern Ireland, Robin Walsh.
Big break: Appointment as Head of Programmes Northern Ireland at the age of 34.
Big mistake: Trusting people is a strength, trusting the wrong people is a mistake.

» **Reading:** *Mainly poetry, it's shorter and more memorable!* **Watching:** *The best documentaries, all news and the X Factor!* **Listening:** *I graze all BBC local radio of course, especially BBC Three Counties. RTE Radio 1 still has a special place - it's the wireless I grew up with.* **Relaxing to:** *Building stone walls in Donegal.* » *Married, 3 children*

James Lowther

27.1.51

36 Golden Square, London W1F 9EE
T 020 7543 4598
E jamesl@mcsaatchi.com

Occupation: Founding Partner, M&C Saatchi

Other positions: Director, British Television Advertising Awards; Trustee, Children in Crisis.
Publications: Contributor to The Copy Book; Contributor to The 20 Immutable Laws of Advertising (and when to break them); one slogan in the Oxford Dictionary of Quotations.
Awards: 3 D&AD silvers; 1 Cannes gold Lion and 3 silver Lions; 1992 ITV Award, best commercial of the year; Campaign Press Awards, Best black and white ad 3 times; Campaign Poster Awards, Best poster of the year twice; Ad in 100 best advertisements; Ivor Novello Award for Music Composition.
Education: Keble College, Oxford
Career highlights: 1977, joined Saatchi & Saatchi as copywriter, worked on campaigns for Castlemaine XXXX, Schweppes, Motorcycles, COI, BR Intercity; 1987, made Joint Creative Director; 1988, Deputy Chairman, oversaw campaigns for launch of National Lottery, Solid Fuel Advisory Service, Campaign for Racial Equality, Le Creuset and Habitat; 1995, left to become Founder and Joint CD of M&C Saatchi, working on Silk Cut, Fosters, BA, Glaxo, Pfizer, COI, Sky Digital; 2000-2005 Chairman.
Mentor: Jeremy Sinclair
Big break: Joining Saatchi & Saatchi.
Big mistake: Waiting eight years until I did.

» **Reading:** *Newspapers by the shovelful, novels and biographies, now shamefully mostly on holidays.* **Watching:** *Have I Got News For You, anything with Jack Dee in it.* **Listening:** *Radio 4, the finest radio station in the world, by a country mile (especially I'm Sorry I Haven't A Clue).* **Relaxing to:** *Playing with my collection of musical instruments, trying to pretend I'm a composer.* » *Married, 4 children*

Kevin Lygo

Channel 4, 124 Horseferry Road, London SW1P 2TX
T 020 7396 4444
E kevin.lygo@channel4.co.uk

Occupation: Director of Television, Channel 4

Other positions: Board Member, Channel 4; Launch Controller, E4; Programme Manager, More4.
Publications: For Channel 4, So Graham Norton, Trigger Happy TV, Top 10s, Smack the Pony, Spaced, Black Books, Da Ali G Show, and The 11 O'clock Show, as well as the now notorious Brass Eye special on paedophilia; At the BBC, The Two Ronnies, Not The Nine O'clock News, They Think It's All Over and Men Behaving Badly.
Awards: 2005 BAFTA winners include Green Wing, Not Only But Always, Omagh, Ramsay's Kitchen Nightmares, Sex Traffic and Shameless.
Career highlights: Head of Independent Commissioning for Entertainment, BBC TV: credits include The Two Ronnies, Not the Nine O'Clock News, They Think It's All Over and Men Behaving Badly. Head of Entertainment and Music, Channel 4: credits include So Graham Norton, Trigger Happy TV, Top 10s, Smack the Pony, Spaced, Black Books, Da Ali G Show, The 11 O'Clock Show, and the now notorious Brass Eye special on paedophilia, 1997-2001; acted as Launch Controller for E4, 2001; Director of Programmes, Five, 2001-03; Director of Television, Channel 4 2003-present: the channel has enjoyed one of its best periods both in terms of ratings and the critical response to its programmes; Channel 4 dominated the BAFTA awards ceremony in 2005, winning 10 awards for programmes broadcast in 2004; other Channel 4 programming highlights include Jamie's School Dinners, Anatomy for Beginners, The Boy Whose Skin Fell Off, Brat Camp, The Government Inspector, Hamburg Cell, Supernanny, You Are What You Eat and hit US imports, Desperate Housewives and Lost; presided over launch of a new daily lunchtime news bulletin and significantly increased the channel's commitment to current affairs, upping the annual run of flagship strand, Dispatches, from 12 to 28 episodes.

Sue Lynas

BBC Broadcasting House, London W1A 1AA
T 020 7765 4630
E sue.lynas@bbc.co.uk

Occupation: Head of Marketing, Communications and Audiences, BBC Radio and Music

Other positions: Various publicity and PR posts - BBC lifer.
Education: St Anne's College, Oxford
Career highlights: Hard to summarise - I enjoy the crisis management as well as the well-executed campaign and the sheer fun of things like the Archers 50th Birthday at St James's Palace. The last few years working with Jenny Abramsky and seeing BBC Radio and Music so fit have been great, but it's a fast-changing world and you can never sit back and relax.
Mentor: No one person - but lucky to have worked, and still be working, with some really clever and talented people - people working for me as well as managers.

» **Reading:** *As much as I can, try to actually read the papers, not just cuts but it's hard to keep up. Then there's the magazines and websites. At least the Guardian and Mail every day.* **Watching:** *Sopranos - every episode. Drama, Newsnight, documentaries, comedy, no sport.* **Listening:** *Not enough hours in the day to keep up with all the BBC services. Naturally listen most to Radios 2, 3, 4 and Five Live, and try to keep across Radio 1 and the digital services. Pressure of time means I rarely listen to non-BBC radio.* **Relaxing to:** *Reading, music, countryside.*

Brian Macarthur

6.2.44

E brian.macarthur@onetel.com

Occupation: Associate Editor, The Times

Other positions: Founder Editor, The Times Higher Education Supplement, 1971-76; Deputy Editor, Sunday Times, 1982-84; Editor, Western Morning News, 1984-85; Founder Editor, Today, 1985-86.
Publications: Eddy Shah: Today and the Fleet Street Revolution; Deadline Sunday: A Life in the Week of The Sunday Times; Despatches from the Gulf War (ed); The Penguin Book of Twentieth Century Speeches; Requiem: Diana, Princess of Wales, 1961-97.
Education: Helsby Grammar; Leeds University, MA (Hon); Open University
Career highlights: Although the launch of Today was not a success, the existence of Today helped to start the Wapping revolution which transformed the ways in which newspapers were written, edited, printed and distributed. All those who knocked Today in 1986 are now practising what Eddy Shah preached. Working as Executive Editor and running the backbench when Harold Evans was editing The Times.
Mentor: The late Ken Donlan, Northern News Editor of the Daily Mail, then of the Sun and briefly editor of the News of the World. Harry Whewell of the Manchester Guardian. Harold Evans.
Big break: Being left editing The Times when Harold Evans and Charles Douglas-Home were both ill for two to three weeks over Christmas and New Year 1981-82.
Big mistake: The Hitler Diaries.

» **Reading:** *Too much non-fiction for my job buying serials and extracts for The Times. Modern novels, history, biography, crime, thrillers.* **Watching:** *News, drama, sport, particularly football.* **Listening:** *Radio 4 and classical music.* **Relaxing to:** *Vegetable gardening, country walking, reading.*
» *Married, 2 daughters by previous wife*

Victoria Macdonald

1.4.66

200 Gray's Inn Road, London WC1X 8XZ
T 020 7833 3000
E victoria.macdonald@itn.co.uk

Occupation: Social Affairs Correspondent, Channel 4 News

Other positions: Channel 4 News; Sunday Telegraph; Daily Telegraph in Sydney; Auckland Star, NZ.
Publications: Mental Health in the Media, Norwich Union Healthcare and Medical Journalists' Association 2004; Broadcast National award.
Education: Epsom Girls Grammar School; Auckland University; Auckland Technical Institute
Career highlights: Causing a row over whether the WHO had proved passive smoking causes lung cancer; revealing Labour wanted to back down from its NHS waiting list manifesto commitment; becoming the first British broadcaster to interview Chief Buthelezi following the death of two of his children from Aids; helping to get a nursing home closed after it was found patients were being abused; revealing hospitals were mistreating suicidal patients.
Mentor: There are a number of people who have helped and inspired me over the years: Jim Tully at the Auckland Star, Martin Ivens at the Sunday Telegraph, and Jon Snow at Channel Four News.
Big break: Coming top of the journalism course at Auckland Technical Institute which gave me the pick of the newspapers I could work on in New Zealand, and of course being given the job of Social Affairs Correspondent on Channel 4 News by Jim Gray.
Big mistake: Not following up on rumours of a fatwa against Salman Rushdie. It was a lesson never forgotten.

» **Reading:** *I am a voracious newspaper reader, like most journalists. I also read a lot of novels and not enough non-fiction. My job also ensures a healthy dose of medical journals have to be read each week.* **Watching:** *I watch Channel 4 News or More4 News. Throughout the day I flick between the BBC and Sky and ITV. In the evening I try to watch Newsnight. I also watch a lot of anything else as long as it does not involve a celebrity chef, redecorating houses or retraining children.* **Listening:** *I listen to the Today programme and to BBC Radio 4 midnight news. I love Jonathan Ross on Radio 2 on Saturday mornings and if I want to sing in the car I switch to Heart or Magic. If I am not at work I try and listen to Kirsty Lang on Front Row.* **Relaxing to:** *Reading, watching television, eating and drinking with friends, going to see bands at smoke-filled venues.*

Michael MacFarlane

14.9.67

35c Marylebone High Street, London W1U 4QA
T 020 7208 9602
E michael.macfarlane@bbc.co.uk

Occupation: Executive Editor, BBC London (Head of Regional and Local Services)

Other positions: Editor, BBC Weekend TV News 2001-03; Election Editor, BBC Radio 2001; Editor, 5 Live Drive 1998-2001.
Education: Glasgow University; City University, London

» *Married, 2 children*

Alastair Machray

20.6.65

Liverpool Echo, PO Box 48, Old Hall Street, Liverpool LG9 3EB
T 0151 472 2507
E suecox@liverpoolecho.co.uk

Occupation: Editor, Liverpool Echo

Other positions: Editor-in-Chief, Trinity Mirror North Wales; Editor, Daily Post; Assistant Editor, Liverpool Echo.
Awards: Tom Cordner Award for sports journalism, 1987.
Education: Glasgow Academy; Greencroft Comprehensive

Career highlights: Appointment to my editor's roles; opening of North Wales children's hospice after chairing appeal; meeting the Royal Family; creation of Welsh Daily Post in 2003.
Mentor: Terry Quinn, Mel Waggitt (ex Chief Sub Newcastle Evening Chronicle), John Griffith (ex Editor Liverpool Echo), Sara Wilde (MD, Trinity Mirror North West).
Big break: Offered trainee reporter's job, aged 18, at Sunderland Echo. Surviving two heart attacks in 2003.
Big mistake: Not splitting English and Welsh Daily Posts in 1995.

» **Reading:** *Liverpool Echo, Daily Mirror, Daily Telegraph.* **Watching:** *X Factor, Phoenix Nights, Newcastle United, cricket, news.* **Listening:** *Talksport, Five Live, Radio Merseyside.* **Relaxing to:** *Golf, family, wine, cooking.* » *Married, 2 children*

Andrew Mackenzie

26.10.74

124 Horseferry Road, London SW1P 2TX
T 020 7306 3680
E amackenzie@channel4.co.uk

Occupation: Commissioning Editor, Factual Entertainment, Channel 4

Other positions: Freelance Producer/Director working for Channel 4 and Five; BBC Producer.
Publications: Broad appealing biographies like The Unseen Eric Morecambe and I Killed John Lennon. Distinctive takes on popular culture like Bring Back Grange Hill and 100 Greatest... Provocative 11pm series and seasons like The Dark Side of Pornography and The Banned Season.
Awards: RTS Sports Documentary of the Year (1999); Broadcast Best Sports Programme (2002).
Education: (BA) University of Liverpool; (PG Dip) University of Central Lancashire
Career highlights: Began TV career at BBC Manchester and joined Channel 4 in May 2003 after several years as a producer / director in London. Credits include The Showbiz Set, The Real Brian Clough and The Real Texas Chainsaw Massacre for Channel 4; Clash of the Titans: Benn V Eubank documentary for the BBC won the RTS Sports Documentary of the Year and The Real Brian Clough won the Broadcast Awards Sports Programme of the Year.
Mentor: Tony Moss, Stuart Cosgrove, me mam.
Big break: Getting a runner's job in the BBC's YEF department in 1991. Working within 'yoof' TV at its wonderfully obnoxious height!

» **Reading:** *The Guardian, the Week, the West Lancashire Evening Gazette and Roy of the Rovers.* **Watching:** *Telly, all of it - through the wonders of Sky+.* **Listening:** *The Wheels on the Bus and other nursery rhyme classics.* **Relaxing to:** *Booze and valium.* » *Single, 2 children*

Kelvin Mackenzie

22.10.46

Highbury House Communications plc, Jordan House, 47 Brunswick Place, London N1 6EB
T 020 7608 6700
E jane.morgan@highburygroup.com

Occupation: Executive Chairman, Highbury House Communications plc

Other positions: Chairman and Chief Executive, Wireless Group plc, 1998-2005.
Career highlights: Editor, the Sun, 1981-94; Managing Director, British Sky Broadcasting, 1994; Director, 1994-98, Gp Managing Director, 1998, Mirror Group plc.

» *Married, 3 children*

Phil Mackenzie

3.5.76

Castle Quay, Manchester M15 4PR
T 0161 288 5000
E phil.mackenzie@thehitsradio.com

Occupation: Manager, The Hits Radio (Emap Digital); Head of Music, Key 103 Manchester

Other positions: Programme Manager, Metro Radio; Presenter and Programme Controller with Radio Investments.
Awards: Nominated for Arqiva award 2005, The Hits.
Education: University of York, B Eng (Hons)
Career highlights: Started on a student show at BBC Radio Cambridgeshire, which led to continuity shifts and shows on Minster FM and Viking FM as a presenter; after university, moved into Sound and Studio Production; Programme Manager at Metro Radio, then back on-air with RIL; now with Emap again in Manchester.
Big break: My first ever radio show at the age of 17 for BBC Radio Cambridgeshire.
Big mistake: Sun.City 103.4 (now Sun FM) back in 1997. Assuming the version of Radiohead Creep on a BBC Top Gear compilation album was the radio edit.

» **Reading:** *Anything that comes recommended, I'm not a big reader so need to know I'm making the effort with ood reason!* **Watching:** *TV drama stuff like Waking The Dead, Lost etc. Fave films would be anything Tarantino.* **Listening:** *Whole cross section, from live bands to dance, and even Classic FM for a bit of variety on a weekend!* **Relaxing to:** *Glass of red wine, dim the lights and something good on the TV.* » *Single (but under the thumb!)*

Laura Mackie

30.1.65

BBC Drama Series and Serials, Centre House, 56 Wood Lane, London W12 7SB
T 020 8941 2156
E laura.mackie@bbc.co.uk

Occupation: Head of Drama Series and Serials, BBC TV

Other positions: Deputy Head of Drama, LWT; Executive Producer, BBC TV.
Publications: Canterbury Tales, Cutting It, Hawking, To The Ends of the Earth, Charles II, North and

South, Bleak House, Flesh and Blood, State of Play.
Awards: 2004 BANFF Mini Series award, Blackpool; 2004 BAFTA Huw Weldon Award, Dunkirk; 2003 BAFTA Best Serial, Charles II; 2003 RTS Best Serial, State of Play; 2002 Comedy-Drama Award, British Comedy Awards, Auf Wiedersehen Pet; 2002 National TV Award, Best New Series, Auf Wiedersehen Pet; 2002 Prix Europa, Flesh and Blood.
Education: Westfield College; London University (BA Hons English)
Career highlights: The last five years in BBC Drama, being enabled to produce the most diverse portfolio of programmes in the industry.
Mentor: Debbie Horsfield (writer)
Big break: Moving from Production Assistant to Script Editor on Making Out.
Big mistake: Not trusting my instincts.

» **Reading:** *All the classic novels we're thinking of adapting, Heat, OK, the Guardian.* **Watching:** *Bodies, EastEnders, Wife Swap, The X Factor.* **Listening:** *Jonathan Ross and Chris Evans on Radio 2, Jonny Vaughan on Capital and Radio 5 Live News.* **Relaxing to:** *Strategically arranged holidays throughout the year, swimming, regular visits to cinema with 12-year-old son.* » *Married, 1 child*

Gordon Macmillan 24.4.63

200 Renfield Street, Glasgow G2 3PR
T 0141 300 3000
E gordon.macmillan@smg.plc.uk

Occupation: Head of News and Current Affairs, Scottish TV

Other positions: Regional Board Member, Scottish TV.
Publications: Scotland Today.
Education: Perth Academy; Aberdeen University
Career highlights: First job was in BBC local radio in Aberdeen; then was a BBC Graduate News Trainee in 1982, moving to Producer BBC News in 1983; moved to Scotland as a producer in 1987, then News Editor in 1990; Chief Assistant to MD BBC Regional Broadcasting in 1995; moved to CNN in Atlanta as Senior Programme Editor in 1996; returned to UK in 1999, as Newsgathering Editor BBC London; in 2000 worked in corporate communications, before joining SMG in 2004.
Mentor: I've been fortunate to work with many people who have taught me so much. My first boss at BBC Radio in Aberdeen, Robert Duncan, was very influential, as were two of the Assistant Editors at BBC News in London, Mike Broadbent and Derek Maude. Each gave me the opportunity to develop and stretch myself.
Big break: Being lucky enough to get onto the BBC traineeship which opened so many doors. There were more than 1000 applications for 12 places.
Big mistake: Leaving the TV industry which I love for four years to try something new which was just not for me.

» **Reading:** *Most of the UK and US major newspapers, political biographies.* **Watching:** *American comedy and drama, all the news channels, classic cinema, documentaries.* **Listening:** *Radio 4 as much as I can and some US radio on the internet.* **Relaxing to:** *Out and about with the family and getting into the countryside at the weekends.* » *Married, 1 child*

Alex Mahon

talkbackTHAMES, 20-21 Newman Street, London W1T 1AL
T 020 7861 8000
E alex.mahon@talkbackthames.tv

Occupation: COO, talkbackTHAMES

Other positions: Commercial and Strategy Director, Fremantlemedia
Publications: talkbackTHAMES productions in 2006 include X Factor, The Bill, Green Wing, Grand Designs, The Apprentice and The IT Crowd.
Education: Imperial College, London
Career highlights: After seven years of rocket science I realised that perhaps a physics PhD was not the ideal career route for someone whose daily highlight was watching This Morning. Magically I then found that knowing nothing about business was an asset in the world of management consultancy and from there became reincarnated as an internet expert (expert being an easy word to apply to anything in the dot.com boom). I fortuitously fell into a television job just before the entire internet world began to crash around my ears.
Mentor: Dale Winton in Supermarket Sweep (from afar).
Big break: Finding out it was legitimate to have a career in something that was actually enjoyable where work could seriously involve reading Heat magazine.
Big mistake: Allowing Heat magazine to be delivered to my assistant before I got to see it.

» **Watching:** *Everything, and almost anything (especially involving cosmetic surgery or an extreme makeover where people cry), and my Blackberry in boring meetings.*

Joe Mahoney 2.3.71

124 Horseferry Road, Victoria, London SW1 2TX
T 020 7306 1065
E jmahoney@channel4.co.uk

Occupation: Head of Consumer Products, Channel 4

Other positions: Senior Commissioning Editor, BBC Video.
Publications: 4DVD, C4 Books, Grand Designs magazine, A Place in the Sun magazine, Channel 4 Shop (online).
Awards: Man of the Match at the 2003 Video Industry 5-a-side tournament.
Education: University of Westminster
Career highlights: From starting as a humble Rights Assistant at the BBC, I have worked in various distribution areas such BBC TV Sales, UK Gold, video distribution, book and magazine publications. A key highlight was being part of turning BBC Video into a £55 million a year turnover business. I recently created the 4DVD label as a self-publishing business on behalf of Channel 4.
Mentor: My probation officer.
Big break: Answering an ad in the Guardian for a Rights Assistant in the BBC's Commercial Rights Department.

Big mistake: Answering an ad in the Guardian for a Rights Assistant in the BBC's Commercial Rights Department.

» **Reading:** *Metro, Guardian, Sunday Times, anything trashy.* **Watching:** *Everything and anything.* **Listening:** *Xfm, Radio 5.* **Relaxing to:** *On a beach at least 5,000 miles away from the UK.* » *Single, no children*

Gerald Main

BBC Radio Suffolk, St Matthew's Street, Ipswich IP1 3EP
T 01473 250000
E gerald.main@bbc.co.uk

Occupation: Managing Editor, BBC Radio Suffolk.

Awards: Sony Gold, Station of The Year 2004; Frank Gillard Awards, Station of the Year 2004.
Education: York University
Career highlights: In three years at BBC Radio Suffolk the station has won major industry awards (Sony Station of the Year) and the audience figures have reached an all-time high. Working, primarily in presentation, for a variety of BBC local stations and occasionally presenting and producing reports for regional TV. Spent two years working for the BBC's Radio Training Unit. During several years freelancing, specialised in media training, corporate video production and presentation work.
Mentor: Greg Dyke was inspirational.
Big break: Getting my first job at BBC Radio Blackburn as a Station Assistant.
Big mistake: My Editor at Radio Blackburn told me I had to watch Coronation Street. 25 years later I am only just beginning to wean myself off it.

» **Reading:** *East Anglian Daily Times, biographies, the net.* **Watching:** *Too much.* **Listening:** *BBC Radio Suffolk, BBC Five Live, Keane, Jimmy Webb, Jamie Cullum.* **Relaxing to:** *Family life, music, red wine, travel, Ipswich Town FC and fly fishing. Trying to master the didgeridoo.*

David Mannion 6.11.54

200 Gray's Inn Road, London WC1X 8HF
T 020 7833 3000
E david.mannion@itn.co.uk

Occupation: Editor-in-Chief, ITV News

Other positions: Editor, Tonight with Trevor; Editor, GMTV; Editor, ITN; Editor, Cook Report; Deputy Editor, Channel 4 News.
Awards: 4 BAFTAs; numerous RTS.
Education: Long Eaton Grammar, Derbyshire
Career highlights: First interview with Nelson Mandela on his release, overseeing coverage of two Gulf wars, de Menezes scoop, bringing news deadlines to current affairs and current affairs production techniques to news.
Mentor: Sir David Nicholas
Big break: Getting a job at ITN in 1979.
Big mistake: I haven't made it yet.

» **Reading:** *History and newspapers.* **Watching:** *Sport and news.* **Listening:** *Radio 4 and Five Live, all music.* **Relaxing to:** *Tennis, cooking.* » *Married*

Grant Mansfield

The Gloucester Building, Kensington Village, Avonmore Road, London W14 8RF
T 020 7103 4000
E Grant.Mansfield@rdfmedia.com

Occupation: Director of Programmes, RDF Media Group plc

Career highlights: Director of Programmes, Granada Productions; Controller of Documentaries, Features and Arts, ITV Network; Managing Editor, BBC Documentaries and Arts.
Mentor: Phillip Chadwick
Big break: Devising and producing Driving School.

» **Relaxing to:** *Running*

Andrew Marr 31.7.59

BBC Television Centre, Wood Lane, London W12 7RJ
T 020 8743 8000
E andrew.marr@bbc.co.uk

Occupation: Journalist, broadcaster and author

Publications: The Battle for Scotland, 1992; Ruling Britannia, 1995; The Day Britain Died, 2000; My Trade: a short history of British journalism, 2004.
Awards: Columnist of the Year, What the Papers Say, 1994; Creative Media Journalist of Year, British Press Awards, 2000; Political Journalist of Year, C4/House Magazine, 2001, 2002; Specialist of the Year, RTS Awards, 2001-02; Best Individual TV Performer, Voice of the Listener and Viewer Awards, 2002; Best TV Performer, BPG, 2002; Richard Dimbleby Award, BAFTA, 2004.
Education: Dundee High School; Craigflower School, Fife; Loretto School, Musselburgh; Trinity Hall, Cambridge
Career highlights: The Scotsman, Trainee and General Reporter, 1982-85, Parliamentary Correspondent, 1985-86; Political Correspondent, the Independent, 1986-88; Political Editor, The Scotsman, 1988; The Economist, 1989-92; the Independent, Political Columnist and Associate Editor, 1992-96; Editor, 1996-98, Editor-in-Chief, 1998; Columnist, the Observer and the Express, 1998-2000; Political Editor, BBC, 2000-05; Columnist, Daily Telegraph, 2000-present; Presenter, Sunday am (BBC One), 2005-present.

» **Relaxing to:** *Reading, painting, talking.*
» *Married, 3 children*

Greg Martin 28.5.68

1 Knightsbridge Green, London SW3
T 020 7656 7674
E greg.martin@jwt.com

Occupation: Creative Director, JWT London

Other positions: Creative Director, Leo Burnett; Creative Director, Saatchi & Saatchi; Art Director, Abbott Mead Vickers.
Awards: Cannes Media Grand Prix; Cannes gold; 4 Cannes silvers; D&AD silver; 2 BTAA silvers; 4 Campaign Press silvers; Creative Circle gold; Clio gold.

Education: Langley Grammar School
Career highlights: Studied at Reading Art College and was tutored by John Gillard. Began advertising career as a junior art director at Ted Bates, then joined Abbott Mead Vickers in 1987, Saatchi & Saatchi in 1998 and Leo Burnett in 2001. Recently joined the new hungry start-up JWT.
Mentor: John Gillard
Big break: Showing my book to Richard Foster and John Horton.
Big mistake: Re-mortgaging my house just before the recession.

» **Reading:** *The Guardian, Angling Times.* **Watching:** *Usually Sky sports.* **Listening:** *Whatever my daughter has just bought.* **Relaxing to:** *Fishing or golf.* » *Married, 1 daughter*

Iain Martin

2.10.71

The Scotsman, Barclay House, 108 Holyrood Road, Edinburgh EH8 8AS
T 0131 620 8626
E imartin@scotsman.com

Occupation: Editor, Scotland on Sunday

Other positions: Fellow, British-American Project.
Education: Castlehead High School; University of Glasgow
Career highlights: Reporter, Sunday Times Scotland, 1993-97; Political Editor, Assistant Editor, Scotland on Sunday, 1997-2000; Political Commentator, Assistant Editor, The Scotsman 2000-01; Deputy Editor, Scotland on Sunday, 2001; Editor, The Scotsman, 2001-04; Editor, Scotland on Sunday 2004-present.

» *Married*

Dave Masterman

1.6.76

60 Kingly Street, London W1B 5DS
T 020 7453 4075
E dave@masterman.org.uk

Occupation: Creative, Bartle Bogle Hegarty

Other positions: Creative, Fallon London; Creative, BMP DDB.
Publications: Double Velvet Soft Factory; BBC Radio 1 Love of Live campaign; the Ben and Jerry's poster campaign; Sony Hollywood says Thank You campaign; Volkswagen press and poster campaigns; Levi's Ice Cream commercial.
Awards: D&AD pencil; BTAA Gold and silver arrows; 2 Cannes Lions; 2 Campaign Poster silvers; 4 Campaign Press silvers; 2 Creative Circle Golds; 3 One Show Pencils.
Education: Bucks College
Career highlights: Being hired at BMP DDB and making a string of award-winning campaigns for Volkswagen, London Transport and Marmite. Moving to Fallon, winning our first D&AD pencil for Radio 1, and creating campaigns for Sony, Skoda and Ben and Jerry's. Making a toilet roll commercial that doesn't have any cute little animals in it. Moving to BBH a year ago and creating campaigns for Levi's, Boddingtons and Lynx.
Mentor: Dave Morris
Big break: Getting a job at BMP DDB.
Big mistake: Not spending enough time with John Webster.

» **Reading:** *The Guardian, books, many and varied.* **Watching:** *Films, voraciously.* **Listening:** *Led Zeppelin, The Today Programme.* **Relaxing to:** *Drumming, cycling through heavy traffic.* » *Living in sin*

Dr Chris Masters

3.5.51

SMG plc, 200 Renfield Street, Glasgow G2 3PR
T 0141 300 3940
E chris.masters@smg.plc.uk

Occupation: Chairman, SMG plc

Other positions: Chair, Festival City Theatres Trust; Senior Independent Director, John Wood Group plc; Non-Executive Director, The Alliance Trust plc, British Assets Trust plc, The Crown Agents. Lay Director, Scottish Chamber Orchestra.
Publications: 43 papers published in the scientific literature together with two patents; advanced text book Homogeneous Transition-metal Catalysis, Chapman Hall 1981.
Awards: CBE
Education: Richmond Grammar School; King's College, University of London; Leeds University
Career highlights: After gaining a PhD from Leeds University in 1971 spent six years in fundamental research with Shell in Amsterdam and two years in business and corporate planning in London. Joined Christian Salvesen in 1979; heavily involved in the company's expansion into North America including the acquisition of Aggreko in 1984; Chief Executive of Christian Salvesen 1987-97; Executive Chairman of Aggreko 1997-2002, during which time the company almost tripled its market capitalisation rising from £435m to £1.1bn; have held a number of chairmanships and non-executive directorships in both the public and private sector including Scottish Opera, Vice Chair 1996-99, Scottish Higher Education Funding Council, Chair 1998-2005 and the Babtie Group, Chair 2002-04; currently Lay Director of the Scottish Chamber Orchestra, Chair of the Festival Theatres Trust, Senior Independent Director of John Wood Group plc and a Non-Executive Director of The Alliance Trust plc, British Assets Trust plc and The Crown Agents; elected a Fellow of the Royal Society of Edinburgh in 1999 and awarded a CBE for contributions to industry in 2002. Appointed Chairman of SMG plc in July 2004.
Mentor: Gerard Fairtlough, previously Managing Director of Shell Chemicals UK and Chief Executive of CellTech plc.
Big break: Having the opportunity to acquire Aggreko in 1984.
Big mistake: No really big one but certainly lots of smaller ones!

» **Reading:** *Mainly non-fiction including historical biographies.* **Watching:** *Drama and current affairs.* **Listening:** *Classical music and opera.* **Relaxing to:** *Listening to Mozart with a good bottle of red wine.* » *Married, 2 daughters*

James Mates

12.8.65

200 Gray's Inn Road, London WC1X 8XZ
T 020 7833 3000
E james.mates@itn.co.uk

Occupation: Senior Correspondent, ITV News

Other positions: Bureau Correspondent in Tokyo, Moscow and Washington.
Education: Marlborough College; Farnham College; Leeds University
Career highlights: Major stories covered include Fall of the Soviet Union, Rwandan Genocide, Invasion of Kosovo, second Gulf War, Monica Lewinsky/Clinton impeachment affair, September 11th, Asian Tsunami.
Mentor: Michael Macmillan, a fine reporter prepared to share everything he knew (almost) with a very pushy young trainee. Sadly no longer practising, but I suspect earning much more money.
Big break: Being the late reporter on a Friday night in 1987 when the Herald of Free Enterprise capsized off Zeebrugge. Stayed on the story until she was righted five weeks later.
Big mistake: Selective memory syndrome kicking in here...

» **Reading:** *Mostly non-fiction and frequently history. But occasionally I surprise myself.* **Watching:** *Very little scheduled TV that isn't a news programme. I love long US drama series on DVD: 24, Six Feet Under, Sopranos.* **Listening:** *Today Programme in the morning, Five Live whenever there's live sport on. Musical tastes are very catholic, although there's never been a decade like the 1970s.* **Relaxing to:** *Ride my bike (sometimes road, mostly mountain), play tennis or some fiercely competitive bridge.* » *Married, 3 children*

Catherine Mayer

23.1.61

Time Magazine, 3rd Floor, Brettenham House, Lancaster Place, London WC2E 7TL
T 020 7322 1047
E Catherine_mayer@timemagazine.com

Occupation: Senior Editor, Time Magazine

Other positions: Formerly 11 years as London Correspondent for the German news weekly, Focus; President, Foreign Press Association in London; Deputy Editor, International Management and Business Traveller; Staff Writer, the Economist.
Education: Schools in the US and UK; Sussex and Freiburg Universities
Career highlights: Not so much highlights as endless feats of logistics: for example, interviewing Gerry Adams at the Felons' Club in Belfast mid-morning, circumnavigating marching season roadblocks to catch a flight in time for a central London screening of Michael Caine's latest movie that afternoon, then catching Caine for a one-to-one later that same day on set in Shepperton; or tracking General Wiranto, then in charge of Indonesian forces, to a military base outside Jakarta, to secure an exclusive an hour before final press deadlines about his political ambitions and the small matter of East Timor.
Mentor: Barbara Beck, now Surveys Editor at the Economist. I was her deputy when she edited International Management - the Journal of European Business. We produced a miracle of fine journalism on a shoestring and despite the best efforts of vacillating publishers. She is wise and calm, always.
Big break: Being naive enough to apply for a staff writer job on the Economist when I was already employed in the marketing department just a few floors below editorial but almost as low as Hades in journalists' perceptions.
Big mistake: Referring to the 'Bush regime' in a live presser with Tony Blair at Downing Street. There was another little interaction with Blair at one of his monthly briefings that still features on TV's Naughtiest Blunders.

» **Reading:** *Time, cover to cover, many times over before we go to press. All other UK papers including tabloids, plus the Frankfurter Allgemeine Zeitung, Focus and Le Monde. Lots of journals. Emails. Popbitch.* **Watching:** *News, news and more news.* **Listening:** *Gang of Four and the sound of my own voice.* **Relaxing to:** *Sorry, does not compute.*

Carolyn McCall

14.9.65

119 Farringdon Road, London EC1R 3ER
T 020 7278 2332
E carolyn.mccall@guardian.co.uk

Occupation: Chief Executive, Guardian Media Group as of 1.08.06

Education: Kent University and London University
Career highlights: Teacher, then risk analyst then researcher for the Guardian; appointed Ad Manager in 1991; Ad Director 1995; Commercial Director 1998 (launching GU in 1999); Managing Director in 2000, and appointed to the Guardian Media Group Board; CEO of Guardian Newspapers Ltd in 2003; launching the Berliner Guardian in 2005; appointed Non-Exec Director of New Look in 1999 (-2004) and currently Non-Exec Director of Tesco (2005-); Chair of Opportunity Now, the UK's leading membership organisation working towards gender equality and diversity in the workplace; President of WACL (2002-03).
Mentor: John Bartle, Jeremy Bullmore, and Caroline Marland.
Big break: Joining the Guardian and launching Wired in the UK (1993).

» *Married, 3 children*

Ian McCulloch

8.12.63

200 Gray's Inn Road, London WC1X 8XZ
T 0207 396 3000
E ian.mcculloch@itv.com

Occupation: Commercial Director, ITV Plc

Other positions: COO, ITV Broadcasting; MD Operations, ITV Broadcasting; MD Operations, Granada Broadcasting; various sales roles.
Education: Esher College
Career highlights: Started at LWT in 1980 and have always been on the commercial side of the business either selling or managing. Completed

two years in Granada Broadband as Commercial Director which, although as a project was ahead of its time, enabled me to gain experience in new media, new distribution and new business models. The last five years have been spent creating and executing a strategic framework built on ROI for the ITV channels.

Mentor: In the early days Ron Miller the Sales Director at LWT and then in the move to a more broadcast-centric role David Liddiment.

Big break: Getting the first job at LWT which saved me from a career in the military, which was my ideal, or the motor trade, which was more likely.

Big mistake: Getting the work-life balance wrong, it cost me my family.

» **Reading:** *Lots of magazines.* **Watching:** *A lot of TV, ITV1 and our other excellent channel offerings.* **Listening:** *iPod.* **Relaxing to:** *By motorcycling as much as I can.* » *Separated, 2 children*

Lawrence McGinty

3.7.52

200 Gray's Inn Road, London WC1X 8XZ

T 07802 216099

E lawrence.mcginty@itn.co.uk

Occupation: Health and Science Editor, ITV News

Publications: MRSA campaign; series on News at Ten from Antarctica.

Awards: Medical Journalists Association 2005; Queen's Silver Jubilee Medal 1989; Association of British Science Writers, 1984; RTS awards for coverage of King's Cross Fire, Zeebrugge Disaster, Drugs Scandal at Barcelona Olympics.

Education: Stand Grammar School; Liverpool University; Sheffield University

Mentor: Bernard Dixon, ex-Editor New Scientist.

Big break: Being offered job on Channel 4 News when it began.

Big mistake: Not believing BSE could spread to humans.

» **Reading:** *Guardian, PG Wodehouse, Georges Simenon.* **Watching:** *Trash to relax, sport.* **Listening:** *Radio 4.* **Relaxing to:** *Follow the priestly advice of Father Jack: 'Drink'. Crosswords. Look at art. Walk in the country (not breaking sweat).* » *Married, no children*

Jill McGivering

15.7.68

World Affairs Unit, Bush House, Aldwych, The Strand, London WC2B 4PH

T 020 7557 2368

E jill.mcgivering@bbc.co.uk

Occupation: Correspondent, BBC World Affairs Unit

Other positions: BBC South Asia Correspondent, Delhi (3 years); BBC Hong Kong/Taiwan Correspondent, Hong Kong (3 years).

Publications: Author of Macau Remembers, OUP 1999.

Awards: Amnesty Human Rights Award, radio (Hong Kong).

Education: King's College, University of London (BA); Queen Mary College, University of London (MA).

Career highlights: Coverage of key events for the BBC, including Hong Kong handover and first years as part of China, East Timor's transition to independence, anti-US/British riots in Beijing, Afghanistan conflict, Indo-Pakistan stand-off, Indian earthquakes (Bhuj and Kashmir) and floods, Iraq.

Mentor: Individual managers at the BBC have given enormous encouragement and support at various stages of my BBC career. For life mentoring, parents always.

Big break: First job in newspapers - for the South China Morning Post in Hong Kong - soon after leaving university, followed, four years later, by being offered a place on the BBC's fast-track trainee scheme back in London.

Big mistake: Not realising early enough the importance of contacts and networking to a successful career in journalism - and that, rightly or wrongly, presentation can be as important as content.

» **Reading:** *Newspapers - I try to keep across the range of UK broadsheets on a daily basis and add Asia-related articles from online editions of the news magazines and Asian newspapers. Non-fiction relevant to Asia. Fiction widely.* **Watching:** *The main news and current affairs programmes/channels on BBC (including News 24 and BBC World). Other news bulletins where time. Drama and documentaries as leisure where possible.* **Listening:** *Radio 4 as often as possible - and for relaxation. BBC World Service for bulletins and current affairs such as Newshour.* **Relaxing to:** *Reading and writing fiction, cinema, dinner for friends.* » *Married, no children*

Declan McGovern

5.1.71

Room 220, BBC Broadcasting House, Ormeau Avenue, Belfast BT2 8HQ

T 028 9033 8294

E declan.mcgovern@bbc.co.uk

Occupation: Editor of Music, BBC Northern Ireland

Other positions: Music Producer, BBC Northern Ireland; Producer, Classic FM; Sound Engineer, CTS Studios.

Publications: Music Programmes on Radio Ulster, Across The Line (youth music), Sounds Classical (classical); Radio 2 Documentaries; Radio 3 Concerts (Ulster Orchestra).

Awards: Celtic Film and TV Awards 2003, Best Radio Documentary; New York Radio Festival Silver Awards for radio docs on Yehudi Menuhin and Leonard Bernstein.

Education: University College Cork (B Mus)

Career highlights: Following a B Mus Degree at Unversity College Cork I worked at CTS studios on productions such as Inspector Morse, Les Miserables and Into The Woods. At Classic FM I produced Susannah Simons' lunchtime show as well as the live music output and outside broadcasts from New York, Brussels and Sydney. At the BBC I am Executive Producer of music programmes and events such as Proms in the Park, Belfast Festival concerts, Laganlive music festival as well as overseeing music output on Radio Ulster and network radio and TV music productions from Northern Ireland.

Mentor: In the past - Michael Bukht, former Programme Controller of Classic FM; Humphrey

Burton, writer and broadcaster; Oliver Macfarlane, Editor BBC Classical Music TV. Currently Lesley Douglas, Controller BBC Radio 2.

Big break: Getting a job at Classic FM when it first started - I was first in the door and thrown in at the deep end ... I got 10 years' experience in the space of five.

Big mistake: No really big one, touch wood, but some silly things like sending a pre-recorded programme to the transmission studio while the CD was still sitting in my CD player!

» **Reading:** *Biographies (Johnny Cash at the moment).* **Watching:** *All kinds of things, drama mainly like Love Soup on BBC and Pure Mule on RTE.* **Listening:** *Radio Ulster all the time, Rob Cowan and Sean Rafferty on Radio 3, Jonathan Ross on Radio 2, World Service when I can't sleep at night.* **Relaxing to:** *In the pub with a nice pint of Guinness.*

» *Single, no children*

John McGurk

13.12.56

The Scotsman, 108 Holyrood Road, Edinburgh EH8 8AS

T 0131 620 8626
E jmcgurk@scotsman.com

Occupation: Editor, the Scotsman

Other positions: Editorial Director, Scotsman Publications (2001-04); Editor, Scotland on Sunday (1997-2001); Editor, Evening News Edinburgh (1995-97); Deputy Editor, Daily Record (1991-1994); Editor, Sunday Sun Newcastle (1989-91); Deputy Editor, Sunday Mail (1988-89).

Publications: The Scotsman

Awards: Scotland on Sunday, UK Sunday Newspaper of The Year 2000 and 1998; Evening News Edinburgh, Scottish Daily Newspaper of the Year 1997.

Education: Tynecastle Senior Secondary; Edinburgh College of Commerce

» *Not married, 2 children*

Mike McKenna

12.3.60

2 Ponsonby Place, London SW1P 4PT

T 07771 974 371
E mike.mckenna@jwt.com

Occupation: Creative Director, J Walter Thompson

Other positions: Writer

Publications: Department of Health Nursing campaign; Multiple Sclerosis Scramble press ad; Heinz tomato ketchup 'can't eat without it' campaign.

Awards: 3 D&AD silvers, Cannes Media Grand Prix; Cannes Press gold; 3 Cannes TV silvers; 2 Campaign Press golds; 2 Creative Circle golds; one Show silver; Campaign Press and Poster silvers (8 or 9).

Education: Clapham College

Career highlights: Messenger at FCB. Junior writer at FCB. Fired from FCB. Went on to work at a number of different agencies (Ted Bates, Butterfield Day, Publicis, Delaney Fletcher, Saatchi & Saatchi). I've always had the good fortune to work with talented people (which probably explains the awards tally). Left Leo Burnett in 2004 to join JWT. Served on numerous awards juries, chaired some too and from 2001 to 2003 was President of the Creative Circle. I've spoken at D&AD, The London Business School, the IPA and the National Film and Television School.

Mentor: Various people; Derek Hass, Derek Day, Dave Droga, Lex Taylor, Roger Kennedy, plus studying anything David Abbot and John Hegarty ever did, the thoughts of George Lois and Bill Bernbach, Tim Delaney and Charles Saatchi.

Big break: Andrew Cracknell giving me my first job at FCB and then FCB giving me the heave-ho a year or two later.

Big mistake: Falling down a cliff whilst working on a pitch for Air France with Dave Dye.

» **Reading:** *Books on film, on design, on boxing, on history, on the Renaissance, on art, on advertising, on Shakespeare. Books about people.* **Watching:** *Sport, movies, politics, programmes on art, cartoons, concerts.* **Listening:** *Classical, indie and eclectic music.* **Relaxing to:** *At home with the family, going to football (Millwall). Visiting the South Bank, movies, music, theatre.* » *Married, 2 children*

Niall McKinney

20.5.78

IPC Media, Stamford Street, London SE1 9LS

T 020 7261 5000

Occupation: Publishing Director, Loaded

Other positions: Marketing Director, IPC Ignite!

Publications: Loaded, Nuts, NME, Uncut.

Awards: Young Marketer of the Year, Marketing Society Awards 2003; Best New Launch, Nuts, Marketing Effectiveness Awards, 2005.

Education: St Anne's College, Oxford

Career highlights: Reversing a 10 year sales decline on the NME in 2003; launching Nuts Magazine in 2004 and prompting feminist demonstrations; for the 'Women, don't expect any help on a Thursday' campaign; turning around Loaded in 2005 and outperforming the market by 40%.

Mentor: Michael Gold

Big break: Realising men's attention spans were shrinking = Nuts magazine!

Big mistake: Agreeing to be the Manager of the Editor of Loaded.

» **Reading:** *Loaded, naturally, and addicted to the Mediaguardian.co.uk.* **Watching:** *West Wing, OC, 24.* **Listening:** *Fashionable indie rock.* **Relaxing to:** *Lengthy sessions in Karaoke box.* » *Partner, no children*

Tim McLoughlin

10.11.72

Screen International, 33-39 Bowling Green Lane, London EC1R 0DA

T 020 7505 8029
E tim.mcloughlin@emap.com

Occupation: Publishing Director, Screen International

Other positions: Group Commercial Controller, DMG World Media; Sponsorship Manager, Daily Mail Ideal Home Show; Sales Manager, Broadcast, the weekly newspaper of the television and radio industries.

Education: Newcastle University
Career highlights: Joined EMAP in 1990, had a great time, left for more money; joined DMG, had a great time; got asked to go back to EMAP to publish Screen. Did. Having a great time.
Mentor: Andrew Watt of UKTV. He's like a walking Wikipedia and lifecoach all rolled into one, and needs very little alchohol to get him started.

» **Reading:** *Modern fiction mostly. Currently working though John McGahern's backlist. Also whatever's brightly stickered with discounts on the front table of any high street bookshop.* **Watching:** *DVDs from Lovefilm.com, I watch very little on the telly.* **Listening:** *Miles Davis, Deep Dish, Joni Mitchell, Ron Sexsmith, Boards of Canada, Led Zeppelin - all sorts really.* **Relaxing to:** *To relax, I drum on my desk with my fingertips.* » *Married, no children*

Conor McNicholas 28.6.77

IPC Media, 25th Floor King's Reach Tower, Stamford Street, London SE1 9LS
T 020 7261 6472
E editor@nme.com

Occupation: Editor, NME

Other positions: Editor, Muzik; News Editor, Mixmag; Account Executive, Maclaurin PR; Features Editor, Ministry Magazine; News Editor, Escape; Staff Writer, CD-ROM Magazine; Treasurer/Co-Editor, Sublime Publications.
Publications: NME, Muzik, Mixmag, Ministry at Ministry of Sound.
Awards: PPA Consumer Magazine Editor Of The Year 2005; BSME Editor Of The Year - Entertainment Magazines 2005.
Education: Belle Vue Boys' School, Bradford; Manchester University
Career highlights: Events that stick in the memory ... launching a magazine with friends while at university and taking it to a distribution of 10,000; being part of the team that secured the Sega Dreamcast account while at Maclaurin PR - the biggest account up for grabs in the games industry at the time; being part of the team at Mixmag that re-gained market leadership and the highest ever sale for the magazine along with the PPA Specialist Magazine Of the Year; taking on the NME and re-establishing it as the most respected, innovative and biggest-selling weekly music magazine in the UK; winning both a PPA and a BSME for Editor Of The Year in 2005.
Mentor: Without question Steve Sutherland, previously Editor of NME, now Editorial Director of IPC Ignite! I simply wouldn't be doing the job I do without his vision, influence and guidance.
Big break: Drunkenly cornering Steve Sutherland at the launch of NME.com in 1995 when I was working on an internet magazine. It meant that when I spotted him at a Pulp gig in Finsbury Park a year later he knew me and asked if I wanted to come in to NME for a couple of weeks.
Big mistake: Telling a particular Managing Director who knew nothing about magazines that he knew nothing about magazines ... I was made redundant soon afterwards. It was a mistake because it meant I never got a chance to resign.

» **Reading:** *Mostly NME.com, MediaGuardian, BBC News Online, the Guardian, Sun, NoTW, Sunday Times, Observer and any newspaper or newspaper magazine supplement I can lay my hands on. I scan any magazine I find but personal favourites are Autocar, Top Gear and Car. Favourite novelists are Umberto Eco, David Mitchell and Iain Banks.* **Watching:** *Any news programme or rolling news service, quality British comedy (Little Britain, Spoons), football on Saturday, well-crafted history, event TV of any kind and, increasingly, any channel with a '4' in the title - More4, ITV4, BBC4 and Channel 4.* **Listening:** *When it's my choice it's usually the latest CDs that have come into the office and been ripped to my iPod, or classic tunes from my iPod that are appropriate to my mood - can be anything from Underworld to Ultrasound, Elton John to John Coltrane. When it's radio it's almost always Radio 1, Xfm and Radio 4, particularly the Today Programme.* **Relaxing to:** *Spending time with my wife, family and friends, good quality booze, driving, fantasising about cars I'll never own, photography, throwing paint on to canvases and looking after a small collection of orchids.* » *Married, 2 children*

John McVay 27.5.64

2nd Floor, 1 Procter Street, London WC1V 6DW
T 020 7067 4363
E john@pact.co.uk

Occupation: Chief Executive, Pact, the Independent Producers' trade association

Other positions: 1983-86, Founding Director, Missing Link Project; 1987-93, Director of Edinburgh Video Training Course and Real Time Media Ltd; 1993-97, Founding Director of Scottish Broadcast and Film Training; 1995-98, Partner of Small Wonder Films, producer of award-winning Tartan Short for BBC Scotland; 1995-97, Director of Glasgow Television Development Fund; 1997, Director of Training and Skills Development at Scottish Screen; 1998-2001, Founding Director of The Research Centre for Television and Interactivity; 1998-2001, Visiting Tutor on Enterprise UK Producers course; 2001-present, Governor of the National Film and Television School; 2001-present, Director of Skillset; 2001-present, Director of the Independent Producers Training Fund.
Awards: Jury Award, Celtic Film and TV festival 1996 for Narance; Indie of the Year 2005.
Education: Firhill High School
Career highlights: Leading a lobbying campaign to convince the UK government and regulators to amend the 2003 Communications Act to allow independent producers to retain the rights in their programmes.
Mentor: Eileen Gallagher from Shed Productions, Stuart Cosgrove from Channel 4, David Frank from RDF, and my Uncle George.
Big break: Convincing a sceptical local authority that it was possible to train disadvantaged kids to work in television in 1983. Doing a John Peel session in 1979.

» **Reading:** *Politics, history, Ian Rankin, John Irving and Trout and Salmon.* **Watching:** *Approx 3 hours of TV per night including Lost, X-Factor, Wife Swap, Spook, Teachers, No Angels, Horizon, Scrapheap Challenge, the Map Man.* **Listening:** *Whatever the kids are into, and my old punk/indie records.* **Relaxing to:** *Sitting in a boat casting a small dry fly to indifferent trout.* » *Long-term partner, 3 children*

Danny Meadows-Klue 17.3.75

34 Kenway Road, Kensington, London SW5 0RR
T 020 7244 9661
E Danny@DigitalStrategyConsulting.com

Occupation: Co-Founder and Chief Executive, European Interactive Advertising Bureau, and Digital Strategy Consulting Group

Other positions: Co-founder and Non-Executive director for the UK Internet Advertising Bureau; Co-chair of the Digital Council at the Institute of Direct Marketing; university lectureships; strategic adviser to banks investing in digital media; Editorial Board of the Journal of Interactive Marketing; Chair of Examinations for the UK's first Diploma in Digital Marketing; various non-executive directorships.

Awards: Internet newspaper of the year (every year as publisher of Telegraph.co.uk); nominated for the first digital BAFTA; nominated twice for the lifetime contribution to the industry; acknowledged by six magazines as being one of the most influential 20 people in the industry; acknowledged by the DTI as one of the 100 founders of the UK online industry.

Education: University of Bristol; Henley Management College

Career highlights: Early dotcom explorer in 94; manager of the Telegraph's online editions from 95; ran search engines, email and online stores; co-founder of the IAB trade body in nine countries; early BBC TV Internet Correspondent; European VP for NBC Internet.

Mentor: Michael Chamberlain was an inspiration while I trained as a newspaper publisher with the Express. Richard Eyre, my chairman at the UK IAB, was a great mentor as we accelerated IABuk.net to become a great trade association.

Big break: In 95 being brought in as the first brand manager for the country's first online newspaper. Telegraph.co.uk was a micro business of just a few people at the time, but we began a rapid expansion to form a digital publishing group.

Big mistake: Not taking equity in the dozens of companies that invited me to along the way!

» **Reading:** *Authors on my desk at the moment: Negroponte, McLuhan, Coupland, Gibson, (William) Mitchell, (Malcolm) Gladwell. Press that I subscribe to: Economist, Harvard Business Review, Wired, New Media Age, Guardian. Websites and blogs: too many!* **Watching:** *I don't have time for traditional TV so tend to dip into whatever is streamed well: the BBC's News at 10 around midnight, some of the US networks. Let's get more of this stuff online! European cinema litters a vast DVD collection.* **Listening:** *For news nothing could beat the excellence and consistency of Today. For classics it's jazz, for contemp it's whichever one of my friends is on tour and needs the support!* **Relaxing to:** *As a master scuba instructor you'll find me heading for the deck of a yacht on a coral reef whenever I get the chance.*

» *Single, no children*

Richard Melman

The History Channel, Grant Way, Isleworth, Middlesex TW7 5QD
T 020 7941 5185
E richard.melman@bskyb.com

Occupation: Channel Director, The History Channel and The Biography Channel

Career highlights: Channel Director for The History Channel and The Biography Channel in the UK, Greece and Africa with responsibility for all aspects of programming, production, acquisition and scheduling; previously Channel Director for the UK arts broadcaster Artsworld; 1998-2000, as Head of Production for Jeremy Isaacs Productions worked on, amongst others, the Emmy award-winning series Millennium and the multi-award winning Cold War for Ted Turner and the BBC; in 1997 launched the BBC/Discovery joint venture channel People and Arts; 1990-94, Head of Production at the independent production company InCA, overseeing and producing commissions for C4 and BBC2.

Mentor: Sir Jeremy Isaacs

» **Watching:** *I love television and watch as much as possible from Iron Chief, a brilliant, totally weird Japanese cooking show, to Newsnight via The Sopranos.*

Sir Christopher Meyer 22.2.44

Press Complaints Commission, 1 Salisbury Square, London EC4Y 8JB
T 020 7353 1248
E kim.baxter@pcc.org.uk

Occupation: Chairman, Press Complaints Commission

Other positions: Chairman, GlobeTel Communications Corporation; Non-executive Director, GKN plc; Non-executive Director, Sanctuary Group.

Publications: DC Confidential, Weidenfeld & Nicolson, 2005.

Awards: Honorary Fellow, Peterhouse, Cambridge, 2001.

Education: Lancing College; Lycée Henri IV, Paris; Peterhouse, Cambridge; School of Advanced International Studies, Bologna

Career highlights: Diplomatic Service; 3rd Secretary, West and Central African Department, 1966-67; 3rd (later 2nd) Secretary, British Embassy, Moscow 1968-70; 2nd, later 1st Secretary, Madrid 1970-73; 1st Secretary, Eastern Europe and Soviet Department, FCO, 1973-76; 1st Secretary, planning staff 1976-78; 1st Secretary, UK Representative to European Community, Brussels 1978-82; headed political section of British Embassy, Moscow, 1982-84; Head, News Dept and Chief FCO spokesman, 1984-88; Visiting Fellow, Center for International Affairs, Harvard, 1988-89; Press Secretary to Foreign Minister Geoffrey Howe and Prime Minister John Major 1993-96; Ambassador to Germany 1997; Ambassador to USA 1997-2003; Chairman, Press Complaints Commission, 2003-present.

» **Listening:** *Jazz.* **Relaxing to:** *Tennis, reading.*

» *Married, 2 sons, 2 stepsons*

Ben Middleton

17.7.81

Mother, Biscuit Building, 10 Redchurch Street, London E2 7DD

T 020 7012 1999
E benj@motherlondon.com

Occupation: Creative, Mother London

Publications: Observer Music Monthly, From Abba to Zappa; Xfm, Welcome to Christian's World; UKTV Style Gardens, Egg.
Awards: 1 gold and 4 silvers, BTAA; 1 gold and 3 silvers, Creative Circle; 3 Campaign posters.
Education: Buckinghamshire Chilterns University College
Career highlights: In our two and a half years here at Mother we've learnt a huge amount. We've worked with the best people and have been given huge oppourtunities. The Abba to Zappa campaign for the Observer Music Monthly and the Welcome to Christian's World campaign for Xfm were great fun to work on.
Mentor: Dave Morris at university; Caroline Pay, Yan Elliot, Luke Williamson, Robert Saville, Mark Waites at Mother.
Big break: Getting a placement at Mother and then doing the Abba to Zappa campaign.
Big mistake: Thinking that teaming up with a Geordie wasn't going to do my head in.

» **Reading:** *Papers, magazines, books, the back of air freshener canisters.* **Watching:** *It depends on what's on. I tend to watch a lot of footie and always get sucked into documentaries and good comedy.* **Listening:** *I try to listen to anything new. Luckily we get sent a lot of music through work so we're usually pretty well stocked.* **Relaxing to:** *Playing golf, it's brilliant - not very cool admittedly, but brilliant.*
» *Single, no children*

Jeremy Miles

24.5.55

Miles Calcraft Briginshaw Duffy, 15 Rathbone Street, London W1T 1NB

T 020 7073 6900
E milesj@mcbd.co.uk

Occupation: Chairman, Miles Calcraft Briginshaw Duffy

Other positions: Member, Marketing Society, 1985; Member, Marketing Group of Great Britain, 2001; Member, Thirty Club, 2005; Director, Sainsbury's, 1985-84; Director, the Economist, 1985-99; Director, BT, 1994-99; Director, BT Global, 1995-99; Vice-Chairman, BT Global, 1998-99.
Awards: 9 Gold Campaign Awards, 24 Silver Campaign Awards, 8 D&AD Silver Pencils, Gold British Television Award, Gold IPA Effectiveness Award.
Education: Gordonstoun; Westminster
Career highlights: Trainee Account Executive, Abbott Mead Vickers BBDO, 1980-85; Co-founder and Chairman, Miles Calcraft Briginshaw Duffy 1999-present.

» **Relaxing to:** *Travel, reading, ballet, watching sport, theatre and film.* » *Married, 1 daughter*

Nick Miles

23.10.58

M:Communications, 1 Ropemaker Street, London EC2Y 9HT

T 020 7153 1535
E miles@mcomgroup.com

Occupation: Co-founder, M:Communications

Other positions: Performed in Death in the Aisles, Nightcap Cambridge Footlights Revues 1979; Directorships, BMP Business Ltd 1985-87; Lowe Bell Financial Ltd 1987-92; Chief Executive, Financial Dynamics Ltd 1992-2001; Chairman, Business Communications International Group, 2001-02; Founder, M: Communications, 2002.
Education: Tonbridge; Corpus Christi College, Cambridge
Career highlights: After Trafalgar House (Express Newspapers, Cunard) joined Good Relations PR business in 1983; hired by Tim Bell in the mid-80s, then hired as CEO of Financial Dynamics in the early 90s; worked on most of the very largest transactions and deals of those times; sold and bought back the business twice before final sale to Cordiant in 2000; left to found M: in 2002.
Mentor: Jimmy Goldsmith (deceased); Tony Good (very much alive).
Big break: Eight months on the beach with my young family in 2002.
Big mistake: Not writing the film I promised myself in 2002; also not climbing up the outside of the Eiffel Tower in 1982 when the opportunity presented itself.

» **Reading:** *Flashman, Waugh, Tolstoy and Zadie Smith.* **Watching:** *House, Lost, rugby, but mostly movies.* **Listening:** *Guitar music, especially Pierre Bensusan.* **Relaxing to:** *With the kids.* » *Married, 3 children*

Jonathan Miller

22.10.66

200 Gray's Inn Road, London WC1X 8XZ

T 020 7430 4606
E jonathan.miller@itn.co.uk

Occupation: Foreign Affairs Correspondent, Channel 4 News

Education: Monkton Combe School; Durham University
Career highlights: Since joining Channel 4 News in 2003, stories covered include the Asian tsunami, the Pakistan earthquake, war in Darfur, Sudan, insurgency in Iraq, revolutions in Georgia and Ukraine and the deaths of Arafat and the Pope; 1998-2003, Documentary Reporter for C4's investigative strand, Dispatches, and foreign affairs series, Unreported World; freelance film-maker and documentary director for C4 and CNN; 1994-1997 BBC Correspondent in Southeast Asia.
Big mistake: Buying C4 News Foreign Editor a camel whip in Sudan.

» **Listening:** *BBC World Service.* » *Married, 1 daughter*

Steve Mitchell 14.7.49

BBC Radio News, Broadcasting House,
Portland Place, London W1A 1AA
T 020 7580 4468
E steve.mitchell@bbc.co.uk

Occupation: Head of Radio News, BBC

Education: Loughborough Grammar School; Manchester University
Career highlights: Reporter, Thompson Newspapers; Reporter, Newcastle Journal; Reporter, South Wales Echo; Reporter, The Times, 1971-74; Producer, BBC; Reporter, Radio Newsroom, and Duty Editor, Today programme, BBC, 1974-84; Deputy Foreign News Editor, 1985; Editor, Parliamentary Output, BBC, 1986-88; Editor, then Managing Editor, Radio Newsroom, BBC, 1988-93; Editor, Radio News Programmes, BBC, 1993-97; Deputy Head, News Progs (Bimedia), 1997-99; Head of Radio News, BBC, 1999-present.

» **Relaxing to:** *Family, reading.* » *Married, 2 children*

Sheila Molnar A long time ago

Private Eye, 6 Carlisle Street, London W1D 3BN
T 020 7437 4017
E sheila.molnar@private-eye.co.uk

Occupation: Managing Director, Private Eye

Publications: Private Eye Magazine; Private Eye Annual; Private Eye Books.
Awards: None
Education: Roehampton Institute
Career highlights: Meeting Peter Cook, working with Ian Hislop and Richard Ingrams. Every Tuesday when a new issue of the Eye is published.
Mentor: Richard Ingrams and Ian Hislop.
Big break: I'm still waiting for that.
Big mistake: Not getting tickets to see Robbie Williams live.

» **Reading:** *Everything and anything - I love books.* **Watching:** *Anything that grabs my attention at the time.* **Listening:** *Pop and classical music, LBC, Clive Bull and Steve Allen.* **Relaxing to:** *Walking the dog and reading crime novels.* » *Married, 1 child*

Steven Moffat 19.11.65

14 Floral Street, London WC2E 9DH
T 020 7632 5281
E fionaw@berlinassociates.com

Occupation: Writer

Other positions: School teacher
Publications: Press Gang (all episodes); Coupling (all episodes); Joking Apart (all episodes); Dr Who (The Empty Child, The Doctor Dances and The Girl In The Fireplace); Murder Most Horrid (Overkill, Dying Live, Elvis, Jesus and Zack).
Awards: Bafta, Press Gang; Royal Television Society Award, Press Gang; Bronze Rose of Montreux, Joking Apart; silver Rose of Montreux, Coupling; British Comedy Award, Coupling; Prix Jeunesse, Exam Conditions.
Education: Glasgow University
Career highlights: I wrote all 43 episodes of Press Gang, a children's series (which I've only to mention in a pub to get bought drinks), all 28 episodes of Coupling, a sitcom which has sold all over the world and has been remade in America and Romania, and three episodes of the new Dr Who series. Having now written on three vaguely culty shows I now have the internet presence of light to middling pornography.
Mentor: Not sure I really have one.
Big break: Sandra Hastie trusting me to write all of Press Gang, as my very first writing job.
Big mistake: I'll tell you when I've finished making mistakes.

» **Reading:** *Not as much as I'd like. But the best book ever is The Time Traveller's Wife by Audrey Niffenegger.* **Watching:** *At the moment, The West Wing, Doctor Who, The X Factor, any Sherlock Holmes, House, Lost, Spooks.* **Listening:** *Classical music mainly, Beethoven and Elgar.* **Relaxing to:** *In hotels with my wife.* » *Married, 2 children*

Professor Fabian Monds 1.11.40

BBC, Broadcasting House, Ormeau Avenue,
Belfast BT2 8HQ
T 028 9033 8000

Occupation: Governor for Northern Ireland, BBC

Other positions: Chairman, BBC Children in Need Trustees; Trustee, UK Teaching Awards, 1999-present.
Publications: Minicomputer Systems, 1979; (with R McLaughlin) An Introduction to Mini and Micro Computers, 1981; The Business of Electronic Product Development, 1984.
Awards: CBE, 1997
Education: Christian Brothers Grammar School, Omagh; Queen's University, Belfast
Career highlights: Visiting Assistant Professor, Purdue University, USA, 1965-66; Lecturer, Queen's University Belfast, 1967-77; Senior Lecturer, Queen's University Belfast, 1977-78; Reader, Queen's University Belfast, 1978-86; Dean, Faculty of Informatics, Magee College, Londonderry, University of Ulster, 1989-93; Provost, Magee College, Londonderry, University of Ulster, 1995-2000; Chairman, Northern Ireland Information Age Initiative, 1999-2002; Chairman, University of Ulster Science Research Parks Ltd, 1999-2002; Chairman, Northern Ireland Industrial Research and Technology Unit, 2000-01; Chairman, Omagh 2010 Task Force, 2001-02; Chairman, Invest Northern Ireland, 2002-05; Chairman, NI Centre for Trauma and Transformation, 2002-present.

» **Relaxing to:** *General aviation.* » *Married, 2 daughters*

Sarah Montague 8.2.66

Today Programme, Room G630, TV Centre, London W12
T 020 8624 9644
E sarah.montague@bbc.co.uk

Occupation: Presenter, Today Programme, Radio 4; Presenter, Hardtalk, BBC World Television

Other positions: Formerly Presenter, Newsnight; BBC Breakfast; BBC News Bulletins; BBC News 24.
Education: Blanchelande College, Guernsey; Bristol University

» *Married, 2 children*

Julie Moore

Haymarket Publishing, 174 Hammersmith Road, London W6 7JP
T 020 8267 4301
E Julie.moore@haynet.com

Occupation: Publishing Director, Marketing, PrintWeek and PrintBuyer

Other positions: Formerly Ad Director and various sales management roles
Publications: Marketing, PrintWeek, PrintBuyer, PRWeek US
Awards: PPA Weekly Business Magazine of the Year, Marketing, 2005; PPA Publisher of the Year, highly commended, 2005; Haymarket Awards, Relaunch of the Year, Marketing, 2005; Gold Medal, Folio Editorial Excellence Award, PRWeek US, 2000; Gold Medal, Folio Circulation Excellence Awards, PRWeek US, 2001; Haymarket Awards, Outstanding Achievement, PRWeek US, 2000.
Career highlights: Two things stand out: the launch of PRWeek in the USA, where I went out as Ad Director and was promoted to Publisher in three months. I stayed running the business for Haymarket for three years and by the end of that period the magazine had achieved a near break-even position, years ahead of business plan. The second was re-launching Haymarket's flagship - Marketing - in 2004. This involved a hugely detailed and far-reaching plan to put some real distance between the two weekly marketing titles. This was achieved in every area from newsstand sales and readership to recruitment advertising and has resulted in winning the coveted PPA Weekly Business Magazine of the Year award in 2005.
Mentor: My old boss, Ruth Dickinson - utterly mad, passionate, hard as nails and great fun.
Big break: Being part of the launch team of PRWeek in New York.
Big mistake: Attempting a right hook to my boss's left jaw.

» **Reading:** *Trillions of magazines, especially food mags, the Guardian and Sunday Times, labels on food and picture captions.* **Watching:** *Not much TV, movies, movies, movies and people.* **Listening:** *The dawn chorus, everything from Gregorian chant to G-Love.* **Relaxing to:** *By satisfying my senses, running and being with my husband.*

Gareth Morgan 12.9.72

The Northern & Shell Building, 10 Lower Thames Street, London EC3R 6EN
T 0871 520 7233
E gareth.morgan@dailystar.co.uk

Occupation: Editor, Daily Star Sunday

Education: Manchester University, BSc (hons), Physics
Career highlights: After a promising start as a rocket scientist for British Aerospace (Army Weapons Division), I ran away and joined the tabloids. Working for Mercury Press, Liverpool; the Daily Star; Sunday Mirror and on to the Daily Star Sunday.
Mentor: The late, great Roger Blyth.
Big break: Getting made redundant by British Aerospace.

» **Reading:** *Every paper, every day and every magazine I can get my hands on.* **Watching:** *Whatever's on.* **Listening:** *Radio 2, Radio 4.* **Relaxing to:** *Watching Wolverhampton Wanderers.* » *Separated, 2 children*

Mike Morgan 12.10.67

The Red Consultancy, 41-44 Great Windmill Street, London W1D 7NF
T 020 7025 6500
E mike.morgan@redconsultancy.com

Occupation: CEO, The Red Consultancy

Publications: Carling Premiership; Nokia Mobile Phone; McDonald's.
Awards: British Association of Industrial Editors, 1992; Woolworths News, Hollis Sponsorship Awards, 1995; Best Sponsorship, Carling Premiership, PRCA Best Consumer Campaign, 1998; PR Week Best Sponsorship, 2000: Nokia PR Week Consultancy of the Year, 2003.
Education: University of East Anglia
Career highlights: Trained at London School of Journalism 1989; joined Paragon Communications in 1990 as a writer; in 1993 after just three years in public relations I was the lead Account Director for the launch of the Carling Premiership, at the time the UK's biggest sports sponsorship, and voted Best Sponsorship 1995; joined Red Consultancy as an Account Director in 1996; won the McDonald's Sport business in 1997 and have worked on the brand continuously since then; promoted to Red Consultancy board in 1999, Managing Director in 2003 and CEO in 2004; launched Red Consultancy, San Francisco 2005.
Mentor: There have been several down the years. Dawn Whiting and Julia Thorn at Paragon Communications, Lesley Brend and David Fuller at The Red Consultancy.
Big break: Being in the office of the London School of Journalism on the day someone rang looking for a junior writer. Literally right place, right time.
Big mistake: I make mistakes all the time. Can't recall an absolute howler but it's only a mouse click away.

» **Reading:** *The Sun, Guardian, Toffeeweb, Private Eye, New Yorker, Holy Moly!* **Watching:** *Football (Everton),*

Seinfeld, Curb Your Enthusiasm, Sopranos, Dad's Army, Carry-On films. **Listening:** *Country rock, country and western, country blues, alt-country.* **Relaxing to:** *Drinking, reading, gym, kids.* » *Married, 2 children*

Piers Morgan

30.3.65

c/o Channel 4, 124 Horseferry Road, London SW1P 2TX

T 020 7396 4444

Occupation: Journalist and broadcaster

Other positions: Co-proprietor, Press Gazette, 2005-present; Presenter, Morgan and Platell (Channel 4) 2004-present. Launching First News, a newspaper for children aged 9-12 years.
Publications: Private Lives of the Stars (1990), Secret Lives of the Stars (1991), Phillip Schofield - To Dream a Dream (1992), Take That - Our Story (1993), Take That - On The Road (1994), The Insider (2005).
Education: Chailey School; Lewes Priory Sixth Form College; Harlow Journalism College
Career highlights: Reporter, Surrey and South London Newspapers, 1987-89; Showbiz Editor, the Sun, 1989-94; Editor, News of the World, 1994-95; Editor, the Mirror, 1995-2004.

» **Relaxing to:** *Cricket, Arsenal FC.* » *Married, 3 sons*

Paul Morley

26.3.57

David Goodwin Associates, 55 Monmouth Street, London WC2H 5DG

T 020 7240 9992
E assistant@davidgodwinassociates.co.uk

Occupation: Writer and broadcaster

Other positions: Panellist, Newsnight Review (BBC2), 2001-present; Consultant, Palm Pictures, 2002-present.
Awards: Honorary Member, Peter Cook Appreciation Society.
Education: Stockport Grammar School; Stockport College of Technology
Career highlights: Writer, NME, 1976-83; Director, Zang Tuum Tumb Records, A&R and Art Director, Frankie Goes to Hollywood (including Relax, biggest selling single of the 1980s); Founder Member, Art of Noise; Consultant, Island Records, 1990-92 (Executive Producer, Vic Reeves' number one single Dizzy); Contributing Editor, Blitz Magazine, 1983-87; Esquire Magazine, 1991-99; TV Critic, New Statesman, 1987-89; the Guardian, 1991-94; GQ Magazine, 1998-99; regular contributor to national newspapers, TV documentaries and radio arts programmes; Co-founder, Service Production Co, 2002; Founder Presenter, The Late Show (BBC2), 1989-91; Writer and Presenter, The Thing Is... (Channel 4), 1989-92; Writer and Director, arts documentaries for BBC; ITV and Channel 4 (including Omnibus on Reeves and Mortimer).

» **Relaxing to:** *Listening, looking, reading, philosophy, hotels, internet, music, waiting.* » *Partner, 1 daughter*

Doug Morris

29.7.66

BBC Radio Cumbria, Annetwell Street, Carlisle CA3 8BB

T 01228 592444
E doug.morris@bbc.co.uk

Occupation: Assistant Editor, BBC Radio Cumbria

Other positions: Assistant Editor, BBC Radio Newcastle; Regional Journalist (NE England and Cumbria), Five Live; BBC News Correspondent.
Education: St George's School, Gravesend, Kent
Career highlights: Now - learning how output is run and how radio stations work. Then - reporting the build-up to the war and reflecting Arab opinion from Jordan February/March 2003. Getting into Belgrade when Milosovic fell. Sleeping out for the fuel protests, foot and mouth, and a report about a man getting stuck in an ironing board.
Mentor: Not a mentor, but a hero - James Cameron.
Big break: The launch of Five Live.
Big mistake: Agreeing to endless early shifts in my early days in local radio.

» **Reading:** *Walking books and cricket magazines. Not enough fiction.* **Watching:** *The Sopranos, Shameless, West Wing, Ashes 2005 DVD.* **Listening:** *Radio - everything I can. Music - Aretha, Otis, lots of soul, Small Faces, ska, The Clash, The Sonics. Online - BBC 7 listen again and Little Stevie's Underground Garage.* **Relaxing to:** *With my family and taking to the Highland hills and beaches.* » *Married, 3 children*

Kylie Morris

18.5.72

518/5 Maneeya Centre, PO Box 43, Ploenchit Road, Patumwan, Bangkok 10330, Thailand

T +66 2 652 0500
E kylie.morris@bbc.co.uk

Occupation: BBC South East Asia Correspondent

Other positions: BBC Kabul Correspondent; BBC Gaza Correspondent.
Awards: Foreign Press Association 2003; Finalist, Sony Awards 2003.
Education: London School of Economics; University of Newcastle, NSW, Australia
Career highlights: Worked for Australian Broadcasting Corporation (ABC) investigative programme, Background Briefing, before joining BBC in 2000. Producer on BBC World Service programme Newshour, and Field Producer for foreign correspondents. In 2001 moved to Gaza to become the BBC's first foreign correspondent based in Gaza City. Left the following year to take up a posting as Kabul Correspondent. Came out of Afghanistan to cover the war in Iraq and embedded with British forces. Made award-winning programme on the fight for Basra. New posting to Bangkok late 2003. Returned to Iraq and covered the Najaf siege in 2004. Late 2005 temporary assignment to Newsnight. Currently based in Bangkok.
Big break: Getting a job with the BBC. Finding great people to work with in the field.
Big mistake: Still working on it.

» **Reading:** *As much as I can. A selection of newspapers,* *normally on the internet, and anything else of note I can get my hands on.* **Watching:** *All news services, and Dr Who DVDs.* **Listening:** *On the road BBC World Service is impossible to beat.* **Relaxing to:** *By occasionally turning off my mobile phone.*

Anne Morrison

18.8.59

MC4 A4, BBC Media Centre, 201 Wood Lane, London W12 7TQ
T 020 8008 2871
E anne.morrison@bbc.co.uk

Occupation: Controller, Network Production, BBC

Other positions: Controller, Documentaries and Contemporary Factual, BBC 2001-06; Controller, Leisure and Factual Entertainment, BBC 2000-01; Head of Features and Events, BBC 1997-2000; Head of Consumer and Leisure, BBC 1996-97; Executive Producer, Crimewatch UK, Crimewatch; File, Taking Liberties, Rough Justice; Producer/ Director on a range of documentaries and factual formats.

Publications: Key TV Productions as Departmental Head: Coast, Great Britons, Live8, The Queen's Jubilee, Dunkirk, The Secret Policeman, The Secret Agent, The Hunt for Britain's Paedophiles, One Life, My Family and Autism, Mischief, My Life as a Child, The Lost World of Mitchell and Kenyon, What Not to Wear, Rogue Traders, Gardeners' World, Antiques Roadshow, Watchdog, Top Gear.

Awards: As Departmental Head; Top Gear, International Emmy; The Secret Policeman, RTS, BAFTA; One Life, Lager, Mum and Me, BAFTA; My Family and Autism, Banff; The Hunt for Britain's Paedophiles, RTS; Dunkirk, BAFTA; Dunkirk, The Soldier's Story, Grierson; What Not to Wear, RTS, Banff.

Education: Richmond Lodge School Belfast; Churchill College, Cambridge

Career highlights: I started my career as a journalist in Belfast and then joined the BBC as a General Trainee in London. I worked as a Film Director on Real Lives and then produced Holiday and Crimewatch UK, becoming Series Producer in 1988. Stints as Executive Producer of Rough Justice, Crimewatch and Taking Liberties followed; in 1994 I was promoted to Head of Features and for the next 11 years led a range of factual in-house production departments. This included 4 years running a combined radio and television department. My area of responsibility in television production increased to include factual formats, events, Bristol and Birmingham factual departments and documentaries. This represented over £100 million of output and around 1000 staff; I took up my current job at the BBC in February 2006 as Controller Network Production to work on the planning of production and management of talent across in-house production and to facilitate the growth in Nations network production.

» **Reading:** *A range of newspapers, Vogue, Heat, slim volumes of poetry and long Victorian novels.* **Watching:** *Anything and everything for work, movies for relaxation.*

» *Married, 1 daughter*

Steve Morrison

3.4.47

All3Media, 87-91 Newman Street, London W1T 3EY
T 020 7907 0177
E information@all3media.com

Occupation: Chief Executive, All3Media

Other positions: Board Member, British Screen Advisory Council, Edinburgh International Film Festival; Governor, National Film and Television School; Director, British Screen Finance; Fellow, Royal Television Society, 1998.

Publications: Granada network credits include: The Spanish Civil War, Disappearing World, China, Scully, The Road to 1984, 28-Up (fourth Seven-Up series); Granada film credits include: The Magic Toyshop, The Fruit Machine, My Left Foot, The Field, Jack and Sarah.

Awards: RTS Award, World in Action; BAFTA, 28-Up; 2 Oscars, My Left Foot; Oscar nominated, The Field, Jack and Sarah.

Education: University of Edinburgh; National Film School

Career highlights: Started career as Radio Producer with BBC Scotland; joined Granada Television to set up Northern Documentary Unit 1974; Producer/Director, World in Action, Head of Regional Programmes, then Head of Features and Documentaries 1987; Founder, Granada Film, 1985; Director of Programmes, 1987-92; Managing Director, Granada Television 1993, LWT 1994-96; Deputy Chief Executive, TV Division, Granada Group plc 1995; CEO, Granada Media plc 1996-2001; CEO, Granada plc 2001-02; Chairman, Granada Sky Broadcasting 1996-2002; Chairman, North West Vision 2003-present; Chief Executive, All3Media 2003-present.

» **Watching:** *Films and theatre.* **Relaxing to:** *Reading, talking and dining, touring delicatessens.* » *Married*

Roger Mosey

5.1.62

BBC Television Centre, Wood Lane, London W12 6RJ
T 020 8743 8000
E Roger.Mosey@bbc.co.uk

Occupation: Director of Sport, BBC

Awards: Today won Sony Gold Awards in 1994 and 1995, British Environment and Media Award and Radio Programme of the Year, Broadcasting Press Guild, 1995; Radio Five Live Sony National Radio Station of the Year, 1998; BBC Television News Programme of the Year awards for Newsnight, 2002 and the Ten O'Clock News, 2004.

Education: Bradford Grammar School; Oxford University

Career highlights: Head of BBC Television News; Editor, Today, Radio 4, 1993-97; Controller, Radio Five Live.

» **Reading:** *Thrillers and political biographies.* **Watching:** *Movies.* **Relaxing to:** *Football, Bradford City fan.*

Chris Moyles

22.2.74

BBC Radio 1, Yalding House,
152-156 Great Portland Street, London W1N 4DJ
T 08700 100 100
E chris.moyles@bbc.co.uk

Occupation: Presenter, Breakfast Show, BBC Radio 1

Awards: Silver Sony Radio Award for DJ of the Year, 1998
Career highlights: Started radio career on Aire FM, Leeds, 1990-91; worked on several other stations including Radio Luxembourg and Capital FM, London, 1991-97; voted as one of the 'Faces for '97' by Sky Magazine; joined Radio 1, 1997; won Silver Sony Radio Award, DJ of the Year, 1998; DJ, Summer Roadshow, 1998; DJ, main compere slot, V98, Leeds, 1998; Front, late afternoon show, Radio 1, 1998; voted DJ of the Year by Sun readers, 1998; DJ, One Big Belly tour, Scarborough, Hunstanton, Weymouth, Paignton and Newquay, 2000; DJ, outside broadcasts from Euro 2000 football tournament in Belgium and Holland, Radio 1, 2000; DJ, One Big Sunday events, Radio 1, 2001; embraced physical fitness in 2003 saying he was 'bored of being fat'; TV work includes Live With Chris Moyles, Five, 2002; The Chris Moyles Show, UK Play, 1999-2000.

Peter Muir

16.11.72

30 Cleveland Street, London W1T 4JD
T 020 7907 6517
E peter_muir@dennis.co.uk

Occupation: Editor, Men's Fitness magazine

Other positions: Managing Editor, Maxim; Chief Sub, Maxim; Chief Sub, Checkout
Awards: 50 metre swimming badge.
Education: Swansea University
Career highlights: Left Reed Business Publishing in 1995 (a definite highlight) and joined Maxim magazine to contribute to the rise of laddist culture (sorry). Moved to Men's Fitness in 2002.
Big break: Being in close proximity to the Editor's chair on Men's Fitness when it became vacant in 2002.
Big mistake: Not leaving Reed Business Publishing sooner.

» **Reading:** *The Week.* **Watching:** *Anything - all TV is great.* **Listening:** *iPod on shuffle mode.* **Relaxing to:** *Sport, drinking with friends, playing with daughter.* » *Married, 1 child*

John Mulholland

16.11.62

The Observer, 3-7 Herbal Hill, London EC1R 5EJ
T 020 7713 3998
E john.mulholland@observer.co.uk

Occupation: Deputy Editor, the Observer

Other positions: Media Editor, the Guardian.
Education: Dublin University; California State University, Sacramento
Career highlights: Overseeing the Observer's switch to mid-size. Seeing the first issues of the new paper roll off the presses after 18 months of work was a huge thrill.

» *Single, 1 child*

James Murdoch

13.12.72

British Sky Broadcasting, Grant Way, Isleworth, Middlesex TW7 5QD
T 0870 240 3000
E tracey.iles@bskyb.com

Occupation: Chief Executive, BSkyB

Other positions: Executive Vice-President, News Corporation, 1999-present.
Education: Horace Mann High School, New York City, Harvard University
Career highlights: Intern, Sydney Mirror, 1987; Cartoonist, the Harvard Lampoon, mid-90s; Founder, Rawkus Records, 1995; joined News Corporation, 1996; Chairman, Festival Records, subsequently Festival Mushroom Records, 1996-2005; Chairman and Chief Executive, Star TV, 2000; Member, Board, One.Tel 1999-2001; Director, then CEO, BSkyB, 2003-present.

» *Married, 2 children*

Rupert Murdoch

11.3.31

Times Newspapers Limited, PO Box 495, Virginia Street, London E1 9XY
T 020 7782 4000
E karen.colognese@newsint.co.uk

Occupation: Chairman and Chief Executive, News Corporation

Other positions: Director, News International; Director, Harper Collins Publishers Ltd, 1989-present; Director, British Sky Broadcasting plc, 1990-present.
Awards: Honorary Fellow, Worcester College, Oxford, 1982.
Education: Geelong Grammar School; Worcester College, Oxford
Career highlights: Chairman and Chief Executive, The News Corporation Ltd; Chairman and President, News America Publishing Inc; Joint Chairman, Ansett Transport Industries, 1982-92; Chairman and CEO, 20th Century Fox to 1996, currently Director; UK newspapers owned include the Sun and The Times.

» *Married, 6 children*

Michael Murphy

26.1.69

2 Oxted Chambers, Station Road East, Oxted, Surrey
T 0870 787088
E michael@friendsreunited.co.uk

Occupation: CEO, Friends Reunited

Other positions: Managing Director, Free Press Group, June 1995; Director, Financial Times, UK, December 1996; World Wide Commercial Director, Financial Times, March 1998; Managing Director, FT Business, March 1999; Chief Operating Officer,

FT.com, August 2000; Chief Operating Officer, Financial Times, October 2001.
Awards: The Sunday Times 2004 Microsoft Tech Track 100, 64th position; the DMA Awards 2004, Other Digital Media, silver; Microsoft Tech Track 100, Best Use of Technology 2004; the Sunday Times PricewaterhouseCoopers Profit Track 100, 84th position; Growing Business Awards 2003, Most Promising Young Company.
Education: St Joseph's Academy, Blackheath, London; Harvard Business School
Career highlights: Prior to my appointment at Friends Reunited, I previously had a 20 year career with Pearson plc, culminating in being Chief Operating Officer of the Financial Times. I left FT in April 2002 to pursue a management buy-out; when this failed to materialise in July 2002, I continued to work with a number of venture capitalists to find a management buy-in opportunity. It was in January 2003 that I finally achieved this, although it was eventually completed without any bank or VC involvement; my last role at the Financial Times Group was Chief Operating Officer of the Financial Times newspaper. Before this I was Chief Operating Officer of FT.com where I helped the site break even and introduced subscription charges; I was also Managing Director of FT Business where I refocused the company as a specialist publisher of market leading magazines whose properties included The Banker and the Investors Chronicle.
Mentor: Stephen Hill, currently CEO, Betfair.
Big break: Buying into Friends Reunited.
Big mistake: Not finding a management buy-out opportunity sooner.

» **Reading:** *James Patterson.* **Watching:** *Sopranos, Waking The Dead, football and golf.* **Listening:** *REM, Seal, Eagles, Simply Red, U2 and David Gray.* **Relaxing to:** *Playing golf.* » *Married, 2 daughters*

Stuart Murphy

7.11.75

RDF Television, The Gloucester Building, Kensington Village, Avonmore Road, London W14 8RF
T 020 7013 4000
E Stuart.Murphy@RDFMedia.com

Occupation: Creative Director, RDF Media

Other positions: Controller, BBC Three; Controller, BBC Choice; Channel Editor, UK Play; Strategic Development Manager, ICG, BBC; Producer, The Big Breakfast; Series Prod, MTV; various prod roles on Great Railway Journeys, comedy docs, Lifeswaps, The Sunday Show, Reportage etc.
Awards: Channel of the Year, 2005, MGEITF; Best Entertainment Channel, 2005, Broadcast Awards; commissioned shows which have won 6 BAFTAs, 15 RTS Awards, 5 British Comedy Awards, 2 BANFF Awards, 5 Rose d'Or, Prix Europa.
Education: St Mary's Menston, Ilkley; Clare College, Cambridge
Career highlights: Launching BBC Three and UK Play; commissioning Flashmob The Opera, Rock Profiles; signing up Dr Tanya Byron, Little Angels.
Mentor: Roly Keating
Big break: Paul Lee suggesting I phone Roly Keating about Radio One TV, which turned into UK Play. Director Steve Smith asking me to do camera scripts when I was a tea boy.
Big mistake: X Ray Vision, MTV show at the Rieperbahn, Hamburg ... rather not talk about it.

» **Reading:** *Political biographies, the Sun.* **Watching:** *As much TV as possible, blockbuster movies.* **Listening:** *Shostakovich, Robbie, Puccini.* **Relaxing to:** *Beers and baths.* » *Single, 2 children*

Susan Murphy

14.7.62

Channel 4, 124 Horseferry Road, London SW1P 2TX
T 020 7306 5369
E smurphy@channel4.co.uk

Occupation: Head of Features, Channel 4 Television

Other positions: Formerly Controller, Factual Entertainment, Channel 5; Commissioning Editor, Factual Entertainment, Channel 4; Executive Producer/Series Producer, Channel 4 Youth Entertainment series.
Education: La Sainte Union Convent; Warwick University
Career highlights: My current job as Head of Features at Channel 4. Being responsible for an important part of the schedule and having the opportunity to work with Gordon Ramsay (GR's F Word and Ramsay's Kitchen Nightmares), Jamie Oliver (Jamie's Great Italian Escape), Kevin McCloud (Grand Designs), and all the other great on-screen talent in C4's Features programming; before that, working at Channel 5 at a key time in its development and being responsible for commissioning some popular pop docs including Michael Jackson's Face. My big break in telly and another highlight was being part of a brilliant team of creative people in Channel 4's Entertainment Department, where I was credited with starting the vogue for Saturday night nostalgia programmes for 20 and 30-somethings including the Top Ten Series and the 100 Greatest Series; in production I worked on a fair few ropey productions but also Series Produced/Exec Produced youth entertainment series such as Passengers and Badass TV. When I started out in television, I couldn't believe my luck when I got a gig as a Film Researcher for Granada Television, working on many GTV shows including the legendary World In Action.
Mentor: Graham Murray, Joanne Wallace, Kevin Lygo.
Big break: Doing maternity cover for Jo Wallace in C4's Entertainment Department and persuading Kevin Lygo to keep me on when Jo returned.
Big mistake: Too many to mention.

» **Reading:** *Philip Roth, James Lee Burke, Mark Burnell, Tess Gerritsen etc.* **Watching:** *Gordon Ramsay, Jamie Oliver, Grand Designs, Simpsons, Supernanny, Brat Camp, all C4 features shows between 8 and 9 pm Tuesday to Thursday, Who Do You Think You Are, Top Gear, Big Brother, X Factor, I'm A Celebrity, obscure music docs on BBC4.* **Listening:** *Joni Mitchell, George and Tammy, Nick Drake, Sandy Denny, Doc Boggs, Dick Gaughan, The Stooges, I'm Sorry I Haven't A Clue.* **Relaxing to:** *Being with my son, friends, reading, music, television.* » *Married, 1 child*

Hamish Mykura 29.3.66

Channel 4, 124 Horseferry Road, London SW1P 2TX
T 020 7306 8283
E hmykura@channel4.co.uk

Occupation: Head of History, Science and Religion, Channel 4

Other positions: Fellow of the Royal Society of Arts.
Publications: Monarchy by David Starkey, Channel 4; Empire by Niall Ferguson, Channel 4; That'll Teach 'Em, Channel 4; What We Still Don't Know, Channel 4; Georgian Underworld season, Channel 4.
Awards: Touching the Void, Best British Film, BAFTA 2004; Georgian Underworld, History Award, RTS Progamme Awards 2003; Tony Robinson, Best Presenter Award, RTS 2005.
Education: Aberdeen University; Manchester University
Career highlights: Getting history and science programmes working together on Channel 4; commissioning That'll Teach 'Em, The Georgian Underworld and Gunther von Hagens on the anatomy of disease on Channel 4; bringing Niall Ferguson's Empire series to Channel 4; directing a BBC2 biography of Liberace that got 4.2 million viewers; producing Peter Snow's swingometer graphics during the 1997 General Election; inventing a new Radio 4 talk show Postcard from Gotham that ran for seven series; getting the first interview with Salman Rushdie since the fatwa on Radio 4; being the occasional voice of Gerry Adams on BBC News during the IRA broadcasting ban.
Mentor: Brian Barron gave me my first break in television. Janice Hadlow gave me the opportunity to make documentaries, and Denys Blakeway revealed the world of independent production.
Big break: Getting on the BBC Production Trainee scheme.
Big mistake: Haven't made it yet.

» **Reading:** *The New Yorker and I'm always happy to be recommended novels.* **Watching:** *Desperate Housewives was this year's treat.* **Listening:** *Radio 4 in moderation.* **Relaxing to:** *I get out of London.* » *Married, 2 children*

Paul Myners 1.4.48

Guardian Media Group, 75 Farringdon Road EC1M 3JY
T 020 7713 4452
E paul.myners@myners.com

Occupation: Chairman, Guardian Media Group

Other positions: Chairman, Council, Tate St Ives, 2001-present; Chairman of Trustees, Tate Gallery, 2003-present; Glyndebourne, 2003-present; Smith Institute, 2003-present; Non-executive Director, Gartmore Global Investors plc (formerly English & Scottish Investors), 1986-present; Guardian Newspapers Ltd, 2001-present; Bank of New York, 2002-present; Bank of England, 2005-present.
Publications: Developing a Winning Partnership, 1995; Creating Quality Dialogue, 1999; Institutional Investment in the UK: a review for HM Treasury, 2001.
Awards: FRSA, 1994; Freeman, City of London, 1996; Honorary LLD, Exeter, 2003.
Education: Truro School, Cornwall; University of London Institute of Education; Stanford School of Business
Career highlights: Daily Telegraph, 1970-74; N M Rothschild & Sons Ltd, 1974-85 (Dir, 1979); Gartmore plc, Chief Executive, 1985-93, 1999-2000; Chairman, 1987-2001; Executive Director, National Westminster Bank, 1997-2000; Deputy Chairman, PowerGen plc, 1999-2001; Orange plc, 1996-99; Coutts Group, 1997-2000; mmO2 plc (formerly BT Wireless), 2001-04; Member, Financial Reporting Council, 1995-2004; Company Law Review Consultative Committee, 1998-2000; Royal Academy Trust, 2000-03; Member, Advisory Council, London Symphony Orchestra, 1993-2003. Trustee, National and Cornwall Maritime Museum Trust, 1998-2004; Charities Aid Foundation, 2003-04.

» **Relaxing to:** *Opera, the work of Cornish artists, the countryside, rugby football.* » *Married, 5 children*

Adam Mynott 22.10.61

c/o BBC News, Television Centre, London W12 7RJ
T 020 8743 8000
E adam.mynott@bbc.co.uk

Occupation: BBC East Africa Correspondent

Other positions: BBC South Asia Correspondent 2001-2004; BBC Sports Correspondent 1998-2004.
Education: Exeter University

» *Married, 3 children*

Clive Myrie 26.8.68

2000 M Street, NW, Washington DC, 20036, USA
T +202 355 1753
E clive.myrie@bbc.co.uk

Occupation: BBC Washington Correspondent

Other positions: BBC Asia Correspondent; BBC News Correspondent.
Awards: Part of team that won a Golden Nymph at 2003 Monte Carlo Television Festival for coverage of Iraq war; Screen Nations Award for services to journalism 2003; nominated twice for Bayeux War Correspondents Award 2001, 2003; nominated twice for Emma Award 2002, 2003; part of team nominated for a BAFTA award for coverage of Mozambique floods 2001.
Education: University of Sussex
Career highlights: Coverage of Hurricane Mitch in the late 1990s, the impeachment of President Clinton in 1998, the Mozambique floods in 2000, the Indian earthquake in 2000, the Football World Cup in Tokyo in 2002, the Iraq war in 2003, the Bali bombings in 2003, and the US Presidential Election in 2004.
Mentor: There have been many who've helped me along the way. I particularly remember the encouragement I received from Roger Mosey and Rod Liddle when I was a reporter on the Today programme on Radio 4.

Big break: Covering the civil strife in Algeria in 1993.
Big mistake: Not keeping a journal while embedded during the Iraq war. Giving up French lessons before O-Level.

» **Reading:** *Documentaries, independent movies.* **Listening:** *Jazz.* **Relaxing to:** *Cinema and listening to jazz.*
» *Married, no children*

Nina Nannar 20.3.71

200 Gray's Inn Road, London WC1X 8XZ
T 020 7430 4071
E Nina.Nannar@itn.co.uk

Occupation: ITN Correspondent

Other positions: Formerly BBC Presenter and Reporter, radio and television. Currently Ambassador, Princes Trust; Ambassador, Sense International; Governor, Staffordshire University; Patron, Commonwealth Tapestry Commission; Patron, DanceEast.
Publications: Arts and Media Correspondent.
Education: Leeds
Career highlights: Oscars 2004, meeting too many amazing people to mention.
Mentor: Parents are my inspiration. Idol is Muhammad Ali.
Big break: Interviewing George Clooney in 2000.
Big mistake: Too many to mention!

» **Reading:** *Presswise the Guardian, Observer, Sun, Mirror and Vanity Fair.* **Watching:** *Avid Coronation Street fan. Never miss Deadwood on Sky.* **Listening:** *Xfm, Jonathan Ross on Radio 2, Five Live for news and sport.* **Relaxing to:** *With my family.*
» *Married, 1 daughter*

James Naughtie 9.8.51

BBC News Centre, London W12 8QT
T 020 8743 8000
E james.naughtie@bbc.co.uk

Occupation: Journalist and radio presenter

Other positions: Laurence M Stern Fellow, Washington Post, 1981; Member, Council, Gresham College, 1997-present; Member, Edinburgh International Festival Trust, 2003-present; Patron, Southbank Sinfonia.
Publications: Editor, Playing the Palace: a Westminster collection, 1984; The Rivals: the intimate story of a political marriage, 2001; The Accidental American, 2004; contributor to newspapers, magazines, journals.
Awards: Personality of the Year, Sony Radio Awards, 1991; Voice of the Listener and Viewer Award for Radio, 2001; Honorary LLD, Aberdeen, 1990; Honorary LLD, St Andrews, 2001; D Univ, Stirling, 2001; Honorary D Litt, Glasgow Caledonian, 2002; Honorary D Litt, Napier, 2002.
Education: Keith Grammar School; Aberdeen University; Syracuse University, New York
Career highlights: Journalist, The Press and Journal, 1975-77; Journalist, the Scotsman, 1977-84; Journalist, the Guardian, 1984-88; Chief Political Correspondent, BBC, including Presenter, The Week in Westminster, 1985-88; Presenter, The World at One, BBC Radio 4, 1988-94; Presenter, Opera News, BBC Radio 3,

1990-93; Presenter, BBC Proms, 1992-present; Presenter, Bookclub, BBC Radio 4, 1998-present; currently Presenter, Today programme and regular election and by-election specials, BBC Radio 4; radio documentaries and series include A Nearby Country, 1991; The Power and the Glory, 1992; The Thin Blue Line, 1993.

» **Relaxing to:** *Books, opera.* » *Married, 3 children*

Bill Neely 22.5.63

200 Gray's Inn Road, London WC1X 8XZ
T 020 7430 4411
E bill.neely@itn.co.uk

Occupation: International Editor, ITV News

Awards: Royal Television Society Award winner (twice); Monte Carlo Gold Nymph Winner Emmy nominations (twice); various Gold (and other) awards at the New York TV News awards.
Education: St. Malachy's College, Belfast
Career highlights: Reporting the fall of the Berlin Wall and the collapse of the Soviet Union over two years; covering several wars including Kosovo, Afghanistan and Iraq 03; six years as Washington Correspondent; three US elections, two World Cups and an Olympic Games; the first Western TV reporter (invited) into KGB Headquarters and the first into the Paris tunnel after the crash that killed Princess Diana; covering the death of Pope John Paul the Second and numerous earthquakes, hurricanes, mudslides, volcanic eruptions and other natural disasters, including the Asian tsumani, the New Orleans flood and the Pakistan earthquake of 2005.
Mentor: The television reporter I most admired until his retirement was Martin Bell. Also then, and now, Paul Davies of ITN.
Big break: Covering the Ballykelly massacre of 1982 was the biggest break of my early career in BBC Radio. Reporting the fall of the Berlin Wall must rank as the biggest break of anyone's career.
Big mistake: Too many and too varied to mention, but nothing - so far - that's landed me in jail or cost a life.

» **Reading:** *Fewer novels than before and more poetry. The Guardian is my base newspaper with the Telegraph as balance and the Observer at weekends. The Economist and, when I have lots of time, the London Review of Books.* **Watching:** *News, and lots of it. Football is my chewing gum TV.* **Listening:** *On Radio, the Today programme, because it's required listening. Once, alas, John Peel, now Melvyn Bragg. As for music, Morrisette, Morrison, Mahler, Cohen, Armatrading and the great glorious Sex Pistols.* **Relaxing to:** *How the hell can I relax with two children and a job like mine? No, I run every day, swim when I can, love movies, family and friends and drink as much fine wine as I can afford and stomach.* » *Married, 2 daughters*

Dawn Neesom 12.12.68

Daily Star, The Northern & Shell Building, 10 Lower Thames Street, London EC3R 6EN
T 0871 520 7474
E dawn.neesom@dailystar.co.uk

Occupation: Editor, Daily Star

Education: Ilford County High School for Girls
Mentor: Peter Hill
Big break: Being made Editor of the Daily Star.

» **Reading:** *Anything and everything.* **Watching:** *Football.* **Listening:** *Talk radio.* **Relaxing to:** *Following West Ham United and running.* » *Married, no children*

Andrew Neil 21.5.49

Glenburn Enterprises, PO Box 584, London SW7 3QY
T 020 7581 1655
E andrew.neil@bbc.co.uk

Occupation: Editor, the Business

Other positions: Chief Executive, Press Holdings Ltd, The Spectator, Apollo; Presenter, The Daily Politics and This Week with Andrew Neil.
Publications: The Cable Revolution, 1982; Full Disclosure, autobiography, 1996; British Excellence, 1998.
Awards: FRSA, 1997
Education: Paisley Grammar School; University of Glasgow
Career highlights: UK and US Correspondent, the Economist, 1973-81; UK Editor, the Economist, 1982-83; Editor, Sunday Times 1983-94. Vital player in Rupert Murdoch's switch to Wapping, 1986; Executive Chairman, Sky TV, 1988-90; Executive Editor, Fox News (New York), 1994; freelance broadcaster, writer, lecturer and media consultant, 1994-present; Columnist, Sunday Times and Daily Mail, 1994-96; Contributing Editor, Vanity Fair, 1994-present; Publisher, Editor-In-Chief and Chief Executive, Press Holdings Ltd (The Scotsman, Scotland on Sunday, Edinburgh Evening News, Scotsman.com and The Business) 1996-present; Chief Executive, The Spectator, Apollo, 2004-present; Co-presenter, The Midnight Hour (BBC 2) 1994-98; Conference Talk (BBC 2), 1996-99; Thursday Night Live (Carlton TV) 1997-2000; Despatch Box (BBC 2), 1998-2002; Presenter: The Andrew Neil Show (BBC 2), 1995-96, The Sunday Breakfast Programme (BBC Radio 5 Live), 1998-2000; The Daily Politics (BBC 2), 2003-present, This Week with Andrew Neil (BBC 1), 2003-present; Lord Rector, University of St Andrews 1999-2002.

» **Relaxing to:** *Dining out in London, New York, Aspen and Côte d'Azur.*

Roger Nelson

28.4.51

Compass House, 22 Redan Place, London W2 4SA
T 020 7229 4400
E roger.nelson@nelsonbostock.com

Occupation: Joint Managing Director, Nelson Bostock Communications

Education: King's College, University of London

» **Watching:** *Only The West Wing.*
» *Married, twin daughters*

Simon Nelson

2.7.73

Room 4402, Broadcasting House, Portland Place, London W1A 1AA
T 020 7765 1403
E simon.nelson@bbc.co.uk

Occupation: Controller, BBC Radio and Music Interactive

Other positions: Head of Strategy, BBC Radio; Brand Development Manager, the Independent; Manager, Dimples Wigs and Toupees.
Publications: www.bbc.co.uk/radio including the BBC Radioplayer; www.bbc.co.uk/music; www.bbc.co.uk/digitalradio; Interactive TV services for Proms, Mozart, Beethoven, Glastonbury; 24/7 interactive TV services on Freeview to support BBC radio stations; BBC download and podcasting trial including Beethoven downloads; coordinate the BBC's DAB digital radio strategy.
Awards: Several Webbys including Best Radio and Best Music Website; 2 interactive BAFTAs; Prix Europa for Internet; AOP Award for Innovation; several Digital Music Awards; World Summit Award for E-Entertainment.
Education: Cambridge University
Career highlights: Developed the BBC's digital radio strategy for all platforms and the new service strategy whilst Strategy Manager and then Head of Strategy for BBC Radio. Then set up the BBC's radio online service including the development of the BBC Radio Player, the BBC's first major move into On Demand. Added responsibility for all digital platforms and for digital music including radio on digital TV and mobiles. Also coordinate the BBC's DAB Digital Radio activities, including as a Director of the Digital Radio Development Bureau. BBC Radio and Music websites now receive 8 million unique users a month and receive over 9 million requests for on-demand content every month.

» *Married, 3 children*

Daniela Neumann

12.11.70

200 Gray's Inn Road, London WC1X 8HF
T 020 7843 8100
E daniela.neumann@itv.com

Occupation: Controller, Commissioned Programmes ITV2 and ITV3

Other positions: Fellow of the Royal Society of Arts; Member of BAFTA.
Education: Westminster Press Journalism College
Career highlights: Producer/Director of factual and factual entertainment programmes including Ibiza Uncovered and Airline. Also Drama Director including The Bill and Emmerdale. Began work at ITV in 2002. Helped make ITV2 one of the fastest growing digital channels.
Mentor: Jim Allen, Director Factual Granada.
Big break: Moving from newspaper reporter to researcher on Crime Monthly at London Weekend Television.
Big mistake: I can't tell you my biggest mistake as it is still a secret, thankfully!

» **Reading:** *The Guardian, Sun, novels ranging from the intelligent to the trashy.* **Watching:** *Everything from the serious to the light-hearted.* **Listening:** *Radio 4, Radio 1, LBC.* **Relaxing to:** *A nice hot bath.* » *One child*

Jackie Newcombe

27.7.64

King's Reach Tower, Stamford Street, London SE1 9LS
T 020 7261 5425
E jackie_newcombe@ipcmedia.com

Occupation: Managind Director of IPC Southbank and Wallpaper

Other positions: Publishing Director, Marie Claire; MD, Cube Contract Publisher; Publishing Director, Now, Woman and Woman's Own, Publisher, Woman and Home and Essentials; Publisher, 19 and Mizz; Ad Director, various titles.
Awards: Player of the match, Nonsuch girls netball circa 1978.
Education: Nonsuch Grammar, Cheam; Loughborough University
Career highlights: Starting my career as a graduate trainee with the best sales team of the 80s - Options; living the whole 80s dream at Carlton Magazines; becoming Ad Director on the launch of Country Homes and Interiors at 24; launching Now magazine; working with our French partners at Groupe Marie Claire.
Mentor: Sue Phipps
Big break: Having Sue Phipps as my mentor.
Big mistake: Not agreeing an agent's fee with Nick Emery (now Worldwide Head of Strategy for WPP) when I gave him his first job in media as a sales exec on Country Homes and Interiors!

» **Reading:** *Marie Claire of course! Times and Observer.* **Watching:** *Sopranos, The Apprentice and Chelsea.* **Listening:** *Radio 4 and Radio 5 are the only constants; all the others come and go.* **Relaxing to:** *Rediscovering the joys of a social life, now that my kids are teenagers.* » *Married, 2 children*

Martin Newland 27.10.65

T 020 7538 6300
E martin.newland@waitrose.com

Occupation: Former Editor, Daily Telegraph

Other positions: Reporter, then Home Editor Daily Telegraph 1989-1998; Deputy Editor, National Post, Canada 1998-2003; 2003-present, Editor Daily Telegraph.
Education: Downside School; Goldsmiths College; Heythrop College, University of London
Mentor: Ken Whyte, Editor in Chief, National Post, now Editor and Publisher Maclean's Magazine, Toronto.
Big break: Getting the chance to launch the Post.
Big mistake: Don't think I have dropped a real clanger yet.

» **Reading:** *Military history, Stephen King.* **Watching:** *All US sitcoms - Frasier etc. Sky news, BBC news and any costume drama going.* **Listening:** *Lou Reed and Velvet Underground, Cohen, Springsteen, Mozart, Verdi, Puccini.* **Relaxing to:** *Martial arts, running, training, TV with the kids on the sofa.* » *Married, 4 children*

Andrew Newman 5.11.73

Channel 4 Television, 124 Horseferry Road, London SW1P 2TX
T 020 7306 6382
E anewman@channel4.co.uk

Occupation: Head Of Entertainment, Channel 4

Other positions: Controller of Entertainment, Five, 2001-03; Head of Programmes, E4, 2000-01; Commissioning Editor, Entertainment, C4 1998-2000.

» *Married, 2 children*

Steve Nicholls 25.12.75

Euro RSCG London, Cupola House, 15 Alfred Place, London WC1E 7EB
T 020 7467 9200
E steve.nicholls@eurorscg.com

Occupation: Senior Copywriter and Art Director, Euro RSCG

Publications: Citroen C4, Transformer; Nissan, Weatherman; Bounty, Strong Housewives; London Underground, unNOTICEd posters; launching bmibaby.
Awards: D&AD silver; BTAA silver; 2 BTAA bronze; Creative Circle gold; 3 Creative Circle silvers; Campaign Poster silver; Cannes bronze. Too many commendations for my liking.
Education: The Kingswinford School; Stourbridge Art College; University of Wolverhampton
Career highlights: Getting hired; winning some awards; being appointed to the board of Partners BDDH, aged 29; making an ad that the Sun rates as 'the best ad ever made', or something.
Mentor: John Lowe, former 3rd year tutor, BA (Hons) Visual Communication course, University of Wolverhampton.
Big break: Getting an award-winning ad out while on a placement at TBWA arranged by John Lowe, through a former student called Trevor Beattie.
Big mistake: Too many to mention.

» **Reading:** *bbc.co.uk/news every 20 minutes; Guardian Unlimited, Times Online, the Sunday Times, Time Out, Popbitch, holymoly, some books.* **Watching:** *Not enough television for this job.* **Listening:** *Squirrels trying to break into my attic.* **Relaxing to:** *Cooking.* » *Married to Sigi, no children yet*

Lindsay Nicholson

National Magazine House, 72 Broadwick Street, London W1F 9EP
T 020 7439 5247
E Lindsay.nicholson@natmags.co.uk

Occupation: Editorial Director, The National Magazine Company

Awards: PPA Consumer Editor of the Year, 1999; Race In Media Award, 2005.
Education: University College London
Career highlights: Studied astrophysics at University College London but turned down jobs in the defence industry as a rocket scientist after winning a place on the Mirror Group Newspapers Training Scheme; switched to magazines, working on titles including Woman's Own, Honey, Living, Best and Woman; Editor, Prima, 1995-99; launched Prima Baby and Your Home; Editor-in-Chief, Good Housekeeping, 1999-2006; appointed Editorial Director of the National Magazine Company, 2006. Probably the only magazine editor who was also a Fellow of the Royal Astronomical Society.
Mentor: Axel Ganz and Terry Mansfield.
Big break: Being appointed Editor of Prima when I was only an Assistant Editor of Woman. I leapfrogged the Deputy bit.
Big mistake: I once did a pink and silver Christmas cover. Never again! There's only one colour at Christmas, and it's red!

» **Reading:** *Everything I can get my hands on - newspapers, books, magazines. I live in terror of being stuck without anything to read.* **Watching:** *American sitcoms, a bit of sci-fi, movies with subtitles.* **Listening:** *Any CD left in the car by my husband or daughter.* **Relaxing to:** *Reading magazines (I can't stop myself) and I like to walk my dogs on Hampstead Heath.* » *Married, 1 daughter*

Mary Nightingale 27.5.67

200 Gray's Inn Road, London WC1X 8XZ
T 020 7833 3000
E mary.nightingale@itn.co.uk

Occupation: Co-presenter, ITV Evening News

Awards: TRIC Newscaster of the Year 2002; TRIC Newscaster of the Year 2004.
Education: Bedford College; London University

» *Married, 2 children*

Anthony Noguera

18.7.73

EMAP, Endeavour House, 189 Shaftesbury Avenue, London WC2H 8JG

T 020 7208 3797
E anthony.noguera@emap.com

Occupation: Editor-in-Chief, EMAP East

Other positions: Editor, Metal Hammer; Editor, FHM; Editor-in-Chief, FHM International; Editor-in-Chief, Arena; Editor-in-Chief, Zoo.
Publications: Arena, Zoo, FHM, Arena Home Plus.
Awards: EMAP Editor Of The Year, 1999; BSME Men's Editor Of The Year, 2000.
Education: Whitefriars, Cheltenham; Birmingham University
Career highlights: After coming to the attention of the national music press for my student fanzine, I edited various best-forgotten music magazines in the mid-90s before joining Sky magazine as a Senior Features Writer in 1998 where I wrote several major cover stories. I joined FHM as Features Editor in November 1995 and became Editor in April 1999. I edited the magazine until September 2001 and am still the only monthly magazine editor in British publishing history to sell a million copies of a single issue. Under me FHM became the best-selling monthly magazine in British history and became famous for, amongst other things, giving Jennifer Lopez her first ever cover story. I was made EMAP Editor Of The Year in 1999 and then British Society of Magazine Editors Editor Of The Year in 2000. I moved to Arena as Editor-in-Chief, in October 2001 (taking the magazine to its most profitable and best-selling issues in more than a decade) and became Editor-In-Chief of EMAP East (overseeing Arena, Arena Homme Plus and Zoo) in August 2005.
Big break: Getting Susie Forbes and Angela Holden at Sky magazine to let me write for the magazine.
Big mistake: Edited the worst magazine cover of all time.

» **Reading:** *Every major men's magazine in the world for work. Every major women's weekly for work. Every major fashion magazine for work. The Week, Viz, Private Eye, the Spectator for pleasure.* **Watching:** *All the usual big-budget US dramas and sitcoms. Especially Arrested Development. Also, Shameless and Nighty Night from the UK.* **Listening:** *Everything from Metallica to Aguilera.* **Relaxing to:** *I edit a magazine and have two children. Relaxing doesn't often come into it.* » *Married, 2 children*

Brigid Nzekwu

12.8.71

c/o Knight Ayton Management, 114 St Martin's Lane, London WC2N 4BE

T 020 7836 5333
E bridgid.nzekwu@itn.co.uk

Occupation: Reporter and Presenter, Channel 4 News

Other positions: Formerly Reporter, Powerhouse, Channel 4; First Edition, Channel 4; Producer, Channel 4 News; Presenter, The Big Breakfast News, Channel 4; Presenter, Five News, Channel 5; Producer, The Big Breakfast News, Channel 4.
Awards: Screen Nation Film & Television Awards, nominated in Favourite Newsreader category, 2005.
Education: Queen Mary College, London
Career highlights: My broadcasting career started in 1997. I had been an electronic publishing consultant but always wanted to work in TV news. I volunteered at a hospital radio station in my spare time, presenting a magazine show and reading the news and I completed a postgraduate broadcasting course at City University in 1997. My first job was as a Producer at ITN on the Big Breakfast News. Getting to present it was a highlight - it was a mad programme, especially the banter with presenter Johnny Vaughan! As a reporter I've worked with children and animals on First Edition - the most memorable piece involved filming with a snake around my shoulders... At Channel 4 News, I've especially enjoyed the buzz of Westminster as a Political Producer working with Gary Gibbon. Now I'm concentrating on reporting and developing my career as a presenter.
Mentor: Peter Barron, now Editor of Newsnight, has been the most influential figure in my career to date. He was Deputy Editor of Channel 4 News when I joined the programme in 1999.
Big break: Standing in for Phil Gayle as Big Breakfast Newsreader when he was struck down with food poisoning. When he left the programme the following year I did the job for a couple of months and then went to work at Channel 4 News.
Big mistake: Nothing big so far, touch wood...

» **Reading:** *I mostly read the Guardian, The Times and Telegraph but I flick through the tabloids at work. Magazine-wise I'm addicted to Grazia and I love InStyle and the Sunday Times Style magazines for fashion tips. The Evening Standard's ES Magazine is also a must. I'm a fan of 20th century French literature since my degree studies.* **Watching:** *Being a bit of a car nut I can't miss Top Gear. I try to see anything in the Bodyshock series on Channel 4 or any health-related programmes, and Desperate Housewives is currently filling the void since Sex & The City left our screens.* **Listening:** *My iPod shuffle has all sorts on it - hip hop, pop and dance music, as well as random tracks by The Gypsy Kings and Portlshead. Some days I'll listen to Classic fm, other days to Kiss fm depending on my mood.* **Relaxing to:** *I'm mad about cars, so I love track days when I've got time. Otherwise listening to music, reading, shopping and cinema - and I'm doing courses in handbag design.* » *Married, no children*

John O'Keeffe 10.11.65

60 Kingly Street, London W1B 5DS
T 020 7453 4247
E john.okeeffe@bbh.co.uk

Occupation: Executive Creative Director, BBH

Other positions: Global Board Member of BBH; Board Member British Television Advertising Association.
Publications: Barnardo's, Heroin Baby; Johnnie Walker, Keep Walking; Levis, Pool Hall (1990 but still a fave - gave The Clash their only number one record).
Awards: D&AD silvers; Cannes golds/silvers; British TV Gold; Ad Age New York Gold; Campaign Press Poster gold/silver for variously NSPCC, BA, Audi, Levis, K Shoes, Barclays, Barnardo's, Lynx, etc; Creative Director of the Year 2003 and 2004 (Campaign Magazine); Featured in FT Most Creative People in the UK 2003.
Education: St John Payne Comprehensive
Career highlights: Moving from Saatchis to BBH.
Mentor: John Hegarty
Big break: John Hegarty saying 'OK, you're in'.
Big mistake: Staying at Saatchi too long.

›› **Reading:** *I get all the dailies but choose the Guardian, Q, and books at random - no favourite author.* **Watching:** *Bottletop Bill (and his best friend Corky). The Fimbles, The Tweenies, Noddy, Pepper Pig and, after Charlotte's gone to bed, The Sopranos.* **Listening:** *Everything I ever bought since I got an iPod. Weren't The Jam brilliant!* **Relaxing to:** *In the park with my wonderful daughter and beautiful wife.*
›› *Married, 1 child and 1 on the way*

Christian O'Connell 1973

Virgin Radio, 1 Golden Square, London W1F 9DJ
T 020 7434 1215
E reception@virginradio.co.uk

Occupation: Presenter, breakfast show, Virgin Radio

Other positions: Presenter, Fighting Talk, BBC Radio Five Live.
Awards: DJ of the Year, Sony Awards, 2004; Sony Gold, Best Breakfast Show, 2003; NTL Commercial Radio Presenter of the Year, 2002; voted best radio show by Campaign Magazine two years running.
Career highlights: Started on breakfast show on Crash, re-launched as Juice 107.6, Liverpool; Presenter, Xfm Breakfast Show, 2001-06; Presenter, Fighting Talk, BBC Radio Five Live, 2004-present; Presenter, Breakfast Show, Virgin Radio, 2006-present.
›› *Married, 1 child*

Jill Offman

Discovery Networks Europe, 160 Great Portland Street, London W1W 5QA
T 020 7462 3600
E Jill_offman@discovery-europe.com

Occupation: Channel Director, Discovery UK

Education: Brandeis University; Columbia University
Career highlights: Independent documentary producer and director; covered the war in Yugoslavia, post-Communist Russia and Courtney Love in the High Arctic, CBC Current Affairs, 1990s; Vice-President of Programming for Discovery Channel, Animal Planet, Civilization and CTV Travel in Canada.

Michelle Ogundehin 6.11.71

64 North Row, London W1K 7LL
T 020 7150 7324
E michelle.ogundehin@hf-uk.com

Occupation: Editor, ELLE Decoration; Director, MO:Studio

Other positions: Editor at Large, ELLE Decoration, 1999-2004; Deputy Editor, ELLE Decoration, 1998-99; Features Director, ELLE Decoration, 1997-98; Senior Editor, Blueprint, 1996; Assistant Editor, Blueprint, 1995-96; Editorial Assistant, Blueprint/Tate Art Magazine, 1994.
Publications: ELLE Decoration Annual Design Awards, this year sponsored by Liberty. Plus for the first time in 2005 I instigated an exclusive designer mug project in aid of the homeless charity Shelter. Alexander McQueen, Lucienne Day, Clements Ribeiro, Johnny Vegas, Daisy de Villeneuve and Gary Hume each designed a limited edition mug for ELLE Decoration. Sold exclusively through Heal's, our project partner. Received publicity in many publications, including the Telegraph, Daily Mail and Time Out; personally, recently profiled in the Independent as a 'Maker of Style'.
Awards: Shortlisted for the Fiona MacPherson New Editor of the Year award 2005.
Education: Bartlett School of Architecture; University College, London
Career highlights: Having trained as an architect, I cut my journalistic teeth 11 years ago on Blueprint Magazine, rising in three years to the position of Senior Editor only to be headhunted to be Features Director at ELLE Decoration, and so began my love affair with the magazine (eight years long and counting!). Promotion to Deputy soon followed, and even when I left a year later to found my own design consultancy, I still maintained a connection to the magazine as its Editor at Large. I was appointed Editor in May 2004.
Mentor: I don't have a specific mentor because I believe everyone has something to teach you. But sometimes that can be how NOT to do things.
Big break: I think you make your own breaks through determination, being good at what you do, and most importantly always being willing to learn and be better.

Big mistake: No such thing as mistakes, only experience gained.

» **Reading:** *The weekend Financial Times, Vanity Fair, Observer, the Week, Condé Nast Traveller, Sight & Sound, Harpers Bazaar, Vogue. Not as many novels as I should, bit addicted to magazines!* **Watching:** *Very little television athough currently loving Lost. Lots of general release movies of all genres except science fiction. Italian films in original language because I'm learning Italian.* **Listening:** *Radio 4 in the mornings. Very varied choice at all other times, including Juice FM (the local station in Brighton, where I live). Currently on the music system at home: Moby, Coldplay, some compilation thing, Zero7, Jack Johnson and Ben Harper.* **Relaxing to:** *Swimming, saunas, travel, sex and baths!*
» *No children*

Joyce Ohajah 25.2.70

200 Gray's Inn Road, London WC1X 8XZ
T 020 7833 3000
E joyce.ohajah@itn.co.uk

Occupation: Newscaster, ITV News

Other positions: Freelance travel writer.
Publications: Supporter of ACLT(African Caribbean Leukemia Trust), ThankYou (Adoption and Fostering Charity), Barnardo's, Mentor for CSV (Community Service Volunteers).
Awards: BT Midlands Journalist of the Year (highly commended) for Windrush: Coming Home; Best Breaking News Story (Society of Professional Journalists, Texas USA) for Immigration Scam.
Education: William Morris School, Walthamstow, London; University of Texas
Career highlights: I worked in the US as a News Reporter and Presenter for NBC and CBS network affiliates covering major stories including hurricanes in North Carolina, the Iraq war and US elections. As Senior Progrmme Editor played a key role in the launch of Westcountry Television in Plymouth. Produced and presented award-winning series in the Midlands on the 50th anniversary of the Empire Windrush, Windrush: Coming Home. First black female News Correspondent and newscaster for ITV.
Mentor: My parents for coming to England from Nigeria in the 1960s and raising a family in the face of adversity - I respect and deeply admire them for what they've achieved. Trevor Macdonald has always been and continues to be an icon. Oprah Winfrey is also a role model for me as one of the most powerful and respected women in broadcasting worldwide.
Big break: Going to the US and getting my first job in TV as a runner and not letting a little thing like a British accent keep me off air. Then coming back to England and not letting a little thing like an American accent keep me off air!
Big mistake: Mispronouncing Phuket on air a few years ago and thinking it hadn't been saved. Only to almost choke on my cocoa two years later when it suddenly reappeared on TV's Most Embarrassing Moments!

» **Reading:** *I read most daily newspapers. I like classic novels. I recently met Alice Walker and am now rereading The Color Purple. I enjoy self-development books, thrillers and autobiographies.* **Watching:** *Apart from News programmes Parkinson is engaging, A Touch of Frost and good TV dramas.* **Listening:** *I am not very loyal, it really depends on my mood - Radio 4, Magic, Heart 106, Choice FM.* **Relaxing to:** *I love musicals and theatre in general, listening and dancing to all types of music especially Cuban salsa and 70s soul, painting and visiting art galleries and simply socialising with family and friends.* » *Single, no children*

Rageh Omaar 19.7.67

BBC Television Centre, Wood Lane, London W12 7RJ
T 020 8743 8000
E Rageh.Omaar@bbc.co.uk

Occupation: Journalist and author

Publications: Revolution Day, The Real Story of the Battle for Iraq (Penguin, 2005).
Awards: Prix Bayeux Award for coverage of the Ethiopian-Eritrean War, 2000; part of BBC team winning Royal Television Society award for the coverage of the fall of Kabul; EMMA for best TV journalist in 2002 and 2003.
Education: Cheltenham Boys' College; Oxford University
Career highlights: Began journalistic career in 1990 as a trainee at The Voice newspaper in Brixton and then moved to City Limits magazine; in 1991 moved to Ethiopia to freelance as a foreign correspondent, much work being broadcast by BBC World Service; in 1992, returned to London as a Producer for Focus on Africa for the World Service at Bush House; 1994-96, worked as a Broadcast Journalist for the World Service and then became a Producer and Reporter for Newshour; 1996, undertook a three-month sabbatical at the University of Jordan, studying Arabic, and was appointed Amman Correspondent in 1997; Developing World Correspondent from 1998 covering stories ranging from drought in Ethiopia to devastating floods in Mozambique; most recently BBC News Africa Correspondent, based in Johannesburg.

» *Married, 2 children*

Steve Orchard 13.4.58

GCap Media, 30 Leicester Square, London WC2H 7LA
T 01793 663083
E steve.orchard@gcapmedia.com

Occupation: Operations Director, GCap Media plc

Other positions: Director, GCAP Media Ltd, 2005-present; other Directorships, GWR Group plc, GWR Radio Services Ltd, GWR International Ltd, Castleform Ltd, The Digital Radio Group (London) Ltd, The Storm (West Midlands) Ltd, Hit 40 UK Ltd, Xfm Manchester Ltd; Member, Sony Radio Academy Awards Organising Committee, 2004.
Awards: Sony Gold winner.
Education: Chadderton Grammar School; St Peter's College, Oxford; National Broadcasting School
Career highlights: Started life as a social worker but became a football reporter whilst still at college and then launched GWR Bristol as Breakfast DJ. Became Programme Controller then MD of GWR Wiltshire, and then Group Programme Director of

GWR. Served as Programme Director of Classic fm and reformatted the station to its current, more accessible position, and pushed the audience through the five million mark for the first time in its history. Appointed to GWR plc board in 1999. Oversaw the launch of GWR's national digital services, Core and Planet Rock. Appointed to GCap plc board in November 2005. Appointed Operations Director GCap when GWR and Capital Group merged in May 2006. Responsible for GCap's local, London and national radio portfolio.
Big break: When Ralph Bernard was auditioning for a breakfast jock to launch the new Bristol station he took time off his own DJ duties as Presenter of Wiltshire Radio's Saturday Supergold - I humbly filled in. During a break in the auditions procession he checked that all was well with his cherished Saturday show and was evidently impressed with what he heard. I got a call at my office and was offered a job as breakfast DJ Bristol. On Friday I was a social worker, by Monday I was a DJ.
Big mistake: I once said that a national commercial station playing classical music had 'no chance'.

» **Reading:** *Quirky novels - just finished Cloud Atlas, and biographies of musicians - currently immersed in Room Full of Mirrors, the Jimi Hendrix story.* **Watching:** *24, Lost and Extras.* **Listening:** *Anything and everything - from Springsteen to Kanye and from Mozart to Nusrat Fateh Ali Khan.* **Relaxing to:** *Playing my 1963 Rockola juke box, watching United, assisting with the kids' homework, reading, and holidays.* » *Married, 2 children*

Sir Anthony O'Reilly 1936

Independent News and Media, Independent House, 191 Marsh Wall, London E14 9RS
T 020 7005 2000

Occupation: Chairman, Independent News and Media plc

Other positions: Chairman and Chief Executive Officer, H J Heinz Company; Chairman, Fitzwilton plc; Non-executive Chairman, Waterford Wedgwood plc; Principal Shareholder, Arcon International Resources plc; Director, the New York Stock Exchange; Chairman, The Ireland Funds of the United States, Canada, Great Britain, Australia, France, Germany, New Zealand, Japan and South Africa.
Education: Belvedere College; University College, Dublin; Incorporated Law Society of Ireland; University of Bradford
Career highlights: Played rugby for Ireland 29 times and for the British and Irish Lions 10 times, including the Test Series winning-British Lions Tour of South Africa in 1955 and the Tour of New Zealand and Australia in 1959, establishing scoring records on both tours; CEO, An Bord Bainne (Irish Dairy Board), 1962-66; Head of the Irish Sugar Company, 1966-69; Managing Director, H J Heinz Company Ltd, England, 1969; Senior Vice-President, North America and Pacific, Heinz World Headquarters, Pittsburgh, 1971; Executive Vice-President and Chief Operating Officer, 1972; President and Chief Operating Officer, Heinz Worldwide, 1973-present.

» *Married, 6 children*

Marie O'Riordan 5.4.64

13th Floor, King's Reach Tower, Stamford Street, London SE1 9LS
T 020 7261 5177
E marie_o'riordan@ipcmedia.com

Occupation: Editor, Marie Claire magazine

Other positions: Production Editor, Deputy Editor, Editor at more! Magazine; Editor ELLE magazine; Group Publishing Director of Emap Youth Market.
Publications: more!, ELLE, Marie Claire.
Awards: Editor of the Year, Emap Awards 1993; Cover of the Year, IPC Awards 2003; Editor of the Year, IPC Awards 2005; Cover of the Year, IPC Awards 2005.
Education: University College, Dublin
Career highlights: Being Editor of Marie Claire magazine.
Mentor: Fiona Gibson, my Editor when I was at more! magazine.
Big break: Getting my first job as Production Editor at more! magazine. I heard about the vacancy via 6 degrees.
Big mistake: Not spotting an insensitive ad in the middle of a very sensitive editorial on Dunblane in time before going to press.

» **Reading:** *1 broadsheet, 1 tabloid, Vanity Fair, lots of novels.* **Watching:** *Everything on HBO and Channel 4.* **Listening:** *Radio 2 and Radio 4.* **Relaxing to:** *Down the pub.* » *Single, no children*

Stuart Outhwaite 27.1.81

Mother, Biscuit Building, 10 Redchurch Street, London E2 7DD
T 020 7012 1999
E stuart@motherlondon.com

Occupation: Advertising Creative, Mother London

Other positions: Paperboy, Leisure Centre Attendant, Barman.
Publications: Observer Music Monthly, Abba to Zappa; XFM, Welcome to Christian's World; UKTV Gardens, Plant Labels; Egg, Tested and Approved by Guinea Pigs.
Awards: 1 gold, 4 silver BTAAs; 1 gold, 3 silver Creative Circles; 3 Campaign Poster Awards.
Education: Buckinghamshire Chilterns University College
Career highlights: Getting a job at Mother. Writing a letter to the Chuckle Brothers asking them to front an Xfm campaign we'd written. An American girl in Cannes.
Mentor: Mike Reeves through high school and sixth form. Dave Morris through uni. Caroline Pay, Yan Elliot, Luke Williamson, Robert Saville and Mark Waites through Mother.
Big break: Observer Music Monthly, Abba to Zappa.
Big mistake: Thinking the Chuckle Brothers would be good front men for Xfm.

» **Reading:** *The Guardian and Observer. Many magazines, not enough books.* **Watching:** *Football on Sky Sports and Bullseye on Challenge TV.* **Listening:** *Five Live and Xfm.* **Relaxing to:** *Do a lot of nothing.* » *Single, no children*

Bill Overton

16.5.73

UBC Media, 50 Lisson Street, London NW1 5DF
T 07970 226210
E bill.overton@classicgolddigital.com

Occupation: Head of Programmes, Classic Gold and freelance projects

Other positions: Radio Presenter; BBC 6 Music Journalist.
Awards: 1999 Sony Silver Award, best news and talk show for Talk Radio; 1992 New York Radio awards, best news anchor for GLR.
Education: Wellington College; Nottingham University
Career highlights: 15 years of varied roles in radio both on and off the air for Talk Radio, Classic Gold and GLR, the highlights of which are yet to come. Repositioning Classic Gold as a mainstream contemporary music station and discarding the baggage of 'oldies' radio. Taking Classic Gold onto a digital platform. Getting away with it.
Mentor: Roger Scott, the great Capital Radio presenter, who made me want to get involved in radio.
Big break: Moving to London and GLR in 1991 to take on the lunchtime show.
Big mistake: Agreeing to front a breakfast show for a station run by Lynne Franks - it was like Ab Fab without the laughs.

» **Reading:** *Independent, Times, Sun, the Word, Empire, Music Week.* **Watching:** *Curb Your Enthusiasm, The Week with Andrew Neil, series on DVD like Murder One as it's impossible to see all episodes when broadcast.* **Listening:** *Xfm, Jonathan Ross, tons of new music every day, www.Gohomeproductions.com.* **Relaxing to:** *Running, trips to the cinema and the company of friends.* » *Single, no children*

Nicholas Owen

11.2.51

200 Gray's Inn Road, London WC1X 8XZ
020 7833 3000
E nicholas.owen@itn.co.uk

Occupation: ITV News Presenter

Other positions: Corporate and charity work.
Publications: Interest in cancer charities, author of Diana the People's Princess and The History of the British Trolleybus.
Awards: RTS for coverage of Diana's death and funeral.
Education: Eventually, West Ewell Secondary Modern
Career highlights: 17 years in newspapers, starting on the local Surrey Mirror, before the Evening Standard, Daily Telegraph, and Financial Times; joined the BBC in 1981, based in the North East, covering general and industrial stories there and nationall;. joined ITN in 1984, working first as Channel Four News Business Correspondent. Later presented Channel 4 News, C4 Midnight Specials during the First Gulf War, and the Parliament Programme; for ITV, presented the whole range of programmes, including News at Ten; Royal Correspondent 1994-2000; Presenter of the ITV Lunchtime News since 2002.
Mentor: Cecil Gegg, my first weekly paper Editor, who instilled journalistic good practice. On TV, Mike Neville, then Presenter of BBC's Look North in Newcastle, taught me so much about presenting.
Big break: Going to the BBC in 1981, and having them take a gamble on an old Fleet Street lad.
Big mistake: Not going into TV much earlier.

» **Reading:** *Every newspaper I can, and as many books too. Recently read and thoroughly enjoyed my first Anthony Trollope.* **Watching:** *TV news (of course), documentaries, movies.* **Listening:** *Today programme in short bursts, Front Row on Radio 4, The World Tonight when I can, Radio 3 and some Classic FM.* **Relaxing to:** *Struggling with golf; walking as much as possible; taking an interest in railways, ancient and modern.* » *Married, 4 children*

Sue Owen

18.3.66

BBC Radio Stoke, Cheapside, Hanley, Stoke on Trent ST1 1JJ
T 01782 208080
E sue.owen@bbc.co.uk

Occupation: Managing Editor, BBC Radio Stoke

Education: Wakefield Girls' High School; Aberystwyth University
Career highlights: 23 years in broadcasting - a mix of both commercial and BBC local radio including Hallam, Chiltern, Hereward and BBC Radio York. Part of the management launch team for 100.7 Heart FM and DNN with Chrysalis. Returned to the BBC as Managing Editor in Stoke in 2002 and won two Gillard golds and a Sony bronze - the station's first awards for a decade.
Mentor: No one individual, but have been inspired by many broadcasters and managers who give heart and soul to the job and always put the listeners first.
Big break: Being advised by my first boss never to say no to a new challenge, change or extra work.
Big mistake: Buying a designer outfit two sizes too small and thinking I'd ever lose enough weight to fit into it.

» **Reading:** *All newspapers but especially the Guardian (for Doonesbury). Anything by Larry McMurtry.* **Watching:** *BBC News, West Wing, Desperate Housewives, Spooks.* **Listening:** *BBC Radio Stoke, Five Live, Radio 2, local commercial competition, Bruce Springsteen CDs.* **Relaxing to:** *Fly fishing, riding, listening to Springsteen, planning and taking holidays.*

Kevin Palmer
29.10.71

30 Leicester Square, London WC2H 7LA
T 020 7766 6000
E kevin.palmer@capitalradiogroup.com

Occupation: Programme Director, Digital Radio, GCap Media plc

Other positions: Group Head of Programmes, Chrysalis Radio; Programme Director, Heart 106.2.
Publications: Responsible for programme output at GCap Media Digital Radio services; Core, Capital Life, Chill, Capital Disney, The Storm.
Awards: Sony Radio Academy gold; Station of the Year, Digital Terrestrial, 2005; Station Promotion, 1998; Breakfast Show, 1997; Number 9 in the Best DJ category, Smash Hits Readers' Poll, 1994.
Education: Yes/No
Career highlights: Reading obituaries on local radio in Ireland (first job); hosting breakfast show on Atlantic 252 in its years as the UK's biggest commercial radio station; being on the launch team of Heart 106.2. Two Station of the Year gongs for Capital Disney.
Mentor: Keith Pringle, Paul Kavanagh, Travis Baxter and Dennis Clark taught me all I know - but not all they know.
Big break: The sudden death of Diana, Princess of Wales, while station bosses at Heart 106.2 were on holiday having left me in charge.
Big mistake: Jumping on the dotcom bandwagon for a spell in 2000.

» **Reading:** *Guardian Unlimited, Pop Justice, Sunday Times, Sneak, Carl Hiaasen.* **Watching:** *Channel 4, Living TV and my West Wing boxed sets.* **Listening:** *Everything on-air, usually at the same time. Nanci Griffith albums when I want to get away from it all.* **Relaxing to:** *The second bottle of Gran Reserva usually does it.* » *Confirmed bachelor, no children*

Andy Parfitt
24.9.58

BBC Radio 1, Yalding House,
152–156 Great Portland Street, London W1N 4DJ
T 08700 100 100
E Andy.Parfittr1@bbc.co.uk

Occupation: Controller, BBC Radio 1

Education: Bristol Old Vic Theatre School; Wharton Business School
Career highlights: Assistant Stage Manager, Bristol Arts Centre, 1978-80; Studio Manager, BBC, 1980-84; Programme Presenter, British Forces Broadcasting Service, 1984; Education Producer, BBC, 1985; Producer, features and magazines including Pick Of The Week and Bookshelf, BBC Radio 4, 1986-89; Launch Assistant Editor, BBC Radio 5, 1989-91; Editor, Breakfast Show, BBC Radio 5, 1991-93; Chief Assistant to the Controller, BBC Radio 1, 1993-94; Editor, BBC Radio 1, 1994-95; Editor, Commissioning and Planning, then Managing Editor, BBC Radio 1, 1995-97; Deputy Controller, BBC Radio 1, 1997; Controller, Radio 1, 1998-present; oversaw conception and launch of BBC 1Xtra, 2002.

» **Relaxing to:** *Running, painting, music.*
» *Married, 2 daughters*

Roger Parry
5.6.57

Clear Channel International, 1 Cluny Mews, London SW5 9EG
T 020 7341 5400
E rogerparry@clearchannelint.com

Occupation: Chairman, Clear Channel International; Chairman, Johnston Press plc; Chairman, Future plc

Other positions: Chairman, Shakespeare's Globe Trust.
Publications: People Businesses, Random House, 1991; Enterprise: The Leadership Role, Profile Books, 2003; co-author Making Cities Work, John Wiley & Sons, 2003.
Awards: Gold Medal, New York Film and TV Festival, 1984.
Education: Jesus College, Oxford (M Lit); Bristol (BSc)
Career highlights: Started out as assistant to Maurice and Charles Saatchi then spent seven years as broadcaster and producer for BBC, ITV and LBC; went to McKinsey for three years to learn how businesses really work; became embroiled in the restructuring of WCRS and Aegis; Went shopping on behalf of Carat to build US business; won and sold LBC radio franchise; Bought into Jazz FM - later sold to Guardian Media Group; bought into the old More O'Ferrall outdoor advertising company and subsequently sold it to Clear Channel; invested some US$ 2 billion for Clear Channel, building the business in Europe and Asia; became Chairman of Johnston Press plc in Edinburgh and also of Future plc in Bath; joined Board of iTouch plc (mobile content) - later sold to For-Side; have now worked in all media except cinema, but always looking for media businesses to invest in.
Big break: Winning LBC radio franchise and subsequently selling the business to Reuters.
Big mistake: Not buying 5% of Yahoo in 1996.

» **Reading:** *William Boyd, Iain Banks, Ian McEwan, and Carl Hiaasen.* **Watching:** *American imports on C4 and C5. Sky News. A movie every week.* **Listening:** *U2, Franz Ferdinand, Red Hot Chilli Peppers, Cat Stevens, Radio 4.* **Relaxing to:** *Skiing, tennis, horseracing, swimming, planting trees.* » *Married, 1 son*

Katherine Parsons

Room 6239, Television Centre, Wood Lane, London W12 7TS
T 020 8624 8619
E katherine.parsons@bbc.co.uk

Occupation: Channel Executive, BBC Three

Other positions: Head of Development, BBC Lifeskills; Senior Producer, BBC Factual Entertaiment; Producer, BBC Docs/History and Community Programmes; Producer, GMTV;

Producer, RDF; Development Consultant, BBC ICG; Producer, Clark TV; Producer, Fuji TV.
Education: University College, London
Career highlights: Being there the night the Berlin Wall opened up. Setting up the first interview with Thatcher after she resigned. All the films I've made in Japan have been unforgettable, but particularly those on Tokyo's red light district. Booking Frankie Vaughan and his entourage to perform in a terraced house in Essex.
Mentor: Stuart Murphy and Jo Clinton Davis. Both are people who support their teams brilliantly and make sure they are steered in the right direction.
Big break: John Willis commissioned our Japan Weekend back in 1991. My colleague and I were very wet behind the ears but came up with an idea that appealed and he went with it on instinct.
Big mistake: Agreeing to dress up as Margaret Thatcher on a Japanese current affairs show and hit a Neil Kinnock lookalike over the head with a leek.

» **Reading:** *Heat, New Statesman, Prospect, Guardian, Observer. 19th century literature.* **Watching:** *Everything, but I do love Lost on Channel 4, Funland on BBC Three, Cribs on MTV, Bleak House on BBC One.* **Listening:** *Soul and funk between 1971-75.* **Relaxing to:** *I cook for England.*

Adam Pasco

12.1.61

Room AG193, Woodlands, 80 Wood Lane, London W12 0TT
T 020 8433 3593
E adam.pasco@bbc.co.uk

Occupation: Journalist

Other positions: Editor, BBC Gardeners' World Magazine; Editorial Director, BBC Easy Gardening and gardening group.
Publications: Collins Complete Garden Manual.
Awards: Editor of the Year, British Society of Magazine Editors, 1998 and 2004.
Education: University of Nottingham
Career highlights: Launching BBC Gardeners' World Magazine in 1991 and working as Editorial Director of BBC Easy Gardening magazine. I have been a keen gardener since childhood and have worked in commercial nurseries, gaining an honours degree in horticulture before becoming a gardening journalist. Won the accolade of 'Editor of the Year' from the British Society of Magazine Editors in both 1998 and 2004. A regular radio broadcaster, I have made numerous television appearances, had a regular column in the Daily Telegraph, and have written for many other magazines and newspapers. I have also contributed to a number of books, including The Collins Complete Garden Manual, Collins Gardeners' Calendar, The Greenfingers Book, and the HDRA Encyclopedia of Organic Gardening.
Big break: Being invited to develop and launch Gardeners' World magazine in 1991.

» **Reading:** *Mainly magazines, including National Geographic.* **Watching:** *Very little.* **Listening:** *BBC Radio 4. I coudn't live without it!* **Relaxing to:** *Apart from gardening, which integrates work and pleasure, I love cooking and baking. I'm also learning to play the piano. In addition, I love magic, and am teaching myself a range of card tricks.* » *Married, 2 children*

Simon Pattern

10.2.67

Queen's Court, Queen's Gardens, Hull HU1 3RH
T 01482 323232
E simon.pattern@bbc.co.uk

Occupation: Managing Editor, BBC Yorkshire and Lincolnshire

Other positions: Senior Presentation Editor, BBC Broadcast; Senior Producer, BBC Radios York and Newcastle.
Publications: BBC Radio Humberside, bbc.co.uk/humber; BBC Open Centre, Hull; BBC Bus, Hull.
Career highlights: Started in independent local radio, moved across to join the BBC as a Programme Assistant in local radio, progressing up to the level of Senior Producer. Moved across to BBC TV to train as a Network Director in the Television Presentation Department and stayed there for 11 years, becoming Senior Presentation Editor for the BBC's main TV services. Returned to local radio to find a better work-life balance - if only I'd known!
Mentor: Tony Fish

» **Listening:** *BBC Radio Humberside, of course!* **Relaxing to:** *Gym and gin!* » *Single*

Allan Pattison

3.5.70

Evo Magazine, Dennis Publishing, 30 Cleveland Street, London W1T 4JD
T 07850 984412
E allanp@evo.co.uk

Occupation: Publisher, evo magazine, Dennis Publishing

Other positions: Launch Director, Evo Publications 1998-2001; Business Development Manager, Consumer Car Titles, EMAP, 1995-98; Client Sales Manager, Consumer Car Titles, EMAP, 1993-95; Advertisement Manager, Times and Observer Regional Newspapers, 1989-93.
Publications: Key publications are Car magazine, Performance Car magazine, Classic Cars magazine, evo.
Awards: PPA Publisher of the Year 2000 (for companies with less than 25 employees); Best New Business Idea/Campaign of the Year, EMAP Awards 1996.
Education: Bushey Hall School, Bushey
Career highlights: Joining together with a group of like-minded media colleagues to create and launch the Evo brand. After convincing a petrolhead entrepreneur to back the business plan, we had just three months to find an office, start a publishing company and launch a must-read car magazine. Each member of the team had at least five roles. My 'bit' included Ads, Finance, Production, Marketing, Circulation, PR and Licensing. You learn a lot this way and the first couple of years were a blur. By the third year evo was starting to challenge the ABCs of established titles and we sold the business to Dennis Publishing in 2001 as a three year earn out. This deal rewarded the original team and

propelled evo into an even faster period of growth as part of the Dennis portfolio. evo now sells 72,000 copies per month and is licensed in six countries including Italy, Greece, Russia, France, Malaysia and Philippines. Creating a strong worldwide brand which serves its target market so well has been rewarding.

Mentor: Richard Branson

Big break: Having the team, timing and funding to launch evo.

Big mistake: No regrets, it's all learning!

» **Reading:** *All magazines, Times, Media Guardian, the Week, Marketing, Sun, Telegraph, Media Week, Boards magazine.* **Watching:** *Sky News, BBC News 24, adventure documentaries, sports and music satellite channels.* **Listening:** *Radio 5 live, Virgin radio.* **Relaxing to:** *Running, mountain biking, windsurfing, golf, the great outdoors, music.*

» *Married, 2 children, Amba and Zachary*

Jeremy Paxman

11.5.50

c/o Capel & Land Ltd, 29 Wardour Street, London W1D 6PS

T 020 7734 2414
E jeremy.paxman@bbc.co.uk

Occupation: Journalist, broadcaster and author

Other positions: Member, Piscatorial Society.

Publications: (Jointly) A Higher Form of Killing: the secret story of gas and germ warfare, 1982; Through the Volcanoes: a Central American journey, 1985; Friends in High Places: who runs Britain?, 1990; Fish, Fishing and the Meaning of Life, 1994; The Compleat Angler, 1996; The English: a portrait of a people, 1998; The Political Animal, 2002.

Awards: Honorary Fellow, St Edmund Hall, Oxford, 2000; Hon LLD Leeds, 1999; Hon DLitt Bradford, 1999; Award for International Current Affairs, RTS, 1985; Award for best personal contribution to television, Voice of Viewer and Listener, 1993, 1998; Richard Dimbleby Award, BAFTA, 1996, 2000; Interview of the Year, RTS, 1997 and 1998; BPG Award, 1998; Variety Club Media Personality of the Year, 1999; Presenter of the Year, RTS, 2001.

Education: Malvern College; St Catharine's College, Cambridge

Career highlights: Reporter, Northern Ireland, 1974-77; BBC TV Tonight, 1977-79; Panorama, 1979-85; The Bear Next Door; Presenter: Breakfast Time, 1986-89; Newsnight, 1989-; Did You See?, 1991-93; You Decide - with Paxman, 1995-96; Start The Week, R4, 1998-2002; Chairman: University Challenge, 1994-present; Times Past, Times Present, R4, 1996.

» **Relaxing to:** *Food, books, fly fishing.*

» *Partner, 3 children*

Andy Payne

28.3.63

Mastertronic Group Ltd, 122 Southwark St, London SE1 0SW

T 07710 141393
E andy.payne@mastertronic.com

Occupation: Chairman, Entertainment Leisure Software Publishers Association

Other positions: Chairman, The Producers; Director, Mastertronic Group; Managing Director, Just Flight.

Publications: I started a magazine called PC Pilot which was sold to Key Publications in 2005. I worked on the million seller The Way of the Exploding Fist for Melbourne House (later bought by Mastertronic, in turn bought by Virgin). I was a key player in the launch of the biggest selling home computer game ever at that time - Domark's Trivial Pursuit. I also launched the UK's premier value games label, PC Gamer Presents (in partnership with Future Publishing) and started the world's biggest flight simulation specialist, Just Flight in 1996.

Awards: Games industry achievement award, 2002.

Education: St Edmund's College, Ware, Herts; London College of Printing

Career highlights: Entering the software industry in 1984, I was responsible for the launch and production of Hill-McGibbon range of educational software for William Collins. Other book publishers quickly utilised my experience and style, amongst them Heinemann (The Fourth Protocol), Macmillan (Trap Door), William Collins (Yes, Prime Minister) and Penguin (Cover to Cover range). I masterminded delivery of games on early 8-bit formats Commodore 64, C16, Spectrum 128, Spectrum 64, Atari 800, Apple II, IBM, Amstrad 464/664/6128, Amstrad PCW, BBC Electron, Atari ST, Sony MSX and Amiga. I formed specialist production company The Producers in April 1988, now part of the Mastertronic Group, which also owns the UK's number one games value specialist Mastertronic Games whose labels comprise PC Gamer Presents, MAD and Sold Out. I have been part of the teams that brought many US-based publishers into Europe, among them Electronic Arts Mindscape, Sierra On-Line, Lucas Arts, Maxis, Interplay, Accolade, 3DO, and Novalogic. I have been involved in over 250 top-30 selling products of which over 40 have hit number one in the charts and have produced over 1000 titles. I am chairman of the ELSPA (Entertainment Leisure Software Publishers Association) Council.

Mentor: My grandfather

Big break: Starting The Producers in 1988 and working with British Telecom's games labels, Rainbird and Firebird.

Big mistake: Not going to art school and seeing my graphic design career through.

» **Reading:** *Books, the internet and the Observer.* **Watching:** *Life on Mars, Test Cricket, Later with Jools, West Wing, live sport.* **Listening:** *Music, too much to list, plus radio - especially sport.* **Relaxing to:** *Playing sport - football and cricket, live music, socialising with friends and taking on interesting challenges.* » *Married, no children*

Jeremy Peat

21.3.49

BBC Broadcasting House, Queen Margaret Drive, Glasgow G12 8DG
T 0141 339 8844
E jeremy.peat@bbc.co.uk

Occupation: BBC National Governor for Scotland

Other positions: Director, the David Hume Institute; Member of the Competition Commission; Visiting Professor, University of Edinburgh; Honorary Professor, Heriot-Watt University; monthly economics column for the Herald newspaper.
Awards: Honorary Doctor of Law, Aberdeen University; Fellow of the Royal Society of Edinburgh; Fellow of the Chartered Institute of Bankers in Scotland.
Education: Bristol University; University College, London
Career highlights: A newcomer to the broadcasting scene, having been appointed - to my great delight - to the BBC Board of Governors on January 1 2005. Previously an economist in the civil service - at home and abroad (Bangkok in the 70s and Botswana in the 80s) - and then Group Chief Economist at the Royal Bank of Scotland (1993-2005). At the BBC I am Chair of the Broadcasting Council for Scotland and the BBC Audit Committee; also Chair of the BBC Pension Fund Trustees.
Big mistake: None as yet - in media.

» **Reading:** *Financial Times, Guardian, Observer, Herald, Scotsman - at different times. Plus a great deal of fiction while travelling between Edinburgh and London in particular.* **Watching:** *A broad range of programmes including a lot of sport - cricket, golf and rugby preferred - plus everything from Casualty to Strictly Come Dancing to Panorama to Dragon's Den; and of course the news.* **Listening:** *Radio Scotland, Radio 4 and Radio 5 Live plus jazz, African jazz in particular.* **Relaxing to:** *Golf, tennis, TV, crosswords, reading detective fiction and walking the dog.* » *Married, 2 grown-up daughters*

Tim Pemberton

10.3.67

BBC Shropshire, 2-4 Boscobel Drive, Heath Farm, Shrewsbury SY1 3TT
T 01743 237024
E tim.pemberton@bbc.co.uk

Occupation: Managing Editor, BBC Shropshire

Other positions: Editor, BBC 2002 Commonwealth Games Radio; Senior Producer, BBC Religion and Ethics.
Publications: Ariel, x-trax, Media Guardian.
Education: Wheelers Lane Boys, Birmingham; Lancaster University
Career highlights: Read Philosophy and Religious Studies at Lancaster University graduating in 1986 with Upper Second Class Honours. Started broadcasting career on University Radio Bailrigg. Training and Development Officer, Macro Films in Birmingham1987-89; Production Trainee for BBC Midlands at Pebble Mill 1989-91; worked for BBC Wales as Religious Producer 1991-94; Producer and then Senior Producer for BBC Religion and Ethics working on Sunday, Good Morning Sunday, Songs of Praise, Heaven and Earth and The Deniece Williams Show, 1994-2001; BBC Commonwealth Games Radio 2001-02; BBC Radio Shropshire 2002 to present. James 'The Godfather of Soul' Brown said 'Tim Pemberton is the best Englishman I know!'
Mentor: Was Owen Bentley (Midlands), and Roy Jenkins (Wales); is Lesley Douglas (Radio 2).
Big break: Landing a producer job at BBC Radio Wales through the then Editor Gaynor Vaughan Jones.
Big mistake: Cutting in to picture South East News while vision mixing the Midlands Today late evening bulletin. Oops. Really launched my career in radio.

» **Reading:** *The Independent and Guardian, Men's Health, Computer Shopper, Home & Garden.* **Watching:** *News, sport, Frasier (how could they kill it off!), Little Britain, lots of DVD films with black actors.* **Listening:** *BBC Radio Shropshire, BBC Radio 5 Live, BBC Radio 4, Beacon Radio, BBC Radio 2, AOL Radio online (playlist generated Smooth Jazz + Urban), MP3 downloads.* **Relaxing to:** *Long-haul holidays - Malaysia, Thailand, Dubai, Tunisia. Where next?* » *Married, no children*

Jerry Perkins

15.8.69

90-92 Pentonville Road, London N1 9HS
T 020 7520 8625
E jerry@developmenthell.co.uk

Occupation: Managing Director, Development Hell Ltd

Other positions: Managing Director, Emap Digital Music; Managing Director, Emap Metro; Publisher of Q, Mojo, Mixmag, Kerrang!, Smash Hits, Select.
Publications: Word magazine.
Education: Devizes Comprehensive; Polytechnic Of Central London
Career highlights: Publishing Q, Mojo and other music magazines at Emap Metro. Running great ad sales teams as Commercial Director of Emap Metro and starting Development Hell Ltd with business partner, David Hepworth.
Mentor: Tom Moloney, Chief Executive, Emap plc.
Big break: Getting a job as Ad Sales Executive at Emap Metro to work on the recently launched Q magazine.
Big mistake: With two friends launching an independent club lifestyle magazine called The Buzz in the late 80s in order to get out of selling lighting and lampshades at Barkers Department Store in Kensington. It lasted two years and took nearly 10 to pay off the debts.

» **Reading:** *The Guardian, the Week.* **Watching:** *Curb Your Enthusiasm, The Simpsons, Nighty Night, QI and any football on TV.* **Listening:** *Everything. Current favourites are Arcade Fire, Jack Johnston, Ben Lee, Joseph Arthur, Rilo Kiley and Richard Hawley.* **Relaxing to:** *Playing pool in 'the den', Ashtanga Yoga, running and when no-one is around, playing the piano.* » *Married, 2 children*

Sir Robert Phillis

4.12.49

Guardian Media Group plc, 75 Farringdon Road, London EC1M 3JY

T 020 7239 9711
E ceoffice@gmgplc.co.uk

Occupation: Chief Executive, Guardian Media Group plc to 31.7.06

Other positions: Non-executive Chairman, All3Media Group Limited; Non-executive Director, ITV plc; Independent Non-executive Director and Honorary Councillor, The Lawn Tennis Association; Chairman, Guardian Newspapers Limited; Chairman, Greater Manchester Newspapers Limited; Chairman, Trader Media Group Limited; Director, Paper Purchase and Management Limited; Director, Real Radio Limited; Director, Jazz FM Limited; Director and Trustee, Television Trust for the Environment, 1985-present; Director and Trustee, Teaching Awards Trust, 2001-present; Fellow of the Royal Society of Arts, 1984; Fellow of the International Visual Communications Association, 2001; Fellow of the Royal Television Society, 1989, Vice-President 1994-2002, Chairman 1989-92.
Publications: Chaired the independent review into the Health of the Programme Supply Market in 2002 for the Independent Television Commission; chaired the Independent Review of Government Communications throughout 2003, report published January 2004.
Awards: Knighthood, 2004; Honorary Professor, Stirling University, 1997; Doctor of Letters, Honoris Causa, Salford University, 1999; Honorary D Litt, City University, London, 2000; Honorary Doctor of Letters, University of Nottingham, 2003; Honorary Fellowship, Cardiff University, 2004.
Education: University of Nottingham
Career highlights: Deputy Director-General of the BBC and Chief Executive BBC Worldwide 1993-97; Managing Director, BBC World Service, 1993-94 and Chairman of BBC Worldwide (which encompasses the World Service, BBC Worldwide Television, BBC Worldwide Publishing and BBC Worldwide Learning) 1994-97; joined ITN as Chief Executive in 1991 from Carlton Communications where I was Group Managing Director from 1987; appointed Managing Director of Central Independent Television in November 1981; moved to Carlton Communications in 1987 but continued as a non-executive director on the Central board until 1991 and was Chairman of Zenith Productions 1984-91; served on the boards of ITN, Independent Television Publications, the Independent Television Companies Association and was Chairman of the ITV Network Programme Committee 1984-86 and Chairman of the ITV Film Purchase Group 1985-87; early career at Thomson Regional Newspapers.
Mentor: Sir Paul Fox, Sir George Russell, and Lord Gavron.
Big break: Being offered the ITV job that no one else wanted, Managing Director, Central Independent Television plc.
Big mistake: Failure to buy Robert Maxwell's stake in Central Television!

» **Reading:** *Guardian, Observer, FT, Economist, Telegraph, political and military history.* **Watching:** *News, news, news, all channels. Bremner, Bird and Fortune, Dead Ringers.* **Listening:** *Radio 4, Today Programme, Mozart, Bach and Handel, Bob Dylan and the Rolling Stones.* **Relaxing to:** *Golf, skiing, wine, gardening, visiting World War I battlefields.*
» *Married, 3 sons*

Peter Phippen

10.2.64

80 Wood Lane, London W12 0TT

T 020 8433 3552
E peter.phippen@bbc.co.uk

Occupation: Managing Director, BBC Magazines

Other positions: Director, BBC Worldwide; Director, Galleon CA (subscription fulfilment); Chairman, Frontline (distribution); Chairman, Origin Publishing; Chairman, BBC Haymarket Exhibitions; Director, Worldwide Media Ltd.
Education: Fitzwilliam College, Cambridge
Career highlights: Joined IPC in 1982; MD, BBC Worldwide, UK 1997; President and CEO, BBC Worldwide Americas Inc 1998; MD, BBC Magazines, 2002.

» **Relaxing to:** *Walking. Triathlons, playing jazz piano, riding motorbikes quickly.* » *Married, 4 children*

Nigel Pickard

10.3.52

RDF Media, The Gloucester Building, Kensington Village, Avonmore Road, London W14 8RF

T 020 7013 4433
E Nigel.Pickard@RDFMedia.com

Occupation: Director of Family and Children's Programmes, RDF Media

Other positions: Formerly Director of Programmes, ITV Network Ltd; Controller CBBC; Controller CiTV.
Education: Truro School and Southampton College of Art
Career highlights: Left art college to become a film editor at 22, moved via floor management to become trainee TV director; worked on broad range of programmes from News to Drama to Entertainment but specialised in Children's Programmes, eventually becoming Controller of Children's for TVS; gained experience in multi-channel as Director of Programmes for the now defunct Family Channel and created Challenge TV with Flextech; David Liddiment offered me role of Controller of CiTV, then moved to Controller BBC and launched two new children's channels - CBeebies and CBBC; took role of Director of Programmes ITV in late 2002.
Mentor: Lewis Rudd, Anne Home, David Liddiment.
Big break: Being offered CiTV job.
Big mistake: Listening to too many people who don't know enough about programming or broadcasting.

» **Reading:** *Varies wildly from magazines to scripts to novels.* **Watching:** *Sport, sport, drama and factual.* **Listening:** *Prefer spoken word to music, so Radio 4 and 5.* **Relaxing to:** *Golf, walking and shooting.* » *Married, 3 children*

John Pidgeon

1.3.47

Ivy Cottage, Wingmore, Elham Valley, Canterbury CT4 6LS
T 01303 840025
E john@wingmoremedia.com

Occupation: Writer and radio producer

Other positions: Head of BBC Radio Entertainment, 1999-2005.
Publications: Slade In Flame
Education: Royal Grammar School, High Wycombe; University of Kent at Canterbury; Slade School; University College
Career highlights: I've been doing this far too long to squeeze those highlights into 200 words.
Mentor: No one person - I've learned from many.
Big break: See career highlights.
Big mistake: Ask me again in six months.

» **Reading:** *Guardian, Observer, Mojo.* **Watching:** *Sport.* **Listening:** *Loud music.* **Relaxing to:** *Gardening, cooking.*
» *Married, 4 children*

Nick Piggott

16.7.76

PO Box 2000, Bristol BS99 7SN
T 020 7911 7300
E nick.piggott@gcapmedia.com

Occupation: Digital Content Manager, GCap Media plc

Awards: CRCA Commercial Radio Award for Technical Innovation 2001, 2003, 2004.
Education: University of Manchester, Institute of Science and Technology (UMIST)
Career highlights: Involved with inception of DAB Digital Radio in UK; launched Core and Planet Rock as UK's first commercial DAB stations; launch of UK's first radio music download service; launch of UK's first interactive SMS requests service; three CRCA awards for Technical Innovation; relaunching Melody FM, Innsbruck, Austria; bidding for a Manchester FM licence in 1992.
Mentor: Dirk Anthony
Big break: The chance to run GWR Group's Digital Project in 1998.
Big mistake: Not spending more on marketing MCR100fm in the run-up to its Manchester FM licence bid in 1990-92.

» **Reading:** *Websites - Guardian Unlimited, The Register, b3ta, The Onion, RAIN. Books - Douglas Adams, Nicholas Negroponte, Malcolm Gladwell, Mark Haddon.* **Watching:** *Virtually nothing.* **Listening:** *Core, GWRfm, Chill, any station playing 80s songs.* **Relaxing to:** *Music, travel, theatre, dance, sailing.* » *Married*

Wendy Pilmer

BBC Television Centre, Wood Lane, London W12 7RJ
T 020 8743 8000
E wendy.pilmer@bbc.co.uk

Occupation: Head of Regional and Local Programmes, BBC North East and Cumbria

Education: Durham University
Career highlights: Joined BBC as Producer for BBC Features in Manchester producing fly-on-the-wall documentaries and features on popular culture for Radio 4; Radio 1, proud occupier of desk next to John Peel and Executive Producer, 1994-97; Head of Presentation, Radio Five Live, 1997-99; Network Manager, BBC Radio 4, and Deputy to the Controller, 1999-2002; Head of Regional and Local Programmes, BBC North East and Cumbria, 2002-present, responsible for regional evening news programme, Look North, and weekly current affairs and political programmes Inside Out and The Politics Show; also in charge of BBC Radio Cleveland, BBC Radio Cumbria and BBC Radio Newcastle, and the four local Where I Live websites.

» **Relaxing to:** *Watching Newcastle United, hill walking.*

Amanda Platell

12.11.57

3rd Floor, 52 Grosvenor Gardens, London SW1W 0AU
T 020 7730 3444
E info@newstatesman.co.uk

Occupation: Columnist, New Statesman

Other positions: Presenter, Morgan and Platell (Channel 4) 2004-present; Columnist, Daily Mail.
Publications: Scandal (1999)
Education: Penrhos Methodist Ladies College; University of Western Australia
Career highlights: Reporter, Perth Daily News 1978-81; Sydney Bureau Chief, Perth Daily News 1983; Subeditor, Sydney Sun, 1984; Harpers Bazaar, 1985; Today Newspaper, 1986; Metropolitan Deputy Editor, London Daily News, 1987; Deputy Editor, Today, 1987-92; (Features, Production Editor 1987), Group Managing Editor, Mirror Group Newspapers, 1993; Director of Marketing, MGN 1993; Marketing Director, Independent, 1993-95; Managing Director, Independent and Independent on Sunday, 1995-96; Editor, Sunday Mirror 1996-97; Editor, Sunday Express, 1998-99; Head of Media, Conservative Party, 1999-2001; Columnist, New Statesman, Daily Mail.

» **Relaxing to:** *Cars, eating out, travelling.*

Jon Plowman

5.7.57

Television Centre, Wood Lane, London W12 7RJ
T 020 8743 8000
E jon.plowman@bbc.co.uk

Occupation: Head of Comedy, BBC TV

Other positions: Head of Comedy Entertainment; Executive Producer; Producer; Freelance Theatre Director.
Publications: The Office (exec); Little Britain (exec); Extras (exec); Absolutely Fabulous (prod and exec); French and Saunders (prod and exec); Bottom (prod); Bit of Fry and Laurie (prod); Gimme Gimme Gimme (prod); Comic Relief (prod and exec); Vicar of Dibley (prod and exec).
Awards: Golden Globe; RTS Fellowship; RTS Award; Golden Rose, Montreux; British Comedy Awards; 2 BAFTAs.
Education: Welwyn Garden City Grammar School; University College, Oxford
Career highlights: Running the most creative comedy department in Britain and having the chance to work with some of the funniest names in the kingdom for a living. Also getting my name on an album by Rufus Wainwright and being Assistant Director to Lindsay Anderson at the Royal Court Theatre, London.
Mentor: Lindsay Anderson, Ronald Eyre, and Francis Matthews.
Big break: My arm in Nacodoches, Texas, and my leg whilst working on the Russell Harty show for the BBC.
Big mistake: Thinking that I know anything about comedy.

» **Reading:** *The Guardian, Evening Standard, Tobias Woolf, Evelyn Waugh, the New Yorker, Attitude.* **Watching:** *Not enough but as much as I can, passions for West Wing, Will and Grace, Family Guy, Love and Death and The Producers.* **Listening:** *Bach, Beethoven, Rufus Wainwright, Nina Simone, Gottschalk, Frank Sinatra, Boyce, Handel, Mozart, James Blunt, Sandy Denny, Mary Chapin Carpenter, Richard Pryor, etc etc.* **Relaxing to:** *A small house in the Pyrenees and a small house in Somerset.* » *Single, no children*

Nick Pollard

15.11.50

Sky News, Unit One, BSkyB, Grant Way, Isleworth, Middlesex TW7 5QD
T 020 7705 3000
E nick.pollard@bskyb.com

Occupation: Head of Sky News

Other positions: Formerly local newspaper reporter in Birkenhead; local radio News Editor; Producer, BBC TV News; Executive Producer, News at Ten (ITN).
Awards: Sky News has won two BAFTAS for best news coverage and numerous RTS and New York Festival awards since 1996.
Education: Birkenhead School; no university
Career highlights: Worked on all the big news stories of the past 25 years including Falklands War, Iranian Embassy siege, Lockerbie air crash, Zeebrugge, fall of Berlin Wall, death of Princess Diana, Kosovo conflict, Omagh bomb, World Trade Centre attacks, Iraq War, Afghan War, Asian tsunami, London bombings, as well as every General Election since 1970.
Mentor: Arthur Johnson, News Editor, Birkenhead News. Sir David Nicholas, Editor and Chief Executive, ITN.
Big break: Being steered towards my local paper by a sympathetic teacher after failing at school.
Big mistake: It's probably just round the corner - that's what keeps me on my toes.

» **Reading:** *Military history - John Keegan and Max Hastings - if you can call two authors incomparable, they are.* **Watching:** *Rolling news all day on five screens in my office, plus The Bill, Sopranos, The Shield (best-kept secret on telly), Dream Team, Liverpool FC winning European trophies.* **Listening:** *Five Live - especially the great Peter Allen.* **Relaxing to:** *Scones and jam in Kew Gardens.* » *Married, 2 children*

David Pollington

30.9.51

The Sunday Post, Albert Square, Dundee DD1 9QJ
T 01382 223131
E dpollington@sundaypost.com

Occupation: Editor, The Sunday Post

Other positions: Deputy Editor; Assistant Editor; News Editor.
Education: Morgan Academy, Dundee

» *Married, 5 children*

Mark Popescu

10.8.64

Room 4631, BBC Television Centre, Wood Lane, London W12 7RJ
T 020 8225 7419
E mark.popescu@bbc.co.uk

Occupation: Editorial Director, BBC News 24

Other positions: Editor, BBC Ten O'Clock News 2001-03; Editor Six O'Clock News, 1999-01; Programme Editor, News at Ten, ITV, 1996-99.
Publications: Relaunch of BBC Six O'Clock News with Huw Edwards, and joint headlines/trails with BBC Nations and Regions as part of integrated newshour; relaunch of Ten O'Clock News with new set, graphics and titles; Deputy Editor Vote '97 - ITV general election programme; Editor, election results day.
Awards: 2003 Broadcast Award, Best News Programme, Ten O'Clock News.
Education: King James College, Henley; Exeter University
Career highlights: Working in the field for ITN on big stories like the collapse of the Iron Curtain and the first Iraq war. Four years at Westminster, with knife-edge votes as John Major's majority slipped away. Introducing more accessible journalism and a new structure to the evening news hour for the Six O'Clock News in spring 1999 and beginning the process of joining up the journalism in the BBC Nations and Regions with that at TVC.
Mentor: Michael Brunson, Political Editor, ITN. Always went after the heart of the story.
Big break: Offered job as guest fixer and tea boy at ITN on the One O'Clock News with Leonard Parkin, in 1987.

Big mistake: Ignoring my instinct on stories which don't smell right.

» **Reading:** *All serious daily papers, Economist, Time and Newsweek, Auto Express.* **Watching:** *News and more news, Arsenal, Waking the Dead, Morse, Top Gear, Spooks.* **Listening:** *Pink Floyd, Clapton, Foo Fighters, Dido.* **Relaxing to:** *Gardening, cheese and wine, walking.*
» *Married, 3 children*

Henry Porter

23.3.53

Vanity Fair, Condé Nast Publications Ltd, 1 Hanover Square, London W1R 0AD
T 020 7499 9080
E daisy.prince@condenast.co.uk

Occupation: London Editor, Vanity Fair

Publications: Lies, Damned Lies and Some Exclusives, 1984; Remembrance Day, 1999; A Spy's Life, 2001; Empire State, 2003; Brandenberg, 2005.
Education: Wellington College; University of Manchester; Perugia University, Italy
Career highlights: Evening Standard, 1979-81; Feature Writer, Sunday Times, 1981-83; Columnist, Sunday Times, 1983-87; Editor, Illustrated London News, 1987-89; Sunday Correspondent Magazine, 1989-90; Executive Editor, Independent on Sunday 1990-91; currently London Editor, Vanity Fair.

» **Relaxing to:** *Walking, painting, art galleries, reading.*
» *Married, 2 daughters*

Richard Porter

Room 2254, BBC Television Centre, Wood Lane, London W12 7RJ
T 020 8743 8000
E richard.porter@bbc.co.uk

Occupation: Head of News, BBC World

Other positions: Editorial Director, BBC World; Editor, BBC Breakfast; Senior Editor, BBC News 24.

» **Listening:** *BBC World - along with 59 million other people around the globe.*

Chris Powell

4.10.43

DDB London, 12 Bishop's Bridge Road, London W2 6AA
T 020 7258 3979
E annouchka.behrmann@ddblondon.com

Occupation: Managing Director, DDB London

Other positions: Non-executive Directorships, Riverside Studios 1989-present; United News and Media plc 1995-present; Britain in Europe 2005-present; President, IPA 1993-95; Chairman, IPPR 2001-present (Trustee 1999-present), National Endowment for Science, Technology and the Arts (NESTA) 2003-present; Deputy Chairman, Riverside Community NHS Trust, 1994-2000; Chairman, Ealing and Hounslow Health Authority, 2000-02; Trustee, Divert 2000-02; Honorary Adviser, Board of International Family Health, 1997-2004.
Education: Canterbury Cathedral Choir School; St Peter's School, York; London School of Economics
Career highlights: Account Management Trainee, Hobson Bates, 1965-67; Account Manager, Wasey's, 1967-69; BMP DDB, joined as Partner and Shareholder 1969, Joint Managing Director, 1975-86; Chief Executive, 1986-98; Chairman, 1999-2003.

» **Watching:** *Theatre.* **Relaxing to:** *Riding, tennis, gardening.*
» *Married, 3 children*

Peter Preston

24.5.42

c/o The Guardian, 119 Farringdon Road EC1 1ER
T 020 7278 2332
E Peter.Preston@guardian.co.uk

Occupation: Columnist, Observer and Guardian; Co-Director, Guardian Foundation

Other positions: Former Editor, Guardian, 1975-95; Chairman, British Executive, International Press Institute.
Publications: Two novels (51st State and Bess) plus numerous columns on newspaper world, based on Guardian experience.
Awards: Four honorary degrees (City, Essex, Leicester, Loughborough); Honorary Fellow, St John's College, Oxford; several times Editor of Newspaper of Year.
Education: Loughborough Grammar School; St John's, Oxford
Career highlights: Had polio at 10, crocked, decided becoming a journalist was almost the only thing I could do; worked on Loughborough Monitor; edited Cherwell at Oxford; three years doing everything on Liverpool Daily Post; joined Guardian in 1963 as Political Reporter, Foreign Correspondent, Education Correspondent, Diary Editor, Features Editor, Night Editor; then Editor for 20 rocky, tumultuous years, culminating in Neil Hamilton and Jonathan Aitken cases; helped buy/save Observer. Very busy keeping busy.
Mentor: Alastair Hetherington, my Guardian predecessor; Charles Wintour, who showed me another approach to editing; Bob Griffiths at school, who taught me to think.
Big break: Reporting wars in Cyprus and Pakistan, because they showed me I could do it.
Big mistake: Too many to list. Most people would say the Sarah Tisdall case, and providing they'd understood the detail of it, I wouldn't argue.

» **Reading:** *Editors don't read for pleasure because they've read 100,000 words a day in the office. Now I just enjoy book reviewing.* **Watching:** *Anything with Bochco or David E Kelley on the TV titles. Plus movies maybe twice a week.* **Listening:** *Tone deaf. I try to sleep during Today between 6.50 and 7.55 am.* **Relaxing to:** *With the internet or eight grandchildren.* » *Married, 4 children*

Matthew Price
7.4.65

BBC Jersey, 18 & 21 Parade Road, St Helier, Jersey JE2 3PL
T 01534 837260
E matthew.price@bbc.co.uk

Occupation: Assistant Editor, BBC Jersey

Other positions: Acting Editor, BBC Jersey; Senior Broadcast Journalist, BBC Radio Jersey; Senior Broadcast Journalist, BBC Radio Devon; Senior Broadcast Journalist, BBC Radio Northampton; Acting Assistant Editor, BBC Radio Cornwall; Acting Assistant Editor, BBC Radio Norfolk; Reporter, BBC Look East; Reporter, BBC East at Westminster.
Awards: Sony Small Station of the Year, BBC Radio Jersey, 2004; Plain English Award, BBC Radio Jersey, 2005.
Education: Nene College, Northampton; Westfield Boys' School, Wellingborough; Oakway School, Wellingborough
Career highlights: I've been based in the Channel Islands for the past five years, working across all three media at BBC Jersey. This is a community that is totally independent from the UK and the EU, has its own government and sets its own laws. The news agenda is both challenging and unique. We're a small team and often find ourselves broadcasting, as well as editing; I've worked entirely in BBC English Regions since joining the BBC full time in 1987 after graduating (BA Combined Studies: Drama, English, History and education); spells at different local radio stations have given me a range of experiences working closely in small communities, whilst two stints in regional television gave me the opportunity to work in front of the camera as well as behind the scenes. In Jersey I get to combine all of these.

» **Reading:** *The Times, Daily Telegraph, Spectator, Private Eye.* **Watching:** *BBC Spotlight Channel Islands, West Wing, Channel 4 News, Newsnight, Frasier, The Simpsons.*
» *Separated, 1 daughter*

Nick Pringle
22.5.80

Leo Burnett, Warwick Building, Kensington Village W14 8HQ
T 07909 990752
E nicholas.pringle@leoburnett.co.uk

Occupation: Art Director and Copywriter, Leo Burnett

Publications: Heinz Pasta, John West, Daz.
Awards: Creative Circle gold 2005; Creative Circle silver 2005; Campaign Poster silver 2005 × 3; D&AD silver nomination 2005; Campaign Press commended 2004; Campaign Press commended 2005; Cannes Finalist 2004; Cannes Finalist 2005 × 2.
Education: University of Sheffield
Career highlights: We have received most press for our Heinz Spiderman Pasta ad and Washington Mutual; amongst other awards we won a silver nomination at D&AD and best use of six sheet advertising in Campaign posters 2005.
Mentor: Nick Hastings, Jim Thornton and Dave Beverley.
Big break: Being given a three-month trial in the creative dept when I was an account manager.
Big mistake: Taking Latin A-level.

» **Reading:** *Trashy papers and www.coolhunting.com.* **Watching:** *Any documentary about music.* **Listening:** *Anything on these record labels: Stones Throw, Ninja Tune, Gamm, Wall of Sound and anything else I'm recommended.* **Relaxing to:** *Scootering round London, gym, climbing and listening to music in the bath.* » *Single, no children*

James Purnell
3.3.74

2-4 Cockspur Street, London SW1Y 5DH
T 020 7211 6303
E james.purnell@culture.gsi.gov.uk

Occupation: Minister for Broadcasting, Creative Industries and Tourism; MP for Stalybridge and Hyde

Other positions: Research Fellow, IPPR; Head of Corporate Planning, BBC; Special Adviser to the Prime Minister on Culture, Media and Sport.
Education: Royal Grammar School, Guildford; Balliol College, Oxford

» *Engaged, no children*

Richard Quest

9.3.66

Turner House, 16 Great Marlborough Street, London W1F 7HS
T 020 7693 1000
E richard.quest@turner.com

Occupation: Correspondent and Anchor, CNN International

Awards: Winner, CWT Business Travel Programme of the Year 2005; Media Personality of the Year, CWT Travel Awards 2005.
Education: University of Leeds; Council of Legal Education
Career highlights: Covering stock market crash in 1987 and 1989; covering launch of the Euro, the last flight of Concorde etc.
Mentor: Paul Gibbs when Business Editor at the BBC.
Big break: Being the late financial reporter in 1987 when the Dow Jones collapsed.
Big mistake: Far too many to mention.

» **Reading:** *In the morning the FT and The Times. The Evening Standard. I try to do the Sunday papers, but frankly these days life is too short.* **Watching:** *The news, obviously. The West Wing.* **Listening:** *Radio 4's Today and PM. BBC World Service. And Magic ... OK ... so I am not cool.* **Relaxing to:** *At 35,000 feet en route to a story. The only way.* » *Single, no children*

Eileen Quinn

23.8.68

3-6 Kenrick Place, London W1U 6HD
T 020 7317 2230
E eileen.quinn@iwcmedia.co.uk

Occupation: Producer, Head of Drama and Company Director, IWC Media

Publications: Meet the Magoons; Coming Up; State of Mind; Bait; The Russian Bride; Love or Money, Seaforth...
Awards: IWC Company Talent Development Award 2005; numerous nominations over the years for Baftas including Best Production and Best Actress for ITV drama, The Russian Bride, 2001; RTS award, Best Actress in Drama Have Your Cake and Eat It, 1997, etc.
Education: Overseas School of Rome; University of California; London University
Career highlights: Joined ITV company Central TV and within two years left to join young indie Initial Films. Became Company Director and Head of Drama within a further two years and produced high end drama, overseeing some £40m worth of production over the next six years. Production highlights during that time include the ten-hour epic drama for BBC1 Seaforth, and the feature film The Hawk starring Helen Mirren. Started my own business Monogram in 1997 where we made among others Imogen's Face for ITV, Bright Hair for BBC1, and The Russian Bride. Sold the company for 20% stake in Wark Clements in 2001, where we made Love or Money for BBC1 and ITV dramas Bait, starring John Hurt, and State of Mind. I now hold 10% in IWC where we make new talent series Coming Up and just made our first comedy Meet the Magoons.
Mentor: Michael Wearing and Fernando Ghia.
Big break: Working for Eric Fellner who let me get on with it.
Big mistake: Not trusting my gut instinct.

» **Reading:** *Dense novels, a hell of a lot of scripts, Italian magazines, Vanity Fair in the bath.* **Watching:** *A little bit of everything and a lot of the news.* **Listening:** *Classical music and opera, Californian mellow mafia and Italian pop.* **Relaxing to:** *I go to Umbria.* » *Divorced, 1 daughter, Lily (10)*

Stephen Quinn

27.12.47

Vogue House, Hanover Square, London W1S 1JU
T 020 7152 3030
E squinn@condenast.co.uk

Occupation: Publishing Director, Vogue; Board Director, Condé Nast

Publications: Launched GQ in 1988, first upmarket magazine for men.
Education: St Kieran's College, Ireland
Career highlights: Publisher, Harpers & Queen 1981; Launch Publisher, GQ 1988; Publishing Director, Vogue 1992.
Mentor: Gordon Brown, first boss IPC magazines.
Big break: Launching GQ against a backdrop of deep scepticism in the industry that men would buy a mag that mixed fashion with general features. It is now our fourth most profitable magazine.
Big mistake: Staying too long in my previous company.

» **Reading:** *Politics, novels, newspapers, mags.* **Watching:** *Thrillers on TV.* **Listening:** *Bob Dylan, John Lee Hooker, The Chieftains, Lyle Lovett, Blues stuff/Irish folk.* **Relaxing to:** *With delightful William, my three-year-old, and with robust Lorcan, my eight-month-old. Taking Matt, Jamie and Fergus, my older sons, to nice restaurants.* » *Married, 2 boys and 3 sons from first marriage*

R

Yvonne Ramsden

21.9.64

IPC Media, King's Reach Tower, Stamford Street, London SE1 9LS
T 020 7261 6408
E yvonne_ramsden@ipcmedia.com

Occupation: Publishing Director, Home Interest

Other positions: Graduate Trainee, British Gas; Marketing Manager, Standbrook Publications; Assistant Publisher, IPC Southbank (Marie Claire, W Journal); Associate Publisher, IPC Connect (Woman, Woman's Realm, Woman's Weekly); Publisher IPC CALM (Classic Cars, Amateur Gardening, Practical Woodworking, New Scientist).
Publications: IPC market leading home portfolio: Ideal Home, Homes & Gardens, Country Homes & Interiors, 25 Beautiful Homes, Livingetc, 25 Beautiful Kitchens.
Awards: Shortlisted PPA Publisher of the Year 1998, 1999 and 2000.
Education: Nottingham University
Career highlights: Having spent 18 years at IPC I have been lucky enough to have worked across many markets and on a variety of magazines but I have found my spiritual home working in Southbank. Key highlights include: rightfully regaining the number one position for Ideal Home in 1999, a position we have held since; launching Livingetc and 25 Beautiful Homes both in 1998 as well as fronting the market-leading portfolio.
Mentor: Isobel McKenzie-Price, ex-Editorial Director Southbank and now Editor of All You for Time Warner in the US.
Big break: When IPC bought Standbrook Publications and I joined the IPC's launch of Marie Claire as Assistant Publisher working for Heather Love.
Big mistake: Spending three years in Southampton with British Gas in the early 80s - I'm sure it's a much nicer place now.

» **Reading:** *Grew up on CS Lewis and Tolkien so naturally moved on to Harry Potter. Just finished all the Dan Browns and currently reading The Insider (Piers Morgan). In terms of magazines, apart from being a home interest junkie I love In-Style.* **Watching:** *I'm a real sucker for whodunits and conspiracy theories, so I have to admit to a diet of CSI, Spooks, Waking the Dead followed by the News.* **Listening:** *Radio 4 in the mornings.* **Relaxing to:** *Having a very energetic five-year-old gives me very little time to relax but I wouldn't have it any other way.* » *Married, 1 child*

Jeff Randall

3.10.54

Telegraph Group, 1 Canada Square, London E14 5AP
T 020 7293 3000
E Jeff.Randall@telegraph.co.uk

Occupation: Editor-at-Large, Telegraph Group

Awards: Financial Journalist of the Year, FT-Analysis, 1991; Business Journalist of the Year, London Press Club, 2001; Sony Gold Award for best radio sports programme, The Bankrupt Game, BBC 5 Live, 2002; Broadcast Journalist of the Year and Decade of Excellence Award, Business Journalist of the Year Awards, 2003; Harold Wincott Award for Best Business Broadcaster, 2004; Communicator of the Year Award, PR Week, 2004.
Education: Royal Liberty Grammar School, Romford; University of Nottingham; University of Florida
Career highlights: Hawkins Publishers, 1982-85; Assistant Editor, Financial Weekly, 1985-86; City Correspondent, Sunday Telegraph, 1986-88; the Sunday Times, Deputy City Editor, 1988-89; City Editor, 1989-94; City and Business Editor, 1994-95; Assistant Editor and Sports Editor, 1996-97; Editor, Sunday Business, 1997-2001; Business Editor, BBC, 2001-05; Director, Times Newspapers, 1994-95; Deputy Chairman, Financial Dynamics Ltd, 1995-96; Columnist, Sunday Telegraph, 2002-04.

» **Relaxing to:** *Golf, horseracing, football.* » *Married, 1 daughter*

Caroline Raphael

Radio 4, Broadcasting House, London W1A 1AA
T 020 7580 4468
E caroline.raphael@bbc.co.uk

Occupation: Commissioning Editor, Drama and Entertainment, BBC Radio 4

Other positions: Head of Radio Drama, Editor Youth Programmes Radio 5; variously Editor, Producer and Script Reader Radio Drama - all at BBC Radio; Theatre Director at Nuffield Theatre Southampton, Royal Exchange Theatre, Bristol Old Vic, Gate Theatre London, Edinburgh Fringe Festival.
Education: Putney High School; Manchester University
Career highlights: Commissioning Little Britain and The League of Gentlemen for BBC Radio 4. First woman Head of Radio Drama. Part of team that set up (and then closed down) the old Radio 5!
Mentor: The late Richard Imison, Deputy Head of Radio Drama and Head of Script Unit when I joined the BBC. Inspiring, passionate, dedicated and very wise.
Big break: Being offered work as Assistant Director at Nuffield Theatre on graduation.
Big mistake: No idea

» **Reading:** *Mainly fiction. Very little reading that is not for work as I also commission Book at Bedtime and The Afternoon Reading. But being paid to read new novels and stories is hardly a chore.* **Watching:** *Comedy across the television networks, new dramas, the news, Coronation Street and EastEnders. At least one episode of any new show whenever possible.* **Listening:** *Radio 4 and Xfm.* **Relaxing to:** *Sleep.* » *Divorced, 1 child*

Sophie Raworth 1.5.68

BBC News, Room 2254, BBC Television Centre, Wood Lane, London W12 7RJ
T 020 8624 9929
E sophie.raworth@bbc.co.uk

Occupation: Presenter, BBC Six O'Clock News

Education: Manchester University; City University, London
Career highlights: Regional Trainee, BBC, 1992; Reporter, Greater Manchester Radio, BBC, 1993-94; Europe Producer for the Regions, Brussels, BBC, 1994; Presenter, BBC Look North, Leeds, 1995; Presenter, BBC Breakfast News, 1997; Presenter, BBC Six O'Clock News, 2003-present; also co-presented the BBC's coverage of State Opening of Parliament, the Queen's Golden Jubilee celebrations, Prince Charles' marriage to Camilla Parker-Bowles, spent a fortnight on the BBC's election bus during the 2005 General Election campaign, regular reporter on Tomorrow's World; also presented Dream Lives, Judgemental and 4×4.

» *Married, 1 daughter*

Deborah Rayner 3.8.64

ITN, 200 Gray's Inn Road, London WC1X 8XZ
T 020 7430 4118
E Deborah.rayner@itn.co.uk

Occupation: Senior Foreign Editor, Channel Four News

Other positions: Commissioning Editor, Independents, C4N; Executive Producer, Independents, C4N.
Publications: Channel Four News
Awards: RTS, Emmy, BAFTA, Amnesty, Rory Peck, Foreign Press Association, New York Festival - C4 awards.
Education: Bristol
Mentor: Sue Inglish and Jon Snow.
Big break: Roof-top producing Snow when Arafat returned to Israel absolutely years ago.
Big mistake: Not spending enough time with family and friends.

» *Single, no children*

Katie Razzall

ITN, 200 Gray's Inn Road, London WC1X 8XZ
T 020 7430 4660
E katie.razzall@itn.co.uk

Occupation: Reporter and Presenter, Channel 4 News

Other positions: Business Producer, Channel 4 News; General Producer, Channel 4 News; ITN News, Trainee Producer; Community Programmes, Carlton TV.
Awards: Award-winning reports as a producer: Enron corruption, Best Broadcast Submission, Business Journalist of the Year Awards; Call centre horrors, Best Campaign, Industrial Society Awards; Dot.com meltdown, Wincott Foundation award for Best Journalism.
Education: Westminster School; Oxford University
Career highlights: My most dramatic career progression was when I arrived for my first TV job, as a Researcher at Carlton TV, to be told that a Producer had left and I'd been promoted before I'd even done a minute's work. Admittedly, I was producing three-minute public access shorts, but it felt incredibly high-powered and fulfilling. Getting onto ITN's trainee scheme was a real break - only four of us were chosen for a year's-worth of invaluable training. But the moment that had the most impact was getting a job at Channel 4 News, having hankered after working here for as long as I can remember. It's allowed me the opportunity to work with the best in the field and be present for some truly dramatic news events - the Milosevic trial, Harold Shipman's conviction, the G8 riots in Genoa. High points must be travelling round India for two weeks by train with Jon Snow, C4 Cameraman Ken McCallum and our fixer for a series of reports for the Channel 4 News in India specials. Also filming in Egypt immediately after September 11th for an entirely different perspective on the attacks on America.
Mentor: Jon Snow - encouraging, inspiring, ever enthusiastic and happy to reverse his opinions entirely if you can persuade him of yours.
Big break: Reporting the murder trial of Trupti Patel while still a Producer and getting the only TV interview with Trupti and Jay Patel after she was cleared so sensationally. I think it finally persuaded my bosses at ITN to give me the reporting job I'd coveted for so long.
Big mistake: Going on honeymoon to Sri Lanka four days before the tsunami hit - although, amidst all the devastation and horror, I found moments of hope and incredible kindness and resilience from so many people. It also taught me, I hope, that the best journalists empathise with the people we interview and never forget our common humanity.

» **Reading:** *All the broadsheets plus Evening Standard, Daily Mirror, the Week, New Statesman, Vogue. I'm an insatiable consumer of fiction, but recently Piers Morgan's diaries have been a source of great amusement.* **Watching:** *Channel 4 News (of course), Newsnight, Sky News, ITV News. Anything by David Attenborough. Costume dramas. American imports. Sky Sports.* **Listening:** *Anything my husband has loaded on my iPod nano. Christina Kulukundis, a great album by my best friend.* **Relaxing to:** *Yoga, poker, sushi, walking in Northumberland, reading cookery books and imagining delicious meals I never manage to make.* » *Married, 1 child*

Philip Reay-Smith 31.5.78

200 Gray's Inn Road, London WC1X 8XZ
T 020 7833 3000
E philip.reay-smith@itn.co.uk

Occupation: Reporter, ITV News

Other positions: Reporter, EuroNews, 2000; Presenter and Reporter, News Direct 97.3FM, 1999; Reporter and News Editor, The Pink Paper, 1995-97.
Education: Shrewsbury School, Shropshire; UCL, London
Career highlights: Going into Iraq with the first troops on the night the ground invasion began in

March 2003. Spending the 2005 general election campaign following all the parties around with a camcorder, demonstrating the behind-the-scenes stage management and spin. Seeing first-hand the events people talk about in the pub.
Mentor: Roger Goode, my first editor, who kept re-writing my pieces until I got a rough idea what I was doing. Bill Dunlop, my first boss in TV, who kept reassuring me that I was doing all right.
Big break: Being sent as an embed with the British military to Iraq. My bosses didn't expect much from the battalion I was with; turned out they spent the war on the front line.
Big mistake: In my first job in 1995, going to my first select committee hearing, grabbing John Reid outside a committee room for a few words, and then entirely misrepresenting Labour party policy in the report I wrote.

» **Reading:** *All the papers, biographies, news websites.* **Watching:** *University Challenge, expensive American drama.* **Listening:** *Radios 1, 4 and 5, Virgin and Magic.* **Relaxing to:** *Driving without a deadline, travelling.* » *Living with partner, no children*

Gail Rebuck

10.2.52

Random House, 20 Vauxhall Bridge Road, London SW1V 2SA
T 020 7840 8888
E grebuck@randomhouse.co.uk

Occupation: Chairman and Chief Executive, The Random House Group Ltd.

Other positions: Publisher, Hamlyn Paperbacks; Publishing Director, Century Hutchinson; Chair, Random House Division, Random Century.
Publications: Launched World Book Day in 1998 and currently chairing the Steering Committee of Quick Reads, the adult literacy initiative to be launched on World Book Day 2006.
Awards: CBE in the 2000 Honours List; Diploma from Wharton Business School; Honorary Doctorates, Universities of Sussex, Exeter and Oxford Brookes; Honorary Fellow, London Business School.
Education: Lycée Français de Londres; University of Sussex
Career highlights: Currently Chairman and Chief Executive of The Random House Group, the UK's leading trade publishing company with over 30 imprints, and publishers of many of the world's best known authors; Trustee of the Institute for Public Policy Research and also a member of the Government's Creative Industry Task Force for 10 years; Non-executive Director of BSkyB; Trustee of the Work Foundation; Member, Council of the Royal College of Art; included in the Financial Times' survey Women in Business: Europe's Top 25 in October 2004 and October 2005.
Mentor: Charles Handy
Big break: Being part of the founding team of Century Publishing.
Big mistake: Too many to mention.

» **Reading:** *As much as I can of what we publish.* **Watching:** *Sky News and choice serials with my daughter.* **Listening:** *My iPod in the gym.* **Relaxing to:** *With difficulty.* » *Married, 2 daughters*

Jenny Reeks

ITV plc, 200 Grays Inn Road, London WC1X 8HF
T 020 7843 8211
E Jenny.Reeks@itv.com

Occupation: Head of ITV Network Drama

Other positions: Senior Executive Producer, BBC; Head of Drama, Red Rooster Film and Television; Head of Drama, Chrysalis Film and Television; Director of Artifax Journalism; teaching; advertising.
Awards: Assorted, for Dramas both produced and commissioned.
Education: Oxford University
Career highlights: Like a proud Mum, a commissioner has highlights every week, but I'm particularly pleased with the schedule fixtures I've helped to introduce: Midsomer Murders, Trial and Retribution, Doc Martin, Life Begins, Foyle's War, Wire in the Blood, Bad Girls, Footballers' Wives, Fat Friends etc. etc. Now I feel bad about the ones I haven't mentioned (so many) - and the wonderful singles and serials like Hillsborough, Reckless, Ahead of the Class, The Second Coming, Bob and Rose, At Home With The Braithwaites, Dirty Filthy Love, Oliver Twist, Forsyte Saga ...
Mentor: I've always been self-reliant. Besides, mentors can often be wrong about somebody else.
Big break: The arrival of Channel 4 at the very moment I and others were setting up an independent TV company (Artifax).
Big mistake: Not having more children.

» **Reading:** *Everything, except for romantic fiction, foreign news pages and things about cruelty to animals.* **Watching:** *Live sport (especially football), reality shows, shock-horror documentaries and old episodes of Bottom and Gimme Gimme Gimme.* **Listening:** *Classic FM, Talksport (though it's very irritating), Van Morrison and Mozart.* **Relaxing to:** *Growing vegetables, making soup, walking dogs, Sunday lunch and too much Sudoku.* » *Divorced, 2 children*

Morgan Rees

8.11.74

National Magazine Company, 33 Broadwick Street, London W1F 0DQ
T 020 7339 4434
E Morgan.rees@rodale.co.uk

Occupation: Editor, Men's Health

Awards: BSME New Editor Of The Year, 2004; Rodale Editor of the Year, 2004; Rodale Editor of the Year, 2005.
Education: Cardiff University
Career highlights: Deputy Editor, Maxim; Associate Editor, Jack and Hotdog; Commissioning Editor, GQ; Editorial Assistant's Assistant, Loaded.
Mentor: James Brown, Dylan Jones, Bill Prince.
Big break: First job at GQ.

» **Reading:** *Books, magazines and newspapers.* **Watching:** *The world go by, attractive women with unattractive men, my weight, my bank balance.* **Listening:** *Good advice, my parents, traffic driving past my flat at two in the morning.* » *Single, no children*

Paul Rees

15.11.71

Q, Mappin House, 4 Winsley Street,
London W1W 8HF
T 020 7182 8000
E paul.rees@emap.com

Occupation: Editor, Q Magazine

Other positions: Reviews Editor, RAW magazine 1992-93; Features Editor, Kerrang! 1994-96; Deputy Editor, Kerrang! 1996-99; Editor, Kerrang! 1999-2002.
Awards: EMAP Magazine Of The Year, 2001; PPA Specialist Magazine Of The Year, 2001; EMAP Performance Cover Of The Year, 2004; EMAP Performance Magazine Of The Year, 2005.
Education: Ounsdale High School, Wombourne; Crewe and Alsager College
Career highlights: Editing both Kerrang! and Q, magazines I bought from their respective first issues has been a highlight in itself; doubling Kerrang!'s circulation within three years was also hugely rewarding, but most satisfying of all has been the last two years on Q, where we have increased our sales (delivering three consecutive year-on-year rises) and market share at a time when all of our competitors have cover-mounted free CDs every month against us. During that time, we've also redesigned the magazine twice, and I believe re-established it not only as the market leader (Q is now Europe's most read music magazine), but revitalised it in terms of both quality and impact.
Mentor: I've been lucky enough to have had three. Steve Morris, who gave me my first job in publishing at Brum Beat, Phil Alexander, under whom I worked on RAW and Kerrang!, and latterly, Marcus Rich.
Big break: Moving to London at the exact time RAW were looking for a Reviews Editor. The large cheque I deposited in their account didn't hurt.
Big mistake: It involved Pink and the words 'Sex Issue', and it still causes me to break out in a cold sweat.

» **Reading:** *Too many magazines to mention. Independent, Guardian and an endless supply of fiction and non-fiction. In my humble opinion, the three greatest books ever written are Harper Lee's To Kill A Mockingbird, John Steinbeck's The Grapes Of Wrath and Mikhail Bulgakov's The Master And Margarita.* **Watching:** *The Sopranos, religiously. News and documentaries, anything by David Attenborough or John Pilger, and movies - this week's top three: It's A Wonderful Life, Casablanca, and Once Upon A Time In America.* **Listening:** *Music of all styles and eras, from Benny Goodman to Bob Dylan to Black Sabbath - each and every day.* **Relaxing to:** *By being with my family or watching West Bromwich Albion FC. The latter is rarely that relaxing, though.* » *Married to Denise, 1 son, Tom*

Allan Rennie

6.7.64

Sunday Mail, One Central Quay, Glasgow G3 8DA
T 0141 309 3403
E a.rennie@sundaymail.co.uk

Occupation: Editor, Sunday Mail

Other positions: Chairman, Scottish Daily Newspapers Society Editors Committee; Chairman, West of Scotland NPF, The Journalists Charity.
Publications: Sunday Mail is Scotland's biggest-selling Sunday. It includes Scotland's best-read magazines Seven Days and Right at Home.
Awards: Newspaper shortlisted in 2004 and 2003 for Cudlipp Award in British Press Awards for Crime Inc and De La Salle investigations.
Education: Kilsyth Academy
Career highlights: Started off as a baker - couldn't make enough dough. Career highlights: Junior Reporter, Springburn Times; Editor, Clydebank Post; Sub-editor, Stirling Observer; Deputy Chief Sub, the Scottish Sun; Deputy Sports Editor/ Features Editor/Assistant Editor, Daily Record, and now.
Mentor: Alice Craig from the Springburn Times and Jack Irvine formerly of the Sun.
Big break: When the Sun phoned me out of the blue and offered me a job as a sub editor for triple the salary. I said 'yes'.
Big mistake: Mistakes, I've made a few ... but then again, too few to mention.

» **Reading:** *Every newspaper every day.* **Watching:** *Will and Grace, Frasier, Lost, Sex and the City, Extras.* **Listening:** *Indie rock and roll and Mylo.* **Relaxing to:** *Running, badminton and going to musicals.* » *Married, 3 children*

Camilla Rhodes

5.5.58

News Magazines Ltd, 1 Virginia Street,
London E98 1SN
T 020 7198 3000
E Camilla.rhodes@newsint.co.uk

Occupation: Chief Executive, News Magazines Ltd

Education: University College, London
Career highlights: Managing Director, the Sun and News of the World; Managing Director, Times Newspapers Ltd.

» *Married, 2 children*

Marcus Rich

22.6.63

Endeavour House, 189 Shaftesbury Avenue,
London WC2H 8JG
T 020 7295 6777
E marcus.rich@emap.com

Occupation: Group Managing Director, Emap Advertising, Metro and Elan

Publications: Q, Mojo, Kerrang, Empire, Smash Hits, Bliss, Sneak, Grazia, New Woman, More, Top Sante.
Education: King Edward 7th Grammar School, Kings Lynn
Career highlights: 1977, fishmonger; 1982, Emap;

1986-92, brief sojourn into advertising; 1994, acquired FHM; 1997, Australia; 1999, New York; 2002, home; May 2005, Emap Advertising.
Mentor: Too many to mention. Everyone contributes a little something.
Big break: First job at Emap in 1982. From fishmonger to media in one easy step!
Big mistake: Supporting West Ham.

» **Reading:** *Q, Mojo, Arena, Grazia, Heat, Match - loyal to the core.* **Watching:** *With the power of Sky+, Curb Your Enthusiasm, Lost, House, Rescue Me, Football First, and a plethora of cooking, gardening and property programmes.* **Listening:** *Kiss, Magic, Kerrang on the radio, but largely the iPod from A Tribe Called Quest to ZZ Top.* **Relaxing to:** *With four kids rarely but wine helps.* » *Married, 4 children*

Ed Richards

1966

Ofcom, Riverside House, 2a Southwark Bridge Road, London SE1 9HA
T 020 7981 3000
E kate.lee@ofcom.org.uk

Occupation: Chief Operating Officer, Ofcom

Other positions: Chief Policy Partner, Ofcom; Member, Board, Donmar Warehouse Theatre, London;
Career highlights: Researcher, Diverse Production Ltd, for Channel 4; Consultant, London Economics Ltd; Adviser to Gordon Brown MP; Controller, Corporate Strategy, BBC; Senior Policy Adviser to the Prime Minister for media, telecoms, internet and e-govt, involved in drafting Communications Bill.

» **Relaxing to:** *Matisse.* » *Married*

Menna Richards

28.2.57

Room 3034, BBC Wales, Broadcasting House, Llandaff, Cardiff CF5 2YQ
T 029 20 322380
E menna.richards@bbc.co.uk

Occupation: Controller, BBC Wales

Other positions: Chair, Board of Governors, Royal Welsh College of Music and Drama.
Awards: Fellow, Royal Television Society.
Education: University of Wales, Aberystwyth
Career highlights: News Reporter, BBC Wales; Current Affairs Reporter/Editor HTV Wales; Head of Factual Programmes, HTV Wales; Director of Programmes, HTV Wales; Director of Broadcasting, HTV Group plc; Managing Director, HTV Wales; Controller, BBC Wales.
Mentor: John Roberts Williams, News Editor. Died 2005.
Big break: Appointed Head of Factual Programmes in 1990. Move from production to management and opportunities to shape output.
Big mistake: Letting some key talent go.

» **Reading:** *Guardian, Western Mail, Golwg, Spectator, contemporary fiction.* **Watching:** *Dr Who, Spooks, West Wing, Little Britain, Strictly Come Dancing.* **Listening:** *Radio Cymru, Radio Wales, Radio 3, Radio 4.* **Relaxing to:** *Family, music, shopping, getting out of the country.* » *Married, 3 stepchildren*

Phil Riley

5.6.63

The Chrysalis Building, Bramley Road, London W10 6SP
T 020 7470 1077
E phil.riley@chrysalis.com

Occupation: Chief Executive, Chrysalis Radio

Other positions: Board Member, CRCA, RAB, DRDB, Rajar.
Education: Loughborough; Columbia Business School
Career highlights: Building Chrysalis Radio into one of the UK's big three radio groups. Taking Heart to number one in both London and the West Midlands.
Mentor: Paul Brown gave me my big break - and he still regrets it!
Big break: Getting a management trainee position in BRMB back in 1980.
Big mistake: Not buying more Chrysalis shares when I joined the company in 1994.

» **Reading:** *The Economist regularly - trashy murder novels on holiday.* **Watching:** *West Wing, The Shield, Lost.* **Listening:** *Heart, Galaxy, LBC, The Arrow (obvious I know) - I do give 5 Live a listen for the sport though!* **Relaxing to:** *Three kids - relax! Actually I ride my bike - it's a strenuous form of relaxation but it seems to work.* » *Married, 3 children*

Tim Riley

11.9.64

AMV BBDO Ltd, 151 Marylebone Road, London NW1 5QE
T 020 7616 3515
E rileyt@amvbbdo.com

Occupation: Writer, Abbott Mead Vickers BBDO

Other positions: Previously worked at BBH, BMP (now DDB London), Leagas Delaney and Simons Palmer.
Publications: Recently Make Poverty History; The Economist; If You Smoke You Stink for the Department of Health; Auschwitz for BBC2.
Awards: D&AD Silvers for Press, Posters and Mixed Media Campaign; quite a few Campaign Press and Poster Awards.
Mentor: Several; Alan Tilby, Alan Curzon, David Watkinson, Chris Palmer, Mark Denton, Tim Delaney and John Hegarty are just a few of them.
Big break: I was lucky. When I began looking for a job in advertising, it was nothing like as tough as it is for people starting out today.
Big mistake: Too numerous to list in the space provided.

» **Reading:** *As much as I can.* **Watching:** *On DVD, Seinfeld, Larry Sanders, The Likely Lads, Porridge. On TV, The Sopranos and BBC4.* **Listening:** *Radio 4, BBC 7 and lots and lots of music.* **Relaxing to:** *See above, plus eating out, cinema, running and football.* » *Single*

Daniel Rivers 8.11.77

200 Gray's Inn Road, London WC1X 8XZ
T 07734 743142
E dan.rivers@itn.co.uk

Occupation: Crime Correspondent, ITV News

Other positions: Freelance presenter on documentaries.
Education: Durham University
Career highlights: I have worked for five years at ITN, during which time I've covered a huge variety of stories. I was one of the first TV journalists into Aceh after the Asian tsunami. I had a series of exclusive reports containing leaked documents relating to the shooting of Jean Charles de Menezes. I was deployed to the Gulf war as an embedded reporter with the Royal Navy in 2003. Before ITN, I worked at Euronews in France, BBC Radio Five Live and BBC local radio.
Mentor: No one in particular, although I've been lucky to have had very good support from a number of colleagues and managers over the years.
Big break: Being on holiday in Australia when the Asian tsunami hit. It gave me the opportunity to report on a huge story, outside of my normal brief.
Big mistake: Staying in local radio too long!

» **Watching:** *News, lots of news.* **Relaxing to:** *Photography, sailing, wine tasting.* » *Married, no children*

James Robbins 20.1.58

Room 2505, BBC Television Centre, Wood Lane, London W12 7RJ
T 020 8624 8550
E james.robbins@bbc.co.uk

Occupation: BBC Diplomatic Correspondent

Other positions: Europe Correspondent, Brussels 1992-97; Southern Africa Correspondent, Johannesburg 1987-92; Reporter, BBC TV News, London 1983-87; Reporter, BBC Northern Ireland 1979-83; BBC News Trainee 1977-79.
Education: Christ Church, Oxford University
Career highlights: Reported the Northern Ireland troubles at their height including the 1981 Maze Prison hunger strikes and the first supergrass trials. Followed the beginnings of reform in South Africa. Witnessed the release of Nelson Mandela from prison in 1990 and conducted the BBC's first interview with him. Charted the rising tensions between Britain and Europe from the Maastricht Summit through the 'beef wars' over BSE to the 1997 General Election. Helped lead the BBC's coverage of the September 11th attacks on America and the wars in Afghanistan and Iraq.

» **Relaxing to:** *With the family, walking and playing tennis, reading, singing, listening to opera and music, and looking out of train windows.* » *Married, 1 child*

Andy Roberts 19.4.78

Emap Radio, Mappin House, 4 Winsley Street, London W1W 8HF
T 020 7182 8525
E andy.roberts@emap.com

Occupation: Group Programme Director, Emap Radio

Publications: Kiss100; Magic 105.4; Kerrang 105.2; Bigcity Network; digital radio stations including Q, Smashhits and Heat; Smashhits Chart/Fresh40 Event radio including UKradio Aid, Live 8, Leaders Live and that 'Egg card' promotion across 60 stations.
Awards: Various radio awards including 12 Sony Awards (including Golds) for various shows, stations and imaging; special award for UKradio Aid; ntl awards for station branding, overall station awards and shows. New York award golds for stations and station sound, and other radio awards for Programmer of the Year, etc.
Career highlights: Originally responsible for the re-invention of Kiss100, hiring Bambam, Robin Banks and tripling Kiss's audience to make it the most listened to station for everyone under 25. Then making it market leader 15-35's in London. Built the Kerrang radio format along with new digital stations including Q, Heat and Smashhits. Created the Smashhits chart and have responsibility for the new set of chart shows on commercial radio, including Fresh40. Involved in UKradioAid, Leaders Live, Live 8 and the creation of 100 grand in 100 minutes, the Egg card promotion across commercial radio. Responsible for A&R-ing various hit records including Frankee Fuck you right back, Ultrabeat Pretty Green Eyes, LMC vs. U2 Take me to the clouds above.
Mentor: Mark Story, Tim Schoonmaker. I've learnt a lot from these guys both professionally and a lot of life stuff.
Big break: Getting into radio, Emap persuaded me not to go to university. They hired me straight from A-levels. I was just in the right place at the right time.
Big mistake: Nothing really that I've done at work. More outside really. I could say I regret not going to uni but I guess I'd never be doing what I'm doing now.

» **Reading:** *Wired magazine, Edge magazine, Empire (Emap's finest publication!), a lot of internet sites, Aintitcool.com, etc, biographies - Don Simpson, George Lucas etc.* **Watching:** *Sky News, Music Vids, DVDs and Discovery Channel. I'm a bad channel hopper and have no attention span. Oh and Dick and Dom, dare I say, although it's for 10-year-olds I find the show genius.* **Listening:** *Loads of internet streamed stations including Z100, Kiss FM, Skyrock and Radio538 Holland. Mostly new music. I don't enjoy listening to radio, I listen and automatically start to analyse the output. Radio kills your favourite songs!* **Relaxing to:** *Eat out, lots, tapas is my vice. Most weeks I'll try and drink the Soho Hotel bar dry. Never works though. I have a studio at home so I'll often play around with tracks, production, etc.* » *Single, no children*

Juliet Roberts

Gardens Illustrated, Origin Publishing, Tower House, Fairfax Street, Bristol BS1 3BN

T 0870 4442611
E julietroberts@originpublishing.co.uk

Occupation: Editor, Gardens Illustrated

Other positions: Deputy Editor, Gardens Illustrated; Subeditor, Radio Times; Publicity Officer, BFI Regional Film Theatre; Assistant Editor, Film; Editorial Secretary, Sight & Sound.
Publications: Gardens Illustrated, Organic Kitchen Garden (published by Conran Octopus).
Awards: They've yet to come.
Mentor: Rosie Atkins, Launch Editor of Gardens Illustrated; Penelope Houston, Editor of Sight & Sound.
Big break: First media job as Editorial Secretary for Sight & Sound magazine published by the British Film Institute.
Big mistake: Staying in a couple of jobs for too long, because I enjoyed them too much.

» **Reading:** *The Week, Guardian, Observer, Saturday Telegraph, The Times, New Scientist, World of Interiors, Kitchen Garden as well as many and varied novels.* **Watching:** *Very little.* **Listening:** *Radio 4.* **Relaxing to:** *Gardening, walking my dog, listening to music, spending time with friends.* » *Single, 1 child*

David Robey
13.1.58

BBC London 94.9, 35c Marylebone High Street, London W1U 4QA

T 020 7224 2424
E david.robey@bbc.co.uk

Occupation: Managing Editor, BBC London 94.9

Other positions: Managing Editor, BBC Radio WM, 1997-99; Managing Editor, BBC Three Counties Radio, 1995-97; Assistant Editor, BBC Radio WM, 1988-95; News Editor, BBC Radio Bedfordshire, 1984-88; Journalist, BBC Radio Nottingham, 1983-84; Journalist, BBC Radio Derby and LBC 1982-83; News Editor and Programme Controller, Centre Radio (Leicester), 1981-82; Deputy News Editor, Radio Hallam (Sheffield), 1978-81; Journalist, Radio Trent (Nottingham), 1977-78; Journalist, Leicester Mercury, 1974-77.
Awards: Numerous Sony Radio Awards, including 1998 Radio Station of the Year for Radio WM; numerous other broadcasting awards, including Race in the Media, EMMA (Ethnic Multicultural Media Awards), Andrew Cross religious broadcasting awards.
Education: Westminster City and Journalism College
Career highlights: Doubling the audience at BBC London 94.9, winning Sony Station of the Year at BBC Radio WM, revamping BBC Three Counties Radio with a fourfold increase in listening, covering the miners' strike in Nottingham, the steel strike and closures in Sheffield, the Yorkshire Ripper inquiry, the Birmingham Six and, most recently, the July 2005 bombings in London.
Mentor: Tony Inchley, late Manager of BBC Radio WM, who developed personality-led, live speech radio for big city BBC local radio stations. Before him, BBC local radio was failing badly in the big cities as it was wedded to the 'down your way' style of the rural stations. Tony realised we needed to be bigger and brasher and it's still working for me today.
Big break: Being given the Managing Editor job at BBC Three Counties Radio (Beds, Herts and Bucks) which was a badly failing station. I was given a free hand to revamp the format and change the presenters, resulting in fourfold increase in listening hours in under two years. It led me back to BBC Radio WM and then on to BBC London 94.9.
Big mistake: Resigning on principle from Centre Radio in Leicester when I was a 27-year-old Acting Managing Director, despite being urged to stay.

» **Reading:** *History, biography and astronomy.* **Watching:** *Not much, but occasionally sport, movies and historical factual and drama documentaries.* **Listening:** *BBC London 94.9! Johnny Cash, Otis Reading, Marvin Gaye, the Rolling Stones, any Blues and current R&B.* **Relaxing to:** *Golf, music, theatre, movies and socialising.* » *Divorced, 4 children*

Dave Robinson
6.8.73

245 Blackfriars Road, London SE1 9UY

T 020 7921 8319
E david.robinson@cmpinformation.com

Occupation: Editor, Pro Sound News Europe (CMPi); Editor, AES Daily News

Other positions: Deputy Editor, Future Music (Future); CD Editor, Total Guitar (Future).
Publications: Redesign/relaunch of PSNE, May 2004; launch of Pro Audio A-Z Directory; pitched Future Publishing on idea for Computer Music magazine, Dec 98; launched in 99 and continues to be successful.
Awards: Insert cycling proficiency gag here.
Education: Birmingham University; York University
Career highlights: Meeting and interviewing musicians and artists I genuinely respect, including Jean-Michel Jarre, Steve Reich, Orbital, 808 State, Tangerine Dream, Talk Talk; being backstage at Nelson Mandela's 46664 concert, and being asked by Yusef Islam (Cat Stevens) to help him with his microphone.
Mentor: Joe Hosken and Phil Ward, both former editors of PSNE.
Big break: A chance phone call to Steve Carey at Future when the company was about to launch Future Music. 'So you are the guy who knows about music techno bollocks, then, are you?' said Mr Carey. Three weeks later, I had my first job there.
Big mistake: Complacency in an interview. Cost me a promotion.

» **Reading:** *Guardian, Empire, Q, BBC website, Chuck Palahniuk, Douglas Coupland, Martin Amis.* **Watching:** *Comedy, news, quiz shows, 24, The Shield. Currently into Arrested Development and Larry David.* **Listening:** *Mindlessly repetitive techno and wall of sound guitar music. And James Taylor.* **Relaxing to:** *By getting sozzled, frankly.* » *Single, no children*

Nick Robinson

5.10.63

BBC Television Centre, Wood Lane, London W12 7RJ
T 020 8743 8000
E Nick.Robinson@bbc.co.uk

Occupation: Political Editor, BBC News

Other positions: Political Editor, ITV News; Presenter, Radio Five Live; Deputy Editor, Panorama and On the Record.
Education: Cheadle Hulme School; University College, Oxford
Career highlights: First broadcasting job was as an unpaid gofer on Piccadilly Radio in Manchester working for a man who's now a BBC colleague - Jim Hancock of BBC North West; joined the BBC as a Production Trainee in 1986 and worked on Brass Tacks, This Week, Next Week, Newsround, Pamela Armstrong Show and Crimewatch UK; joined On the Record as an Assistant Producer, becoming Deputy Editor, then moved to Panorama as Deputy Editor for 3 years. During the 1992 General Election campaign was Editor of The Vote Race, a special series examining the marketing of politics and America's influence on British campaigning; in 1996 moved in front of the camera to become a Political Correspondent, covering the General Election for BBC Radio in 1997; News 24's Chief Political Correspondent 1999-2002; returned to the BBC after spending just under 3 years as Political Editor of ITV News; BBC's Political Editor, 2005-present.
Mentor: Inspired to go into broadcasting by the legendary Today Programme presenter Brian Redhead, a family friend.

» *Married, 3 children*

Paul Robinson

31.12.56

Disney Channel, Building 12, 566 Chiswick High Road, London W4 5AN
T 020 8222 2563
E paul.robinson@disney.com

Occupation: Vice-President and Managing Director, Disney Channel UK

Other positions: Judge, BAFTA Awards; Judge, Sony Radio Awards, 1996-present; Member, Radio Academy, 1985; Vice-President, Macmillan Nurses; School Governor, Kempston Rural; Member, Institute of Management, 1985.
Awards: RTS, 1998
Education: Camberley Grammar School; Manchester University; University of Bradford School of Management
Career highlights: Presenter, ILR, 1970s; Programme Director, Chiltern Radio Network, 1987-90; Head of Programmes, BBC Radio 1, 1990-94; Head of Strategy and Development, BBC, 1994-96; Managing Director, Talk Radio UK, 1996-98; Vice-President and Managing Director, Disney Channel UK, 1998-present.

» **Relaxing to:** *Golf, gardening, popular music, providing taxi service for my children!* » *Married, 2 children*

Hugh Robjohns

The Institute of Broadcast Sound, PO Box 932, Guildford GU4 7WW
T 01905 381725
E editor@lineup.biz

Occupation: Editor, Line Up magazine

Other positions: Technical Editor, Sound On Sound.
Education: University College, Swansea
Career highlights: Graduated with Honours from Swansea, University College Wales in 1983 after reading Electronics and Electrical Engineering; joined BBC as Video Engineer in 1983, but transferred to Operations in 1984; progressed through numerous departments within the BBC, mainly specialising in Sound, Picture Editing and related activities. Became Lecturer in Audio Operations at BBC Wood Norton in 1990. Took voluntary redundancy in 1997; joined SOS Publications in 1997 to launch Sound Pro magazine. Became Technical Editor of Sound On Sound 1998 and continue in that role today; also appointed Editor of Line Up magazine in 2000 (Line Up is the Journal of the Institute of Broadcast Sound), and continue in that role as well.

Tim Rogers

8.3.65

200 Gray's Inn Road, London WC1X 8XZ
T 020 7833 3000
E tim.rogers@itn.co.uk

Occupation: North of England Correspondent, ITV News

Other positions: Moscow Correspondent; Wales and West of England Correspondent.
Awards: Voted BT Welsh TV Reporter of the Year in 1994 while working for BBC Wales TV current affairs programme Week In Week Out; won the 1996 BT Welsh Radio News Broadcaster of the Year for work on Eye of Wales, a radio current affairs programme; same broadcast earned a National Sony Radio Award in 1997.
Education: Ysgol Maes Garmon, Mold; North West Independents Printing and Publishing Training Group
Career highlights: Started as junior reporter in weekly newspapers in Chester and Ellesmere Port, then on to Liverpool Daily Post and Echo before moving into BBC local radio in 1985 at Radio Clwyd. Moved on to Reporter, Producer and Chief News Assistant with BBC Wales in Cardiff, later Reporter/Presenter of Week in Week Out current affairs series and Presenter, Wales Today. Joined ITN in 1997as Wales and West of England Correspondent - reporting on path to devolution, foot and mouth crisis in South West and fuel protests. As Moscow Correspondent covered war in Afghanistan, post 9/11 and conflict in Iraq. As North of England Correspondent major stories included murder of GMP detective Stephen Oake, the drowning of 21 Chinese cocklers in Morecambe Bay, and the 7/7 suicide bombers from West Yorkshire.

Mentor: David Nicholas, former Editor of BBC Wales, Week In Week Out. At ITN, too many to mention.

» **Reading:** *As many newspapers as I can, but always the Guardian, Telegraph, Mail and Times.* **Watching:** *As many TV news programmes as possible ... always good to see what the other sides are up to. For entertainment - movie addict, but on TV it has to be David Jason, in anything, particularly Frost.* **Listening:** *Radio Five Live from dawn till dusk - and beyond. R4 for the dramas and Archers. iPod for broad musical tastes and audiobooks for travelling.* **Relaxing to:** *Walking the hills in Wales, with dog.* » *Divorced*

Michael Rohowski

10.11.67

Carl Bertelsmann Strasse 29, 33311 Guetersloh, Germany

T +49 5241 80 71021
E michael.rohowski@lycos-europe.com

Occupation: Chief Sales Officer, Lycos Europe

Other positions: MD, Bertelsmann Direct (Coron); Senior Engagement Manager, McKinsey & Co.
Awards: Outstanding Exam Karlsruhe (Prädikatsexamen in engineering); Dean's List Los Angeles (MBA).
Education: University of Southern California, Los Angeles; University Karlsruhe
Career highlights: Consultant at McKinsey, working in Germany for four years, Netherlands for one year, Australia/New Zealand for two years, focused on media and heavy industry; moved to Bertelsmann Direct Sales organisation, leading sales (through independent agents) in Austria and Switzerland; took over Coron Group (ex-Holtzbrink) within Bertelsmann Direct Sales; moved to Lycos Europe as Head of European Business Development, promoted to Chief Sales Officer (member of management team) in 2004.
Mentor: Christoph Mohn (Lycos Europe), Paul Bernhard Kallen (Burda).
Big break: Becoming a father. Signing a rather significant contract for Lycos Europe with the Yahoo group.
Big mistake: Leaving Australia - Sydney is simply lovely.

» **Reading:** *Everything I can get a hold of - literally.* **Watching:** *Hardly anything except for sports (Bayern Munich).* **Listening:** *Talk radio.* **Relaxing to:** *Playing Lego with my three-year-old son.* » *Married, 1 child*

Jane Root

18.5.57

Discovery Communications Inc, One Discovery Place, Silver Spring, MD 20910, USA

Occupation: Executive Vice-President and General Manager, Discovery

Other positions: Member, Executive Committee, Edinburgh International Television Festival, and Chair, 1995.
Publications: Pictures of Women: sexuality (1981); Open the Box: about television (1983).
Education: London College of Printing; University of Sussex
Career highlights: Freelance journalist and film critic with Cinema of Women, 1981-83; Press Officer and Catalogue Author, Edinburgh Film Festival, 1981-84, also with BFI 1982-83; Writer and Researcher, Open the Box Beat Productions,1983; Lecturer in Film Studies, University of East Anglia, 1981-84; Co-creator, Media Show, 1986; Co-founder, Wall to Wall Productions, 1987; Head of Programme Development and Joint Managing Director, Wall to Wall Productions, 1987-96; Head, Independent Commissioning Group and Head Factual, BBC, 1997-98; Controller, BBC 2, 1999-2004; Executive Vice-President and General Manager, Discovery Channel USA, 2004-present.

» **Relaxing to:** *Reading, travel*

Susan Rose

Ideal Home, King's Reach Tower, Stamford Street, London SE1 9LS

T 020 7261 6474
E susan_rose@ipcmedia.com

Occupation: Editor, Ideal Home

Other positions: Editor, Your Home; Editor, Perfect Home; Editor, The London Magazine; Editor, In Britain.
Education: Dr Challoner's High School
Career highlights: Launching The London Magazine. Relaunching Your Home magazine, which was promptly sold. The format remains the same, however, and is still one of top 5 selling homes magazines in UK. Highlight of career is being appointed Editor of Britain's number one homes magazine.
Mentor: I've learned something from everyone I've worked with, even when I haven't realised it at the time.
Big break: Being 'spotted' at Perfect Home. I was a freelance writer/sub there and was called in to the publisher's office one day, expecting to be told I was no longer needed. She offered me a year's contract to edit the title.
Big mistake: If you are creative, there are always things you try that don't work. If you learn from it, it's not a mistake. In life, I regret being so eager to get on with my career that I skipped university. It wouldn't have been a career advantage, but I missed three years of being young.

» **Reading:** *30-40 UK and international homes and lifestyle magazines a month, 1-2 newspapers a day (usually Independent, Daily Mail, Evening Standard) and a book a month, if I'm lucky. Unlike my TV tastes, which are very undemanding, I'm finicky about my literature, non-fiction and fiction.* **Watching:** *Very little, I don't sit down at home until 9pm. I channel-hop until I find something totally unchallenging to wash over me for an hour before the news.* **Listening:** *Soulful stuff - Thea Gilmore, Israel Kamakawiwo'ole are two of my favourites.* **Relaxing to:** *Long, fast walks with my 3 dogs.* » *Married, 2 children*

Claudia Rosencrantz

23.6.59

ITV Network Centre, 200 Gray's Inn Road, London WC1X 8HF
T 020 7843 8105
E Claudia.Rosencrantz@itv.com

Occupation: Network Controller, Entertainment, ITV plc

Awards: The Dame Edna Experience (series 2) nominated for British Academy Award; Night on Mount Edna, Golden Rose of Montreux, 1991; Popstars, Silver Rose of Montreux, 2001; Pop Idol, Best Entertainment Programme, TRIC Awards, 2002; I'm A Celebrity Get Me Out of Here, BAFTA Award 2003; Woman of the Year 2003; FRTS 2004.
Education: Queen's College, London
Career highlights: Picture Editor/Journalist 1979-86, Telegraph Sunday Magazine, Sunday Magazine, Elle; TV Researcher: Aspel and Company, Sunday Sunday, The Trouble with Michael Caine, An Audience with Victoria Wood, Dame Edna Experience (LWT, 1986); Producer, The Dame Edna Experience (series 2) 1989; Incredibly Strange Film Show, A Late Lunch with Les (Channel 4) 1990; An Audience with Jackie Mason, A Night on Mount Edna (LWT) 1991; Dame Edna's Hollywood (NBC), Edna Time (Fox), Elton John - Tantrums and Tiaras; Producer/Director, Two Rooms, Creator/ Producer, Dame Edna's Neighbourhood Watch (LWT), 1992; Executive Producer, Don't Forget Your Toothbrush (Channel 4), 1994; Features Dept BBC (responsible for Out of This World and Prisoners in Time) 1994-95; Controller Network Entertainment ITV 1995-present (responsible for 600 programmes a year including WWT BAM, Ant and Dec's Saturday Night Take-Away, Popstars, Pop Idol, I'm A Celebrity Get Me Out of Here).

» Unmarried

Jonathan Ross

17.11.60

BBC Radio 2, Western House, 99 Great Portland Street, London W1A 1AA
T 020 7765 5712
E jonathan.ross@bbc.co.uk

Occupation: Broadcaster

Other positions: Compere, the British Comedy Awards, 1991-present ; Host, Bafta Awards.
Publications: The Incredibly Strange Film Book (Simon and Schuster, 1995); Jonathan Ross Uncensored (Bantam, 2002).
Awards: Sony Award for Music Presentation, 2000; Radio Programme of the Year, TRIC Awards, 2000; Radio Personality of the Year, TRIC Awards, 2001; 2 Sony Awards for work in the radio industry, 2003; voted the most powerful man in broadcasting, 2005; OBE, 2005.
Education: School of Slavonic and East European Studies (now merged UCL), London
Career highlights: Researcher, Loose Talk, RPM Productions; Researcher, Solid Soul; Co-founder, Channel X (with Alan Marke), 1987-95; television work, Presenter, The Last Resort, Channel X/ Channel 4, 1987-91; Presenter, The Incredibly Strange Film Show, Channel X/Channel 4, 1988-89; Presenter, One Hour With Jonathan Ross, Channel X/Channel 4, 1990; Presenter, For One Week Only, Channel X/Channel 4, 1991; Host, Wogan, BBC One for two weeks on two separate occasions, 1991; Tonight With Jonathan Ross, Channel 4, 1991-94; Co-host, Gag Tag, BBC One, 1996; Presenter, Mondo Rosso, BBC Two, 1996; Presenter, The Late Jonathan Ross, ITV, 1996; Presenter, In Search Of..., ITV, 1996-97; Presenter, The Big Big Talent Show, ITV, 1996-97; Presenter, It's Only TV But I Like It, BBC One, 1999-2001; Presenter, Friday Night with Jonathan Ross, BBC One, 2001-present; Presenter Film Programme, BBC Two, 2001-present; radio work, filled in for Janice Long on Radio 1 for two weeks, 1987; Host, flagship show, Radio Radio (forerunner to Virgin Radio), 1988; Regular Contributor, Loose Ends, Radio 4, 1987-89; Host, The Jonathan Ross Show, Virgin Radio, 1998; Presenter, Saturday morning show, BBC Radio 2, 1999-present.

» Married, 3 children

Viscount Rothermere

3.12.67

Daily Mail and General Trust plc, Northcliffe House, 2 Derry Street, London W8 5TT
T 020 7938 6613
E chairman@chairman.dmgt.co.uk

Occupation: Chairman, Daily Mail and General Trust plc

Career highlights: Newspaper career began at the International Herald Tribune in Paris; Managing Director, Courier Printing and Publishing, 1993-97; Deputy, then Managing Director, Evening Standard 1997-98; Chairman, Daily Mail and General Trust plc, Chairman, Associated New Media 1998-present.

» Married, 4 children

Paul Rothwell

15.6.65

Gorgeous House, 11 Portland Mews, London W1F 8JL
T 020 7287 4060
E paul@gorgeous.co.uk

Occupation: Managing Director and TV Producer, Gorgeous Enterprises

Publications: Sony Playstation, Mountain; Levi's, Twist; Reebok, Sofa; Guinness, Snails.
Awards: BTA Craft Awards, Best Produced TV Commercial 2004, 2002, 2001, 2000; Gorgeous, BTA Production Company of the Year × 3, Campaign Magazine Production Company of the Year × 3, Gunn Report Most Awarded TV Commercials Production Company in the World 1999-2004.
Education: Mill Hill School; Peterhouse, Cambridge
Career highlights: Studied architecture at Cambridge; 1983, joined FCB Advertising as Trainee Account Manager; 1984, BMP Advertising as Producer; 1988, Paul Weiland Film Co as Producer; 1996, Ridley Scott Associates as Joint Managing Director; 1997, Gorgeous Enterprises as Partner/Managing Director.
Mentor: Parents, Sheila and Miles.

Big break: Work experience at BMP Advertising.
Big mistake: Forgetting it
» **Reading:** *Guardian, Sunday Times.* **Watching:** *Sport, news, Spooks, 24, films.* **Listening:** *My wife, good advice.* **Relaxing to:** *Keeping busy, gardening, kitesurfing.*
» *Married, 2 children*

Caroline Rowland

14.5.72

8 Ganton Street, London W1F 7QP
T 020 7479 7010
E caroline@new-moon.co.uk

Occupation: Group Managing Director, New Moon Television Ltd

Other positions: Partner, Moongate Films Ltd
Publications: London 2012 Olympic Bid films, Make Britain Proud and Inspiration.
Awards: IVCA Grand Prix Award 2005 for Make Britain Proud, the official London 2012 Olympic Bid film; 12 other 2005 IVCA Awards in various production categories; included in Who's Who of Britain's Young Entrepreneurs.
Education: Rhodes University
Career highlights: Being involved in bringing the Olympics to London is without question the highlight of my career - in fact, probably my life! The honour of being appointed to make the films, the privilege of working with Lord Coe and his team and the euphoria of London being selected may well go unsurpassed!
Mentor: My Dad
Big break: Dialling the wrong number a week after setting up New Moon and being commissioned to produce films for Walkers and Pepsi by the exec who picked up the call.
Big mistake: Assuming I'd never make mistakes.
» **Reading:** *Heat, Variety, Management Today and film scripts.* **Watching:** *Desperate Housewives, ER, The West Wing, movies.* **Listening:** *Robbie Williams, Sheryl Crow, whatever is on shuffle.* **Relaxing to:** *Horseriding, golf, swimming, skiing, diving.* » *Married, no children*

Jonathan Rugman

16.11.69

ITN, 400 N Capitol Street, Suite 899, Washington DC 20001, USA
T 020 7833 3000
E jonathan.rugman@itn.co.uk

Occupation: Washington Correspondent, Channel 4 News

Other positions: Business Correspondent, Channel 4 News; Producer, Lion Television Ltd; Reporter, File on 4, BBC Radio 4; Istanbul Correspondent, the Guardian and the Observer; Turkey Correspondent, BBC World Service.
Publications: Ataturk's Children - Turkey and the Kurds (Cassell, 1996).
Awards: Work Foundation Broadcaster and TV Awards; Business Journalist of the Year, Broadcast and Retail Awards; Harold Wincott Foundation, Broadcaster Award, co-winner British Environment Media Award; Royal Television Society Midlands Award; Radio Programme, British Social Services Media Awards.
Education: Bradfield College; Cambridge University
Big break: A news traineeship at the BBC.
» **Reading:** *New York Times, Washington Post, Newsweek, Weekly Standard, New York Review of Books, New Yorker, Mother Jones, the Observer.* **Watching:** *Nightly News (NBC), Commander in Chief (ABC), The West Wing (NBC), Newsnight (CNN), Today Show (NBC).* **Listening:** *National Public Radio.* **Relaxing to:** *With my family.* » *Married, 3 children*

Alan Rusbridger

29.12.53

119 Farrington Road, London EC1R 3ER
T 020 7239 89644
E Alan.Rusbridger@guardian.co.uk

Occupation: Editor, The Guardian

Other positions: Executive editor, the Observer. Scott Trust. Dir, GMG, GNL. Chairman National Youth Orchestra.
Awards: Editor of the Year, 1996, 2001. WTPS Judges Award 2005, Newspaper of the Year, 1996, 1997, 2005.
Education: Magdalene College, Cambridge
Career highlights: Reporter, Cambridge Evening News. Reporter and Diary Editor, Guardian. TV critic, Observer. Washington Correspondent, London Daily News. Launch editor, Guardian Weekend, G2. Deputy Editor, Guardian 1994. Editor, 1995- Launched GU. Launched Berliner Guardian 2005.
Mentor: Fulton Gillespie, Chief Reporter, Cambridge Evening News.
Big break: Reporter, Guardian, 1979.
Big mistake: Becoming a TV critic.
» **Reading:** *Too many newspapers.* **Watching:** *Newsnight, C4 News and films.* **Listening:** *Radio 3 and anything my daughters insist on.* **Relaxing to:** *Playing music or golf.*
» *Married, 2 children*

Julian Rush

24.2.53

ITV Broadcasting, 200 Gray's Inn Road, London WC1X 8HF
T 020 7430 4661
E julian.rush@itn.co.uk

Occupation: Science Correspondent, Channel 4 News

Awards: RTS Home News Award, Paddington rail crash Investigation, 1999; RTS Home News Award, exclusive on cracked rail as cause of Hatfield rail crash, 2000; several British Environment Media Awards as Producer with former Channel 4 News Science Correspondent, Andy Vetch.
Big break: Getting the tip-off that the government's 'dodgy dossier' justifying the Iraq war had been plagiarised from the work of a PhD student was great! Finding the thesis online and seeing the proof in black and white was incredible!
Big mistake: A long time ago in local radio, playing hospital requests - it wasn't a good idea to play Wide Eyed and Legless for a pensioner who'd just had a leg amputated!

Michael Russoff

27.7.77

16 Hanbury Street, London E1 6QR
T 020 7194 7000
E michael.russoff@wk.com

Occupation: Currently consulting at Wieden + Kennedy; Freelance Advertising Writer, Art Director, Creative Director

Other positions: Fish and Chip Shop Assistant; Guinness Book of Records Researcher.
Publications: Honda Grrr, Yakult, Nike.
Awards: Cannes Grand Prix, Honda Grrr; Titanium Lion, Honda Grrr; Journalists' Award, Honda Grrr; D&AD gold, Grrr; Use of Music in TV & Cinema, gold, Grrr; TV over 60 seconds, silver, Grrr; Use of Music in TV & Cinema, silver, Grrr; TV over 60 seconds, silver, Grrr; Animation in TV & Cinema, silver, Grrr; Art Direction in TV & Cinema, silver, Grrr; Cinema, silver, Grrr; Direction in Cinema, silver, Grrr; Radio silver, Grrr; Radio EPICA D'Or, Honda Grrr; Andy's Grandy, Honda Grrr; Automotive, One Show, Honda Grrr; gold, Consumer TV, Over 30 seconds Max 90 seconds; Clio Automotive, Honda Grrr, gold; Creative Circle, Honda Grrr, gold; Best Idea in 60 seconds or over, gold; Best Cinema Commercial, gold; Best TV Commercial, gold; Best Use of Music, gold; Best Use of Animation, platinum overall: BTAA, Honda Grrr; ITV Best Commercial of the Year, gold; Best less than 90 seconds, gold; Vehicles, gold; Commercials shown in Cinemas as well as TV; and a few more...
Education: City of London School; Goldsmiths; University of London
Career highlights: Started at Mother in 1998; left in 1999 on the day of the eclipse (not sure if that's significant but it felt like it was at the time); freelanced at W+K London where I worked on Nike, winning two Campaign Press Awards; worked at W+K Amsterdam and Portland on projects for Siemens, Nike; came back to London and worked on the Honda pitch. Wrote the Honda Grrr ad, also composing the song; currently at W+K making the new Honda Civic ad.
Mentor: Robert Saville, Tony Davidson and Kim Papworth.
Big break: Writing the words 'Hate Something, Change Something' down on a piece of paper.
Big mistake: Choosing the wrong director once. It was a horrible experience. I completely misjudged the guy. I've never done that again.

» **Reading:** *The backs of cereal packets, toilet graffiti, other people's shopping lists that are left behind in supermarket baskets.* **Watching:** *Couples in high-street doorways who are obviously having the 'break-up' conversation, Big Brother, the mass audition rounds of X Factor.* **Listening:** *People behind me on the bus, the blood rushing through my ear when my head's against the pillow, my instinct.* **Relaxing to:** *I write music and garden.* » *Single but in love*

John Ryan

4.9.72

BBC, Oxford Road, Manchester M60 1SD
T 0161 244 43002
E john.ryan@bbc.co.uk

Occupation: Managing Editor, BBC Greater Manchester Radio

Education: Sandhurst School, Berkshire
Career highlights: Managing Editor, BBC Radio Leeds 2004-05; Marketing Manager, BBC English Regions 2001-04; Managing Editor, BBC Radio Northampton 1999-2000; Managing Director, CTFM Canterbury 1997-99.

» **Reading:** *Douglas Coupland, the Guardian, Details, Attitude, City Life.* **Watching:** *Six Feet Under, old and new Dr Who, Property Ladder, The Apprentice, League of Gentlemen.* **Listening:** *Everything except Radio 4.*
Relaxing to: *Too rarely. Playstation, shopping, cinema.*
» *Single, no children*

Charles Saatchi

9.6.43

M&C Saatchi, 36 Golden Square, London W1F 9EE
T 020 7543 4500
E charlessi@mcsaatchi.com

Occupation: Founder, M&C Saatchi

Other positions: Patron of the arts
Publications: Successful campaigns in the UK include Silk Cut cigarettes and the promotion of Margaret Thatcher through the slogan Labour Isn't Working.
Education: Christ's College, Finchley
Career highlights: Founder, Saatchi and Saatchi, 1970; Founder, M&C Saatchi; art collector and owner of the Saatchi Gallery; Sponsor of the Young British Artists.

» **Listening:** *Elvis Presley, Little Richard and Chuck Berry.* **Relaxing to:** *Collecting, from Superman comics and cigarette cards to jukeboxes and modern art.* » *Married, 3 children*

Clare Salmon

13.5.67

200 Gray's Inn Road, London WC1X 8HF
T 020 7843 8064
E clare.salmon@itv.com

Occupation: Director of Marketing and Commercial Strategy, ITV plc

Other positions: Director, Freeview; Director, Alliance Trust plc and Second Alliance plc; Director, Marketing Society.
Education: Cambridge University
Career highlights: I joined ITV in January 2005 and am Director of Marketing and Commercial Strategy. I am also on the Board of Freeview and the Alliance Trust plc which is a large Scottish Investment Trust, and on the Management Board of the Marketing Society. I joined Centrica in 2000 as Marketing Director of British Gas Services, then becoming Sales and Marketing Director of the AA and subsequently Managing Director of AA Financial Services. My previous roles include eight years at Prudential where I was Consumer Marketing Director and European Marketing Director of Avis. I worked as a Management Consultant with Boston Consulting Group in Spain and London and spent two years at the Industrial Society setting up a Small Business Unit.
Mentor: My mentors have included two former CEOs of Prudential - Nick Newmarch and Sir Peter Davis. The AA's Managing Director, Roger Wood. Julia Cleverdon in Absentia, and of course, my mother.
Big break: Meeting a woman called Julia Middleton in the lift when I was 21 - she offered me a job at the Industrial Society, having read some article I'd written.
Big mistake: Spraying the floor with Tampax at a job interview when I reached for a pen - 'my earplugs!' I exclaimed ... I didn't get the job.

» **Reading:** *Fiction - everything from Balzac to Rohinton Mistry, Horse and Hound (I have two horses), Cycling Weekly (I am an ex-racing cyclist), the Week, OK, Economist and Grazia.* **Watching:** *ITV drama!* **Listening:** *My daughter Jessica's laughter.* **Relaxing to:** *Riding horses and bikes, travelling to eccentric destinations, drinking champagne, reading books and going to the flicks.* » *Single, 1 child*

Matt Salmon

21.5.75

The National Magazine Co Ltd, 72 Broadwick Street, London W1F 9EP
T 020 7312 3721
E matt.salmon@natmags.co.uk

Occupation: Group publishing Director, Prima Group

Other positions: Publisher, Prima and Prima Baby; PPA Marketing Board Member.
Education: St Joseph's College, Ipswich; University of Portsmouth
Career highlights: Joined National Magazines on the graduate entry scheme and worked in a number of central departments. Moved onto the brand side of the business in 2000 as the Advertising Director for She Magazine; took advertising responsibility for the Prima Group after the G&J acquisition. Progressed to Publisher in 2004, taking on the complete commercial responsibility for both titles; joined the PPA Marketing Board in 2005.
Mentor: Austyn Hallworth, former Sales Director, NatMag Director, Publisher of House Beautiful and Harpers & Queen.
Big break: Moving from NatMag Direct to become the Advertisement Director on She in 2000.
Big mistake: Allowing Terry Mansfield to publish an advertisement with me dressed as a doctor delivering a baby - to promote Prima Baby's ABC!

» **Reading:** *The Economist, Times and Auto Express.* **Watching:** *Top Gear and occasionally Coronation Street!* **Listening:** *Broad music collection, from Shed Seven to Embrace. Will once again be found at V and Isle of Wight Festivals.* **Relaxing to:** *As much tennis as time (and weather) will permit.* » *Married to Lisa, no children*

Anthony Salz

30.6.50

Freshfields Bruckhaus Deringer, 65 Fleet Street, London EC4Y 1HS
T 020 7936 4000
E Anthony.Salz@bbc.co.uk

Occupation: Vice-Chairman, Board of Governors, BBC

Publications: Contributor to various legal books and journals.
Awards: Honorary Doctor of Laws, Exeter University, 2003; Business in the Community Ambassador Award from the Prince of Wales for work on homelessness and education; FRSA, 1996
Education: Summerfields School, Oxford; Radley College; Exeter University
Career highlights: Solicitor, admitted 1974; Kenneth Brown Baker Baker, 1972-75; joined Freshfields,

1975, Partner, 1980, Senior Partner, 1996-2000; seconded to Davis Polk & Wardwell, New York, 1977-78; Member, Tate Gallery Corporate Advisory Group, 1997-present (Chairman, 1997-2002); Director, Tate Foundation, 2000-present; Habitat for Humanity GB, 2004-present; Trustee, Paul Hamlyn Foundation, 2005-present; Trustee, Eden Project, 2001-present; member, Business in the Community's Business Action on Homelessness Executive Forum; Director, Habitat for Humanity GB; Vice-Chairman, BBC, 2004-present.

» **Relaxing to:** *Travelling, art, theatre, golf, fishing and Southampton FC.* » *Married, 3 children*

Bruce Sandell

23.6.70

Dennis Publishing, 30 Cleveland Street, London W1T 4JD

T 020 7907 6454
E bruce_sandell@dennis.co.uk

Occupation: Managing Director, Dennis Consumer

Other positions: Publishing Director, Maxim; Member, Executive Board, DPL UK.

Publications: Bizarre; Inside Edge and its associated contract-publishing businesses; Maxim; Men's Fitness; Poker Player; Total Gambler; Viz.

Awards: Best Total Communications Programme, Maxim's Little Black Book, Campaign Media Awards, 2005.

Education: Haydon School, Northwood, Middlesex

Career highlights: I worked at IPC for 13 years, starting as an A-level Trainee. I worked my way up through the ad team, then became IPC's youngest Publisher (at the time) on Muzik magazine. I went on to publish Uncut and NME - the magazine that drew me to the company originally. I left IPC in 2000 to join IFG - James Brown's start-up company - where we launched two magazines and acquired three from John Brown Publishing. Then, in 2003, Dennis Publishing acquired IFG and I moved on to Maxim and Men's Fitness. Recently I have taken on the role of MD of the Dennis consumer division. I have been lucky enough to work on five launches so far - without doubt one of the most exciting and rewarding things you can do in publishing. And not many people get the chance to work on a magazine phenomenon that changes a market forever. Loaded did, and being involved in its inception was fantastic experience and brilliant fun (shame it is now a shadow of its former self). There are a couple of launches that sadly didn't make it, but the experience on them is almost more valuable than with the successes.

Mentor: At IPC it was Editor-in-Chief Alan Lewis, who is one of the great unsung heroes of magazine publishing. He was behind all the great products I worked on there, and without him Loaded would never have been the massive success it became. Plus, he is a fellow soul boy.

Big break: Becoming a publisher at IPC on Muzik magazine aged 26 - probably still one of their youngest ever.

Big mistake: Taking eight of my highest-spending record company and club advertisers on a jolly to Prague - they took full advantage of all that great city could offer. Complete mayhem ensued, and I had a very difficult job explaining my expenses on returning...

» **Reading:** *I am a magazine junkie, with over 20 subscriptions and a house full of magazines - I get all the men's magazines for work, and Uncut, Mojo, NME, Straight No Chaser and Record Collector to feed my music obsession, along with many others.* **Watching:** *I do not spend a huge amount of time watching TV - but when I do it is normally Spongebob Squarepants (with my daughter), or if I do get any time to myself it would be CSI.* **Listening:** *I collect original 60s/70s soul singles and LPs.* **Relaxing to:** *Spending time with my family, cycling, listening to and searching for obscure American soul records.* » *Married, 1 daughter*

Daniel Sandford

16.9.70

Room 1264, BBC Television Centre, Wood Lane, London W12 7RJ

T 020 8624 9019
E daniel.sandford@bbc.co.uk

Occupation: Home Affairs Correspondent (TV), BBC News

Other positions: Rome Correspondent, BBC News; Health Correspondent, BBC News.

Education: Magdalen College School; Southampton University

Career highlights: Joined ITN in January 1989 in the computer graphics department. Programmed 1992 election graphics. Then switched to journalism by way of the ITN Graduate Trainee course. Worked as Home Affairs Producer (Dunblane massacre), South Africa Producer (fall of Mobutu) and General Reporter before moving to the BBC in 1998. As BBC Health Correspondent covered the Bristol Royal Infirmary Inquiry and the NHS reforms. As BBC Home Affairs Correspondent covered the London bombings of 2005. BBC Rome Correspondent.

Mentor: Stewart Purvis, then Editor-in-Chief at ITN who encouraged me to switch from computer graphics to journalism. Fran Unsworth, Richard Clark and Chris Rybczynski at the BBC who helped me move from producer to correspondent.

Big break: Being taken seriously at ITN when I said I wanted to change career to become a journalist.

Big mistake: Taking too long to start doing what I love - eyewitness reporting for television news.

» **Reading:** *All the newspapers, Private Eye, the Economist.* **Watching:** *BBC1 News, ITV News, News 24, Sky News, Newsnight.* **Listening:** *The Today Programme, Front Row, In Our Time, Five Live.* **Relaxing to:** *On holiday with a book.* » *Married, no children*

Sham Sandhu

3.12.71

Five, 22 Long Acre, London WC2E 9LY

T 020 7550 5555
E sham.sandhu@five.tv

Occupation: Controller, Special Events and Pop Features, Five

Other positions: Member, Council, RTS 2000-present; Member, Edinburgh International Television Festival Executive Committee, 2004-present.

Awards: Member, BAFTA
Education: Ashmole School, London; St Catherine's College, Oxford
Career highlights: Production Trainee, Features Department, BBC, 1994-96; Assistant Producer, Watchdog and Crimewatch, BBC, 1996-97; Director and Producer, Blue Peter and Live and Kicking, BBC, 1997-99; Development Planner, BBC One, 1999-2000; Head of New Media and New Channels, BBC Production, 2000-01; Controller, Interactive Programming, Five, 2001-02; Controller, Youth and Music Programmes, Five, 2002-04; Controller, Special Events and Pop Features, Five, 2002-04.
» **Relaxing to:** *Skiing, television, photography, 1950s Scandinavian design.*

Marc Sands 12.12.63

Guardian Newspapers Ltd, 119 Farringdon Road, London EC1 3ER
T 020 7278 2332
E marc.sands@guardian.co.uk

Occupation: Marketing Director, Guardian Newspaper Ltd

Other positions: Brand Director, ONdigital.
Awards: Campaign Press and Poster, silver and gold; D&AD silver; Campaign Direct; IPA Effectiveness.
Education: UCS; Pembroke College, Cambridge; Bradford Management Centre
Mentor: Nigel Yates (school geography teacher).
Big break: Being part of the start up of ONdigital.
Big mistake: Being part of the start up of ONdigital.
» **Reading:** *All the newspapers except the Daily Mail. The New Yorker and Arseblog.* **Watching:** *Channel 4 News, Arsenal, You've Been Framed, anything on More 4.* **Listening:** *Radio 4, Radio 5 and iPod playlists.* **Relaxing to:** *Playing the guitar, watching live music.* » *Married, 2 children, Aldo and Emil*

Sarah Sands 1961

T 020 7538 5000
E hazel.gilbertson@telegraph.co.uk

Occupation: Consulting Editor, Daily Mail

Other positions: Editor, Sunday Telegraph
Publications: Novels, Playing the Game (Pan, 2004); Hothouse (Pan, 2005).
Career highlights: Trainee News Reporter, the Sevenoaks Courier; Editor, Londoner's Diary, London Evening Standard; Features Editor, London Evening Standard; Associate Editor, London Evening Standard; Deputy Editor, Daily Telegraph 1996, later assuming responsibility for Saturday edition; Editor, the Sunday Telegraph 2005-present.
» *Married, 3 children*

Angela Sarkis 6.1.55

BBC Broadcasting House, Portland Place, London W1A 1AA
T 020 8743 8000
E angela.sarkis@bbc.co.uk

Occupation: Governor, BBC

Other positions: Adviser, Social Exclusion Unit, Cabinet Office, 1997-present; Member, House of Lords Appointments Commission, 2000-present; Member, Council, Howard League for Penal Reform, 1998-present; Member, Housing and Neighbourhood Committee, Joseph Rowntree Foundation, 1997-present; Chair, NCVO Diversity Project.
Awards: CBE, 2000
Education: Cottesmore School, Nottingham; Clarendon College of Further Education, Nottingham; Leeds University; Leicester University
Career highlights: Probation Officer, Middlesex Probation Service, 1979-89; Trustee, Single Homeless Housing Project, NW10, 1980-87; Trustee, Learie Constantine Youth Club, NW2, 1980-90; Trustee, Single Mothers Project, NW10, 1984-90; Trustee, Tavistock Youth Club, NW10, 1985-90; Unit Manager, Brent Family Services Unit, 1989-91; Assistant Director, Intermediate Treatment Fund, 1991-93; Director, DIVERT Trust, 1993-96; Member, Council, Evangelical Alliance, 1995-99; Member, Leadership Team, Brentwater Evangelical Church, 1990-94; Trustee, Institute of Citizenship Studies, 1995-97; Member, Committee, Association of Charitable Foundations, 1995-99; Trustee, BBC Children in Need, 1995-2002; Trustee, Notting Hill Housing Trust, 1995-97; Vice-President, African and Caribbean Evangelical Alliance, 1996; Governor, BBC, 2002-present.
» *Married, 2 children*

Sue Saville

200 Gray's Inn Road, London WC1 8XZ
T 020 7430 4402
E sue.saville@itn.co.uk

Occupation: Medical Correspondent, ITV News

Other positions: Chief Correspondent, GMTV 1993-98; Reporter, BBC Breakfast News; Reporter, BBC South; BBC News Trainee; Reporter, Hong Kong Commercial Radio.
Publications: Reported and produced The Ice Patrol documentary on Britain's latest Antarctic vessel.
Awards: Medical Journalists' Association to ITV News team for MRSA campaign.
Education: Dorking County Grammar School (became The Ashcombe School); St Hilda's College, Oxford; Centre for Journalism Studies, Cardiff
Career highlights: Covering key medical issues such as bird flu, MRSA, cancer treatments, obesity and school dinners; hitting the ground running on breaking stories like the assassination of Israel's Yitzhak Rabin, the civil war in Rwanda, war and peace in Northern Ireland; scoops such as an unplanned live interview with Nelson Mandela on

a visit to Britain; fun stuff like an interview on the wing from a shared paraglider while jumping off the cliffs at Alum Bay.

» *Married, 2 children, boy and girl*

Dame Marjorie Scardino 25.1.47

Pearson plc, 80 Strand, London WC2R 0RL
T 020 7010 2300
E kathie.skillen@pearson.com

Occupation: Group Chief Executive, Pearson plc

Other positions: Non-executive Director, Nokia Corporation; member of various charitable and advisory boards including Carter Center Georgia, V&A; European Corporate Governance Institute, 2002.
Awards: Winner, Pulitzer Prize, 1983.
Education: Baylor University, Texas; George Washington University Law School, University of San Francisco Law School.
Career highlights: Partner, Brannen Wessels Searcy, law firm Savannah Georgia 1975-85; Publisher, The Georgia Gazette, 1978-85; President, Economist Newspaper Group Inc, New York 1985-92; Chief Executive, the Economist Group plc, London 1992-96; Group Chief Executive, Pearson plc, 1997-present.

» *Married, 3 children*

David Scott 26.8.58

25 Moreton Place, Pimlico, London SW1V 2NL
T 07831 311 074
E david.scott@rackenford.com

Occupation: Consultant

Education: Wellington College
Career highlights: 1972-81 Chartered Accountant, Peat Marwick Mitchell; 1981-88 Finance Controller, Channel 4; 1988-97 Finance Director, Channel 4; 1997-2002 Managing Director, Channel 4; 2002-05, Deputy Chief Executive, Channel 4.
Mentor: Jeremy Isaacs, Justin Dukes and Michael Grade.

» *Married, 2 children*

Jane Scott

Five TV, 22 Long Acre, London WC2E 9LY
T 020 7550 5555
E jane.scott@five.tv

Occupation: Director of Marketing, Channel Five Broadcasting Limited

Other positions: Controller, TV Strategy and Marketing, BBC; Marketing Director, Financial Times; Marketing Manager, The Telegraph Group.
Education: University of Edinburgh; London Business School
Career highlights: At Five, leading the new branding strategy and working in tandem with Five's Director of Programming to ensure our vision, brand values and tone of voice are completely aligned; at the BBC, leading the refreshed re-branding and launch of the BBC's digital portfolio; at the FT, devising and launching the FT Mastering series, starting with FT Mastering Management.
Mentor: Different people at different times.
Big break: Moving to The Telegraph Group (without any prior media experience).
Big mistake: Giving my sanction to run a very, very expensive ad my instinct told me was just not right - never again!

» **Reading:** *Fiction, the Week, Sunday press, the daily cuts.* **Watching:** *As much as I can.* **Listening:** *As above.* **Relaxing to:** *Family, friends, country, cooking, eating, piano, riding, reading...*

Sebastian Scott 2.8.65

Princess Productions, Whiteleys Building, 151 Queensway, London W2 4SB
T 020 7985 1901
E Sebastian.Scott@princestv.com

Occupation: Joint CEO, Princess Productions, Princess Talent Management, Princess North, Ten Tonne Productions

Other positions: Executive Producer, Planet 24; Executive Producer, BBC TV; Reporter, LWT Sunday productions.
Publications: Network 7, Big Breakfast, Don't Forget Your Toothbrush, Light Lunch, Show Me the Money, Jailbreak, The Wright Stuff, Model Behaviour, Back to Reality, Ruby, The Restaurant (NBC), Date my Mom (MTV USA), Friday Night Project, Office Monkey.
Awards: RTS award, Show Me the Money.
Education: Bristol University
Career highlights: Reporter on Network 7; Foreign Correspondent Eyewitness (LWT); Launch Editor and then Executive Producer, The Big Breakfast; started own company in 1997; Princess Productions is now one of the UK's ten largest independent production companies.
Big break: Becoming a reporter on Network 7.

» **Reading:** *Independent, Sun.* **Watching:** *Reality, comedy, US imports.* **Relaxing to:** *Travel.* » *Single, no children*

James Scroggs

MTV, Hawley Crescent, London NW1 8TT
T 020 7284 7777
E scroggs.james@mtvne.com

Occupation: Vice-President, Marketing, MTV

Other positions: Judge, D&AD Awards, Music Video, 2005
Career highlights: Senior Brand Manager, ITV Digital, instrumental in creating Al and Monkey advertising campaign; Vice-President, Marketing, MTV, 2002-present.

Richard Scudamore
11.8.59

FA Premier League, 11 Connaught Place W2 2ET
T 020 7298 1607
E rdonnelly@fapl.co.uk

Occupation: Chief Executive, Football Association Premier League

Education: Kingsfield School, Bristol; Nottingham University
Career highlights: Regional Director, BT Yellow Pages, ITT World Directories, 1981-89; Managing Director, Newspaper and Media Sales Ltd, Ingersoll Publications, 1989-90; Thomson Corporation, Newspaper Group Sales and Marketing Director, 1991-94; Assistant, then Managing Director, Scotsman Publications, 1994-95; Senior Vice-President, North America, 1995-98; Chief Executive and Director, Football League Ltd, 1998-99.

» **Relaxing to:** *Golf, music, children, and of course football.*
» *Married, 5 children*

Judith Secombe
21.6.67

Hachette Filipacchi UK Ltd, 64 North Row, London W1K 7LL
T 020 7150 7606
E judith.secombe@hf-uk.com

Occupation: Publisher, Red and Psychologies magazines

Other positions: Publisher, CosmoGIRL! and Cosmopolitan Hair & Beauty, National Magazine Company; Commercial Director, Women's Home and Lifestyle Group, National Magazine Company; Publisher, Gardens Illustrated and Waitrose Food Illustrated, John Brown Publishing.
Education: King's College, University of London
Career highlights: Being part of the team that turned Food Illustrated into Waitrose Food Illustrated.
Mentor: John Thater and Tim Brooks at Media Week in 1987.
Big break: Getting out of retail and into media in 1987.
Big mistake: Not going straight from university into media.

» **Reading:** *The Daily Telegraph, Vanity Fair, The Garden.* **Watching:** *Almost anything on Living TV.* **Listening:** *Radio 4.* **Relaxing to:** *In my garden.* » *Married, 2 children*

Adrian Serle
20.5.76

Kerrang House, 20 Lionel Street, Birmingham B3 1AQ
T 0845 053 1052
E adrian.serle@kerrangradio.co.uk

Occupation: Managing Director, Kerrang Radio UK

Other positions: Sales Director, Hallam FM; Media Director, Radio Works.
Awards: Music Week station of the year; 18 industry recognised awards in first 12 months Kerrang has been on air.
Education: University of the West of England
Mentor: I enjoyed working with Gus MacKenzie (now MD at Key 103) who taught me a great deal, but my most loyal ongoing sounding board and confidante is my wife ... she should be paid a fortune!
Big break: Being involved with such a huge brand as Kerrang, and being involved in helping to shape its future is a real privilege, and probably one of the highlights so far.
Big break: There have been several, but I am trying to cut back on them now...

» **Reading:** *Just finished Piers Morgan's diaries, he sounds like an interesting character!* **Watching:** *I don't get a lot of time to watch much television.* **Listening:** *The radio.* **Relaxing to:** *Mess about with the kids, play rugby, enjoy time with my wife, although not necessarily in that order.* » *Married, 3 children*

Samir Shah
29.1.52

Juniper Communications Ltd, 47-49 Borough High Street, London SE1 1NB
T 020 7407 9292
E juniper@junipertv.co.uk

Occupation: CEO, Juniper Communications Ltd

Other positions: Trustee, Victoria and Albert Museum; Chairman, Runnymede Trust; Trustee, The Medical Foundation; Fellow, RTS; Member, BAFTA.
Publications: The Great Plague; Invitation to a Hanging; The Difference; Playing the Race Card; Iraq - the Reckoning; When Black Became Beautiful; Dirty Race for the White House; Great British Asian Invasion; Thatcher, the Downing Street Years; Eastern Eye.
Awards: OBE, New Year Honours, 2000; RTS, The Politics Show; RTS, Invitation to a Hanging; RTS, The Great Plague; RTS, Thatcher, the Downing Street Years; RIMA, I'm Not a Racist But...; Screen Nation Award, Bare Knuckle Boxer, When Black Became Beautiful.
Education: Latymer Upper School; University of Hull; St. Catherine's College, Oxford
Career highlights: My television career began at LWT in the early 80s; LWT (including working on Eastern Eye, Weekend World, Credo, The London Programme), 1979-87; BBC Head of Current Affairs TV (i/c Panorama, Question Time, The Money Programme, Assignment, Public Eye), 1987-94; Head of Political Programmes TV & Radio (i/c Pol newsroom, Midnight Hour, Week in Westminster, On the Record), 1994-98; CEO, Juniper Communications (The Great Plague, Invitation to a Hanging, When Black Became Beautiful, Iraq - the Reckoning), 1998-present.
Mentor: Jane Hewland of Hewland International.
Big break: Being poached from LWT by the BBC.
Big mistake: Being poached and losing out on the LWT millions.

» **Reading:** *All dailies/weeklies.* **Watching:** *24, all Manchester United matches, anything new at least once.* **Listening:** *The Today Programme, The Incredible String Band, Van Morrison.* **Relaxing to:** *Watching Manchester United.* » *Married, 1 child*

Simon Shaps
10.9.56

London Television Centre, Upper Ground SE1 9LT
T 020 7843 8000
E Chief Executive, Granada

Occupation: Magdalene College, Cambridge

Career highlights: Researcher, Thames TV, 1982-83; London Weekend Television, Researcher, 1983-90; Head of Current Affairs, 1990-93; Controller, Factual Programmes, 1993-96; Director of Programmes, 1996-97; Director of Programmes, Granada TV, 1997-2000; Managing Director, Granada Productions, 2000; Granada Broadband, 2000-01; Managing Director, then Chief Executive, Granada Content, 2001-04.

» *Married*

Alison Sharman
18.3.65

200 Gray's Inn Road, London WC1X 8HF
T 020 7843 8132
E alison.sharman@itv.com

Occupation: Director, Factual and Daytime, ITV

Other positions: Controller, CBBC; Controller, BBC Daytime; Series Producer, BBC Factual.
Education: Newcastle-upon-Tyne Polytechnic
Mentor: Mark Thompson, Peter Salmon.
Big break: Researcher, BBC Holiday.
Big mistake: Not listening to the Today Programme.

» **Reading:** *The Sun, Guardian, Economist, the Week, Vanity Fair.* **Watching:** *A huge amount!* **Listening:** *My iPod.* **Relaxing to:** *Running, eating and boating.* » *Married, 2 children*

Johnny Sharp
14.9.73

Front, Jordan House, 47 Brunswick Place, London N1 6EB
T 020 7608 6406
E johnny.sharp@hhc.co.uk

Occupation: Acting Editor, Front magazine

Other positions: Freelance writer for the Guardian, Mojo, Q, Kerrang!, Time Out, Bizarre, Four Four Two, Champions, and whoever else will have me.
Publications: I personally invented Britpop and then killed it in cold blood.
Awards: Most improved player, Beverley Minster School U-11s, 1980; 27th sexiest male, NME readers' poll, 1998.
Education: Beverley Grammar School, East Yorks; Warwick University
Career highlights: Being threatened with a bottle-related assault by Verve singer Richard Ashcroft outside Barcelona's Nou Camp stadium before the 1999 European Cup Final as a result of a long-held grudge from a 200-word review I did of the band in 1992. Almost as good as that was interviewing James Brown for Loaded (godfather of soul, not the former editor of that publication) where he told me 'You have soul in your semen' because my parents would probably have been listening to his music when I was conceived. He also advocated that powerful men should be allowed to have as many as five wives, and put salt in his beer.
Mentor: First one was Steve Lamacq at NME, who hired me with the proviso that I shorten my reviews and stop talking about myself. Then Simon Williams, who was his successor at the live reviews desk at NME, and Steve Sutherland, who was Editor throughout my time there, and changed his mind every five minutes while swearing a lot, as I myself now do as an editor.
Big break: Being nicknamed 'Johnny Cigarettes' in the playground by kids who would send me out to the corner shop to get ciggies because I was the tallest in the class. If I hadn't had such a bloody ridiculous name less people would have bothered reading what I wrote.
Big mistake: Too many to mention. But writing in an early review of Oasis that they had no songs and 'If they didn't exist no one would want to invent them' was a touch wide of the mark in hindsight. Also I should have changed my name back to my real one far earlier than I did, because no one knows who I am any more.

» **Reading:** *The Guardian, Mirror, NME, Mojo, Kerrang!, Viz, Private Eye, Bizarre, Four Four Two, Champions, United We Stand, plus the usual internet tat.* **Watching:** *Soaps, although EastEnders makes me want to eat caustic soda. Other than that, comedy, Soccer am, Hitler and serial killer docs. Big Brother, I'm a Celebrity, Wife Swap.* **Listening:** *Everything. I've just got one of these iPod things. I tend to favour miserable Leonard Cohen type singer-songwriters, loud traditional rock music, slightly homosexual-friendly pop and the usual concensus indie fare. I never listen to the radio.* **Relaxing to:** *I tend to drink. It's obviously fatal to associate drinking and relaxation but what can you do? I'm just a slave to the rhythm of our stinking ale-soaked culture. I play and watch football and that is quite relaxing in its own way, because it's totally unrelated to any other concerns you may have in life – it's like an alternative existence that ultimately doesn't mean that much. I find playing so relaxing that I actually think about imaginary football games to get to sleep. What a sad indictment of the state of our national game.*
» *Married, no children*

Chris Shaw
19.6.57

Channel 5 Broadcasting Ltd, 22 Long Acre, London WC2E 9LY
T 020 7421 7123
E chris.shaw@five.tv

Occupation: Senior Programme Controller, Channel 5

Education: Westminster School; Balliol College, Oxford
Career highlights: Trainee, LBC, 1980-81; Bulletin Editor, Independent Radio News, 1981-85; Chief Subeditor, ITN, 1987-89, including Writer, 1985-87; Senior Producer, Sky News, 1990-91; Foreign and Home News Editor, Channel 4 News, ITN, 1992-93; Programme Editor, News at Ten, ITN, 1993-96; Editor, ITN News Service for Channel 5, 1996-98; Controller of News, Current Affairs and Documentaries, Channel 5 Broadcasting, 1998-2001; Senior Programme Controller, Channel 5 Broadcasting, 2001-present.

» **Relaxing to:** *Travel, watching football, archaeology.*
» *Married*

Robin Shenfield

21.1.60

The Mill, 40-41 Great Marlborough Street, London W1F 7JQ
T 020 7287 4041
E sam@the-mill.com

Occupation: Chief Executive, Mill Digital Media

Other positions: Managing Director, The Mill
Awards: None personally but many for The Mill including the Academy Award for Gladiator and numerous D&AD yellow pencils for contributing to some of the best advertising in the world.
Education: University of Bradford
Career highlights: With our Oscar-winner Tim Burke, bringing home the 2001 Academy Award for Visual Effects for Gladiator to a rousing reception from The Mill. Working with Ridley Scott on Gladiator and Black Hawk Down, with Tony Scott on Enemy of The State, with George Miller and Doug Mitchell on Babe: Pig in the City, with Chris DeFaria on the riotous Cats and Dogs and with Warner Brothers on the first two Harry Potter films. In 1990, being given the opportunity to help create a ground-breaking new visual effects business for advertising, film and television called The Mill.
Mentor: James Morris, Chairman of the Irish Film Board and of Irish Broadcaster TV3.
Big break: I was rescued from a dead-end trade magazine to work on the trade weekly, Broadcast.
Big mistake: It involves people still working in the feature film visual effects business and so is best glossed over.

» **Reading:** *Random selections from Amazon.* **Watching:** *Dr Who, QI and Arsenal!* **Listening:** *Radio 4 and the contents of my iPod.* **Relaxing to:** *With my family, especially on Camber Sands in the winter.*
» *Married, 2 children*

Bob Shennan

18.3.62

Radio Five Live, Television Centre, Wood Lane, London W12 7RJ
T 020 8624 8956
E bob.shennan@bbc.co.uk

Occupation: Controller, BBC Radio Five Live, Sports Extra and BBC Asian Network

Education: Lancaster Royal Grammar School; Corpus Christi College, Cambridge
Career highlights: Journalist, Hereward Radio, 1984-87; Producer, Radio Sport, BBC, 1987-90; Assistant Editor, Radio Sport, BBC, 1990-92; Editor, Radio Sport, BBC, 1992-94; Head, Radio Sport, BBC, 1994-97; Head of Sport, TV and Radio, BBC, 1997-2000; Controller, Five Live, BBC, 2000-present.

» **Relaxing to:** *Sport, literature, children.*
» *Married, 3 children*

John Shone

20.7.49

Bryngwilla House, Gledrid, St Martins, Oswestry SY10 7AY
T 01691 778375
E john.shone@tesco.net

Occupation: Freelance journalist and media consultant

Other positions: Casual shifts for BBC Wales; running Border Media; formerly News Organiser, BBC Wales, Wrexham; News Editor, BBC Radio Shropshire; North Wales Manager/News Editor, HTV Wales; Manager, BBC Radio Clwyd.
Publications: Newspapers: Fishing News, Grocers' Gazette, Flintshire Leader; Broadcasting: BBC Nationwide, Radio Wales, Radio Clwyd, HTV Wales, BBC Radio Shropshire.
Awards: 1972 J R Freeman News Reporter of the Year, Wales; NUJ News Reporter of the Year North Wales and North West England for campaign to save Shotton steelworks from closure.
Education: Castell Alun High School, Hope, near Wrexham
Career highlights: Began career in 1960 as copy boy on Daily Herald/Sporting Life; managed to secure trainee's job in Fleet Street as reporter/sub with Fishing News after phoning the editor every day for a fortnight; two awards in 1972 helped me land a job with BBC Nationwide; in 1981 the BBC gave me my own radio station to run, BBC Radio Clwyd, the first 'opt out' station on mainland Britain, broadcasting for two and a half hours a day.
Mentor: Newspapers: the late Tom Batty, former News Editor, Grocers' Gazette. Broadcasting: Gareth Bowen, (father of BBC's Jeremy Bowen), who was my Editor in charge of Good Morning Wales.
Big break: Joining BBC Nationwide when it was pulling in 12 million viewers a night! Working with Ron Neil, John Morrell, Keith Clement, Sue Lawley, Bob Wellings, Frank Bough and Michael Barratt was a great experience and I learnt so much from them about broadcasting.
Big mistake: Possibly turning down a job with the Daily Mail in Manchester. My head was turned by TV, and I've always wondered how my newspaper career would have developed if I'd taken up the offer.

» **Reading:** *Guardian, Independent, Mail, Sunday Times, political biographies, thrillers - anything and everything!* **Watching:** *I'm addicted to news and current affairs programmes, national and regional. I also enjoy historical dramas such as the current Rome and Egypt, plus repeats of old comedy series such as Open All Hours, Dad's Army, Porridge etc.* **Listening:** *I take myself off to Ambridge every Sunday morning - my weekly date with The Archers helps me through the tedium of ironing shirts. Desert Island Discs, the News Quiz and I'm Sorry I Haven't a Clue. I also listen to Radio Wales and Radio Shropshire.* **Relaxing to:** *Outings to the North Wales coast and countryside; holidays in Spain; walking with my partner in the lovely countryside around our home on the Shropshire-Wales border; reading. Having retired from the BBC in July 2005, I'm still learning to wind down!*
» *Divorced, living with partner, Juliet, 2 children*

Alexandra Shulman 13.11.57

Vogue Magazine, Vogue House, Hanover Square, London W1R 1JU
T 020 7499 9080
E ashulman@condenast.co.uk

Occupation: Editor, Vogue

Other positions: Trustee, National Portrait Gallery, 1999-present; Trustee, Arts Foundation, 2001-present.
Awards: PPA Editor of the Year, 1997; Vogue, Consumer Magazine of the Year, PPA Awards, 2001; Editors' Editor of the Year, British Society of Magazine Editors Awards, 2004; OBE, 2005.
Education: St Paul's Girls' School; Sussex University
Career highlights: Tatler, Commissioning Editor, 1982-84; Features Editor, 1984-87; Sunday Telegraph, Editor, Women's Page, 1987; Deputy Editor, 7 Days magazine, 1987-88; Features Editor, Vogue, 1988-90; Editor, GQ, 1990-92; Editor, Vogue, 1992-present; Director, Condé Nast Publications, 1997-2002.

» *Divorced, 1 son*

Chris Sice

MTV, Hawley Crescent, London NW1 8TT
T 020 7284 7777

Occupation: Business Manager, MTV Interactive

Career highlights: Former Commercial Manager, dotmusic; Business Manager, MTV Interactive, 2000-present.

John Simpson 10.8.48

World Affairs Unit, TV Centre, Wood Lane, London W12 7RJ
T 020 8743 8000
E john.simpson@bbc.co.uk

Occupation: BBC Foreign Affairs Editor

Other positions: Political Editor; Diplomatic Editor; Foreign Correspondent in Dublin, Brussels and Johannesburg; started with BBC as half-pay Sub-editor in 1966.
Publications: Strange Places, Questionable People (1998) - autobiography; A Mad World, My Masters (2000) - tales of travel; News From No Man's Land (2002) - nature of reporting; The Wars Against Saddam (2003); Days From Another World - a 1940s childhood (2005). All published by Macmillan.
Awards: RTS Journalist of the Year (twice) plus four other RTS awards; two BAFTAs; International Emmy; Peabody; Bayeux war correspondents' award; Golden Nymph award, Cannes film festival.
Education: St Paul's School, London; Magdalene College, Cambridge
Career highlights: Covered 36 wars and insurgencies, reported from 118 countries, interviewed 130 heads of state and government including Khomeini, Gadaffi, Gorbachev, Mandela, Sharon and Mugabe. Covered Iranian revolution, 1978-79; Israeli invasion of Lebanon, 1982; fall of Argentine junta, 1983; Tiananmen Square massacre, fall of Berlin Wall, and revolutions in Czechoslovakia and Romania, 1989; release of Nelson Mandela, 1990; first Gulf War from Baghdad, coup against Gorbachev and resulting collapse of Soviet Union, 1991; drugs trade and human rights abuse in Peru and Colombia; Bosnian war, 1992-95; the end of apartheid in South Africa, 1994; NATO bombing of Kosovo and Serbia from Belgrade; the victory, rule and collapse of Taliban in Afghanistan, 1996-2001; invasion of Iraq, 2003.
Mentor: Martha Gellhorn
Big break: Deciding to ignore BBC instructions and flying from Paris to Tehran in Ayatollah Khomeini's plane in 1979.
Big mistake: Identifying the wrong Gemayel brother as newly elected President of Lebanon, 1982; the right one was murdered two weeks later and the other one became President after all. Other mistakes include agreeing to present 9 O'Clock News.

» **Reading:** *Social and political history and eighteenth and nineteenth century fiction by choice; back of cornflakes packet if necessary.* **Watching:** *Not much television, lots of movies.* **Listening:** *BBC World Service, Radio Three, an iPod packed with music of various kinds.* **Relaxing to:** *Ferretting round in old bookshops, hanging out at Chelsea Arts Club.*

» *Married, 2 daughters by 1st marriage, 1 son by 2nd marriage*

Charles Sinclair 4.4.48

Northcliffe House, 2 Derry Street, London W8 5TT
T 020 7938 6614
E charles.sinclair@dmgt.co.uk

Occupation: Group Chief Executive, Daily Mail and General Trust plc

Other positions: Director, Euromoney Institutional Investor plc, 1985-present; Director, Schroders plc, 1990-2004; Director, Reuters Group plc, 1994-2005; Director, SVG Capital plc, 2005; Chairman of Trustees, Minack Theatre Trust, Porthcurno, Cornwall, 1985-present.
Education: Winchester College; Magdalen College, Oxford
Career highlights: ACA, 1974; VSO, Zambia, 1966-67; Dearden Farrow, California, 1970; joined Associated Newspapers Holdings, 1975; Assistant Managing Director and Member, Main Board, 1986; Managing Director, 1988 (Associated Newspapers Holdings became a wholly-owned subsidiary of Daily Mail and General Trust, 1988).

» **Relaxing to:** *Opera, fishing, skiing.* » *Married, 2 sons*

Gilly Sinclair 19.7.57

Chat, IPC Magazines, King's Reach Tower, Stamford Street, London SE1 9LS
T 020 7261 6560
E gilly_sinclair@ipcmedia.com

Occupation: Editor, Chat magazine

Other positions: Fellow of the Royal Society of Arts; Editor, Woman's Weekly; Editor, GMTV magazine; Editor, Family Circle.
Awards: IPC's Magazine of the Year 2001, while editing Woman's Weekly.

Education: Brentwood County High School; Harlow College
Career highlights: Getting it right! When an issue comes together so well that it leaps off the shelf. It's not every week, but when it happens, yup, it's a highlight.
Big break: Becoming Deputy Editor on Family Circle in 1990. I still think cracking a Deputy Ed's job is the toughest thing.
Big mistake: Undoubtedly still to come.

» **Reading:** *Anything and everything from the FT to coffee jars...* **Watching:** *Currently Spooks and Waking the Dead - loved the new Dr Who.* **Listening:** *Music, music, music ... Gershwin to gorillaz; Elgar to eels. Radio 4 and 2.* **Relaxing to:** *Music, gardening, reading, with a good glass of wine...* » *Divorced, no children*

Hardeep Singh Kohli

22.1.73

c/o Miriam James, Casarotto Ramsay & Associates, National House, 60-66 Wardour Street, London W1V 4ND
T 020 7287 4450
E agents@casarotto.uk.com

Occupation: Writer, Director, Presenter, Performer and budding Town Planner.

Awards: BAFTA, RTS, 100 metres swimming badge.
Education: St Aloysius College, Glasgow; Glasgow University Law School
Career highlights: That I seem to have a career is a highlight.

» **Reading:** *Guardian, Observer and BBC News weather reports.* **Watching:** *Bodies, West Wing, Late Review, any new comedy and most new drama.* **Listening:** *Five Live somewhat obsessively and increasing amounts of Radio 4: Front Row, Dead Ringers, Any Questions and the constant surprise that is the afternoon play...* **Relaxing to:** *I was hoping you might tell me...* » *Married*

Alan Smith

24.3.71

113-114 Shoreditch High Street, London E1 6JN
T 020 7749 7500
E info@nexusproductions.com

Occupation: Director, based at Nexus Productions

Publications: Directed Honda Grr; NSPCC Speech Bubble; Observer Music Monthly Abba to Zappa; Littlest Elf sequence from Lemony Snicket's A Series of Unfortunate Events; Thunderbirds film title sequence; sketches for Monkey Dust.
Awards: Include Cannes Grand Prix 2005; BTAA Best Commercial 2005; BTAA Craft Best Animation 2004/5; 2 D&AD Golds 2005; 2005 Grandy.
Education: Forest of Dean Grammar; Leicester Poly, RCA
Career highlights: Met Adam Foulkes at the Royal College of Art in 1994. Directed together since graduating, working initially mostly on music promos, then commercials and broadcast work.
Mentor: We work very closely with our producer Chris O'Reilly who usually steers us in the right direction.
Big break: We were asked to direct sequences for U2's giant Popmart Tour visuals just after leaving college.
Big mistake: You learn everything on the job so you're bound to make mistakes. We once shot one of the biggest bands in Britain then just as the lead singer was about to begin we cut to some random animated nonsense. It never got aired.

» **Reading:** *Whatever's got a good cover.* **Watching:** *Regional news and the Simpsons.* **Listening:** *Playlist includes Psapp, Lucky Pierre, Midlake, Tunng, My Computer, Arcade Fire, Flotation Toy Warning.* **Relaxing to:** *I go to work (I've got three kids).* » *Married, 3 children*

Craig Smith

22.2.71

174 Hammersmith Road, London W6 7JP
T 020 8267 4341
E craig.smith@haynet.com

Occupation: Editor, Marketing

Publications: Power 100 - most influential people in marketing (June); Biggest Brands (August); Agencies of the Year (December).
Awards: PPA Weekly Business and Professional Magazine of the Year (2005-06).
Education: Manchester University
Career highlights: Relaunching Marketing in 2004 in an A4 format, achieving a circulation of 50,412 or 25% higher than the nearest competitor, gaining record preference scores and winning the PPA Business Magazine of the Year award.
Mentor: My predecessor, Conor Dignam, now editor of Broadcast. Taught me a lot about news judgement and people skills - the latter not necessarily by example.
Big break: Always being one career move behind people who had a short attention span.
Big mistake: Still hoping to make it.

» **Reading:** *bbc.co.uk/mobile, FT, Sun, Metro, Marketing Week, Campaign, Business Life, Real Business, Observer, Sunday Times. Tragically, little time for books.* **Watching:** *West Wing, Lost, Scrubs, Tour de France given the choice. I never am, so it's more often Thomas the Tank Engine, Maggie and Beast, Max and Ruby, Dora the Explorer...* **Listening:** *Whatever's playing on Xfm. The Today Programme when I'm feeling guilty about listening to Xfm.* **Relaxing to:** *Pruning my bonsai trees, cycling, skiing. My life coach says I'm not a team player - can't imagine why.* » *Happily co-habiting, 2 children*

Elizabeth Smith

16.8.40

CBA, 17 Fleet Street, London EC4Y 1AA
T 020 7583 5550
E elizabeth@cba.org.uk

Occupation: Secretary-General, Commonwealth Broadcasting Association

Other positions: Controller, English Programmes, BBC World Service
Publications: Commonwealth Broadcaster
Awards: OBE
Education: Edinburgh University
Career highlights: Secretary-General of the Commonwealth Broadcasting Association since 1994; 1987-94 Controller (Director) of English Programmes for the BBC World Service; 1984-87 Head of Current Affairs for the World Service, following posts as Deputy Editor, Consumer

Programmes, BBC Radio, and as a news and current affairs producer for BBC TV; 1979-81 Senior Assistant, BBC Secretariat, involved in broadcasting policy and Advisory Groups; began in the BBC as a Studio Manager in Glasgow in 1958 and then became a news and current affairs producer in first Radio and then TV; Trustee of the Voice of the Listener and Viewer; Honorary Secretary of the Elizabeth R Broadcasting Fund and a Fellow of the UK's Radio Academy; on the Advisory Committee of the Rory Peck Trust, and a Trustee of the Commonwealth Human Rights Initiative.

›› **Reading:** *History, biography, newspapers.* **Watching:** *News, documentaries.* **Listening:** *Radio 4, BBC World Service, Radio 5.* **Relaxing to:** *Gardening, walking, reading.*
›› *Married, 2 children*

Godric Smith 29.3.65

Prime Minister's Office, 10 Downing Street, London SW1A 2AA
T 020 7219 4272
E godric.smith@pmo.gov.uk

Occupation: Head of Strategic Communications, Prime Minister's Office

Education: Perse School, Cambridge; Worcester College, Oxford
Career highlights: Appeals Manager, SANE, 1988-91; Senior Information Officer, 1991-94, Chief Press Officer, 1995, Department of Health; Deputy Press Secretary, 1998-2001; Prime Minister's Official Spokesman, 2001-03; Prime Minister's Office, 1996-present.

›› **Relaxing to:** *Watching Cambridge United, family.*
›› *Married, 2 sons*

Graham Smith 24.9.59

Five TV, 22 Long Acre, London WC2E 9LY
T 020 7550 5555
E graham.smith@five.tv

Occupation: Controller of Comedy, Five TV and Paramount Comedy

Other positions: Commissioning Editor, Entertainment and Comedy, Channel Four; Editor, New Comedy, BBC TV.
Education: Epsom School of Art
Career highlights: I started as a Journalist with NME before moving to Channel 4 in 1985 to work on The Tube, The Last Resort with Jonathan Ross, and later became Music Producer on BBC2's The Late Show; in 1989, I joined Noel Gay Television as Producer on a number of series including Juke Box Jury for BBC2. Within two years, I set up my own independent production company, TV21, producing projects that included Viva Cabaret for C4, and also worked with Open Mike Productions, developing programmes including The Jack Dee Show; in 1996, I became Commissioning Editor for Entertainment and Comedy at C4, managing TFI Friday, Graham Norton, The Harry Hill Show, Armstrong & Miller, Comic Strip Presents and Spaced; after a year as Head of Entertainment Development at Carlton TV, I became a freelance producer and consultant on projects including An Audience with Tom Jones (LWT), before being appointed Executive Producer/Head of Development for the BBC's New Comedy Entertainment Department in 2000, responsible for commissions across all the BBC terrestrial and digital channels. In June 2002, I was promoted to Acting Editor for New Comedy. Productions included Little Britain and the Mark Steel Lectures; in August 2004 I was appointed as Controller of Comedy at Five TV and Paramount Comedy.
Mentor: Paul Jackson, Tony Orsten and Stuart Cosgrove.
Big break: Working for Paul Jackson, becoming Commissioning Editor at Channel Four.
Big mistake: Spending £200K of Channel Four money on a doomed pilot.

›› **Reading:** *Independent, Mirror, the Week.* **Watching:** *Curb Your Enthusiasm, Thick Of It, Porridge, Woody Allen movies.* **Listening:** *Vaughan Williams, Arctic Monkeys and a lot in between.* **Relaxing to:** *Go to football, cook, buy art.*
›› *Married, 4 daughters*

Matt Smith

Sky News, Grant Way, Isleworth TW7 5QD
T 020 7705 3000
E matt.smith@bskyb.com

Occupation: Entertainment Correspondent, Sky News

Other positions: Formerly Programme Editor, BBC Liquid News; Senior Reporter, Radio 1 Newsbeat; Reporter, BBC GLR; Reporter, BBC Radio Kent; Reporter, Radio Mercury.
Education: University of Westminster
Career highlights: I started my reporting life driving a battered Vauxhall Astra radio car around the hot and happening news patch of Surrey and North East Hampshire. Then it got swapped for a Peugeot at BBC Kent, and a beaten up-Montego estate at BBC GLR in London. Now you'll probably find me in the back of a Mercedes Sprinter satellite van, cutting a piece for Sky News. The vehicles may have changed but the pressure to hit the deadline never goes away. As Sky News' Entertainment Correspondent, I cover showbiz, films, music and media stories for the channel. Since joining Sky in 2003, I've interviewed a conveyor belt of Hollywood stars, covered the Oscars four times, as well as reporting live from the Golden Globe awards, the Brits, the BAFTAs, and the Venice and Cannes film festivals. Prior to joining Sky News, I was a Programme Editor and a Reporter on the BBC's daily entertainment TV show, Liquid News. While at Liquid News, I covered a wide range of showbiz stories, building up a huge working knowledge of film, TV and music. I produced specials on the Oscars and George Harrison, as well as following Eminem and Oasis on tour to Japan and reporting live from Tokyo. My experience also includes 8 years as a BBC Reporter, covering major news stories like the Docklands Bomb and reporting live from the funeral route of Diana, Princess of Wales. I've also reported live from all over the UK and most of Europe - investigating

drug dealing in Ayia Napa, child prostitution in Prague and gangster rappers in Germany.

Mentor: A BBC Reporter called Paul Greer who used to work at Radio Solent in Southampton. He told me to be a reporter because it would save me having to get a proper job.

Big break: My foot after falling down the stairs at home. I wasn't drunk, I was decorating.

Big mistake: Making fun of a group of flower arrangers in a piece for a very earnest BBC local radio station I was freelancing at. I was told politely never to come back again.

» **Reading:** *Papers: Daily Telegraph for news coverage, Sun/Mirror/Star for entertainment stories. Trade mags: Variety, Hollywood Reporter and Broadcast. Websites: BBC News online, mediaguardian.co.uk, entnews.co.uk for the stuff I can report on. Popbitch and HolyMoly for the stuff I can't. Mags: Total Film, Q, NME, Guitarist and Bass Guitar Magazine. I'm a pretend rock star on weekends, playing bass in an indie/rock covers band - www.spacehopperband.co.uk.* **Watching:** *Sky News, or I'd get fired. MTV2, VH2 and BBC2. Basically, anything with a '2' in it. In truth, I surf the music channels and tape anything that has live bands on. One day, I'm hoping somebody might phone me up and offer me a job playing bass on a world tour, so I watch and learn all the basslines just in case.* **Listening:** *Good indie guitar bands. Recent favourites include Hard-Fi, Maximo Park and Athlete. Mourn the loss of Shed Seven. Also like funk and jazz, the stuff without the beard and sandals.* **Relaxing to:** *Horizontally, with my eyes closed.*

Neil Smith

1965

Telewest Global, Export House, Cawsey Way, Woking, Surrey GU21 6QX
T 01483 750900
E pressoffice@telewest.co.uk

Occupation: Vice-President and Chief Financial Officer, Telewest

Career highlights: Positions at Somerfield plc, including Deputy Finance Director, 1994-2000; joined Telewest Communications as Group Financial Controller, 2000; Finance Director, Consumer Sales Division, Telewest Communications, 2000-02; Deputy Group Finance Director, Telewest Communications, 2002-03; Vice-President and Chief Financial Officer, Telewest, 2003-present.

Sarah Smith

23.11.72

200 Gray's Inn Road, London W1T 3PH
T 020 7833 3000
E sarah.smith@itn.co.uk

Occupation: Presenter, More4 News

Other positions: Presenter Channel 4 News; Correspondent, Channel 4 News; Reporter, 5 News; Producer, BBC Newsnight.

Awards: International Emmy award for coverage of Madrid Bombings 2004.

Education: Boroughmuir High School, Edinburgh; University of Glasgow

» *Single, no children*

Steve Smith

1.6.70

AFM Lighting, 12 Waxlow Road, London NW10 7NU
T 020 8233 7200
E steve.smith@afmlighting.com

Occupation: Managing Director, AFM Group

Other positions: Director, British Television Advertising Awards.

Publications: Provided lighting on the last 4 James Bond films, Star Wars, Lord of The Rings, Charlie and the Chocolate Factory and many more! Also hundreds of commercials, music videos, TV dramas, etc.

Education: University of life!

Career highlights: Became involved in the film and TV industry by accident aged 18. Managed my first Lighting Co at 19 knowing very little but never letting anyone down. Moved on in 1992 to join up with Andy Martin at AFM Lighting. Went on to expand from a small UK-based Film and TV Lighting company into an international group of facilities companies providing lighting, studios, cameras and grip in locations including London, Prague, Cape Town, Johannesburg and Sydney. I now manage the AFM Group with a fantastic management team. I also commit time to various industry working groups including the UK Film Council, The Production Guild and The British Television Advertising Awards to name a few.

Mentor: I've never had any in particular. I have always enjoyed watching and learning from a diverse range of businesses and find that learning from other people's mistakes doesn't cost me money.

Big break: I've always been quite fortunate. There are a number of occasions in my business life when I felt like I was the special one as Jose would say. In my personal life, marrying Cathy last year!

Big mistake: Marrying my first wife.

» **Reading:** *Various trade mags including Screen International, Campaign and The Hollywood Reporter. I also enjoy entertaining books by the likes of Dan Brown.* **Watching:** *Obviously I'm a bit of a film fan but also can't get enough football, much to the dismay of my wife.* **Listening:** *Many different kinds of music, far too many to list. Also find myself listening to the likes of Talksport which I find thoroughly entertaining.* **Relaxing to:** *Going for long walks and meals out with my wife. Love playing golf but have little time to indulge.* » *Married, 1 child from first marriage*

Stuart Smith

17.9.53

Centaur Publishing, St Giles House, 49-50 Poland Street, London W1F 7AX
T 020 7970 4000
E stuart.smith@centaur.co.uk

Occupation: Editor, Marketing Week

Other positions: Chairman of the Judges, Marketing Week Effectiveness Awards.

Education: City of Bath Boys' School; Wadham College, Oxford; University of Sussex

Career highlights: Joined Marketing Week as Subeditor, 1982; Editor, 1988-present.

» **Relaxing to:** *Skiing, reading, riding.* » *Married, no children*

Stuart Smith

Haymarket House, 28/29 Haymarket,
London SW1Y 4SP
T 020 7344 1338
E stuart.smith@edelman.com

Occupation: CEO, Edelman London

Career highlights: Head of Communications at the Audit Commission; Director of Corporate Practice, Edelman, 1999-2003; Deputy CEO and Joint CEO, Edelman, 2003-05; CEO, Edelman London, 2005-present.

Susy Smith 16.8.61

The National Magazine Company,
72 Broadwick Street, London W1F 9EP
T 020 7439 5294
E susy.smith@natmags.co.uk

Occupation: Editor, Country Living magazine and Coast magazine

Publications: Farmer Wants a Wife campaign from 1999 to present; Enterprising Rural Women campaign from 2001 to present; anti-packaging campaign launched 2005; Reduce the Commute (anti-work miles campaign) launched 2005.
Awards: BSME Innovation of the Year 1999 for Farmer wants a Wife Campaign; British Environment and Media Awards 2003 for Best Coverage of environmental issues by a consumer magazine; PPA Consumer Lifestyle Magazine of the Year 2004.
Education: Grosvenor High School, Belfast; Central School of Art and Design, studied graphic design
Career highlights: First job was Designer on My Guy magazine; Designer on Ideal Home magazine; Homes and Decorating Assistant on Homes and Gardens magazine; Style Editor on In Store magazine; Freelance Style Consultant; Style Editor/Associate Editor House Beautiful magazine; Editor Country Living magazine; Editor Country Living and Coast magazine.
Mentor: Terence Whelan at IPC Magazines and Pat Roberts-Cairns at Natmags.
Big break: Getting my first job on My Guy: I'd wanted to work on magazines since I was 12. I knew once I was in, I'd make it.
Big mistake: Leaving my car aerial up on entering a car wash and getting out of the car when the machine was operational to try to retrieve it. Result: driver's door ripped off and very wet car interior!

» **Reading:** *The Week, Gardens Illustrated, endless gardening books, poetry anthologies, popular fiction and all the competitive magazines in Country Living's market. Oh yes – and Tisted Tales, our great village magazine.* **Watching:** *ER, Gardener's World, period dramas, natural history programmes.* **Listening:** *60s singles on our Ami Continental jukebox, pop compilations in the car, Radio 4.* **Relaxing to:** *Gardening, dog-walking and birdwatching.* » *Married, twin girls aged 7*

Lisa Smosarski 15.2.81

Endeavour House, 189 Shaftesbury Avenue,
London WC2H 8JG
T 020 7208 3478
E lisa.smosarski@emap.com

Occupation: Editor, Bliss

Other positions: Editor, Smash Hits; Editor, mykindaplace.com; Entertainment Editor, New Woman.
Education: London College of Printing
Career highlights: Editor of Bliss magazine since February 2005; first editorship was on pop music title, Smash Hits for two and a half years, leaving with a 10% increase in sales; previously launch editor of mykindaplace.com (the most successful website for teenage girls), Entertainment Editor for New Woman and a contributor to many UK magazines; also wrote an advice book for teenage girls, The Smart Girls' Guide to Friends.
Big break: Landing my first job as Junior Writer on Bliss on the day I finished university.

» **Reading:** *I really will read anything! I love non-fiction books on anything a bit spooky and weird, books crammed with facts, Dan Brown-esque thrillers, books about the media world (from Devil Wears Prada to How to Lose Friends and Alienate People) and a good pile of chick-lit too. Oh, and don't forget the magazines!* **Watching:** *I'm a real TV bore - I love it all. My current favourites are Most Haunted, the OC, Desperate Housewives, Lost, any soap, Saturday Kitchen (that's a favourite), Body Hits, Friends, Will and Grace, anything on Living TV.* **Listening:** *At the moment I'm listening to Razorlight, White Stripes, Kaiser Chiefs, Keane, U2. I never like to be far from a bit of classic soft rock or a power ballad either!* **Relaxing to:** *Usually with a bottle of wine or by making whatever I've just watched on Saturday Kitchen (not very succesfully).* » *Single, no children*

Jon Snow 29.9.51

Channel 4 News, 200 Gray's Inn Road,
London WC1 8XZ
T 020 7833 3000
E jon.snow@itn.co.uk

Occupation: Main Presenter, Channel 4 News

Publications: Shooting History, HarperCollins, 2004.
Awards: RTS Journalist of the Year, 1980; RTS Presenter of the Year, 1994 and 2002.
Education: Liverpool University
Career highlights: Have reported from Afghanistan to Zimbabwe, interviewed Mandela, Reagan, Gorbachev, Thatcher etc; Reporter, LBC 1973-76; Reporter, ITN News at Ten 1976-89.
Mentor: Nigel Ryan, David Nicholas and Jim Gray.
Big break: Getting hired by LBC.

» **Reading:** *New Yorker, New York Review of Books, New Statesman, Country Life, Time, FT, Guardian, Telegraph.* **Watching:** *Newsnight.* **Listening:** *Radio 3, Radio 4, Bach, Brahms, Stones.* **Relaxing to:** *Watercolour painting.* » *Partnered, 2 children*

Sarah Solftley

24.11.68

BBC Radio Devon, PO Box 1034, Plymouth
T 01752 260323
E sarah.solftley@bbc.co.uk

Occupation: Assistant Editor, BBC Radio Devon and Devon Online

Other positions: BBC South West Diversity Representative; Trustee, Chestnut Appeal for Prostate Cancer.
Awards: Lead the BBC Radio Devon Chestnut Appeal, which raised £1,000,000 for the specialist treatment of prostate cancer; executive produced Twelve Days, an innovative radio drama project with the Theatre Royal, Plymouth; launched Breeze, a new talent scheme for the South West with the Arts Council to identify and support 12 arts and media projects from the community.
Career highlights: Helping our listeners and viewers raise £1,000,000 for the Chestnut Appeal, the power of local radio! Launching Breeze, the creative talent scheme, and teaching children the joys of film making as part of the Breeze project; working with the Theatre Royal, Plymouth to bring original drama to the airwaves; running digital storytelling workshops in the community; there are too many moments to mention, but these projects are in the forefront of my mind as they are pieces of work I have been recently involved in.
Mentor: Ros Henry, a former camerawoman who shared the joy of broadcasting with me and gave me my first real break in the industry.
Big break: Being offered a place on the BBC's trainee journalism scheme.
Big mistake: Turning down a great job offer.

» **Reading:** *The Guardian, Observer, the classics, Philip Roth, Robert Littell, Isabel Allende, Arthur Ransome.* **Watching:** *Newsnight, the Culture show, films.* **Listening:** *BBC Radio Devon, Radio 4, Late Junction on Radio 3, any radio drama.* **Relaxing to:** *Sailing, body-boarding, going to the movies, reading, travelling.*

Ranjit Sondhi

22.10.50

BBC Television Centre, Wood Lane, London W12 7RJ
T 020 8743 8000
E ranjit.sondhi@bbc.co.uk

Occupation: BBC Governor, English Regions

Other positions: Senior Lecturer; Chairman, NHS Trust; Trustee, National Gallery.
Publications: Various academic publications on community and identity.
Awards: CBE; DUniv (Hon).
Education: Bedford School, University of Birmingham
Career highlights: Degree in Theoretical Physics; Community and Youth Worker; Member of the Independent Broadcasting Authority and the Radio Authority; Chairman of Refugee Employment Training and Education Council; Deputy Chairman of Commission for Racial Equality; Member of Lord Chancellor's Advisory Forum on Legal Education and Conduct; Senior Lecturer in Community and Youth Studies; Trustee of National Gallery; Chairman of Heart of Birmingham NHS Primary Care Trust; BBC Governor with special responsibility for the English Regions.

» **Reading:** *Modern and classical literature, the Guardian.* **Watching:** *The news, comedy, satire, drama and history programmes.* » *Married, 2 children*

Jon Sopel

23.5.63

Room 2624, Stage 6, Television Centre, London W12 7RJ
T 020 8743 8000
E jon.sopel@bbc.co.uk

Occupation: Presenter, Politics Show, BBC1; Senior Presenter, BBC News 24

Publications: Biography of Tony Blair, published 1995.
Education: Southampton University
Career highlights: In the past year I have presented programmes from Sri Lanka after the tsunami, New Orleans after Hurricane Katrina and was in Rome for the Pope's death; for the Politics Show we took the programme to Alabama for an exclusive joint interview with Condoleezza Rice and Jack Straw; before becoming a full time presenter I was the BBC's Paris Correspondent during the presidential elections there, and in that time reported on the war in Afghanistan and Iraq; until 1999 I was the BBC's Chief Political Correspondent on News 24.
Mentor: The usuals: John Cole when I was at Westminster, and as producers of great telelvision, Martin Bell and Brian Barron.
Big break: Becoming Paris Correspondent. Being paid to live and work in one of the most beautiful cities in the world often just felt too good to be true.
Big mistake: Too numerous to mention.

» **Reading:** *A mix of current novels and worthy biographies.* **Watching:** *Sport (more or less any kind), virtually anything that comes out of HBO, documentaries and am struggling with a hopeless addiction to news.* **Listening:** *Eclectic mix of 70s West Coast, punk/2 tone of the early 80s and selected Britpop.* **Relaxing to:** *Running across Hampstead Heath, drinking red wine, theatre and cinema.*

Sir Martin Sorrell

14.2.45

WPP Group plc, 27 Farm Street, London W1J 5RJ
T 020 7408 2204
E fmcewan@wpp.com

Occupation: Group Chief Executive, WPP

Other positions: Non-executive Director, Colefax & Fowler Group plc, 1997-present; Member, Board, NASDAQ, 2001-present; Chairman, Advisory Group, KPMG, 2002-present; Member, ATP Marketing Advisory Board, 2001-present; International Advisory Board, CBI, 2002-present; Special Adviser, Loyalty Management UK Ltd, 2003-present; Special Adviser, Modern Apprenticeship Taskforce, DfES, 2003-present; Member, Energy and Technology Board, 2002-present; Member, Advisory Board,

International Graduate School of Management, University of Navarra, Spain, 1989-present; Deans Advisory Council, Boston University School of Management, 1998-present; Member, Board of Directors of Associates, Harvard Business School, 1998-present; Member, Board, Indian School of Business, 1998-present; Member, Panel 2000, 1998-99; Member, Council for Excellence in Management and Leadership, 1999-present; Ambassador for British Business, 1997-present; Member, Board and Committee, Special Olympics, 2000-present; Corporate Advisory Group, Tate Gallery, 2000-present; Member, Board, Media Center, Museum of TV and Radio, New York, 2002-present; Governor, London Business School, 1990-present, Deputy Chairman, 1998-present; Vice-President, National Deaf Children's Society; Member, National Appeal Board, NSPCC; Trustee, Cambridge Foundation, 1990-present; RCA Foundation, 1999-present; Patron, Queen Charlotte's Appeal, Hammersmith Hospital, 1999-present; Patron, Christ's College, Cambridge; Honorary Patron, Cambridge University Jewish Society, 2002-present.

Education: Haberdashers' Aske's School; Christ's College, Cambridge; Harvard Graduate School of Business

Career highlights: Consultant, Glendinning Associates, Connecticut, 1968-69; Vice-President, Mark McCormack Organisation, London, 1970-74; Director, James Gulliver Associates, 1975-77; Group Financial Director, Saatchi & Saatchi, 1977-86; Founder and Chairman, WPP, 1986-present.

» **Relaxing to:** *Skiing, cricket.* » *Married, 3 sons*

Mike Soutar

9.11.70

King's Reach Tower, Stamford Street, London SE1 9LS

T 020 7261 6489
E mike_soutar@ipcmedia.com

Occupation: Editorial Director, IPC Media

Awards: PPA Magazine Of The Year, FHM, UK, 1997; Advertising Age Magazine Of The Year, Maxim, USA, 2000; Sony gold, Kiss FM, 1999; BSME Launch Of The Year, Nuts, 2004.

Education: Glenrothes High School

Career highlights: Left school at 17 and started off writing the horoscopes and the beauty page for Secrets, a magazine for elderly ladies published by DC Thomson; became the Pop Editor of Jackie; was the world's worst Press Officer at Virgin Records for a year until sacked; persuaded Smash Hits to give me a junior writer job in 1988 and was Editor by 1991, aged 24; became Editor of FHM in 1994 (circ 50k per month); left that in 1997 (circ 500k per month); was MD of Kiss FM in London; got poached to be Editor-in-Chief of Maxim in 1999. Presided over doubling of sales from one million per month to just over two million; joined Board of IPC in late 2000 as MD of Ignite Division; became group Editorial Director in 2003; launched Nuts, Pick Me Up and TV Easy between 2004 and today.

Mentor: Maggie Dun at DC Thomson; Mark Ellen and David Hepworth at Emap; Sly Bailey at IPC; Norm Pearlstine at Time Inc. and lots of other brilliant people who I won't embarrass further here.

Big break: Getting the sack from Virgin Records. I was too proud to admit I was hopeless and could have wasted years there if somebody hadn't made the decision for me.

Big mistake: Made loads of stupid mistakes, have very few regrets.

» **Reading:** *Biographies, Iain Banks books, every magazine I possibly can.* **Watching:** *Sky Sports News.* **Listening:** *Radio 4 and Kiss FM.* **Relaxing to:** *I hang out with my family.*
» *Married to Beverly, 2 children Jai (18) and Alfie (14)*

Justine Southall

4.1.62

National Magazine Company, 33 Broadwick Street, London W1F 0DQ

T 020 7312 3838
E Justine.southall@natmags.co.uk

Occupation: Group Publication Director, National Magazine Company

Other positions: Formerly Launch Publisher, eve Magazine; Group Commercial Director, Fashion and Beauty Group, IPC; Advertising Director, Marie Claire.

Education: Essex University

Career highlights: Worked on Marie Claire for eight years culminating in its highest ever ABC and market share performances to date; launched eve magazine in 2000, the only major launch that year (out of six) that has survived and succeeded; took Company to four in the young women's market and grew circulation by 40%; in 2005 launched new SHE, the first time a completely new launch concept was brought to market in an existing brand shell.

Mentor: Heather Love, Jackie Newcombe.

Big break: Becoming Advertising Director of Marie Claire.

» **Reading:** *Currently reading Ninetail Fox by John Courtney Grimwood.* **Watching:** *Boston Legal, Location Location Location, Grand Designs and Simpsons.* **Listening:** *At the moment Gill Scott Heron.* **Relaxing to:** *Walking, playing and wine!* » *Married, 2 children*

Simon Spanswick

14.1.66

PO Box 141, Cranbrook TN17 9AJ

T 020 7993 2557
E simon.spanswick@aib.org.uk

Occupation: Chief Executive, The Association for International Broadcasting

Other positions: Launch of Switch Digital, London's second commercial DAB Digital Radio multiplex; Managing Editor of The Channel, the quarterly publication of The Association for International Broadcasting.

Education: King Edward VII School, Lytham; Newport Grammar School, Essex

Career highlights: I have worked in broadcasting since 1981 when I first started freelancing for the BBC; in 1986 I joined the BBC fulltime, working in BBC Monitoring, then Corporate Affairs and finally the World Service; moved to WRN as Director, Corporate Affairs; led the WRN-run project that developed the world's first portable DAB Digital Radio and launched WRN's German-language

service; appointed Launch Director for Switch Digital, the DAB Digital Radio multiplex operator mostly owned by Kelvin Mackenzie's Wireless Group; have led the AIB, the industry association for international broadcasting, since 2000.
Mentor: John Tusa
Big break: Breaking into the BBC fulltime in 1986.
Big mistake: Allegedly upsetting Kelvin Mackenzie.

» **Reading:** *Economist, Telegraph, Guardian, Spectator, FT.* **Watching:** *Good drama, Spooks, for example, and good comedy. English-language output of AIB members, like DW-TV.* **Listening:** *BBC Radio 3, BBC World Service, Radio Sweden and other AIB members.* **Relaxing to:** *Gardening in our new home in the Kent countryside, walking (leisurely, not speed), cycling (gently, not racing).* » *Married, 1 child*

Patrick Spence 15.10.71

Room C401, BBC Centre House, Wood Lane, London W12 7RJ
T 020 8576 1664
E patrick.spence@bbc.co.uk

Occupation: Head of Drama, BBC Northern Ireland

Other positions: Head of Development and Executive Producer, BBC Drama Series; Head of Development, Pearson Television; Script Editor, Cracker, for Granada.
Publications: Lilies, The Innocence Project, The Amazing Mrs Pritchard, Messiah, Murphy's Law, Shakespeare Contemporary Adaptations, Waking the Dead.
Awards: None yet
Education: Exeter, BA Hons Latin
Career highlights: Too early to describe anything that significant. I am very proud of having been involved in the Shakespeare Adaptations, and to have convinced the channel to commission Waking the Dead as a pilot in 1999, despite their enormous reservations. But the three recent commissions for Lilies, The Innocence Project and The Amazing Mrs Pritchard are easily my most exciting and hopeful moments to date.
Mentor: Mal Young was, though will continue to be an influence.
Big break: Getting my first job as a script editor on Cracker.
Big mistake: Agreeing to try to rescue Harbour Lights the week it went into production.

» **Reading:** *Everything I can get my hands on.* **Watching:** *Spooks, Bodies, West Wing, Curb Your Enthusiasm.* **Listening:** *Radio 4 in the car, Underworld on my iPod.* **Relaxing to:** *Bike up mountains.* » *Single, no children*

James St Aubyn 7.6.54

The Manor Office, West End, Marazion, Cornwall TR17 0EF
T 01736 719933
E james@manor-office.co.uk

Occupation: Chairman, UKRD Group

Other positions: Chairman, Pirate FM; Chairman, Armada Productions; Governor, University College, Falmouth; Trustee, Hall for Cornwall; Chairman, Frank Copplestone Trust.
Education: Eton; Oxford
Career highlights: Merchant banker for twelve years with spells in New York and Tokyo; subsequently consultant to or investor in developing businesses in financial, leisure, media or retail sectors; Founder Chairman of Pirate FM which went on air in 1992 and was a Sony Station of the Year in 2003; Chairman of UKRD Group since it was formed in 1994 by the merger of Pirate with its largest shareholder; oversaw both UKRD's rapid expansion and its subsequent long march to reach profitability; joint owner of Armada Productions which has variously produced or invested in theatre and radio plays; since 2003 have lived in family home on St Michael's Mount in West Cornwall; in partnership with my wife, operate under licence from the National Trust the visitor business on St Michael's Mount, which attracts over 200,000 people each year.
Mentor: No one person.
Big break: Being invited to lead the applicant group which won the first ILR licence for Cornwall.
Big mistake: Not somehow holding onto and enlarging UKRD's share in Manchester and Yorkshire regional radio licences.

» **Reading:** *Modern fiction, with a weakness for detective stories. Collect Wisdens.* **Watching:** *Dr Who, Spooks, This Week.* **Listening:** *UKRD stations or Radio 4.* **Relaxing to:** *Watching cricket. Sudoku or other mind games. Waging war on ivy on St Michael's Mount.* » *Married, 4 children*

Emer Stamp 2.5.79

DDB London, 12 Bishops Bridge Road, London W2 6AA
T 020 7258 4458
E emer.stamp@ddblondon.com

Occupation: Advertising Art Director, DDB London

Other positions: Sailing, windsurfing and kayak instructor.
Publications: Co-creator of the Travelocity ad campaign starring Alan Whicker.
Awards: Some gold ones, some silver ones and some bronze ones (which if I polish hard enough look like gold ones).
Education: Buckinghamshire Chilterns University

» *Single, no children*

Sara Stephenson 5.6.66

Company, 96 Woodstock Road, Chiswick, London W4 1EG
T 020 7439 5000
E sara.stephenson@natmags.co.uk

Occupation: Publisher, Company magazine

Other positions: Formerly Group Commercial Director, Young Women's Group; Group Advertisement Director, Cosmopolitan; Senior Sales Exec, Sunday Times.
Education: Huyton College, Liverpool; King Alfred's College, Winchester
Career highlights: I entered the media world, like many others, by accident. A mediocre degree in History and English didn't set me up for much but reluctant to return to my home town of Wigan,

I scoured the Guardian and was determined to convince Haymarket publishing I was destined for a career in ad sales. My strategy worked and a month after graduating I was moving to London to start work on the well-known Direction magazine, much to the relief of my father. There I learnt d.i.p.a.d.a and the joys of closing issues, from there it was to Murdoch Magazines, then News International and finally to Nat Mags where I have spent the last 10 happy years.

Mentor: Simon Kippin, Publishing Director Glamour and Chris Hughes, Publishing Director Easy Living. Chris coaxed me away from newspapers into the wonderful world of glossies, I missed the boys but that aside, have never looked back. They both taught me that you're only ever as good as your team, the importance of attending the opening of an envelope, that people buy people, and always maintain a sense of humour, we don't save lives.

Big break: Being promoted to Group Commercial Director, Young Women's Group responsible for revenues into Cosmopolitan, Cosmo Girl, Company, She and Zest Magazines.

Big mistake: A karaoke performance at a News International leaving do. I've never sung live since!

» **Reading:** *Company magazine, and every other magazine, the Daily Telegraph, Sunday Times.* **Watching:** *Not much.* **Listening:** *Radio 4 and all kinds of music.* **Relaxing to:** *Over several glasses of wine and dinner with friends.*

» *Married, 2 children*

Ali Stevens

24.4.72

64-65 North Road, St Andrews, Bristol BS5 6AQ
T 0117 9428491
E a.stevens@venue.co.uk

Occupation: Associate Editor, Folio Magazine

Other positions: Reporter, Eastern Counties Newspapers; Researcher, BBC Bristol and HTV; Producer, Peachey Films.

Awards: Kodak Award for a short film called The Sobering; First Cut Award for a short film called Matter of Taste; Editor of Batteries Not Included, a gift guide supplement for Venue Magazine, which won Northcliffe's best supplement award 1992.

Education: University of East Anglia

Career highlights: As a cub reporter for ECN in 1992 I instigated an aid campaign to help the people of the former Yugoslavia displaced by the war. I travelled to Serbia and Bosnia tracking delivery of aid and sending daily reports to the Eastern Daily Press. Film-wise, I won a Kodak award to shoot a short in 35MM. Magazine-wise, I'm thrilled to see Folio grow; circulation has doubled and it's a joy to edit, and a perfect part-time position to combine with motherhood.

Big break: A commission from HTV to make a 30-minute documentary about the free party scene in the South West. After that I secured private funding to set up a film production company, and relished every moment of producing three short films.

» **Reading:** *Quality fiction, biographies and popular science (environment, evolution, biology, health). Weekend newspapers.* **Watching:** *Channel 4, mostly. Films, ocasionally.* **Listening:** *Radio 1, 4 and 6, Chill on DAB digital.* **Relaxing to:** *Cooking, visiting people and places, reading, watching TV.*

» *Married, 1 child*

Alastair Stewart

200 Gray's Inn Road, London WC1X 8XZ
T 020 8833 3000
E alastair.stewart@itn.co.uk

Occupation: News Anchor/Presenter, ITN

Other positions: Industrial Correspondent; Washington DC Correspondent.

Awards: RTS Presenter of the Year, 2004.

Education: St Augustine's Abbey School; Bristol University

Career highlights: Trained at Southern ITV from 1976 having been Deputy President of NUS; joined ITN in 1980 as Industrial Correspondent; began newscasting in the mid-80s, sub-anchored various major events, notably the fall of the Berlin Wall; went to USA as Washington Correspondent in 1990; sub-anchored coverage of Gulf War for three months from Saudi Arabia; joined Carlton-Granada in 1992 to present London Tonight and various regional and network programmes; rejoined ITN in 2004 to present on ITV News Channel, London Tonight and various network bulletins; frequent presenter of budgets, general elections and state occasions including opening of parliament and weddings; no barmitzvahs to date.

Mentor: Sir Alastair Burnet, simply the best.

Big break: Appearing as Deputy President of the NUS on Southern ITV's local news show in 1976 - they offered me a job!

Big mistake: Accepting their offer instead of going into politics and ruling the world.

» **Reading:** *Too many newspapers (Indy is favourite!) and not enough novels.* **Watching:** *Too much news, anything with Rik Mayall, the Rolling Stones or Helen Mirren in and not enough documentaries.* **Listening:** *A very catholic range from Beethoven to the Rolling Stones, Villa-Lobos to Pink Floyd. And the phone.* **Relaxing to:** *We live on a farm and I have lots of CDs by the above artists: it's a mix of both.*

» *Married, 4 children*

Ian Stewart

4.8.60

Edinburgh Evening News, 108 Holyrood Road, Edinburgh EH8 8AS
T 0131 620 8703
E smarshall@scotsman.com

Occupation: Editor, Edinburgh Evening News

Education: Royal High School, Edinburgh; Napier College, Edinburgh

Career highlights: Royal Marines, 1979-82; Nottingham Evening Post, 1986-91; The Scotsman, 1991-98; Scottish Daily Mail, 1998-99; Scotland on Sunday, 1999-2001.

» **Relaxing to:** *Mountain biking, reading, cigar smoking.*

» *Married, 2 children*

Charlotte Stockting

Wellington House, 69-71 Upper Ground, London SE1 9PQ
T 020 7667 8745
E charlotte.stockting@hellomagazine.com

Occupation: Publisher, HELLO! and hellomagazine.com

Other positions: Publisher, Elle and Elle Decoration; Marketing and Research Director, Carlton Screen Advertising; Marketing Director, TAG Heuer, Oris, Maurice Lacroix; Media Buyer, Saatchi & Saatchi.
Publications: Favourite Mag (other than HELLO!) Vanity Fair; Favourite TV Ad, Combover for Hamlet Cigars; Favourite Radio Ad, Archers for Volvo Motors; Favourite Poster Campaign, I think, therefore IBM.
Awards: None
Education: Ashford School for Girls, Kent; Coventry and Kingston
Career highlights: Becoming publisher of my favourite weekly magazine, in 2000!
Mentor: Currently my boss, of course. Previously Sue Phipps, publisher of Options and Country Homes & Interiors.
Big break: Getting a job in the media department of Saatchi & Saatchi - I have Nick Lockett to thank for that!
Big mistake: Too many to mention.

» **Reading:** *See above.* **Watching:** *Anything on C5 after 9pm, and EastEnders.* **Listening:** *Radio 4 Breakfast.* **Relaxing to:** *What's that?* » *Married, no kids but a dog which might as well be!*

Mark Story 10.5.55

Mappin House, 4 Winsley Street, London W1W 8HF
T 020 7975 8100
E mark.story@emap.com

Occupation: Managing Director, Kiss and Q Radio

Awards: Sony Award winner; New York Radio Gold Medal; Premios Ondos Gold winner; Fellow, Radio Academy, 1999.
Education: Dublin High School; School of Law, Trinity College, Dublin
Career highlights: Producer, RTE Radio 1978-83; Senior Producer, Capital Radio 1983-88, BBC Radio 1 1988-90; Programme Director, Piccadilly Radio 1990-95, Virgin Radio 1995-97; Managing Director, Magic 105.4 1998-present, Kiss 100 FM 1999 and Magic 105.4fm.

» **Relaxing to:** *Collecting oriental art.*

Sir Peter Stothard 28.2.51

TLS, Times House, 1 Pennington Street, London E98 1BS
T 020 7782 4960
E peter.stothard@the-tls.co.uk

Occupation: Editor, The Times Literary Supplement

Other positions: Formerly Editor of The Times, 1992-2002.
Publications: Book, Thirty Days, A Month at the Heart of Blair's War, 2003.
Awards: What The Papers Say Editor of the Year, 1999.
Education: Brentwood School, Essex; Trinity College, Oxford
Career highlights: BBC Trainee (failed), 1974-75; Sunday Times Business and Political Reporter (one year off for industrial dispute), 1979-81; Times Features Editor and Chief Leader Writer, 1983-86; Times Deputy Editor, 1986-92; Times US Editor, 1989-92; Times Editor, 1992-2002; Editor of The Times Literary Supplement, 2002-present.
Mentor: Sir Harold Evans
Big break: Reporting the contents of the radical 1981 budget before the Cabinet knew about it - in the days when budgets did not leak as they do today.
Big mistake: One or two staff appointments best left unspecified.

» **Reading:** *Ancient and modern literature.* **Watching:** *Birds.* **Listening:** *Miles Davis.* **Relaxing to:** *Not as easily as I would like.* » *Married, 2 children*

Edward Stourton 25.11.61

c/o Today, Television Centre, White City, London W12 7RJ
T 020 8624 9644
E Edward.Stourton@bbc.co.uk

Occupation: Presenter of Today programme, Sunday programme and BBC current affairs and religious programmes

Other positions: Author
Publications: Worked for Correspondent, Assignment, Panorama, Analysis and produced many stand-alone programmes and series for BBC television and radio. Written work includes Absolute Truth (pub 1998) and In the Footsteps of St Paul (pub 2004).
Awards: Sony gold, best radio current affairs programme 1998; Sony bronze, News Broadcaster Award, 2003; Amnesty Award, best television current affairs programme 2000.
Education: Ampleforth College, York; Trinity College, Cambridge
Career highlights: Working on Channel Four News in its first days - when everyone thought it would fold. Covering America in the final years of the Reagan presidency, working as Diplomatic Editor for ITN during a period of exceptionally intense international activity (the end of the Cold War, the Gulf War, the wars in the former Yugoslavia, the Maastricht negotiations in Europe)

and covering pretty much every international story that was going. All Radio 4 series that I have done and Today almost every morning I do it.

Mentor: Pass

Big break: Becoming Washington Correspondent for Channel Four News at 27.

Big mistake: Exclusively killing off Abu Nidal on the air (he was in fact very much alive).

» **Reading:** *As many new novels as possible, some biography - once in a while I give myself a dose of good poetry.* **Watching:** *Not much - Channel Four News regularly, good drama and comedy, BBC 2 current affairs and history.* **Listening:** *Lots - the radio dial seldom moves from Radio 4 (the World at One a daily appointment) and on CD mostly choral works (requiems a particular favourite) and trash from the early 1970s.* **Relaxing to:** *Gardening, skiing, playing tennis, swimming, reading, eating and talking.* » *Married, 3 children*

Janet Street-Porter 27.12.46

c/o Emma Hardy, Princess Television, Princess Studios, Whiteleys, 151 Queensway, London W2 4SB

T 020 7985 1917

E talent@princesstv.com

Occupation: Journalist, broadcaster and TV producer

Other positions: Editor-at-Large, Independent Newspapers; President, Ramblers' Association, 1994-96.

Publications: (With Tim Street-Porter) The British Teapots (1985); Scandal (1983); As the Crow Flies: A Walk from Edinburgh to London - in a Straight Line (1998); Coast to Coast: From Dungeness to Weston-super-Mare and Cardiff to Conwy (1998); Baggage: My Childhood (2004).

Awards: BAFTA award for originality, 1988; Prix Italia, opera, The Vampyr, 1993; Honorary FRIBA; FRTS, 1994.

Education: Lady Margaret Grammar School; Architectural Association

Career highlights: Writer, Petticoat Magazine, 1968; Daily Mail, 1969-71; Evening Standard, 1971-73; Contributor, Queen, Vogue, etc; Presenter, LBC Radio, 1973; TV Presenter for LWT 1975-81 including London Weekend Show; Saturday Night People; Around Midnight; Six O'Clock Show; produced and devised series 1981-88 including Twentieth Century Box; Get Fresh; Bliss; Network 7; Head of Youth and Entertainment Features, BBC TV, 1988-94; Head of Independent Production for Entertainment, 1994; Managing Director, Live TV, Mirror Group, 1994-95; Editor, the Independent on Sunday, 1999-2001; TV Presenter, Design Awards, BBC 2; J'Accuse, C4 (1996); Travels with Pevsner, BBC 2 (1997); Coast to Coast, BBC 2 (1998); The Midnight Hour, BBC 2 (1998); As the Crow Flies, BBC 2 (1999); All the Rage, one-woman show, Edinburgh Festival 2003, tour 2004.

» **Relaxing to:** *Walking, modern art.* » *Divorced*

Sir Howard Stringer

Royal Television Society, 5th Floor, Kildare House, 3 Dorset Rise, London EC4Y 8EN

T 020 7822 2810

E info@rts.org.uk

Occupation: Vice-President, Royal Television Society

Other positions: Chairman and Chief Executive Officer, Sony Corporation; Board Director, Sony Corporation; Board Member, Sony BMG Music Entertainment; Chairman, American Film Institute Board of Trustees; Member, Board of Trustees, Museum of Television and Radio (USA); Board Member, InterContinental Hotels Group; Board Member, New York/Presbyterian Hospital, American Theatre Wing; Board Member, American Friends of the British Museum; Board Member, Corporate Leadership Committee of the Lincoln Center for the Performing Arts.

Publications: Award-winning programmes include The Rockefellers, The Palestinians, A Tale of Two Irelands, The Defense of the United States, The Boat People, The Boston Goes To China, The Fire Next Door, The CIA's Secret Army.

Awards: U.S. Army Commendation Medal, meritorious achievement, service in Vietnam (1965-67); as Executive Producer, CBS Reports documentary unit 1981-84, 31 Emmys, 4 Peabody Awards, 3 Alfred I du Pont-Columbia University Awards, 3 Christopher Awards, 3 Overseas Press Club Awards, 1 ABA Silver Gavel, 1 Robert F Kennedy Grand Prize; 9 individual Emmys as a writer, director and producer; International Radio and Television Society's Foundation Award, 1994; First Amendment Leadership Award, Radio & Television News Directors' Foundation, Washington, DC, 1996; Broadcasting and Cable Hall of Fame, 1996; Knight Bachelor, 1999; UJA-Federation of New York, Steven J Ross Humanitarian Award, 1999; Royal Television Society, Welsh Hall of Fame, 1999; Public Service Award, Phoenix House, 2002; Honorary Fellow, Merton College, Oxford; Honorary Fellow, Welsh College of Music and Drama; Honorary Doctorate, London Institute, 1993.

Education: Oxford University

Career highlights: Writer, Director and Producer, CBS, 1974-76; Executive Producer, CBS Reports documentary unit, 1976-81 (see awards); Executive Producer, CBS Evening News, 1981-84; President, CBS News, 1986-88; President, CBS 1988-95; Chairman and CEO, Tele-TV, 1995-97; joined Sony, 1997; Chairman and Chief Executive Officer, Sony Corporation, 2005-present.

» *Married, 2 children*

James Studholme
10.2.60

Blink Productions, 181 Wardour Street,
London W1F 8WZ
T 020 7494 0747
E info@blinkprods.com

Occupation: Proprietor, Blink Productions, Blinkink and Colonel Blimp

Publications: In chronological order, Persil, Skinhead; Yorkie, Rock Chunk; Terrence Higgins Trust, Hopping Pecker; Guinness, Chain; Whiskas, Insights; Freelander; Drink/Drive, Dave; X Box, Ear Tennis; Orange, Dance.
Awards: Numerous D&AD Pencils, Cannes Lions, BTAA Arrows etc; Campaign Magazine Production Company of the Year, 1997.
Education: Eton; Reading University
Career highlights: Mostly the list above. Getting a New Zealand Woolboard Shearing Certificate. Starting to produce at 23 for Dick 'the first straw is the last straw' McNeil. Working with Tony Kaye. Learning how not to run a company from Tony. Starting Blink with Bob Lawrie. Finding Doug Foster, Ivan Zacharias, Dominic Murphy, Blue Source and Dougal Wilson amongst others. Travelling to places I never would have seen otherwise. Working with BMP. Assembling the gang we presently are. Founding Stink. Selling Stink. Seeing Stink succeed. Working with John Hassay and Colonel Blimp. Starting Blinkink. Finding Pleix, Lynn Fox, Ben Hibon, Simon Willows and Ruari Robinson. Starting Furlined in Santa Monica with Diane McArter.
Mentor: My Dad and Ray Walledge.
Big break: Becoming the librarian and inventing the library at MPC on 10th February 1982.
Big mistake: I never ever make mistakes.

» **Reading:** *The Week, Daily Telegraph (mostly from the back).* **Watching:** *Not enough.* **Listening:** *Masses, songs mostly, 70s and 80s, alt country, folk.* **Relaxing to:** *Go to Devon.*
» *Married, 3 children*

Richard Sutcliffe
25.11.72

Jordan House, 47 Brunswick Place, London N1 6EB
T 020 7608 6500
E Richard.sutcliffe@smdpublishing.co.uk

Occupation: Managing Editor, Front and Hotdog

Other positions: Formerly Editor, X-Ray magazine; Publishing Director, Jockey Slut and Sleazenation magazines.
Publications: X-Ray magazine.
Awards: 3 Magazine Design Awards for Sleazenation.
Education: Notre Dame, Sheffield
Career highlights: Successfully launching X-Ray with no money into a crowded market, and keeping a number of magazines afloat while Highbury went down the pan were two of the hardest but ultimately most satisfying achievements.
Mentor: Almost everyone I've ever worked with.
Big break: Becoming Publishing Director of Jockey Slut and Sleazenation.
Big mistake: Putting the wrong barcode on a cover and costing the company thousands to get it stickered over.

» **Reading:** *Private Eye, media and sport websites, the Observer, Sun and loads of magazines for work.* **Watching:** *Wall-to-wall comedy and football.* **Listening:** *Radio 5, at least a couple of hours a day and music the rest of the time.* **Relaxing to:** *A lot of gigs and extended DVD sessions.*
» *Single, no children*

Alex Sutherland
29.01.59

Five TV, 22 Long Acre, London WC2E 9LY
T 020 7550 5555
E alex.sutherland@five.tv

Occupation: Commissioning Editor, History Programming, Five TV

Other positions: Deputy Commissioning Editor, Science and Current Affairs Programmes, Channel 4; before that I was an Executive Producer, Series Producer and Producer/Director in TV, and before that I was Media Correspondent for the Sunday Times and a print journo on trade mags for the film and TV industries.
Awards: As Director, Indie award for best documentary for Loss of the Marchioness, a Dispatches Special for Channel 4, 1993; The Wincott Business Programme award for Hamleys for Channel 4, 2001 (as Executive Producer).
Education: Many (my father was in the diplomatic service and dragged us round the world); latterly Sherborne School for Girls; Bedales; York University; City University, London
Career highlights: As a TV director, winning an award for 'best documentary' for the first film I directed, The Loss of the Marchioness, for C4, and directing the film which exposed the two paediatric cardiac surgeons in the Bristol Royal Infirmary heart scandal, a story which reverberates within the NHS today; as a commissioner, commissioning the documentary How the Twin Towers Fell for C4, which got the highest audience for a factual programme that year, and at Five, commissioning Fighter Plane Dig...Live! a 90-minute live show during which we found the remains of the WW2 plane which saved Buckingham Palace during the Battle of Britain, and coming up with the series Big Ideas that Changed the World in which world leaders and thinkers, including Mikhail Gorbachev and Desmond Tutu, told the histories of Communism, Christianity and other influential ideas in history.
Mentor: David Lloyd - formerly Head of News and Current Affairs at Channel 4. He gave me my first break as a TV Producer/Director.
Big break: Getting a freelance job at the Sunday Times, from Screen International, the trade mag where I'd cut my journalistic teeth, and being given the chance to make my first TV documentary (the Loss of the Marchioness) through my own company soon after I moved into TV.
Big mistake: More missed opportunity, not getting to make what became 1900 House, one of the most successful factual formatted shows for Channel 4, after my independent company developed the idea a year earlier for the channel.

» **Reading:** *Guardian, Observer and Sun (delivered daily), Radio Times, digested TV press cuttings, and at last, now my kids can play on their own on holiday, books!*

Watching: *Newsy stuff, BBC News and Newsnight regularly, property shows like Grand Designs, factual formats like Who Do You Think You Are, comedy like In The Thick Of It, occasionally a drama like Life on Mars, Celebrity Big Brother, and Dick and Dom in da Bungalow with my kids.* **Listening:** *Radio 4 (mostly), Radio 2 (occasionally), Radio 1 and Heart FM (very occasionally).* **Relaxing to:** *With great difficulty. I recite 'thinking, thinking' during Yoga – which is supposed to stop you thinking.* » *Married, 2 children*

Emma Swain
10.6.63

Room 6060, BBC Television Centre, Shepherds Bush, London W12 7RJ
T 020 8576 7142
E emma.swain@bbc.co.uk

Occupation: Commissioner, Specialist Factual, BBC TV

Other positions: Freelance director
Publications: Egypt, Coast, Springwatch, Big Cat Diary, Should I Worry About.
Education: St Martin's School of Art
Career highlights: Freelance director for many years making films for BBC and C4, credits include science series Labours of Eve (about reproductive technology) and The Limit (extreme engineering), as well as films for Comic Relief and even a film about mothers-in-law; since working in Specialist Factual, executive produced series for BBC One on Space (with Sam Neill), pre-natal medicine (Life Before Birth) and The Secrets of Happiness; moved from development in BBC Science to the role of Deputy Commissioner; Commissioner for Specialist Factual since April 2002; commissioning Science, History, Business and Natural History for BBC One, Two, Three and Four from in-house and independent suppliers. Recent commissions include British Isles: A Natural History; Pompei; British Battlefields; Little Angels; Seven Wonders of the Industrial World; Should I Worry About...?; Coast; Springwatch.
Mentor: Carl Hawlam, Glenwyn Benson, and Jana Bennett.
Big break: My first directing job, for Comic Relief.
Big mistake: Directing and sound recording a film New Zealand key contributor sync in gale-force winds without a wind-shield on the mic.

» **Reading:** *Novels, magazines.* **Watching:** *Almost anything.* **Listening:** *Handel opera arias, Keith Jarrett and Alison Goldfrapp.* **Relaxing to:** *Long lunches with friends and children.* » *Cohabiting, 2 children*

Christy Swords
8.5.73

London TV Centre, Upper Ground SE1 9LT
T 020 7261 3951
E christy.swords@itv.com

Occupation: Director of Regulatory Affairs, ITV plc; Managing Director, ITV London

Other positions: Political Consultant, GPC/Prima Europe; Researcher/Assistant Producer, NHK TV.
Education: Wimbledon College; Oxford University

» *Married, 2 children*

T

Professor Richard Tait
22.5.47

Bute Building, Cardiff University, Cardiff CF10 3NB
T 029 2087 4430
E richard.tait@bbc.co.uk

Occupation: Governor, BBC

Other positions: Professor of Journalism and Director of the Centre for Journalism Studies, Cardiff University; Trustee, John Schofield Memorial Trust; Member, Advisory Board, Kurt Schork Memorial Fund; Former Member, Government Communications Review Group.
Awards: CBE, 2003; FRTS, 1996; Fellow, Society of Editors, 2002.
Education: Bradfield College; New College, Oxford
Career highlights: Researcher, Money Programme, BBC, 1974-75; Producer, Nationwide, BBC, 1976-82; Editor, People and Power, BBC, 1982; Editor, Money Programme, BBC 1983-85; Editor, Newsnight, BBC, 1985-87; Editor, General Election Results Programme, BBC, 1987; Editor, Channel Four News, ITN, 1987-90; Editor, Channel Four programmes, 1990-95; Editor-in-Chief, ITN, 1995-2002; Member, International Board, IPI, 1998-present, Vice-Chairman, 2000-present; Member, Advisory Board, International News Safety Institute, 2003-present; Governor, BBC, 2004-present.

» **Relaxing to:** *History, ballet, opera, tennis, skiing.*
» *Married, 1 daughter*

Steve Taschini
18.12.61

269 Banbury Road, Oxford OX2 7DW
T 08459 311444
E Steve.Taschini@bbc.co.uk

Occupation: Executive Editor, BBC Oxford

Career highlights: Worked in BBC Local Radio since 1985, left to present for Sky News and BBC Regional TV News in 1996; rejoined BBC Radio Cumbria in 1998; Managing Editor BBC Radio Kent 2000-02; Business Manager BBC English Regions 2002-04.
Big break: Getting a freelance contract with BBC Radio Merseyside in 1985.
Big mistake: Staying in one place too long (13 years).

» **Reading:** *Most newspapers, historical and semi-factual novels.* **Watching:** *Films, news, documentaries, Never Mind the Buzzcocks, Open All Hours, Game On, Last Orders, Two Pints of Lager and a Packet of Crisps, Dinner Ladies, Discovery Wings...* **Listening:** *Radio Oxford, R4, R2, R1, local commercial and other BBC local radio stations when travelling.* **Relaxing to:** *Travelling, eating out, watching TV, reading, maintaining my Jaguar XK8, gardening, fixing things, car boots, collecting antiques.*

Ceri Thomas

11.7.76

AG192, 80 Wood Lane, London W12 0TT
T 020 8433 1651
E ceri.thomas@bbc.co.uk

Occupation: Editor, Easy Gardening magazine

Publications: Easy Gardening magazine
Education: University of Reading
Career highlights: Since leaving university with a degree in horticulture, I've been lucky enough to pursue a career in gardening magazines. I started as a garden writer for EMAP, then moved to the BBC where I've been a garden writer, website editor and now magazine editor.
Big break: Getting my first job by doing work experience in my Easter holiday before leaving university.

» **Reading:** *Grazia and Easy Living, plus all of the gardening titles.* **Watching:** *EastEnders, Property Ladder, Grand Designs.* **Listening:** *The Archers, The Today Programme and random Radio 4.* **Relaxing to:** *At home with my husband and dog, plus weekly trips to the cinema.* » *Married, no children*

Mark Thomas

2.3.71

1 Canada Square, London E14 5AP
T 020 7293 3614
E m.thomas@mgn.co.uk

Occupation: Editor, the People

Other positions: Deputy Editor, Sunday Mirror; Assistant Editor, the Mirror; Features Editor, the Mirror; Chief Reporter, News of the World, the People.
Education: Rutlish School, London
Career highlights: Being on Sunday newspapers during the John Major 'back to basics' era when it was almost impossible to find a minister with his wife; working for Piers Morgan first at the News of the World and later at the Mirror - a roller-coaster ride at times! And finally being made Editor of the People, my first national newspaper.
Big break: Getting my first job at Fleet Street News Agency - launch pad for so many into Fleet Street.

» *Married, 4 children*

David Thompson

19.7.54

1st Floor, 1 Mortimer Street, London W1T 3JA
T 020 7735 0251
E david.thompson@bbc.co.uk

Occupation: Head of BBC Films

Other positions: Documentary Producer and Director, BBC; Exec Producer, BBC Drama; English and General Studies teacher, Bedales School.
Publications: As a Producer, numerous television films including Shadowlands, The Firm, Road, Conspiracy, The Gathering Storm. As an Executive Producer in film and television reponsible for over 60 films including Billy Elliott, Iris, Dirty Pretty Things, My Summer of Love, A Cock and Bull Story and Mrs Henderson Presents.
Awards: Include 3 British Academy Awards; 3 Emmys; 1 International Emmy; 2 Golden Globes; 2 Golden Nymph Monte Carlo Television Festival Awards; an ACE Award. As Executive Producer, responsible for films which have won many other awards including an Oscar and 4 British Academy Awards for new talent.
Education: Charterhouse School; St Catherine's College, Cambridge
Career highlights: Winning a table tennis competition aged 12 and Emmys and BAFTAs, but most of all working with new talent and bringing productions to fruition.
Mentor: Alan Clarke had a major influence on me, and also William Nicholson.
Big break: Getting offered a job at the BBC Drama Department to set up and run a series of new films called Screenplay.
Big mistake: Failing to set up as an independent producer when I had the opportunity!

» **Reading:** *Mainly on holiday, novels for which the film rights have already gone, and far too many scripts.* **Watching:** *Lots of movies and mainly comedy on television, and some brilliant documentaries.* **Listening:** *Classical music and also very loud sounds from my son's recording studio.* **Relaxing to:** *Tennis and alcohol, sometimes together.* » *Married, 2 children*

Graeme Thompson

24.12.60

ITV Tyne Tees, Television House, The Watermark, Gateshead NE11 9SZ
T 0191 404 8760
E graeme.thompson@itv.com

Occupation: Managing Director and Controller of Programmes, ITV Tyne Tees

Other positions: Chair, Live Theatre, Newcastle; Chair, Royal Television Society North East and Borders Centre; Board Director, Northern Film and Media.
Publications: As Producer/Executive Producer: North East Tonight with Mike Neville, Dr Rock's Guide to Hollywood, Waiters (drama), Girls Club (drama), He's Done It! (Jonny Wilkinson profile for ITV), Hard is the Road (music documentary), The Dales Diary, The Way We Were, Wilfred (short film).
Awards: RTS awards Best Regional News Programme; New York Festival Award, Dr Rock's Guide to Hollywood.
Education: Boldon School; Darlington College
Career highlights: Reporter, Berrows Newspapers 1976-79; Express and Star 1979-83; BBC Radio York 1983-87; Producer, Radio 4 1987-88; News Editor, Yorkshire Television, 1989-92; Producer, Tyne Tees Television 1993-95; Head of News, TTTV 1995-97; Director of Broadcasting 1997-2003; Managing Director 2003-.
Big break: Joining the BBC.
Big mistake: Too many to mention!

» **Reading:** *Thrillers, Private Eye, Guardian, Darlington and Stockton Times, Empire.* **Watching:** *News, movies, musicals, documentaries and football.* **Listening:** *Jazz, Sinatra, Broadway soundtracks, the Today Programme and The Archers.* **Relaxing to:** *Watching football, writing pantomimes and keeping up with my children.* » *Married to Alyson, 3 children*

Jeremy Thompson

Sky News, Grant Way, Isleworth TW7 5QD
T 020 7705 3000
E Jeremy.Thompson@bskyb.com

Occupation: Presenter, Sky News Live at 5

Other positions: Africa Correspondent; Chief USA Correspondent, Sky News; Chief Sports Correspondent, Asia Correspondent and Africa Correspondent, ITN; North of England Correspondent, BBC TV News.
Awards: Two News Emmys; 4 RTS awards; 2 Baftas; TRIC Satellite/Digital TV Personality of the Year 2004.
Education: Sevenoaks School; King's, Worcester

» **Reading:** *Cambridge Evening News Reporter; BBC Radio and TV; ITN; Sky News.* » *Married, 2 sons, 4 grandchildren*

Mark Thompson 31.7.57

BBC Television Centre, Wood Lane, London W12 7RJ
T 020 8743 8000
E mark.thompson@bbc.co.uk

Occupation: Director-General, BBC

Other positions: Chairman, Edinburgh International Television Festival, 1996.
Publications: At BBC Two, drama including Our Mutual Friend, The Cops, Amongst Women, Shooting the Past; entertainment and comedy including I'm Alan Partridge, The Fast Show, The Royle Family, Big Train; factual, arts and leisure programmes including The Nazis - A Warning from History, Storyville, Naked, Back to the Floor, and Ground Force.
Education: Stonyhurst College, Lancashire; Merton College, Oxford
Career highlights: Editor, Oxford University newspaper, Isis; Production Trainee, BBC, 1979; assisted in launch of Watchdog, 1981; assisted in launch of Breakfast Time, 1983; Output Editor, Newsnight, 1985; Editor, Nine O'Clock News, 1988; Editor, Panorama 1990; Head of Features, 1992; Head of Factual Programmes, 1994; Controller, BBC Two, 1996; Director, National and Regional Broadcasting, BBC, 1999; Director of Television, BBC, 2000; Chief Executive, Channel 4, 2001-04; Director-General, BBC, 2004-present.

» **Relaxing to:** *Flying aircraft.* » *Married, 3 children*

Sean Thompson 24.9.70

Wieden + Kennedy, 16 Hanbury Street E1 6QR
T 020 7194 7012
E sean.thompson@wk.com

Occupation: Creative Director and Senior Copywriter, Wieden + Kennedy

Publications: Honda Grrr commercial and integrated; Honda Everyday commercial; Honda Dreams commercial; Honda CrazySensible campaign; Aiwa Worldwide launch; Nike Run London integrated campaign; Sony PlayStation TV campaign; Sony PlayStation Le Petit Chef; Nike Do Running Campaign; Crisis Homeless Charity press campaign...
Awards: 2 gold D&AD Pencils; 12 silver D&AD Pencils; 1 Cannes Grand Prix; 1 Cannes titanium award; 1 Cannes Journalist's Award; 7 Cannes Lions; 1 British Television ITV Best Commercial of the Year; 5 gold BTA Awards; 2 gold One Show Awards; 1 silver; 1 platinum Creative Circle; 9 golds; 1 Andy Best in Show...
Education: Gunnersbury Catholic School; Newcastle College of Art and Design
Career highlights: Starting at CDP at 19 years of age, keeping my head down writing trade ads; getting fired from CDP and retiring from advertising at 22; getting back into the business thanks to my ex-CDP colleague, David Horry; teaming up with my long-time Creative Partner Ros Sinclair; winning our first D&AD Pencil; moving back to CDP; getting hired at Simon's Palmer; winning loads more awards working on Nike and the early days of PlayStation; becoming a Group Head; joining Leagas Delaney as a Creative Director; leaving Leagas Delaney; joining Fallon; getting fired from Fallon; going freelance on my own, doing all my own planning, strategies, account handling, art direction, copywriting whilst working for practically every creative and not so creative agency in town; finally joining an agency where it was all about to happen, rather than had happened, Wieden and Kennedy; breaking away from traditional media; winning awards for integrated.
Mentor: I'd have to say Soichiro Honda. A bit of a strange one, but the more I learn about the man's maverick nature the more I admire him. He was after all the person who sprayed the local tax men with a water cannon every single morning until they reduced his tax bill. Genius.
Big break: Winning a week's work experience at CDP in a competition at Newcastle College, which eventually turned into a job.
Big mistake: I don't regret any of it. I've worked for some of the biggest bastards in the business but I've learnt something from every single one of them (including how not to do it).

» **Reading:** *The internet (all day long), the odd contemporary novel, the Guardian (crawler), the Word, the Gruffalo (every night), in-flight magazines, (I'm forever tearing out articles from all over the place intending to stick them into scrapbooks).* **Watching:** *Queens Park Rangers Football Club, animation, films, documentaries, rubbish TV like Lost.* **Listening:** *Funk, soul, jazz, dance, hip-hop, easy listening, power ballads.* **Relaxing to:** *Doesn't sound very macho, but a candlelit bath with lavender oil does the trick.* » *Married, 1 child*

Alexander Thomson 22.12.60

Channel 4 News, ITN, 200 Gray's Inn Road, London WC1X 8XZ
T 020 7430 4601
E alex.thomson@itn.co.uk

Occupation: Presenter and Chief Correspondent, Channel 4 News

Publications: A wide variety of articles in journals and press of many years particularly on media issues. A number of reports on foreign news

stories in various nationals when on assignment. A travel book.
Education: Cranbourne Comprehensive, Basingstoke; Queen Mary's Sixth Form, Basingstoke; University College, Oxford; Cardiff School of Journalism
Career highlights: Reporter, Channel 4 news; Reporter, BBC Northern Ireland 'Spotlight' current affairs programme.
» *Single, 2 children*

Brian Thomson
21.11.18

D C Thomson, 2 Albert Square, Dundee DD1 9QJ
T 01382 223 131
E tstewart@dcthomson.co.uk

Occupation: Director, D C Thomson & Co. Ltd

Awards: Hon. DLitt, Abertay, Dundee, 2002.
Education: Charterhouse School
Career highlights: War service 1939-45; 1st Fife and Forfar Yeomanry, on Staff, DAQMG 1st Armoured Division, North Africa and Italy, 1943-44; GSO2 Instructor, Staff College, Haifa, 1944-46; Lt-Col, Fife and Forfar Yeomanry TA, 1953-56; DC Thomson & Co Ltd, 1937; Director, John Leng & Co Ltd, 1948-present; Southern Television, 1959-88; Alliance Trust and Second Alliance Trust, 1961-89; DL Fife, 1988.
» **Relaxing to:** *Golf, shooting.* » *Widower, 5 children*

Gordon Thomson
13.1.72

Time Out, Universal House, 251 Tottenham Court Road, London W1T 7AB
T 020 7813 6118
E gordonthomson@timeout.com

Occupation: Editor, Time Out magazine

Awards: Shortlisted, BSME New Editor of the Year award, 2005.
Education: University of Glasgow
Career highlights: Deputy Editor, Observer Sport Monthly; Senior Editor, Maxim magazine; Assistant Producer, Sky Sports News; Researcher, Fantasy World Cup (1998 Skinner and Baddiel show); Freelance Writer, Marie Claire, men's mags, Sunday Times, Four Four Two, among others; Contributor, Goal magazine.
Mentor: Dave Cottrell, Editor of the sadly defunct Goal magazine (IPC). A brilliant journalist who somehow managed to be the friend of the staff and their boss at the same time, an incredibly tricky thing to pull off. He always knew instinctively when to be funny in print, which he did wonderfully, and when to play it straight. A great writer too and showed me that the detail in journalism is crucial (his captions were always superb). Made me feel like I could do whatever I wanted to do, and gave me an enormous amount of freedom to do it.
Big break: Getting a foot in the door at Goal without any writing or journalistic experience - a magazine with an incredible wealth of talent; I soaked it all up. Or else being appointed Deputy Editor of Observer Sport Monthly - working in a newspaper environment for two years was fascinating after years in magazines and I learned a great deal about editing copy as well as making some great contacts.
Big mistake: Two years working in TV production. I was trying to be jack of all trades. Stick to what you are good at, that's what I learned.
» **Reading:** *Modern American literature, I'm a huge fan of Paul Auster; Follow Follow (Rangers fanzine), Guardian, Observer, Indie, Uncut, the Word, all the predictable blokey stuff!* **Watching:** *Not a great deal. Shameless, Peep Show, Newsnight, Sky sports, Rangers TV.* **Listening:** *Wide range of tastes, particular interest in folk, country, Americana, northern soul, new wave. Artists? Dylan, Talking Heads, John Martyn, Ryan Adams, Bowie, Tom Waits, Teenage Fanclub, Roddy Frame etc.* **Relaxing to:** *Listening to music, watching bands, cinema, eating out, theatre, showing the kids London, spending time with family.*
» *Married, 3 children*

Robert Thomson
11.3.61

Times House, 1 Pennington Street, London E98 1TT
T 020 7782 5000
E denise.renner@thetimes.co.uk

Occupation: Editor, The Times

Publications: The Judges: a portrait of the Australian judiciary, 1986; (jointly) The Chinese Army, 1990; (Editor) True Fiction, 1998.
Education: Royal Melbourne Institute of Technology
Career highlights: Finance and General Affairs Reporter, The Herald, Melbourne, then Sydney, 1979-83; Senior Feature Writer, Sydney Morning Herald, 1983-85; Financial Times, Beijing Correspondent, 1985-89; Tokyo Correspondent, 1989-94; Foreign News Editor, 1994-96; Assistant Editor, then Editor, Weekend FT, 1996-98; Managing Editor based in New York, 1998-2002; Chairman, Arts International, 2001-02; Director, Society of American Business Editors and Writers, 2001-02.
» **Watching:** *Cinema.* **Relaxing to:** *Reading, tennis.*
» *Married, 2 sons*

Nick Thorogood
5.7.72

ITV, 200 Gray's Inn Road, London WC1X 8HF
T 020 7843 8132
E lucy.campbell@itv.com

Occupation: Editor, ITV Day

Other positions: Head of Lifestyle Channels, UKTV; Development Executive, BBC Birmingham; Freelance Programme Director.
Education: Bournemouth
Career highlights: Worked on the rebrand of ITV Day and was part of the team that brought Jeremy Kyle, Paul O'Grady and various new titles to the channel; I created two channels for UKTV and saw UKTV Style become one of the top 10 channels; I have also worked on programmes for all terrestrial channels and the leading satellite channels.
Mentor: William G Stewart
Big break: Assistant Studio Manager on 15-1.

Big mistake: Stepping on Stephanie Beacham.

›› **Reading:** *The Guardian, Daily Mail, Mirror, Private Eye, the Week and Heat.* **Watching:** *From 0600-2400 I consume as much TV as I can - in particular I am fascinated by lifestyle and daytime programming. To relax I enjoy crime dramas, soap operas and light entertainment.* **Listening:** *Talking books, speech radio and I have an undefinable music collection.* **Relaxing to:** *Socialising, music, entertainment and TV.*

Nicholas Thorpe

4.2.64

c/o World Affairs Unit, BBC News, Wood Lane, London W12 7RJ

T +36 209 538 284
E nick.thorpe@bbc.co.uk

Occupation: BBC Correspondent, Budapest

Other positions: Contributions to newspapers, including the Guardian.
Publications: From Our Own Correspondent, Profile Books, 2005; Un-Earth, stories from Bosnian war, 2004 (theatre); The Vineleaf and the Rose, 2002 (film); Vigilance, 1997 (film); The Fairy Island, 1993 (film); Tearing Down the Curtain - the Observer Book of the Revolutions in Eastern Europe (1990).
Education: Reading, Berks; Dakar, Senegal; Freiburg, FRG
Career highlights: I was the first western journalist based in Hungary, in 1986. I covered the collapse of Communism throughout eastern Europe, including the revolutions in Romania, Czechoslovakia and East Germany. Then the break-up of Yugoslavia, and some of the wars that resulted. In 1993 I also covered the UNTAC elections in Cambodia. Since 2001, I have travelled extensively in Turkey and the Middle East for the BBC.
Mentor: Istvan Siklos, the former Head of the BBC Hungarian Section.
Big break: Covering the aftermath of the riots in Brasov, Romania, in 1987, and taking Silviu Brucan's statement to the West.
Big mistake: Becoming a journalist.

›› **Reading:** *Books on religion, especially Christianity and Islam, novels, poetry.* **Watching:** *Films, especially Tarkovsky, Paradzhanov, Jim Jarmusch and Mike Leigh.* **Listening:** *BBC Radio, Hungarian jazz saxophonist Mihaly Dresch, and a lot of other music.* **Relaxing to:** *Playing with my children, growing vegetables, running, walking.* ›› *Married, 5 boys*

Simon Tiffin

Esquire, National Magazine House, 72 Broadwick Street, London W1F 9EP

T 020 7439 5000
E simon.tiffin@natmags.co.uk

Occupation: Editor, Esquire magazine

Awards: Editor of the Year (Men's Magazines), BSME Awards 2003.
Career highlights: Chief subeditor and sports editor, GQ; Deputy Editor, GQ Active, 1996-98; Editor, GQ Active, 1998-2001; Deputy Editor, Harpers & Queen 2001-03; Editor, Esquire, 2003-present.

Sir Ray Tindle

9.10.30

The Old Court House, Union Road, Farnham, Surrey GU9 7PT

T 01252 735667
E wendy.craig@internet-today.co.uk

Occupation: Chairman and Editor, Tindle Newspapers Ltd

Publications: The press today and tomorrow.
Awards: CBE, OBE, DL, Knighthood.
Education: Torquay Grammar School; Strand School
Career highlights: I have been in the newspaper industry for 58 years following service in the wartime army, and am now the proprietor of over 200 newspaper titles and ten radio stations; I started as a dogsbody on a small local weekly after serving in the 1st Battalion of the Devonshire Regiment in the Far East, attaining the rank of Captain; I was elected President of the Newspaper Society - the industry's highest honour - in 1971, and am also a Fellow of the Chartered Institutes of Secretaries, Arbitrators and Journalists; in 1985 I became Master of the Worshipful Company of Stationers and Newspaper Makers; HRH The Prince of Wales showed a personal interest in a scheme I founded in 1984 to assist the unemployed. When unemployment was at its peak the ten Tindle Enterprise Centres operated 100 units providing rent-free premises for out-of-work people trying to start up a business or to become self-employed. The first Centre was formally opened in 1985 by the then Prime Minister, Margaret Thatcher.
Mentor: H R Davies, Director of the Newspaper Society.
Big break: The 1950 newspaper strike in London.
Big mistake: Not buying the Surrey Advertiser.

›› **Reading:** *Newspapers and crime fiction.* **Watching:** *Comedy.* **Listening:** *News.* **Relaxing to:** *Veteran cars.*
›› *Married to Beryl, 1 son, Owen*

Ben Tollett

7.12.72

DDB London, 12 Bishops Bridge Road, London W2 6AA

T 020 7258 3979
E ben.tollett@ddblondon.com

Occupation: Copywriter, DDB London

Other positions: Copywriter at KesselsKramer, Mother, Leagas Delaney and MCBD.
Awards: Are really nice things to have. I'd like more.
Education: University of Wales, Cardiff
Career highlights: Co-wrote the Travelocity ad campaign starring Alan Whicker.
Big mistake: Falling backwards off the stage at an awards show.

›› **Reading:** *Books, magazines, newspapers, ads, DVD covers, as much as I can (which never feels like enough).* **Watching:** *My back, news programmes, comedy programmes, films, documentaries, music videos. And far too many rubbish adverts.* **Listening:** *Radio 4.* **Relaxing to:** *With friends and alcohol.* ›› *Single, no children*

Deborah Tonroe
21.7.73

Marshall Mill, Marshall Street, Leeds LS11 9YJ
T 0113 367 4600
E deborah.tonroe@orange.co.uk

Occupation: Head of Commercial Development Multimedia Operations, Orange UK

Other positions: Head of Sport, Orange UK; Head of Commercial Development, PA; New Media Executive Producer, the Web Connection, Hong Kong; Business Development Manager, American Express, Hong Kong.
Education: Sheffield Hallam University

» *Married, no children*

Tim Toulmin
20.1.79

1 Salisbury Square, London EC4Y 8JB
T 020 7353 1248
E tim.toulmin@pcc.org.uk

Occupation: Director, Press Complaints Commission

Other positions: Acting Director, PCC, Jan-March 2004; Deputy Director, PCC, 2000-03.
Education: Repton School; Peterhouse, Cambridge

» *Single, no children*

Ed Tranter
18.5.73

St Giles House, 50 Poland Street, London W1F 7AX
T 020 7970 4318
E ed.tranter@centaur.co.uk

Occupation: Publisher, Marketing Week

Education: The Skinners School for Boys
Career highlights: My career followed the standard sales route as a Classified Exec on Printing World nine years ago and involved moving to Dotprint as an Online Sales Exec and then a move to Paper Europe as Display Manager. Centaur has definitely been the highlight with New Media Age being both an exciting marketplace and a great title. Marketing Week is a huge role and hopefully the highlights are still to come!
Mentor: I've been fortunate to work with a number of inspirational individuals in my career so far, many of whom are at Centaur, but all in all too many to name! Other than that, Bertie Wooster has always led a lifestyle I feel I was designed for, though as a Christian Jesus has to be the role model.
Big break: The Classified Ad Manager at Miller Freeman misreading my CV for a graduate interview - I don't have a degree - and after discovering the fact, interviewing me anyway. She chucked a rock on the desk and said "sell me that" ... very old school!
Big mistake: I still maintain not my fault ... however we decided to run an Awards book of the night with the magazine the day after the event, and by a printer's error we ended up distributing on the morning of the event. We managed to stop most of the copies going out, but not before most agencies, the BBC, FT and the Guardian had received their copies!

» **Reading:** *Marketing Week obviously! The Times, Guardian on Monday, Independent on Wednesday. Anything by P G Wodehouse, C S Forester or Homer (not Simpson).* **Watching:** *I'm a West Wing addict but I'm also a big fan of historical-based movies with casts of thousands, Gladiator, Spartacus etc.* **Listening:** *I have a fairly eclectic mix of musical tastes, though I only tend to listen to music in the car or during dinner. My current car selection is Stereophonics, Dandy Warhols, James Blunt (current favourite), Aerosmith, Pink Floyd and Bob Marley.* **Relaxing to:** *I don't know if relaxing will be on the menu with a new baby, but currently holidays with my wife Ali, walking, reading, eating out, going out with friends, watching films or DVDs and driving.* » *Married, 1 child*

Jane Tranter
18.3.67

D305 Centre House, 56 Wood Lane, London W12 7SB
T 020 8576 8133
E jane.tranter@bbc.co.uk

Occupation: Controller of Drama Commissioning, BBC

Other positions: Head of Drama Serials, BBC; Executive Producer, BBC Film; Executive Producer and Commissioning Editor, Carlton TV.
Publications: The Lost Prince, State of Play, Bleak House, The Canterbury Tales, Shakespeare Re-told, To The Ends of the Earth, Rome, Spooks, Cutting It.
Awards: The Way We Live Now, Warriors, Care (as Executive Producer).
Education: Kingswood School, Bath; King's College London
Career highlights: The past four years of being part of a team that has changed the face of BBC drama, making it distinctive and pluralistic.
Mentor: The writing and acting community.
Big break: Becoming Assistant Script Editor on Casualty series 4.
Big mistake: Not being offered Shameless. Not being able to achieve more impact for Outlaws, Conviction and Bodies.

» **Reading:** *Scripts and more scripts, but also newspapers and magazines, novels for potential adaptation, and biographies for relaxation.* **Watching:** *Everything dramatic, but obsessively News 24.* **Listening:** *My husband's choice from his ludicrously vast music collection, currently liking The Soweto String Quartet, Silje Nergaard and Johnny Cash.* **Relaxing to:** *With my family, doing the housework, drinking too much.* » *Married, 2 children*

Janice Turner 18.3.60

BECTU, 373-377 Clapham Road, London SW9 9BT
T 020 7346 0900
E jturner@bectu.org.uk

Occupation: Editor, Stage Screen & Radio magazine

Other positions: Diversity Officer, BECTU
Publications: Stage Screen & Radio, the journal of the Broadcasting Entertainment Cinematograph & Theatre Union (BECTU); set up the film and broadcasting industry diversity initiative Move on Up, a BECTU initiative run in partnership with the industry.
Awards: TUC Equality Award.
Education: Dartington College of Arts
Career highlights: While at South magazine in the 1980s, covered conflicts in the Middle East and North Africa; as Editor of Stage Screen & Radio ran many campaigns in the magazine such as exposing deferred payment contracts on low-budget films as a rip-off, working hours, theatre/lottery funding, pay; as Diversity Officer (in addition to Editor's role) set up the Move on Up initiative on behalf of BECTU's Black Members Committee which by early 2006 had facilitated almost 1,000 one-to-one meetings between industry executives and black and minority ethnic film and broadcasting industry professionals. The aim was that the new contacts, in a contacts-driven industry, would lead to new opportunities and jobs. A survey indicated success. The initiative continues. For the first event in 2003 BECTU was awarded the TUC Equality Award in 2004.

» *Married, 1 child*

Sophie Turner Laing 7.9.60

British Sky Broadcasting Ltd, Grant Way, Isleworth, Middlesex TW7 5QD
T 020 7805 8271
E sophie.turner-laing@bskyb.com

Occupation: Deputy Managing Director, Sky Networks

Awards: Women in Film and TV Business Award 2004.
Education: Oakdene; University of life
Career highlights: Variety Club Events Co-ordinator, 1979-80; KM Campbell, Assistant to Managing Director, 1980-82; Henson International TV, Sales Director, 1982-89; HIT Entertainment plc, Joint Founder and Deputy MD, 1989-95; Vice President, Broadcasting, Flextech TV, 1995-98; BBC Controller, Programme Acquisitions, 1998-2003; Acting Head of Business Affairs, 1998; Acting Director of Marketing, 2001; Acting Director of Television, 2002; BSkyB Director of Film Channels and Acquisitions, 2003-04.
Mentor: Dawn Airey
Big break: Having lunch with Mark Grenside and persuading him that I would make a great PA.
Big mistake: Not trusting my instincts on programming and people.

» **Reading:** *Everything.* **Watching:** *Everything, especially films and US series. 24 top of the list.* **Listening:** *Anything my son downloads onto my iPod.* **Relaxing to:** *Escape to France.*
» *Married, 2 children*

U

Laurie Upshon 22.5.54

Upshon Media Limited, Willow Court, Kemerton, Tewkesbury GL20 7JN
T 01386 725615
E laurie@upshon.com

Occupation: Media Consultant, Upshon Media Limited

Other positions: Director, Central Broadcasting plc; Controller of News and Operations, ITV Central; Executive Producer, News and Current Affairs, TVS; Features Editor, Southern TV; Subeditor, Press Association; Assistant Group Editor, Stratford Express Group; Political Editor, Newham Recorder; Chief Subeditor, Newham Recorder.
Publications: ITV 50th anniversary exhibition, Birmingham Museum and Art Gallery, 2005; No Turning Back, Colloquium IEE, 1995.
Awards: Royal Television Society Baird Medal; Fellow, Royal Television Society; Newsworld innovation award; Worldfest Flagstaff International Film Festival Gold Award for Breaking News; RTS National Awards for Regional News (×3); RTS Geoffrey Parr Award for Technical Innovation; RTS Midlands Centre Awards (×4).
Education: St Peter's Merrow, near Guildford
Career highlights: Controller of News and Operations at ITV Central from 1990-2005; October 2005 awarded Royal Television Society's top honour, the Baird Medal, for outstanding contribution to the Television Industry; joined Central in 1985 as Editor of Central News West, became Head of News in 1989 and then Controller; joined the Central board in 1993; started in newspapers in London and joined Southern Television in 1976; part of the launch team of TVS in 1981, setting up the South East news service. At Central, responsible for creating Britain's first automated newsroom at Abingdon, winning the Royal Television Society Award for technological innovation; received an international technical innovation award from Newsworld; won RTS national awards for Daily News Programming, and the gold award at the Worldfest Flagstaff International Film Festival.
Mentor: Bob Southgate, former Controller of News and Current Affairs at TVS, then Central.
Big break: Joining the TVS launch team in 1981.
Big mistake: Could have made a great newspaper reporter had I not followed the management route early on.

» **Reading:** *The heavy papers, Waugh, Le Carré, Deighton, de Bernières, Harris, Heller, Ludlum, Lee, sporting biogs.* **Watching:** *Cricket is only appointment to view, other sports, all news channels, West Wing, ER, NYPD Blue, QI, Have I Got News etc for entertainment.* **Listening:** *Today programme, Five Live Drive programme, Radio Gloucestershire (when my son's on), mainly classical CDs, some 60s for nostalgia.* **Relaxing to:** *Music, fishing, cricket, watching sports, golf (not the way I play), walking on Bredon Hill, reading.* » *Married, 3 children*

Sebastian Usher 16.9.67

27 Lock Road, Ham Common, Richmond, London TW10 7LQ
T 020 8948 5119
E susher_6@hotmail.com

Occupation: BBC World Media Correspondent

Other positions: North Africa Correspondent, BBC; Middle East Analyst, BBC; Arab Affairs Editor, BBC; Senior Editor, Euronews.
Publications: Arab Media and the Death of Hariri, essay in book 2005; various From Our Own Correspondents looking at Islamic extremism in Middle East in past few years; series of articles for Al Hayat on Beirut during 1980s; stories and poems published in various magazines over past 15 years in Britain and abroad.
Awards: None that I'm aware of.
Education: New College, Oxford University
Career highlights: Reporting on hostage crisis in Beirut in mid-80s; reporting on Saudi Arabian life and culture in late 80s; reporting on post-break of the Soviet Union in Poland and Hungary in early 90s; writing series on Muslim traces in Eastern Europe for Al Hayat; reporting from Kosovo, Macedonia, Belgrade during Yugoslav wars; being insulted by Edward Heath in Whitehall while working in features department at WS BBC; working for Arabic Service at BBC while not fully understanding Arabic; editing the news at Euronews when Diana died; returning to Beirut to the Ottoman house I shared with Brian Keenan and from which he was kidnapped after 14 years for From Our Own Correspondent; reporting on Hezbollah in the south of Lebanon days after 9/11; editing the World Service news programme during the 2nd Iraq war; reporting from Casablanca on the bombings there in 2003; looking at the role TV has played in changes in Ukraine, Georgia, Lebanon, Iraq and so on in past year and a half as World Media Correspondent.
Mentor: I was never really very good with mentors, but it was the writing of James Baldwin, Norman Mailer and Saul Bellow in the 60s that made me want to be some kind of journalist.
Big break: Getting taken on by the BBC Arabic Service in 1995 without having to take a language test, which would have shown the shortcomings in my Arabic.
Big mistake: Nothing really stands out, but lots of missed opportunities due to a mixture of arrogance, insecurity and sloth.

» **Reading:** *New York Review of Books, New Yorker, Vanity Fair, Village Voice, Salon, Al Hayat, Corriere della Sera, El Pais, Liberation, most British newspapers.* **Watching:** *Far too much.* **Listening:** *I rarely have the radio on as I like to listen to my own music in the car or at home, but as a child I used to love driving home with the Sunday play on on Radio 4, a pleasure that I've just recently rediscovered.* **Relaxing to:** *Walking and cycling by the river and in Richmond Park and travelling just for the sake of it; also, growing pointlessly exotic plants in my garden that struggle to survive.* » *Married, 2 children*

Adam Uytman 30.8.1978

20 Lionel Street, Birmingham B3 1AQ
T 07834 311 003
E adam.uytman@kerrangradio.co.uk

Occupation: Programme Director, Kerrang! Radio

Other positions: Head Of Music, Music Manager, Producer, Presenter.
Awards: Kerrang! Radio has won 3 Sony Awards, Music Week Best Radio Station, various Arqiva and BRAs.
Education: Glasgow University
Career highlights: Starting off presenting a rock show on community radio at the age of 15, music radio has been my passion since an early age. Whilst studying at Glasgow University, most of my time was spent working on student radio and other projects around the area, as well as working for record company BMG for two years; in 1999 I became part of the launch team of regional station Beat 106 covering Central Scotland, with various different on-air roles and also working as Station Producer. By 2001 I was promoted to the role of Music Manager, responsible for programming the music at the station; in 2004, I moved out of Scotland to become the launch Head of Music at Kerrang! 105.2 in the West Midlands, also responsible for programming the music on Kerrang! Radio UK; most recently, in June 2005, I was promoted to Programme Director for both stations - so far taking the national station to a high of 1,214,000 listeners across the UK.
Mentor: Andrew Jeffries, I worked under him at Beat 106 and Kerrang! Radio.
Big break: Becoming PD at Kerrang! Radio.
Big mistake: I don't regret anything in my career so far!

» **Reading:** *Music magazines mostly.* **Watching:** *Whatever my girlfriend makes me!* **Listening:** *A mix of all styles, but predominantly rock music.* **Relaxing to:** *Listen to music, watch TV, go on holiday.* » *Common law partner*

Adrian van Klaveren

1.1.66

Room 5601, BBC Television Centre, Wood Lane, London W12 7RJ
T 020 8576 8937
E adrian.van-klaveren@bbc.co.uk

Occupation: Deputy Director and Controller of Production, BBC News

Other positions: Head of Newsgathering, BBC News; News Editor, Newsgathering, BBC News; Head of Local Programmes, BBC West Midlands; Deputy Editor, Newsnight; Deputy Editor, Nine O'Clock News; Senior Producer, Panorama.
Education: Bristol Grammar School; St John's College, Oxford
Career highlights: Inevitably governed by news events. Being in Washington as 9/11 happened; making a quick turnround Panorama about Margaret Thatcher's fall; overseeing coverage of Diana's death and funeral; editing the Nine O'Clock News for stories such as the death of John Smith, the Windsor Castle fire and the Iraqi invasion of Kuwait. Producing coverage of Reagan/Gorbachev summits, events such as Lockerbie, Hillsborough and the first East German elections.
Mentor: I have to say Richard Sambrook, because I've followed him into five different jobs.
Big break: Being chosen for the BBC's News Trainee scheme.
Big mistake: Putting Jeremy Paxman in a mock football dug-out on Newsnight.

» **Reading:** *Novels - Kazuo Ishiguro, Sebastian Faulks. Political biographies, almost anything within reason about sport.* **Watching:** *The West Wing, Grand Designs, Little Britain.* **Listening:** *Johnnie Walker, Five Live, The Archers, American singer-songwriters.* **Relaxing to:** *Cricket, movies and spending time with the children.* » *Married, 2 children*

John van Vroenhoven

14.8.75

8th Floor, 1 Stephen Street, London W1T 1AL
T 020 7462 9200
E john.vanvroenhoven@lycos-europe.com

Occupation: Managing Director, Portal, Lycos UK

Other positions: Managing Director Central Countries, Netherlands, Italy and Spain.
Education: Business School, Eindhoven
Career highlights: Promoted to MD Netherlands in 2003, interim MD Lycos portal France and creator of centralisation plan for country organisations Netherlands, Italy and Spain; in current position responsible for strong portal growth UK.
Big break: Reversing the declining traffic trend for Lycos UK.
Big mistake: Underestimation of the strong social law in France.

» **Reading:** *Management and marketing books, industry magazines, newspapers and I love to read the Jeremy Clarkson books.* **Watching:** *Top Gear, Lost.* **Listening:** *My iPod filled with a very broad range of music, especially Latin.* **Relaxing to:** *By cooking a five-course meal while having a glass of quality champagne.* » *Married, no children*

Simon Veksner

2.5.72

DDB London, 12 Bishops Bridge Road, London W2 6AA
T 020 7258 4419
E simon.veksner@ddblondon.com

Occupation: Advertising Creative, DDB London

Publications: Various campaigns for Volkswagen, the Guardian, Budweiser.
Awards: Cannes Grand Prix; D&AD Pencil; Campaign Press gold; Campaign Poster gold.
Education: Oxford University
Career highlights: Highlight was winning the Cannes Grand Prix in 2004 for a print ad for Volkswagen Polo - it's the one with the American policemen taking cover behind a Polo. The ad also won a Clio in Miami - which is a rather nice place to go to pick up an award...
Mentor: Jeremy Craigen, creative director at DDB London. Plus I learned a lot from David Hume.
Big break: Getting hired at DDB London by former Creative Director Larry Barker. I love this place. We have a crappy old building and nowhere near as funky an image as agencies called things like Zebedee, Xtreme, Bang! or Mother... but we win more creative awards than they do.
Big mistake: I don't mind making mistakes, it's a good way to learn. Seems to be how I learn, anyway...

» **Reading:** *All the newspapers and magazines, a lot of novels, plus psychology and philosophy books.* **Watching:** *Basically Channel 4, Match of the Day, and lots of DVDs - LoveFilm is brilliant.* **Listening:** *My daughter.* **Relaxing to:** *Not easy. My wife can always find me something to do...*
» *Married, 2 children*

Sue Vertue

Hartswood Films, Twickenham Film Studios, The Barons, Twickenham, Middlesex TW1 2AW
T 020 8607 8736
E suevertue@hartswoodfilms.co.uk

Occupation: Producer, Hartswood Films

Publications: Mr Bean, The Vicar of Dibley, Gimme Gimme Gimme, The Last Englishman, Coupling, Carrie and Barry, Supernova.
Awards: Banff Comedy Award, Hospital!; British Comedy Award, Coupling; silver Rose of Montreux, Coupling; International Emmy, The Vicar of Dibley.
Education: Oxford Poly, now Brookes University
Career highlights: The first award that we won for Coupling was in Montreux. We'd had a great week at the festival anyway and so to win an award at the end was fantastic. I had the opportunity for the first time to thank my husband for being not only a great husband and dad but a pretty nifty writer as well.
Mentor: Beryl Vertue, my mother (and my boss) is very much my mentor. I have watched her work over the years and she has always followed the

belief of 'honesty is the best policy'. She has always been firm but fair and is very welcoming to people who are new to the industry and need some guidance.

Big break: When I was a Production Manager at Tiger Aspect, Peter Bennett Jones gave me my first producing break with the second series of Mr Bean. A very nice one to cut my teeth on but unfortunately it rather spoilt me on what to expect the overnights for a programme should be.

Big mistake: I'm sure others could point at many but as I can't really think of one offhand, I have a dreadful feeling that I've yet to make it. I think sometimes not going with my gut instinct however and carrying on regardless never really helps.

» **Reading:** *Because we've got two young children - mostly Mr Men, Horrid Henry, or about 25 pages of a really good book on holiday is about all I manage to have time for. Last great book I read was The Time Traveller's Wife.* **Watching:** *I try to watch a little bit of everything but still tend towards American dramas such as The West Wing and House. Obviously I watch Little Angels and Supernanny in the hope it will make me a better parent. Sometimes we decide to watch an old series from beginning to end on DVD and see how well it's dated. I Claudius was the last one.* **Listening:** *Sadly I think I've got a bit middle aged and classical. Also like Katie Melua, James Blunt kind of stuff. The great thing about an iPod though is that you can set it on random and get a quick blast of all kinds of music. Radio stations - Heart, Kiss Fm or Radio 4.* **Relaxing to:** *There doesn't seem to be an awful lot of spare time to relax at the moment but any chance we get, Steven and I like to go away to a hotel for the night (without the kids), have a meal, nice wine and a lie in.* » *Married, 2 children*

Matthew Vincent

28.10.66

96 Speed House, Barbican, London EC2Y 8AU
T 020 7382 8607
E matthew.vincent@ft.com

Occupation: Editor, Investors Chronicle

Publications: Contributor of articles to various financial journals.

Education: Salvatorian College, Harrow Weald; University of Manchester

Career highlights: Production assistant, BBC TV, 1988-89; Staff writer, Stately Homes and Gardens, 1989-90; Money, 1990; Moneywise magazine, staff writer, 1990-92; Chief Subeditor / Associate Editor, 1992-95; Editor, 1995-2000; Head of Content, Investors Chronicle Online and FT Business, 2000-02; BBC TV reporter, Short Change, 1994; presenter, Pound For Pound, 1998.

» **Relaxing to:** *Poetry, cricket, sherry.*

Jeremy Vine

17.5.65

Radio 2, BBC London W1A 1AA
T 020 7765 0585
E jeremy.vine@bbc.co.uk

Occupation: Presenter, Jeremy Vine Show, Radio 2

Other positions: Reporter, Coventry Evening Telegraph; BBC News Trainee; Reporter, Today, Radio 4; BBC Political Correspondent; BBC Africa Correspondent; Newsnight Presenter.

Awards: Speech Broadcaster of the Year, 2005, Sony Awards; Silver Nymph at Monte Carlo; Amnesty International Radio Award, 1999.

Education: Epsom College; Durham University

Career highlights: Began with traineeship at the Coventry Evening Telegraph; 1987, joined the BBC; 1989, reporter on Radio 4's Today Programme; 1993-97, Lobby Correspondent based at Westminster; moved on to Johannesburg as the BBC's Africa Correspondent, a stint including an April 1999 exclusive on South African police brutality, the fly-on-the-wall film of the Brixton Flying Squad in Johannesburg won the Silver Nymph at Monte Carlo, rocked the police service in South Africa and sparked uproar across the country: 22 officers were suspended and two convicted as a result of the footage. From Our Own Correspondent piece on Civilian, a former child soldier in Sierra Leone, won an Amnesty International Radio Award in June 1999; during the 2001 UK election campaign, travelled the length of Britain in a 1976 Volkswagen camper van, a journey declared one of the highlights of the election by the Sun. Peter Mandelson famously stormed out of the van in Hartlepool after being asked whether Chancellor Gordon Brown was having a perfect election campaign.

» *Married, 1 child*

Bruce Waddell
18.3.59

Daily Record, 1 Cental Quay, Glasgow G3 8DA
T 0141 309 3000
E m.collins@dailyrecord.co.uk

Occupation: Editor, Daily Record

Education: Graeme High School, Falkirk; Napier University
Career highlights: Reporter, Journal and Gazette, Linlithgow, 1977-87; News Subeditor, the Scottish Sun, 1987-90; Deputy Editor, Sunday Scot, 1991; Marketing Executive, Murray International, 1991-92; Features Subeditor, the Sun, 1992-93; Deputy Editor, the Scottish Sun, 1993-98.

» **Relaxing to:** *Football, classic cars, cinema, golf.*
» *Married, 1 son*

Rebekah Wade
27.5.68

The Sun, 1 Virginia Street, London E98 1SN
T 020 7782 4000
E Rebekah.wade@the-sun.co.uk

Occupation: Editor, the Sun

Other positions: Founder member and President, Women in Journalism.
Education: Appleton Hall, Cheshire; Sorbonne, Paris
Career highlights: Features Editor, Associate Editor, Deputy Editor, News of the World, 1989-98; Deputy Editor, the Sun, 1998-2000; Editor, News of the World, 2000-03.

» *Married*

Veronica Wadley
29.2.56

Evening Standard, Northcliffe House, 2 Derry Street, London W8 5EE
T 020 7938 7007
E veronica.wadley@standard.co.uk

Occupation: Editor, Evening Standard

Other positions: Previously Deputy Editor, Daily Mail, 1998-2002; Associate Editor, Daily Mail, 1995-98; Deputy Editor, Daily Telegraph, 1994-95; Assistant Editor, Daily Telegraph, 1989-94; Features Editor, Daily Telegraph, 1986-89; Mail on Sunday, 1982-86; Sunday Telegraph Magazine 1978-81; Condé Nast Publications 1971-74.
Education: Benenden School, Kent

» *Married, 2 children*

Glenn Waldron
2.6.81

i-D Magazine, 124 Tabernacle Street, London EC2A 4SA
T 020 7490 9710
E glenn.waldron@i-dmagazine.co.uk

Occupation: Editor, i-D Magazine

Publications: Writing for i-D, Vogue, the Guardian etc. Trend reporting for MTV.
Education: University of Nottingham; Plymouth College
Career highlights: Editing i-D Magazine, contributing to a variety of fine publications and seeing one of my articles taught on the school syllabus (my Mum was particularly proud).
Mentor: Avril Mair and Terry Jones.
Big break: The first one.
Big mistake: No big ones ... yet.

» **Reading:** *Anything by Muriel Spark or Graham Greene, and Grazia, obviously.* **Watching:** *Documentaries, cookery programmes and reality shows about unruly teenagers.* **Listening:** *At the moment Devandra Banhart, Sigur Ros, Kate Bush, old folk.* **Relaxing to:** *Not consuming.* » *Unmarried*

Angus Walker
19.2.74

Press Gallery, House of Commons, Westminster SW1A 0AA
T 020 7430 4991
E angus.walker@itn.co.uk

Occupation: Political Correspondent, ITV News

Mentor: Ed Boyle, former Political Editor, Westcountry TV.
Big break: My first scoop for Westcountry TV - an exclusive interview with the fortune teller who'd picked 2.7-million-pound-winning lottery numbers by holding a North Devon OAP's key ring and 'getting vibrations'.
Big mistake: Not spotting that the water bottled by Coke was in fact just that: water, from a tap in South London!

» **Reading:** *A lot.* **Watching:** *A lot.* **Listening:** *The Voice of Experience.* **Relaxing to:** *With friends.* » *Single, 2 children*

Mark Walker
14.4.67

26-27 Castlereagh Street, London W1H 5DL
T 020 7706 4100
E mark.walker@smoothfm.com

Occupation: Programme Director, Smoothfm London

Other positions: Head of Music; Presenter; Newsreader.
Education: Forest School For Boys, Winnersh, Berks
Career highlights: Started at the new County Sound Radio in Surrey in 1983, presented the late show and then moved to breakfast; first station move was to Southern Sound (as it was called then) to present breakfast. Loved Brighton and still live there today. In 1991 I moved to Jazz FM as breakfast show presenter and now here I am back with the station as PD of the new smoothfm; in

between I spent the time as Head of Music at Ocean FM in Hampshire and as a Newsreader at BFBS.
Mentor: Phil Miles taught me loads in the beginning when I thought I knew best.
Big break: Getting a call from John Simons and being given a big London radio station to play with. Moving Jazz FM to smoothfm has been one of the most exciting things I've ever done.
Big mistake: Getting a little worse for wear in my first week as PD and singing Sex Bomb very badly to some very powerful people in the industry. Not done Karaoke since.

» **Reading:** *Guardian and tons of books on the train.* **Watching:** *Addicted to Corrie, hate reality TV.* **Listening:** *smoothfm and favourite ever band Prefab Sprout.* **Relaxing to:** *Leave London at the weekends for Brighton, where you can never get bored!* » *Single, no children*

Richard Walker

Sunday Herald, 200 Renfield Street, Glasgow G2 3QB
T 0141 3027800
E richard.walker@sundayherald.com

Occupation: Editor, Sunday Herald

Other positions: Deputy Editor, Sunday Herald; Deputy Features Editor, Daily Record; Spectrum Production Editor, Scotland on Sunday.

» *3 children*

Steven Walker

7.4.61

Scotsman Publications Limited, 108 Holyrood Road, Edinburgh EH8 8AS
T 0131 6208620
E nmcdonald@scotsman.com

Occupation: Managing Director, Scotsman Publications Ltd

Other positions: Council Member, Scottish Daily Newspaper Society.
Education: Broughton School
Career highlights: Sales Representative, Edinburgh Evening News, 1986-88; Group Sales Executive, Thomson Regional Newspapers, 1988-90; Highland Advertising Manager, Press and Journal, 1990-91; General Advertising Manager, Daily Record and Sunday Mail, 1991-95; Scotsman Publications Ltd, Advertising Director, 1995-98; Assistant Managing Director, 1998-99.

» **Watching:** *Sports.* **Relaxing to:** *Outdoor pursuits.*
» *Married, 1 son*

Richard Wallace

12.6.65

1 Canada Square, London E14 5AP
T 020 7293 3000
E r.wallace@mirror.co.uk

Occupation: Editor, Daily Mirror

Tim Ward

2.1.69

2 Oxted Chambers, Station Road East, Oxted, Surrey
T 0870 7870881
E tim@friendsreunited.co.uk

Occupation: Marketing Director, Friends Reunited

Other positions: Marketing Director, Financial Times.
Awards: The Sunday Times 2004 Microsoft Tech Track 100, 64th position; The DMA Awards 2004, Other Digital Media, silver; Microsoft Tech Track 100, Best Use of Technology 2004; The Sunday Times PricewaterhouseCoopers Profit Track 100, 84th position; Growing Business Awards 2003, Most Promising Young Company.
Education: Chetham's School of Music; Trinity College of Music
Career highlights: I joined Friends Reunited in June 2003 from the Financial Times; prior to this I spent majority of my career to date in telecoms, including BellSouth, Mercury one2one and from 1993 to 2000 with Vodafone UK. At the FT, achievements included introducing subscription to FT.com; at Vodafone achievements included the early years of marketing and distribution of pre-paid mobiles in the UK.
Mentor: Several, but most notably David Jones at Vodafone.
Big break: Giving up playing the French horn as a career.
Big mistake: No really big ones, but loads of small to medium.

» **Reading:** *90% pulp fiction, 10% pseudo-intellectual.* **Watching:** *West Wing and films.* **Listening:** *My wife's advice.* **Relaxing to:** *Drink.* » *Married, 1 son*

Kirsty Wark

3.2.55

Black Pepper Media Limited, St Georges Studios, 93-97 St Georges Road, Glasgow G3 6JA
T 0141 353 8438
E kirsty.wark@blackpeppermedia.com
kirsty.wark@bbc.co.uk

Occupation: Television journalist and presenter

Other positions: Fronts a variety of current affairs, arts and cultural programmes; presenter on Newsnight since 1993; main presenter on Newsnight Review. Cultural travel show, Tales From Europe, is in its third series. Writes occasional articles and is currently working on a novel.
Education: Edinburgh University

» *Married to the independent producer Alan Clements, 2 teenage children.*

William Watt
6.1.73

Dennis Publishing, 30 Cleveland Street, London W1T 4JD
T 020 7907 6472
E will_watt@dennis.co.uk

Occupation: Publisher, Viz comic, Bizarre magazine

Awards: None, thank goodness. No desire to meet Jimmy Carr.
Education: King's School, Macclesfield; King's School, London
Career highlights: Viz 25th anniversary party. All-in wrestling, Nicholas Parsons, The Ukulele Orchestra and the Cuban Brothers. I first kissed my wife. Publishing the Profanisaurus books.

» **Reading:** *Viz, Private Eye, Guardian Weekly, the Week, the Nation (US).* **Watching:** *The Thick of It, films.* **Listening:** *Today programme, Smooth fm.* **Relaxing to:** *Playing chess and football.* » *Married, 1 child*

Mary Wear
5.4.64

AMV BBDO Ltd, 151 Marylebone Road, London NW1 5QE
T 020 7616 3449
E wearm@amvbbdo.com

Occupation: Advertising Copywriter, Abbott Mead Vickers BBDO

Publications: Yellow Pages Haircut, Messy Flat; DfT Lucky; Famous Grouse campaign.
Awards: Gold Lion, Cannes 2004; silver Lions Cannes 2005, 2004, 2003; BTA Gold 1999; others.
Education: Kent University
Career highlights: Combining award-winning and happy career with increasing number of children.
Mentor: Dave Trott from Gold Greenlees Trott circa 1987.
Big break: Getting a job working for Dave Trott at Gold Greenlees Trott.
Big mistake: Don't know if it was a mistake but I did take a drastic pay cut in 1990 to work for a not terribly great place.

» **Reading:** *Carl Hiaasen, Jerome K Jerome, Jay McInerney, Scott Fitzgerald. Nothing by Dan Brown.* **Watching:** *University Challenge, Green Wing, Nighty Night, anything with Ricky Gervais in.* **Listening:** *Terry Wogan.* **Relaxing to:** *Crossword, dancing with the family, cooking and eating.* » *Married, 4 children*

Tina Weaver
17.6.65

1 Canada Square, Canary Wharf, London E14 5AP
T 020 7293 3000
E catriona.irvine@mgn.co.uk

Occupation: Editor, Sunday Mirror

Other positions: Chair, Women in Journalism
Career highlights: Deputy Editor, the Mirror; Editor, Sunday Mirror, 2001-present

Justin Webb
4.1.65

c/o World Affairs Unit, BBC Television Centre, Wood Lane, London
T 001 202 223 2050
E justin.webb@bbc.co.uk

Occupation: BBC Chief Washington Correspondent

Other positions: BBC Europe Correspondent; Presenter, Breakfast News.
Education: London School of Economics
Career highlights: As a radio and TV foreign affairs correspondent I covered the Bosnian civil war, the first Gulf war, the collapse of the Soviet Union, the first democratic elections in South Africa, and, best of all, a coup in the Maldives...
Mentor: Kate Adie - I admire her guts and her writing ability.
Big break: Probably being on my way to Enniskillen in November 1987 to make a feature for the Today Programme when the Remembrance Day bomb went off.
Big mistake: I once asked David Blunkett - live on Breakfast News - if he could see me! It had been a long morning...

» **Reading:** *The Wall Street Journal and the New York Times.* **Watching:** *Rugby videos.* **Listening:** *Radio WTOP (Washington DC news radio station).* **Relaxing to:** *Going to the office (I have 3 young children).* » *Married, 3 children*

Richard Webb
1959

1 Canada Square, Canary Wharf, London E14 5AP
T 020 7293 3000

Occupation: Manging Director, Mirror Group Newspapers

Career highlights: Deputy Managing Director, Optimedia; Advertising Director, the Sun and News of the World, 1995-2000; General manager, the Sun and News of the World, 2000-05; Managing Director, Mirror Group Newspapers, 2005-present.

Romilly Weeks
16.12.77

200 Gray's Inn Road, London WC1X 8LW
T 020 7833 3000
E Romilly.Weeks@itn.co.uk

Occupation: Royal Correspondent, ITV News

Other positions: News Correspondent, ITV News; Reporter, ITV News; Reporter/Presenter, News Direct Radio.
Education: St Paul's Girls' School; Edinburgh University
Career highlights: Most memorable assignment was the five weeks I spent embedded with the army during the war in Iraq; most entertaining assignment was covering the Royal ski trip to Klosters when Prince Charles let slip his opinions on the Palace press pack.
Big break: Being sent to cover the last Gulf War.

» **Reading:** *Novels for pleasure, newspapers for work.* **Watching:** *ITV News, Newsnight, C4 News.*

Listening: *Radio 4.* **Relaxing to:** *By getting out of range of the news desk, failing that, yoga and riding.* » *Single, no children*

Paul Welling

2.2.73

Discovery Networks Europe, Discovery House, Chiswick Park Building 2, 566 Chiswick High Road, London W4 5YB

T 020 8811 3000
E paul_welling@discovery-europe.com

Occupation: Vice-President and Channel Director, Discovery Real Time, Discovery Travel and Living

Other positions: Various media roles including Head of On Air Presentation and Promotions, Discovery Networks Europe; prior to TV I was a chartered surveyor.
Publications: Superhomes for Discovery Travel and Living, The Caravan Show, Wheeler Dealers and Build Buy or Restore? for Discovery Real Time. Looking forward to The Ultimate House for Real Time in 2006.
Awards: Promax US Platinum award for the on-air look for Discovery Home & Leisure.
Education: University of East London
Career highlights: Helping to launch and brand the on-air for Discovery Europe's network of 10 channels across the UK and Europe over the course of several years; growing Discovery Home and Leisure into the highest rating cabsat lifestyle channel of 2004; launching and running three of Discovery Networks three lifestyle channels in the UK - Discovery Real Time, Discovery Real Time, Extra and Discovery, Travel and Living.
Mentor: Peter Weil, who now runs our Latin American programming division was one of the most extraordinary and encouraging people I have ever worked with.
Big break: Being given Home and Leisure to run for Discovery Networks Europe three years ago.
Big mistake: Eating seafood whilst visiting our office in New Delhi.

» **Reading:** *Novels by the ton, as many magazines as possible and Sunday newspapers.* **Watching:** *Channel 4, a lot of cabsat and our multichannel competitors - most telly folk don't watch enough TV.* **Listening:** *Radio 1 in the car on the way to work, Radio 4 on the way home.* **Relaxing to:** *A glass of wine, a good book, Thai food with friends or by escaping to the country.* » *Single, no children*

Mark Wells

21.6.71

The London Television Centre, Upper Ground, London SE1 9LT

T 020 7261 3458
E mark.wells@itv.com

Occupation: Controller of Entertainment, Granada

Other positions: Previously Controller of Entertainment at Carlton, prior to that Executive Producer, Entertainment at LWT and Senior Producer, Entertainment at BBC.
Education: King Edward VI School, Birmingham; University of Lancaster
Career highlights: The highlight of my career to date is leading the premier Entertainment Department in Britain at Granada, where I am fortunate to work with a diverse portfolio that includes Parkinson, Ant and Dec's Saturday Night Takeaway, The Paul O'Grady Show, Stars in their Eyes, University Challenge, It'll Be Alright on the Night and the Brit Awards ... in the words of the song, 'who could ask for anything more?'.
Mentor: David Liddiment
Big break: My biggest break was probably being made a Producer in Granada's Entertainment Department in Manchester the day before my 25th birthday. It was genuinely the happiest day of my career, and the beginning of an adventure that I've relished.
Big mistake: An over-ambitious project called ITV's Year of Promise in May 2000. There was too much programming, too little to spend, and I mistakenly didn't devote enough of my time to it. It passed without incident but unnoticed.

» **Reading:** *On weekdays The Times, Guardian and Sun. At weekends the Sunday Times. The rest of the time Entertainment Weekly, Vanity Fair, OK!, Heat, the Week and The Stage. Also lots of biographies and occasional popular history.* **Watching:** *Everything on Saturday nights on ITV1 or BBC1. I also enjoy Coronation Street, I'm A Celebrity, America's Next Top Model, Newsnight, Question Time, football on Sky Sports, American network news on CNBC and lots of Sky News or News 24.* **Listening:** *Radio 4, Classic FM, Heart 106.2, Capital, Kiss, Radio Five Live and occasionally Radio 2.* **Relaxing to:** *Reading, walking in the countryside, lying down in a darkened room.* » *Single, no children*

Mark Westaby

27.6.59

Portfolio Group, Russell Chambers, The Piazza, Covent Garden, London WC2E 8AA

T 020 7240 6959
E mark.westaby@portfoliocomms.com

Occupation: Director, Portfolio Group; Portfolio Communications; Metrica.

Other positions: Immediate past Chairman of the Association of Media Evaluation Companies (AMEC); Chairman of the education committee for AMEC.
Publications: Contributed to various books; published paper How PR Works, Specifically Media Relations in AdMap; Major awards for mummy, the Inside Story for Silicon Graphics (SGI).
Awards: PR Week Best Consultancy (although a long time ago now); CIPR Award for Industry and Technology; PRCA Award for Best Technology Campaign.
Education: Brunel University
Career highlights: An engineering graduate of Brunel University, I'm really a frustrated academic (I was offered various PhDs) but there's not enough money in university research! Having decided engineering was not for me I became the youngest Board Director of Countrywide Communications (now Porter Novelli) in 1987; I then left Countrywide in 1990 and in 1993 joined Portfolio Communications. I was subsequently a founding member of The Portfolio Group, which is now one of the country's largest independent PR organisations. I also founded Portfolio Group company Metrica, which is now one of the largest media evaluation, research and planning

companies in Europe, if not the world; I was Chairman of the Association of Media Evaluation Companies (AMEC) for four and a half years until the end of 2004, and I'm now founding the Institute of Communication Research, Planning and Evaluation (ICRPE) to support the development and training of research, planning and evaluation of professionals.

Mentor: Alan Butler, for whom I have the greatest respect and to whom I owe a great deal. Also Peter Hehir, who taught me a lot (and regularly called me 'petulant').

Big break: Being made redundant in 1993 and joining a couple of industry friends. I never looked back and we subsequently became The Portfolio Group.

Big mistake: Joining the company I was with after Countrywide and before Portfolio, but then I learnt a lot - mainly how NOT to do things!

» **Reading:** *I usually have half a dozen books on the go. My main interests are academic books on psychology, neuroscience, econometrics, statistics and mathematical modelling (I know, I'm a sad case). I also read a lot of popular science, but never fiction. Also an avid reader of research and academic papers, especially around market research and communication theory. Other books include cricket and football, plus magazines on gardening, the home, etc.* **Watching:** *Sport, mainly cricket and football. I love documentaries, history programmes, satirical comedy and Newsnight. Also, well-written comedy dramas and Midsomer Murders. Can't stand soaps.* **Listening:** *Very broad range of musical taste from opera through to contemporary rock, jazz and pop. Also love to listen to dance music, very loud, when on my own in my car.* **Relaxing to:** *We own a holiday home, which is a lovely 17th century thatched cottage in Yorkshire. I love being there and pottering around. I also enjoy gardening, sport (watching), socialising and music. I love being with my family, but I'm not sure it counts as 'relaxing'...* » *Married, 1 child*

Mark Whall

7.5.60

Broadcasting House, Abington Street,
Northampton NN1 2BH

T 01604 231900
E mark.whall@bbc.co.uk

Occupation: Programmes Editor, BBC Radio Northampton

Other positions: News Editor, Programme Producer, Programme Presenter, News Reader.

Education: Sussex University

Career highlights: I've produced and presented every mainstream programme in local radio; spent two years as a News Editor and am now Programmes Editor.

Mentor: Paul Needle, former ILR Station Manager, formerly Senior Lecturer in Broadcast Journalism at City University, London, and former BBC Producer. Now retired.

Big break: Being offered a five-minute 'new technology' spot on a fledgling and short-lived commercial radio station despite having no previous broadcasting experience: a case of a steep learning curve!

Big mistake: In a pacy 'newsbeat style' news programme headline sequence I was supposed to read 'and the hunt for the British Rail killer continues...' Instead, I grandly announced 'and the hunt for the British Rail killer cunt continues...!'

» **Reading:** *Books and occasionally newspapers. I've even been known to read toilet cubicle walls.* **Watching:** *Television and people.* **Listening:** *The voices in my head.* **Relaxing to:** *Flying - I'm an accomplished pilot with many thousands of hours in command and owner of two aircraft. I also enjoy foreign travel.* » *Single parent, 3 children*

Adrian Wheeler

5.11.49

GCI UK, New Bridge Street House,
30-34 New Bridge Street, London EC4V 6BJ

T 020 7072 4000
E awheeler@gciuk.com

Occupation: Chief Executive, GCI Group

Other positions: Chairman, PRCA 1998-2000; Court Assistant, Guild of PR Practitioners 2000-present; member, Marketing Society.

Awards: FCIPR 1998 (memb 1972).

Education: Dulwich College; Clare College, Cambridge

Career highlights: Director, Brian Dowling Ltd, 1974-76 (executive, 1971-74); Managing Director, Sterling Public Relations, 1976-87; chief executive, GCI Group London, 1998-99 (managing director, 1994-98); chief executive, GCI UK 1999-present; chaiman, GCI Europe 2001-present.

» **Relaxing to:** *Skiing, sailing, tennis.* » *Married, 2 children*

Lynda Wheeler

21.12.73

Unit 1.4 Shepherds Building, Charecroft Way,
London W14 0EE

T 020 7471 6900
E lynda.wheeler@wisdengroup.com

Occupation: Publisher of The Oldie and The Wisden Cricketer

Other positions: Publisher for John Brown Citrus Publishing; Subscriptions, Merchandise and Books Manager for JBCP; Book Publisher for Ministry of Sound.

Publications: Have worked on a variety of publications - Viz, Bizarre, Fortean Times, Gardens Illustrated, Classic FM mag, Bare, Wisden Cricket Monthly.

Awards: PPA subscriptions magazine of the year for smaller publishers.

Education: Maidenhead college of FE

Career highlights: My first job in publishing was as Merchandise Assistant for Viz. It was selling over a million copies an issue so it was an exciting time. Watching our books get to number one in the bestsellers list was amazing. I worked my way through the ranks and got my first publisher job on Wisden Cricket Monthly which picked up a BSME award. I knew nothing about cricket at the time, but thankfully everyone around me made up for that. Getting to publish The Oldie and The Wisden Cricketer, two very different magazines, has been a great experience.

Mentor: John Brown has always been very supportive of me and has helped me gain the experience I needed to get where I am now. I owe a lot to him.

Big break: Getting my first job in publishing. I had no idea that the tiny company I joined was going to grow into one of the biggest publishing companies in the UK. It was a great training ground.

Big mistake: I still have sleepless nights over a book that was printed with the wrong price on the cover.

» **Reading:** *I've just finished The Time Traveller's Wife by Audrey Niffenegger and before that I was reading Beryl Bainbridge. Am also a bit partial to a bit of Iain Banks.* **Watching:** *Too much television.* **Listening:** *I have a diverse taste in music but hate heavy rock and boy bands with passion.* **Relaxing to:** *Days out with friends, lazy lunches, playing with my daughter, yoga and swimming.* » *Living with partner and two children*

Francis Wheen 22.1.57

c/o PFD, Drury House, 34-43 Russell Street, London WC2B 5HA

T 020 7344 1000
E cmacarthur@pfd.co.uk

Occupation: Author and journalist

Publications: Das Kapital, (Atlantic, 2006); How Mumbo-Jumbo Conquered the World (Fourth Estate, 2004); Idiot Proof: a Short History of Modern Delusions, (2004); The Irresistible Con: The Bizarre Life of a Fraudulent Genius, (2004); Who Was Doctor Charlotte Bach?, (Short Books, 2002); Hoo-Hahs and Passing Frenzies, (Atlantic, 2002); The Soul of Indiscretion: Tom Driberg, Poet, Philanderer, Legislator and Outlaw - His Life and Indiscretions, (Fourth Estate, 2001); Biography of Karl Marx, (Fourth Estate, 1999); Lord Gnome's Literary Companion (Editor, 1996); The Chatto Book of Literary Cats, (Chatto, 1993); Tom Driberg: His Life and Indiscretions, (Chatto and Windus, 1990); Battle for London, (Pluto Press, 1985); Television: A History, (Ebury Press, 1984); The Sixties (Century, 1982).

Awards: Columnist of the Year, 1997; George Orwell Prize, 2003; Isaac Deutscher Memorial Prize, 2000

Education: Harrow School; Royal Holloway College, University of London

Career highlights: Writer for Oz magazine before progressing to the Guardian, Vanity Fair and Private Eye (Street of Shame); diarist on many newspapers and magazines including the New Statesman, the Independent and the Mirror; Book reviewer, Gay News; Theatre Critic, Today; News Editor, New Socialist; Contributing Editor, Tatler; Presenter, News-Stand, BBC Radio 4; appearances on ITV's What the Papers Say, BBC2's Have I Got News For You.

» **Reading:** *P G Wodehouse*

Ronnie Whelan 10.6.56

Wellington House, 69-71 Upper Ground, London SE1 9PQ

T 020 7667 8721
E annie.bowman@hellomagazine.com

Occupation: Editor, Hello!

Other positions: Layout Designer, Ideal Home; Deputy Art Director, Options magazine; Art Director/Associate Editor, Woman's World; Art Director, Hello! Magazine.

Publications: Ideal Home, Options, Woman's World, Hello!

Awards: PPA Runner-Up, Designer of the Year Award for Woman's World.

Education: St Martin's Secondary Modern School

Career highlights: My career highlights have been going from Junior Secretary on Ideal Home to Junior Layout Designer, then going to the launch of Options Magazine as Senior Designer, winning an award for what I did on Woman's World, getting the extra title of Associate Editor on Woman's World, and becoming Editor of Hello! magazine.

Mentor: There have been many people who have influenced me greatly, but my original mentor was Monica Tyson, Editor of Ideal Home.

Big break: Getting the position of Junior Layout Designer on Ideal Home.

Big mistake: Leaving a package of original copy and photographs which was ready to go to press on the train. I worked for a PR company, publishing house journals, and in those days, there were no computers. My boss had to produce most of the material again! I have never forgotten this experience and I have never left anything on a train again!

» **Reading:** *All tabloid newspapers, some fashion magazines.* **Watching:** *Reality TV shows!* **Listening:** *CD UK, Jools Holland and soul music.* **Relaxing to:** *Pottering in local shops and going out to eat.* » *Widowed, 3 stepchildren*

Victoria White 2.3.76

72 Broadwick St, London W1F 9EP

T 020 7312 3774
E victoria.white@natmags.co.uk

Occupation: Editor, Company Magazine

Other positions: Deputy Editor, Company; Deputy Editor, B; LA Bureau Chief Pacific Publications; Editor, Inside TV Australia; Features Editor, Inside Soap.

Education: University of Sussex

Career highlights: Being involved in the launch of the National Television Awards while working at Inside Soap, personal highlights include the entire time spent working at Inside Soap as I met my best friends there and loved every minute of hanging out with soap stars in improbable situations! Working in both Australia and the US was a great challenge and highlights there include covering the Emmys, Golden Globes and the Oscars. And interviewing George Clooney! Being editor of Company is the highlight of my career.

Mentor: My first bosses from those Inside Soap days, Vicky Mayer and Katie Eckberg.
Big break: Getting a job on Inside Soap having done two weeks' work experience on its sister title TV Hits.
Big mistake: Writing and publishing an entire feature about Ruby Wax based around the fact that she was presenting the BAFTAs - she wasn't, Angus Deayton was!

» **Reading:** *Chick lit and cook books.* **Watching:** *Coronation Street religiously, Extreme Home Makeover, The Apprentice USA, Waking the Dead, The X Factor, Dr Who, Grand Designs.* **Listening:** *Blue's Greatest Hits on a loop.* **Relaxing to:** *Wine usually helps.* » *Married, 1 child*

Brian Whittaker 26.6.63

BBC Worldwide Ltd, Woodlands, 80 Wood Lane, London W12 0TT
T 020 8433 1663
E brian.whittaker@bbc.co.uk

Occupation: Group Publisher, BBC Magazines

Publications: Homes & Antiques, Good Homes and How To Be Better Off magazines
Awards: Sales Team Of The Year at Nat Mags whilst Director Of Corporate Sales.
Education: Middlesex University; Sevenoaks School
Career highlights: Telesales, Guardian Newspaper; Launch of Fitness Magazine; at Company Magazine rose from Ad Manager to Publisher in 1989; first Director of Corporate Sales for National Magazine Company managing international, classified, regional and the major display advertisers, grew revenues and market share significantly; Publisher Of Country Living and improved profit of title by 50% in three years; Publishing Director, British Film Institute; Director, Highbury Leisure (previously SPL); Publisher Europe and Australia for IMP for subscription partworks for food, gardening and home.
Mentor: Simon Kippin who took me on at Company Magazine and who remains a good mentor today.
Big break: Becoming Publisher of Company Magazine in my twenties, the youngest Publisher at Nat Mags.
Big mistake: Not preparing for an advertising meeting where I asked a Media Buyer (Jimmy Wild) what was going on with his accounts - and he said you tell me! 'If you had had the courtesy to read your predecessor's notes (which I had not!) you would know,' and with that he sent me away with a flea in my ear.

» **Reading:** *Novels - most recently enjoyed American Boy and am an avid Wilkie Collins fan. Like the Telegraph although not its politics.* **Watching:** *Period dramas, Randall & Hopkirk when it was on, recently Martin Scorsese doc on Bob Dylan, Monarchy with David Starkey, Ten O'Clock News, Have I Got News For You, and Dr Who.* **Listening:** *Front Row, Jonathan Ross Saturday morning show, Today Programme, Afternoon Theatre, Sounds of the Sixties, Radio 2 and Radio 3 sometimes.* **Relaxing to:** *Theatre, cinema - especially international movies and photography (have been on trips to Chile, Tuscany and Romania recently).* » *Married, 2 children*

Libby Wiener 3.3.63

ITV News, Press Gallery, House of Commons, London SW1A 1AA
T 020 7430 4991
E libby.wiener@itn.co.uk

Occupation: Political Correspondent, ITV News

Other positions: Royal Correspondent, ITV News; Australia Correspondent, ITN; Europe Correspondent, ITN; Home Affairs Correspondent, ITN.
Education: Leeds University
Career highlights: Reporting on the collapse of the Soviet Union and withdrawal of the Red Army from the Baltic States. Subsequently reporting on political crises surrounding the birth of the European Union. In Australia, filming ecological damage to Great Barrier Reef. Back in the UK in 2000 as Royal Correspondent following Prince William's emergence into public life and Camilla's rehabilitation. Campaign Correspondent with the Conservatives during the 2005 General Election.

» *Married, 3 children*

David Willey 18.10.36

1A Piazza Collegio Romano, Rome 00186
T +39 339 232 6283
E ddw@tim.it

Occupation: BBC Rome Correspondent

Publications: Italians, BBC Publications 1984; God's Politician, Faber & Faber, 1992.
Awards: OBE
Education: Queens' College, Cambridge
Career highlights: Longest serving BBC Foreign Correspondent. Reported from more than 70 countries during career spanning 40 years.
Mentor: Tony Lawrence, former BBC Far East Correspondent.
Big break: Jetting around the world during 26 years following Pope John Paul's travels.
Big mistake: Not learning Chinese.

» **Reading:** *Roman inscriptions.* **Watching:** *Heimat.* **Listening:** *Private Passions.* **Relaxing to:** *In my country house on the rim of an extinct volcano overlooking Lake Bracciano.* » *Living with partner, 1 child from former marriage*

Gwyneth Williams 15.7.57

Room 1200, BBC White City, London W12 7TS
T 020 8752 7303
E gwyneth.williams@bbc.co.uk

Occupation: Head of BBC Radio Current Affairs; Editor, Reith Lectures.

Other positions: Talks Writer, Producer, Editor and Executive Editor at BBC on different networks and programmes; Research Assistant at the Overseas Development Institute.
Publications: Third World Political Organisations, Macmillan 1981, second edition 1987; The Contemporary Political Dictionary of Southern

Africa, Routledge, 1988 (co-author with Brian Hackland).
Awards: Various programme awards including Sony, Amnesty, Mental Health.
Education: St John's High School, Pietermaritzburg, South Africa; St Hugh's College, Oxford
» *Married, 2 children*

Stuart Williams 24.12.76

Emap Metro, Mappin House, 4 Winsley Street, London W1W 8HF
T 020 7182 8858
E stuart.williams@emap.com

Occupation: Publishing Director, Q, MOJO and Kerrang! Magazines

Other positions: Head of Marketing, Emap Performance music magazines; International Account Manager, Seymour International.
Publications: Q, MOJO, Kerrang! Magazines; Q, MOJO and Kerrang! Awards.
Awards: Media Brand of the Year for Kerrang!; Q campaigns published in the D&AD Yearbook; QTV launch campaign won numerous awards; PPA International Mag of the Year for MOJO.
Education: University of Kent at Canterbury; University of Vienna, Austria
Career highlights: A four-year degree in Chemistry convinced me that a career in music media was the only logical choice; two years working in circulation and export sales at Haymarket and Emap led me to Emap Metro in 1997, working in the marketing department of the men's and music magazines; the subsequent eight years have seen huge changes in the music market. From the boom in digital music to the explosion in the live and festival scene, it is an extraordinary time to be working in the music media. Emap has led the field in extending powerful brands into new media and my personal highlight is having seen Kerrang! transform from a magazine which sold 40,000 copies a week into a many-tentacled powerhouse of youth media, connecting with over five million people a month. I believe we have established a culture of rock music which hitherto never existed in the UK. In doing so we have presented music fans with an alternative to the dance and pop culture which dominated the country for decades. This career has also allowed me to drink absinthe with Marilyn Manson, kiss Kate Bush and spill beer over Bill Clinton. Nice work if you can get it.
Mentor: Emap is full of inspirational people. Phil Alexander, Paul Rees, Paul Brannigan and Dave Henderson never cease to amaze me with their knowledge, craft and obsession with producing amazing magazines. Their record collections would dwarf John Peel's (RIP). On the business side, Tim Schoonmaker was a real visionary.
Big break: Being given the chance to take Kerrang! and Q into new media. Launching our music TV channels and winning a radio licence for Kerrang! in the West Midlands gave the opportunity to give the UK a real rock media alternative.
Big mistake: The launch of Kingsize magazine, a great idea at the wrong time. Well, maybe not. Spent months working on the name rather than what would fill up the other 147 pages. I also regret wearing a Frankie Howerd T-shirt on Blockbusters.
» **Reading:** *All music mags, Vanity Fair, Private Eye, Dazed, the Grauniad, The Onion, Flight International, weezer.com, nicksfix.com, blabbermouth.net, tightbutloose.com.* **Watching:** *Six Feet Under (RIP), Black Books, Arrested Development, Tittybangbang, Catherine Tate, Nighty Night, Newsnight, Letterman, Kerrang! TV, endless pointless films at the ICA, hours and hours of DVD extras.* **Listening:** *Metal, emo, screamo, stoner, goth, punk, industrial, classic rock, electronica, americana, post-grunge, early post-alt.country, fado, prog and Desert Island Discs.* **Relaxing to:** *Tennis, travel and flying a small Cessna.*

John Willis

BBC TV, White City Building, 201 Wood Lane W12 7TS
T 020 8752 6501
E john.willis@bbc.co.uk

Occupation: Director, BBC Factual and Learning

Awards: British Academy Award, Johnny Go Home; International Emmy, Rampton - The Secret Hospital; Royal Television Society Gold Medal for Creative Contribution to Television, 2001.
Career highlights: Began career at Yorkshire Television, subsequently Controller of Documentaries and Current Affairs, including documentary series First Tuesday; Controller of Factual Programmes, Channel 4 Television, including Cutting Edge, True Stories and Secret History, 1988-93; Director of Programmes, Channel 4 Television, including Father Ted, Rory Bremner, The Politician's Wife, Four Weddings and a Funeral and Trainspotting, 1993-; Chief Executive, United Productions, including Hornblower, Oliver Twist and several Paul Watson documentaries; represented United on the Boards of both Channel 5 and Independent Television News; Managing Director, United Productions and London Weekend Television; Managing Director, Granada's International Production; Vice-President in charge of National Programmes, WGBH, Boston, Massachusetts, including award-winning programmes Frontline, Nova, American Experience and ExxonMobil Masterpiece Theatre, 2002-03; Director of Factual and Learning, BBC, 2003-present; Member, Creative Board, BBC, 2004-present.

Andrew Wilson 14.11.1960

Sky News, Grant Way, Isleworth, Middlesex TW7 5QD
T 020 7705 3000
E Andrew.Wilson@bskyb.com

Occupation: US Correspondent, Sky News

Other positions: Middle East Correspondent, Moscow Correspondent.
Awards: 2002 gold, The Intifada; 1999 silver, Russia, the weapons trade; Royal Television Society, Best Coverage of a Breaking Story, Sky News, Kosovo, 1999.
Education: Clifton College; Sandhurst; Sheffield University

Career highlights: It's all about being in the right place when things happen. I've managed a few, including the fall of the Berlin wall, the taking of Kuwait in the first Gulf War, the NATO advance through Kosovo, the Russian bombardment of Grozny, and the Northern Alliance advance into Kabul. Add to that a US Presidential election and the aftermath of the tsunami in Thailand; but there are human moments too. I'll never forget the East German cop embracing his Western counterpart at the top of two ladders. I'll never forget the young Albanian girl who broke her self-imposed silence to describe her escape from Serb paramilitaries who killed the rest of her family. I'll never forget the young Arab teenager who lost her eye playing with an unexploded cluster bomb, or the two Palestinian girls we saw come back from school to find their home destroyed. Indelible memories that dwarf our own experience.
Mentor: Abbas the Magnum Photographer for his consistent alternative approach, and Bruce Gyngell for his innate understanding of the television business.
Big break: Being a German speaker on shift in a UK newsroom in November 1989.
Big mistake: Turning down that job in the investment bank all those years ago! Just kidding.

» **Reading:** *Papers by day, books by night. Rarely the latest must-read. Yes to Amis, Waugh, and Mailer; no to the Da Vinci Code and Bridget Jones.* **Watching:** *Living abroad for so long, the pickings are slim. I watch complete series when they're out on DVD. Lots of online shopping required.* **Listening:** *Teenage sons' compilations to stay in touch. They bring the Nine Inch Nails, I offer JJ Cale and Talking Heads in return. But Van Morrison still rides with me at the cutting edge.* **Relaxing to:** *One of those series above, and the cinema at every possibility. Also whatever the great outdoors offers where I'm living. Off-roading in the West Bank desert, sledging in Moscow, river hikes in Virginia.* » *Married, 3 children*

Jane Wilson

10.6.71

30 Leicester Square, London WC2H 7LA
T 020 7766 6000
E jane.wilson@gcapmedia.com

Occupation: Communications Director, GCap Media plc

Education: Glasgow Caledonian University
Career highlights: After graduating, I had a few temporary positions including a fun stint in the marketing department of Celtic FC; my first opportunity came from a Ford dealer chain where I was promoted through the ranks from Marketing Executive to a Board position; following a merger and redundancy, I was offered a temporary job in corporate affairs at SMG plc. After two weeks they asked me to stay and soon I experienced lots of corporate activity including the acquisition of Virgin Radio, and this set me on my current career path; I moved to London as Account Director of a small financial PR consultancy and later joined Capital Radio as Communications Director. An amazing three years here has involved a number of high-profile communications issues ranging from presenter changes, acquisitions, board changes, a merger and the post-merger integration programme; I have also been lucky enough to have led the successful bid for the new analogue licence for our Xfm brand in Manchester, the first win in the company's 30-year history; following Capital's merger with GWR in May 2005, I was appointed Communications Director for GCap Media and now manage Media Relations, IR, Internal Communications and Public Affairs.
Mentor: As Chief Executive of Capital Radio, David Mansfield has been a great mentor over the past three years since I joined the company and really helped champion me through the merger process which created GCap Media.
Big break: Biggest break was at the age of 27, being appointed Marketing Director of a Scottish Ford dealership with a position on the board - my first really senior job. A great opportunity to get operations experience in a results-driven environment and the first merger I was involved with!
Big mistake: Can't think of one in particular but I think mistakes happen when I don't trust my instincts.

» **Reading:** *I get most industry news delivered as press cuttings every morning. I read the media trades, the FT for market news and the MediaGuardian website for quick updates. Outside work, I read design and fashion magazines.* **Watching:** *I tend to watch DVDs at home - love watching Curb Your Enthusiasm and Seinfeld. My other half is a news junkie so there's usually a news channel on.* **Listening:** *Working for a radio group, we listen to radio all day in the office. Xfm, Capital Gold, Capital Radio and Classic FM - depending on who gets to the radio first!* **Relaxing to:** *I love music and get to attend lots of Xfm gigs as well as listening to a huge CD collection at home. I have a passion for shoes and have just completed a shoe design course. I am looking forward to the next course in shoe making.* » *Living with partner, no children*

Michael Wilson

20.4.49

BskyB, Grant Way, Isleworth, Middlesex TW7 5QD
T 020 7797 2199
E Michael.Wilson@bskyb.com

Occupation: Business and Economics Editor, Sky News

Awards: Television Business Journalist of the Year, 2005; Freeman of the City.
Education: Scarborough High School for Boys; King's College, London
Career highlights: Getting a job at, and working with the news and current affairs teams at Thames Television; starting The City Programme in 1986; being in at the beginning of GMTV and making a 1,000,000-strong news audience between 6 and 7am. Being a founder member of Sky's television revolution and staying with it. So far.
Mentor: Oscar Petersen
Big break: Pretending I was a member of the ACTT and NUJ and getting a TV reporter's job.
Big mistake: Not being in Barcelona when Manchester United completed the treble.

» **Reading:** *As much as I can.* **Watching:** *People who reply honestly to this question.* **Listening:** *Rhythm and blues and jazz.* **Relaxing to:** *Running and playing the above.* » *Married, 1 child*

Nick Wilson

21.4.49

Five TV, 22 Long Acre, London WC2E 9LY
T 020 7550 5555
E nick.wilson@five.tv

Occupation: Controller Children's Programmes, Five TV

Publications: Playschool, Choc a Bloc, Wide Awake Club, WACADAY, Dappledown Farm, Hit Man and Her, Snobs, Milkshake, Shake.
Awards: TRIC Best Children's Programme, Wide Awake Club, 1987; BAFTA nomination, Wide Awake Club, 1986; Chicago International Children's Film Festival, Best Short Drama, Snobs (creator).
Education: Manchester University; Buxton College
Career highlights: First landmark four fantastic years directing/producing/writing Playschool with icons like Derek Griffiths, Brian Cant and Chloe Ashcroft. Later creating/directing and producing Wide Awake Club for TVAM - a series that clocked over three million viewers regularly at 8am! Launching and running Clear Idea Television - very successful independent production company later torpedoed by ITV franchise changes! Thanks, Mrs Thatcher. Being part of the Channel Five launch team and developing from scratch a market leading pre-school Children's brand, Milkshake, plus the multi award winning Shake strand for older children. Creating and co-writing children's drama, Snobs, Five's most successful children's programme outside of pre-school and winner of Chicago Children's Film Festival Live Action prize.
Mentor: Cynthia Felgate and Bruce Gyngell.
Big break: I've been very lucky! My first job came as a result of meeting Chris Pye at Midnight in Manchester. I benefited from upheaval at TVAM after their first year on air, and I joined the pitch writing team for the successful Five bid after a BAFTA presentation when I was unemployed.
Big mistake: A recent commission and trusting the wrong people during a short stint at a multi-channel broadcaster.

» **Reading:** *Scripts, a huge variety of novels and some biography.* **Watching:** *Films, epic TV drama, football and 'intelligent' comedy (like Curb Your Enthusiasm).* **Listening:** *Bob Marley, Blondie, Eagles, Dido, Green Day, Busted, Kirsty McCall.* **Relaxing to:** *Fly-fishing, tennis, family, Southampton FC.* » *Married, 5 children*

Nicholas Witchell

24.9.57

Room 5550, BBC TV Centre, London W12 7RJ
T 020 8624 9047
E nick.witchell@bbc.co.uk

Occupation: BBC Royal and Diplomatic Correspondent

Awards: Sony Radio Academy Award 2002.
Education: Leeds University (LLB)
Career highlights: Joined BBC as a News Trainee in 1976; Reporter, BBC Northern Ireland, 1979-82; Reporter, BBC TV News London, 1982-84; Ireland Correspondent, 1984; Presenter, BBC TV Six O'Clock News, 1984-89; Presenter, BBC Breakfast News, 1989-94; Diplomatic Correspondent, 1995-98; Royal and Diplomatic Correspondent, 1998-present.

» *Separated, 2 children*

John Witherow

21.1.56

1 Pennington Street, London E98 1ST
T 020 7782 5640
E john.witherow@sunday-times.co.uk

Occupation: Editor, the Sunday Times

Other positions: Reuters, London and Madrid; The Times, Home and Foreign Reporter; attachment to the Boston Globe; the Sunday Times, Defence Correspondent, Diplomatic Correspondent, Focus Editor, Foreign Editor, Head of News.
Education: Bedford School; University of York
Career highlights: Editing a great newspaper for 10 years and working with some of the best journalists in Britain. During the last decade we have taken the circulation of the Sunday Times to a 20-year high in an ever more competitive market, created not one but three colour magazines, started Home, Driving and Travel, provided the best foreign reporting of any newspaper, launched the biggest Sports section, enhanced a superlative Business section, delivered some great scoops that spoiled numerous breakfasts, and cheered up a lot of people.
Mentor: Andrew Neil
Big break: It should have been covering the Falklands war for The Times, but I was outflanked by Max Hastings and a buffoon from the Ministry of Defence. Otherwise it was becoming Focus Editor on the Sunday Times, my first taste of editing and one that was to prove intoxicating.
Big mistake: Not thumping Piers Morgan when the News of the World stole our serialisation of Jonathan Dimbleby's biography of Prince Charles.

» **Reading:** *Most newspapers and weeklies, early page proofs (just to keep section editors on their toes), books on current affairs, tennis ladders, tide timetables.* **Watching:** *Newsnight, Question Time, Grand Designs, Lost, historical documentaries and dramas, and I've yet to find a replacement for Sex and the City.* **Listening:** *The Today Programme, preferably when John Humphrys is in the chair. Damon Albarn's forays into Malian music and Gorillaz.* **Relaxing to:** *Trying, with ever-growing frustration, to play tennis well, and the occasional foray out to sea.* » *Married, 3 children*

Mark Wnek

19.2.59

Lowe New York, 150 East 42nd Street, New York, NY 10017, USA
T +1 212 605 8000

Occupation: Creative Director, Lowe Worldwide

Awards: Awards and commendations, D&AD, Cannes, Campaign Press, Eurobest, Epica, Creative Circle and Clio Awards.
Education: Dulwich College; Gonville & Caius College, Cambridge, Massachusetts
Career highlights: Freelance journalist / English teacher, Spain, 1980-82; Copywriter, Ogilvy & Mather, 1982-85; Senior Writer and Board Director, Ogilvy & Mather, 1985-90; Senior Writer and Board Director, Lowe Howard-Spink Advertising, 1990-94; Executive Creative Director and

Managing Partner, Euro RSCG Wnek Gosper Advertising, 1994-2003; Member, Board, Euro RSCG Worldwide 1996-2003; Co-founder, Ben Mark Orlando 2004; Chairman and Chief Creative Officer, Lowe New York, 2005-present.

Sir Terry Wogan

3.8.38

c/o Jo Gurnett, 2 New Kings Road, London SW6 4SA
T 020 7736 7828
E info@jgpm.co.uk

Occupation: Television and Radio Presenter

Publications: Banjaxed, 1979; The Day Job, 1981; To Horse, To Horse, 1982; Wogan on Wogan, 1987; Wogan's Ireland, 1988; Is It Me? (autobiography), 2000.
Awards: Pye Radio Award, 1980; Radio Industries Award, Radio Personality 3 times, TV Personality, 1982, 1984, 1985, 1987; TV Times TV Personality of the Year, 10 times; Daily Express Award, twice; Carl Alan Award, 3 times; Variety Club of Great Britain, Special Award, 1982; Variety Club of Great Britain, Showbusiness Personality, 1984; Radio Personality of last 21 yrs, Daily Mail National Radio Awards, 1988; Sony Radio Award, 1993, 1994 (Best Breakfast Show), 2002; Radio Programme of the Year, TRIC Award, 1997; Honorary Doctorate, University of Limerick, 2004; Radio Broadcaster of the Year, Broadcasting Press Guild awards, 2005; Knighthood, 2005.
Education: Crescent College, Limerick; Belvedere College, Dublin
Career highlights: After leaving college worked for 5 years in banking; joined RTE as Announcer, 1963; Senior Announcer, 1964-66; various programmes for BBC Radio, including Midday Spin, 1965-67; Late Night Extra, BBC Radio, 1967-69; The Terry Wogan Show, BBC Radio 1, 1969-72; The Terry Wogan Show, BBC Radio Two, 1972-84 and 1993-present; television shows include Lunchtime with Wogan, ATV, 1972-73; Come Dancing, BBC, 1973-79; Song for Europe, BBC; The Eurovision Song Contest, BBC, 1972-present; Blankety-Blank, BBC, 1979-83; Children in Need, BBC, 1980-present; Wogan's Guide to the BBC, 1982-present; Wogan; Terry Wogan's Friday Night; Auntie's Bloomers, BBC, 1991-present; Wake Up To Wogan, Radio 2, 1993-present; Do the Right Thing, BBC, 1994; Auntie's Sporting Bloomers, BBC; Wogan's Island, BBC, 1994; Points of View, BBC, 1999-present; The Terry and Gaby Show, BBC, 2003.

» **Relaxing to:** *Tennis, golf, swimming, reading, writing.*
» *Married, 3 children*

Mark Wood

28.3.52

ITN, 200 Gray's Inn Road, London WC1X 8XZ
T 020 7430 4332
E mark.wood@itn.co.uk

Occupation: Chairman and CEO, ITN

Other positions: Chairman, Museums, Libraries and Archives Council.
Education: Gillingham Grammar; Leeds University; Warwick University; Oxford University
Career highlights: Joined Reuters as Trainee Journalist in 1976; Correspondent in Vienna 1977-78, East Berlin 1978-81, Moscow 1981-85, Bonn 1985-87 (as Bureau Chief, Reuters Germany); Editor, Europe, 1987-89; Reuters Editor-in-Chief, 1989-2000; Member, Reuters plc Board, 1989-1996; Managing Director, Reuters Content Partners, 2000-02; Chairman, ITN, 1998-present; Executive Chairman 2002-03, Chief Executive 2003-present; Chairman, Library and Information Commission, 2000-02; Chairman, Museums, Libraries and Archives Council, 2002-present.
Mentor: Sidney Weiland, Reuters veteran Bureau Chief in Vienna in the 1970s/80s.
Big break: Getting sent to cover East Germany at the height of the Cold War.
Big mistake: What I thought was a tremendous scoop on the death of a senior member of the Soviet leadership. Got front pages all over the world. He then reappeared a day later.

» **Reading:** *History, biography and modern politics - anything by Beevor, Ferguson, Holland, Garton Ash.* **Watching:** *ITV News and Channel 4 News.* **Listening:** *Radio 4, Virgin and Classic fm.* **Relaxing to:** *With my two children, going to museums and galleries or going to Spurs.*
» *Separated, 2 children*

Lisa Woodman

2.2.76

1-5 Wandsworth Road, London SW8 2LN
T 020 7526 3244
E Lisa.woodman@bigissue.com

Occupation: Publisher, Big Issue magazine

Education: North London Collegiate School; Leeds University
Career highlights: Writing on spec to the Big Issue about a sales exec job, and getting a call back six months later saying they'd kept my CV on file and now had a vacancy! Being promoted to Ad Manager within a couple of years. Having left to go to the Guardian, being approached and asked to return to the Big Issue as Publisher.
Big break: Being offered the position of Ad Manager after only having been at the Big issue for a couple of years.

» **Reading:** *The Guardian and Observer.* **Watching:** *BBC breakfast news.* **Listening:** *Xfm, CDs.* **Relaxing to:** *I don't very often!* » *Unmarried, no children*

Richard Woolfe

15.8.66

160 Great Portland Street, London W1W 5QA
T 020 7299 5000
E richard_woolfe@flextech.co.uk

Occupation: Director of Television, LIVINGtv, LIVINGtv2 and Ftn

Other positions: 2003-04, Director of Programming, Bravo; 1999-2001, Head of Entertainment Planet 24; 1998, Editor, Entertainment Programmes, Granada Television; 1996-97, Real Television; 1991-96, Entertainment and Features Producer, BBC; 1986-91, Producer, That's Life, BBC1.
Publications: That's Life, Producer; rebranding and new strategic direction for LIVINGtv culminating in Broadcast Channel of the Year award; pioneering paranormal, pink and plastic surgery programming

with Most Haunted, Queer Eye and Extreme Makeover UK.
Awards: Industry Player of the Year, Edinburgh TV Festival, 2005; 4th, Strictly Come Dancing, Edinburgh TV Festival, 2005; Broadcast Channel of the Year (LIVINGtv), 2005; Childine Award for Services to Children, 2005; Consumer Journalist of the Year, 1991; New York Festivals, Queer Eye for the Straight Guy UK, International Programming and Production, Reality TV, 2004.
Education: Brighton College; Hebrew University, Jerusalem; Manchester Poly
Career highlights: I shall always be very proud of the fact that when I worked on That's Life! as a producer I was responsible for jailing three paedophiles and I changed the law - as a parent now I think that's pretty important. Working at LIVINGtv has been an amazing experience - transforming the channel from a downmarket daytime housewives' channel to a cool entertainment brand has been hard work but worth it all. Winning Broadcast Channel of the Year was fantastic.
Mentor: David Liddiment, Esther Rantzen, Lisa Opie, MD Flextech Television.
Big break: Getting a job on That's Life as a researcher after receiving 106 rejection letters!
Big mistake: Turning down a format identical to Wife Swap before Channel 4 aired the show.

» **Reading:** *Guardian, The Times, Heat, Broadcast, Observer, Sunday Times, Sun, Daily Mail, Campaign, Media Week, biographies and historical books.* **Watching:** *Everything! From GMTV to Newsnight, from X Factor to Strictly Come Dancing - and everything on LIVINGtv of course!* **Listening:** *Radio 4, Radio 5, Radio 2, Smooth FM, Xfm.* **Relaxing to:** *Restaurants, theatre, wine, learning to salsa dance!* » *Married to Hilary, 2 children, Elise and Daniel*

Chris Wright

7.9.44

Chrysalis Group plc, The Chrysalis Building, Bramley Road, London W10 6SP
T 020 7221 2213
E chris.wright@chrysalis.com

Occupation: Chairman, Chrysalis plc

Other positions: Chairman, QPR FC 1996-2001; Chairman and majority shareholder, London Wasps Holdings / RFC 1996-present; Chairman and majority shareholder, Portman Film and TV, 2004-present.
Awards: CBE, 2005
Education: King Edward VI Grammer School, Louth; University of Manchester; Manchester Business School
Career highlights: Formed Ellis Wright Agency with Terry Ellis in 1967, changed name to Chrysalis, 1968; Chairman, 1985-present; built Chrysalis into a leading independent music company with artists such as Blondie, Jethro Tull, Ten Years After and Sinead O'Connor; sold original record label to Thorn EMI in 1991, but retained publishing interests; Led group's expansion into radio and book publishing.

» **Relaxing to:** *Tennis, breeding racehorses, food and wine.*
» *Married, 4 children*

Helen Wright

12.2.71

200 Gray's Inn Road, London WC1X 8XZ
T 020 7833 3000
E helen.wright@itn.co.uk

Occupation: Social Affairs Correspondent, ITV News

Other positions: News Correspondent; Health Correspondent; Education Correspondent.
Publications: Cot death mother cases (Sally Clark / Angela Cannings / Donna Anthony); Family court campaign; Anti-bullying campaign.
Education: University of Wales Institute of Science and Technology
Career highlights: I started out as a trainee in a local radio newsroom in West Yorkshire before joining Yorkshire TV, then ITN. I've worked as a reporter, correspondent and newscaster in both regional and national ITV newsrooms. I've also written, directed and produced regional documentaries, and worked on numerous films for the Tonight with Trevor McDonald programme.

» **Reading:** *For pleasure, modern fiction. For work, newspapers. For fun, Vogue.* **Watching:** *Films, plays, and most of the US TV drama series C4 shows.* **Relaxing to:** *A quiet dinner with my partner David.* » *Living with partner*

Peter Wright

13.8.53

Mail on Sunday, Northcliffe House, 2 Derry Street, Kensington, London W8 5TT
T 020 7938 6000
E peter.wright@mailonsunday.co.uk

Occupation: Editor, Mail on Sunday

Education: Marlborough College; Clare College, Cambridge
Career highlights: Reporter, Evening Post, Echo, Hemel Hempstead 1975-78; Daily Mail, reporter 1979; assistant news editor, 1979-85; associate news editor (foreign), 1985-86; assistant features editor, 1986-88; editor, Femail, 1988-91; assistant editor (features), 1991-92; associate editor, 1992-95; deputy editor, 1995-98; editor, Mail on Sunday 1998-present.

» *Married, 4 children*

Roger Wright

1956

Broadcasting House, Portland Place, London W1A 1AA
T 020 7765 2523
E Roger.Wright@bbc.co.uk

Occupation: Controller, BBC Radio 3

Other positions: Freelance arts writer and broadcaster; Member, Arts Council Music Panel; President, Students' Union, 1977-78.
Publications: (With M Finnissy) New Music 1989, 1989.
Education: Chetham's School, Manchester; Royal Holloway College, University of London
Career highlights: Manager, then Director, British Music Information Centre, 1978-87; Senior Producer, BBC Symphony Orchestra, 1987-89;

Artistic Administrator, Cleveland Orchestra, 1989-92; Executive Producer, then Vice-President, Deutsche Grammophon, 1992-97; Head of Classical Music, BBC, 1997-98.

» *Married, 2 children*

Caroline Wyatt 22.4.71

BBC Paris Bureau, 155 Rue du Faubourg-St Honoré, 75008 Paris, France
T 00 33 1 56 88 50 30
E caroline.wyatt@bbc.co.uk

Occupation: BBC Paris Correspondent

Other positions: BBC Moscow Correspondent 2000-03; BBC Berlin Correspondent 1999-2000; BBC Bonn Correspondent 1997-99; BBC Berlin Reporter.
Education: University of Southampton; City University; Rutgers University
Career highlights: Moving to Berlin to cover Germany after the fall of the Berlin Wall - it was fascinating. Later on, covering the 'Desert Fox' campaign in Iraq in 1998, the war in Afghanistan in 2001/2002, travelling and reporting on the former Soviet Union including Chechnya, embedding with British troops to cover the Iraq war in 2003. Living in Paris and reporting on France is the current highlight - especially covering the all-important champagne harvest...
Mentor: Linda Christmas, my tutor at City University post-graduate journalism course.
Big break: Joining the BBC in 1991.
Big mistake: Not anything I'd like to share here!

» **Reading:** *Everything and anything, from John Banville to 19th century novels to the back of a cornflakes packet, if there's nothing else to read. On a daily basis, several newspapers - British and French, tabloid and broadsheet - and news magazines.* **Watching:** *Pretentious French films and anything by Pedro Almodovar. Mainly foreign films. On TV - the news, and films.* **Listening:** *Again, anything and everything from Françoise Hardy to speed garage....* **Relaxing to:** *When I'm asleep.* » *Single, no children*

Y

Lucy Yeomans 1.11.70

Harpers & Queen Magazine, 72 Broadwick Street, London W1F 9EP
T 020 7439 5533
E lucy.yeomans@natmags.co.uk

Occupation: Editor, Harpers & Queen

Awards: FRSA
Education: University of St Andrews
Career highlights: Editor, Boulevard magazine, Paris, 1993-95; Literary Editor and Features Editor, the European, 1995-98; Features Editor, Deputy Editor and Acting Editor, Tatler, 1998-2000; Features Director, Vogue; Editor, Harpers & Queen, 2000-present.

» **Relaxing to:** *Theatre, horse-riding, music, poetry.*

Jan Younghusband 9.5.58

124 Horseferry Road, London SW1 2TX
T 020 7306 8283
E jyounghusband@channel4.co.uk

Occupation: Commissioning Editor, Arts and Performance, Channel 4 Television

Other positions: Freelance Producer; Production Manager in opera and theatre; Author.
Awards: Loads!
Education: Portsmouth High School; Millfield School; University of London
Career highlights: Trained in opera production at Glyndebourne. Line produced in theatre, National Theatre, West End, several years in arts television specialising in classical music, and lately the arts in general. Author of three books, one of which became a film.
Mentor: Tom Waits
Big break: Meeting Janey Walker.
Big mistake: Not meeting Janey Walker sooner.

» **Reading:** *Contemporary fiction and biography.* **Watching:** *Loads of TV, and especially history films, current affairs, and feature films.* **Listening:** *Music of all genres. The radio.* **Relaxing to:** *Spending time with my son.* » *Single, 1 child*

Z

Fareed Zakaria

20.1.64

Newsweek International, 251 West 57th Street,
New York, NY 10019

T 212 445 4672
E fareed.zakaria@newsweek.com

Occupation: Editor, Newsweek International

Other positions: Managing Editor, Foreign Affairs
Publications: Three books, including The Future of Freedom, which has been translated into 18 languages; several cover stories for Newsweek including 'Why They Hate US' three weeks after 9/11.
Awards: Overseas Press Club, National Press Club, Deadline Club, National Headliner, etc.
Education: Yale University; Harvard University
Mentor: The first were two prominent editors in India, where I grew up: Khushwant Singh and Girilal Jain.
Big break: Getting hired as Managing Editor of Foreign Affairs straight out of graduate school. I was 28, my predecessor was probably 58.
Big mistake: Oh God, I've made too many to count.

» **Reading:** *Mostly non-fiction these days. I'd like to read more fiction.* **Watching:** *Anything on video.* **Listening:** *Western and Indian classical, and jazz.* **Relaxing to:** *Music, reading, sports, and children.* » *Married, 2 children*